LAW, POLITICS
AND THE
JUDICIAL PROCESS
IN CANADA

LAW, POLITICS
AND THE
JUDICIAL PROCESS
IN CANADA
THIRD EDITION

F. L. MORTON, ed.

UNIVERSITY OF
CALGARY
PRESS

University of Calgary Press
2500 University Drive NW
Calgary, Alberta
Canada T2N 1N4
www.uofcpress.com

National Library of Canada Cataloguing in Publication Data

Law, politics and the judicial process in Canada

Includes index.
ISBN 1-55238-046-7

1. Courts — Canada. 2. Judicial process — Canada. 3. Poliltical questions
   and judicial power — Canada.
I. Morton, F. L. (Frederick Lee), 1949-

KE8200.Z85L39 2001   347.71'012 C2001-911196-7   KF8700.ZA2L39 2001

 We acknowledge the financial support of the Government of Canada
through the Book Publishing Industry Development Program (BPIDP) for
our publishing activities.

 The Canada Council for the Arts
Le Conseil des Arts du Canada

Printed and bound in Canada by Friesens.
∞ This book is printed on acid-free paper.

Page, cover design, and typesetting by Kristina Schuring.

Table of Contents

4

Judicial Recruitment and Selection 117

5

Judicial Independence, Ethics, and Discipline 169

6

Access to Judicial Power 255

7

Interest Groups and Litigation   301

8

Fact Finding in the Courts   363

9

Prcedents, Statutes, and Legal Reasoning   387

10

11

12

13

Reconciling Judicial Review and Constitutional Democracy

Appendices

* Reprinted elsewhere in the book.

Preface

2002 marks the twentieth anniversary of the *Canadian Charter of Rights and Freedoms*. I completed the first edition of this book in May, 1984, the month the Supreme Court issued its first *Charter* decision. In the preface to that first edition, I speculated that the adoption of the *Charter* was going to "force the Canadian judiciary into a much more explicit political function than it had previously exercised." This was indeed speculation. No one knew at the time what the *Charter* would hold. The impact – if any – of the *Charter* would be a function of judicial interpretation and choice. Given our judges' history of deference to elected governments and provincial opposition to the *Charter* (especially Quebec's), there were ample reasons to suspect no more than modest deviation from the *status quo ante*.

Today, twenty years down the road into "Charterland," Canadians live in a different legal and political world. There have been more than four hundred *Charter* cases decided by the Supreme Court of Canada and thousands more by lower courts. The list of public policies shaped by the courts' interpretation of the *Charter* is long and still growing: aboriginal rights and land-claims, abortion, bilingualism, capital punishment, criminal procedure, electoral distribution, family law, gay rights, immigration and refugee determination, judicial ethics, judicial salaries, labour law, Quebec separatism, pornography, prisoner voting rights, Sunday closing laws.

While the Supreme Court's *Charter* decisions are the most visible and often dramatic indicators of the impact of the *Charter*, they represent only the tip of the iceberg of *Charter*-induced activities. The courts' *Charter* activism has been both a cause and an effect of numerous other changes in the legal and political systems: the docket and decision-making procedures of the Supreme Court, judicial appointments, law schools, legal scholarship, interest group activity, and government expenditures. These changes are recounted in the revised introductions to each chapter and the twenty-seven new readings that have been selected for the third edition. The merits of these changes have become a topic of growing debate, a debate reflected in many of the new readings chosen for the third edition.

In a 1991 study of judicial activism in ten different democracies, Canada was ranked second only to the United States.[1] England, the model followed by Canadian jurists until recently, was ranked ninth. Had the same survey been done twenty years ago, when the Canadian Court was still "the quiet court in the unquiet country," Canada would have taken its place next to the mother country. No longer! Indeed, a strong case can now be made that the Supreme Court of Canada is more activist than the contemporary American Supreme court. The heydays of American judicial activism are long gone, stopped if not reversed by the judicial appointments of more recent Republican presidents and senates.

In the preface to the first edition, I also hazarded the observation that the study of the judicial process in Canada had been relatively neglected because it was "too political for law professors but too legal for political scientists." There is hardly any danger of this today. The *Charter* has dissolved any bright-line distinction between law and politics and produced a new generation of political scientists who are analyzing and writing about judicial politics. The works of some of these new scholars are included in this new edition.

I am indebted to many people who assisted in the production of this third edition. I would like to thank all the contributing authors, without whom there would be no book. In particular, I would like to thank Glenn Blackett and Adrian Ang, graduate research assistants who worked long hours in the preparation of the manuscript and without whom I would not have finished. Finally, I want to thank the staff at the University of Calgary Press, especially John King, my capable and patient editor. For any errors of omission or commission, I take full responsibility.

---

1 Kenneth Holland, *Judicial Activism in Comparative Perspective* (London: Macmillan, 1991).

The Rule of Law in the Canadian Constitution

On December 4, 1946, Frank Roncarelli was informed by the Quebec Liquor Commission that the liquor licence for his Montreal restaurant had been revoked "forever." Mr. Roncarelli had not violated any Liquor Commission guidelines, nor had he been charged with or convicted of any criminal wrongdoing. The licence was revoked because, as Mr. Roncarelli and indeed everyone else knew, Maurice Duplessis, the Premier of Quebec, wanted to punish him for his membership in and financial support of the Jehovah's Witnesses. The Jehovah's Witnesses are an evangelizing, fundamentalist protestant sect, who had outraged Duplessis and the French Catholic majority in Quebec through their outspoken criticisms of the Catholic Church and its priests. The Duplessis government had begun a campaign of legal harassment against the Witnesses by arresting them for distributing their printed materials without a licence. Roncarelli frustrated this plan by regularly providing bail money for his arrested fellow-believers, who would then return to the streets. Roncarelli thus became a special target of the harassment policies of the Quebec government.

After a thirteen-year legal battle, the Supreme Court of Canada finally ruled that the government of Quebec's treatment of Roncarelli had been arbitrary and illegal. Moreover, Duplessis could not hide behind the civil immunity normally enjoyed by state administrators under Quebec law. By grossly abusing his administrative discretion, Duplessis was deemed to have acted outside the law and was thus subject to being sued by Roncarelli for damages[1] (Reading 1.1). A majority of the Court held that in Canada there is a general right not to be punished by the arbitrary exercise of government power. A government, federal or provincial, can only move against an individual in accordance with known rules, and the Duplessis government had failed to meet this standard. In so ruling, the Supreme Court

---

1 For an excellent account of both the Roncarelli Case and the larger conflict between the Jehovah's Witnesses and the Quebec government, see William Kaplan, *State and Salvation: The Jehovah's Witnesses and Their Fight for Civil Rights* (Toronto: University of Toronto Press, 1989).

re-asserted one of the fundamental principles of the "unwritten constitution" of Canada – "the rule of law."

The Roncarelli case was just the most recent chapter in a living tradition that can be traced back through the nineteenth-century writings of A.V.C. Dicey (Reading 1.4); the American *Declaration of Independence* of 1776 (Reading 1.3); the political theory of the seventeenth-century philosopher John Locke (Reading 1.2); and back to the fields of Runnymede in June of 1215, when the English nobles forced King John to sign *Magna Carta* and to agree to rule *per legem terrae* – according to the laws of the land.[2]

Magna Carta marked the beginning of the "rule of law" tradition. The "Glorious Revolution of 1688" deposed the Stuart kings and established the supremacy of Parliament over the Crown. This landmark event initiated the practice of government that we now take for granted (too much so!) – representative government, or government by consent of the governed.

The second reading is from the writings of John Locke, often referred to as the "theorist of the Glorious Revolution." Locke's *Second Treatise on Government*, first published in 1690, has been the most influential defence and advocacy of "government by consent," or liberal democracy, ever written. In it, we find not only a defence of "government by consent of the governed," but also a restatement of the principle of *per legem terrae*. Locke explicitly declares that even the new sovereign, the legislature, must rule "by declared and received laws ... interpreted by known authorized judges."

A careful reading of the passage from Locke reveals that, in addition to these procedural restrictions, he imposes a second major restriction on the legislative, or "law-making," power of the state – "the law of Nature." This substantive restriction means that, not only must laws be duly enacted and fairly administered, but also that the laws themselves must not violate the "natural rights" of individuals that exist by the "law of Nature." This law of nature is understood to transcend human society and to exist independently of the positive law of any given state.

This double limitation on just government was given its most striking and memorable articulation in the American *Declaration of Independence* of 1776, written primarily by Thomas Jefferson (Reading 1.3). The Americans justified their revolution, and subsequently founded their new republic, on the

---

2 The full text of s.39 of Magna Carta reads as follows: "No freeman shall be taken or (and) imprisoned or disseised or outlawed or exiled or in any way destroyed, nor will we go upon him nor send upon him, except by the lawful judgement of his peers or (and) by the law of the land." This 700 year-old rule is the direct ancestor of the 1982 *Charter of Rights and Freedoms*, whose preamble declares: "Whereas Canada is founded upon principles that recognize the supremacy of God and the rule of law." Section 7 of the *Charter* essentially restates the modern formulation of *per legem terrae*, that no person can be deprived of his life, liberty, or security of the person, except according to the due process of law. Sections 8 through 15 then elaborate specific aspects of due process.

two fundamental principles of Locke's political theory: that "all men are by Nature equal," and that they possess "certain inalienable (i.e., natural) rights." There is a critical tension between these two fundamental concepts of equality and liberty. The principle of natural equality essentially means that no person (or group of persons) is so inherently superior as to rule others without their consent. This banishes the traditional claims of priests, kings, and nobles to rule on the basis of their alleged natural superiority, and replaces it with government by consent of the governed. In practice, this has meant some form of "majority rule" democracy. The principle of natural rights means that a just government cannot violate these rights, since the very purpose of government is to secure such rights. The tension arises from the fact that "majority rule" does not always produce laws that respect the rights of individuals or groups that are not part of the majority.

This tension is more of a theoretical problem than a practical one. Most of the time, the combined practice of "government by consent" and "the rule of law" is a strong guarantee that the twin requirements of equality and liberty will both be met. It is unlikely that a governing majority will ever (knowingly) consent to policies that are destructive of their rights. The "rule of law" provides additional safeguards by detering rulers from pursuing ends and using means that "they would not like to have known by the people, and own not willingly."[3] But what happens when the majority consents to laws that are destructive of the natural rights of a minority? What happens when government by the "consent of the governed" no longer "secures these rights"? Neither Locke nor Jefferson answered this question. The practical problem of reconciling "majority rule" with "minority rights" was left to the founders of new liberal democracies such as the United States and Canada.

Historically, there have been two principal approaches to giving institutional expression to the principles of equality and liberty in modern liberal democracies: the British parliamentary or Westminster model and the American "separation of powers" model. Because of two major differences in the parliamentary and American systems, the courts in each system have very different functions and characteristics. The American model is ultimately based on and organized by a single basic document – a written constitution. This single document sets down in writing "the rules governing the composition, powers and methods of operation of the main institutions of government, and the general principles applicable to their relations to the citizens."[4] By contrast, the Westminster model is based on an "unwritten constitution" – a combination of historically important statutes, the common law, and numerous unwritten conventions and usages. (In 1998, Britain took a step in the direction of the American model by making the *European Convention on Human Rights* justiciable in British courts. See below.)

---

3 See Locke, *The Second Treatise*, Ch. 1. Reading 1.2.

4 Sir Ivor Jennings, *The Law and the Constitution*. 5th ed. (London: University of London Press, 1959), p. 33.

The second difference is that the "written constitution" of the Americans includes an enumeration of the fundamental rights and liberties of the individual against government, known collectively as the *Bill of Rights*. While individuals enjoy basically the same rights and freedoms under the British parliamentary model of democracy, they are not "spelled out" in any single, basic document of government, i.e., they are not "constitutionally entrenched."

The result of these two differences is that, under the American model of democracy, the courts, and especially the Supreme Court, play a more explicit and influential political role. Ever since the 1803 case of *Marbury v. Madison*, American courts have assumed the function of interpreting and enforcing "constitutional law" just as they do all other law. This "judicial review" of legislative and executive actions is intended to ensure that the latter conform to the procedures and limitations laid down in the Constitution. If government laws and actions do not conform, the court declares them to be "unconstitutional," invalid and therefore without legal effect.

It is easy to see how, in theory at least, combining the American practice of judicial review with an entrenched bill of rights resolves the tension between liberty and equality, majority rule and minority rights. If the majority enacts a law that infringes a person's constitutional right, the individual can go to court and ask the judges to strike down the law as unconstitutional. This approach to protecting civil liberties was particularly effective in promoting racial justice in American society during the 1950s and 1960s. While the more "democratic" (majoritarian) institutions of government refused to take action, the American Supreme Court used the Bill of Rights guarantee of "equal protection of the laws" to strike down the legal barriers of racial discrimination in American society. However, as the American Supreme Court expanded its "judicial activism" into more and more areas of public policy and local government, serious questions began to arise about the "undemocratic" character of its use of judicial review. In protecting the "individual rights" side of the liberal equation, the Court was perceived as neglecting and even violating the equality requirement of government by consent of the governed.[5]

The British model of parliamentary supremacy combined with the "rule of law" tradition avoids this problem. There are no written constitutional prohibitions for the British courts to enforce against Parliament, and the courts do not interpret or enforce constitutional conventions, the "unwritten constitution."[6] The critics of parliamentary democracy, however, contend that it is prone to the opposite problem – that there is no adequate mechanism

---

5 This problem is the subject of Chapter 13.

6 The Canadian Supreme Court's decision in the 1981 *Constitutional Amendment Reference* was contrary to this generally accepted practice and is probably best understood as an exception to an otherwise still valid rule.

to protect individuals or minorities from democratic majorities that violate their rights. While this may be true in theory, in practice it has not proven to be a serious problem in either Great Britain or Canada. While Canada's civil liberties record is far from perfect,[7] it remains much better than the vast majority of modern nation states.

The key to the practical success of the British parliamentary system is conveyed in the reading from Dicey on "the rule of law," and especially his quotation from Tocqueville (Reading 1.4). Comparing the governments of England and Switzerland, Tocqueville observed that, "In England there seems to be more liberty in the customs than in the laws of the people," while the opposite holds for Switzerland. For both Tocqueville and Dicey, the British condition is far preferable. For, in the long run, the customs, habits, beliefs – the moral quality public opinion – of a society is a more dependable guarantee of just laws than the "paper barriers" of constitutional "guarantees." Put very simply, a written constitution cannot "guarantee" that the laws of a democratic society will be any more just or fair than the people who make up that society.

The government of Canada was basically modelled after the British parliamentary system. The one important exception is the federal form of the union of the Canadian provinces, and the defining of the forms and limits of this union in a single, written document – the *British North America Act, 1867*, now known as the *Constitution Act, 1867*. This aspect of Canadian government is especially important for the courts because it has thrust upon them the function of judicial review, or "umpire" of the federal system.[8] Federalism aside, both levels of government in Canada were formed after the Westminster model, which meant parliamentary supremacy within their respective spheres of jurisdiction.

Accordingly, Canada, until very recently, followed the British approach to the protection of civil liberty – parliamentary supremacy combined with "the rule of law," and a healthy self-confidence in the basic sense of fairness and toleration for diversity in the Canadian people. Inevitably the proximity of the United States has prompted constant comparisons. One of the most eloquent and forceful defences of the Anglo-Canadian approach to protecting civil liberties was given by the dean of Canadian political science, R. MacGregor Dawson. In discussing the various components of Canada's unwritten constitution, Dawson argued:

> The mere fact that a constitutional doctrine is not explicitly enunciated and formally committed to writing may affect the external appearance but not disturb the genuineness or force of that doctrine. Thus the broad tolerance which will permit differences of opinion and will disapprove of punitive

---

7 See Thomas Berger, *Fragile Freedoms: Human Rights and Dissent in Canada* (Vancouver, BC: Clarke, Irwin, and Co., 1981).
8 This is the subject of Chapter 10.

or repressive measures against the dissenters is of as great constitutional significance and may conceivably under some circumstances afford an even more assured protection than an explicit guarantee of freedom of speech, written into a constitution, yet with no solid conviction behind it.[9]

The force of Dawson's argument notwithstanding, Canadian political leaders have been increasingly attracted to the American approach to protecting civil liberties. In 1960, the Diefenbaker government enacted the Canadian *Bill of Rights*. It took the form of a statute, not a constitutional amendment, and applied only to the federal government and not to the provinces.[10] Partly because of dissatisfaction with this document and partly in response to political developments within Canada during the 1970s, the Trudeau government undertook a major program of constitutional reform in 1980. Prime Minister Trudeau's constitutional agenda included "patriating" the *B.N.A. Act*, an amending formula, and a new *Charter of Rights* that applied to both levels of Canadian government. After a year and a half of political maneuvering, confrontation, and finally compromise, modified versions of all three objectives were achieved.

The adoption of a constitutionally entrenched *Charter of Rights* (reproduced in Appendix C) fundamentally altered the Canadian system of government by placing explicit limitations on the law-making power of both levels of government. Parliament was no longer supreme; the Constitution was. Or almost. The *Charter* was not adopted in its original "pure" form. Attachment to the tradition of parliamentary supremacy, combined with provincial suspicion and opposition, forced an important compromise. Added in the eleventh hour of constitutional negotiations between the federal government and the provinces, section 33 of the *Charter* allows both levels of government to "override" certain *Charter* provisions if they deem it necessary. Parliamentary supremacy was thus preserved, albeit in a qualified form.

In 1998, the United Kingdom took a step in the direction of its two former North American colonies by incorporating the *European Convention for the Protection of Human Rights and Fundamental Freedoms* into English domestic law. This legislation allows the rights enumerated in the European Convention to be asserted and adjudicated in British courts. However, UK political leaders were reluctant to abandon their 300-year tradition of parliamentary sovereignty. In the end, they chose not to give British courts the power to declare laws invalid. Instead, the courts are instructed to interpret legislation in accordance with the Convention "as far as it is possible." However, if a judge finds a irreconcilable conflict between a statute and a provision of the Convention, the most the judge can do is issue a

---

9 R. MacGregor Dawson, *The Government of Canada*. 4th ed. (Toronto: University of Toronto Press, 1963), p. 70.

10 This is discussed in greater detail in Chapter 11.

"declaration of incompatibility." This "finding" does not invalidate the law in question or prevent it from being enforced. However, it triggers a "fast track" procedure for Parliament to remedy the legal problem identified by the courts. In the final analysis, however, it rests with the government of the day whether or how to respond to a "declaration of incompatibility."

At the outset of the twenty-first century, Canada finds itself somewhere between the British and American models of liberal democracy. Each nation has given its courts a role in interpreting and enforcing constitutional rights but have structured the division of labour between courts and legislatures differently. In each instance, elected governments can have the final word, but with different degrees of difficulty. For the Americans to reverse a Supreme Court ruling on their Bill of Rights requires either a constitutional amendment or "packing the Court" with new appointments committed to overturning the disputed precedent. While there are several examples of both, neither occurs frequently. In theory, Canadian governments are armed with a more usable "check" on perceived judicial error – the section 33 "notwithstanding" clause. In practice, Canadian governments other than Quebec have been increasingly reluctant to invoke their section 33 power. However, they have used the less drastic remedy of simply re-enacting the impugned legislation with amendments. In the UK, a judicial declaration of incompatibility does not alter the legal status quo, so it remains at the discretion of the government of the day whether or how to respond.

As a result, the debate over which form of liberal democracy is best designed to protect the liberties of its citizens remains very much alive. The truth of this debate lies somewhere between the two contending positions, for as Dawson pointed out: "Written law and the conventions will normally complement one another and each becomes necessary to the proper functioning of the other."[11] The implications of these different divisions of labour between courts and legislatures is the focus of the "dialogue theory" discussed in chapter 13. While this debate is ongoing, there is one undisputed fact about the effect of enumerating individual rights in a written constitution: it thrusts the courts, and the judges who constitute them, into a more explicit and influential political role.

How to strike the right balance between legislatures and courts is a long-standing issue. The power of judges is also influenced by a more recent debate: whether constitutional rights (and thus judicial review) apply only to what the government does or whether they extend to the actions of private citizens and businesses. This new debate is the focus of Thomas Bateman's contribution in Reading 1.6.

Traditional liberal constitutionalism drew a sharp distinction between the public and the private, between state and civil society. The purpose of constitutionalism (and especially constitutional rights) was to protect the latter from the former. Constitutional rights applied only to "state action" – laws

---

11 Dawson, p. 71.

passed by legislators, executive orders and the conduct of "state agents" such as the police. By placing written (and thus judicially enforceable limits) on what (and how) the state may do, liberal constitutionalism sought to enhance the sphere of individual freedom (civil society) by limiting the scope of state powers. Liberal constitutionalism thus conceived of rights as "negative" – rights against government. So conceived, constitutional rights – and thus judicial review – do not apply to "private" actions – relationships in the home, the workplace or between neighbours. While this was the original understanding behind the 1982 Canadian *Charter of Rights*, Bateman analyzes how the Supreme Court has chipped away at this understanding and advanced – but not yet embraced – a post-liberal constitutionalism that applies to both state and civil society.

1.1

Roncarelli v. Duplessis
Supreme Court of Canada (1959)

The judgment of Rand and Judson JJ. was delivered by RAND J.: – The material facts from which my conclusion is drawn are these. The appellant was the proprietor of a restaurant in a busy section of Montreal which in 1946 through its transmission to him from his father had been continuously licenced for the sale of liquor for approximately 34 years; he is of good education and repute and the restaurant was of a superior class. On December 4 of that year, while his application for annual renewal was before the Liquor Commission, the existing licence was cancelled and his application for renewal rejected, to which was added a declaration by the respondent that no future licence would ever issue to him. These primary facts took place in the following circumstances.

For some years the appellant had been an adherent of a rather militant Christian religious sect known as the Witnesses of Jehovah. Their ideology condemns the established church institutions and stresses the absolute and exclusive personal relation of the individual to the Deity without human intermediation or intervention.

The first impact of their proselytizing zeal upon the Roman Catholic church and community in Quebec, as might be expected, produced a violent reaction. Meetings were forcibly broken up, property damaged, individuals ordered out of communities, in one case out of the province, and generally, within the cities and towns, bitter controversy aroused. The work of the Witnesses was carried on both by word of mouth and by the distribution of printed matter, the latter including two periodicals known as "The Watch Tower" and "Awake", sold at a small price.

In 1945 the provincial authorities began to take steps to bring an end to what was considered insulting and offensive to the religious beliefs and feelings of the Roman Catholic population. Large scale arrests were made of young men and women, by whom the publications mentioned were being held out for sale, under local by-laws requiring a licence for peddling any kind of wares. Altogether almost one thousand of such charges were laid. The penalty involved in Montreal, where most of the arrests took place, was a fine of $40, and as the Witnesses disputed liability, bail was in all cases resorted to.

The appellant, being a person of some means, was accepted by the Recorder's Court as bail without question, and up to November 12, 1946, he had gone security in about 380 cases, some of the accused being involved in repeated offences. Up to this time there had been no suggestion of impropriety; the security of the appellant was taken as so satisfactory that at times, to avoid delay when he was absent from the city, recognizances were signed by him in blank and kept ready for completion by the Court officials. The reason for the accumulation of charges was the doubt that they could be sustained in law. Apparently the legal officers of Montreal, acting in concert with those of the Province, had come to an agreement with the attorney for the Witnesses to have a test case proceeded with. Pending that, however, there was no stoppage of the sale of the tracts and this became the annoying circumstance that produced the volume of proceedings.

On or about November 12 it was decided to require bail in cash for Witnesses so arrested and the sum set ranged from $100 to $300. No such bail was furnished by the appellant; his connection with giving security ended with this change of practice; and in the result, all of the charges in relation to which he had become surety were dismissed.

At no time did he take any part in the distribution of the tracts: he was an adherent of the group but nothing more. It was shown that he had leased to another member premises in Sherbrooke which were used as a hall for carrying on religious meetings: but it is unnecessary to do more than mention that fact to reject it as having no bearing on the issues raised. Beyond the giving of bail and being an adherent, the appellant is free from any relation that could be tortured into a badge of character pertinent to his fitness or unfitness to hold a liquor licence.

The mounting resistance that stopped the surety bail sought other means of crushing the propagandist invasion and among the circumstances looked into was the situation of the appellant. Admittedly an adherent, he was enabling these protagonists to be at large to carry on their campaign of publishing what they believed to be the Christian truth as revealed by the Bible; he was also the holder of a liquor licence, a "privilege" granted by the Province, the profits from which, as it was seen by the authorities, he was using to promote the disturbance of settled beliefs and arouse community disaffection generally. Following discussions between the then Mr. Archambault, as the personality of the Liquor Commission, and the chief prosecuting officer in Montreal, the former, on or about November 21, telephoned to the respondent, advised him of those facts, and queried what should be done. Mr. Duplessis answered that the matter was serious and that the identity of the person furnishing bail and the liquor licencee should be put beyond doubt. A few days later, that identity being established through a private investigator, Mr. Archambault again communicated with the respondent and, as a result of what passed between them, the licence, as of December 4, 1946, was revoked.

In the meantime, about November 25, 1946, a blasting answer had come from the Witnesses. In an issue of one of the periodicals, under the heading "Quebec's Burning Hate," was a searing denunciation of what was alleged to be the savage persecution of Christian believers. Immediately instructions were sent out from the department of the Attorney-General ordering the confiscation of the issue and proceedings were taken against one Boucher charging him with publication of a seditious libel.

It is then wholly as a private citizen, an adherent of a religious group, holding a liquor licence and furnishing bail to arrested persons for no other purpose than to enable them to be released from detention pending the determination of the charges against them, and with no other relevant considerations to be taken into account, that he is involved in the issues of this controversy.

The complementary state of things is equally free from doubt. From the evidence of Mr. Duplessis and Mr. Archambault alone, it appears that the action taken by the latter as the general manager and sole member of the Commission was dictated by Mr. Duplessis as Attorney-General and Prime Minister of the province; that that step was taken as a means of bringing to a halt the activities of the Witnesses, to punish the appellant for the part he had played not only by revoking the existing licence but in declaring him barred from one "forever," and to warn others that they similarly would be stripped of provincial "privileges" if they persisted in any activity directly or indirectly related to the Witnesses and to the objectionable campaign. The respondent felt that action to be his duty, something which his conscience demanded of him; and as representing the provincial government his decision became automatically that of Mr. Archambault and the Commission....

... In these circumstances, when the *de facto* power of the Executive over its appointees at will to such a statutory public function is exercised deliberately and intentionally to destroy the vital business interests of a citizen, is there legal redress by him against the person so acting? This calls for an examination of the statutory provisions governing the issue, renewal and revocation of liquor licences and the scope of authority entrusted by law to the Attorney-General and the government in relation to the administration of the Act....

... The provisions of the statute, which may be supplemented by detailed regulations, furnish a code for the complete administration of the sale and distribution of alcoholic liquors directed by the Commission as a public service, for all legitimate purposes of the populace. It recognizes the association of wines and liquors as embellishments of food and its ritual and as an interest of the public. As put in Macbeth, the "sauce to meat is ceremony," and so we have restaurants, cafés, hotels and other places of serving food, specifically provided for in that association.

At the same time the issue of permits has a complementary interest in those so catering to the public. The continuance of the permit over the years, as in this case, not only recognizes its virtual necessity to a superior class restaurant but also its identification with the business carried on. The provisions for assignment of the permit are to this most pertinent and they were exemplified in the continuity of the business here. As its exercise continues, the economic life of the holder becomes progressively more deeply implicated with the privilege while at the same time his vocation becomes correspondingly dependent on it.

The field of licenced occupations and businesses of this nature is steadily becoming of greater concern to citizens generally. It is a matter of vital importance that a public administration that can refuse to allow a person to enter or continue a calling which, in the absence of regulation, would be free and legitimate, should be conducted with complete impartiality and integrity; and that the grounds for refusing or cancelling a permit should unquestionably be such and such only as are incompatible with the purposes envisaged by the statute: the duty of a Commission is to serve those purposes and those only. A decision to deny or cancel such a privilege lies within the "discretion" of the Commission; but that means that decision is to be based upon a weighing of considerations pertinent to the object of the administration.

In public regulation of this sort there is no such thing as absolute and untrammelled "discretion," that is that action can taken on any ground or for any reason that can be suggested to the mind of the administrator; no legislative Act can, without express language, be taken to contemplate an unlimited arbitrary power exercisable for any purpose, however capricious or irrelevant, regardless of the nature or purpose of the statute. Fraud and corruption in the Commission may not be mentioned in such statutes but they are always implied as exceptions. "Discretion" necessarily implies good faith in discharging public duty; there is always a perspective within which a statute is intended to operate; and any clear departure from its lines or objects is just as objectionable as fraud or corruption. Could an applicant be refused a permit because he had been born in another province, or because of the colour of his hair? The ordinary language of the legislature cannot be so distorted.

To deny or revoke a permit because a citizen exercises an unchallengeable right totally irrelevant to the sale of liquor in a restaurant is equally beyond the scope of the discretion conferred. There was here not only revocation of the existing permit but a declaration of a future, definitive disqualification of the appellant to obtain one: it was to be "forever." This purports to divest his citizenship status of its incident of membership in the class of those of the public to whom such a privilege could be extended. Under the statutory language here, that is not competent to the Commission and *a fortiori* to the government or the respondent: *McGillivray* v. *Kimber*. There is here an administrative tribunal which, in certain respects, is to act in a judicial manner; and even on the view of the dissenting justices in *McGillivray*, there is liability: what could be more malicious than to punish this licencee for having done what he had an absolute right to do in a matter utterly irrelevant to the *Liquor Act*? Malice in the proper sense is simply acting for a reason and purpose knowingly foreign to the administration, to which was added here the element of intentional punishment by what was virtually vocation outlawry.

It may be difficult if not impossible in cases generally to demonstrate a breach of this public duty in the illegal purpose served; there may be no means, even if proceedings against the Commission were permitted by the Attorney-General, as here they were refused, of compelling the Commission to justify a refusal or revocation or to give reasons for its action; on these questions I make no observation; but in the case before us that difficulty is not present: the reasons are openly avowed.

The act of the respondent through the instrumentality of the Commission brought about a breach of an implied public statutory duty toward the appellant; it was a gross abuse of legal power expressly intended to punish him for an act wholly irrelevant to the statute, a punishment which inflicted on him, as it was intended to do, the destruction of his economic life as a restaurant keeper within the province. Whatever may be the immunity of the Commission or its member from an action for damages, there is none in the respondent. He was under no duty in relation to the appellant and his act was an intrusion upon the functions of a statutory body. The injury done by him was a fault engaging liability within the principles of the underlying public law of Quebec: *Mostyn* v. *Fabrigas*, and under art. 1053 of the *Civil Code*. That, in the presence of expanding administrative regulation of economic activities, such a step and its consequences are to be suffered by the victim without recourse or remedy, that an administration according to law is to be superseded by action dictated by and according to the arbitrary likes, dislikes and irrelevant purposes of public officers acting beyond their duty, would signalize the beginning of disintegration of the rule of law as a fundamental postulate of our constitutional structure. An administration of licences on the highest level of fair and impartial treatment to all may be forced to follow the practice of "first come, first served," which makes the strictest observance of equal responsibility to all of even greater importance; at this stage of developing government it would be a danger of high consequence to tolerate such a departure from good faith in executing the legislative purpose. It should be added, however, that that principle is not, by this language, intended to be extended to ordinary governmental employment: with that we are not here concerned.

It was urged by Mr. Beaulieu that the respondent, as the incumbent of an office of state, so long as he was proceeding in "good faith," was free to act in a matter of this kind virtually as he pleased. The office of Attorney-

General traditionally and by statute carries duties that relate to advising the Executive, including here, administrative bodies, enforcing the public law and directing the administration of justice. In any decision of the statutory body in this case, he had no part to play beyond giving advice on legal questions arising. In that role his action should have been limited to advice on the validity of a revocation for such a reason or purpose and what that advice should have been does not seem to me to admit of any doubt. To pass from this limited scope of action to that of bringing about a step by the Commission beyond the bounds prescribed by the legislature for its exclusive action converted what was done into his personal act.

"Good faith" in this context, applicable both to the respondent and the general manager, means carrying out the statute according to its intent and for its purpose; it means good faith in acting with a rational appreciation of that intent and purpose and not with an improper intent and for an alien purpose; it does not mean for the purposes of punishing a person for exercising an unchallengeable right; it does not mean arbitrarily and illegally attempting to divest a citizen of an incident of his civil status….

1.2

Of the Extent of the Legislative Power
John Locke, *The Second Treatise* (1690)
Cambridge and New York: Cambridge University Press, 1960. Edited by Peter Laslett.
Reprinted with permission.

The great end of Mens entring into Society, being the enjoyment of their Properties in Peace and Safety, and the great instrument and means of that being the Laws establish'd in that Society; the first and fundamental positive Law of all Commonwealths, is the establishing of the Legislative Power; as the first and fundamental natural Law, which is to govern even the Legislative itself, is the preservation of the Society, and (as far as will consist with the publik good) of every person in it. This Legislative is not only the supream power of the Commonwealth, but sacred and unalterable in the hands where the Community have once placed it;…

… Though the Legislative, whether placed in one or more, whether it be always in being, or only by intervals, tho' it be the Supream Power in every Common-wealth; yet,

First, It is not, nor can possibly be absolutely Arbitrary over the Lives and Fortunes of the People. For it being but the joynt power of every Member of the Society given up to that Person, or Assembly, which is Legislator, it can be no more than those persons had in a State of Nature before they enter'd into Society, and gave up to the Community … Their Power in the utmost

Bounds of it, is limited to the publik good of the Society. It is a Power, that hath no other end but preservation, and therefore can never have a right to destroy, enslave, or designedly to impoverish the Subjects. The Obligations of the Law of Nature, cease not in Society but only in many Cases are drawn closer, and have by Humane Laws known Penalties annexed to them, to inforce their observation. Thus the Law of Nature stands as an Eternal Rule to all Men, Legislators as well as others ...

... Secondly, The Legislative, or Supream Authority, cannot assume to its self a power to Rule by extemporary Arbitrary Decrees, but is bound to dispense Justice, and decide the Rights of the Subject by promulgated standing Laws, and known Authoris'd Judges. For the Law of Nature being unwritten, and so no where to be found but in the minds of Men, they who through Passion or Interest shall mis-cite, or misapply it, cannot so easily be convinced of their mistake where there is no establish'd Judge: And so it serves not, as it ought, to determine the Rights, and fence the Properties of those that live under it, especially where every one is Judge, Interpreter, and Executioner of it too, and that in his own Case: And he that has right on his side, having ordinarily but his own single strength, hath not force enough to defend himself from Injuries, or to punish Delinquents. To avoid these Inconveniencies which disorder Mens Properties in the state of Nature, Men unite into Societies, that they may have the united strength of the whole Society to secure and defend their Properties, and may have standing Rules to bound it, by which every one may know what is his. To this end it is that Men give up all their Natural Power to the Society which they enter into, and the Community put the Legislative Power into such hands as they think fit, with this trust, that they shall be govern'd by declared Laws, or else their Peace, Quiet, and Property will still be at the same uncertainty, as it was in the state of Nature.

Absolute Arbitrary Power, or Governing without settled standing Laws, can neither of them consist with the ends of Society and Government, which Men would not quit the freedom of the state of Nature for, and tie themselves up under, were it not to preserve their Lives, Liberties and Fortunes; and by stated Rules of Right and Property to secure their Peace and Quiet ... And therefore whatever Form the Common-wealth is under, the Ruling Power ought to govern by declared and received Laws, and not by extemporary Dictates and undetermined Resolutions. For then Mankind will be in a far worse condition, than in the State of Nature, if they shall have armed one or a few Men with the joynt power of a Multitude, to force them to obey at pleasure the exorbitant and unlimited Decrees of their sudden thoughts, or unrestrain'd, and till that moment unknown Wills without having any measures set down which may guide and justifie their actions. For all the power the Government has, being only for the good of the Society, as it ought not to be *Arbitrary* and at Pleasure, so it ought to be exercised by *established and promulgated Laws*: that both the People may know their Duty, and be safe and secure within the limits of the Law, and the Rulers too kept within their due bounds, and not to be tempted, by the Power they have in their hands, to imploy it to such purposes, and by such measures, as they would not have known, and own not willingly.

... Thirdly, The Supream Power cannot take from any Man any part of his Property without his own consent....

... Fourthly, The Legislative cannot transfer the Power of Making Laws to any other hands. For it being but a delegated Power from the People, they, who have it, cannot pass it over to others. The People alone can appoint the Form of the Commonwealth, which is by Constituting the Legislative, and appointing in whose hands that shall be.

... These are the Bounds which the trust that is put in them by the Society, and the Law of God and Nature, have set to the Legislative Power of every Commonwealth, in all Forms of Government.

First, They are to govern, by promulgated establish'd Laws, not to be varied in particular Cases, but to have one Rule for Rich and Poor, for the Favourite at Court, and the Country Man at Plough.

Secondly, These Laws also ought to be designed for no other end ultimately but the good of the People.

Thirdly, they must not raise Taxes on the Property of the People, without the Consent of the People, given by themselves, or their Deputies. And this properly concerns only such Governments where the Legislative is always in being, or at least where the People have not reserv'd any part of the Legislative to Deputies, to be from time to time chosen by themselves.

Fourthly, The Legislative neither must nor can transfer the Power of making Laws to any Body else, or place it anywhere but where the People have.

1.3

The Declaration of Independence
Thomas Jefferson (1776)

When in the course of human events, it becomes necessary for one people to dissolve the political bands which have connected them with another, and to assume among the Powers of the earth, the separate and equal station to which the Laws of Nature and of Nature's God entitle them, a decent respect to the opinions of mankind requires that they should declare the causes which impell them to the separation.

We hold these truths to be self-evident, that all men are created equal, that they are endowed by their Creator with certain unalienable Rights, that among these are Life, Liberty and the pursuit of Happiness. That to secure these rights, Governments are instituted among Men, deriving their just powers from the consent of the governed, that whenever any Form of Government becomes destructive of these ends, it is the Right of the

People to alter or to abolish it, and to institute new Government, laying its foundation on such principles and organizing its powers in such form, as to them shall seem most likely to effect their Safety and Happiness. Prudence, indeed, will dictate that Governments long established should not be changed for light and transient causes; and accordingly all experience hath shown, that mankind are more disposed to suffer, while evils are sufferable, than to right themselves by abolishing the forms to which they are accustomed. But when a long train of abuses and usurpations, pursuing invariably the same Object evinces a design to reduce them under absolute Despotism, it is their right, it is their duty, to throw off such Government, and to provide new Guards for their future security....

1.4

The Rule of Law
A.V.C. Dicey
The Law of the Constitution, 7th ed. (1885), London: MacMillan. 1908, ch. 4. Reprinted with permission.

Two features have at all times since the Norman Conquest characterised the political institutions of England.

The first of these features is the omnipotence or undisputed supremacy throughout the whole country of the central government. This authority of the state or the nation was during the earlier periods of our history represented by the power of the Crown. The King was the source of law and the maintainer of order. The maxim of the Courts, *tout fuit in luy et vient de lui al commencement*, was originally the expression of an actual and undoubted fact. This royal supremacy has now passed into that sovereignty of Parliament which has formed the main subject of the foregoing chapters.

The second of these features, which is closely connected with the first, is the rule or supremacy of law. This peculiarity of our polity is well expressed in the old saw of the Courts, "*La ley est le plus haute inheritance, que le roy ad; car par la ley il même et toutes ses sujets sont rulés, et si la ley ne fuit, nul roi, et nul inheritance sera.*"

This supremacy of the law, or the security given under the English constitution to the rights of individuals looked at from various points of view, forms the subject of this part of this treatise.

Foreign observers of English manners, such for example as Voltaire, De Lolme, Tocqueville, or Gneist, have been far more struck than have Englishmen themselves with the fact that England is a country governed, as is scarcely any other part of Europe, under the rule of law; and admiration or astonishment at the legality of English habits and feeling is nowhere better expressed than in a curious passage from Tocqueville's writings, which compares the Switzerland and the England of 1836 in respect of the spirit which pervades their laws and manners.

"I am not about," he writes, "to compare Switzerland with the United States, but with Great Britain. When you examine the two countries, or even if you only pass through them, you perceive, in my judgment, the most astonishing differences between them. Take it all in all, England seems to be much more republican than the Helvetic Republic. The principal differences are found in the institutions of the two countries, and especially in their customs (*moeurs*)."…

> The Swiss do not show the love of justice which is such a strong characteristic of the English. Their Courts have no place in the political arrangements of the country, and exert no influence on public opinion. The love of justice, the peaceful and legal introduction of the judge into the domain of politics, are perhaps the most standing characteristics of a free people.

> Finally, and this really embraces all the rest, the Swiss do not show at bottom that respect for justice, that love of law, that dislike of using force, without which no free nation can exist, which strikes strangers so forcibly in England.

> I sum up these impressions in a few words.

> Whoever travels in the United States is involuntarily and instinctively so impressed with the fact that the spirit of liberty and the taste for it have pervaded all the habits of the American people, that he cannot conceive of them under any but a Republican government. In the same way it is impossible to think of the English as living under any but a free government. But if violence were to destroy the Republican institutions in most of the Swiss Cantons, it would be by no means certain that after rather a short state of transition the people would not grow accustomed to the loss of liberty. In the United States and in England there seems to be more liberty in the customs than in the laws of the people. In Switzerland there seems to be more liberty in the laws than in the customs of the country.

Tocqueville's language has a twofold bearing on our present topic. His words point in the clearest manner to the rule, predominance, or supremacy of law as the distinguishing characteristic of English institutions. They further direct attention to the extreme vagueness of a trait of national character which is as noticeable as it is hard to portray. Tocqueville, we see, is clearly perplexed how to define a feature of English manners of which he at once recognises the existence; he mingles or confuses together the habit of self-government, the love of order, the respect for justice and a legal turn of mind. All these sentiments are intimately allied, but they cannot without confusion be identified with each other. If, however, a critic as acute as Tocqueville found a difficulty in describing one of the most marked peculiarities of English life, we may safely conclude that we ourselves, whenever we talk of Englishmen as loving the government of law, or of the supremacy of law as being a characteristic of the English constitution, are using words which, though they possess a real significance, are nevertheless to most persons who employ them full of vagueness and ambiguity. If therefore we are ever to appreciate the full import of the idea denoted by the term "rule, supremacy, or predominance of law," we must first determine precisely what we mean by such expressions when we apply them to the British constitution.

When we say that the supremacy or the rule of law is a characteristic of the English constitution, we generally include under one expression at least three distinct though kindred conceptions....

... It means, in the first place, the absolute supremacy or predominance of regular law as opposed to the influence of arbitrary power, and excludes the existence of arbitrariness, of prerogative, or even of wide discretionary authority on the part of the government. Englishmen are ruled by the law, and by the law alone; a man may with us be punished for a breach of law, but he can be punished for nothing else.

It means, again, equality before the law, or the equal subjection of all classes to the ordinary law of the land administered by the ordinary Law Courts; the "rule of law" in this sense excludes the idea of any exemption of officials or others from the duty of obedience to the law which governs other citizens or from the jurisdiction of the ordinary tribunals; there can be with us nothing really corresponding to the"administrative law" (*droit administratif*) or the "administrative tribunals" (*tribunaux administratifs*) of France. The notion which lies at the bottom of the "administrative law" known to foreign countries is, that affairs or disputes in which the government or its servants are concerned are beyond the sphere of the civil Courts and must be dealt with by special and more or less official bodies. This idea is utterly unknown to the law of England, and indeed is fundamentally inconsistent with our traditions and customs.

The "rule of law," lastly, may be used as a formula for expressing the fact that with us the law of the constitution, the rules which in foreign countries naturally form part of a constitutional code, are not the source but the consequence of the rights of individuals, as defined and enforced by the Courts; that, in short, the principles of private law have with us been by the action of the Courts and Parliament so extended as to determine the position of the Crown and of its servants; thus the constitution is the result of the ordinary law of the land.

General propositions, however, as to the nature of the rule of law carry us but a very little way. If we want to understand what that principle in all its different aspects and developments really means, we must try to trace its influence throughout some of the main provisions of the constitution. The best mode of doing this is to examine with care the manner in which the law of England deals with the following topics, namely, the right to personal freedom; the right to freedom of discussion; the right of public meeting; the use of martial law; the rights and duties of the army; the collection and expenditure of the public revenue; and the responsibility of Ministers. The true nature further of the rule of law as it exists in England will be illustrated by contrast with the idea of *droit administratif*, or administrative law, which prevails in many continental countries. These topics will each be treated of in their due order. The object, however, of this treatise, as the reader should remember, is not to provide minute and full information, *e.g.* as to the *Habeas Corpus* Acts, or other enactments protecting the liberty of the subject; but simply to show that these leading heads of constitutional law, which have been enumerated, these "articles," so to speak of the constitution, are both governed by, and afford illustrations of, the supremacy throughout English institutions of the law of the land. If at some future day the law of the constitution should be codified, each of the topics I have mentioned would be dealt with by the sections of the code.

1.5

The Independence of the Judiciary
W.R. Lederman

This article is reprinted as Reading 5.1.

1.6

Liberal versus Post-liberal Constitutionalism:
Applying the *Charter* to Civil Society

Thomas M.J. Bateman
Political Studies, Augustana University College

Introduction

In their study of the new politics of the Canadian *Charter of Rights and Freedoms*, F.L. Morton and Rainer Knopff contend that a revolution is afoot, led, with active state assistance, by a coterie of interest groups and professional castes they call the "Court Party." They muster persuasive evidence to demonstrate that this political configuration has permeated not only the departments of the state but also the offices of the academy and the pages of the law journals.

Revolutions require more than the storming of the palace. They require a fundamental alteration of the principles of the regime. A revolution changes the moral fabric of the polity, reorienting citizens' habits and preferences. Is there evidence that the Court Party has proceeded beyond the occupation of the palace toward an alteration of the lives of citizens? In other words, have *Charter* norms penetrated civil society – those myriad institutions like family, workplace, church, school, and fraternal associations – where people live outside of the direct influence of the state?

This question begs others. What is the purpose of a *Charter* anyway? At bottom, is the *Charter* designed to limit action the state can take with respect to civil society and individual citizens? Or is it intended to announce a set of norms for all of society to embody? In one sense, these questions pose a false choice, since a constitution seeking to limit the scope of state action reflects principles informing the shape and purpose of a polity. But in another sense the questions imply a distinction between two different understandings of constitutionalism. The first, traditional liberal constitutionalism, distinguishes state from society and understands the constitution as a way to protect the latter from the former. The second is a more recent twentieth century variant urging the application of constitutional principles of liberty, equality, and due process on institutions regardless of their connections to the state.

The Supreme Court of Canada has been divided on the purpose of the *Charter*. More basically, it has been divided on the kind of constitutionalism the *Charter* should embody. Early *Charter* decisions reflect a traditional constitutionalism. But later decisions became longer, more complex, more riven with dissents based on divergent interpretive principles. One of the sources of divisions was a disquiet about traditional liberal constitutionalism. Decisions in the late 1980s and 1990s began to hint at a new understanding of the *Charter*. Judges are increasingly willing to apply the *Charter* to institutions beyond the state, and increasingly disposed to apply *Charter* norms "into" society, converting informal relationships into more formal, rule-bound ones based on judicially articulated principles of fairness, non-discrimination, and individual autonomy. However, the Court has not abandoned liberal constitutionalism for the new version. It goes back and forth, sensitive, apparently, to the circumstances of particular cases and to changes in Court personnel. If and when the Supreme Court of Canada finally drops liberal constitutionalism for a new post-liberal constitutionalism, the *Charter* revolution will have approached its consummation.

Post-Liberal Constitutionalism

Liberal constitutionalism is a set of political attitudes, an ideology, centred on the notion that legitimate government is limited, controlled government. Constitutionalism in the end is a counsel of political restraint on the part of all institutions of government. Constitutional government is constrained in what it can and should do. It is premised on a distinction between state and society. While a properly functioning society needs government to maintain order, enforce contracts, protect against external military threat, and address various forms of market failure, society functions best when citizens are free from the vicissitudes of arbitrary, ill-considered state meddling. Of course, ambitious and unscrupulous persons are found in government as well as civil society, and so the problem arises as to how the government not only can control excesses in civil society but also excesses of its own. And because the state has a monopoly on the legitimate use of coercion, it presents a unique threat to society. State power can threaten society as much as preserve it.

Constitutions are addressed to this problem. Constitutional mechanisms are all about "countervailance": power can only be checked by power, and the properly constructed constitution provides a set of checks and balances ensuring that the power of one state actor or state institution can be checked by the countervailing power of another. The doctrine of the "separation of powers" (more accurately, separate institutions sharing powers), for which the American Constitution is justly famous, is a cardinal constitutional idea. A judicially enforced bill of rights, of more recent vintage, is another.

In the beginning, bills of rights were intended to declare an absolute limit to what the state could do. They were a defence of individual persons and civil society against illegitimate state action. As the franchise was expanded and governments became sensitive to majority opinion, the bill of rights was upheld as an important bulwark against the reckless rule of the majority. So bills of rights were about the protection of property against expropriation, the protection of the due process rights (like the presumption of innocence until proven guilty) of accused offenders against overzealous police, and the protection of eccentric writers and religionists against majoritarian pressures to conform. In all these cases, the bill of rights marked out a region of non-interference around civil society beyond which the state was not to trespass. This liberal constitutionalism both reflected and supported a distinction between private and public realms. If you want to exclude women from your fraternal organization's membership, the liberal constitutionalist may resent your sexism but would defend your right to discriminate in this fashion in your private dealings.

Liberal constitutionalism has been attacked in a variety of ways. Critics argue that it relies on a right-wing ideology stressing the self-correcting, utility-maximizing wonders of the market which empirical evidence fails to confirm. When democratically elected governments sought to address market failure and unacceptable inequalities of wealth, judges in the early twentieth century vetoed such policies on increasingly anachronistic liberal constitutionalist principles, claiming employment matters were private relations beyond the reach of government. It is also claimed that the distinction between public and private realms is likewise an ideological construction that historically reinforced the subordination of women. Power is a problem not just of the state but of all manner of institutions: corporations, unions, and families. Confining principles of equality, liberty, and due process to the public, governmental realm does nothing to liberate women imprisoned in the domestic, "private" realm beyond the reach of such constitutional principles.

Criticisms like these led some to discard the liberal constitutionalist enterprise altogether. Others sought to revise liberal constitutionalism, to develop a new kind of constitutionalism which would provide the intellectual and moral foundation for the application of judicially enforced constitutional norms to institutions of civil society. The primary virtue of this new constitutionalism is that the application of constitutional norms "downward" into society need not await the action of the government. As the political history of liberal democracies of the twentieth century indicates, the line between state and society, public and private, has become fluid, subject to the willingness of state action to convert a formerly private matter into a public matter subject to legislative control. But what if the state refuses so to act?

Post-liberal constitutionalism is the solution. Judges need not await the formation of positive public policy. At the urging of a group or even an individual litigant, the private can be converted into the constitutional, subject to constitutional norms. For the new constitutionalists, the problem becomes: what regions of private choice should be exempt from judicial inquiry? If I must serve food at my restaurant to anyone who enters, can I nonetheless be allowed to decide on my marriage partner based on my racist preference for people of a certain skin colour or cultural background? Or are such manifestations of discriminatory preference incompatible with a democratic society, which requires the universal application of equality norms?

Constitutionalism and the Canadian *Charter*

An early draft of the Canadian *Charter* contained what is called an application provision, a section indicating what entities were bound by the terms of the *Charter*. *Charter* application is a threshold litigants initially have to clear before the courts can hear a *Charter* claim. The draft provision was crucially ambiguous and seemed to declare that not only government but "all matters within the authority of" government would be caught by *Charter* rights. According to three participants in the patriation debate,

> Since all the things that private citizens do are within the legislative jurisdiction of one level of government or another, the wording of the new application section turned the *Charter* not only into a constitutional document which restrained government, but a constitutional set of norms relating to the whole of social activity within the country. This was a radical transformation of the nature of the *Charter*.

Before the final draft was approved by the premiers, section 32 of the *Charter* was reworded to allay fears that the *Charter* was designed to apply to civil society institutions as well as the state proper. Representatives of the federal Department of Justice testifying before a special parliamentary committee on the constitution in 1981 were fairly clear that the *Charter* was to conform to the principles of a traditional constitutionalism: it would bind the government, not the whole of society. So settled did this issue seem to be that several constitutional scholars could insist immediately after the *Charter's* entrenchment that it was a liberal constitutionalist instrument. As late as 1992, responding to suggestions that the *Charter* was transferring major social policy powers to the courts and undermining democracy in Canada, Peter Russell stressed the constraints on judicial decision making, a major one being the limits of *Charter* application:

> ... the *Charter* applies only to governments and legislatures. *Charter* rights and *Charter* freedoms can be claimed only against the actions of governments or legislatures. However the main barrier to full enjoyment or exercise of some rights, particularly equality rights, is not government action but government inaction in responding to problems emanating from the private sector and the very structure of society.

Russell's confidence is misplaced. While the Supreme Court of Canada has not rejected liberal constitutionalism, it is in the throes of a clash of constitutionalisms, uncomfortable with aspects of liberal constitutionalism but apparently wary of the consequences of traveling the new path of universal application of constitutional norms.

Toward a Post-Liberal Constitutionalism

The Supreme Court's *Charter* jurisprudence reveals several means by which liberal constitutionalism has been challenged: the expansion of the definition of "government" for the purposes of section 32 interpretation; the application of "*Charter* values" to the development of private law; and the development of a doctrine of "inaction" and "underinclusivity" in respect to section 15 equality rights claims. These mechanisms often arise together in the same cases but are analytically distinct and will be treated as such.

Defining "Government"

Section 32 of the *Charter* declares in part that the *Charter* applies "to the parliament and government of Canada ... and to the legislature and government of each province." How do we define government? In the era of the administrative state in which public expenditures consume over 40 percent of the GDP, it is hard to discern where the state stops and society begins. Equally, it is hard to determine when state influence over an entity becomes so overwhelming that the entity is then subsumed under the definition of government for the purposes of section 32. And is it possible for a part of an entity to be governmental for the purposes of section 32, while other parts of an entity escape *Charter* application?

Such issues were squarely presented to the Supreme Court for the first time in *McKinney* v. *University of Guelph* (1990). Eight university professors were subject to mandatory retirement according to university policies or collective agreements negotiated with faculty associations. They did not want to retire so they challenged (unsuccessfully) the mandatory retirement policy on the basis that it constituted age discrimination contrary to section 15 of the *Charter*. A crucial issue was whether the *Charter* applied to universities. For the majority, Gerard LaForest argued that universities are not sufficiently governmental to be caught by the *Charter*. Though they receive public moneys, are established by legislation, and are subject to myriad rules and regulations, they are, he wrote, independent civil society institutions. In order for an entity to be considered "government" for the purposes of section 32, there must be a clear nexus between government and the entity, and the entity must be subject to control and compulsion. It must be an instrument of public policy.

While universities did not qualify under this test, the Court has ruled that other entities like community colleges do fall within the *Charter's* reach. Even community-based organizations like an Ontario sexual assault counseling centre was considered to be subject to the *Charter* by virtue only of its receipt of government grants.

Even if an entity is considered non-governmental, it may still be caught by the *Charter*. In *Stoffman* (1990), the Court held that the Vancouver General Hospital is not subject to the *Charter*. But in *Eldridge* (1997), the Court, in partial retreat, held that while an entity *in toto* may not be governmental, some of the acts which it performs may. Accordingly, the failure to provide interpretation services for deaf patients was considered contrary to section 15 of the *Charter*.

In addition, insofar as human rights legislation affects employment matters in private organizations, those matters are indirectly subject to *Charter* scrutiny. Human rights legislation, like all other legislation, is clearly subject to *Charter* scrutiny and courts have brought it into conformity with the *Charter* when they have found it constitutionally wanting. Even when a court has defined an institution to be non-governmental for purposes of *Charter* application, if the impugned activity (e.g., employment) of that institution is governed by human rights laws, then the *Charter* applies to the entity indirectly through the instrumentality of that law.

For example, in the *McKinney* case just discussed, whatever the status of universities for the purposes of *Charter* application, the fact that universities as employers are subject to the constraints of human rights legislation means that they are indirectly subject to *Charter* values. Universities are subject to human rights law; human rights law is subject to the *Charter*; ergo, universities are subject, albeit indirectly, to the *Charter*.

The *Charter* and Private Law

While legislation as positive acts of government are clearly subject to *Charter* scrutiny, courts do not simply interpret legislation. They are the custodians of the common law, a massive body of legal rules developed incrementally on a case-by-case basis independently of the legislative action of government. Legislation in an area of common law regulation has the effect of superceding common law rules; in the absence of state action, the common law prevails. Common law rules govern relationships between private persons – persons as contractors for goods or services or as tortfeasors, for example. Common law as a result is often called private law.

Should private law conform to *Charter* rights? The Supreme Court has been definitive on the point: yes and no. In the early, complicated case of *Dolphin Delivery* (1986), the Court was faced with a challenge to the constitutionality of a common law ban on secondary picketing. If a union is striking against company *A*, and *A* tries to stay in business by subcontracting its work out to company *B*, can the union conduct "secondary picketing" of *B*? While labour legislation has overturned much of the common law of employment, the legislation governing this particular case was silent on the matter. The union objected that the common law restriction on secondary picketing was contrary to the *Charter's* protection of freedom of expression.

The Supreme Court, seeming to endorse liberal constitutionalist ideals, said that the *Charter* does not apply to the private law, even though private law is enforced by the courts which, on a common sense reading, are state institutions: "To regard a court order as an element of governmental intervention necessary to invoke the *Charter* would ... widen the scope of *Charter* application to virtually all private litigation." This was considered unacceptable. But the devil was in the details. First, the Court indicated, the *Charter* applies to private law when the government is party to a dispute. Second, as Justice McIntyre wrote for the Court:

> Where ... private party "A" sues private party "B" relying on the common law and where no act of government is relied upon to support the action, the *Charter* will not apply. I should make it clear, however, that this is a distinct issue from the question whether the judiciary ought to apply and develop the principles of the common law in a manner consistent with the *fundamental values* enshrined in the Constitution. The answer to this question must be in the affirmative. In this sense, then, the *Charter* is far from irrelevant to private litigants whose disputes will be decided at common law.

So while *Charter rights* may not apply to private legal disputes, *Charter values* do. Subsequent case law suggests that there is precious little difference in practice between *Charter* rights and *Charter* values. When the Court wanted to alter common law rules to make them more egalitarian, *Charter* values enabled it to do so. In *Salituro* (1991), the common law rule that a person was incompetent to testify against his or her spouse was altered, with reliance upon *Charter* values, to allow that spouses irreconcilably separated were competent to do so.

In *Dobson* (1999), the Court was asked to develop tort law to allow a child to sue its mother for injuries sustained in a car accident *prior* to being born. Since the case raised the issue of the rights of a (yet) unborn child against his or her mother, *Dobbs* had implications for the issue of abortion. (LEAF, for example, intervened against the claim of the child.) Here a majority of the Court held that, among other things, the *Charter* value of gender equality militated against such a development.

Charter values constitute a package of interpretive possibilities for judges more limitless than even the vaguely worded provisions of the *Charter* themselves. Litigants may be forgiven for their inability to guess whether *Charter* values will work for them or against them when they approach the bench. They can be assured, though, that regardless of positive state legislative action, the *Charter* will reach their private legal disputes.

State Inaction and Underinclusivity

Liberal constitutionalist theory suggests that the *Charter* is triggered only when the state acts. In the absence the state action, the *Charter* does not apply. This comports with the previous discussion of the common law; whatever is not made a matter of public law remains the province of the common law. This view obviously constrains *Charter* application. And for critics of liberal constitutionalism, this is precisely the problem. For them, *Charter* norms, if they are to be given society-wide application, must be enforced by courts whether or not the state acts. At the distant but logical extreme, this implies a full-scale jurocracy, with popularly elected legislatures becoming irrelevant for public policy purposes.

The Courts have not gone this far. But they have not shied away from declaring that when the state does enact programs that provide benefits to citizens, it cannot leave out persons who can claim the protection of section 15 of the *Charter*. In its 1999 ruling in *Law* v. *Canada*, the Court declared, "Underinclusive ameliorative legislation that excludes from its scope the members of a historically disadvantaged group will rarely escape the charge of discrimination."

It is worth pausing to consider the significance of this. Almost all of the thousands of laws and policies enforced by the state single out certain groups of people for special treatment. In this sense, almost every public policy discriminates against someone. Post-secondary students are entitled to tax deductions denied non-post-secondary students. Murderers are treated differently under the Criminal Code than are those convicted of manslaughter. Parents who send their children to daycares can claim favourable tax treatment while those who forego income to stay at home with their children cannot. Older people are entitled to state benefits to the exclusion of younger people. The ability to marry is confined to heterosexuals and monogamists. Adults are not allowed to have sex with children. Incestuous relationships are excluded from definitions of family. The list goes on. The point is that public policy is almost always selective. When is selectivity constitutionally benign and when is it constitutionally offensive?

In *Schachter* (1992), the father of a newborn sought parental leave benefits provided under the terms of the UI act. Benefits were available to natural mothers and adoptive parents but not natural fathers. Schachter claimed a section 15 violation. He won.

In *Miron* v. *Trudel* (1995), the issue was the restrictive definition of spouse in an insurance policy. Trudel was injured by an uninsured driver and as a result could no longer support his common law wife and family. His only recourse was to apply for benefits from his common law wife's insurance plan. The plan was held to extend to legally married spouses only. A 5–4 majority of the Supreme Court found this unconstitutionally underinclusive of common law spouses, granted the *Charter* claim, and read in common law spouse.

The *Eldridge* case, discussed earlier, concerned the failure of medical authorities acting under the terms of B.C. legislation to provide sign language interpretation services to deaf persons receiving medical care in that province. Eldridge was a deaf, pregnant woman to whom publicly funded signing services were denied because authorities did not consider them "medically required services" under the legislation. For a unanimous Court, LaForest found sign language interpretation so closely intertwined with the effective provision of medical services that it falls within the legislative definition of "medically required services." That provision, wrote LaForest, "impugns the state's failure to correct even those disadvantages it has not itself created." As an effects-oriented protection, section 15 prohibits "adverse effects of a facially neutral benefits scheme." Section 15 "makes no distinction between laws that impose unequal burdens and those that deny unequal benefits."

Perhaps the greatest strides have been made in relation to the equality rights of homosexuals. In *Knodel* v. *British Columbia* (1991), the issue before the B.C. Court of Appeal was the "restrictive" heterosexual definition of spouse in an employee benefits package for nurses. The homosexual partner of a nurse sought benefits on the nurse's death and was refused. The court found that definition of spouse to be unconstitutionally underinclusive of homosexual relationships. When the government "takes on an obligation and provides a benefit, section 15(1) makes denial of that benefit to other groups questionable." To remedy the defect, the court defined spouse inclusively.

The Supreme Court added sexual orientation to section 15's list of prohibited grounds of discrimination in *Egan* (1995) but narrowly upheld the heterosexual definition of spouse for the purposes of eligibility of spousal benefits under the Old Age Security Act. But in *Vriend* (1998), two years later, the Court rendered a stunning victory for homosexuals. Delwin Vriend was an instructor at a private Christian university college; when it was learned that he was gay, he was relieved of his duties. He protested to the Alberta Human Rights Commission but was told that the AHRC could not help him because the legislation did not prohibit discrimination on the basis of sexual orientation. Vriend then turned his sights on the Alberta government, alleging in court that the legislation was unconstitutionally underinclusive of this particular prohibited ground of discrimination. In other words, while the Alberta government acted to prohibit employment discrimination on some grounds (e.g., sex, age, colour, religion), it failed to include sexual orientation in that list. It therefore deprived Vriend and other homosexuals of the benefit of Alberta's human rights policy. The Supreme Court agreed with Vriend, and "read in" (i.e., judicially added) sexual orientation to the *Alberta Human Rights Act.*

Vriend provokes several questions. First, what if the state intended to leave sexual orientation out of the legislation? This was an easy question to answer. The Court heard evidence that the Alberta legislature considered and rejected proposed amendments to the law to add sexual orientation. For the Court, this was evidence enough that the legislature "acted" (though not in the form of legislation) to exclude homosexuals from a state benefit. Second, does *Vriend* mean that human rights legislation must mirror the protections of section 15 of the *Charter*? It seems so, Supreme Court comments in *Vriend* notwithstanding. An interesting problem with this is that section 15 prohibits discrimination on the basis of group characteristics that are unlisted in the provision. The courts since 1989 have added a few "analogous" grounds like citizenship and sexual orientation. It would seem that human rights legislation would be subject to judicial amendment each time the courts add a new prohibited ground to section 15 of the *Charter*. Critics claimed that this aspect of *Vriend* violated the principles of both federalism and democratic accountability.

Buoyed by their victory in *Vriend*, homosexual advocacy groups pressed the courts to declare unconstitutional underinclusive definitions of spouse in Ontario's *Family Law Act*. Ontario's NDP government in the early 1990s introduced legislation to give homosexual couples in conjugal relationships many of the same rights (and obligations) accorded heterosexual ones. That controversial legislation was defeated in a free vote by the legislature. But what cannot be done by the legislature may be done through the courts. *In M.v.H.* (1999), the Supreme Court essentially enacted the earlier legislation. The Court ruled that the omission of the right to sue for spousal support (in the event of a breakdown of a same-sex relationship) meant that the Family Law Act discriminated against homosexuals, contrary to section 15 of the *Charter*.

In the political economy of recognition and dignity, *M.v.H.* signals a major shift of political resources to homosexual advocacy groups. For all but one justice in the majority, evidence of legislative opposition to the extension of spousal rights to homosexuals did not figure in the section 15 analysis. It was simply the underinclusion of homosexual couples and the effects on their circumstances that governed the case.

...

Section 15 jurisprudence in the 1990s has been concerned in part with the development of an underinclusivity doctrine. In its section 15 jurisprudence, the Supreme Court has rejected the older notion that it is state action that triggers *Charter* review. It has not yet accepted the full logic of such a move, which is to enforce a constitutional standard of public policy in the complete absence of evidence of state action.

...

Conclusion

When and if the Court does adopt such a post-liberal understanding of constitutionalism, the *Charter* revolution of which Morton and Knopff have written would be consummated.

1.7

Key Terms

Concepts

"the rule of law"
per legem terrae
natural right theory of government
"All men are by nature equal"
natural law
positive law
"written constitution"
"limited government"
liberal constitutionalism
post-liberal constitutionalism
civil society
judicial review
"unwritten constitution"
"declaration of incompatibility"
parliamentary or Westminster form of democracy
"Separation of powers" or American form of democracy
judicial independence
under-inclusive
state action

Institutions, Events and Documents

Magna Carta (1215)
Habeas Corpus Act (1679)
"Glorious Revolution of 1688"
John Locke, *Second Treatise on Government* (1690)
Declaration of Independence (1776)
Constitution of the United States of America (1788)
U.S. Bill of Rights (1790)
Constitution Act, 1867 (British North American Act, 1867)
A.V.C. Dicey, *The Law of the Constitution* (1885)
Roncarelli v. *Duplessis* (1959)
1960 *Canadian Bill of Rights*
Canadian Charter of Rights and Freedoms (1982)
European Convention for the Protection of Human Rights
    and Fundamental Freedoms (1950)
Eldridge v. *British Columbia* (1997)
Vriend v. *Alberta* (1998)

Political Jurisprudence 2

This chapter addresses a deceptively simple set of questions. What do judges do? Do they just interpret and apply the law? Or, in the process of interpreting and applying the law, do the judges also "make law"? If the answer to this second question is yes, then how do courts differ from legislatures? Ultimately, these questions take on a normative character: Should judges restrict themselves to declaring what the law is, as determined by statute and precedent? Or if a judge finds the relevant statutes and precedents inadequate or even "wrong," is the judge free to "make new law"?

These are old and much-debated questions, and they have been given very different answers by scholars and judges. There is some truth in each of these conflicting answers because the character of the judicial process varies from nation to nation, and within a single nation. What is true of trial courts is not applicable to appeal courts, and what is true for torts and contracts does not apply to constitutional law. Different judges on the same court may conduct themselves according to different judicial philosophies. Professor Ian Greene's research suggests such differences between courts and among judges currently exist in Canada (Reading 5.7).

Canadian legal and political thought has traditionally held that judges do not, and should not, "make law" in any significant sense. "The law" has been portrayed as something that already exists "out there," and the role of the judge is merely to find or "discover" its meaning and declare it to the interested parties. This view of judicial decision-making is known as the "declaratory model" and is closely associated with the British common law tradition from which it evolved. In both Britain and Canada, this view of the judges as exercising "neither force nor will, but only judgement," has been reinforced by the practice of parliamentary supremacy and the theory of legal positivism.

The parliamentary model of government stresses that only the representative legislature can "make law" because only the elected legislators have the consent of the people to govern. This understanding of just laws comes directly from the equality-consent dimension of liberal political theory, as articulated by John Locke in the preceding chapter. According to its logic, it would be unjust and unjustifiable for judges to "make law," since judges are neither representative of nor responsible to the citizenry. This precise and limiting understanding of the judicial function has been reinforced by the theory of legal positivism. Legal positivism defines law as "the command of the sovereign," in this case, the Queen in Parliament. This definition stresses the form and function of the law, not its content. The notion of judicial law-making is logically incompatible with this view.

Note that contemporary British jurists such as Professor Conor Gearty no longer subscribe to a strict theory of legal positivism (Reading 5.8). Writing in 2001, Gearty acknowledged a law-making function for British judges in their development of the common law and in statutory interpretation. Still, Gearty stresses the interstitial and incremental nature of such judicial law-making. Consistent with British legal tradition, Gearty also expresses concerns about the expansion of judicial law-making under the newly adopted *European Convention of Human Rights*. Stressing concerns about the unrepresentative character of the British judiciary and (the lack of) accountability, Gearty declares his "strong hankering for a very limited judicial function." This view was dominant in Canadian legal culture in the 1960s and 1970s and explains the judges' reluctance to do much with the 1960 *Bill of Rights*. In the decade following the adoption of the *Charter of Rights*, however, this traditional view of the judicial function has been marginalized.

The "declaratory model" of judging is drawn from British experience. This explains both its original dominance of Canadian jurisprudence and also its more recent decline. Greene's research (Reading 5.7) indicates that a majority of Canadian judges still view their work as "finding not making law," but that this is hardly a unanimous view. As we saw in Chapter One, Canada differs from Great Britain by being a federal not a unitary state, and by having the boundaries of federalism defined in a "written constitution" – the *Constitution Act, 1867*.[1] Because of this difference, Canadian courts and judges have had to fulfill an important function unknown in British legal experience – judicial review. Since its creation in 1875, the Supreme Court of Canada has acted as the "neutral umpire" of the federal division of powers between Ottawa and the provinces.

A constitutional law of federalism is political in a way other kinds of law are not. It defines and therefore limits the law-making powers of rival levels of government. Questions of constitutional law often arise in the context of heated political struggles between Ottawa and one or more provinces. Political passions run high, and all of Canada awaits the Court's decision with interest. Major government policy often hangs in the balance. In such circumstances, it becomes difficult to believe that judges are not aware of the policy consequences of their "legal" decisions and that these decisions are not influenced by the anticipation of their consequences. Indeed,

---

1 Originally known and still commonly referred to as the *British North America Act*.

in 1985, the former Chief Justice of the Supreme Court of Canada, Brian Dickson, cautioned his fellow judges against adopting a "mechanical legalism," advising them instead to "be aware of the underlying principles and practical consequences of questions before [them], paying close attention to the policy aspects of each issue."[2] Under these circumstances, final appeal courts inevitably come to be regarded as hybrid institutions, part-judicial, part-political.

In view of this dimension of Canadian law, it is not surprising that Canadian jurists began to be attracted by the "legal realism" theory of judging that had developed in the United States in the early decades of this century. The Americans had lived with the practice of judicial review since 1803. Moreover, the American Supreme Court not only exercised judicial review over the boundaries of federalism but also enforced the more absolute limitations of the *Bill of Rights*. By the end of the nineteenth century, the U.S. Supreme Court had come to play an influential role in the major political issues of the day. The traditional "declaratory model" of judging, inherited with the common law from Great Britain, seemed to provide a less and less satisfactory explanation of what American courts and judges were actually doing in the area of constitutional law. A new generation of American jurists began to rethink and reformulate the relationship between judges and law. Through the writings of men like Oliver Wendell Holmes, Benjamin Cardozo, and Roscoe Pound, the "legal realism" theory of judging was developed.

The legal realists stressed the creative and personal connection between judges and law. Holmes declared that the law is "the prophecies of what the courts will do in fact, and nothing more pretentious."[3] Pound and Cardozo extended Holmes's critique by elaborating the subjective, personal dimension of judging. The key to this analysis was the "unfinished" quality of law, and the resulting discretion and freedom of the judge to give the law its practical meaning when applied to a novel set of circumstances.

The inescapably personal dimension of judging is explored in former Justice Bertha Wilson's discussion of the question, "Will women judges make a difference?" (Reading 2.5). Writing in 1990, Justice Wilson argued that, in certain areas of "judge-made law," gender does make a difference and claimed that women judges bring a "uniquely feminine perspective" to certain issues.

Wilson's claims are partially supported by Candice White's subsequent research (Reading 2.6). White did a statistical study of the *Charter* voting records of what at the time (1997) were the three women judges to have

---

2 "Dickson discourages mechanical legalism," *The Globe and Mail*, Oct. 5, 1985, A4. This message seems somewhat inconsistent with Dickson's opinion in the 1976 case of *Harrison* v. *Carswell* (see Reading 2.2) and suggests that Dickson may have changed his mind.

3 *Harvard Law Review* 10 (1897), p. 39.

served on the Supreme Court of Canada: Justices Wilson, Claire l'Heureux-Dubé, and Beverley McLachlin. White's study found no significant gender differences in *Charter* cases dealing with legal rights; some differences in the fundamental freedoms cases; and very significant differences in the equality rights cases. In the latter, the three women justices' mean level of support for equality claims was two and half times higher than the mean for the male judges – 67 per cent versus 26 per cent. White also found that the three women justices were almost twice as likely to write dissenting opinions than their male counterparts (21 per cent versus 11 per cent).

American studies of gender differences in judging confirmed similar trends but also found that (for federally appointed judges) the partisan affiliation of the president making the appointments is also a relevant factor. This is not surprising, given the sharp conflict over federal judicial appointments between Republicans and Democrats since the U.S. Supreme Court's *Roe* v. *Wade* abortion decision in 1973. The Democrats have favoured judges who espouse a "noninterpretivist" approach to constitutional interpretation while the Republicans have supported judges with a "strict constructionist" (i.e., interpretivist) philosophy.

Justice Wilson's acceptance of the argument that the gender of a judge may influence his or her decisions reveals the extent to which legal realism has triumphed. However, acceptance of the legal realist view still leaves open the question whether this is desirable or should be encouraged, especially in appeal court judges and especially in the area of constitutional law. The first generation of legal realists were almost all supporters of judicial self-restraint and deference to legislative judgments, while today many of their followers support a more activist exercise of judicial review.

The preceding example of Justice Wilson notwithstanding, Canadian jurists were initially unreceptive to the theory of judicial realism, which they considered an American idiosyncrasy. Predictably, it was the constitutional law decisions of Canada's first final court of appeal – the Judicial Committee of the Privy Council (JCPC) – that provoked the first appearance of judicial realism in Canadian legal and political thought. Beginning in the 1890s, the JCPC made a series of important constitutional decisions that progressively narrowed the scope of the legislative powers of the federal government. This trend reached a climax in the mid-thirties, when the Privy Council struck down a number of federal "New Deal" programs designed to cope with the economic and social devastation of the Great Depression. This provoked an angry reaction among some Canadian leaders, culminating in the *O'Connor Report* (1939) to the Senate, which advocated the abolition of appeals to the JCPC. The *O'Connor Report* argued that questions of Canadian constitutional law could be better answered by Canadian judges, judges with first-hand familiarity with the political and economic realities of Canadian life. Implicit in this argument was a tacit acceptance of the legal realist view that the personal background and political formation of a judge is an important factor in his legal decision-making. Because the goal of this movement was to make the Supreme Court the final court of appeal "of and for Canadians," it came to be known as "judicial nationalism."[4]

In 1949, appeals to the JCPC were abolished, and the Supreme Court of Canada became the final and exclusive court of appeal for Canada. But this has not stopped the debate over the nature of the judicial process in Canada. The adoption in 1960 of the *Bill of Rights* stimulated new debate on this old issue. The broadly worded prohibitions of the *Bill of Rights* – such as freedom of religion and equality before the law – seemed to invite and even require judicial choice and creativity in giving them practical application. By and large, the Canadian judiciary declined this invitation. Stressing the statutory (as opposed to constitutional) character of the 1960 *Bill of Rights* and the absence of any explicit qualification of the tradition of parliamentary supremacy, the Supreme Court gave a limited and traditional interpretation to the bill's major provisions. Partly in response to the courts' cautious use of the *Bill of Rights*, it was superseded in 1982 by the *Charter of Rights and Freedoms*. A constitutionally entrenched document that applies to both levels of government, the *Charter* raises the issue of proper judicial decision-making in an even more pointed and pressing manner.

The competing views of proper judicial conduct are the subject of Paul Weiler's 1967 article, "Two Models of Judicial Decision-Making" (Reading 2.1). One – the "adjudication of disputes" model – stresses the traditional understanding of the judicial function and the institutional characteristics that distinguish the judicial process from the legislative process. Weiler's second model, the "policy-making" model, asserts that there is no essential difference between judges and legislators, that "they make policy, or legislate, through essentially the same mode of reasoning."

Weiler's two models are not coterminous with the declaratory and judicial realist theories of judging. While most informed observers now reject the declaratory model of judging, acceptance of judicial realism does not require acceptance of Weiler's "policy-making" model. While conceding that the personal characteristics of judges do influence their legal choices, many Canadian commentators continue to stress the "interstitial" character of judicial law-making. They argue that, while some judicial law-making may be an inevitable by-product of judicial interpretation, it is and should remain secondary to the main function of adjudication of disputes. While this prescription for minimizing the law-making potential of judges may seem to rob the courts of influence, Peter Russell argues that it may do more to preserve judicial authority. Russell notes that the *O'Connor Report* and the increased acknowledgment of judicial power in Canadian legal culture resulted in a loss of authority for the Supreme Court in Quebec. "Just as nationalist Canadian

---

4 See Peter H. Russell, "Judicial Power in Canada's Political Culture," in *Courts and Trial: A Multidisciplinary Approach*, ed. M.L. Friedland (Toronto: University of Toronto Press, 1975), p. 75. This article was reprinted in the first edition of this book.

jurists denounced the British judges for their insensitive interpretation of the Canadian constitution, nationalist lawyers in Quebec resumed their protest against the Supreme Court of Canada's insensitive interpretation of Quebec's Civil Code."[5] Russell's thesis that "less may be more" is especially relevant to judicial decision-making under the 1982 *Charter of Rights*. While the *Charter* clearly expands the potential for judicial law-making, the section 33 legislative override explicitly arms governments with a power to fight back against perceived abuses of judicial review. Is it by accident that Quebec has had more statutes declared invalid under the *Charter* than any other province and has also been the province to make the most use of the section 33 override?[6]

Weiler's model provides a conceptual framework through which we can better understand the differences between Canadian, British, and American judicial process, and better evaluate recommendations that Canadian judges adopt a greater "policy-making" role. The "two models" analysis also demonstrates that different institutional consequences follow from the two different conceptions of judging. Traditional Canadian practices regarding judicial recruitment, judicial independence, jurisdiction, access to the courts, judicial fact-finding, and modes of legal argument – were all premised on the understanding that judges do not, and should not, "make law." As Canadian judges have moved away from the "adjudication of disputes" approach and toward a greater "policy-making" role, especially since the 1982 adoption of the *Charter*, the continued adequacy of traditional institutional practices has been challenged. Weiler's elaborations of the different institutional consequences of the two models are not included in this chapter but are discussed in the introductions to the subsequent chapters. We can thus use Weiler's analytical framework to understand the traditional aspects of the judicial process and to evaluate the changes that have occurred in recent decades.

The next two readings demonstrate the contemporary character of the debate over the proper role of the judiciary in Canadian law and politics. In the 1976 case of *Harrison* v. *Carswell*, we find a sharp disagreement over proper judicial role between the then Chief Justice of Canada, the late Bora Laskin, and his successor as Chief Justice, Brian Dickson (Reading 2.2). The principal difference between Dickson's majority opinion and Laskin's dissent is not about the law but about the limits of the Supreme Court's responsibility. Both agree that there is a serious legal problem raised by the *Harrison* case. Laskin argues that the Supreme Court should solve it, while Dickson maintains that law reform is the business of the legislatures not the courts.

Michael Mandel's analysis of the Supreme Court's decision in the 1981 *Patriation Reference* provides strong evidence to support the judicial realist school (Reading 2.3). The Supreme Court's decision in the *Patriation Reference* was arguably the most important it has ever made. It broke the political deadlock between the federal government and eight of the ten provinces

---

5 Russell, p. 75.
6 See Readings 11.5 and 13.3.

and led to the adoption of the *Constitution Act, 1982*, of which the *Charter of Rights* was an integral part. At stake was whether Prime Minister Trudeau's plan to "patriate" the constitution unilaterally – that is, add an amending formula and the *Charter* to the Constitution without first obtaining the consent of all the provinces – was constitutionally permissible. While it was generally agreed that constitutional convention required the unanimous consent of the provinces for a formal amendment of this magnitude, it was also agreed that constitutional conventions were political matters and could not be recognized or enforced in courts of law. The federal lawyers argued that unilateral amendment was both constitutional (i.e., there was no convention of unanimity) and "legal" (i.e., even if there were such a convention, it could not be enforced by the courts). The opposing provinces argued that Trudeau's unilateralism was both unconstitutional and illegal (i.e., that it violated the convention and that the convention could be enforced by the courts). In the end, a sharply divided Supreme Court split the difference and ruled that the federal government's plan was "unconstitutional but legal."

Mandel shows that the division of the judges closely followed their political and regional affiliations. The three judges from Quebec all agreed that unilateralism was unconstitutional. The two judges who said that Trudeau's plan was both unconstitutional and illegal were Tory appointees from provinces that opposed the Liberal plan (Alberta and Nova Scotia). The three judges who took the other extreme – that unilateralism was both legal and constitutional – were all Trudeau appointees, two from Ontario, a province that supported the Trudeau initiative. Of the seven-judge coalition that held unilateralism was legal, six were Trudeau appointees. "If we were paying attention," writes Mandell, this "gave us a good idea of what Canada could expect with the *Charter*."

Sixteen years later, the Supreme Court was called on again to broker a constitutional dispute between Ottawa and Quebec. In the *Quebec Secession Reference* (Reading 2.4), the Court was asked by the federal government whether Quebec had a right to secede unilaterally from Canada; that is, based on winning a Quebec-only referendum on secession and without any consent from or negotiations with the rest of Canada.

Unlike the *Patriation Reference*, in this case, the Court was unanimous. Thus, there were no (visible) disagreements among the justices that tracked along provincial or party-of-appointment lines. Does this mean that the *Quebec Secession Reference* was decided on strictly legal grounds and that the justices' political sympathies played no role? This seems unlikely since the Court's ruling hardly mentions the relevant constitutional texts (the amending provisions in Section 38-41 of the *Constitution Act, 1982*). Rather, the Court "discovered" four new "foundational constitutional principles" – democracy, federalism, the rule of law, and the protection of minorities – that it said underlie written constitutional rules and practice.

Skeptics have pointed out that, if the Court had used the same four "foundational principles" to decide the 1981 *Patriation Reference* or the 1982

Quebec Veto Reference , the results would have been different. Since only two of ten provinces were supporting Trudeau's unilateral initiative in 1981, this presumably would have failed the federalism principle. The following year, after Ottawa and all nine English-speaking provinces had consented to the *Constitution Act, 1982*, the Quebec government challenged its constitutional validity. At the time, the Supreme Court rejected Quebec's claim. However, if Quebec had been able to invoke the "protection of minorities" principle announced in 1998, presumably it would have prevailed in 1982.

Why in 1998 did the Supreme Court resort to unwritten "constitutional principles" that contradicted two of its most important constitutional precedents affecting Quebec? Again, the answer seems to be political logic rather than legal logic. If the Court had simply followed precedent and the relevant written rules of constitutional amendment, its ruling would have been a crushing defeat for the separatist Parti Québécois government, which would have then denounced the Court as a biased and illegitimate lackey of the federal Liberal party. Instead, the Court used the newly discovered unwritten "constitutional principles" to craft a compromise decision. Significantly, when the Court released its decision, both Ottawa and the PQ government in Quebec claimed they had won. (See the Introduction to Chapter 10 for additional discussion of this case.) In this way, the Court preserved its credibility and authority, especially in Quebec.

Perhaps the best way to understand the Court's ruling is as an application of Professor James Gibson's legal realist definition of judicial decisions as "a function of what judges prefer to do, tempered by what they ought to do, but constrained by what they perceive is feasible to do." In other words, judicial decisions – especially those involving constitutional law – are often a composite of law, politics, and policy.

2.1

Two Models of Judicial Decision-Making
Paul Weiler
Canadian Bar Review 46 (1968), 406-471. Reprinted with permission.

I. Introduction

The philosophy of the judicial process will soon be of great practical significance for the Canadian legal scene. The traditional, inarticulate, legal positivism of Canadian lawyers and judges is rapidly becoming outmoded by recent developments. First, the determination of our new Prime Minister [*Ed. note*: In 1968 Pierre Trudeau had just been elected Prime Minister.] to achieve an entrenched Bill of Rights will, of necessity, confer on the courts the power and the duty to make fundamental value judgments which cannot flow mechanically and impersonally from the language of the document.

Second, the British House of Lords has decided to change its long-standing rule that its earlier precedents could not be overruled. Presumably, and hopefully, the Canadian Supreme Court will continue to imitate slavishly its English counterpart by following this decision. Third, Canadian scholarship about the Supreme Court has begun to utilize some of the advanced techniques of the behavioural sciences in order to study judicial decision-making. Two related developments should follow. Our judges will grow increasingly conscious of the freedom and the responsibility they have to develop and alter the law. Both academics and the public will become aware of the fact of judicial power and then go on to question its legitimacy.

It is only too true that we will be decades behind the same course of developments in our neighbour to the south. There is a favourable cast to this situation. We have available to us a significant body of American experience, and of jurisprudential reflection concerning it, which we can use in intelligently understanding and evaluating the process of change that the Canadian judicial process is likely to undergo. Moreover we can choose between at least two, substantially different conceptions of judicial decision-making which have been elaborated in some detail in American legal thinking. One theory characterizes the judicial function as, essentially, the "adjudication of disputes" within the legal system. The other holds that at least some courts are primarily engaged in "policy-making," in a manner largely indistinguishable from the other political agencies in our society. It is my intention to draw together, in a systematic way, these two very sophisticated theories, to show the conclusions which flow from the insights that lie at the root of each "model," and to indicate the important problems which, as yet, detract from the adequacy of each. In doing so, I shall also record the significance of many apparently unrelated phenomena within the Canadian judicial system.

What theoretical significance do I attach to the use of these models? Sociological theory tells us that the position of judge in any society carries with it a set of shared expectations about the type of conduct that is appropriate to that position. These expectations have reference not only to the proper *physical* behaviour of one who occupies that position but also to the mode of reasoning to be used in making his judicial decisions. There are several possible decision-making roles that can be proposed by society for its judges, each having different supporting reasons for their acceptance. Two of these roles are the subject of this article, "adjudicator" and "policy-maker." Both embody fundamental value choices for the society which, presumably, are made after some consideration of these competing justifications. Once the choice is made, the expectations that are connected with this one role must be shared by at least a substantial majority of the participants within the system in order that it have some institutional stability. Finally, the institutional position of the judge is reciprocally connected with society's wishes about how they should behave in their decision-making capacity. It is this connection between the role we give to our judges and the design of the structure within which they operate that the two models are intended to display.

Hence, the function of each model is to trace the institutional implications of each of these fundamental value judgments about the appropriate mission of the judge. One model is based on the value judgment that judges should make policy choices as a political actor; the other assumes it is desirable that judges confine their activity to the settlement of private disputes. As we shall see, there are real differences in the social arrangements which are most compatible with these two distinctive judgments about the appropriate judicial role. We should be able to verify the existence of these proposed differences in actual practice, or in recommendations about changes in the existing system. Moreover, not only do these theoretical models serve as a framework for explanations of how judges do behave, they also assist our appraisal of how judges ought to behave.

Finally, the use of these two schematic representations of the judicial process should serve to illuminate a significant moral problem that has surfaced recently in American legal discussion of the role of the judiciary. Once an institution has gained inertial force and power as a result of shared expectations about how it is and ought to operate, it is then available as an instrument for serving social purposes that are not compatible with the original model. Is it legitimate for those who believe in an alternative model of judicial behaviour to make covert use of the existing organization? To what extent will such "parasitic" utilization of one version of the judicial process induce actual changes in the existing system which make it more compatible with the form that naturally flows from a new conception of appropriate judicial decision-making? To these, and other problems, this article is addressed in a preliminary way.

II. The Adjudication of Disputes Model

The two models whose traits I am going to describe both agree in rejecting the viability and the desirability of the traditional Anglo-Canadian model of judicial decision-making. The latter suggests that a judge decides his cases by the somewhat mechanical application of legal rules which he finds *established* in the legal system. They are, in this sense, *binding* on him completely apart from his own judgment as to their fitness. This theory has a historical, if not a logical, relationship with the dictates of an Austinian, positivist conception of law and a rigid notion of the division of powers. The "adjudication of disputes" model shares, to some extent, the assumption that judges have a distinctive and limited function. However, it emphatically denies the conclusion that it is *possible* for a judge to be purely passive, and *desirable* that he makes decisions without a necessary exercise of his judgment about what the law ought to be.

As was stated earlier the purpose of the model is to show the necessary inter-relationship between the function which judicial decision-making is primarily intended to perform, the institutional characteristics which are implied by such a function, and the qualities in judicial decision-making which flow naturally from this institutional background. In short, the job we give judges to perform determines the design of the judicial process; the nature of the structure influences the manner in which judges carry out their tasks; the form of judicial action limits the issues judges may appropriately resolve. Hence the adjudication model rejects the tacit assumption, often made, of "institutional fungibility." The latter holds that the same substantive policies can and should be achieved in the same undifferentiated way, whatever be the organizational form in which various actors are allowed to strive for these ends. To the contrary, the specific institutional form of adjudication, by comparison with that of legislation, for instance, limits both the goals for which judges should strive and the means they should use for achieving these goals.

To summarize the model very briefly, it conceives of the judge as the adjudicator of specific, concrete disputes, who disposes of the problems within the latter by elaborating and applying a legal regime to facts, which he finds on the basis of evidence and argument presented to him in an adversary process. The body of rules and principles which are to govern the private conduct of the participants in the legal order are largely settled by forces outside adjudication, although the judge does play a collaborative role in articulating and elaborating these principles. However, the primary focus of adjudication is the settlement of disputes arising out of private line of conduct, by evaluating such conduct in the light of established rules and principles. As we shall see, the whole institutional structure of adjudication – its incidence, access to it, the mode of participation in it, the bases for decision, and the nature of the relief available in it – are all defined by and flow naturally from this function. The key elements within the adjudicative model are (1) settlement of disputes, (2) the adversary process and (3) an established system of standards which are utilized in the process to dispose of the disputes.

Settlement of Concrete Disputes

The first characteristic of "adjudication" is that it has the function of settling disputes (between private individuals or groups, or the government and the individual). These disputes are not future-oriented debates over general policy questions, although, as we shall see, the latter can enter into the final resolution of the problem. Rather, the disputes which are necessary to set the process of adjudication in motion involve "controversies" arising out of a particular line of conduct which causes a collision of specific interests. There is no *logical* or *factual* necessity about this proposition. There can be exceptions and the question of defining the limits of the adjudicative function can be difficult and debatable in the marginal areas….

… To summarize, a court should confine itself to settling concrete, private disputes between individuals who apply to the adjudicator for the resolution of their problem.

An Adversary Process

An adversary process is one which satisfies, more or less, this factual description: as a prelude to the dispute being solved, the interested parties have the opportunity of adducing evidence (or proof) and making arguments to a disinterested and impartial arbiter who decides the case on the basis of this evidence and these arguments. This is by contrast with the public processes of decision by "legitimated power" and "mediation-agreement," where the guaranteed private modes of participation are voting and negotiation respectively. Adjudication is distinctive because it guarantees to each of the parties who are affected the right to prepare for themselves the representations on the basis of which their dispute is to be resolved.

The Need for Standards

... Why does the institution of adjudication require the existence of standards for decision? Of what type are these standards and what does it mean to say that they "exist"? Taking these questions in reverse order, in order that standards "exist," there must be a shared consensus between the adjudicator and the parties about what the standards are which the former is going to apply. Secondly, the parties must reasonably have expected, at the time they acted, that these standards would be used to evaluate their private conduct. Of course, some legal rules can be directed only to the arbiter himself dealing with purely remedial problems. We draw our standards from the legal order which regulates private conduct because a primary objective of the use of adjudication is to preserve the viability of this legal order by settling authoritatively the disputes arising within it. Successful adjudication requires that there be a shared consensus about these rules, especially insofar as they can be utilized to evaluate the conduct of the parties which gives rise to the dispute.

In order that adjudicative decisions be characterized by the quality of rationality which is a prerequisite for their moral force and acceptability, the arbiter must have some principles which he can utilize in explaining to himself and to the parties his reasons for deciding one way or the other. The arbiter is under a duty to articulate a reasoned basis for his decision (whether or not he writes an opinion), because he is not conceded the power of *enactment*. He is not considered to have a *legitimate* power to exercise a discretion to settle a matter just because it needs settling, and without giving reasons for deciding on the particular disposition he selects. Hence, he cannot merely confront an undifferentiated factual situation and decide by an intuitive "leap in the dark." He needs a set of ordering principles which enable him to make sense of the situation and abstract those relevant facets of it which can be organized into a reasoned argument.

Second, the adjudicative process can have the enhanced quality of rationality, which derives from its focusing on a specific, concrete dispute for decision, only if there are standards or principles which enable the adjudicator to single out the relevant, problematic facets of the situation on which he is going to concentrate his attention. If there is no framework of settled principles within which he can operate, and every aspect of every situation is always open to question, then the adjudicator will not be able to focus his attention on unresolved problems. Thus, he will not be able to attain a significantly higher quality of rationality in the solution which he produces for the problem.

Thirdly, to the extent that adjudication entails adversary participation, the presentation of proofs and arguments to the arbiter, the process is meaningless unless the parties can know before their preparation and presentation of the case the principles and standards which the arbiter is likely to find relevant to his disposition of the dispute. It is impossible to make an intelligent argument "in the air" and without any idea of which factors are considered relevant by the person whom one's argument is attempting to persuade. If a relatively passive attitude is necessarily conducive to impartiality (although this does not exclude some reciprocal clarification of views), and a high degree of rationality in result thus depends directly on the quality of the preparations and representation by each side, then a consensus of standards is needed in order that intelligent alternative positions are established and that an adequate "joinder of issue" results....

III. The Judicial Policy-Maker Model: The Judge as Political Actor

A second distinctive model of the judicial process has been developed in recent years, largely by American political scientists. Of course, it is not original in recognizing the inescapable fact that judicial decisions must involve the creative exercise of a court's judgment. It builds on the work of American Legal Realism, which showed that the mechanical application of rigid, automatic rules does not and cannot dispose of individual cases. Men, as judges, decide cases and this activity is one for which they are personally responsible.

However, as we have seen, the "adjudication" model also begins with this assumption. Judges must collaborate with other bodies in society in the development and elaboration of the law "as it ought to be." Yet this collaborative role is institutionally distinctive. The creative articulation of new legal rules is limited and incremental; it is based on a moving background of established legal principles; it is related to the dispute-settling focus of courts because the new rule must be appropriate for retrospective application to the facts giving rise to the instant case; finally, the adoption of the new rule must be justified in a reasoned opinion which establishes the probable "rightness" of the new rule. This whole set of limitations on judicial law-making is necessary in order to *legitimate* the final product. However, this legitimacy does not require a mechanical deduction of the rule from legal premises in which it somehow pre-exists, as in a "brooding omnipresence in the sky."

The reasoning in the opinion is not of a logical-deductive type. Yet, it is supposed to be sufficiently communicable that it is open, in principle at least, to prior vicarious participation by the parties in the adversary process.

Many political scientists, by contrast, believe that judges should be perceived as political actors, continuously engaged in the formulation of policy for society. To say that judges are political actors is not simply to assert the truism that they are part of the governmental system, "authoritatively allocating values in society." Nor is it characteristic of only this model that judges exercise personal judgment in each decision they make and that no conclusions are automatic. What is distinctive is the thesis that judges make policy, or legislate, through essentially the same mode of reasoning as other actors in the governmental system. Moreover, at least for some courts, such political action is becoming, and is seen to be becoming, their primary concern, and adjudication of disputes is growing secondary.

Legislators have traditionally been contrasted with courts by the fact that society considers it acceptable for them to justify authoritative policy-making by reference to their own value preferences, or the interests of those who support or have access to them. Legislators do not feel institutionally committed to the formulation of new legal rules only if they can be justified by a reasoned opinion relating the development to accepted doctrinal premises. This model suggests that some courts also are not, and should not be, so institutionally committed.

The quality of political decision-making both influences and reflects the make-up of the institution within which it is carried on. If, as, and when judges become candid policy-makers, courts will take on a "political" character, and judges will be subjected to "political" pressures. The new orientation of the "policy-making" model should render appropriate for judges the same analysis that is applied to other political actors, as regards the recruitment of the men who make these decisions, the timing of their policy pronouncements, the influences brought to bear on the court, both internally and externally, and the success which attends its policy promulgation. The new model explains, in an illuminating way, many recent judicial phenomena that have followed the proposal and adoption of the new political role by some courts in some legal system. Moreover, it shows the linkage of the various components in the judicial systems, as it becomes redesigned for its new institutional function. I shall compare the new model with the old, showing the changes we may expect in the existing system if and when judges turn from adjudication to concentrate on policy-making. I will not be interested in empirical proof, by scalogram analysis or otherwise, that courts do or do not make decisions based on "policy," rather than "law." Assuming that judges may internalize the role of "political actor" rather than "adjudicator," I hope to make clear the institutional significance of this fact....

IV. Conclusion

I do not believe it is possible yet to decide which of these models expresses a more appropriate role for judges in our society. Nor does either version furnish a type of litmus test for discovering the nature of our present system. Probably, the various judiciaries in the common law are based on different mixtures of each role, however contradictory they may appear in the abstract. Our models are "ideal types," furnishing us with distinctive angles of vision on the same judicial reality, thus allowing us a more profound understanding and evaluation of tendencies within the existing system. Moreover, these two artificial constructs of the judicial process show us the practical significance of two as yet unresolved problems in legal philosophy. Is rational and communicable decision-making possible in choosing between social values? Is judicial choice about values that favour one interest over another a fair institution within a democracy?

In conclusion, I should emphasize my belief that the judicial process in Canada fits neither model as regards the appropriate mode of reasoning, although it is organized more or less along adjudicative lines. In fact, common law judging in Canada has truly been a wasteland of arid legalism, one that is only beginning to be relieved by a profounder vision of the scope of judicial action. For this reason alone, I am just as dubious about the desirability of judicial review of legislative action as about the present review of administrative action. Perhaps the proposal for a Canadian Bill of Rights should await the advent of judges who are products of a different legal education. It seems safe to predict that they will have been schooled in some version of the philosophies of judicial decision-making which I have sketched.

2.2

Harrison v. Carswell
Supreme Court of Canada (1976)

> [In this case the Supreme Court was faced with a dispute between Harrison, the manager of a shopping centre in Winnipeg, and Carswell, a striking employee of one of the stores in the shopping centre. Carswell was participating in a lawful strike and was picketing on the sidewalk in front of her employer's store. Harrison informed her that picketing was not permitted in any area of the shopping centre, and asked her to leave. Carswell refused, and was arrested and convicted of petty trespass. The legal issue at stake in this case was the conflict between the traditional rights of private property (protected by the law of trespass) and the right to strike.]

The judgment of Laskin C.J. and Spence and Beetz J.J. was delivered by THE CHIEF JUSTICE (dissenting) – I would be content to adopt the reasons of Freedman C.J.M. and, accordingly, to dismiss this appeal without more if I did not feel compelled, in view of the course of argument, to add some observations bearing on the decision of this Court in *Peters* v. *The Queen* dismissing an appeal from the judgment of the Ontario Court of Appeal. The observations I am about to make about the *Peters* case carry into two areas of concern respecting the role of this Court as the final Court in this country in both civil and criminal causes. Those areas are, first, whether this Court must pay mechanical deference to *stare decisis* and, second, whether this Court has a balancing role to play, without yielding place to the Legislature, where an ancient doctrine, in this case trespass, is invoked in a new setting to suppress a lawful activity supported both by legislation and by a well-understood legislative policy....

... This Court, above all others in this country, cannot be simply mechanistic about previous decisions, whatever be the respect it would pay to such decisions. What we would be doing here, if we were to say that the *Peters* case, because it was so recently decided, has concluded the present case for us, would be to take merely one side of a debatable issue and say that it concludes the debate without the need to hear the other side.

I do not have to call upon pronouncements of members of this Court that we are free to depart from previous decisions in order to support the pressing need to examine the present case on its merits.

The judgment of Martland, Judson, Ritchie, Pigeon, Dickson, and de Grandpré, J.J. was delivered by Dickson J.

... The submission that this Court should weigh and determine the respective values to society of the right to property and the right to picket raises important and difficult political and socio-economic issues, the resolution of which must, by their very nature, be arbitrary and embody personal economic and social beliefs. It raises also fundamental questions as to the role of this Court under the Canadian constitution. The duty of the Court, as I envisage it, is to proceed in the discharge of its adjudicative function in a reasoned way from principled decision and established concepts. I do not for a moment doubt the power of the Court to act creatively – it has done so on countless occasions; but manifestly one must ask – what are the limits of the judicial function? There are many and varied answers to this question. Holmes J. said in *Southern Pacific Co.* v. *Jensen*, at p. 221: "I recognize without hesitation that judges do and must legislate, but they can do it only interstitially; they are confined from molar to molecular actions." Cardozo, *The Nature of the Judicial Process* (1921), p. 141, recognized that the freedom of the judge is not absolute in this expression of his review:

> This judge, even when he is free, is still not wholly free. He is not to innovate at pleasure. He is not a knight-errant, roaming at will in pursuit of his own ideal of beauty or of goodness. He is to draw his inspiration from consecrated principles.

The former Chief Justice of the Australian High Court, Sir Owen Dixon, in an address delivered at Yale University in September 1955, "Concerning Judicial Method," had this to say:

> But in our Australian High Court we have had as yet no deliberate innova-
> tors bent on express change of acknowledged doctrine. It is one thing for a
> court to seek to extend the application of accepted principles to new cases
> or to reason from the more fundamental of settled legal principles to new
> conclusions or to decide that a category is not closed against unforeseen
> instances which in reason might be subsumed thereunder. It is an entirely
> different thing for a judge, who is discontented with a result held to flow
> from a long accepted legal principle, deliberately to abandon the principle
> in the name of justice or of social necessity or of social convenience. The
> former accords with the technique of the common law and amounts to no
> more than an enlightened application of modes of reasoning traditionally
> respected in the courts. It is a process by the repeated use of which the law
> is developed, is adapted to new conditions, and is improved in content. The
> latter means an abrupt and almost arbitrary change.

Society has long since acknowledged that a public interest is served by permitting union members to bring economic pressure to bear upon their respective employers through peaceful picketing, but the right has been exercisable in some locations and not in others and to the extent that picketing has been permitted on private property the right hitherto has been accorded by statute. For example, s. 87 of the *Labour Code of British Columbia Act*, 1973 (B.C.) (2nd Sess.), c. 122, provides that no action lies in respect of picketing permitted under the Act for trespass to real property to which a member of the public ordinarily has access.

Anglo-Canadian jurisprudence has traditionally recognized, as a fundamental freedom, the right of the individual to the enjoyment of property and the right not to be deprived thereof, or any interest therein, save by due process of law. The Legislature of Manitoba has declared in *The Petty Trespasses Act* that any person who trespasses upon land, the property of another, upon or through which he has been requested by the owner not to enter, is guilty of an offence. If there is to be any change in this statute law, if *A* is to be given the right to enter and remain on the land of *B* against the will of *B*, it would seem to me that such a change must be made by the enacting institution, the Legislature, which is representative of the people and designed to manifest the political will, and not by the Court.

2.3

Re Constitution of Canada, 1981:
The Patriation Reference

Michael Mandel
The Charter of Rights and the Legalization of Politics in Canada (Toronto: Wall and
Thompson, 1988), 24–34. Reprinted with permission.

[The constitutional reference cases of 1981 were] the third and by far most
important aspect of the provincial counterattack. Three of the opposing provincial governments, Manitoba, Quebec, and Newfoundland, referred the
question of the constitutionality of the federal proposal to their provincial
supreme courts. But this was "constitutionality" with a difference. For in
addition to the ordinary questions governments ask courts concerning matters of constitutional *legality*, each government asked a separate question
about whether it was consistent with constitutional *convention* (understood
as meaning, roughly, a historically recognized norm of political behaviour)
for the federal government to approach the UK Parliament over such substantial provincial opposition.

Of course, everyone knew that the government's plan was *not* consistent
with constitutional convention. What was extraordinary was to ask the
courts to say so. Courts had sometimes ruled on conventions where doing
so was necessary to resolve a question of law, but they had *never* done so
where, as in this case, the supposed convention was completely detached
from any legal question. Why?

The technical distinction between conventions and laws is that conventions are *unenforceable* in the courts. This means that the courts will not
authorize the use of force to obtain obedience to conventions. But they will
with laws. Why is this important? Because this regulation or authorization
of the use of official force, this law *enforcement*, is not merely one of the
functions of courts among many. It is their defining characteristic. Courts
do not distinguish between the legal and the illegal in a vacuum or as an
end it itself. Their determinations are a crucial part of the legitimate use
of force in the modern state. The practical activity of the use of force by
the state requires an institution capable of finally, efficiently, and authoritatively determining its legitimacy in any given case. The very idea of legality
requires such an institution. That institution is the courts. Their word is law.
But we do not need only one institution authorized to determine right and
wrong or historical practice. Quite the contrary. We can do without "official" moralities and "official" histories. For a court to recognize a convention that by definition it will nevertheless not enforce is to do something
that *anyone* has the authority to do. A court's opinion on the matter has
no more formal, judicial, legal, or whatever-you-choose-to-call-it, authority

than yours, mine, Pierre Trudeau's or René Lévesque's. If it is more persuasive, this is a political fact, not a legal one.

So when the courts were asked a separate question on constitutional convention, they were asked something outside of the realm of law and judging. Nevertheless, there was little reluctance on their part to answer it. Only one judge out of 22 refused out of a sense of judicial propriety. [*Ed. note*: The figure of 22 judges includes those who initially heard the reference in the Courts of Appeal.] As for the answers to the various questions, the three appellate courts were hopelessly divided, with Manitoba and Quebec (over dissents) in favour, and Newfoundland (unanimously) opposed. Of the 13 appellate judges who heard the cases, seven found in favour of the federal government and six against it. There was no avoiding referring the whole matter to the Supreme Court of Canada....

The arguments before the Supreme Court of Canada by a battery of constitutional lawyers in *Re Constitution of Canada* took only five days of late April 1981, amid what court historians claim was the most concentrated public attention in its history. However, the Court took the entire summer to prepare its decision, which was ready for release on September 28. Far from being reticent about its new role, the Court seemed eager for it, even too eager. It broke yet another tradition by allowing TV cameras into the courtroom for the first time, but the effect was ruined when one of the judges tripped a sound cable rendering the Chief Justice's reading of the judgment inaudible. What he had to say was hardly the stuff of high television ratings anyway. It was a dry recitation of the various questions put to the Court and their technical answers, confusing even for lawyers. The Supreme Court had many lessons to learn in public relations. What the decision would mean in political terms was also unclear at first. It was interpreted differently according to which side of the issue and which side of the Quebec border one was on. Quebec's *Le Devoir* headline was one way of looking at it: "Legal but unconstitutional," while Ontario's *Globe and Mail* headline was another: "PM's bid 'offends' but is legal." Both were technically correct: the legality of the plan was affirmed by a vote of seven judges to two, and its inconsistency with constitutional convention by a vote of six to three. A lot of the confusion came from the shifting alignments on the Court with some judges dissenting on one question yet joining the majority on the other. But closer examination shows the political logic of the decision. The Court voted almost perfectly along political and regional lines:

Judge	Province	Appointed	Legal	Conventional
Laskin	Ontario	Trudeau	Yes	Yes
Estey	Ontario	Trudeau	Yes	Yes
MacIntyre	B.C.	Trudeau	Yes	Yes
Dickson	Manitoba	Trudeau	Yes	No
Beetz	Quebec	Trudeau	Yes	No
Lamer	Quebec	Trudeau	Yes	No
Chouinard	Quebec	Trudeau	Yes	No
Martland	Alberta	Diefenbaker	No	No
Ritchie	Alberta	Diefenbaker	No	No

This was a transparently political decision and gave us a good idea, if we were paying attention, of what Canada could expect with the *Charter*.

The reasoning of the judges was as revealing as their voting pattern. Of the two questions, the legality question was probably the easiest. As we have seen, for a court to hold an act of government illegal is, at least implicitly, to prohibit it. The majority argued that, however unconventional the federal government's action might be, there was nothing in the decided cases or the statutes authorizing a court actually to interfere with what was, after all, a mere request made by the Canadian Parliament to the UK Parliament. Whatever impact such a request might in fact have, it had no legal effect without a law being passed by the sovereign UK Parliament. Where could a court get the authority to *prohibit* a *request*? Furthermore, given the fact that the entire legal structure of Canada depended on a British enactment, what legal authority could a Canadian court have to refuse to recognize an amendment to the *BNA Act* by the Parliament that enacted it in the first place, however that amendment came to be proposed? The minority's answer was that the Court should, in effect, make up the authority so as to protect the fundamental federal structure of Canada. Courts had made things up before.

There was logic on both sides and certainly a lack of precedent had become increasingly unimportant to this court – that very day it would do a most unprecedented act. But to hold this action illegal, even if technically possible, would have been reckless on the part of the Court. What if Parliament were unable to achieve an agreement through patently unreasonable provincial intransigence? The Court would then have set up an insuperable legal obstacle to a constitutional amendment and would have found itself confronting an already popular plan (the *Charter*) as well as what could turn into a popular strategy (unilateralism). If, in such an event, Parliament went ahead despite the illegality, the Court would have had its *order* ignored with a consequent loss of prestige. And what then? Could it actually refuse to enforce the law once it returned? Shades of Roosevelt and 1937! Besides, it was unnecessary to go this far in light of the Court's answer on the convention question.

That there was a convention requiring more provincial consent than the federal government had obtained could not really be challenged. In fact, the historical record was that no amendments had been passed without the consent of *all* of the provinces affected, and this record strongly implied that this was indeed recognized as binding on the federal government. Indeed, the only legitimate questions concerned the requirement of unanimity and the Quebec veto. There was in fact no dissent from anyone on the Court that constitutional convention required more provincial support than had been obtained. What is intriguing about the convention question has nothing to do with the answers given to it nor the arguments offered by majority and minority for their respective conclusions. What is intriguing is the way the convention question was interpreted by each side, the way the answers of each side were presented, and, most intriguing of all, *that it was even answered*.

First, the way the question was interpreted. When it asked whether "the consent of the provinces" was necessary, did it mean *all* of the provinces or merely *some* of them? Each side interpreted this differently, but in the way that best suited its point of view on the outcome. It was as obvious to the majority that the question did *not* mean to refer to *all* of the provinces as it was to the minority that it *did*.

> Majority:
> It would have been easy to insert the words "all" into the question had it been intended to narrow its meaning. But we do not think it was so intended.

> Minority:
> From the wording of the questions and from the course of argument it is clear that the questions meant the consent of all the Provinces.... There is no ambiguity in the questions before the Court.

The only thing that was really clear, of course, was that if the majority wanted to cast doubt on the plan and the minority to approve it, interpreting the question in their respective ways made it easier for each side to achieve its respective goal. If they were only interested in the truth, each side would have given answers to each possible interpretation of the question. If this is not coincidence enough, there are the very obvious attempts by each side to give maximum impact to its respective position. The minority, which found the plan not contrary to constitutional convention, but nevertheless knew itself to have lost this issue, *minimized* the general importance of conventions:

> We cannot...agree with any suggestion that the non-observance of a convention can properly be termed unconstitutional in any strict or legal sense.... In a federal State ... constitutionality and legality must be synonymous, and conventional rules will be accorded less significance than they may have in a unitary State such as the United Kingdom.

> With conventions or understandings he [the lawyer and law teacher] has no direct concern. They vary from generation to generation, almost from year

to year.... The subject ... is not one of law but of politics, and need trouble no lawyer or the class of any professor of law.

The majority, on the other hand, went to great lengths to *maximize* the significance of its holding that the federal resolution, though legal, was contrary to convention: "[W]hile they are not laws, some conventions may be more important than some laws." Indeed, the majority went about as far as it could in this direction when it declared that conventions "form an integral part of the constitution and the constitutional system":

> That is why it is perfectly appropriate to say that to violate a convention is to do something which is unconstitutional although it entails no direct legal consequences. But the words "constitutional" and "unconstitutional" may also be used in strict legal sense, for instance with respect to a statute which is found *ultra vires* or unconstitutional. The foregoing may perhaps be summarized in an equation: constitutional conventions plus constitutional law equal the total Constitution of the country.

But one does not have to look any further for proof of the political nature of the case than to the fact that the Court agreed to answer the convention question at all. And this is the only point upon which it was unanimous! Remember that there was no precedent for the Court ruling on a convention question divorced from any legal question. Indeed, according to the Court's own definition, conventions "are not enforced by the courts." So, answering the convention question at all was out of line with the role of courts as ordinarily conceived. In answering the convention question, the Supreme Court of Canada acted "outside its legal function and [attempted] to facilitate a political outcome." It "intervened as another political actor, not as a court of law." What was the Court's defence of this action? The majority devoted a separate section of its reasons to the issue, but nothing it said really answered the question. We were told that the question was important (though "not confined to an issue of pure legality... It has to do with a fundamental issue of constitutionality and legitimacy") and that courts should not "shrink" from answering a question "on account of the political aspects." But these are reasons for answering a *legal* question with political implications, not for answering a political question that has nothing to do with law. The minority argued that they had to answer because the majority answered, but also because the case was "unusual" and there had been extensive argument on the convention question. Perhaps the judge who came the closest to the truth was the Chief Justice of Manitoba, quoted by the majority in the Supreme Court, who said that the question "calls for an answer, and I propose to answer it." Put another way, the reasons given by the various judges to justify their willingness to answer the convention question, and characterized by one commentator as "inadequate" as, no doubt, technically they were, amounted to no more and no less than that they were answering it because they were *expected* to answer it.

Can anyone doubt that they were right about this? Outside of scholarly criticism of the legal credentials of the decision and the dangers such political behaviour might cause the Supreme Court, not a peep of political criticism was heard of the decision to answer the question. And, while it is impossible to say what would have happened had the convention question not been answered or had it been answered differently, it is clear that with the Court decision as it was, the federal government had no political hope of going ahead without at least another round of negotiations. For one thing, the NDP informed the government that it would now vote against the resolution without a new conference. In Britain, too, the decision was regarded as decisive.... The *Guardian* reported that even with strenuous Thatcher sponsorship, the Bill would now have a tough time. Though the outcome would obviously have been impossible to predict with certainty, it is clear that there would have been a serious battle in the British Commons and House of Lords had the federal government tried to go ahead with its original plan after the judgment.

But most important of all was that the whole *Charter* enterprise depended for its success on reverence for the Court. The reason Trudeau wanted the *Charter* in the first place was to use it against the unilingual tendencies of provincial governments in areas beyond federal control. He needed it now to use against the popular language legislation of the PQ government of Quebec. The idea was to entrench English language rights which directly contradicted the PQ's *Bill 101* so that the courts, ultimately the Supreme Court, would strike down the law as violating the *Charter of Rights*. Trudeau was going to trump democracy by claiming a greater legitimacy for the Supreme Court of Canada than for any mere government. How could he criticize the Court for going too far today when he needed it to go all the way tomorrow?

So the Supreme Court's decision all but forced the First Ministers' conference that began on November 2, 1981. In fact, it practically determined its outcome. This was due partly to the holding on legality, because the knowledge that a unilateral federal gambit would be legal and enforceable gave the provinces an extra incentive to be conciliatory and even to break ranks to achieve individual objectives. But most important of all to the final outcome was the clear indication given by both majority and minority on the convention question that constitutional convention did not require the unanimous, or even near unanimous, assent of the provinces. Both sides let everyone know that they would approve of much less. For the minority judges, the denial of a unanimity requirement was part and parcel with their dissent, but this would have been a fragile predictor without some expression on the question by the majority judges, and express themselves they did, once again completely without judicial excuse:

> It was submitted by counsel for Manitoba, Newfoundland, Quebec, Nova Scotia, British Columbia, Prince Edward Island and Alberta that the convention does exist [and] that it requires the agreement of all the Provinces....
>
> Counsel for Saskatchewan ... submitted that the convention does exist and requires a measure of provincial agreement....
>
> We wish to indicate at the outset that we find ourselves in agreement with the submissions made on this issue by counsel for Saskatchewan.
>
> ...
>
> It seems clear that while the precedents taken alone point at unanimity, the unanimity principle cannot be said to have been accepted by all the actors in the precedents.
>
> ...
>
> It would not be appropriate for the Court to devise in the abstract a specific formula which would indicate in positive terms what measure of provincial agreement is required....
>
> It is sufficient for the Court to decide that at least a substantial measure of provincial consent is required.... Nothing more should be said about this.

The Court had said more than enough already. It had introduced a completely "new element" into the equation, an element that was emphasized by the Premiers of both British Columbia and Saskatchewan (two *opposing* provinces) in their televised opening speeches to the First Ministers' conference on November 2. It was this element that made possible the ultimate exclusion of Quebec, the only province with truly irreconcilable differences with Ottawa, differences over entrenched minority language rights, not only Trudeau's bottom line but actually his *raison d'être*. It is clear that these specific rights, which in their precision and prolixity read more like a tax statute than a constitution, were the only non-negotiables for Trudeau. The grand rights and freedoms of "conscience," "association," "fundamental justice," "equality," and so on, which granted a purely general supervisory jurisdiction over legislation to the courts, were expendable. Trudeau said as much after the referendum. And he proved it in the resulting constitution where none of these grand individualistic rights would be so precious as to be immune from legislative veto by use of s.33, the "notwithstanding" clause. By contrast, language rights would be immune, and at the same time, they would automatically render null and void the language of education provisions of the PQ's *Bill 101*, the centrepiece of its program to make the French language *the* language of Quebec.

In other words, unanimity among provinces and the federal government was simply not achievable so long as Trudeau and Lévesque had to sign the same document. The freedom from unanimity which the Supreme Court presumed to grant made possible the only conceivable agreement, one that would exclude Quebec. Furthermore, the "deliberate vagueness" of the Court's formula gave the other provinces more than enough incentive to jump on the federal bandwagon lest they be isolated with English Canada's anathema. This seems in fact to have been what determined Manitoba's capitulation. It was the only other province with a real interest in opposing entrenched language rights (because of its relatively large and linguistically mistreated French minority) and, because of this, the only other province firmly opposed to a *Charter* at the time of the conference (Alberta had made its deal with the federal government on energy prices in September). An accord excluding Quebec did not necessarily entail the sneakiness of the night of November 4–5, 1981, during which, with all parties but Quebec involved, the compromise that was to be Canada's constitution was worked out and then presented as a *fait accompli* to a shocked René Lévesque the next morning at breakfast. That there would be an accord, however, and that it would exclude Quebec was as about as inevitable as these things ever get.

The Court's role in the ultimate making of the deal and in its general contours was, therefore, a rather large one. Furthermore, the script required it consciously to stride outside of its judicial confines and directly into the political arena. But this, as we have tried to show, was not a random occurrence. For most of the century, everything, and more and more nearly everyone, had been grooming the Court for this part. In fact, the most obvious thing about the decision to answer the convention question was that this thoroughly non-traditional decision of the Court concerned the adoption of a law – a constitutionally entrenched *Charter of Rights and Freedoms* – that would invest the judiciary with essentially the same thoroughly non-traditional function, namely judging the *legitimacy* of jurisdictionally valid legislation. The *Charter of Rights and Freedoms* in fact transformed the Court into an institution charged with making the very sort of judgments which it made on the convention issue – though such judgments would henceforth be made under the formally satisfying umbrella of constitutional authority. So if we want to know why the Court would accept such a non-traditional role in determining the outcome of a major political crisis and why its acceptance of this role would in turn be accepted by all the other actors, the answer is that it would have been strange indeed for the Court, standing on the threshold of its new era, to have been too prudish to engage in the very kind of activity that would characterize that era, or to have been criticized for doing so. The decision on the convention should be regarded as the inauguration of a new era in which the judiciary is to play a central role in the political life of this country. The triumph of the legalization of politics can be dated, then, not from the formal entrenchment of the *Charter of Rights and Freedoms* on April 17, 1982, but from the decision on the convention question in *Re Constitution of Canada* some seven months earlier.

2.4

Reference re the Secession of Quebec
Supreme Court of Canada (1998)

The Court –

I. Introduction

This Reference requires us to consider momentous questions that go to the heart of our system of constitutional government.... In our view, it is not possible to answer the questions that have been put to us without a consideration of a number of underlying principles.... Only once those underlying principles have been examined and delineated may a considered response to the questions we are required to answer emerge.

The questions posed ... read as follows:

1.   Under the Constitution of Canada, can the National Assembly, legislature or government of Quebec effect the secession of Quebec from Canada unilaterally?
2.   Does international law give the National Assembly, legislature or government of Quebec the right to effect the secession of Quebec from Canada unilaterally? In this regard, is there a right to self-determination under international law that would give the National Assembly, legislature or government of Quebec the right to effect the secession of Quebec from Canada unilaterally?
3.   In the event of a conflict between domestic and international law on the right of the National Assembly, legislature or government of Quebec to effect the secession of Quebec from Canada unilaterally, which would take precedence in Canada?

Before turning to Question 1, as a preliminary matter, it is necessary to deal with the issues raised with regard to this Court's reference jurisdiction.

II. The Preliminary Objections to the Court's Reference Jurisdiction

The *amicus curiae* [for Quebec] argued that s.101 of the *Constitution Act, 1867* does not give Parliament the authority to grant this Court the jurisdiction provided for in s.53 of the *Supreme Court Act*, R.S.C., 1985, c.S-26. Alternatively, it is submitted that even if Parliament were entitled to enact s.53 of the *Supreme Court Act*, the scope of that section should be interpreted to exclude the kinds of questions the Governor in Council has submitted in this Reference. In particular, it is contended that this Court cannot answer Question 2, since it is a question of "pure" international law over which this

Court has no jurisdiction. Finally, even if this Court's reference jurisdiction is constitutionally valid, and even if the questions are within the purview of s.53 of the *Supreme Court Act*, it is argued that the three questions referred to the Court are speculative, of a political nature, and, in any event, are not ripe for judicial decision, and therefore are not justiciable.

[*Ed. note:* The Court rejects the first two objections to its hearing this reference.]

C. Justiciability

It is submitted that even if the Court has jurisdiction over the questions referred, the questions themselves are not justiciable. Three main arguments are raised in this regard:

(1) the questions are not justiciable because they are too "theoretical" or speculative;

(2) the questions are not justiciable because they are political in nature;

(3) the questions are not yet ripe for judicial consideration.

In the context of a reference, the Court, rather than acting in its traditional adjudicative function, is acting in an advisory capacity. The very fact that the Court may be asked hypothetical questions in a reference, such as the constitutionality of proposed legislation, engages the Court in an exercise it would never entertain in the context of litigation. No matter how closely the procedure on a reference may mirror the litigation process, a reference does not engage the Court in a disposition of rights. For the same reason, the Court may deal on a reference with issues that might otherwise be considered not yet "ripe" for decision.

Though a reference differs from the Court's usual adjudicative function, the Court should not, even in the context of a reference, entertain questions that would be inappropriate to answer. However, given the very different nature of a reference, the question of the appropriateness of answering a question should not focus on whether the dispute is formally adversarial or whether it disposes of cognizable rights. Rather, it should consider whether the dispute is appropriately addressed by a court of law. As we stated in *Reference re Canada Assistance Plan (B.C.)* [1981]:

> ... In exercising its discretion whether to determine a matter that is alleged to be non-justiciable, *the Court's primary concern is to retain its proper role within the constitutional framework of our democratic form of government*.... In considering its appropriate role the Court must determine whether the question is purely political in nature and should, therefore, be determined in another forum or *whether it has a sufficient legal component to warrant the intervention of the judicial branch*. [Emphasis added.]

Thus the circumstances in which the Court may decline to answer a reference question on the basis of "non-justiciability" include:

(i)   if to do so would take the Court beyond its own assessment of its proper role in the constitutional framework of our democratic form of government or

(ii) if the Court could not give an answer that lies within its area of expertise: the interpretation of law.

As to the "proper role" of the Court, it is important to underline, contrary to the submission of the *amicus curiae*, that the questions posed in this Reference do not ask the Court to usurp any democratic decision that the people of Quebec may be called upon to make. The questions posed by the Governor in Council, as we interpret them, are strictly limited to aspects of the legal framework in which that democratic decision is to be taken. The attempted analogy to the U.S. "political questions" doctrine therefore has no application. The legal framework having been clarified, it will be for the population of Quebec, acting through the political process, to decide whether or not to pursue secession. As will be seen, the legal framework involves the rights and obligations of Canadians who live outside the province of Quebec, as well as those who live within Quebec.

As to the "legal" nature of the questions posed, if the Court is of the opinion that it is being asked a question with a significant extralegal component, it may interpret the question so as to answer only its legal aspects; if this is not possible, the Court may decline to answer the question. In the present Reference the questions may clearly be interpreted as directed to legal issues, and, so interpreted, the Court is in a position to answer them.

Finally, we turn to the proposition that even though the questions referred to us are justiciable in the "reference" sense, the Court must still determine whether it should exercise its discretion to refuse to answer the questions on a pragmatic basis.

Generally, the instances in which the Court has exercised its discretion to refuse to answer a reference question that is otherwise justiciable can be broadly divided into two categories. First, where the question is too imprecise or ambiguous to permit a complete or accurate answer.... Second, where the parties have not provided sufficient information to allow the Court to provide a complete or accurate answer:

There is no doubt that the questions posed in this Reference raise difficult issues and are susceptible to varying interpretations. However, rather than refuse to answer at all, the Court is guided by the approach advocated by the majority on the "conventions" issue in *Reference re Resolution to Amend the Constitution* [1981] 1 S.C.R. 753 (*Patriation Reference*), at pp. 875–76:

If the questions are thought to be ambiguous, this Court should not, in a constitutional reference, be in a worse position than that of a witness in a trial and feel compelled simply to answer yes or no. Should it find that a question might be misleading, or should it simply avoid the risk of misunderstanding, the Court is free either to interpret the question ... or it may qualify both the question and the answer....

The Reference questions raise issues of fundamental public importance. It cannot be said that the questions are too imprecise or ambiguous to permit a proper legal answer. Nor can it be said that the Court has been provided with insufficient information regarding the present context in which the questions arise. Thus, the Court is duty bound in the circumstances to provide its answers.

III. Reference Questions

A. Question 1

Under the Constitution of Canada, can the National Assembly, legislature or government of Quebec effect the secession of Quebec from Canada unilaterally?

(1) Introduction

As we confirmed in *Reference re Objection by Quebec to a Resolution to Amend the Constitution* [1982], "The *Constitution Act, 1982* is now in force. Its legality is neither challenged nor assailable." The "Constitution of Canada" certainly includes the constitutional texts enumerated in s.52(2) of the *Constitution Act, 1982*. Although these texts have a primary place in determining constitutional rules, they are not exhaustive. The Constitution also "embraces unwritten, as well as written rules," as we recently observed in the *Provincial Judges Reference*, Finally, as was said in the *Patriation Reference*, the Constitution of Canada includes

> the global system of rules and principles which govern the exercise of constitutional authority in the whole and in every part of the Canadian state.

These supporting principles and rules, which include constitutional conventions and the workings of Parliament, are a necessary part of our Constitution because problems or situations may arise which are not expressly dealt with by the text of the Constitution. In order to endure over time, a constitution must contain a comprehensive set of rules and principles which are capable of providing an exhaustive legal framework for our system of government. Such principles and rules emerge from an understanding of the constitutional text itself, the historical context, and previous judicial interpretations of constitutional meaning. In our view, there are four fundamental and organizing principles of the Constitution which are relevant to addressing the question before us (although this enumeration is by no means exhaustive): federalism; democracy; constitutionalism and the rule of law; and respect for minorities. The foundation and substance of these principles are addressed in the following paragraphs. We will then turn to their specific application to the first reference question before us.

(2) Historical Context: The Significance of Confederation

In our constitutional tradition, legality and legitimacy are linked. The precise nature of this link will be discussed below. However, at this stage, we wish to emphasize only that our constitutional history demonstrates that our governing institutions have adapted and changed to reflect changing social and political values. This has generally been accomplished by methods that have ensured continuity, stability and legal order.

Because this Reference deals with questions fundamental to the nature of Canada, it should not be surprising that it is necessary to review the context in which the Canadian union has evolved. To this end, we will briefly describe the legal evolution of the Constitution and the foundational principles governing constitutional amendments. Our purpose is not to be exhaustive, but to highlight the features most relevant in the context of this Reference.

Confederation was an initiative of elected representatives of the people then living in the colonies scattered across part of what is now Canada. It was not initiated by Imperial *fiat*. In March 1864, a select committee of the Legislative Assembly of the Province of Canada, chaired by George Brown, began to explore prospects for constitutional reform. The committee's report, released in June 1864, recommended that a federal union encompassing Canada East and Canada West, and perhaps the other British North American colonies, be pursued. A group of Reformers from Canada West, led by Brown, joined with Etienne P. Taché and John A. Macdonald in a coalition government for the purpose of engaging in constitutional reform along the lines of the federal model proposed by the committee's report.

An opening to pursue federal union soon arose. The leaders of the maritime colonies had planned to meet at Charlottetown in the fall to discuss the perennial topic of maritime union. The Province of Canada secured invitations to send a Canadian delegation. On September 1, 1864, 23 delegates (five from New Brunswick, five from Nova Scotia, five from Prince Edward Island, and eight from the Province of Canada) met in Charlottetown. After five days of discussion, the delegates reached agreement on a plan for federal union.

The salient aspects of the agreement may be briefly outlined. There was to be a federal union featuring a bicameral central legislature. Representation in the Lower House was to be based on population, whereas in the Upper House it was to be based on regional equality, the regions comprising Canada East, Canada West and the Maritimes. The significance of the adoption of a federal form of government cannot be exaggerated. Without it, neither the agreement of the delegates from Canada East nor that of the delegates from the maritime colonies could have been obtained.

Several matters remained to be resolved, and so the Charlottetown delegates agreed to meet again at Quebec in October, and to invite Newfoundland to send a delegation to join them. The Quebec Conference began on October 10, 1864. Thirty-three delegates (two from Newfoundland, seven from New Brunswick, five from Nova Scotia, seven from Prince Edward Island, and twelve from the Province of Canada) met over a two and a half week period. Precise consideration of each aspect of the federal structure preoccupied the political agenda. The delegates approved 72 resolutions, addressing almost all of what subsequently made its way into the final text of the *Constitution Act, 1867.* These included guarantees to protect French language and culture, both directly (by making French an official language in Quebec and Canada as a whole) and indirectly (by allocating jurisdiction over education and "Property and Civil Rights in the Province" to the provinces). The protection of minorities was thus reaffirmed.

Legally, there remained only the requirement to have the Quebec Resolutions put into proper form and passed by the Imperial Parliament in London. However, politically, it was thought that more was required. Indeed, Resolution 70 provided that "The Sanction of the Imperial and *Local Parliaments* shall be sought for the Union of the Provinces on the principles adopted by the Conference." [emphasis added]

Confirmation of the Quebec Resolutions was achieved more smoothly in central Canada than in the Maritimes. In February and March 1865, the Quebec Resolutions were the subject of almost six weeks of sustained debate in both houses of the Canadian legislature. The Canadian Legislative Assembly approved the Quebec Resolutions in March 1865 with the support of a majority of members from both Canada East and Canada West. The governments of both Prince Edward Island and Newfoundland chose, in accordance with popular sentiment in both colonies, not to accede to the Quebec Resolutions. In New Brunswick, a general election was required before Premier Tilley's pro-Confederation party prevailed. In Nova Scotia, Premier Tupper ultimately obtained a resolution from the House of Assembly favouring Confederation.

Sixteen delegates (five from New Brunswick, five from Nova Scotia, and six from the Province of Canada) met in London in December 1866 to finalize the plan for Confederation. To this end, they agreed to some slight modifications and additions to the Quebec Resolutions. Minor changes were made to the distribution of powers, provision was made for the appointment of extra senators in the event of a deadlock between the House of Commons and the Senate, and certain religious minorities were given the right to appeal to the federal government where their denominational school rights were adversely affected by provincial legislation. The British North America Bill was drafted after the London Conference with the assistance of the Colonial Office, and was introduced into the House of Lords in February 1867. The *Act* passed third reading in the House of Commons on March 8, received royal assent on March 29, and was proclaimed on July 1, 1867. The Dominion of Canada thus became a reality.

There was an early attempt at secession. In the first Dominion election in September 1867, Premier Tupper's forces were decimated: members opposed to Confederation won 18 of Nova Scotia's 19 federal seats, and in the simultaneous provincial election, 36 of the 38 seats in the provincial legislature. Newly-elected Premier Joseph Howe led a delegation to the Imperial Parliament in London in an effort to undo the new constitutional arrangements, but it was too late. The Colonial Office rejected Premier Howe's plea to permit Nova Scotia to withdraw from Confederation. As the Colonial Secretary wrote in 1868:

> The neighbouring province of New Brunswick has entered into the union in reliance on having with it the sister province of Nova Scotia; and vast obligations, political and commercial, have already been contracted on the faith of a measure so long discussed and so solemnly adopted.... I trust that the Assembly and the people of Nova Scotia will not be surprised that the Queen's government feel that they would not be warranted in advising the reversal of a great measure of state, attended by so many extensive consequences already in operation.

The interdependence characterized by "vast obligations, political and commercial", referred to by the Colonial Secretary in 1868, has, of course, multiplied immeasurably in the last 130 years.

Federalism was a legal response to the underlying political and cultural realities that existed at Confederation and continue to exist today. At Confederation, political leaders told their respective communities that the Canadian union would be able to reconcile diversity with unity. It is pertinent, in the context of the present Reference, to mention the words of George-Etienne Cartier:

> [TRANSLATION] When we are united, he said, we shall form a political nationality independent of the national origin or the religion of any individual. There are some who regretted that there was diversity of races and who expressed the hope that this distinctive character would disappear. The idea of unity of races is a utopia; it is an impossibility. A distinction of this nature will always exist, just as dissimilarity seems to be in the order of the physical, moral and political worlds. As to the objection based on this fact, that a large nation cannot be formed because Lower Canada is largely French and Catholic and Upper Canada is English and Protestant and the interior provinces are mixed, it constitutes, in my view, reasoning that is futile in the extreme.... In our own federation, we will have Catholics and Protestants, English, French, Irish and Scots and everyone, through his

efforts and successes, will add to the prosperity and glory of the new confederation. We are of different races, not so that we can wage war on one
another, but in order to work together for our well-being.

The federal-provincial division of powers was a legal recognition of the
diversity that existed among the initial members of Confederation, and
manifested a concern to accommodate that diversity within a single nation
by granting significant powers to provincial governments. The *Constitution
Act, 1867* was an act of nation-building. It was the first step in the transition from colonies separately dependent on the Imperial Parliament for
their governance to a unified and independent political state in which different peoples could resolve their disagreements and work together toward
common goals and a common interest. Federalism was the political mechanism by which diversity could be reconciled with unity.

A federal-provincial division of powers necessitated a written constitution which circumscribed the powers of the new Dominion and Provinces
of Canada. Despite its federal structure, the new Dominion was to have "a
Constitution similar in Principle to that of the United Kingdom" (*Constitution
Act, 1867*, preamble). Allowing for the obvious differences between the governance of Canada and the United Kingdom, it was nevertheless thought
important to thus emphasize the continuity of constitutional principles,
including democratic institutions and the rule of law; and the continuity of
the exercise of sovereign power transferred from Westminster to the federal
and provincial capitals of Canada.

After 1867, the Canadian federation continued to evolve both territorially
and politically. New territories were admitted to the union and new provinces were formed. In 1870, Rupert's Land and the Northwest Territories
were admitted and Manitoba was formed as a province. British Columbia
was admitted in 1871, Prince Edward Island in 1873, and the Arctic Islands
were added in 1880. In 1898, the Yukon Territory and in 1905, the provinces
of Alberta and Saskatchewan were formed from the Northwest Territories.
Newfoundland was admitted in 1949 by an amendment to the *Constitution
Act, 1867*. The new territory of Nunavut was carved out of the Northwest
Territories in 1993 with the partition to become effective in April 1999.

Canada's evolution from colony to fully independent state was gradual.
The Imperial Parliament's passage of the *Statute of Westminster, 1931* (U.K.),
22 & 23 Geo. 5, c. 4, confirmed in law what had earlier been confirmed in fact
by the Balfour Declaration of 1926, namely, that Canada was an independent
country. Thereafter, Canadian law alone governed in Canada, except where
Canada expressly consented to the continued application of Imperial legislation. Canada's independence from Britain was achieved through legal
and political evolution with an adherence to the rule of law and stability.
The proclamation of the *Constitution Act, 1982* removed the last vestige of
British authority over the Canadian Constitution and re-affirmed Canada's
commitment to the protection of its minority, aboriginal, equality, legal

and language rights, and fundamental freedoms as set out in the *Canadian Charter of Rights and Freedoms.*

Legal continuity, which requires an orderly transfer of authority, necessitated that the 1982 amendments be made by the Westminster Parliament, but the legitimacy as distinguished from the formal legality of the amendments derived from political decisions taken in Canada within a legal framework which this Court, in the *Patriation Reference,* had ruled were in accordance with our Constitution. It should be noted, parenthetically, that the 1982 amendments did not alter the basic division of powers in ss.91 and 92 of the *Constitution Act, 1867,* which is the primary textual expression of the principle of federalism in our Constitution, agreed upon at Confederation. It did, however, have the important effect that, despite the refusal of the government of Quebec to join in its adoption, Quebec has become bound to the terms of a Constitution that is different from that which prevailed previously, particularly as regards provisions governing its amendment, and the *Canadian Charter of Rights and Freedoms.* As to the latter, to the extent that the scope of legislative powers was thereafter to be constrained by the *Charter,* the constraint operated as much against federal legislative powers as against provincial legislative powers. Moreover, it is to be remembered that s.33, the "notwithstanding clause," gives Parliament and the provincial legislatures authority to legislate on matters within their jurisdiction in derogation of the fundamental freedoms (s.2), legal rights (ss.7 to 14) and equality rights (s.15) provisions of the *Charter.*

We think it apparent from even this brief historical review that the evolution of our constitutional arrangements has been characterized by adherence to the rule of law, respect for democratic institutions, the accommodation of minorities, insistence that governments adhere to constitutional conduct and a desire for continuity and stability. We now turn to a discussion of the general constitutional principles that bear on the present Reference.

(3) Analysis of the Constitutional Principles
(a) Nature of the Principles

What are those underlying principles? Our Constitution is primarily a written one, the product of 131 years of evolution. Behind the written word is an historical lineage stretching back through the ages, which aids in the consideration of the underlying constitutional principles. These principles inform and sustain the constitutional text: they are the vital unstated assumptions upon which the text is based. The following discussion addresses the four foundational constitutional principles that are most germane for resolution of this Reference: federalism, democracy, constitutionalism and the rule of law, and respect for minority rights. These defining principles function in symbiosis. No single principle can be defined in isolation from the others, nor does any one principle trump or exclude the operation of any other.

Our Constitution has an internal architecture, or what the majority of this

Court in *OPSEU* v. *Ontario (Attorney General)* [1987] 2 S.C.R. 2, called a "basic constitutional structure." The individual elements of the Constitution are linked to the others, and must be interpreted by reference to the structure of the Constitution as a whole. As we recently emphasized in the *Provincial Judges Reference*, certain underlying principles infuse our Constitution and breathe life into it. Speaking of the rule of law principle in the *Manitoba Language Rights Reference, supra*, at p. 750, we held that "the principle is clearly implicit in the very nature of a Constitution." The same may be said of the other three constitutional principles we underscore today.

Although these underlying principles are not explicitly made part of the Constitution by any written provision, other than in some respects by the oblique reference in the preamble to the *Constitution Act, 1867*, it would be impossible to conceive of our constitutional structure without them. The principles dictate major elements of the architecture of the Constitution itself and are as such its lifeblood.

The principles assist in the interpretation of the text and the delineation of spheres of jurisdiction, the scope of rights and obligations, and the role of our political institutions. Equally important, observance of and respect for these principles is essential to the ongoing process of constitutional development and evolution of our Constitution as a "living tree," to invoke the famous description in *Edwards* v. *Attorney-General for Canada* [1930]. As this Court indicated in *New Brunswick Broadcasting Co.* v. *Nova Scotia (Speaker of the House of Assembly)* [1933] Canadians have long recognized the existence and importance of unwritten constitutional principles in our system of government.

Given the existence of these underlying constitutional principles, what use may the Court make of them? In the *Provincial Judges Reference*, we cautioned that the recognition of these constitutional principles (the majority opinion referred to them as "organizing principles" and described one of them, judicial independence, as an "unwritten norm") could not be taken as an invitation to dispense with the written text of the Constitution. On the contrary, we confirmed that there are compelling reasons to insist upon the primacy of our written constitution. A written constitution promotes legal certainty and predictability, and it provides a foundation and a touchstone for the exercise of constitutional judicial review. However, we also observed in the *Provincial Judges Reference* that the effect of the preamble to the *Constitution Act, 1867* was to incorporate certain constitutional principles by reference…. In the *Provincial Judges Reference*, we determined that the preamble "invites the courts to turn those principles into the premises of a constitutional argument that culminates in the filling of gaps in the express terms of the constitutional text."

Underlying constitutional principles may in certain circumstances give rise to substantive legal obligations (have "full legal force," as we described it in the *Patriation Reference*), which constitute substantive limitations upon government action. These principles may give rise to very abstract and general obligations, or they may be more specific and precise in nature.

The principles are not merely descriptive, but are also invested with a powerful normative force, and are binding upon both courts and governments. "In other words," as this Court confirmed in the *Manitoba Language Rights Reference*, "in the process of Constitutional adjudication, the Court may have regard to unwritten postulates which form the very foundation of the Constitution of Canada." It is to a discussion of those underlying constitutional principles that we now turn.

(b) Federalism

It is undisputed that Canada is a federal state. Yet many commentators have observed that, according to the precise terms of the *Constitution Act, 1867*, the federal system was only partial. This was so because, on paper, the federal government retained sweeping powers which threatened to undermine the autonomy of the provinces. Here again, however, a review of the written provisions of the Constitution does not provide the entire picture. Our political and constitutional practice has adhered to an underlying principle of federalism, and has interpreted the written provisions of the Constitution in this light. For example, although the federal power of disallowance was included in the *Constitution Act, 1867*, the underlying principle of federalism triumphed early. Many constitutional scholars contend that the federal power of disallowance has been abandoned.

In a federal system of government such as ours, political power is shared by two orders of government: the federal government on the one hand, and the provinces on the other. Each is assigned respective spheres of jurisdiction by the *Constitution Act, 1867*. It is up to the courts "to control the limits of the respective sovereignties." In interpreting our Constitution, the courts have always been concerned with the federalism principle, inherent in the structure of our constitutional arrangements, which has from the beginning been the lodestar by which the courts have been guided.

This underlying principle of federalism, then, has exercised a role of considerable importance in the interpretation of the written provisions of our Constitution. In the *Patriation Reference*, we confirmed that the principle of federalism runs through the political and legal systems of Canada. Indeed, Martland and Ritchie JJ., dissenting in the *Patriation Reference*, considered federalism to be "the dominant principle of Canadian constitutional law." With the enactment of the *Charter*, that proposition may have less force than it once did, but there can be little doubt that the principle of federalism remains a central organizational theme of our Constitution. Less obviously, perhaps, but certainly of equal importance, federalism is a political and legal response to underlying social and political realities.

The principle of federalism recognizes the diversity of the component parts of Confederation, and the autonomy of provincial governments to develop their societies within their respective spheres of jurisdiction. The federal structure of our country also facilitates democratic participation by distributing power to the government thought to be most suited to achieving the particular societal objective having regard to this diversity. The scheme of the *Constitution Act, 1867*, it was said in *Re the Initiative and Referendum Act* [1919], was

> not to weld the Provinces into one, nor to subordinate Provincial Governments to a central authority, but to establish a central government in which these Provinces should be represented, entrusted with exclusive authority only in affairs in which they had a common interest. Subject to this each Province was to retain its independence and autonomy and to be directly under the Crown as its head.

More recently, in *Haig v. Canada* [1993], the majority of this Court held that differences between provinces "are a rational part of the political reality in the federal process." It was referring to the differential application of federal law in individual provinces, but the point applies more generally….

The principle of federalism facilitates the pursuit of collective goals by cultural and linguistic minorities which form the majority within a particular province. This is the case in Quebec, where the majority of the population is French-speaking, and which possesses a distinct culture. This is not merely the result of chance. The social and demographic reality of Quebec explains the existence of the province of Quebec as a political unit and indeed, was one of the essential reasons for establishing a federal structure for the Canadian union in 1867. The experience of both Canada East and Canada West under the *Union Act, 1840*, had not been satisfactory. The federal structure adopted at Confederation enabled French-speaking Canadians to form a numerical majority in the province of Quebec, and so exercise the considerable provincial powers conferred by the *Constitution Act, 1867* in such a way as to promote their language and culture. It also made provision for certain guaranteed representation within the federal Parliament itself.

Federalism was also welcomed by Nova Scotia and New Brunswick, both of which also affirmed their will to protect their individual cultures and their autonomy over local matters. All new provinces joining the federation sought to achieve similar objectives, which are no less vigorously pursued by the provinces and territories as we approach the new millennium.

(c) Democracy

Democracy is a fundamental value in our constitutional law and political culture. While it has both an institutional and an individual aspect, the democratic principle was also argued before us in the sense of the supremacy of the sovereign will of a people, in this case potentially to be expressed by Quebecers in support of unilateral secession. It is useful to explore in a summary way these different aspects of the democratic principle.

The principle of democracy has always informed the design of our constitutional structure, and continues to act as an essential interpretive consideration to this day. A majority of this Court in *OPSEU* v. *Ontario*, confirmed that "the basic structure of our Constitution, as established by the *Constitution Act, 1867*, contemplates the existence of certain political institutions, including freely elected legislative bodies at the federal and provincial levels." As is apparent from an earlier line of decisions emanating from this Court, including *Switzman* v. *Elbling* [1957], *Saumur* v. *City of Quebec* [1953], *Boucher* v. *The King* [1951], and *Reference re Alberta Statutes* [1938], the democracy principle can best be understood as a sort of baseline against which the framers of our Constitution, and subsequently, our elected representatives under it, have always operated. It is perhaps for this reason that the principle was not explicitly identified in the text of the *Constitution Act, 1867* itself. To have done so might have appeared redundant, even silly, to the framers. As explained in the *Provincial Judges Reference*, it is evident that our Constitution contemplates that Canada shall be a constitutional democracy. Yet this merely demonstrates the importance of underlying constitutional principles that are nowhere explicitly described in our constitutional texts. The representative and democratic nature of our political institutions was simply assumed.

Democracy is commonly understood as being a political system of majority rule. It is essential to be clear what this means. The evolution of our democratic tradition can be traced back to the *Magna Carta* (1215) and before, through the long struggle for Parliamentary supremacy which culminated in the English *Bill of Rights* in 1688-89, the emergence of representative political institutions in the colonial era, the development of responsible government in the 19th century, and eventually, the achievement of Confederation itself in 1867. "[T]he Canadian tradition," the majority of this Court held in *Reference re Provincial Electoral Boundaries* (Sask.) [1991], is "one of evolutionary democracy moving in uneven steps toward the goal of universal suffrage and more effective representation." Since Confederation, efforts to extend the franchise to those unjustly excluded from participation in our political system – such as women, minorities, and aboriginal peoples – have continued, with some success, to the present day.

Democracy is not simply concerned with the process of government. On the contrary, as suggested in *Switzman* v. *Elbling*, *supra*, democracy is fundamentally connected to substantive goals, most importantly, the promotion of self-government. Democracy accommodates cultural and group identities: *Reference re Provincial Electoral Boundaries*. Put another way, a sovereign people exercises its right to self-government through the democratic process. In considering the scope and purpose of the *Charter*, the Court in *R.* v. *Oakes* [1986] 1 S.C.R. 103, articulated some of the values inherent in the notion of democracy:

> The Court must be guided by the values and principles essential to a free and democratic society which I believe to embody, to name but a few,

respect for the inherent dignity of the human person, commitment to social justice and equality, accommodation of a wide variety of beliefs, respect for cultural and group identity, and faith in social and political institutions which enhance the participation of individuals and groups in society.

In institutional terms, democracy means that each of the provincial legislatures and the federal Parliament is elected by popular franchise. These legislatures, we have said, are "at the core of the system of representative government": *New Brunswick Broadcasting, supra*. In individual terms, the right to vote in elections to the House of Commons and the provincial legislatures, and to be candidates in those elections, is guaranteed to "Every citizen of Canada" by virtue of s.3 of the *Charter*. Historically, this Court has interpreted democracy to mean the process of representative and responsible government and the right of citizens to participate in the political process as voters (*Reference re Provincial Electoral Boundaries, supra*) and as candidates (*Harvey v. New Brunswick (Attorney General)* [1996]). In addition, the effect of s.4 of the *Charter* is to oblige the House of Commons and the provincial legislatures to hold regular elections and to permit citizens to elect representatives to their political institutions. The democratic principle is affirmed with particular clarity in that section 4 is not subject to the notwithstanding power contained in s.33.

It is, of course, true that democracy expresses the sovereign will of the people. Yet this expression, too, must be taken in the context of the other institutional values we have identified as pertinent to this Reference. The relationship between democracy and federalism means, for example, that in Canada there may be different and equally legitimate majorities in different provinces and territories and at the federal level. No one majority is more or less "legitimate" than the others as an expression of democratic opinion, although, of course, the consequences will vary with the subject matter. A federal system of government enables different provinces to pursue policies responsive to the particular concerns and interests of people in that province. At the same time, Canada as a whole is also a democratic community in which citizens construct and achieve goals on a national scale through a federal government acting within the limits of its jurisdiction. The function of federalism is to enable citizens to participate concurrently in different collectivities and to pursue goals at both a provincial and a federal level.

The consent of the governed is a value that is basic to our understanding of a free and democratic society. Yet democracy in any real sense of the word cannot exist without the rule of law. It is the law that creates the framework within which the "sovereign will" is to be ascertained and implemented. To be accorded legitimacy, democratic institutions must rest, ultimately, on a legal foundation. That is, they must allow for the participation of, and accountability to, the people, through public institutions created under the Constitution. Equally, however, a system of government cannot survive through adherence to the law alone. A political system must also possess legitimacy, and in our political culture, that requires an interaction between the rule of law and the democratic principle. The system must be capable of reflecting the aspirations of the people. But there is more. Our law's claim to legitimacy also rests on an appeal to moral values, many of which are imbedded in our constitutional structure. It would be a grave mistake to equate legitimacy with the "sovereign will" or majority rule alone, to the exclusion of other constitutional values.

Finally, we highlight that a functioning democracy requires a continuous process of discussion. The Constitution mandates government by democratic legislatures, and an executive accountable to them, "resting ultimately on public opinion reached by discussion and the interplay of ideas" (*Saumur* v. *City of Quebec*). At both the federal and provincial level, by its very nature, the need to build majorities necessitates compromise, negotiation, and deliberation. No one has a monopoly on truth, and our system is predicated on the faith that in the marketplace of ideas, the best solutions to public problems will rise to the top. Inevitably, there will be dissenting voices. A democratic system of government is committed to considering those dissenting voices, and seeking to acknowledge and address those voices in the laws by which all in the community must live.

The *Constitution Act, 1982* gives expression to this principle, by conferring a right to initiate constitutional change on each participant in Confederation. In our view, the existence of this right imposes a corresponding duty on the participants in Confederation to engage in constitutional discussions in order to acknowledge and address democratic expressions of a desire for change in other provinces. This duty is inherent in the democratic principle which is a fundamental predicate of our system of governance.

(d) Constitutionalism and the Rule of Law

The principles of constitutionalism and the rule of law lie at the root of our system of government. The rule of law, as observed in *Roncarelli* v. *Duplessis* [1959], is "a fundamental postulate of our constitutional structure." As we noted in the *Patriation Reference*, "[t]he 'rule of law' is a highly textured expression, importing many things which are beyond the need of these reasons to explore but conveying, for example, a sense of orderliness, of subjection to known legal rules and of executive accountability to legal authority." At its most basic level, the rule of law vouchsafes to the citizens and residents of the country a stable, predictable and ordered society in which to conduct their affairs. It provides a shield for individuals from arbitrary state action.

In the *Manitoba Language Rights Reference*, this Court outlined the elements of the rule of law. We emphasized, first, that the rule of law provides that the law is supreme over the acts of both government and private persons. There is, in short, one law for all. Second, we explained, at p. 749, that "the rule of law requires the creation and maintenance of an actual order of positive laws which preserves and embodies the more general principle of normative order." It was this second aspect of the rule of law that was primarily at issue in the *Manitoba Language Rights Reference* itself. A third aspect of the rule of law is, as recently confirmed in the *Provincial Judges Reference*, that "the exercise of all public power must find its ultimate source in a legal rule." Put another way, the relationship between the state and the individual must be regulated by law. Taken together, these three considerations make up a principle of profound constitutional and political significance.

The constitutionalism principle bears considerable similarity to the rule of law, although they are not identical. The essence of constitutionalism in Canada is embodied in s.52(1) of the *Constitution Act, 1982*, which provides that "[t]he Constitution of Canada is the supreme law of Canada, and any law that is inconsistent with the provisions of the Constitution is, to the extent of the inconsistency, of no force or effect." Simply put, the constitutionalism principle requires that all government action comply with the Constitution. The rule of law principle requires that all government action must comply with the law, including the Constitution. This Court has noted on several occasions that with the adoption of the *Charter*, the Canadian system of government was transformed to a significant extent from a system of Parliamentary supremacy to one of constitutional supremacy. The Constitution binds all governments, both federal and provincial, including the executive branch (*Operation Dismantle Inc.* v. *The Queen* [1985]). They may not transgress its provisions: indeed, their sole claim to exercise lawful authority rests in the powers allocated to them under the Constitution, and can come from no other source.

An understanding of the scope and importance of the principles of the rule of law and constitutionalism is aided by acknowledging explicitly why a constitution is entrenched beyond the reach of simple majority rule. There are three overlapping reasons.

First, a constitution may provide an added safeguard for fundamental human rights and individual freedoms which might otherwise be susceptible to government interference. Although democratic government is generally solicitous of those rights, there are occasions when the majority will be tempted to ignore fundamental rights in order to accomplish collective goals more easily or effectively. Constitutional entrenchment ensures that those rights will be given due regard and protection. Second, a constitution may seek to ensure that vulnerable minority groups are endowed with the institutions and rights necessary to maintain and promote their identities against the assimilative pressures of the majority. And third, a constitution may provide for a division of political power that allocates political power amongst different levels of government. That purpose would be defeated if one of those democratically elected levels of government could usurp the powers of the other simply by exercising its legislative power to allocate additional political power to itself unilaterally.

The argument that the Constitution may be legitimately circumvented by resort to a majority vote in a province-wide referendum is superficially persuasive, in large measure because it seems to appeal to some of the same principles that underlie the legitimacy of the Constitution itself, namely, democracy and self-government. In short, it is suggested that as the notion of popular sovereignty underlies the legitimacy of our existing constitutional arrangements, so the same popular sovereignty that originally led to the present Constitution must (it is argued) also permit "the people" in their exercise of popular sovereignty to secede by majority vote alone. However, closer analysis reveals that this argument is unsound, because it misunderstands the meaning of popular sovereignty and the essence of a constitutional democracy.

Canadians have never accepted that ours is a system of simple majority rule. Our principle of democracy, taken in conjunction with the other constitutional principles discussed here, is richer. Constitutional government is necessarily predicated on the idea that the political representatives of the people of a province have the capacity and the power to commit the province to be bound into the future by the constitutional rules being adopted. These rules are "binding" not in the sense of frustrating the will of a majority of a province, but as defining the majority which must be consulted in order to alter the fundamental balances of political power (including the spheres of autonomy guaranteed by the principle of federalism), individual rights, and minority rights in our society. Of course, those constitutional rules are themselves amenable to amendment, but only through a process of negotiation which ensures that there is an opportunity for the constitutionally defined rights of all the parties to be respected and reconciled.

In this way, our belief in democracy may be harmonized with our belief in constitutionalism. Constitutional amendment often requires some form of substantial consensus precisely because the content of the underlying principles of our Constitution demand it. By requiring broad support in the form of an "enhanced majority" to achieve constitutional change, the Constitution ensures that minority interests must be addressed before proposed changes which would affect them may be enacted.

It might be objected, then, that constitutionalism is therefore incompatible with democratic government. This would be an erroneous view. Constitutionalism facilitates – indeed, makes possible – a democratic political system by creating an orderly framework within which people may make political decisions. Viewed correctly, constitutionalism and the rule of law are not in conflict with democracy; rather, they are essential to it. Without that relationship, the political will upon which democratic decisions are taken would itself be undermined.

(e) Protection of Minorities

The fourth underlying constitutional principle we address here concerns the protection of minorities. There are a number of specific constitutional provisions protecting minority language, religion and education rights. Some of those provisions are, as we have recognized on a number of occasions, the product of historical compromises. As this Court observed in *Reference re Bill 30, (Ont.)* [1987], and in *Reference re Education Act (Que.)* [1993], the protection of minority religious education rights was a central consideration in the negotiations leading to Confederation. In the absence of such protection, it was felt that the minorities in what was then Canada East and Canada West would be submerged and assimilated.... Similar concerns animated the provisions protecting minority language rights, as noted in *Société des Acadiens du Nouveau-Brunswick Inc.* v. *Association of Parents for Fairness in Education* [1986].

However, we highlight that even though those provisions were the product of negotiation and political compromise, that does not render them unprincipled. Rather, such a concern reflects a broader principle related to the protection of minority rights. Undoubtedly, the three other constitutional principles inform the scope and operation of the specific provisions that protect the rights of minorities. We emphasize that the protection of minority rights is itself an independent principle underlying our constitutional order. The principle is clearly reflected in the *Charter*'s provisions for the protection of minority rights. See, e.g., *Reference re Public Schools Act (Man.)* [1993], and *Mahe* v. *Alberta* [1990].

The concern of our courts and governments to protect minorities has been prominent in recent years, particularly following the enactment of the *Charter*. Undoubtedly, one of the key considerations motivating the enactment of the *Charter*, and the process of constitutional judicial review that it entails, is the protection of minorities. However, it should not be forgotten that the protection of minority rights had a long history before the enactment of the *Charter*. Indeed, the protection of minority rights was clearly an essential consideration in the design of our constitutional structure even at the time of Confederation: *Senate Reference*. Although Canada's record of upholding the rights of minorities is not a spotless one, that goal is one towards which Canadians have been striving since Confederation, and the process has not been without successes. The principle of protecting minority rights continues to exercise influence in the operation and interpretation of our Constitution.

Consistent with this long tradition of respect for minorities, which is at least as old as Canada itself, the framers of the *Constitution Act, 1982* included in s.35 explicit protection for existing aboriginal and treaty rights, and in s.25, a non-derogation clause in favour of the rights of aboriginal peoples. The "promise" of s.35, as it was termed in *R.* v. *Sparrow* [1990], recognized not only the ancient occupation of land by aboriginal peoples, but their contribution to the building of Canada, and the special commitments made to them by successive governments. The protection of these rights, so recently and arduously achieved, whether looked at in their own right or as part of the larger concern with minorities, reflects an important underlying constitutional value.

(4) The Operation of the Constitutional Principles in the Secession Context

Secession is the effort of a group or section of a state to withdraw itself from the political and constitutional authority of that state, with a view to achieving statehood for a new territorial unit on the international plane. In a federal state, secession typically takes the form of a territorial unit seeking to withdraw from the federation. Secession is a legal act as much as a political one. By the terms of Question 1 of this Reference, we are asked to rule on the legality of unilateral secession "under the Constitution of Canada." This is an appropriate question, as the legality of unilateral secession must be evaluated, at least in the first instance, from the perspective of the domestic legal order of the state from which the unit seeks to withdraw. As we shall see below, it is also argued that international law is a relevant standard by which the legality of a purported act of secession may be measured.

The secession of a province from Canada must be considered, in legal terms, to require an amendment to the Constitution, which perforce requires negotiation. The amendments necessary to achieve a secession could be radical and extensive. Some commentators have suggested that secession could be a change of such a magnitude that it could not be considered to be merely an amendment to the Constitution. We are not persuaded by this contention. It is of course true that the Constitution is silent as to the ability of a province to secede from Confederation but, although the Constitution neither expressly authorizes nor prohibits secession, an act of secession would purport to alter the governance of Canadian territory in a manner which undoubtedly is inconsistent with our current constitutional arrangements. The fact that those changes would be profound, or that they would purport to have a significance with respect to international law, does not negate their nature as amendments to the Constitution of Canada.

The Constitution is the expression of the sovereignty of the people of Canada. It lies within the power of the people of Canada, acting through their various governments duly elected and recognized under the Constitution, to effect whatever constitutional arrangements are desired within Canadian territory, including, should it be so desired, the secession of Quebec from Canada. As this Court held in the *Manitoba Language Rights Reference, supra,* at p. 745, "The Constitution of a country is a statement of the will of the people to be governed in accordance with certain principles held as fundamental and certain prescriptions restrictive of the powers of the legislature and government." The manner in which such a political will could be formed and mobilized is a somewhat speculative exercise, though we are asked to assume the existence of such a political will for the purpose of answering the question before us. By the terms of this Reference, we have been asked to consider whether it would be constitutional in such a circumstance for the National Assembly, legislature or government of Quebec to effect the secession of Quebec from Canada *unilaterally*.

The "unilateral" nature of the act is of cardinal importance and we must be clear as to what is understood by this term. In one sense, any step towards a constitutional amendment initiated by a single actor on the constitutional stage is "unilateral." We do not believe that this is the meaning contemplated by Question 1, nor is this the sense in which the term has been used in argument before us. Rather, what is claimed by a right to secede "unilaterally" is the right to effectuate secession without prior negotiations with the other provinces and the federal government. At issue is not the legality of the first step but the legality of the final act of purported unilateral secession. The supposed juridical basis for such an act is said to be a clear expression of democratic will in a referendum in the province of Quebec. This claim requires us to examine the possible juridical impact, if any, of such a referendum on the functioning of our Constitution, and on the claimed legality of a unilateral act of secession.

Although the Constitution does not itself address the use of a referendum procedure, and the results of a referendum have no direct role or legal effect in our constitutional scheme, a referendum undoubtedly may provide a democratic method of ascertaining the views of the electorate on important political questions on a particular occasion. The democratic principle identified above would demand that considerable weight be given to a clear expression by the people of Quebec of their will to secede from Canada, even though a referendum, in itself and without more, has no direct legal effect, and could not in itself bring about unilateral secession. Our political institutions are premised on the democratic principle, and so an expression of the democratic will of the people of a province carries weight, in that it would confer legitimacy on the efforts of the government of Quebec to initiate the Constitution's amendment process in order to secede by constitutional means. In this context, we refer to a "clear" majority as a qualitative evaluation. The referendum result, if it is to be taken as an expression of the democratic will, must be free of ambiguity both in terms of the question asked and in terms of the support it achieves.

The federalism principle, in conjunction with the democratic principle, dictates that the clear repudiation of the existing constitutional order and the clear expression of the desire to pursue secession by the population of a province would give rise to a reciprocal obligation on all parties to Confederation to negotiate constitutional changes to respond to that desire. The amendment of the Constitution begins with a political process undertaken pursuant to the Constitution itself. In Canada, the initiative for constitutional amendment is the responsibility of democratically elected representatives of the participants in Confederation. Those representatives may, of course, take their cue from a referendum, but in legal terms, constitution-making in Canada, as in many countries, is undertaken by the democratically elected representatives of the people. The corollary of a legit-imate attempt by one participant in Confederation to seek an amendment to the Constitution is an obligation on all parties to come to the negotiating table. The clear repudiation by the people of Quebec of the existing con-stitutional order would confer legitimacy on demands for secession, and place an obligation on the other provinces and the federal government to acknowledge and respect that expression of democratic will by entering into negotiations and conducting them in accordance with the underlying con-stitutional principles already discussed.

What is the content of this obligation to negotiate? At this juncture, we confront the difficult inter-relationship between substantive obligations flowing from the Constitution and questions of judicial competence and restraint in supervising or enforcing those obligations. This is mirrored by the distinction between the legality and the legitimacy of actions taken under the Constitution. We propose to focus first on the substantive obli-gations flowing from this obligation to negotiate; once the nature of those obligations has been described, it is easier to assess the appropriate means of enforcement of those obligations, and to comment on the distinction between legality and legitimacy.

The conduct of the parties in such negotiations would be governed by the same constitutional principles which give rise to the duty to negotiate: fed-eralism, democracy, constitutionalism and the rule of law, and the protection of minorities. Those principles lead us to reject two absolutist propositions. One of those propositions is that there would be a legal obligation on the other provinces and federal government to accede to the secession of a prov-ince, subject only to negotiation of the logistical details of secession. This proposition is attributed either to the supposed implications of the demo-cratic principle of the Constitution, or to the international law principle of self-determination of peoples.

For both theoretical and practical reasons, we cannot accept this view. We hold that Quebec could not purport to invoke a right of self-determination such as to dictate the terms of a proposed secession to the other parties: that would not be a negotiation at all. As well, it would be naive to expect that the substantive goal of secession could readily be distinguished from the practi-cal details of secession. The devil would be in the details. The democracy principle, as we have emphasized, cannot be invoked to trump the prin-ciples of federalism and rule of law, the rights of individuals and minori-ties, or the operation of democracy in the other provinces or in Canada as a whole. No negotiations could be effective if their ultimate outcome, secession, is cast as an absolute legal entitlement based upon an obligation to give effect to that act of secession in the Constitution. Such a foregone conclusion would actually undermine the obligation to negotiate and render it hollow.

However, we are equally unable to accept the reverse proposition, that a clear expression of self-determination by the people of Quebec would impose *no* obligations upon the other provinces or the federal government. The continued existence and operation of the Canadian constitutional order cannot remain indifferent to the clear expression of a clear majority of Quebecers that they no longer wish to remain in Canada. This would amount to the assertion that other constitutionally recognized principles necessarily trump the clearly expressed democratic will of the people of Quebec. Such a proposition fails to give sufficient weight to the underlying constitutional principles that must inform the amendment process, including the principles of democracy and federalism. The rights of other provinces and the federal government cannot deny the right of the government of Quebec to pursue secession, should a clear majority of the people of Quebec choose that goal, so long as in doing so, Quebec respects the rights of others. Negotiations would be necessary to address the interests of the federal government, of Quebec and the other provinces, and other participants, as well as the rights of all Canadians both within and outside Quebec.

Is the rejection of both of these propositions reconcilable? Yes, once it is realized that none of the rights or principles under discussion is absolute to the exclusion of the others. This observation suggests that other parties cannot exercise their rights in such a way as to amount to an absolute denial of Quebec's rights, and similarly, that so long as Quebec exercises its rights while respecting the rights of others, it may propose secession and seek to achieve it through negotiation. The negotiation process precipitated by a decision of a clear majority of the population of Quebec on a clear question to pursue secession would require the reconciliation of various rights and obligations by the representatives of two legitimate majorities, namely, the clear majority of the population of Quebec, and the clear majority of Canada as a whole, whatever that may be. There can be no suggestion that either of these majorities "trumps" the other. A political majority that does not act in accordance with the underlying constitutional principles we have identified puts at risk the legitimacy of the exercise of its rights.

In such circumstances, the conduct of the parties assumes primary constitutional significance. The negotiation process must be conducted with an eye to the constitutional principles we have outlined, which must inform the actions of *all* the participants in the negotiation process.

Refusal of a party to conduct negotiations in a manner consistent with constitutional principles and values would seriously put at risk the legitimacy of that party's assertion of its rights, and perhaps the negotiation process as a whole. Those who quite legitimately insist upon the importance of upholding the rule of law cannot at the same time be oblivious to the need to act in conformity with constitutional principles and values, and so do their part to contribute to the maintenance and promotion of an environment in which the rule of law may flourish.

No one can predict the course that such negotiations might take. The possibility that they might not lead to an agreement amongst the parties must be recognized. Negotiations following a referendum vote in favour of seeking secession would inevitably address a wide range of issues, many of great import. After 131 years of Confederation, there exists, inevitably, a high level of integration in economic, political and social institutions across Canada. The vision of those who brought about Confederation was to create *a unified country*, not a loose alliance of autonomous provinces. Accordingly, while there are regional economic interests, which sometimes coincide with provincial boundaries, there are also national interests and enterprises (both public and private) that would face potential dismemberment. There is a national economy and a national debt. Arguments were raised before us regarding boundary issues. There are linguistic and cultural minorities, including aboriginal peoples, unevenly distributed across the country who look to the Constitution of Canada for the protection of their rights. Of course, secession would give rise to many issues of great complexity and difficulty. These would have to be resolved within the overall framework of the rule of law, thereby assuring Canadians resident in Quebec and elsewhere a measure of stability in what would likely be a period of considerable upheaval and uncertainty. Nobody seriously suggests that our national existence, seamless in so many aspects, could be effortlessly separated along what are now the provincial boundaries of Quebec.... In the circumstances, negotiations following such a referendum would undoubtedly be difficult. While the negotiators would have to contemplate the possibility of secession, there would be no absolute legal entitlement to it and no assumption that an agreement reconciling all relevant rights and obligations would actually be reached. It is foreseeable that even negotiations carried out in conformity with the underlying constitutional principles could reach an impasse. We need not speculate here as to what would then transpire. Under the Constitution, secession requires that an amendment be negotiated.

The respective roles of the courts and political actors in discharging the constitutional obligations we have identified follows ineluctably from the foregoing observations. In the *Patriation Reference*, a distinction was drawn between the law of the Constitution, which, generally speaking, will be enforced by the courts, and other constitutional rules, such as the conventions of the Constitution, which carry only political sanctions. It is also the case, however, that judicial intervention, even in relation to the *law* of the Constitution, is subject to the Court's appreciation of its proper role in the constitutional scheme.

The notion of justiciability is, as we earlier pointed out in dealing with the preliminary objection, linked to the notion of appropriate judicial restraint. We earlier made reference to the discussion of justiciability in *Reference re Canada Assistance Plan*:

> In exercising its discretion whether to determine a matter that is alleged to be non-justiciable, the Court's primary concern is to retain its proper role within the constitutional framework of our democratic form of government.

In *Operation Dismantle, supra,* at p. 459, it was pointed out that justiciability is a "doctrine ... founded upon a concern with the appropriate role of the courts as the forum for the resolution of different types of disputes." An analogous doctrine of judicial restraint operates here. Also, as observed in *Canada (Auditor General)* v. *Canada (Minister of Energy, Mines and Resources)* [1989]:

> There is an array of issues which calls for the exercise of judicial judgment on whether the questions are properly cognizable by the courts. Ultimately, such judgment depends on the appreciation by the judiciary of its own position in the constitutional scheme.

The role of the Court in this Reference is limited to the identification of the relevant aspects of the Constitution in their broadest sense. We have interpreted the questions as relating to the constitutional framework within which political decisions may ultimately be made. Within that framework, the workings of the political process are complex and can only be resolved by means of political judgments and evaluations. The Court has no supervisory role over the political aspects of constitutional negotiations. Equally, the initial impetus for negotiation, namely a clear majority on a clear question in favour of secession, is subject only to political evaluation, and properly so. A right and a corresponding duty to negotiate secession cannot be built on an alleged expression of democratic will if the expression of democratic will is itself fraught with ambiguities. Only the political actors would have the information and expertise to make the appropriate judgment as to the point at which, and the circumstances in which, those ambiguities are resolved one way or the other.

If the circumstances giving rise to the duty to negotiate were to arise, the distinction between the strong defence of legitimate interests and the taking of positions which, in fact, ignore the legitimate interests of others is one that also defies legal analysis. The Court would not have access to all of the information available to the political actors, and the methods appropriate for the search for truth in a court of law are ill-suited to getting to the bottom of constitutional negotiations. To the extent that the questions are political in nature, it is not the role of the judiciary to interpose its own views on the different negotiating positions of the parties, even were it invited to do so. Rather, it is the obligation of the elected representatives to give concrete form to the discharge of their constitutional obligations which only they and their electors can ultimately assess. The reconciliation of the various legitimate constitutional interests outlined above is necessarily committed to the political rather than the judicial realm, precisely because that reconciliation can only be achieved through the give and take of the negotiation process. Having established the legal framework, it would be for the democratically elected leadership of the various participants to resolve their differences.

The non-justiciability of political issues that lack a legal component does not deprive the surrounding constitutional framework of its binding status, nor does this mean that constitutional obligations could be breached without incurring serious legal repercussions. Where there are legal rights there are remedies, but as we explained in the *Auditor General's* case, and *New Brunswick Broadcasting*, the appropriate recourse in some circumstances lies through the workings of the political process rather than the courts.

To the extent that a breach of the constitutional duty to negotiate in accordance with the principles described above undermines the legitimacy of a party's actions, it may have important ramifications at the international level. Thus, a failure of the duty to undertake negotiations and pursue them according to constitutional principles may undermine that government's claim to legitimacy which is generally a precondition for recognition by the international community. Conversely, violations of those principles by the federal or other provincial governments responding to the request for secession may undermine their legitimacy. Thus, a Quebec that had negotiated in conformity with constitutional principles and values in the face of unreasonable intransigence on the part of other participants at the federal or provincial level would be more likely to be recognized than a Quebec which did not itself act according to constitutional principles in the negotiation process. Both the legality of the acts of the parties to the negotiation process under Canadian law, and the perceived legitimacy of such action, would be important considerations in the recognition process. In this way, the adherence of the parties to the obligation to negotiate would be evaluated in an indirect manner on the international plane.

Accordingly, the secession of Quebec from Canada cannot be accomplished by the National Assembly, the legislature or government of Quebec unilaterally, that is to say, without principled negotiations, and be considered a lawful act. Any attempt to effect the secession of a province from Canada must be undertaken pursuant to the Constitution of Canada, or else violate the Canadian legal order. However, the continued existence and operation of the Canadian constitutional order cannot remain unaffected by the unambiguous expression of a clear majority of Quebecers that they no longer wish to remain in Canada. The primary means by which that expression is given effect is the constitutional duty to negotiate in accordance with the constitutional principles that we have described herein. In the event secession negotiations are initiated, our Constitution, no less than our history, would call on the participants to work to reconcile the rights, obligations and legitimate aspirations of all Canadians within a framework that emphasizes constitutional responsibilities as much as it does constitutional rights.

It will be noted that Question 1 does not ask how secession could be achieved in a constitutional manner, but addresses one form of secession only, namely unilateral secession. Although the applicability of various procedures to achieve lawful secession was raised in argument, each option would require us to assume the existence of facts that at this stage are unknown. In accordance with the usual rule of prudence in constitutional cases, we refrain from pronouncing on the applicability of any particular constitutional procedure to effect secession unless and until sufficiently clear facts exist to squarely raise an issue for judicial determination.

(5) Suggested Principle of Effectivity

In the foregoing discussion we have not overlooked the principle of effectivity, which was placed at the forefront in argument before us. For the reasons that follow, we do not think that the principle of effectivity has any application to the issues raised by Question 1. A distinction must be drawn between the right of a people to act, and their power to do so. They are not identical. A right is recognized in law: mere physical ability is not necessarily given status as a right. The fact that an individual or group can act in a certain way says nothing at all about the legal status or consequences of the act. A power may be exercised even in the absence of a right to do so, but if it is, then it is exercised without legal foundation. Our Constitution does not address powers in this sense. On the contrary, the Constitution is concerned only with the rights and obligations of individuals, groups and governments, and the structure of our institutions. It was suggested before us that the National Assembly, legislature or government of Quebec could unilaterally effect the secession of that province from Canada, but it was not suggested that they might do so as a matter of law: rather, it was contended that they simply could do so as a matter of fact. Although under the Constitution there is no right to pursue secession unilaterally, that is secession without principled negotiation, this does not rule out the possibility of an unconstitutional declaration of secession leading to a *de facto* secession. The ultimate success of such a secession would be dependent on effective control of a territory and recognition by the international community. The principles governing secession at international law are discussed in our answer to Question 2.

In our view, the alleged principle of effectivity has no constitutional or legal status in the sense that it does not provide an *ex ante* explanation or justification for an act. In essence, acceptance of a principle of effectivity would be tantamount to accepting that the National Assembly, legislature or government of Quebec may act without regard to the law, simply because it asserts the power to do so. So viewed, the suggestion is that the National Assembly, legislature or government of Quebec could purport to secede the province unilaterally from Canada in disregard of Canadian and international law. It is further suggested that if the secession bid was successful, a new legal order would be created in that province, which would then be considered an independent state.

Such a proposition is an assertion of fact, not a statement of law. It may or may not be true; in any event it is irrelevant to the questions of law before us. If, on the other hand, it is put forward as an assertion of law, then it simply amounts to the contention that the law may be broken as long as it can be broken successfully. Such a notion is contrary to the rule of law, and must be rejected.

B. Question 2

Does international law give the National Assembly, legislature or government of Quebec the right to effect the secession of Quebec from Canada unilaterally? In this regard, is there a right to self-determination under international law that would give the National Assembly, legislature or government of Quebec the right to effect the secession of Quebec from Canada unilaterally?

[*Ed. Note:* The Court answers "no" to this question.]

C. Question 3

In the event of a conflict between domestic and international law on the right of the National Assembly, legislature or government of Quebec to effect the secession of Quebec from Canada unilaterally, which would take precedence in Canada?

In view of our answers to Questions 1 and 2, there is no conflict between domestic and international law to be addressed in the context of this Reference.

IV. Summary of Conclusions

As stated at the outset, this Reference has required us to consider momentous questions that go to the heart of our system of constitutional government. We have emphasized that the Constitution is more than a written text. It embraces the entire global system of rules and principles which govern the exercise of constitutional authority. A superficial reading of selected provisions of the written constitutional enactment, without more, may be misleading. It is necessary to make a more profound investigation of the underlying principles that animate the whole of our Constitution, including the principles of federalism, democracy, constitutionalism and the rule of law, and respect for minorities. Those principles must inform our overall appreciation of the constitutional rights and obligations that would come into play in the event a clear majority of Quebecers votes on a clear question in favour of secession.

The Reference requires us to consider whether Quebec has a right to *unilateral* secession. Those who support the existence of such a right found their case primarily on the principle of democracy. Democracy, however, means more than simple majority rule. As reflected in our constitutional jurisprudence, democracy exists in the larger context of other constitutional values such as those already mentioned. In the 131 years since Confederation, the people of the provinces and territories have created close ties of interdependence (economically, socially, politically and culturally) based on shared values that include federalism, democracy, constitutionalism and the rule of law, and respect for minorities. A democratic decision of Quebecers in favour of secession would put those relationships at risk. The Constitution vouchsafes order and stability, and accordingly secession of a province "under the Constitution" could not be achieved unilaterally, that is, without principled negotiation with other participants in Confederation within the existing constitutional framework.

The Constitution is not a straitjacket. Even a brief review of our constitutional history demonstrates periods of momentous and dramatic change. Our democratic institutions necessarily accommodate a continuous process of discussion and evolution, which is reflected in the constitutional right of each participant in the federation to initiate constitutional change. This right implies a reciprocal duty on the other participants to engage in discussions to address any legitimate initiative to change the constitutional order. While it is true that some attempts at constitutional amendment in recent years have faltered, a clear majority vote in Quebec on a clear question in favour of secession would confer democratic legitimacy on the secession initiative which all of the other participants in Confederation would have to recognize.

Quebec could not, despite a clear referendum result, purport to invoke a right of self-determination to dictate the terms of a proposed secession to the other parties to the federation. The democratic vote, by however strong a majority, would have no legal effect on its own and could not push aside the principles of federalism and the rule of law, the rights of individuals and minorities, or the operation of democracy in the other provinces or in Canada as a whole. Democratic rights under the Constitution cannot be divorced from constitutional obligations. Nor, however, can the reverse proposition be accepted. The continued existence and operation of the Canadian constitutional order could not be indifferent to a clear expression of a clear majority of Quebecers that they no longer wish to remain in Canada. The other provinces and the federal government would have no basis to deny the right of the government of Quebec to pursue secession, should a clear majority of the people of Quebec choose that goal, so long as in doing so, Quebec respects the rights of others. The negotiations that followed such a vote would address the potential act of secession as well as its possible terms should in fact secession proceed. There would be no conclusions predetermined by law on any issue. Negotiations would need to address the interests of the other provinces, the federal government, Quebec and indeed the rights of all Canadians both within and outside Quebec, and specifically the rights of minorities. No one suggests that it would be an easy set of negotiations.

The negotiation process would require the reconciliation of various rights and obligations by negotiation between two legitimate majorities, namely, the majority of the population of Quebec, and that of Canada as a whole. A political majority at either level that does not act in accordance with the underlying constitutional principles we have mentioned puts at risk the legitimacy of its exercise of its rights, and the ultimate acceptance of the result by the international community.

The task of the Court has been to clarify the legal framework within which political decisions are to be taken "under the Constitution," not to usurp the prerogatives of the political forces that operate within that framework. The obligations we have identified are binding obligations under the Constitution of Canada. However, it will be for the political actors to determine what constitutes "a clear majority on a clear question" in the circumstances under which a future referendum vote may be taken. Equally, in the event of demonstrated majority support for Quebec secession, the content and process of the negotiations will be for the political actors to settle. The reconciliation of the various legitimate constitutional interests is necessarily committed to the political rather than the judicial realm precisely because that reconciliation can only be achieved through the give and take of political negotiations. To the extent issues addressed in the course of negotiation are political, the courts, appreciating their proper role in the constitutional scheme, would have no supervisory role.

We have also considered whether a positive legal entitlement to secession exists under international law in the factual circumstances contemplated by Question 1, i.e., a clear democratic expression of support on a clear question for Quebec secession. Some of those who supported an affirmative answer to this question did so on the basis of the recognized right to self-determination that belongs to all "peoples." Although much of the Quebec population certainly shares many of the characteristics of a people, it is not necessary to decide the "people" issue because, whatever may be the correct determination of this issue in the context of Quebec, a right to secession only arises under the principle of self-determination of peoples at international law where "a people" is governed as part of a colonial empire; where "a people" is subject to alien subjugation, domination or exploitation; and possibly where "a people" is denied any meaningful exercise of its right to self-determination within the state of which it forms a part. In other circumstances, peoples are expected to achieve self-determination within the framework of their existing state. A state whose government represents the whole of the people or peoples resident within its territory, on a basis of equality and without discrimination, and respects the principles of self-determination in its internal arrangements, is entitled to maintain its territorial integrity under international law and to have that territorial integrity recognized by other states. Quebec does not meet the threshold of a colonial people or an oppressed people, nor can it be suggested that Quebecers have been denied meaningful access to government to pursue their political, economic, cultural and social development. In the circumstances, the National Assembly, the legislature or the government of Quebec do not enjoy a right at international law to effect the secession of Quebec from Canada unilaterally.

Although there is no right, under the Constitution or at international law, to unilateral secession, that is secession without negotiation on the basis just discussed, this does not rule out the possibility of an unconstitutional

declaration of secession leading to a *de facto* secession. The ultimate success
of such a secession would be dependent on recognition by the international
community, which is likely to consider the legality and legitimacy of secession having regard to, amongst other facts, the conduct of Quebec and
Canada, in determining whether to grant or withhold recognition. Such recognition, even if granted, would not, however, provide any retroactive justification for the act of secession, either under the Constitution of Canada or
at international law.

The reference questions are answered accordingly.
Judgment accordingly.

2.5

Will Women Judges Really Make a Difference?
Justice Bertha Wilson

This article is reprinted as Reading 4.4.

2.6

Gender Differences on the Supreme Court
Candace C. White
This reading is excerpted from Candace C. White's M.A. thesis, "Gender Differences in the
Supreme Court" (University of Calgary, 1998)

The Design and Methodology of the Statistical Study

A statistical study conducted by F.L. Morton, P.H. Russell and T. Riddell in
1995 inquires into the topic, *inter alia,* of divisions and ideological differences
among Justices sitting on the Supreme Court of Canada…. The authors examine gender as an incident of judicial voting behaviour and conclude that,
"gender alone is not a reliable predictor of a Judge's *Charter* voting record."

The current study proposes to update and expand on the Morton et al. article and demonstrate that, if not an exclusive predictor of a Justice's voting
behaviour, there is at least some correlation between voting and gender on the
Supreme Court of Canada. The data … incorporate the Morton et al. data set
of 195 *Charter* decisions and updates this set of cases by including a further 85
decisions rendered by the Supreme Court between the beginning of January,
1993 and ending with the month of June, 1996 for a total of 280 cases….

...

The first part of the study compared the percentage of *Charter* support between the male and female Justices of the Supreme Court of Canada for each of the three sub-categories of legal issue…. The results of the cross-gender comparison are summarized in Tables 1 to 3 divided into the three *Charter* issues examined, legal rights, fundamental freedoms and equality rights. For each issue studied, the tables show the total number of supporting votes for each justice and provides a statistical mean for the whole field as well as a mean of support for the men as compared to the women.

Table 1 – Legal Rights

	Percentage of Support	Total Number Cases
Wilson	**57.50%**	**80**
Chouinard	50.00%	12
Estey	47.83%	23
Lamer	45.51%	156
Sopinka	42.62%	122
Dickson	38.36%	73
LaForest	36.91%	149
LeDain	37.93%	29
Cory	37.86%	103
McLachlin	**37.74%**	**106**
Mean	**37.70%**	**1297**
Beetz	35.14%	37
Iacobucci	34.15%	82
Gonthier	33.00%	109
Major	32.61%	46
L'Heureux-Dubé	**23.28%**	**116**
McIntyre	22.22%	54
Mean Supported by Men	37.79%	995
Mean Supported by Women	37.42%	302

Table 1 summarizes the data for legal rights by calculating the number of cases on which each respective Judge rendered a positive decision and then establishing an average rate of support by the Court in order to achieve a ranking in overall support. The results … in Table 1 reveal that Madame Justice Wilson is the highest supporter of *Charter* claims relating to legal rights, well above the Court average with Justice McIntyre being well below the Court average. Madame Justice McLachlin exhibits an average level of support for these claims while Madame Justice L'Heureux-Dubé finishes near the bottom in the second last position in support of legal rights claims. These results indicate that a gender difference does not exist. This finding is further evidenced by the proximity of the statistical means representing support by the men versus support by women….

Table 2 – Fundamental Freedoms

	Percentage of Support	Total Number Cases
Wilson	**60.87%**	**23**
McLachlin	**61.11%**	**18**
Beetz	50.00%	10
Major	40.00%	5
McIntyre	36.36%	11
Lamer	36.36%	22
Sopinka	36.00%	25
Mean	**34.00%**	**250**
Chouinard	33.33%	2
Cory	30.00%	20
Dickson	28.57%	21
Iacobucci	25.00%	10
L'Heureux-Dubé	**23.08%**	**26**
LaForest	22.58%	31
Gonthier	21.05%	19
Estey	00.00%	1
LeDain	00.00%	6
Mean Supported by Men	29.51%	183
Mean Supported by Women	46.27%	67

The results summarized in Table 2 … provide support for the claim that there is a gender difference…. The women Justices on the Supreme Court of Canada appear to be significantly more sympathetic with fundamental freedoms claims than their male counterparts. Madame Justices Wilson and McLachlin are both well above the overall judicial mean of support…. Madame Justice L'Heureux-Dubé, on the other hand, appears in the bottom third of supporters for fundamental freedoms claimants. This difference might be partially explained by the fact that L'Heureux-Dubé sat on more of these decisions than Wilson or McLachlin and may have reviewed different issues in combination with the fundamental freedoms claim, which she favoured….

Of particular note from Table 2, however, is the difference between the average rate of support for the men Justices and the women Justices. This comparison … reveals that the women of the Court are almost 50% more likely to support fundamental freedoms claims than are the men….

Table 3 represents the sharpest distinction between voting patterns for men and women…. All three of the women top the list as the strongest supporters of a *Charter* argument based on the equality rights sections. The data [for mean support] … also indicate that the women are more than twice as likely as the men to support an equality claim.

Table 3 – Equality Rights

	Percentage of Support	Total Number Cases
McLachlin	**75.00%**	**8**
L'Heureux-Dubé	**71.43%**	**14**
Wilson	**50.00%**	**8**
Beetz	50.00%	2
Estey	50.00%	2
Chouinard	n/a	0
Cory	45.45%	11
Iacobucci	44.44%	9
Lamer	36.36%	11
Mean	**35.20%**	**125**
Dickson	25.00%	8
LaForest	17.65%	17
Sopinka	16.67%	12
Gonthier	15.38%	13
LeDain	n/a	0
Major	00.00%	6
McIntyre	00.00%	4
Mean Supported by Men	25.53%	94
Mean Supported by Women	66.67%	30

... The results of the current study would seem to suggest that for equality rights claims and to a lesser extent, fundamental freedoms, there is a gender difference on the Supreme Court of Canada. Morton et al. noted in their 1995 study that L'Heureux-Dubé "occupies two different wings of the Court depending on the issues." This conclusion is further born out by the current study because Madame Justice L'Heureux-Dubé stands out against McLachlin and Wilson on the issues of legal rights and fundamental freedoms as being one of the least supportive of the Court for these claims. The writer posits that this phenomenon is best explained by an examination of L'Heureux-Dubé's legal writing and predicts that she most closely approximates a consistent "feminist" position (i.e. a position which ranks women's concerns and interests higher against competing rights claims).

...

Patterns of Dissenting Judgments between the Men and the Women on the Court

As a final comparison, the study gauge[d] the judicial disposition of the women of the Supreme Court of Canada versus the men through measuring the frequency of dissenting opinions. This measurement is intended to establish a yardstick for judicial independence, which ... might also be indicative of gender difference.... The study took the total number of times an individual member dissented divided by the total number of decisions on which he or she deliberated within the selected set of 280 *Charter* cases. The results are summarized in Table 4.

Table 4 – Rates of Dissent

	Percentage of Dissent	Total Number Cases
L'Heureux-Dubé	**21.82%**	**165**
Wilson	**20.87%**	**115**
McLachlin	**18.80%**	**133**
McIntyre	15.94%	69
Mean	**11.78%**	**1689**
Cory	10.45%	134
Lamer	9.95%	191
Gonthier	9.63%	135
Sopinka	9.49%	158
LaForest	9.00%	200
Iacobucci	7.84%	102
Estey	7.69%	26
Major	7.02%	57
Beetz	5.88%	51
Dickson	5.83%	103
LeDain	2.86%	35
Chouinard	0.00%	15
Mean Dissent for Men	11.29%	1276
Mean Dissent for Women	20.58%	413

The figures in Table 4 provide perhaps the most startling contrast between the male and female members of the Supreme Court of Canada because it illustrates very clearly that the women of the Court demonstrate a greater willingness to contradict the majority, just as Morton et al. found in their 1995 study. The aggregate averages [reveal] that ... the women are almost twice as likely to dissent [as] the men on the Court. Moreover, Wilson, L'Heureux-Dubé and McLachlin are so close together in their respective rates of dissent while the rest of the field is well below these rates....

... Morton contends that a study of dissenting voting patterns reveals and reflects the existence of shared judicial philosophy. His 1992 study concludes, for instance, that Justices Wilson and McIntyre dissented most frequently, although they had never dissented together. The results of the current study indicate that Wilson and L'Heureux-Dubé dissent most often for the women while McIntyre shows the highest predisposition toward favouring a dissenting position for the men on the Court. The ... polarization of male and female dissent on the Court provides a strong argument for gender-based differences in judicial decision-making.

Conclusions Based on the Data

...

In addition to these gender differences, there are also notable differences among the three women of the Supreme Court. According to the calculations in the study, Madame Justice Wilson remains the most consistently supportive member of the Court for all three categories of *Charter* rights, although she slips behind L'Heureux-Dubé and McLachlin on equality claims. L'Heureux-Dubé and McLachlin are especially interesting because they align themselves diametrically on legal rights issues, and to a lesser extent fundamental rights, so that McLachlin appears more supportive of the individualistic position represented by legal rights arguments. Alternatively, this difference could be explained by the fact that McLachlin appears to apply the traditional rules of evidence and the fundamental principles of justice in a judicially restrained manner in order to ensure that only the guilty are convicted. On the other hand, L'Heureux-Dubé tends to represent what might be referred to as a more "communitarian perspective" by interpreting legal issues and fundamental freedoms in light of the greater social context and potential impact on otherwise disadvantaged members of society.

The data collected in this study appear to support the conclusion that, like the American studies, there is a gender difference on the Supreme Court of Canada which is not universally apparent across the spectrum of issues tested. This gender difference manifests itself most visibly when the issue being deliberated by the court is a "woman's" issue, that is, it speaks more to women's lived experience than it does perhaps to men's experience…. The empirical findings of the study alone do not provide sufficient data to determine whether the statistical gender difference is coincidental or supports the larger proposition that women judges view the world differently than their male colleagues.

2.7

Key Terms

Concepts

declaratory model of judging
legal positivism
legal realism
judicial nationalism
adjudication of disputes model of judging
policy-making model of judging
adversary process
power vs. authority
constitutional law
constitutional convention
"unconstitutional but legal"
"unilateral declaration of independence" (UDI)
"foundational constitutional principles"
"a clear majority on a clear question"
"duty to negotiate"

Institutions, Events and Documents

Judicial Committee of the Privy Council (JCPC)
O'Connor Report (1939)
Abolition of Appeals to JCPC (1949)
Harrison v. *Carswell* (1976)
Re Constitution of Canada, 1981 (Patriation Reference)
Quebec Secession Reference (1998)

The Canadian Judicial System 3

A distinctive feature of the Canadian judicial system is its unitary character. This distinguishes it from other federal nations such as the United States, which has a "dual court system." A dual court system parallels the division of legislative powers along federal lines by creating federal courts for federal law and state courts for state law. While the Canadian founders adopted the logic of federalism for the distribution of legislative authority, they did not apply it to the judiciary. They created a single judicial system to interpret and to apply both federal and provincial laws.

The unitary character of the Canadian judicial system is illustrated by the judicial flowchart (Figure 1) in Reading 3.3. Both civil law, which is mainly provincial in origin, and criminal law, which is exclusively federal in origin, move from trial to appeal through the same system of courts. This unitary character of the Canadian judicial system is politically significant because it can mitigate the centrifugal forces of federal-provincial politics. Rather than accentuating regional differences, it promotes a continuity and uniformity of legal policy across the nation. However, the federal monopoly over appointing superior court judges, combined with long periods of Liberal Party dominance in Ottawa, have led some provinces – notably Quebec and Alberta – to demand that the power to appoint section 96 court judges be transferred to the provinces. In the United States, all state court judges are selected by the state, either by executive appointment, election, or some combination of both. However, Ottawa has shown no interest in this proposal.

The unitary character of the Canadian judicial system is reinforced by the fact that it is the shared responsibility of both levels of government. The legal framework for this joint-responsibility is laid out in sections 92(14) and 96 to 101 of the *Constitution Act, 1867* (see Reading 3.2). Section 92 allocates to the provinces the powers to make laws that provide for the "constitution, maintenance, and organization of provincial courts." Section 96 provides that the federal government "shall appoint the judges of the superior, district, and county courts in each province." These provisions create a joint federal-provincial responsibility for the section 96 courts, which are created and maintained by the provinces but whose judges are appointed by the federal government.

In the judicial hierarchy, there are two additional tiers of courts beside the section 96 or superior courts. Below are the section 92 courts, so-called because they are created, maintained, and staffed wholly by the provincial governments, pursuant to section 92(14) of the *Constitution Act*. In most provinces, these courts are entitled "provincial courts" and are the modern-day successors to the old Magistrates or Police courts. Above the section 96 courts is the Supreme Court of Canada, which, pursuant to section 101 of the *Constitution Act*, is created, maintained, and staffed wholly by the federal government. This allocation of responsibility for the different tiers of the judicial system is illustrated in the diagram in Figure 1 of Reading 3.3.

Section 92 Courts

The section 92 courts can be described as both the least important and the most important courts in Canada. Their lack of status stems from their position as the lowest rung in the Canadian judicial hierarchy. They serve principally as trial courts for less serious offences and as courts of preliminary inquiry for more serious offences. Their decisions are always subject to review and reversal by "higher" courts. On the other hand, these courts are critically important because of the high volume of litigation that they process each year. Described as the "workhorse" of the Canadian judicial system, the provincial courts handle over ninety per cent of all criminal litigation. For most Canadians, "a day in court" means a day in provincial court. The quality of justice in Canada is thus directly affected by the quality of the provincial court system. As a result of the somewhat belated recognition of their importance, there has been a conscious effort in the past several decades to improve the salaries and training of provincial court judges, the efficiency of court administration, and even the physical setting of courtrooms and courthouses. The criminal law jurisdiction of the provincial courts is illustrated in the flowchart in Reading 3.4 (Figure 2). Provincial courts hear all provincial offences and summary conviction offences and conduct all preliminary inquiries. In addition, they hear indictable offences under section 483 of the Criminal Code, some indictable offences of election, and cases under the *Young Offenders Act*. Their civil law jurisdiction includes issues of minor civil claims and family law.

The Section 96 Superior, County, and District Courts

Each province has a two-tier system of superior courts: a trial court of general criminal and civil jurisdiction and a corresponding appeal court.[1] The names of these courts vary from province to province, but their constitutional status is the same. In Alberta, Manitoba, and Saskatchewan, these

---

1 While Ontario has County and District Courts, most provinces have amalgamated them with the trial division of the superior court.

courts are the Court of Queen's Bench and the Court of Appeal. In Quebec, they are called the Superior Court and the Court of Appeal. In most of the other provinces, they are distinguished as the trial division and appellate division of the province's Supreme Court. The judges in both courts are appointed by the federal government.[2]

The Court of Queen's Bench (or Trial Division of the Supreme Court) is generally regarded as the cornerstone of the Canadian court system. Its prestige flows from its very broad criminal and civil jurisdiction and the fact that it is derived from the English superior courts of common law and equity. W. R. Lederman argues that the independence of these courts is part of the "unwritten constitution" inherited from Great Britain and that they could not be abolished or significantly altered without doing violence to the fundamental order of Canadian government (see Reading 5.1).

The criminal jurisdiction of the Court of Queen's Bench includes the trial of all indictable offences under section 427 of the Criminal Code and indictable offences by election. It also hears appeals from all summary conviction offences (see Figure 2 in Reading 3.4). The Court of Queen's Bench is clearly the most important civil law court. It hears divorces, separations, and guardianship disputes and all civil disputes whose monetary claims are too large for small claims courts. It also hears appeals from juvenile and family courts and from some provincial administrative boards and tribunals.

The Court of Appeal of the province (or Appellate Division of the Supreme Court) is the highest court in the province. It sits principally to hear appeals from the Court of Queen's Bench on questions of law, and its decisions are binding on all other courts within the province (unless overturned on appeal to the Supreme Court of Canada). The Court of Appeal of each province also hears references from the provincial government. The chief justice of the Court of Appeal serves as the chief justice of the province.

Supreme Court of Canada

At the summit of the judicial pyramid sits the Supreme Court of Canada. Since appeals to the Judicial Committee of the Privy Council were abolished in 1949, the Supreme Court has served as the final court of appeal for all matters of Canadian law. Its creation was authorized but not required by section 101 of the *Constitution Act, 1867*. Parliament, after considerable debate, exercised that power and enacted the *Supreme Court Act* in 1875.[3]

The Supreme Court has jurisdiction to hear appeals on all questions of criminal and civil law from the provincial courts of appeal and also accepts appeals from the Federal Court. Since 1975, the Court grants "leave to appeal" in a civil case only if it raises an issue of national concern or public

---

2 Prince Edward Island does not have a separate appeal court. Appeals are heard by the Chief Justice and two judges who did not participate in the trial.
3 See Jennifer Smith, "The Origins of Judicial Review in Canada," Reading 10.1.

importance, so that the Court now has considerably more control over the content and size of its docket than before. In Reading 3.1, the late Chief Justice Bora Laskin argues that the increasingly discretionary character of the Supreme Court's appellate jurisdiction changes the nature of the Court's function from that of traditional appellate review to one of "supervisory control." This represents a change of emphasis from concern for the individual case to overseeing the consistent development of Canadian law, especially in issues of public importance and national concern. As Ian Bushnell has observed,

> In the role of simply another review court, it is the litigant who is afforded access, and he brings the legal issue with him; when the court fulfills a lawmaking function, it is the legal problem that determines access, and the litigant is brought along with it.[4]

Gaining control of its docket has been one of the most important factors in the Supreme Court's rise in political prominence over the past two decades. As Professor Roy Flemming (Reading 12.2) explains, this reform has allowed the Supreme Court to "set its own agenda" rather than having to take whatever appeals happen to come along. This constitutes a significant new strategic asset for Supreme Court justices who want to influence the outcome of leading political controversies of the day. The number of appeals by right dropped dramatically after 1975, while the number of cases accepted "by leave" of the Court soared (see Reading 11.7). Applying the maxim that "you are what you do," Professor Peter McCormick concludes that the Supreme Court has changed its function from that of an arbiter of economic disputes to a criminal and *Charter* adjudicator.[5] Significantly, McCormick found that the origin of this shift occurred under the leadership of former Chief Justice Bora Laskin, the leading advocate of giving the Court control of its own docket (see Reading 3.1).

In the two decades preceding 1975, private law cases (mostly lawsuits between businesses) made up more than fifty per cent of the Court's caseload. That figure began dropping immediately following the reform, and today these kinds of cases constitute less than twenty per cent. On the other side of the ledger, the Court has used its new discretion to hear many more criminal law cases, a category that represented only fifteen per cent of the Court's case load prior to 1975. Since the reform, criminal cases jumped to over twenty per cent on the Laskin Court (1973–1984); thirty-seven per cent on the Dickson Court (1984–1990); and over forty per cent on the Lamer Court (1990–1999). The other major new component of the Court's caseload

---

4 S. I. Bushnell, "Leave to Appeal Applications to the Supreme Court of Canada: A Matter of Public Importance," *Supreme Court Law Review* 3 (1982), p. 488.

5 The following figures are all from Peter McCormick, *Supreme at Last: The Evolution of the Supreme Court of Canada* (Toronto: James Lorimer, 2000).

is *Charter of Rights* cases. In the two decades since the *Charter* became justiciable (1982), *Charter* cases have come to account for approximately twenty per cent of the Court's decisions each year.

This does not mean that the Court accepts every *Charter* case that asks for leave to appeal. Professor Roy Flemming's recent study of Supreme Court "agenda setting" found that the Court still rejects four out of every five leave applications that it receives, including *Charter* cases. More important in granting leave are factors like new legal issues, conflicting decisions by lower courts, and dissenting opinions in the lower court decision being appealed. (Reading 12.2).

While the Supreme Court can now pick and choose which appeals to hear, there are several exceptions. One is the reference procedure, by which the federal government can ask the Court for an "advisory opinion" on any question of constitutional or statutory law. While the number of references has decreased as a proportion of the total number of cases heard annually by the Court, they frequently represent the most important cases (see Readings 5.6, 6.1, 10.6, and 10.7).

The original *Supreme Court Act* authorized the appointment of six judges and required that two of the six be from Quebec. This was deemed necessary to accommodate Civil Law appeals from Quebec. Not to be outdone by her provincial rival, Ontario demanded equal treatment, and eventually a custom of having two Ontario judges on the Court came into being. In 1927, the size of the Court was increased to seven judges, and again in 1949 to nine. The number of Quebec and Ontario judges was increased to three, Quebec's by law and Ontario's by custom. Again by custom, the three remaining vacancies are normally filled by one judge from the Atlantic provinces and two from the western provinces. This *de facto* practice of regional representation on the Supreme Court attests to its perception as an important "political" institution in the process of national government.

The Supreme Court is presided over by a Chief Justice, the highest judicial officer of Canada. Over time, customs developed to govern the appointment of the Chief Justice. A pattern of alternating the position between English-Canadian and French-Canadian judges developed and also of appointing the most senior judge in terms of service within each of these groups. Both of these customs were broken by Prime Minister Trudeau. In 1973, he appointed Bora Laskin, who had served considerably less time on the court than several other anglophone members. In April of 1984, Trudeau again broke with tradition by appointing another anglophone, Brian Dickson, to succeed Laskin. These appointments cast doubt on the continued validity of these traditions. However, in 1989, upon Dickson's retirement, Prime Minister Mulroney elevated puisne justice Antonio Lamer, the senior Quebec francophone on the Court, to the Chief Justiceship. When Lamer retired in 2000, Prime Minister Chrétien appointed the anglophone judge with the most years of service, the current Chief Justice Beverley McLachlin. The Lamer and McLachlin appointments suggest that there is still vitality in both conventions.

Because the Supreme Court was not constitutionally entrenched, Parliament could technically abolish it at any time. Many commentators have argued that this impugned the independence and thus the status of the Court. It was illogical, they argued, that the institution responsible for enforcing the constitution protections against governments was not itself constitutionally protected. There was an attempt to change this situation in 1982. The *Constitution Act, 1982*, Section 41(d), declares that the composition of the Supreme Court (nine judges with three from Quebec) can only be changed by the unanimous consent of all the provinces and the federal government. Section 42 requires that any changes to the Supreme Court other than its composition be done according to the new amending formula. These changes were intended to eliminate the Court's potential vulnerability to Parliament but confused the situation by "constitutionalizing" an arrangement that existed only by statute, the *Supreme Court Act*. These provisions thus "put the cart before the horse." Some scholars argued that the effect of the 1982 amendments was to constitutionally entrench the entire *Supreme Court Act*, while others argued that the amendments could have no effect until or unless the Supreme Court itself was made part of the formal constitution.

The 1987 *Meech Lake Accord* proposed to resolve this confusion by explicitly constitutionalizing the existence of the Supreme Court. Sections 101(a) to (e) of the *Meech Lake Accord* would have constitutionally entrenched the existence of the Supreme Court and its basic function; the number of judges (a chief justice plus eight others); the requirement that three of the judges come from Quebec; the qualifications, tenure and mode of payment (the same as section 96 court judges, as protected by sections 99 and 100 of the *Constitution Act, 1867*); and the method of appointment.[6] With the exception of appointments, the proposed changes were largely symbolic, providing formal constitutional status for what had previously existed as a matter of constitutional convention. The appointment procedure proposed under the *Meech Lake Accord* was both novel and controversial. It would have left the appointment power with the federal government but required that all new appointments to the Supreme Court be made from nomination lists submitted by the provinces. This issue is discussed further in the introduction to Chapter 4. In the end, however, the *Meech Lake Accord* failed to be ratified, so none of these amendments took effect. The ambiguities created by the 1982 amendments remain unresolved.

Federal Court of Canada

In addition to authorizing the creation of the Supreme Court, section 101 of the *Constitution Act, 1867*, also allows "for the establishment of any additional courts for the better administration of the laws of Canada." If it chose

---

6 See Peter H. Russell, "The Supreme Court Proposals in the Meech Lake Accord," *Canadian Public Policy* 14 (Sept. 1988), pp. 93–106.

to, Parliament could use this authority to create an entirely new tier of federal courts, similar to those of the United States. In practice, it has not done so, creating instead only two federal courts of specialized jurisdiction. In 1875, Parliament created the Exchequer Court. In 1970, it was renamed the Federal Court and was given an expanded jurisdiction. The original jurisdiction of the Exchequer Court consisted of a collection of specialized areas of federal law – admiralty law, copyright and trademark law, income and estate tax law, and citizenship and immigration law. It also heard civil claims against the Crown.

In 1970, the new Federal Court inherited this jurisdiction and, in addition, was given the function of supervising federal administrative law. The Federal Court has both a trial and an appellate division. The federal administrative law area has been hived off from the rest of the judicial system and made the special responsibility of the Federal Court. There is the possibility of leave to appeal to the Supreme Court from all Federal Court decisions. In 1983, Parliament created a new section 101 court, the Tax Court of Canada. It hears appeals from Revenue Canada, and its decisions may be appealed to the Federal Court.

Judicial Committee of the Privy Council

Prior to Confederation, the Judicial Committee of the Privy Council (JCPC) served as the final court of appeal for the courts of all the British colonies, including Canada. It continued in this capacity under section 129 of the *Constitution Act, 1867*. The Privy Council served as final court of appeal for the entire British Empire. It was not a part of the regular English court system and did not hear appeals from English courts. It consisted of five judges drawn mainly from the law lords in the House of Lords.

Even after the Supreme Court was created in 1875, appeals to the Privy Council remained. In addition to appeals from Supreme Court decisions, there were also appeals from the Court of Appeal of each province. This latter possibility, known as a *per saltum* appeal, allowed parties to effectively bypass the Supreme Court of Canada and reduced its prestige and influence. The decisions of the Privy Council played a major role in shaping the constitutional development of Canada. Its interpretations of the federal division of powers significantly diminished the authority of the federal government while expanding that of the provinces. As discussed in the preceding chapter, this trend reached a climax during the 1930s and provoked a reaction against the continued role of the Privy Council in Canadian public affairs. This "judicial nationalism" movement culminated in the abolition of appeals to the Privy Council in 1949. However, its pre-1949 decisions remain an important part of Canadian law, especially in the areas of federalism (see Reading 10.4).

3.1

The Role and Functions of Final Appellate Courts:

The Supreme Court of Canada

Chief Justice Bora Laskin
Canadian Bar Review 53 (1975), 469–81. Reprinted with permission.

I

... I look upon the functions of the Supreme Court of Canada as those that arise out of its jurisdiction; the definition of its role depends on how that jurisdiction is exercised, how it uses its final appellate authority having regard to the kind and range of cases that come before it. The interaction between jurisdiction and role is obvious; and, inevitably, the judges' view of their role is bound to undergo definition and redefinition in the day-to-day grind of the court's business and in the periodic changes of its membership. One can envisage judges of the Supreme Court having some differences of opinion, probably slight ones, on the court's functions; any differences about its role are likely to be more serious.

II

The starting point for any consideration of the Supreme Court's functions and its role is that fact, a surprising one I am sure to foreign students of federalism, that the Supreme Court of Canada has no constitutional base. This marks it off immediately from such kindred courts as the Supreme Court of the United States and the High Court of Australia. The Supreme Court of Canada is a statutory creation of the Parliament of Canada under the power given that Parliament by section 101 of the British North America Act to constitute, maintain and organize "a general Court of Appeal for Canada." The size of the court, its jurisdiction, its procedure, indeed all questions touching its operation as a general court of appeal, an appellate court in short without any declared right to original jurisdiction, were left to the Government and Parliament of Canada to prescribe.

The size of the court, originally composed of six judges, with a seventh added in 1927 and two more added in 1949 upon the abolition of all appeals to the Privy Council from any appellate court in Canada, testifies both to population and regional growth in Canada, to the expansion of the business of the court and to its ultimate grave responsibility as a final appellate court. Of significance in its structure and operations was the provision of a quorum for sittings of the court, the number being fixed at five upon the creation of the court and remaining constant despite increase in its overall size. There could not, and even today there cannot be more than one Bench for the hearing of appeals; and I am thankful that this precludes having two Supreme Courts of Canada. Perhaps the only power a Chief Justice has is to assign the Bench for the hearing of appeals. Since my personal preference is to have the full court sit, and since the recent change in our jurisdiction enables the court to be selective in the cases that it will hear, I will not view with any regret the surrender of the power of assignment which, in any event, has been exercised with regard to the opinions of the other members of the court as to whether a panel of five or the full court should be assigned in any particular appeal.

The jurisdiction of the court, the scope of its appellate authority, was undoubtedly the most important matter that faced the Government and Parliament of Canada in creating the court in 1875. A number of models were available for consideration. There was the model of a national appellate court, functioning like an English appellate court, or like the House of Lords, with general jurisdiction (be it as of right or by leave) not limited to any class or classes of cases. There was, second, the model of a purely federal court, with an appellate jurisdiction limited to matters within or arising out of the exercise of federal legislative powers, including the validity of that exercise, but excluding constitutional issues arising under provincial legislation in view of the fact that appeals then lay directly to the Privy Council from provincial courts of appeal. There was, third, the model of a federal appellate court having also comprehensive appellate jurisdiction in all constitutional matters as ultimate Canadian expositor of the constitution, albeit there was a further appeal to the Privy Council. This was the model offered by the Supreme Court of the United States. There was, fourth, the model of a purely constitutional court and, fifth, the model of a federal and a constitutional court, with separate chambers for each of these functions, in adaptation of the chamber system found today in the *Cour de Cassation* of France.

Happily, in my view, the first model was chosen, thus adapting to federal Canada a system of appellate adjudication operative in unitary Great Britain but familiar to Canadians of Bench and Bar. To have adopted the federal model represented by the Supreme Court of the United States or some other such model, would have required at least consideration of, if not actual establishment of a system of federal courts of original jurisdiction. A dual court system such as obtains in the United States was resisted in Canada, save for the establishment of an Exchequer Court with a limited jurisdiction, and of Admiralty Courts. It was in the character of concurrent appointment as Exchequer Court judges that the judges of the Supreme Court of Canada were invested with original jurisdiction but this ceased when the Exchequer Court was set up on a separate base in 1887, ending a short first life and beginning a second one with a judge wholly its own, but with more added over the succeeding years.

Although the jurisdiction of the Exchequer Court was extended considerably when it was translated into the Federal Court of Canada in 1970, the latter is still a court of limited jurisdiction in federal matters. A serious and, in my view, unfortunate as well as an unnecessary upheaval in our Canadian system of judicature would result if the Government and Parliament of Canada moved now to federalize it at the level of original and intermediate appellate jurisdiction by withdrawing such jurisdiction in all federal matters from the provincial courts and reposing it in a federal court structure.

The Parliament of Canada has power to that end under section 101 of the British North America Act, the same section which authorized the creation of the Supreme Court of Canada. In authorizing as well (in its words) "the establishment of any additional Courts for the better administration of the laws of Canada," the section may be said to reflect some incongruity. On the one hand, it enabled Parliament to establish a "general," a truly national court of appeal whose authority was not limited to federal matters – the telling word is "general" – and, on the other hand to establish federal courts limited to jurisdiction in federal matters. To have exercised both grants of authority to the full, in the light of the fact that at Confederation in 1867 there were developed provincial courts habituated to adjudicate on matters that after Confederation were in terms of legislative power distributed between the central and provincial legislatures, would have created, and would now certainly create great tensions in federal-provincial relations. We can do without adding to those that already exist, although I am bound to add that tension to some degree is a by-product of federalism.

Parliament did exercise its authority to the full in establishing the Supreme Court of Canada in 1875 and in reconstituting the court in 1949 upon the abolition of all appeals in Canadian causes to the Privy Council. This makes good sense to me so long as the provincial courts are left, as they now are, to administer federal law as well as provincial law, indeed federal common law as well as provincial common law, save to the limited extent that judicial jurisdiction in federal matters has been reposed in the Federal Court of Canada, which has both a trial division and an appeal division in respect of those matters.

If there was any thought-out rationale for investing the Supreme Court of Canada with appellate authority from all provincial appellate courts, and in respect of provincial as well as federal matters cognizable in those courts, it was posited and, in my view, may be said to rest today on the following factors. First, there was and is the fact that particular litigation frequently involves issues that engage both federal and provincial matters which provincial courts have continued to handle without difficulty, and forum problems are, in general, avoided notwithstanding the hived-off jurisdiction of the Federal Court. Its jurisdiction is, on the whole, fairly distinct and has hitherto not created any intractable difficulties in forum selection, although some such questions have arisen. Second, there was and is the fact that the common law is largely the same in all the provinces outside of Quebec and that, subject to legislative changes, it ought to have a uniform operation in all those provinces, thus avoiding some possible conflict of laws problems; and, moreover, even in Quebec there are branches of the common law, as for example in the field of public law, that were and are common to it and to the other provinces of Canada. Third, there was and is the fact that many important branches of law, such as the criminal law, the law of negotiable instruments, the law of bankruptcy, the law of shipping, railway law, the law of patents and copyright have a national operation because they fall within exclusive federal competence; and even though they may interact in some respects with some aspects of the common law their interpretation and application must necessarily be uniform, and perhaps all the more so because of the interaction. Fourth, constitutional adjudication, involving the resolution of disputes as to the scope and reach of federal and provincial legislative powers must necessarily end in a court that can speak authoritatively for the whole of Canada, and I may add here that there is equally a case to be made for final uniform resolution of questions touching the operation of public authorities.

Thus it was that upon the establishment of the Supreme Court of Canada we had in the main a one-stream two-tier system of appeals like that in Great Britain, although that country did not have to contend with federalism as we know it in Canada. To some extent, there is a three-tier system in respect of Ontario cases by reason of the recent establishment there of an intermediate appellate court, with a limited jurisdiction, operating between courts of first instance and the Ontario Court of Appeal. Should this innovation spread to other provinces it would not alter the force of the considerations which led to the establishment of the Supreme Court of Canada as a national court. Its character does not depend on the system of appeals within the judicial structure of any one or more provinces but, rather on how far beyond adjudication on federal matters and on constitutional matters its jurisdiction should extend.

The Government and the Parliament of Canada saw no need to water down the broad authority given to establish "a general Court of appeal for Canada"; and Parliament emphasized the breadth of its power by generous scope, especially in civil cases, for appeals as of right, appeals which the Supreme Court of Canada was obliged to hear, however local or private were the issues that they raised. This was appellate review in a traditional sense as distinguished from what I would term supervisory control.

Until the beginning of this year [1975] when appellate review was replaced by supervisory control (leave now being required in all non-criminal cases and in most criminal cases before an appeal will be entertained on the merits), appeals as of right in civil cases formed a large part of the Supreme Court's case load. I think this was one of the factors that led some scholarly students of the Supreme Court's work to urge federalization of its jurisdiction. Other factors were also raised in support of this position, such as the virtue of allocating judicial power along the same lines as legislative power, and the merit of leaving to final adjudication in the provincial courts legal issues reflecting local conditions and those based on provincial or municipal legislation.

I think that the amendments recently made to the Supreme Court's jurisdiction, making a previous requirement of leave (whether from the Supreme
Court or the provincial appellate court) the general rule, have blunted the
case that could formerly have been made and was made for limiting the
Supreme Court of Canada to federal and constitutional issues. The four-
pronged rationale which I mentioned earlier in this address as supporting
a final appellate court with a general national jurisdiction is not, in my
opinion, cogently answered by those who would reduce the court to a federal and constitutional institution. Still less is it answerable now that the
Supreme Court is a supervisory tribunal rather than an appellate tribunal in
the traditional sense. As a supervisory tribunal, it is fully able and would be
expected to resist interference in purely local or private issues, and it is in
fact enjoined to do so by the statutory formula which prescribes the requirements that must be met in order to obtain leave. The case for leave must
be one with respect to which "the Supreme Court is of the opinion that any
question involved therein is, by reason of its public importance or the importance of any issue of law or any issue of mixed law and fact involved in such
question, one that ought to be decided by the Supreme Court or is, for any
other reason, of such a nature or significance as to warrant decision by it."

The discretion given to the court under the foregoing formula is obvious,
but it is a necessary control over the flow of cases that have already been
before two courts. Now, even more in its supervisory role than in its heretofore more traditional appellate role, the Supreme Court's main function is
to oversee the development of the law in the courts of Canada, to give guidance in articulate reasons and, indeed, direction to the provincial courts and
to the Federal Court of Canada on issues of national concern or of common
concern to several provinces, issues that may obtrude even though arising
under different legislative regimes in different provinces. This is surely the
paramount obligation of an ultimate appellate court with national authority. It is only under this umbrella that it can, in general, be expected to be
sensitive to the correctness of the decisions in particular cases, whether they
be between private litigants only or involve some government as a party.

I think I can risk saying that the mere fact that any level of government or
any government agency is involved in a particular case is no more telling
in favour of leave to appeal than the fact that litigation is private necessarily tells against the granting of leave. The issues in contention and, indeed,
the issues which will be determinative of the appeal, however there may be
others of importance in the case, and not the character of the parties, will
guide the court in the exercise of its power to grant or refuse leave. Even
where the court may be disposed to grant leave, it may do so, not at large,
but by defining the specific question or questions on which it is prepared to
have the case come forward.

III

I turn now to more debatable questions respecting the Supreme Court's exercise of its jurisdiction, questions going to its role as Canada's highest and final court on all justiciable matters. Two considerations affect any assessment of that role. One has to do with the kind of business that comes and will come before the court; the second has to do with the collegiality of the court, with the blend of individual independence of the judges *inter se* and their institutional responsibility. The bulk of the court's business is, and is likely to continue to be, the interpretation and application of statutes, some of which, as for example, parts of the Criminal Code and of the Quebec Civil Code, to take two illustrations, have long ago taken on what I may term a common law appearance. Two statutes, one, the British North America Act (and its amendments), only formally of that character (since it is Canada's chief written constitution), and the second, the Canadian Bill of Rights, a quasi-constitutional enactment are not, for interpretative purposes "statutes like other statutes" (to adopt well-known phraseology); and there is little doubt, certainly none in my mind, that the judicial approach to them, compelled by their character, has been different from that taken with respect to ordinary legislation. The generality of their language and their operative effect compel an approach from a wider perspective than is the case with ordinary legislation, especially legislation that is more precisely formulated.

The collegiality of the court touches a matter that may have a greater interest for the academic component of this assembly than for the practising Bar or members of the judiciary. It is theoretically open to each member of the Supreme Court of Canada, as it is theoretically open to each member of any appellate court, to write reasons in every case in which the member sits. Practical and institutional considerations militate against this; and so it is that when bare concurrences are filed with reasons proposed by a colleague, they may suggest some shift of position by the concurring judge who does not choose to write separate reasons, a shift on some matter subsidiary to or connected with the disposition of the main issue to which the concurrence was given.

Bare concurrences ought not to be taken as representing unqualified endorsement of every sentence of the reasons concurred in. Contextual approval, yes; and approval of the result, of course. After all the scrutiny and conferring on a set of proposed reasons are over, and after changes have been made in language and organization by the writer so far as he is willing to accommodate himself to the views of his colleagues, there may still remain in some colleague some questions about some parts of the reasons. However, he may decide on balance that there is no point in writing his own. In short, it is far safer and surer, if one would assess how a judge discharges his duties and how he regards his role and the role of the court, to assess him on what he himself writes and not on all of what is written by a colleague with whom he concurs in some particular case or cases.

There is no question that seems to have been as continuously and as strenuously considered, in relation to all courts and judges, and more particularly in relation to judges and courts of ultimate authority, as their law-making role. The Supreme Court of Canada began life at about the time Langdell and his case-law approach to the discovery of the "true legal rule" revolutionized legal studies in the United States. On the English side, before the nineteenth century was out the House of Lords had sanctified its own position as the expositor of the one true rule which, once declared, was alterable only by legislation. A quarter of a century later Cardozo was to tell us that at its highest reaches the role of the judge lay in creation and not in mere discovery. In this country, and perhaps in England too, we were inclined to think that creativity applied to what had not been previously considered and determined but, that accomplished in the highest court, creativity was spent and change was only for the legislature or for the constitutional amending process, as the case might be....

... Controversy has now ceased on the law-making role of judges, especially of judges of a final appellate court. Laymen may beg the question by consoling the dissenting judges of a divided court with the remark, "too bad the law was against you," but judges and lawyers know better. The late Lord Reid helped to bury the declaratory theory by remarking in a speech delivered in 1971 that law is not some known and defined entity secreted in Aladdin's cave and revealed if one uses the right password. We do not believe in fairy tales any more, said Lord Reid, and Lord Diplock did not doubt, when speaking for the Privy Council in an Australian appeal in 1974, that "when for the first time a court of final instance interprets [a statute] as bearing one of two or more possible meanings ... the effect of the exercise of its interpretative role is to make law." Such controversy as there is today in judicial law-making in a final court concerns the appropriateness of the occasion or of the case for enunciating a new rule of law and, even more important, the appropriateness of the occasion or of the case for upsetting an existing rule and substituting a different one in its place.

Neither here nor in any of the countries whence come our distinguished guests is *stare decisis* now an inexorable rule for our respective final courts. In this country, what appeared to be at times an obsessiveness about it came partly at least from our link with English law which also involved the ascendancy of English courts, so that *stare decisis* amounted to a form of ancestor worship. We are now able to view it as simply an important element of the judicial process, a necessary consideration which should give pause to any but the most sober conclusion that a previous decision or line of authority is wrong and ought to be changed. Such a conclusion is not likely to be arrived at by any judge or number of judges without serious reflection on its conformity or consistency with other principles that are part of the institutional history or the institutional patterns of the court. None of us operates without constraints that are both personal and institutional, born of both training and experience and of traditions of the legal system of which the court is a part.

When everything considered relevant has been weighed and an overruling decision commends itself to a judge, he ought not at that stage to stay his opinion and call upon the legislature to implement it. This is particularly true in respect of those areas of the law which are judge-made, and to a degree true in respect of those areas where legislation is involved which is susceptible of a number of meanings. A final court must accept a superintending responsibility for what it or its predecessors have wrought, especially when it knows how little time legislatures today have (and also, perhaps, little inclination) to intrude into fields of law fashioned by the courts alone, although legislatures may, of course, under the prodding of law reform agencies and of other public influences, from time to time do.

The role of the courts, the role of a final court, in the interpretation of legislation, bringing into play the relation between the legislative and the judicial arms of government, is of a different dimension, in my view, than the role played in the promulgation of judge-made law. The dimension comes from the dominant political and legal principle under which our courts operate, which is that, constitutional issues apart, Parliament and the provincial legislatures are the supreme, certainly the superior law-making bodies. On constitutional issues, issues concerning the division of distribution of legislative power, the courts, and ultimately the Supreme Court of Canada, have the final word (subject to constitutional amendment). This is a critical role, so critical for exercises of legislative and governmental power at both the central and provincial level as to put every Supreme Court decision in this field, whatever it be, into the political mill. Yet it is a role which the court cannot eschew if we believe in constitutional order, any more than can any final court with constitutional jurisdiction in a federal state. There is no other instrument with final authority available for this role. It is of course possible (and indeed there are known examples) for the central and provincial governments to avoid constitutional determinations in the Supreme Court of Canada by entering into co-operative arrangements which do not call for any test of constitutional competence. In this way they may hold some of the tensions in their relations in equilibrium, so long as those arrangements last. The fact that such arrangements exist at all underlines the delicate nature of the Supreme Court's constitutional jurisdiction. Of course, it must proceed with caution in that field but, that having been said, it brings the same independent judgment to bear on constitutional questions as on other matters that are brought before it, fully conscious, however, that there are no more important public issues submitted to its adjudication than those that arise out of alleged conflicts of legislative authority.

The stakes in interpretation and application of ordinary legislation may not be as high because here the courts play not an ascendant role but rather more of a complementary one. The judges, no less than others in society, owe obedience to legislation which they may be called upon to interpret and apply; they have a duty to respect the legislative purpose or policy whatever be their view of its merit. Judges subscribe to this proposition, and then may be seen to proceed to differ on what the purpose or policy is, or to differ on whether the legislation or some part of it is apt to realize the purpose. This is not the time nor the place to enlarge on the variety of approaches to legislative interpretation which in close cases can lead to different results in respect of the same piece of legislation. In the majority of cases where legislation is a factor in the litigation, there is no such difficulty in interpretation as to require the particular expertise of a lawyer or a judge. Where that special competence is necessary, the judges owe it to the enacting legislature as well as to the litigants to expose the legal reasoning which underlies their decisions.

The public expectation is, I suspect, of a somewhat different order. Since so much of the legislation that comes before the courts and before the Supreme Court of Canada involves controls or limitation of the social conduct or business behaviour of persons or classes of persons or corporations, either by direct penal sanction or by supervision of administrative agencies, those affected may look to the courts for some wider exposition than a strict regard for legal issues would warrant. Is the policy a desirable or a workable one? Is the administrative structure fair? Is the procedure fair, are the decisions supported by reasons that are disclosed to the affected persons? There is no invariable stance that a court takes on these questions. Where it has deemed it proper to pronounce on policy (as it has on occasion) it has done so with prudence, and, generally, when prompted by difficulties that reside in the interpretation and application of the legislation. Fairness of administrative procedure is more confidently dealt with by the courts because what is compendiously called "natural justice" has long been regarded as involving legal issues for their consideration.

Natural justice, embracing the right to notice of possibly adverse action, the right to be heard or to make representations before being adversely affected, and the right to be judged by an impartial tribunal, is a central feature of an evolved political and legal tradition which sees the courts as wielders of protective authority against an invasion of the liberty of the individual by government or its agencies. Text books, periodical literature and the everyday press reinforce this tradition, and thus strengthen the public expectation that the courts, and especially the Supreme Court of Canada, will speak out on the matter. The enactment of the Canadian Bill of Rights as a federal measure, and operative only at that level, has fed that expectation. It is well to recall that judges of the Supreme Court spoke strongly on aspects of individual liberty in the *Alberta Press* case, the *Switzman* case, the *Roncarelli* case, and in other cases too, without the back-up or the direction of the Canadian Bill of Rights, which became effective only in 1960. It was able to do so because the avenues for recognizing individual rights or civil liberties had not been closed by competent legislation, nor did any relevant legislation as interpreted by the judges of the Supreme Court preclude them. Legislation may however appear to be preclusive in some areas of civil liberties, and if interpreted with that result the judicial duty of fidelity to legislation as superior law must be acknowledged whatever be the consequences, although the acknowledgment may be accompanied by an expression of regret or even of remonstrance that the legislation went so far.

The Canadian Bill of Rights has now provided a legislative measure and standard of protection of civil liberties but, in the generality of some of its language, it adds to the dilemmas of interpretation which are so often evident in civil liberties cases. Its direction may be clearer in some cases than it is in others, or clearer to some judges in some cases than to others. Each charts his own course here, as in the other roles that he is called upon to play in the discharge of his judicial duties and, indeed, in determining what roles he should take on.

This, however, is simply another aspect of the side discretion opens to a judge of a final appellate court. There may be differences about the scope of the discretion, but there cannot be any dispute about its existence. As I said at the beginning of my remarks, each judge puts his own questions and supplies his own answers and, in yielding ground to institutional considerations, he does so according to his own assessment of what they demand.

3.2

Constitution Act, 1867, **Sections 96–101**

VII. – Judicature.

96. The Governor General shall appoint the Judges of the Superior, District, and County Courts in each Province, except those of the Courts of Probate in Nova Scotia and New Brunswick.

97. Until the laws relative to Property and Civil Rights in Ontario, Nova Scotia, and New Brunswick, and the Procedure of the Courts in those Provinces, are made uniform, the Judges of the Courts of those Provinces appointed by the Governor General shall be selected from the respective Bars of those Provinces.

98. The Judges of the Courts of Quebec shall be selected from the Bar of that Province.

99. (1) Subject to subsection two of this section, the Judges of the Superior Courts shall hold office during good behavior, but shall be removable by the Governor General on Address of the Senate and House of Commons.

(2) A Judge of a Superior Court, whether appointed before or after the coming into force of this section, shall cease to hold office upon attaining the age of 75 years, or upon the coming into force of this section if at that time he has already attained that age.

100.   The Salaries, Allowances, and Pensions of the Judges of the Superior, District, and County Courts (except the Courts of Probate in Nova Scotia and New Brunswick), and of the Admiralty Courts in Cases where the Judges thereof are for the Time being paid by Salary, shall be fixed and provided by the Parliament of Canada.

101.   The Parliament of Canada may, notwithstanding anything in this Act, from Time to Time provide for the Constitution, Maintenance, and Organization of a General Court of Appeal for Canada, and for the Establishment of any additional Courts for the better Administration of the Laws of Canada.

3.3

The Canadian Judicial System

Figure 1 represents the Canadian judicial system as it exists in Alberta. The names of the "section 92" and "section 96" courts vary from province to province. In Alberta, they are called the Provincial Court and the Court of Queen's Bench, respectively. In Ontario, by contrast, the same courts are known as the High Court of Justice and the Court of Appeal. Together, they constitute the trial and appellate divisions of the Supreme Court of Ontario. Also, note that in Alberta there no longer are county and district courts, as they were amalgamated with the Court of Queen's Bench in 1979. The vertical arrows indicate the paths of appeal. The left-diagonal and right-diagonal hatch-marks indicate section 92 and section 101 courts, respectively. The cross-hatched area represents the section 96 courts and the joint responsibility of the two levels of government.

The Criminal Court Process

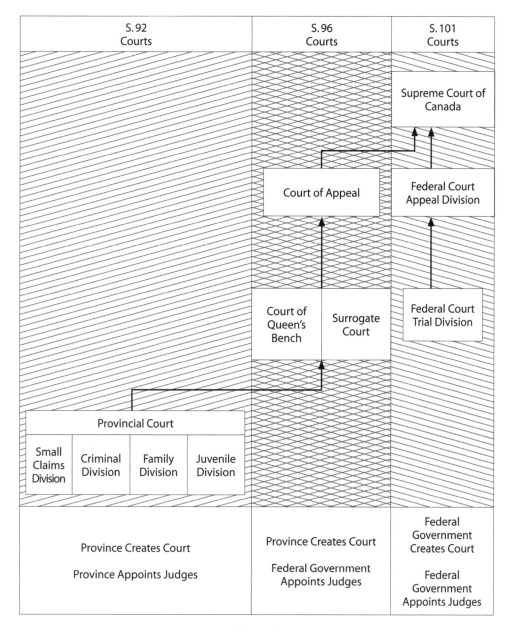

Figure 1

3.4

The Criminal and Civil Court Processes

The Criminal Court Process

Provincial Court

- First appearance court on all matters
- Trial of all municipal Bylaws (Summary)
- Trial of all Provincial Statutes (Summary)
- Trial of some Federal Statutes:
  - All summary conviction offences
  - All s. 483 CCC offences
  - All s. 484 CCC offences
    And other Federal Statute Indictable offences where accused has elected trial by Provincial Court Judge
    ...
- Preliminary Inquiry on all s. 484 CCC offences and Federal Statutes where accused has elected trial in higher court
- Preliminary Inquiry on all s. 427 CCC offences

Court of Queen's Bench

- Trials of s. 484 CCC offences and other Federal Statutes after preliminary inquiry in Provincial Court
- Trials of s. 427 offences after preliminary inquiry in Provincial Court
- Appeals of Summary conviction matters from provincial Court – heard by one Justice

Court of Appeal

- All appeals from Court of Queen's Bench

Figure 2

The Criminal Court Process

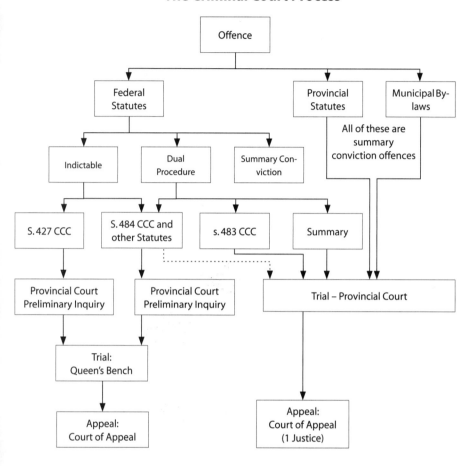

Figure 3

1. Election of Procedure (Summary or Indictable) belongs to the Crown
2. Election of Trial method belongs to accused
3. May be Court composed of Judge alone or Judge and Jury

The Civil Court Process

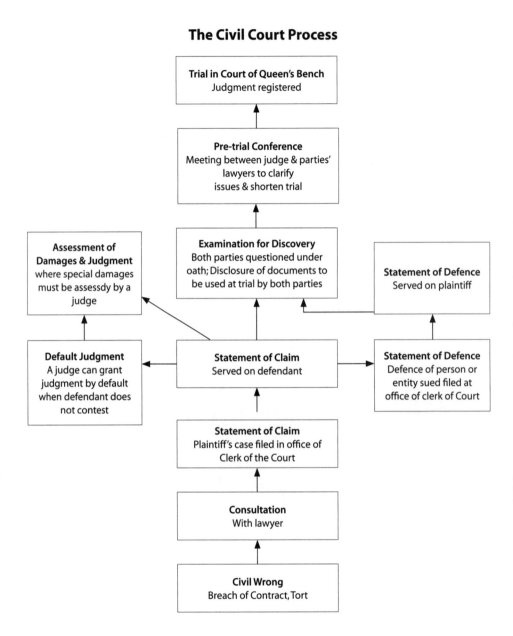

Figure 4

3.5
Key Terms

Concepts

unitary court system
dual court system
section 92 courts
section 96 courts
civil law
criminal law
administrative law
Common Law system
Civil Law system (Quebec)
indictable offence
summary conviction offence
preliminary inquiry
discretionary appellate jurisdiction
supervisory vs. appellate function
"per saltum appeal"

Institutions, Events, and Documents

Provincial Court
Court of Queen's Bench
Court of Appeal
Supreme Court of Canada (1875)
Federal Court of Canada (1970)
Exchequer Court (1875-1970)
Judicial Committee of the Privy Council
Constitution Act, 1982 (provisions relating to Supreme Court of Canada)
Meech Lake Accord (provisions relating to Supreme Court of Canada)

Judicial Recruitment and Selection

4

Under the *Constitution Act, 1867*, judicial appointments are made by the two different levels of government to three different levels of courts. Pursuant to section 101, the federal government is responsible for appointing all judges of the Supreme Court of Canada (nine), the Federal Court (twenty-five), and the Tax Court (twenty-five). In addition, the federal government appoints all the judges of the "section 96 courts" (just over 1,000) even though the latter are created and maintained by the provinces. This is one of the distinctive features of Canada's unitary judicial system. Vesting the appointment power with the new federal government was intended to insure the independence of the provincial superior courts from local politics or prejudice. It is also a legacy of British imperial rule and (some of) the Canadian founders' desire to subordinate provincial governments to Ottawa. As provincial governments have achieved a more equal status in the Canadian federal system, this continuing federal monopoly has become a point of political conflict (see "Saskatchewan Judges Affair," below). Finally, the provincial governments appoint all the judges (about 1,500) of the provincial courts created pursuant to section 92 of the *Constitution Act, 1867*. As of 2002, there are approximately 2,500 judges in Canada. Interestingly, this represents a fifty per cent increase since 1982, the year the *Charter* was adopted. During the same time period, Canada's population grew by less than twenty per cent.

Appointment Procedures

Federal judicial appointments are made by the Cabinet on the advice of the Minister of Justice, except for chief justices,[1] who are recommended by the prime minister. While final responsibility for appointments remains with the minister of justice, under the reforms adopted in 1988, an ongoing

---

1 In addition to the Chief Justice of the Supreme Court of Canada and the Federal Court, the prime minister appoints a separate chief justice for the Court of Appeal and the superior trial court of each province except P.E.I., which has only one chief justice.

search for appropriate candidates is carried on by the Commissioner for Federal Judicial Affairs. The commissioner solicits suggestions from a nationwide network of contacts. Judges, bar associations, law schools, members of Parliament, and provincial office-holders are all encouraged to recommend individuals for judicial appointment. The commissioner conducts a preliminary investigation to insure that candidates possess the required technical qualifications[2] and then refers their names to the appropriate provincial or territorial committee for screening. Each provincial (and territorial) committee consists of five persons (including at least one non-lawyer) and is responsible for assessing whether the candidate possesses the required qualifications for appointment. The committee can give only two assessments – "qualified" or "not qualified" – and must be prepared to give reasons for any negative assessments. It should be noted that this procedure applies only to new appointments to the federal bench. The government's decision to elevate a sitting judge to a higher judicial office is not subject to review by a provincial screening committee.

The procedures for judicial appointments to "section 92 courts" vary from province to province. In several, there are no judicial councils and the appointment of provincial judges is left to the discretion of the attorney general. Others have some form of judicial council based on one of two basic models: a screening committee or a nominating commission. The difference is the stage at which the government uses an independent, non-governmental body to assess potential candidates. In the first, the attorney general conducts the initial recruitment and then refers his or her candidate to an independent body for assessment. If approved, the government then proceeds with the appointment. The 1988 federal practice is a modified version of this model, since the provincial committees are limited to a screening function.

The alternative model is the nominating commission, which actually conducts the initial recruitment as well as screening and then presents the government with a list of approved nominees from which it must choose. This is the practice in Ontario, British Columbia, and Alberta, where each province's Judicial Council receives applications for provincial court judgeships. (In Ontario, this body is called the Ontario Judicial Appointments Advisory Committee.) After reviewing the credentials of the applicants, the Judicial Council recommends individuals to the provincial attorney general. If the attorney general disagrees with the Council's recommendation, he or she is free to request another. The difference between these two approaches lies in the extent to which they allow political influence. The Ontario, Alberta, and B.C. governments can only make appointments from a pool of candidates who have already been selected by an independent body, while, under the screening model, the government is initially unrestricted and only uses the independent committees to confirm choices that the attorney general has

---

2 That the person is a member of a provincial or territorial bar association and has a minimum of ten years experience as a practising lawyer and/or judge.

already made. This latter procedure gives the party that forms the government a much freer hand to favour party members and supporters when making appointments to the bench.

Politics versus Professionalism

The judicial selection process in all common law nations manifests a tension between judicial expertise and political influence. With the exception of certain final courts of appeal, the trend in recent decades has been to institute reforms that favour judicial expertise and reduce the degree of political influence. The most obvious manifestation of this is the long-established practice of appointing rather than electing judges. In theory, the potential for undue political influence is also limited by review of nominations by independent screening commissions, and reduced still further by merit selection nominating committees. In practice, it turns out to be more difficult to reduce political influence in the appointment process. In Ontario, for example, the Conservative government of Premier Mike Harris (1995–2001) became unhappy with the perceived political bias of the recommendations of the Ontario Judicial Appointments Advisory Committee. The Ontario Judicial Appointments Committee was created in 1989 by a Liberal government and had Professor Peter Russell as its first chair. Under the succeeding NDP government (1991–95), the chair passed to Judy Rebick, a former president of the National Action Committee on the Status of Women (NAC) and well-known feminist advocate. The Harris government requested the Council to send its judicial nominations in groups of two or three so that the government would have some choice in making a final appointment.

This emphasis on insulating judicial selection from partisan politics is premised on the assumption that judges and judging are not "political" in the way legislators and legislating are and therefore that judges need not be politically accountable. (Judges of course are political in the sense that they usually accept [and enforce] the underlying political principles and beliefs of a society.) Impartiality is an essential ingredient of judicial authority, and the selection process is structured to preserve the perception of the judges as impartial arbiters. A non-political selection process assumes a non-political court. According to Weiler's "two models" theory, if the function of a judge is limited to adjudicating disputes, the only prerequisite for appointment is the necessary legal training, accompanied by good moral character and steady work habits.

While the assumptions associated with an adjudicative court were generally true of the common law tradition out of which Canada's legal system has evolved, they became strained with the introduction of written constitutional law and its corollary, judicial review. For reasons discussed in Chapters 1 and 2, courts charged with interpreting constitutionally entrenched restrictions on democratic legislatures affect public policy more directly than courts whose functions are limited to resolving disputes arising under common law and statutes. To the extent that this occurs, the original rationale for excluding political considerations from the selection process is weakened. At the extreme is Weiler's "policy-making court." "Rather than focusing on legal ability and training as the key elements in judicial qualifications," writes Weiler,

> the policy-making model holds that a person's political program and abilities should be most important. In fact, the logic of the system demands that these be evaluated in some manner other than an apolitical appointment process. Instead, judges should either be directly elected, or the various groups whose interests are affected by the judges' decisions should have some more formalized and legitimized form of participation in the making of the selection.[3]

While Weiler's model is theoretical, it reflects a fundamental norm of liberal democracy: that the governors should be accountable to the governed. It also captures what American political scientist V. O. Key has described as "an iron rule of politics": "where power rests, there influence will be brought to bear."[4]

Evidence supporting this axiom is most evident in the politicization of judicial selection that has developed in the United States, where judicial review was invented and where the fact of judicial "law-making" has long been acknowledged. Under many state constitutions in the U.S., judges are selected through public elections. In California, the judges of the state's Supreme Court are initially appointed by the governor but after nine years must face a "confirmation vote" in a general election. In 1986, three judges, including the chief justice, were rejected by the California voters because they were perceived as blocking the majority will on capital punishment. Even though American federal judges are still appointed, strong political forces shape these appointments, especially appointments to the Supreme Court. While these practices may seem unacceptable by traditional Canadian standards, they are consistent with a more "political" judicial function.

"Politics" can enter the judicial appointment process in four distinct (albeit sometimes overlapping) forms: patronage, regional representation, ethnic or group representation, and ideological compatibility. Such political appointments tend to reflect the contours of political division and the distribution of influence in the larger society. As such, they vary from country to country, and within the same country over time. In Canada, for example, patronage has declined as a major factor in Supreme Court appointments, while group representation and ideological compatibility have become more important.

---

3 Paul Weiler, "Two Models of Judicial Decision-Making," *Canadian Bar Review* 46 (1968), p. 406.

4 V. O. Key, *Politics, Parties and Pressure Groups* (New York: Thomas Y. Crowell, 1958), p. 154.

Note also that a single judicial appointment can encompass several of these political factors simultaneously. American President George Bush's 1991 appointment of Clarence Thomas to the U.S. Supreme Court, for example, represented considerations of both ideology (Thomas was a judicial conservative) and group representation (Thomas, an African-American, replaced Justice Thurgood Marshall, the first and only African-American to serve on the U.S. Supreme Court). Similarly, Brian Mulroney's 1987 appointment of Claire L'Heureux-Dubé to the Supreme Court of Canada provided symbolic representation for both francophones and women.

Patronage – appointment as a reward for past service to or support of a party – is the oldest, most common, and best known form of political influence in judicial appointments in all common law nations. Sir Robert Megarry reports that political patronage was the dominant factor in British judicial appointments until the post-war era (Reading 4.2). Similarly, in Canada, patronage has been a dominant factor in both federal and provincial judicial appointments since before Confederation. Since the 1960s, the Canadian Bar Association has lobbied both levels of government to curb the influence of patronage.

At the "section 92 court" level, patronage was once the dominant criterion for appointment. As recently as 1971, a study of Ontario found that, after twenty-five years of Progressive Conservative rule, most "section 92" provincial court magistrates were past or present supporters of the Progressive Conservative party. The institution of provincial judicial councils has reduced the practice of judicial patronage, especially in provinces such as British Columbia, Ontario, and Alberta, where the councils are true "nominating commissions."

Patronage has been equally pronounced in the federal government's appointment of judges to section 96 courts. Depending on whether "political" was defined strongly (holding office) or weakly (running for office), studies have found that, prior to World War II, anywhere from fifty to eighty per cent of federally appointed judges had "political careers" prior to their appointment and that appointments followed party lines eighty to ninety per cent of the time. The same studies show that patronage declined significantly after World War II but did not disappear.[5]

In 1966, dissatisfaction with the continuing effects of patronage on the quality of federal judicial appointments led the Canadian Bar Association to create the "Committee on the Judiciary" to provide a non-partisan source of advice to the federal government on judicial appointments. The CBA committee would receive the names of potential nominees from the minister of justice, review the candidate's record, and then rate the candidate as "well qualified, qualified, or not qualified." Under this program, which operated

---

5 These studies are discussed in greater detail in Peter H. Russell, *The Judiciary in Canada: The Third Branch of Government* (Scarborough, ON: McGraw-Hill Ryerson, 1987), pp. 114–15.

from 1967 until 1988, no candidates receiving an unqualified rating were appointed. The CBA Committee on Judiciary was replaced by the 1988 reforms (described above) by provincial screening committees.

A succession of Liberal ministers of justice during the 1970s is generally credited with improving the quality of federal judicial appointments. John Turner initiated the practice of systematically collecting names and background information of potential judicial nominees before openings occurred, and this practice was formalized by his successor, Otto Lang, through the creation of a Special Advisor on Judicial Affairs. By consulting widely and constantly updating the list of potential nominees, the office of the Special Advisor was credited with further improving the quality of federally appointed judges.

Notwithstanding improvements in the quality of appointments, the Trudeau government continued to use its judicial appointments to section 96 courts to reward its members and supporters. In 1982, this practice provoked an angry reaction by the newly elected Progressive Conservative party of Premier Grant Devine in Saskatchewan. Devine's attorney general, Gary Lane, accused Ottawa of "stacking the courts with partisan appointees" and declared that he "wants more consultation on appointments, not just a phone call after the fact."[6] To protest the Liberals' alleged abuse of patronage in judicial appointments in Saskatchewan, the Devine government began reducing the number of section 96 judgeships by eliminating positions as they became vacant through death or retirement, thereby denying Ottawa the opportunity to make appointments. As recounted by Jeffrey Simpson (Reading 4.1), this stalemate, known as the "Saskatchewan Judges Affair," was not resolved until the defeat of the Liberals in the federal elections in 1984. The newly elected Conservative government informally agreed to consult more closely with the provinces before making superior court appointments. Because of these kinds of tensions, there have been recurrent suggestions that the constitution be amended to transfer "section 96" appointments to the provinces. However, no one gives these proposals any serious chance of being adopted, at least while the Liberal Party controls Ottawa. The patronage benefits of section 96 court appointments are too valuable a political asset for the federal government to give up.

The patronage issue again became the focus of public attention following a series of judicial appointments occasioned by Pierre Trudeau's resignation as leader of the Liberal Party and prime minister in 1984. Before leaving, Trudeau appointed three of his former cabinet ministers to the Federal Court, one without any prior review by the CBA Committee on the Judiciary. Several other Liberal politicians were also appointed to provincial superior courts.

The 1984 Trudeau appointments were widely criticized in the press. Brian Mulroney, the new leader of the Progressive Conservative party, exploited the judicial patronage issue in the 1984 federal election and promised

---

6 *Calgary Herald*, April 11, 1984, p. A5.

change if elected. The incident also led to new studies by the Canadian Association of Law Teachers (CALT) and the Canadian Bar Association. In 1985, both the CALT and CBA issued reports recommending reform. While the details varied, both reports recommended a process in which an independent nominating commission would recruit and screen potential candidates and then create lists from which the minister of justice would be expected to make appointments. The Mulroney government took these reports under consideration.

In 1988, when the Mulroney government announced its new judicial appointments procedures, it paid lip service to the CALT and CBA reports. Close scrutiny, however, reveals that the 1988 reforms represented only a half-step in the direction of reform. The novel element was the transfer of the recruitment function from the Judicial Affairs Advisor, who worked within the justice minister's personal office, to the judicial affairs commissioner. The latter has the rank and status of a deputy minister and is thus more independent than the now defunct judicial affairs advisor. The new provincial and territorial committees, however, are not true nominating commissions. Their function remains essentially that of screening names of candidates provided to them by the commissioner, who, when all is said and done, remains an employee of the federal government. To date, there has been no systematic study to assess the impact of the 1988 reforms.

The 1989 study of Peter Russell and Jacob Ziegel (Reading 4.3) suggests why the Mulroney government did not rush to embrace the recommendations of the CBA and CALT. Contrary to their promises of reform during the 1984 campaign, it turned out that the Mulroney government did not practice what it preached. Of the 228 federal judges appointed during the first Mulroney government (1984–88), forty-eight per cent were found to have associations with the Progressive Conservative party. While eighty-six per cent received a good or better rating from the CBA Committee on the Judiciary, of the thirteen who did not, ten had Tory political connections. Russell and Ziegel conclude that there was only "marginal improvement" in the judicial selection process during the Mulroney government's first term, that political patronage remained "pervasive," and that the 1988 reforms did "little to address the basic flaws in the appointing system."

Other forms of political influence in judicial appointments – such as regional or ethnic group representation – tend to reflect the political sociology of a nation. Canada has a long tradition of ethnic and regional representation in the judicial appointments to the Supreme Court. The legal guarantee of three justices from Quebec is technically justified by the Court's appellate jurisdiction over Quebec's civil law, but it also symbolizes the "distinct" status of Quebec and the French people in Canadian politics. The French–English dualism of Canadian political experience has also manifested itself in the tradition of alternating the appointment of the chief justice between an anglophone and a francophone, as explained in Reading 3.0.

Similarly, the convention of *de facto* geographical representation on the

Supreme Court testifies to the strong influence of regionalism in Canadian politics. Significantly, this is not a Canadian idiosyncrasy. For the first century of the United States, geographical representation in appointments was considered essential for maintaining the legitimacy of the Supreme Court and the national government. By tradition, there was a "Southern seat," a "New England seat," and later a "Western seat" on the Court. In nineteenth-century American politics, as in contemporary Canadian politics, this practice was a symptom of the relative weakness of the central government and its attempt to reassure the provinces / states that their "special circumstances" could receive a "sympathetic hearing" in the national court of appeal.

This comparative perspective helps illuminate a new dimension of the politics of judicial appointments in Canada. The American convention of geographic representation fell into disuse as regionalism ceased to be a dominant factor in American politics. It was replaced, in part, by a new practice of ethnic or "group" representation. Twentieth-century American politics has witnessed the development of the traditions of a Catholic seat (1894), a Jewish seat (1916), a black seat (1967), and more recently a woman's seat (1981). While none of these practices have been treated as absolutely binding, they reflect the emergence of the various groups as potentially powerful voting blocs within the American electorate. Presidents seeking re-election have sought to improve their chances by making judicial appointments that demonstrate solidarity or sympathy with these groups.

British jurist Conor Gearty reports that similar concerns about demographic diversity and a "representative" judiciary are taking hold in Great Britain as their judges undertake their new role of interpreting the *European Convention on Human Rights* (Reading 5.8). In Canada, there is ample evidence that the same dynamic of group representation is taking hold. As noted above, French Canadians have always been represented on the Supreme Court through the three legally required appointments from Quebec. However, with the appointments of Justice Bastarache from New Brunswick in 1997 and Justice Arbour from Ontario in 1999, Prime Minister Chrétien ensured that there will be a francophone majority on the Court for at least two decades (assuming both serve until the compulsory retirement age of 75). This prospect has provoked political grumbling in parts of English-speaking Canada.

More recently, in 1982, Prime Minister Trudeau set a precedent by appointing Bertha Wilson, the first woman ever to serve on the Supreme Court of Canada. Prime Minister Mulroney subsequently appointed two more women to the highest Court: Claire l'Heureux-Dubé (1987) and Beverley McLachlin (1989). When Justice Wilson retired in 1991, feminists lobbied unsuccessfully to have her replaced by another woman. However, the number of female justices on the Supreme Court returned to three when Prime Minister Chrétien appointed Louise Arbour to replace retiring Justice Peter Cory in 1999. Given the high profile of the sexual equality issue in contemporary Canadian politics, it seems that the convention of having at least three women justices is here to stay. Mulroney also appointed the first Ukrainian-Canadian, John Sopinka (1988) and the first Italian-Canadian, Frank Iacobucci (1991). While it seems unlikely that these appointments will lead to a convention of a Ukrainian- or Italian-Canadian seat, they symbolically reinforce the policy of multiculturalism. (A complete list of both chief and puisne judges is found in Appendices D and E.)

The fourth form of political influence in judicial appointments is political program or ideology. The influence of ideology is most pronounced in final courts of appeal exercising judicial review over written constitutions. It is generally recognized that political compatibility has been a dominant factor in presidential appointments to the U.S. Supreme Court since its origins. The ideological dimension of U.S. Supreme Court appointments is most obvious in the years following a "watershed" or critical election,[7] during which a newly elected president and his party in Congress face a Supreme Court still dominated by the appointments of the preceding regime. Recognizing that their policy agenda is or may be threatened by a hostile Court, these presidents have exercised their power of appointment to "pack the court" with judges who support their political program. Republican President Abraham Lincoln did this following his election in 1860. Following his re-election in 1936, President Franklin D. Roosevelt packed the Court with supporters of the Democrats' "New Deal" programs to protect them from judicial attack. The Reagan–Bush appointments of "strict constructionists" during the 1980s were the most recent example of this political trend. In the 2000 U.S. elections, Democratic candidate Al Gore tried to make the prospect of more Republican appointments to the Supreme Court an issue against his adversary George W. Bush. While Bush eventually won, his judicial appointments are being closely scrutinized by Senate Democrats and liberal advocacy groups.

While "court packing" in its more dramatic form is mainly an American phenomenon, appointments to the constitutional courts in Europe tend to follow party lines very closely. Canada has been different in this regard, at least until recently. Patronage, not ideology, was the dominant factor in appointments to the Supreme Court of Canada through 1949 (Reading 4.1). Since the *Victoria Charter* of 1971, a majority of the provinces have lobbied for increased provincial participation in the appointment process and constitutional entrenchment of the convention of regional representation.[8] While their advocates argued that these changes would guarantee a more

---

7 The most important watershed elections were the election of Jefferson and the Democrats in 1800; Lincoln and the Republicans in 1860; Franklin Delano Roosevelt and the Democrats in 1932; and Ronald Reagan in 1980. In each of these general elections, what had been the dominant national party lost the White House and one or both houses of Congress to what had been the minority national party.

8 See Peter H. Russell, "Constitutional Reform of the Judicial Branch," *Canadian Journal of Political Science* 17, no. 2 (1984), pp. 227–52.

"representative" court, critics protested that a provincial veto over Supreme Court appointments would amount to the rejection of "the basic principle of the judicial process: that judges are judges of the issue, not partisans of the parties to the issue."[9]

Such criticisms notwithstanding, in 1987, the Mulroney government accepted these reforms in the hope that they would increase the legitimacy and authority of the Supreme Court, thus making it a more effective vehicle of "intrastate federalism" – the representation of regional interests within the institutions of the national government. The 1987 *Meech Lake Accord* proposed that the federal government be required to appoint Supreme Court judges from lists submitted by the provinces. Since the *Meech Lake Accord* would have also required three judges from Quebec, this provision would have forced Ottawa and Quebec to reach an agreement on appointments. With the other provinces, Ottawa would have had more flexibility. If the list submitted by one province was unacceptable, the federal government could turn to a different province from the same region. (This possibility would in turn encourage a provincial government to submit candidates whose credentials were acceptable.)

This proposal for the provincial nomination of Supreme Court appointments was one of the controversial elements of the *Meech Lake Accord*. Critics alleged that it would allow provincial governments to mould the political orientation of the Court's decision-making in a decentralist direction, thereby weakening the country and also subverting the potential for an expansive interpretation of the *Charter of Rights*. Defenders of this proposal argued that it was consistent with the spirit of equality of the two levels of government in Canadian federalism and that provincially nominated judges were likely to be as ideologically diverse on *Charter*-related issues as any other set of nominees.[10]

In the end, the *Meech Lake Accord* was defeated by an odd alliance that consisted mainly of small-c conservatives and small-l liberals – human rights, native rights, feminist, civil libertarian, and environmental groups. Most of these latter groups have been beneficiaries of the *Charter* and the new politics of rights that it has generated. The defeat of the *Meech Lake Accord* may be seen as the defeat – perhaps temporary – of the politics of federalism by the politics of rights.

The beginning of the influence of the "politics of rights" on appointments to the Supreme Court can be traced back to the appointment of Bora Laskin as Chief Justice in 1973. At this time, the Supreme Court was being criticized by civil libertarian lawyers and law professors for its traditional and cautious interpretation of the 1960 *Bill of Rights*. Laskin had proven himself as the

---

9 E. D. Fulton, as reported in G. M. Stirling, "A Symposium of the Appointment of Judges," *Alberta Law Review* 2 (1973), p. 301.

10 See Peter H. Russell, "The Supreme Court Proposals in the Meech Lake Accords," *Canadian Public Policy* 14 (Sept. 1988), pp. 93, 99.

Court's leading civil libertarian and judicial activist since his appointment in 1970, but tradition dictated that the most senior judge in terms of service on the Court be chosen Chief Justice. Prime Minister Trudeau broke with this tradition and chose Laskin, much to the delight of the Court's civil libertarian critics. There were rumours that several of the more senior judges who had been passed over might resign in protest, but this never materialized.

The enactment of the *Charter of Rights* in 1982 clearly enhanced the potential for Supreme Court judges to influence public policy and has elicited growing interest in the ideological orientation of appointments to the Court, especially from interest groups with a policy stake in *Charter* interpretation. For example, during 1981–82, in anticipation of the enactment of the *Charter*, the National Action Committee on the Status of Women (NAC) began to lobby for the appointment of a woman "acceptable to our purposes" to the Supreme Court of Canada.[11] This campaign bore fruit in March, 1982, when Prime Minister Trudeau appointed Bertha Wilson to the Supreme Court. Several months later, NAC honoured Justice Wilson by awarding her with a special medallion commemorating the fiftieth anniversary of the "Persons Case" (Reading 10.2). Justice Wilson went on to become the Supreme Court's leading practitioner of judicial activism during the first decade of the *Charter*. Justice Wilson's activism was best exemplified by her outspoken defence of the right of a woman to choose an abortion in her concurring opinion in the Court's 1988 *Morgentaler* decision, which struck down the *Criminal Code* restrictions on abortion.

The *Morgentaler* decision caught Canadians by surprise and alerted them to the new power exercised by judges under the *Charter*. As Peter Russell observed at the time,

> Filling Supreme Court vacancies ... has always been a little bit political in a subterranean way, and now it will be right at the surface [with] the political interest groups lobbying and pressing the appointing authorities to put people on the court of their persuasion.[12]

Russell's prediction was fulfilled almost before he finished making it. The *Morgentaler* decision was criticized by Angela Costigan, counsel for Choose Life Canada, a national pro-life lobby group, as "the expression of personal opinion by the judges." Costigan allowed that in the future her group would try to influence the appointment of judges who shared its position. Norma Scarborough, president of the Canadian Abortion Rights League (CARAL), responded by declaring that, while her group had never tried to influence judicial appointments in the past, it would if necessary in the future. "We

---

11 "NAC Memo," Committee Report, September, 1981, Justice Committee, p. 5; "NAC Memo," March, 1981, Justice Committee Report, p. 4.

12 "Public to Demand Say in Court Appointments," *Lawyers Weekly*, February 12, 1988, p. 1.

are going to protect our position as much as possible," she declared.[13] When Justice Estey announced his intention to retire several months later, Member of Parliament James Jepson, an outspoken pro-life Tory back-bencher, declared, "We now have a chance to put men and women on the bench with a more conservative point of view." While emphasizing that he had never lobbied for a judicial appointment before, Jepson continued:

> But this one seems to have caught the people's attention. Unfortunately, with the *Charter* that Trudeau left us, we legislators do not have final power. It rests with the courts.... You have seen the battling in the United States for the [most recent] Supreme Court nominee. Well, it doesn't take a rocket scientist to see we have the same situation here now.[14]

At the time, Jepson's comments represented a sharp break with Canadian practice. In retrospect, they marked the beginning of a growing demand for greater transparency and public participation in Supreme Court appointments.

On April 17, 1992, the tenth anniversary of the *Charter*, Chief Justice Antonio Lamer waded into this debate by observing that, "I don't think the American process is a good one." While he did not rule out the possibility of change, he stressed that:

> What we must be very careful not to do is to politicize the process. That's what the Americans have done. We've worked very hard to depoliticize the process. We started 25 or 30 years ago, and I think we have succeeded. You know, I was appointed to this court by Mr. Trudeau. I was appointed Chief Justice by Mr. Mulroney. I don't think there is any love lost between the two of them.[15]

This argument was hard to square with the Chief Justice's earlier remark in the same interview that "the *Charter* has changed our job descriptions." Prior to the *Charter*, Lamer observed, judges were trained and expected just "to apply" and, if necessary, "to interpret" laws. "But with the *Charter*," he continued:

> We are commanded to sometimes judge the laws themselves. It is [a] very different activity, especially when one has to look at Section 1 of the Charter [the reasonable limitations clause], which is asking us to make what is essentially what used to be a political call.[16]

---

13 Ibid.
14 Reduced Role for Politicians Urged in Naming of Judges," *The Globe and Mail*, May 16, 1988, A1.
15 *The Globe and Mail*, April 17, 1992, A17.
16 Ibid.

Lamer seemed to admit that under the *Charter* the Court is now engaged in a function similar to that of the U.S. Supreme Court, yet continued to cling to a British-style appointment process associated with an adjudicatory court. The danger of this hybrid approach is that, rather than preventing the politicization of the appointment process, it will just drive the politics underground, beyond pubic knowledge or scrutiny.

An incident pursuant to Justice LaForest's retirement in 1997 suggests that this is precisely what has been happening. In an interview shortly after he retired, Justice LaForest became the first Supreme Court justice to support public nomination hearings. In September, 1997, it came to light that EGALE, Canada's leading gay rights advocacy group, was actively lobbying the upper echelons of the Chrétien government for a replacement who would be more supportive of their litigation campaign (Reading 4.6). Critics such as F. L. Morton (Reading 4.6) claimed that this showed that the appointment process was already politicized and that holding public hearings for judicial nominees would simply democratize the process. A month later, a francophone lawyer from New Brunswick, Michèle Bastarache, was appointed to the Court. Less than a year later (April, 1998), he joined a majority of the Court in the *Vriend* decision, a major constitutional victory for gay rights and EGALE.

Several months later, the influential editor of the *Globe and Mail*, William Thorsell, condemned the practice of choosing judges "in secret" and called for broader public input and debate in appointing Supreme Court judges (Reading 4.7). Thorsell was particularly concerned that the judge chosen to replace LaForest, Michèle Bastarache, was "heavy with political baggage." Bastarache was a former partner in the prime minister's old law firm; the former co-chair of the national "Yes Committee" for the Charlottetown Accord Referendum; and a 1993 election advisor to the federal Liberal party. Thorsell echoed Morton's concern (made before the Bastarache appointment) that the appointment was unduly influenced by the Chrétien government's interest in the outcome of the then pending *Quebec Secession Reference* (Reading 2.4).

Stung by mounting public criticism, in December, 1998, Prime Minister Chrétien defended the existing appointment process. "American-style public confirmation hearings before appointing Supreme Court justices," Chrétien wrote, "would limit the choice of excellent candidates as many would not wish to undergo the ordeal of public and partisan-motivated attacks." And it would be wrong, he added, "if the underlying objective was to shape the court's decision-making process through partisan questioning."[17]

The issue returned the following year when Justice Peter Cory retired and the speculation (and behind-the-scenes lobbying) about his replacement

---

17 Jean Chrétien, "A question of merit: ensuring quality and commitment in High Court appointments," *National* (Canadian Bar Association) (December, 1998), p. 15.

began anew. This time, the *National Post* weighed in and took aim at the prime minister's defence of the status quo: "If judges cannot withstand the heat of an open selection process, how can they expect to determine highly controversial cases that will certainly invite attacks from their critics."[18] The *Post* editorial went on to specifically oppose the appointment of either Louise Arbour or Rosalie Abella, two women from the Ontario Court of Appeal, because of their alleged proclivities for judicial activism. It then endorsed Ontario Justice David Doherty whom it described as a "criminal law genius" and "resistant to the creeping expansionism of the Charter." "Judge Doherty," the editorial concluded dryly, "is not, admittedly a woman; but no one's perfect." This ongoing and growing debate is the focus of Professor Jacob Ziegel's more scholarly treatment in Reading 4.8. Ziegel concludes that a more transparent and accountable appointment process would be more compatible with the Supreme Court's new role under the *Charter*.

A related development is the push for the appointment of more women judges to all levels of the Canadian judiciary. At the beginning of the decade of the 1980s, only three per cent of the federally appointed judges were women. This figure rose to ten per cent by 1990 and twenty-five per cent by 2002. Since 1982, there have been three women appointed to the Supreme Court of Canada (to fill nine vacancies). The Russell and Ziegel study found that 17.5 per cent of the Mulroney judicial appointments (1984–88) were women.

The Ontario Judicial Appointments Advisory Committee was given an explicit "employment equity" mandate at its creation in 1989. During its first six years of operation, thirty-nine per cent of Ontario's 111 judicial appointments were women – increasing the percentage of women provincial judges in Ontario from three per cent to twenty-two per cent. In addition, three of these new judges were aboriginal, ten from racial minorities, and eight francophones – including Canada's first aboriginal woman judge, Ontario's first black woman judge and Canada's first East Asian woman judge.[19] While there is certainly no longer any controversy over an "equal opportunity" appointments policy, there are critics of "employment equity" measures who argue merit – not gender – should be the only relevant criterion of appointment (Reading 4.5).

The push for more female judges raises the question of whether "women judges will make a difference" (Reading 4.4). In a widely publicized speech in 1990, Justice Bertha Wilson argued that certain areas of judge-made law reflect the gender bias of a male judiciary and that women judges will

---

18 "Judging the judges," *National Post*, June 5, 1999, A15 (unsigned editorial).

19 Justice Maryka Omatsu, "On Judicial Appointments: Does Gender Make a Difference?", in Joseph F. Fletcher, ed., *Ideas in Action: Essays on Politics and Law in Honour of Peter Russell* (Toronto: University of Toronto Press, 1999), p. 177.

bring a "uniquely feminine perspective" to bear on certain issues of legal interpretation. She also suggested that "some aspects of criminal law in particular cry out for change since they are based on presuppositions about the nature of women and women's sexuality that in this day and age are little short of ludicrous." While Justice Wilson did not specify what these aspects were, many assumed, based on her own votes and written opinions, that she was referring to abortion and prostitution.

Justice Wilson's speech provoked a strong protest by REAL (Realistic, Equal and Active for Life) Women, a conservative women's group, that subsequently filed a complaint with the Canadian Judicial Council. REAL Women's complaint argued that there is no necessary connection between gender and political views and that Justice Wilson was in fact advancing feminist teachings and policy under the guise of gender equality:

> Women in Canada do not all think alike. The views of vocal feminists (scholars or otherwise) do not represent the views of all Canadian women. The failure of Madame Justice Wilson to either understand this point or alternatively, fail to accept the fact that all women (not to mention men) do not agree with the feminist interpretation of law, is in itself deeply disturbing and indicative of her inability to properly carry out her duties to impartially and objectively interpret the law.[20]

The Canadian Judicial Council found that the complaint did not justify a formal investigation, and rejected it.

This incident is indicative of a growing controversy between feminists and their critics over the judiciary. The same dispute has arisen over the recent practice of "education seminars" on gender bias issues for judges, a policy that Justice Wilson also endorsed in her 1990 speech. The Canadian Judicial Centre, established in 1988 to provide continuing education courses for judges, has begun to include seminars on gender bias in judging. Most of the materials used for these seminars have been prepared by law professors associated directly or indirectly with LEAF(Reading 7.2). This connection has fuelled allegations that the Canadian Judicial Centre has become "an indoctrination centre for feminist thought."[21] Gwen Landolt, president of REAL Women, said she respects the right of feminists to use the *Charter* to advance their policy objectives but objects to what she maintains is their privileged access to judges: "We're saying, if you've got an argument to make, line up like everyone else and make your case in court."[22] In 1991, the

---

20 Letter to the Canadian Judicial Council from Lettie Morse, President, REAL Women, February 13, 1990.

21 "Political Correctness Undermines Judicial System: Reader," Letter to the editor from C. Gwendolyn Landolt, *Lawyer's Weekly*, August 2, 1991, p. 5.

22 "Justice and Gender," *Alberta Report*, February 26, 1990, p. 35.

Alberta Provincial Judges Association passed a resolution protesting judicial education programs that provide "unilateral views on socio-political sensitization issues."[23]

The Centre has defended the utility of gender bias seminars and continues to offer them. In 1992, the then federal minister of justice, Kim Campbell, rejected the recommendation of the National Action Committee on the Status of Women (NAC) to make them mandatory. To require attendance at any such seminar, the justice minister explained, would infringe the principle of judicial independence.[24] This policy was challenged in the wake of the "McClung Affair" (Reading 5.4). Commenting on the Canadian Judicial Council's decision to reprimand but not remove Judge McClung, Kathleen Mahoney, a law professor at the University of Calgary who has contributed to the development of the gender-bias seminars, commented that "the federal government should not appoint or promote judges unless they have taken gender sensitivity courses to root out anti-female bias in the courts."[25]

From a political science / judicial process perspective, feminist support for gender-bias seminars for judges is analogous to the efforts of American feminists to prevent judges like Robert Bork from being appointed, except that this "lobbying" occurs after the appointment and is directed at the appointee rather than the appointers. The common denominator of both tactics is the perception that judges can and do use their discretion in interpreting constitutional rights to alter public policy. Since there is no opportunity to exert influence prior to the appointment, such as the hearings of the Senate Judiciary Committee in the U.S., Canadian interest groups are forced to seek access after the appointment. These "special education" seminars for judges provide just such a forum. Nor is it surprising that conservative groups have protested this "privileged audience" with the judges. Since presumably other Canadian interest groups would also welcome the opportunity to educate judges on their views of "the public interest," it will be interesting to see whether this practice is expanded or eliminated.

To conclude, there have been somewhat contradictory trends in judicial selection in Canada during recent decades. Based on the decline in patronage appointments, Sir Robert Megarry predicted further depoliticization of judicial selection in Canada along the lines of the British experience that he describes (Reading 4.2). But when Megarry was writing (1973), British judges had never exercised judicial review of a federal constitution nor interpreted an entrenched charter of rights. British judges had thus never become embroiled in the "constitutional politics" or "politics of rights" that

---

23 David Vienneau, "Some judges balking at anti-sexism training," *The Toronto Star*, Dec. 10, 1991, B1, B8.

24 "Mandatory Training of Judges Rejected by Justice Minister," *The Globe and Mail*, April 11, 1992, A6.

25 "McClung reprimanded for critical remarks made at L'Heureux-Dubé," *National Post*, May 22, 1999, A4.

result from judicial review. Writing in 2001, after Britain's adoption of the *European Convention of Human Rights*, Conor Gearty reports that this appears to be changing (Reading 5.8). In Canada, this political dynamic was captured by Peter Russell's 1982 prediction that a principal effect of the *Charter* would be "its tendency to judicialize politics and to politicize the judiciary."[26] Certainly the growing debate over the appointment process and other court-related controversies over the last decade support Russell's prediction. Patronage considerations might well be replaced by political considerations of a more ideological nature.

On the other hand, the availability of the section 33 legislative override may neutralize the "court packing" tendencies of calculating politicians and interest groups. If a government finds a judicial interpretation of the *Charter* legally wrong, politically unacceptable, or both, it can always invoke the section 33 "notwithstanding" power to overrule the judges' "mistake." This is a much more direct and precise way of dealing with such decisions than the blunt (and uncertain) method of "court packing." Presumably U.S. President Franklin D. Roosevelt would have felt no need to "pack" the U.S. Supreme Court during the 1930s if he had a power like the section 33 legislative override. With this consideration in mind, it remains to be seen whether the *Charter of Rights* will produce a more ideologically charged appointment process to the Supreme Court of Canada.

4.1

Patronage in Judicial Appointments
Jeffrey Simpson
The Spoils of Power: The Politics of Patronage (Toronto: Collins, 1988), 300–310. Reprinted with permission.

… Broadly speaking, the further down the judicial hierarchy, the more obvious the evidence of patronage. The Supreme Court of Canada, for example, is now completely devoid of patronage, or even of the tinge of partisan appointments…. Supreme Court appointments were not always so pure. A scholarly history of the Supreme Court makes clear that partisanship joined religion and region – and merit, when available – as indispensable criteria for Supreme Court appointments until the immediate post-war years. When Louis St. Laurent became prime minister in 1949, the court contained seven justices, four of whom had had extensive political ties to the Liberal party. St. Laurent himself appointed justices from a mixture of non-political and political backgrounds, the most obvious being long-time Liberal cabinet

---

26 Peter H. Russell, "The Effect of the Charter of Rights on the Policy-Making Role of Canadian Courts," *Canadian Public Administration* 25, (1982), p. 1.

minister Douglas Abbott. But partisanship appeared to wane throughout subsequent years as prime ministers increasingly sought advice from the legal fraternity before making Supreme Court appointments. Twenty-two of forty Supreme Court judges appointed before 1949 had previously been politicians; since then, only two of twenty-two justices had entered politics.

That sharp decline in previous political experience of Supreme Court justices is partly – but only partly – reflected further down the hierarchy. The Canadian Bar Association said as recently as 1985 that "there is ample scope for the functioning of a political patronage system without applying it to judicial appointments." The association declared itself satisfied that patronage had been rooted out of the Supreme Court, but it worried about patronage elsewhere in the judiciary, especially in the Federal Court, whose members are appointed by Ottawa. Writing after Prime Minister Pierre Trudeau sent three former ministers (Mark MacGuigan, Bud Cullen and Yvon Pinard) to the Federal Court as part of his 1984 orgy of patronage appointments, the association remarked, "at present, this court is perceived by many, rightly or wrongly, as a government-oriented court because so many former politicians and federal officials have been appointed to it." The association added, "as to appointments to the Federal Court of Canada, political favouritism has been a dominant, though not sole, consideration; many appointees have been active supporters of the party in power."

Trudeau's parting gesture also featured the appointment of two other Liberal MPs and a defeated Liberal candidate to lower courts. These appointments fitted a familiar Trudeau pattern for patronage. A professor of law before entering politics, Trudeau took considerable care in his early years in office to temper patronage in making senior judicial appointments. This was consistent with other intermittent efforts to change traditional assumptions about patronage. But such efforts declined in intensity as his years in office wore on, so that by the end of his sixteen years as prime minister Trudeau was practising patronage as relentlessly as his predecessors.

The association also analysed federal appointments to higher courts in the provinces – so-called section 96 courts – and concluded that political favouritism still existed in Alberta, Manitoba, Newfoundland, and Ontario, and that it remained a "dominant" but not exclusive consideration in New Brunswick, Nova Scotia, Prince Edward Island, and Saskatchewan. That the three Maritime provinces appeared on the association's list was not surprising; there the traditions of political patronage have persisted longer than almost anywhere else in Canada. But Saskatchewan's inclusion might raise a few eyebrows, until one remembers that Saskatchewan was the fiefdom of Otto Lang, Trudeau's minister of justice and a former dean of the University of Saskatchewan law school.

Lang and his successor Mark MacGuigan scattered prominent or low-profile Liberals throughout the Saskatchewan judiciary, including former party leaders, MLAs, defeated candidates and loyal party workers. This propensity for appointing Liberals to Saskatchewan courts led directly to a *contretemps* with the Conservative government of Premier Grant Devine. The provincial Conservatives, eager dispensers of patronage themselves, became sufficiently riled by Liberal appointments to the bench, and by Ottawa's refusal to consult the provincial government before making appointments, that they tried to restrict Liberal opportunities for patronage. In 1982 the provincial government passed an order-in-council reducing the number of judges on the Saskatchewan Court of Appeal from seven to five.

For the next two years, open warfare raged between the provincial Conservative government and the Trudeau Liberals. The provincial cabinet passed another order-in-council closing down each vacancy on the Court of Queen's Bench, so that its strength fell from thirty to twenty-four. Only the election of the Mulroney Conservatives ended the impasse. With Conservatives in Regina and Ottawa, the provincial party quickly restored the judicial positions, and filled some of them with prominent supporters such as George Hill and Irving Goldenberg, former presidents of the Saskatchewan Conservative party. The Saskatchewan experience of the 1980s mirrored that of Newfoundland in 1960 when Liberal premier Joey Smallwood, rebuffed by the federal Conservatives in his demand for control of judicial appointments, refused to proclaim legislation creating a new position on the provincial Supreme Court.

The Bar Association's 1985 review of judicial appointments gave provincial governments better marks than it gave the federal government. In five provinces – Alberta, British Columbia, Newfoundland, Quebec, and Saskatchewan – the association thought "political favouritism has played no part in appointments." In Manitoba, favouritism played "some part" in appointments, whereas in those hardy patronage perennials – New Brunswick, Prince Edward Island and Nova Scotia – the association found that "most appointees have been active supporters of the party in power."

That 1985 review, sparked by Trudeau's parting orgy of patronage and his failure to consult the bar before making Yvon Pinard's appointment, flowed from the association's decades-long campaign to squeeze patronage from the process of selecting judges. Moral suasion was about the association's only weapon for many years, although it helped the association's case when its president, R.B. Bennett, became prime minister in 1930 and tried to set a better example in selecting Supreme Court justices. But the concept of formal consultation with the legal community had to await the arrival of Trudeau as minister of justice in 1967.

Trudeau became the first minister of justice to seek an opinion of the Canadian Bar Association's National Council on the Judiciary before appointing a judge. This practice continued when John Turner became minister of justice in the first Trudeau government, and Turner is fairly credited with having improved the quality of judicial appointments across the country. In 1972, a special adviser on judicial appointments was named in the minister's office. These reforms sprang both from Trudeau's own convictions as a professor of law and from intermittent attempts to change some traditional conventions of patronage in his early years in office. In five provinces – Alberta, British Columbia, Newfoundland, Ontario, and Saskatchewan – attorneys-general now formally consult provincial judicial councils before making appointments, while in Quebec the attorney-general consults a nominating committee. British Columbia's *Provincial Court Act* even requires the cabinet to appoint only persons recommended by the judicial council.

Pressure from the bar, then, has been among those restricting the incidence of political patronage on judicial appointments. Some numbers illustrate the point. Will Klein studied federally appointed judges in Manitoba, Ontario, and Quebec from 1905 to 1970. He found that nearly ninety-five percent of former politicians appointed to Ontario courts by Liberal governments were Liberals, and eighty-one percent appointed by Conservative governments were Conservatives. But he also discovered that although forty-three percent of all Laurier's appointments had contested elections, only twenty-one percent of Trudeau's (up to 1970) had done so. Klein concluded that "political activities prior to appointment to the bench have been common to about a third of the judges appointed in Manitoba, Ontario, and Quebec between 1905 and 1970 but that ... proportion of judges with electoral experience has diminished through these years."

What Klein could not measure was the partisanship of appointees who had participated in politics other than by running in elections or serving in legislatures. It was a key omission, since many judicial appointees have been active party supporters without ever having entered electoral politics. His general conclusion that political considerations in judicial appointments have waned over this century was supported by Guy Bouthillier, who examined the careers of appointees to the Quebec Court of Appeal from 1867 to 1972. Bouthillier found that the proportion involved in politics had dropped from over seventy-eight percent between Confederation and World War I to twenty-two percent since World War II. But remember that these sorts of studies undoubtedly underestimate, often considerably, the partisan factor in appointments. They trace only electoral careers, and forget that many judges with the proper political credentials never ran for office. For example, one study in the early 1950s found that in six provinces all judges were supporters of the party in power at the time of their appointment. In the four other provinces, the percentage of party supporters ranged from seventy percent to eighty-seven percent. And a survey for the Association of Canadian Law Teachers in 1966 concluded, "All but a few of the judges appointed during the period were affiliated with the party in power at the time of their appointment, and most were actively engaged in politics.

The practice still continues. For example, Prime Minister Joe Clark appointed five judges to the Superior Court for the Montreal district. All had Conservative credentials: Claude Gérin, who ran unsuccessfully against Liberal kingpin Marc Lalonde; Gérard Trudel, a Conservative organizer; Maurice Mercure, a former Union Nationale candidate and Conservative organizer; Bernard Flynn, who worked for Clark and his predecessor Robert Stanfield; and Claude Nolin, former president of the Conservative party in Quebec.

4.2

Judicial Appointments in Great Britain
Sir Robert Megarry
From G.M. Stirling, "A Symposium of the Appointment of Judges," *Alberta Law Review 2*
(1973), 279–309. Reprinted with permission.

… First, I must make a brief disclaimer. Naturally I shall say nothing that comes from any confidential source; I merely recount what is generally known or believed by the English Bar, or is the public domain. That said, I may begin with the formal details of appointment to the Bench in England. It is briefly told. There are three main categories of judges, and I give the figures in round numbers. First, there is the High Court and above (Court of Appeal and House of Lords), with a total of 100. Second, there are 125 county court judges; and third, there are 50 stipendiary magistrates. That makes a total of 275. All are appointed by the Crown on the Advice of the Lord Chancellor or, in the case of the Court of Appeal and House of Lords, the Prime Minister. The responsibility for this advice is individual and not collective; it is not a Cabinet matter. The Prime Minister is generally believed to consult closely with the Lord Chancellor before making his recommendations, and so it is the Lord Chancellor who in substance is the great appointer to the Bench.

The *Judicature Act, 1925*, s.12, replacing provisions in the *Judicature Act, 1873*, and the *Act of Settlement, 1700*, provides that judges of the Supreme Court (that is, the High Court and Court of Appeal) hold office "during good behaviour, subject to a power of removal by the Crown" on an address presented to His Majesty by both Houses of Parliament. No English judge has ever been removed under these provisions, but in 1830 Sir Jonah Barrington, a judge of the Court of Admiralty in Ireland, was removed for misconduct and malversation in office. That is all. County court judges and stipendiary magistrates are in effect removable by the Lord Chancellor for inability or misbehaviour. I know of only one such removal. In 1851 Judge Ramshay had become very eccentric indeed, and after a hearing he was removed from office. From his chambers in the Temple he continued to send letters to court officials asserting that he was still the judge, and adjourning the court, but all to no avail; and *quo warranto* proceedings against his successor failed…. So we have little experience in this field that would assist you. At the same time, it is said that there have been some instances – a very few – in which the Lord Chancellor and others have encouraged a resignation; but that is a little different. Other and more subtle forces, and not least, association with the Bar, and the influence of the Inns of Court, do much to sustain the judge in England on the difficulties of his office.

Retirement? This is now mandatory at 75 for High Court judges and above, at 72 for county court judges, and at 70 for stipendiary magistrates. Machinery for discipline? Nil. Training? Nil. And so on that I seem to be of very little use to you. Yet I think that we have been merely looking at the tip of the iceberg. We must look a little below the surface if we want to get a balanced picture. Let me mention, as briefly as may be, seven factors which help to show the realities.

1. There are relatively few appointments to be made. With a population for England and Wales approaching 50 million, there are a little less than 100 judges of High Court level and above to do all the trial and appellate work; and that comes to two judges per million of population. At the same level, Canada had roughly five and a half times as many judges per million population, and about three times as many at the county court level; if one ignores the size of the population and takes absolute figures, yours are of the order of 250 and 160 as compared with our 100 and 125....

2. The field from which appointments are made is much smaller in England than in Canada. Three main factors play their part; specialization of function, specialization of subject-matter, and age. The first lead primarily refers to the division of our legal profession into barristers and solicitors. Of a total legal profession of some 28,000 or 29,000, less than about 2,600 are practising barristers. With certain exceptions at the lower levels, all appointments are made from the Bar, the branch of the profession that lives out its professional life in the courts. There is then the further division of barristers into Q.C.'s and juniors. Of the 2,600 practising barristers, rather less than 300 are Q.C.'s; and appointments to the High Court are nearly always made from among practising Q.C.'s. In fact, the field of choice is smaller than that, because after discounting those who are approaching retirement or have not been very successful, probably there are some 150 or 200 who do the great bulk of the work; and it is from them that the appointments will be made.

In England, of course, silk is a reality and not merely an honour. A junior who takes silk takes his professional life in his hands, for he has to give up all his smaller work, including settling pleadings, and, being unable to appear in court without a junior, must confine himself to the bigger cases; and the number of these is limited. A junior does not lightly apply for silk, and silk is not to be had for the asking. It is believed that something like four out of five applications fail. Solicitors play an important part in this field. Nobody will be appointed a Q.C. unless many solicitors, on a basis of trial and error, have acquired a faith in his abilities as an advocate; and no Q.C. will get much work unless many more solicitors have faith in his forensic abilities at the higher level of silk. The collective judgment of solicitors thus plays a large part in selecting the field of possible candidates for the Bench. Solicitors judge from knowledge and experience, too; unlike the lay client, they will not confuse a flashy but incompetent display with a restrained but skilled performance.

I need say little about specialization of subject-matter. Barristers tend to specialize in work which usually finds its way into one or other of the three Divisions of the High Court, Chancery, Queen's Bench, and Probate, Divorce and Admiralty (soon to become the Family Division); and within those broad divisions there are often specialist sub-divisions. This, of course, narrows the field. A Queen's Bench judge dies; who will be appointed in his place? You may be sure that it will not be a Q.C. who normally practises in the Chancery Division.

As for age, there is in practice a limited range for appointment. Looking at recent years, the average age for appointment to the High Court comes out at about 52 for the Probate, Divorce and Admiralty Division, 53 or 54 for the Queen's Bench Division, and 55 or 56 for the Chancery Division. The youngest age at which anyone has been appointed to the High Court this century is 42 and the oldest 65 (though I cannot forbear from mentioning that Sir Salathiel Lovell began his five years in the Court of Exchequer when he was 89; but that was in 1708). The normal effective range of ages is from the late forties to the late fifties. Again, this restricts the field of choice.

Let me take a melancholy but practical example. Suppose that, overwhelmed by the hospitality that I have been receiving here (and that is far from a remote possibility), I keel over and die before your eyes. A successor to my seat in the Chancery Division will then have to be appointed. Well, this does not look very difficult. In the *Law List* there is a list of the Q.C.'s who practise specially in the Chancery Division. There are 28 names there. Some of the more senior are over the age at which appointment is probable; others are too young or too inexperienced. There are other considerations, too, and in the end probably most lawyers who have any familiarity with the Chancery Division would agree upon the handful of names, perhaps two, three or even four, from which the appointment would almost certainly be made. The Chancery Division is small, with only ten judges, and the field is more open in the Queen's Bench Division, with some 45 judges. But even so, in most cases the question must come down to one of choosing from a very small number of possibilities; and this must usually make the process of appointment far less complex than it must be in some other jurisdictions.

3. Most judges have had some trial runs on the Bench before being appointed. Your chairman touched on this a short while ago when he mentioned what Henry Cecil had said in his book. It is common for a potential judge to be appointed a Commissioner of Assize for a period of four, six or eight weeks at a time; and during this period he has the temporary status of a High Court judge. Again, many a barrister sits three or four times a year as a Recorder, or Chairman or Deputy Chairman of Quarter Sessions, spending perhaps some twenty days a year as a judge in criminal cases too serious for the magistrates and not serious enough for a High Court judge. Although the prime purpose of these activities is to get the work done, there is great value in the incidental result that it becomes known what sort of a judge the barrister is likely to make if he is appointed to the Bench. Nobody can really tell how anyone will behave as judge until he has been seen performing as a judge. Being a judge is so different from being an advocate, not least in that the advocate knows which side he is on. There have been many instances of Commissioners of Assize demonstrating their suitability for judicial office,

and in other instances demonstrating just the opposite, for a wide variety of reasons. Men react to the stresses of the Bench in remarkably different ways. Like the elephant, the judicial quality is easily recognizable but very difficult to define; and so this is one of the fields in which "Try it and see" becomes an important adage. By way of footnote, I may add that until 1933 Scotland even had a trial run for each newly appointed judge of the Court of Session *after* his appointment; but this had become a mere formality.

I would attach very little value to any formal training for judicial office. I do not see how you can effectually train a man to be a judge. You can, of course, teach a man the technique of driving a car; but it is the man and not his training that predominantly determines whether he uses wisely and tolerantly the skills that he has acquired, or whether he is a foolish and aggressive driver. The judicial quality is something that the man has or has not got; and whatever training may do to improve the native quality, it cannot graft a judicial temperament on to barren stock.

4. The Lord Chancellor, the great appointer of judges, is an active judge himself. He is a Cabinet Minister, of course, but he is far from being that alone. He is necessarily someone of a sufficient judicial stature to enable him to preside over the House of Lords, and command the respect of the other law lords. He does not merely sit in an office and in Parliament, but lives and moves in the world of law. He has long known many of the senior members of the Bar, and of course in the House of Lords he listens to many arguments. There is, therefore, much that he can decide upon his own first-hand knowledge, and not merely upon report.

5. Judges live and work with the Bar. If you are near the Inns of Court in London at lunch-time on any day during term, you will see that at about one p.m. most of the judges of the High Court and Court of Appeal and many of the practising members of the Bar are on their way to the halls of their Inns of Court for lunch. Each judge will be a bencher of his Inn, and the senior Q.C.'s and some of the senior juniors (you will know what I mean) will also be benchers. All lunch together on a basis of equality, whether judge, silk or junior. Seniority as a bencher depends on seniority of election, and is unaffected by judicial office. The atmosphere is one of ease and friendliness; and informal though this is, it has a constitutional importance. It is in these regular and informal contacts that we find so much of value rubbing off on each other. It tends to prevent the judges from becoming pompous and overbearing; and not only is the judge constantly reminded of his own days at the Bar, but also the silk or junior finds himself absorbing overtones of the Bench. A civilizing atmosphere spills over into the courts, and sweetens the acerbities of the contest. This association contributes towards a firmness of moral tone throughout the administration of the law, and provides a nursery for the future judge.

6. It is rare for an appointment to the High Court to be refused. The prevailing tone is that it is of paramount importance to the country that the standard of the Bench should be maintained at the highest possible level,

and that if a barrister is offered an appointment to the Bench, this shows that the Lord Chancellor thinks him the most suitable person to be appointed. Whatever the individual feelings may be, the need to maintain the standard of the Bench impels acceptance.

7. Last, and in some ways the most important, is the fact that 25 years ago politics dropped almost completely out of appointment to the English Bench. The effect of political considerations in making judicial appointments is certainly not something to be exclusively attributed to Lord Halsbury while he was Lord Chancellor, interesting though some of his appointments were. Long before his time, and for many years after it, the general belief was that a career in Parliament was a powerful aid to appointment to the Bench; and there were many appointments that gave colour to this belief. The normal road to many of the highest offices in the law, too, was not by successful service as a puisne judge but by becoming Attorney-General or Solicitor-General. The Attorney-General of the day was regarded as having something of a right to the Chief Justiceship of the Common Pleas when it fell vacant. It was his "pillow," and when in 1880 that office in effect became merged in the Chief Justiceship of the Queen's Bench as the Lord Chief Justiceship of England, some regarded that office as having become the pillow. Later events tended to support that view; and although the emphasis on politics was probably lessening, down to the war of 1939–45 the position was substantially unaltered.

The change can almost be pinpointed. On January 21, 1946, Viscount Caldecote, C.J., a former Solicitor-General, Attorney-General and Lord Chancellor, resigned, and Lord Goddard, a law lord, was appointed Chief Justice in his place. Lord Goddard was a lawyer through and through, with no more than a faint brush with politics in his youth; and he had moved steadily up from the King's Bench to the Court of Appeal and then to the House of Lords. Within a fortnight, on February 1, 1946, Sir Donald Somervell, a former Tory Attorney-General, was appointed to a seat in the Court of Appeal, even though the Government in power from 1945 to 1951 was a Labour government. These two appointments seem to have set the seal on the change. Politics were out, and such politics as were in were bi-partisan. During the six years of the Labour government, Lord Jowitt, as Lord Chancellor, was responsible for the appointment of over half the entire Bench; and yet not until towards the end of the time did he make any appointment to the High Court from the MPs supporting his own party, and then only one. In 1958 Lord Goddard retired as Chief Justice, and despite political contenders, the appointment made was of Lord Parker, a Lord Justice with no political career. When Lord Parker retired this year, again the appointment as Chief Justice went to a non-political member of the Court of Appeal, Lord Widgery; and each of these appointments was made while a Tory government was in power. With that unanimity of performance, there is good reason to believe that each of the two major political parties is at least agreed on the proper approach to judicial appointment today.

I am not saying that to have been in politics is today an actual disqualification for appointment to the Bench; but I do say that to be an active supporter of the party in power no longer seems to be an asset of any real weight. Experience in public affairs, especially in Parliament, may be a factor of great value in moulding a man's character and giving him breadth of vision; the Bench would be the poorer without some who have this background. But it has ceased to matter much whether the candidate for appointment is a supporter or opponent of the party in power. With the withering of partisan claims to appointment has come another change. For over twenty years nearly all appointments to the Court of Appeal and House of Lords have been by way of promotion from the High Court, and not *per saltum* from the Bar. A vacancy in the Court of Appeal will be filled from the ranks of the High Court judges whose judicial abilities are known. No longer is there the problem of trying to guess the probable performance of a giant of the Bar as a Lord Justice of Appeal, and trying to compare that guess with a reasoned estimate, based on experience of how a High Court judge of, say, five years standing would do in the Court of Appeal.

Those, then, are the seven factors that I wanted to put before you. Perhaps I may add some comments on two final matters. First, there is the actual process of appointment to the Bench. On this, I speak with no certain knowledge, but on guesses which I hope are intelligent. The Lord Chancellor's Office is in effect a small government department, with a staff of some two dozen lawyers. By a mysterious system of osmosis and grape-vines, I would expect the Lord Chancellor and his staff to have a pretty good idea about all that is going on in the legal world. If at any given moment you were to ask the Lord Chancellor whether X or Y or Z is likely to be appointed a judge when a vacancy occurs, and he were willing to answer, I should expect him to be able to say, then and there, that X is a strong candidate, that Y is a possible, and that Z is a nonstarter. You will remember how small the English Bar is, how few English silks there are, and how small the country is. Only a very small part of the population lives more than 250 miles from London.

Despite the background of knowledge of the Bar, the Lord Chancellor may be expected to consult the Chief Justice and the Master of The Rolls (who presides over the Court of Appeal) when a vacancy occurs; and if it is in the Chancery Division or the Probate, Divorce and Admiralty Division, he may well consult the head of that Division as well. Whether those consulted ever have or take the initiative, suggesting that A or B is better than X and Y who are under consideration, I cannot say. I should doubt if there are rules or even conventions; I should expect everything to be highly informal or, if you like, very English. When the *Courts Act, 1971*, comes into force there will be many changes, some of them important; but I do not think that they will alter the essence of what I have been saying.

Secondly, perhaps I may be mildly historical. On at least some views it is possible to discern four stages in the part played by politics in appointments to the Bench, each stage merging into the next. In the first stage, party politics may play so large a part that some of those appointed fall short of the standards that the office demands. In the second stage, political claims do no more than give some preference among those who are fully qualified for appointment; of three candidates with not much to choose between them, the supporter of the party in power will be preferred to the political opponent or the politically inert. Without being unduly cynical, it is possible to observe that there are times when a government may prefer the sight of a political opponent sitting non-politically on the Bench to the sight of him in vigorous opposition in the legislature. The third stage comes when the political opponent has prospects of appointment which, other things being equal, are on a par with those of a political supporter, or nearly so. At the fourth stage politics have ceased to play any real part. Appointments are made very largely from the ranks of those who have made law and not politics their life.

As I indicated, England seems to have reached this fourth stage in 1946. Where Canada is I must leave you to say; if I had to guess, from what I have read and heard recently my surmise would be that it is somewhere about the third stage, or not far short of it. I repeat that I would not suggest that politics should disqualify. In considering suitability for the Bench a strong case can be made for the wide-ranging span of a statesman's career as against the restricted vision of a technically superb lawyer; the old jibe is that law sharpens the mind by narrowing it. But not all politicians are statesmen, nor do all fine lawyers have minds that are closed to the wider issues of life – not by a long chalk. In the end, the question, as in so many fields, is one of balance, within the national genius....

4.3

Mulroney's Judicial Appointments and the New Judicial Advisory Committees

Peter H. Russell and Jacob S. Ziegel

University of Toronto Law Journal 41 (1991), 4–37. Reprinted with permission.

The data we have collected on the Mulroney government's first-term judicial appointments [1984–1988] are presented in [this section]....

First, we should note the distribution of the 228 judicial appointments.... By far the bulk of these appointments, over 90 percent, is to the section 96 courts, that is, the provincial and territorial courts presided over by federally appointed judges....

... Of the 228 appointments, 67 were promotions within the judicial system.... [T]here is a promotional ladder from the highest provincial trial court (the General Jurisdiction Trial Court) to the Court of Appeal, and then to the

Supreme Court of Canada. Indeed, over half of the appointments to the provincial courts of appeal were "elevations" from the superior trial court. It is pleasantly surprising to find that as many as 13 judges were promoted from the lower provincial courts and that these were spread across the country. In the past such promotions have been very rare. Perhaps their increased frequency reflects the improvements many of the provinces have made in their method of selecting judges....

... [Women comprised 17.5 percent of the appointees, and these appointments were spread] proportionately among the various positions and levels. Certainly this is a clear improvement over the situation at the beginning of the decade, when Pauline Jewett reported to the House of Commons that only three percent of the federally appointed judiciary were women.... [this] suggest[s] a conscious effort at affirmative action to redress the gender imbalance on the bench.

It would appear that this move towards appointing more women judges has not been at the expense of merit. All but one of the 13 appointees whose professional reputation were in the lower of categories – "fair" or "weak" – were men. It is indeed an "old boys network" that enables less qualified lawyers to obtain appointments....

... We turn now to information about the political background of the appointees. We ... organized this information ... by placing each appointee in one of five categories: those with a major involvement with the Conservative party, those with a minor involvement or association with that party, those with no known political affliation, those who with a minor involvement with an opposition party, and those with a major involvement or association with an opposition party. A major involvement with a party includes running for elected office under the party's banner, serving as a party official or "bagman," and active involvement in election or leadership campaigns. [Lesser partisan associations include] minor constituency work, financial contributions, and close personal or professional associations with party leaders....

... The appointment of a lawyer associated with an opposition party may well be politically motivated. There are well-known incidents in Canadian history where a political opponent received an appointment in order to make it easier to elect a government member in the appointee's constituency....

... [What our "political background" data do] show is that patronage, or "political favouritism," to use the CBA's phrase, continued to have a major influence on judicial appointments during the first Mulroney government. One hundred and eight of the appointees, just under half of the total number (47.4 percent), had a known political association with the Conservative party. For just under a quarter (24.1 percent), the involvement was considered strong. Mr. Mulroney's government, it would appear, so far as judicial appointments are concerned, did not exercise its options much differently from the Trudeau/Turner Liberal government....

... In five provinces – Manitoba, New Brunswick, Nova Scotia, Prince

Edward Island, and Saskatchewan – the percentage of appointees with a known connection to the Conservative party ranges from P.E.I.'s 71.5 percent to Manitoba's 87.5 percent. These findings closely resemble the CBA committee's findings on judicial appointments from 1978 to 1985. [It] reported that in New Brunswick, Nova Scotia, Prince Edward Island, and Saskatchewan "political favouritism has been a dominant, though not the sole, consideration; most appointees have been active supporters of the party in power." ... [P]olitical favouritism has not been concentrated on appointments to the lowest level. On the contrary, the percentage of appointees with ties to the Conservative party was greater – over half – among those appointed to the provincial courts of appeal and the superior courts than to the county or district courts, where it was 39.6 percent. In this respect our results differ from those of the CBA committee, which found that under the Trudeau and Clark governments the influence of political favouritism was generally greater at the county and district court level.

... While the influence of political favouritism is less marked [in regard to promotion], it is still strong: 29 of the 66 judges and one court administrator who were promoted by the Mulroney government were known to have had an involvement or association with the Conservative party, while 11 had opposition party affiliations....

This observation is disturbing. Judicial promotions have always been a delicate issue. In the common law world some observers have expressed concern that the desire for promotion may colour an appointee's conduct on the bench so that he or she will be well thought of by the appointing authority.... Our data show, however, that promotions are frequent and not necessarily based on merit, and that some may well have a political flavour. In the next section we note that promotions have been excluded from the reformed judicial appointing process....

... On the whole, the persons appointed by the Mulroney government in its first term appear to be well regarded within the profession. Nearly a quarter of them are considered outstanding, and 86.3 percent are considered at no less than good. [Interestingly,] appointees with a strong political profile, at either end of the spectrum, were not rated as highly as those with weak political connections: for example, only 19.2 percent of appointees with strong Conservative party connections were rated as outstanding, compared with 30.9 percent with weak Conservative party linkages, and 41.7 percent for appointees with slight opposition party linkages. However, these differences become much smaller when the percentages for outstanding and outstanding/good reputations are combined in each of the categories. Only 13 appointees, 6.1 percent of those appraised, were considered by both assessors to be either fair or weak.

On the basis of this part of our research, some might question the need to reform the traditional appointing system.... But we think there are at least three reasons for dissatisfaction....

First, it should be noted that among the most poorly regarded appointees

– those considered fair or weak – there is a disproportionately large number with political connections to the government – 10 out of 13, or nearly 76.9 percent....

Second, we believe Canadians should strive for a system that is designed so far as possible to appoint not simply persons who will make acceptable judges but those who are best qualified for judicial service....

Third,... [t]here is also the danger of producing a judiciary which is ideologically imbalanced. Canadians have reasons to be especially sensitive to this danger, now that their judges are playing such a significant policy-making role in interpreting the *Charter of Rights and Freedoms.* We should be looking for a reasonable balance in the political and philosophical perspectives represented on the bench....

Finally, but not least,... there is a highly subjective component in assessing the merits of appointees, a difficulty that argues strongly in favour of using committees to assess candidates for judicial office. With the benefit of hindsight we now also recognize that our categories were too broad and that there is a large gap between an "outstanding" appointee and a "good" one....

... Based on the analysis of the data and other developments described in this report, our conclusions are that only marginal improvements were made in the system of selection of judges by the Mulroney government during its first term of office. Political patronage in judicial appointments was still pervasive....

The federal government's much delayed response to the CALT and CBA recommendations was deeply disappointing and does little to address the basic flaws in the judicial appointing system.... The fact remains that the new committees are essentially toothless. They are not authorized to rank candidates, they have no staff to assist them to do well the limited task assigned to them, and they are not even required (nor, for the most part do they have the resources) to interview candidates before determining whether or not they are qualified for judicial office....

The committees face the further invidious task of being asked to give five reasons for not deeming a candidate suitably qualified and of having their assessments reversed on appeal by the minister of justice. Most disturbing of all, the new screening process will not prevent the federal government from continuing to promote candidates on political and personal grounds or to appoint even highly qualified candidates for the wrong reasons. There is an almost irresistible inference that the wish to cling to political patronage power, if not for the sake of the patronage then for the power itself, is the federal government's primary reason for refusing to allow the advisory committees the right to rank candidates.

4.4

Will Women Judges Really Make a Difference?
Justice Bertha Wilson
Osgoode Hall Law Journal 28, no. 3 (1990), 507–22. Reprinted with permission.

… Many have criticized as totally unreal the concept that judges are some-how superhuman, neutral, above politics and unbiased, and are able to completely separate themselves from their personal opinions and pre-dispositions when exercising their judicial function.…

In his text, *The Politics of the Judiciary*, Professor Griffith caused a furor in legal and judicial circles in the United Kingdom when he questioned whether the English judiciary were capable of impartiality. He stated that for a judge to be completely impartial he or she would have to be like a political, economic and social eunuch and have no interests in the world outside the court. Because this is impossible, Griffith concludes that impar-tiality is an ideal incapable of realization. He says of the English judiciary:

> These judges have by their education and training and the pursuit of their profession as barristers acquired a strikingly homogeneous collection of atti-tudes, beliefs, and principles which to them represents the public interest.

The public interest, in other words, is perceived from the viewpoint of their own class. Chief Justice Nemetz has suggested that Professor Griffith's views may have some validity in Canada too, more particularly, Professor Griffith's view that judicial attitudes towards political and social issues reflect the lack of a proper understanding of the view of labour unions, minorities and the under-privileged.

Judge Rosalie Abella (Chair of the Ontario Law Reform Commission) also doubts that judicial impartiality is a realistic requirement. In her arti-cle, "The Dynamic Nature of Equality," she emphasizes that "[e]very deci-sion-maker who walks into a courtroom to hear a case is armed not only with the relevant legal texts but with a set of values, common experiences and assumptions that are thoroughly embedded." [*Ed. note*: In March, 1992 Justice Minister Kim Campbell announced Judge Abella's appointment to the Ontario Court of Appeal.]

Judge Shientag refers to the fact that many judges believe that they have acted with the cold neutrality of an impartial judge when, in fact, they have completely failed to examine their prejudices and biases. He points out that the partiality and prejudice with which we are concerned is not overt, not something tangible on which the judge can put his or her finger. Yet by fail-ing to appreciate this many judges are lulled into a false sense of security. Judge Sheintag emphasizes that progress will only be made when judges recognize this condition as part of the weakness of human nature. Then "[h]aving admitted the liability to prejudice, unconscious for the most part, subtle and nebulous at times, the next step is to determine what the judge, with his trained mind, can do to neutralize the incessant play of these obscure yet potent influences." Judge Sheintag concludes that "the judge who realizes, before listening to a case, that all men have a natural bias of mind and that thought is apt to be coloured by predilection, is more likely to make a conscientious effort at impartiality and dispassionateness than one who believes that his elevation to the bench makes him at once the dehumanized instrument of infallible logical truth."

But what has all this got to do with my subject: "Will women judges really make a difference?" It has a great deal to do with it and whether you agree or not will probably depend on your perception of the degree to which the existing law reflects the judicial neutrality or impartiality we have been discussing. If the existing law can be viewed as the product of judicial neutrality or impartiality, even though the judiciary has been very substantially male, then you may conclude that the advent of increased numbers of women judges should make no difference, assuming, that is, that these women judges will bring to bear the same neutrality and impartiality. However, if you conclude that the existing law, in some areas at least, cannot be viewed as the product of judicial neutrality, then your answer may be very different.

Two law professors at New York University, Professor John Johnston and Professor Charles Knapp, have concluded, as a result of their studies of judicial attitudes reflected in the decisions of judges in the United States, that United States judges have succeeded in their conscious efforts to free themselves from habits of stereotypical thought with regard to discrimination based on colour. However, they were unable to reach a similar conclusion with respect to discrimination based on sex and found that American judges had failed to bring to sex discrimination the judicial virtues of detachment, reflection and critical analysis which had served them so well with respect to other areas of discrimination.

They state:

> "Sexism" – the making of unjustified (or at least unsupported) assumptions about individual capabilities, interests, goals and social roles solely on the basis of sex differences – is as easily discernible in contemporary judicial opinions as racism ever was.

Professor Norma Wikler, a sociologist at the University of California, has reviewed a number of other studies of judicial attitudes by legal researchers and social scientists. These studies confirm that male judges tend to adhere to traditional values and beliefs about the "natures" of men and women and their proper roles in society. The studies show overwhelming evidence that gender-based myths, biases and stereotypes are deeply embedded in the attitudes of many male judges as well as in the law itself. Researchers have concluded that gender difference has been a significant factor in judicial decision-making, particularly in areas of tort law, criminal law and family law. Further many have concluded that sexism is the unarticulated underlying premise of many judgments in these areas, and that this is not really surprising having regard to the nature of the society in which the judges themselves have been socialized.

... So, where do we stand in Canada on this matter? As might be expected, feminist scholars in Canada have over the past two decades produced a vast quantity of literature on the subject, some of it very insightful, very balanced and very useful, and some of it very radical, quite provocative and probably less useful as a result. But all of it, it seems, is premised, at least as far as judicial decision-making is concerned, on two basic propositions: one, that women view the world and what goes on in it from a different perspective from men, and two, that women judges, by bringing that perspective to bear on the cases they hear, can play a major role in introducing judicial neutrality and impartiality into the justice system.

Talking my own personal experience as a judge of fourteen years' standing, working closely with my male colleagues on the bench, there are probably whole areas of the law on which there is no uniquely feminine perspective. This is not to say that the development of the law in these areas has not been influenced by the fact that the lawyers and the judges have all been men. Rather, the principles and the underlying premises are so firmly entrenched and so fundamentally sound that no good would be achieved by attempting to re-invent the wheel, even if the revised version did have a few more spokes in it. I have in mind areas such as the law of contract, the law of real property and the law applicable to corporations. In some other areas of the law, however, I think that a distinctly male perspective is clearly discernible. It has resulted in legal principles that are not fundamentally sound and that should be revisited when the opportunity presents itself. Canadian feminist scholarship has done an excellent job of identifying those areas and making suggestions for reform. Some aspects of the criminal law in particular cry out for change; they are based on presuppositions about the nature of women and women's sexuality that, in this day and age, are little short of ludicrous.

But how do we handle the problem that women judges, just as much as their male counterparts, are subject to the duty of impartiality? As was said at the outset, judges must not approach their task with preconceived notions about law and policy. They must approach it with detachment and, as Lord MacMillan said, purge their minds "not only of partiality to persons but of partiality to arguments." Does this then foreclose any kind of "judicial affirmative action" to counteract the influence of the dominant male perspective of the past and establish judicial neutrality through a countervailing female perspective? Is Karen Selick, writing recently in *The Lawyers Weekly*, correct when she argues that offsetting male bias with female bias would only be compounding the injustice? Does the nature of the judicial process itself present an insuperable hurdle so that the legislatures rather than the courts must be looked to for any significant legal change?

In part this may be so. Certainly, the legislature is the more effective instrument for rapid or radical change. But there is no reason why the judiciary cannot exercise some modest degree of creativity in areas where modern insights and life's experience have indicated that the law has gone awry. However, and this is extremely important, it will be a Pyrrhic victory for women and for the justice system as a whole if changes in the law come only through the efforts of women lawyers and women judges. The Americans were smart to realize that courses and workshops on gender bias for judges, male and female, are an essential follow-up to scholarly research and learned writing. In Canada, we are just beginning to touch the fringes.

... The Canadian Judicial Council and the Canadian Judicial Centre have both recognized the need for judicial education in this area and will include gender issues in their summer seminars for judges this year. I understand that the Centre hopes to subsequently present the program in a number of locations across the country, and the course materials will be available to all Canadian judges. I heartily endorse this initiative. It is a significant first step towards the achievement of true judicial neutrality. But it is only a first step and there is a long way to go.

I return, then, to the question whether the appointment of more women judges will make a difference. Because the entry of women into the judiciary is so recent, few studies have been done on the subject. Current statistics, however, show that just over nine percent of federally appointed judges are women; it is reasonable to assume that more and more women will be appointed to the Bench as more and more women become licensed to practice law. Will this growing number of women judges by itself make a difference?

The expectation is that it will, the mere presence of women on the bench will make a difference. In an article "The Gender of Judges," Suzanna Sherry (an Associate Law Professor at the University of Minnesota) suggests that the mere fact that women are judges serves an educative function; it helps to shatter stereotypes about the role of women in society that are held by male judges and lawyers, as well as by litigants, jurors and witnesses.

... Some feminist writers are persuaded that the appointment of more women judges will have an impact on the process of judicial decision-making itself and on the development of the substantive law. As was mentioned earlier, this flows from the belief that women view the world and what goes on in it from a different perspective from men. Some define the difference in perspective solely in terms that women do not accept male perceptions and interpretations of events as the norm or as objective reality. Carol Gilligan (a Professor of Education at Harvard University) sees the difference as going much deeper than that. In her view, women think differently from men, particularly in responding to moral dilemmas. They have, she says, different ways of thinking about themselves and their relationships to others.

In her book, *In a Different Voice*, Gilligan analyses data she collected, in

the form of responses from male and female participants in a number of different studies. These responses, she submits, support her central thesis that
women see themselves as essentially connected to others and as members
of a community; men see themselves as essentially autonomous and independent of others. Gilligan makes no claim about the origins of the differences she describes. She does, however, use the psychoanalytical work of
Dr. Nancy Chodorow as a starting point. Chodorow postulates that gender
differences arise from the fact that women do the mothering of children.
Because the gender identity of male children is not the same as their mothers, they tend to distance and separate themselves from their mothers'
female characteristics in order to develop their masculinity. Female children,
on the other hand, define themselves through attachment to their mothers.
Masculinity is therefore, according to Gilligan, defined through separation
and individualism; femininity is defined through attachment and the formation of relationships. The gender identity of the male, she submits, is threatened by relationships while the gender identity of the female is threatened
by separation.

Gilligan's work on conceptions of morality among adults suggests that
women's ethical sense is significantly different from men's. Men see moral
problems as arising from competing rights; the adversarial process comes
easily to them. Women see moral problems as arising from competing obligations, the one to the other; the important thing is to preserve relationships,
to develop an ethic of caring. The goal, according to women's ethical sense
is not seen in terms of winning or losing but, rather, in terms of achieving
an optimum outcome for all individuals involved in the moral dilemma. It
is not difficult to see how this contrast in thinking might form the basis of
different perceptions of justice.

There is merit in Gilligan's analysis. In part, it may explain the traditional
reluctance of courts to get too deeply into the circumstances of a case, their
anxiety to reduce the context of the dispute to its bare bones through a complex system of exclusionary evidentiary rules. This is one of the characteristic features of the adversarial process. We are all familiar with the witness
on cross-examination who wants to explain his or her answer, who feels that
a simple yes or no is not an adequate response, and who is frustrated and
angry at being cut off with a half-truth. It is so much easier to come up with
a black and white answer if you are unencumbered by a broader context
which might prompt you, in Lord MacMillan's words, to temper the cold
light of reason with the warmer tints of imagination and sympathy.

Gilligan's analysis may explain also the hostility of some male judges to
permitting interveners in human rights cases. The main purpose of having
interveners is to broaden the context of the dispute, to show the issue in a
larger perspective or as impacting on other groups not directly involved in
the litigation at all. But it certainly does complicate the issues to have them
presented in polycentric terms.

... One of the important conclusions emerging from the Council of

Europe's Seminar on Equality between Men and Women held in Strasbourg last November is that the universalist doctrine of human rights must include a realistic concept of masculine and feminine humanity regarded as a whole, that human kind *is* dual and must be represented in its dual form if the trap of an asexual abstraction in which human being is always declined in the masculine is to be avoided. If women lawyers and women judges through their differing perspectives on life can bring a new humanity to bear on the decision-making process, perhaps they *will* make a difference. Perhaps they will succeed in infusing the law with an understanding of what it means to be fully human.

4.5

A "Gender Patronage" for Judges?
Rob Martin
The Lawyers Weekly, March 29, 1991, 5. Reprinted with permission.

Nothing ever really seems to change. To be sure, we are constantly presented with the illusion of change, especially in an economy based on consumption. But it is mostly illusion, appearance. The substance of things tends to remain the same. Take judicial appointments. The Canadian way has been to use patronage as the main – not the only, but the main – basis for appointing people to the Bench. Loyal service to the party in power has been the most important qualification for a judgeship. The tradition of patronage appointments is a long, if not particularly honourable, one. It predates Confederation.

The Canadian Bar Association, to take but one example, has been criticizing patronage since 1916. In 1985 it even produced a report about the whole business. The report observed:

> There has been a long history of patronage appointments by both major parties in Canada. Although there have been some commendable exceptions, the practice of appointing the party faithful to the Bench has been all too common.

From time to time various political leaders have denounced patronage and promised to put the bad old days behind us. Success has been limited. Pierre Trudeau first gained national prominence in 1966 as Minister of Justice in the government of Lester Pearson. He announced his determination to end patronage and make judicial appointments on merit. The determination didn't last long. Trudeau resigned as prime minister in 1984. His departure was accompanied by an orgy of patronage appointments which was shocking, even by Canadian standards. A small horde of Cabinet ministers, terrified at the prospect of their party's impending electoral debacle, went to their reward on the Bench. [*Ed. note*: see Reading 4.1.]

Brian Mulroney promised to do better. He didn't. A 1989 study of judicial appointees during Mulroney's first four years in office concluded that 48 percent were known supporters of the Progressive Conservative party. [*Ed. note*: See Reading 4.3.] An ostensibly new system for making federal judicial appointments was instituted in 1988. But its newness is more apparent than real. The final authority over appointments remains in political hands.

Well, what's the problem with patronage appointments? Obviously, not all are, or have been, bad. Long service to a political party should not disqualify someone from holding judicial office. But should it be the most important consideration? The real problem lies in the failure of patronage appointments to address, or even raise, the question of an individual's fitness to be a judge. Politics, not merit, determines the decision.

The problem is compounded because we don't really know what we are looking for in judges. We have never, probably because we are inured to patronage appointments, determined what qualities make people fit to be judges and how we might go about assessing those qualities. But if we regard judging as important, we should concede that patronage is not the ideal basis for electing judges. Merit, however we eventually decide to define it, should take precedence over politics.

All of which brings me to the new Ontario government's approach to appointing judges. Once again, we have the illusion of change. The reality is business as usual. Upon taking office as attorney-general, Howard Hampton announced his determination to have more women judges in Ontario. He went to the point of saying he was prepared to look outside the province if enough women who were members of the Ontario Bar could not be found. These statements were followed up with letters to many women lawyers inviting them to apply for judgeships. And Hampton has been true, more or less, to his word. At my count he has made 18 judicial appointments since taking office. Eleven of these have been women.

So what's my problem? I'm certainly not opposed to women judges. And I'm definitely not worried about lowering the quality of the Provincial Court Bench in Ontario – a virtually impossible task, I would think. And I'm even prepared to accept some of Hampton's appointees may turn out to be competent judges. No, the point is that Hampton is continuing the dismal Canadian tradition of politics over merit. The announced basis for his appointments is the gender of the people chosen, not their ability or qualifications. I don't believe it's much of a step forward to replace party loyalty with gender as the basis for choosing judges. Gender is as much a political consideration as is party loyalty. Neither relates directly to an individual's fitness to be a judge.

In our federal and provincial public services we go through an elaborate ritual of assessing people's ability and qualifications before they can be appointed. Might we not devote the same care to picking judges?

4.6

To Bring Judical Appointments Out of the Closet

F.L. Morton

The Globe and Mail, Monday September 22, 1997, A15

The Sept. 13 memo by EGALE (Equality for Gays and Lesbians Everywhere) on the Internet should be the final nail in the coffin for the current closed and secret appointments process to the Supreme Court of Canada. It should also persuade the government to scuttle its current search for a new justice and postpone it until after the Quebec/UDI reference has been heard.

Justice Minister Anne McLellan (and others) have defended the current process on the grounds that a public parliamentary hearing on the government's nominee would "politicize" the process. As evidence, they trot out the spectre of the Judge Robert Bork and Clarence Thomas hearings before the Senate judiciary committee in the United States. The EGALE memo shows that the process is already politicized, except that entry is limited to a select group of insiders.

The gay lobby, represented by EGALE, obviously has a seat at the table. The writer of the memo already knows who is on the government's short-list and clearly expects to receive a hearing on who is and is not acceptable to his constituency. Whatever access EGALE has, LEAF – the litigation arm of the organized feminist movement – has more.

Larger, better-funded and better connected, LEAF (Women's Legal and Education Action Fund) has been an active player in the Supreme Court appointments game since the retirement of Bertha Wilson in 1990. Jeffrey Simpson, writing in his book, *Faultlines: Struggling for a Canadian Vision*, recounts how LEAF mounted an all-court press to try to get feminist legal braintruster and super-litigator Mary Eberts appointed to replace Ms. Wilson. The Eberts campaign "was fought behind the scenes through letters, phone calls and personal representations to the PMO, cabinet ministers and officials in the Department of Justice."

We can be assured that other political interests who increasingly depend on the courts to protect and promote their interests are also vying for similar access.

This criticism is directed at the government. EGALE, LEAF and others certainly have the right to lobby for a judge who is positively inclined toward their constituencies and concerns. But so do those who think Canadians would be better served by a judge who is supportive of traditional Judeo-Christian morality and who recognizes the important role of intact families in cultural transmission from one generation to the next. Why is one set of interests at the table but not the others?

What is at stake here is nothing less than the accountability of governments

To: EGALE-l@EGALE.ca
From: john@EGALE.ca
Subject: Supreme Court appointment
Date: Sat, 13 Sept. 1997

Hi Everyone,

I need some detective work by some of our folks there in the Atlantic.

As most of you will be aware, Justice [Gérard] La Forest is retiring from the Supreme Court of Canada. This is good news, since La Forest has consistently ruled against glb equality issues, taking the considered position that marriage is by nature heterosexual, always has been and always will be, so where's the discrimination in not recognizing our relationships?

We lost the last big Supreme Court challenge [*Ed. note: Egan* v. *Canada*] by 5 judges to 4. Needless to say, it is vitally important for our communities that La Forest be replaced by someone more committed to equality issues. The Minister of Justice and the PM will replace him by another judge from the Atlantic provinces.

We now have a fairly good idea of who the main contenders for the position are, but need some background info on these candidates so that we know which ones are most likely to be supportive and which ones should be avoided. I'm reluctant to post the actual names of the candidates to this list, because of the possibility that there may be anti-glb "lurkers" on the list, waiting to hear our trade secrets. Usually, this isn't a problem, since EGALE doesn't really have any secrets – our "agenda" is well-known: we'd like equality, and we'd like it now. Since we also do a lot of public education work, we're usually quite happy to describe our activities to anyone who'll listen, and, in fact, many who won't. In this case, however, although I'm hardly giving anything away by saying that EGALE is interested in the issue, I think it would be imprudent to release the actual names.

Anyway, what I'd suggest is that anyone who is plugged into the Atlantic legal community (both academic and practicing/judicial) please E-mail me privately at john@EGALE.ca. We can then enter into conversation and determine what, if anything, can be done to support the appointment of a more suitable Supreme Court Justice.

Thanks, everyone

John

for the appointments they make. Given a ruling party's working majority in the House of Commons, a parliamentary committee will never have the power to block its appointments the way the U.S. Senate occasionally does. Rather, an open hearing before a parliamentary committee would educate the public in advance of what sort of judge a government has nominated, and force it to accept responsibility for its decision. Critics protest this would "politicize" the process. The process is already politicized. A public hearing would simply democratize it.

What deals are being struck between the EGALE–LEAF lobbyists and the Chrétien government? It has been widely reported that the cabinet is obsessed with making an appointment of someone who will "get it right" on its upcoming reference on the legality of a Quebec unilateral declaration of independence. What price is the government willing to pay for the right vote? Will they concede a gay-feminist vote in return for an anti-Quebec-UDI vote? This would certainly be fine by EGALE and LEAF.

You say the Chrétien government would never be so cynical? Excuse me, but it has already amended the *Judges Act* to allow Federal Court judge Danièle Tremblay-Lamer, second wife of Supreme Court Chief Justice Antonio Lamer, to collect his pension as well as hers if he predeceases her. This was not allowed 12 months ago.

In the administration of justice, the appearance of fairness is as important as the reality. The EGALE memo in the context of the government's UDI reference to the Supreme Court has destroyed this appearance. Just the possibility of a secret deal being struck has poisoned the appointment.

The only proper course of action – one advocated by The Globe editorial page even before this new revelation – is for the government to postpone the next appointment until after the Supreme Court hears the oral argument in the Quebec reference (scheduled for December [1997]), and then launch a new appointments process that includes a public hearing before a parliamentary committee.

4.7

What to Look For, and Guard Against, in a Supreme Court Judge

William Thorsell
The Globe and Mail, Saturday December 20, 1997, D6.

The politicization of the Supreme Court of Canada from internal and external sources has become a subject of intense discussion in widening circles. No wonder.

Canadians are growing much more aware of the power judges exercise on matters of stark personal interest through interpreting the 1982 *Charter of Rights and Freedoms*: the right to assisted suicide; the rights of the unborn fetus; the right to public services for the disabled; the right to equality in family law for gay and lesbian couples; rights to privacy and security from unreasonable search and seizure; the right to free speech and freedom of the press – and soon, probably, the status of "compassionate homicide" in criminal law.

By narrow margins in some cases, judges have made important rulings in these fields, creating precedents under the still-young *Charter* that will bind their successors, lower courts and legislatures for years. Quite suddenly, we have come to realize how important the personal assumptions of judges are about law and democracy, yet we have no say in who they are.

The traditional process by which judges are chosen is entirely hostile to the public's interest. The choosing goes on in secret, with no opportunity for public input or debate. The appointment is simply announced by the Minister of Justice, and then greeted with hosannas by deferential legal experts who will be exposed to the new judge's power for decades to come.

Assuming a judge's basic competence, our fundamental concern should be the candidate's attitude to our legislatures. That attitude should be both respectful and demanding.

It should be respectful of the power of democratic legislatures to make law. For example, if Alberta's legislature has excluded sexual orientation from its human-rights act, even though the *Charter* protects homosexuals from discriminatory laws, the court should be very hesitant to declare Alberta's act unconstitutional for what it does not say. In common parlance, the court should shy away from "reading into law" provisions that do not exist there. It is the constitutionality of laws that do exist, rather than of laws that do not, that is the proper province of the courts.

Some Supreme Court judges disagree forcefully with this view, and are quite prepared to legislate from the bench in good causes. We need no more of such judges, because our democratic process can stand no more of them.

On the other hand, the court should impose a high hurdle of skepticism in allowing legislatures to make laws that offend fundamental rights and freedoms. The *Charter* allows for "reasonable" legal limits on basic rights, but the court is the ultimate judge of what reasonable means. The onus must be heavy on lawmakers to demonstrate "reason," and that onus must come from the court.

Finally, because the Supreme Court is the highest constitutional arbiter, its judges should not carry excess political baggage in federal- provincial affairs. Former Alberta premier Peter Lougheed, for example, would not be a good choice for the court on that ground (as he himself would surely insist).

The external political threat to the Supreme Court comes in the current reference by the federal government on Quebec's right to declare independence. Allan Rock brought this question forward when he was justice minister, asking the court's opinion on a hypothetical situation. There is nothing in law or before any legislature for the court to consider, as there was in 1981, when the court was asked to assess the constitutionality of Ottawa's patriation bill before Parliament.

Mr. Rock's reference has a political purpose: to influence public opinion in Quebec before the next referendum. This should have been enough for the court to decline Mr. Rock's invitation to express its non-binding view, even without this week's potent application by the lawyer arguing for Quebec that the court lacks legal jurisdiction to consider the matter in any case.

The dubiousness of Mr. Rock's reference on Quebec is exacerbated by Prime Minister Jean Chrétien's recent appointment of Mr. Justice Michel Bastarache to the Supreme Court. Judge Bastarache was a colleague in Mr. Chrétien's law firm, former co-chairman of the national Yes committee for the Charlottetown Accord, and a 1993 election adviser to the federal Liberal Party – a good man, no doubt, but heavy with political baggage.

We must reform the appointment process for the Supreme Court (and other senior courts) to eliminate the sole discretion of the Prime Minister and Minister of Justice. Their power to appoint judges is an arbitrary measure of the greatest provocation, which should be neither advised nor consented to by any subject who is truly loyal to the Chief Magistrate.

The integrity of the Supreme Court and our democratic process requires much broader participation in fashioning the court, with a sharp eye for judges who accept their appropriate place in the scheme of public affairs.

4.8

Merit Selection and Democratization of Appointments to the Supreme Court of Canada
Jacob S. Ziegel
The original version of this study was published in the Institute for Research on Public Policy's (IRPP) special series on "Courts and Legislatures," in *Choices,* 5, no. 2 (June, 1999). The full-text version can be accessed through the IRPP's website: www.irpp.org.

Introduction

The long simmering debate over the appropriate method of appointing judges to the Supreme Court of Canada in the *Charter* era has flared up again over the past year. It is safe to assume that the debate will continue to attract the attention of Supreme Court watchers until a more satisfactory method of appointment is adopted than the present.

The current resurgence of interest is illustrated, among others, by the following events. In Alberta and elsewhere in Canada, right wing politicians have long been critical of the activist role of the Supreme Court. The criticism mounted last year with the Supreme Court's decision in the *Vriend* case declaring Alberta's Human Rights Code to be in violation of the equality provision in the *Charter* because it discriminated against gays and lesbians. Critics urged the Klein government to use the override provision in the *Charter* to reverse the Supreme Court's judgement, although the province eventually decided against it. Then, much more recently, Justice McClung's unprecedented public outburst over Justice L'Heureux-Dubé's criticisms of his judgement in the *Ewanchuk* case sparked a vigorous media debate on gender issues in the Supreme Court and Justice L'Heureux-Dubé's gender philosophy.

Not surprisingly, these events have encouraged editorialists and politicians to renew their calls for greater transparency in the appointment of Supreme Court judges. Members of the Supreme Court have also been drawn into the debate. Last September, shortly after announcing his retirement from the Court, Justice Gérard V. La Forest indicated his support for some sort of confirmation procedure for appointments of Supreme Court judges. On the other hand, in a similar but more recent interview following the announcement of his retirement, Justice Peter Cory expressed strong opposition to any confirmation procedure that included questioning of nominees for appointment about issues likely to come before the Court. In a subsequent address to law students, Justice Frank Iacobucci also expressed his hostility to a public confirmation procedure.

Meanwhile, reacting to common knowledge in the Toronto legal community that supporters of John Laskin and Rosie Abella, both members of the Ontario Court of Appeal, had actively lobbied for their favoured candidate to succeed Justice John Sopinka on the Supreme Court, Chief Justice Lamer publicly rebuked both factions for engaging in conduct that, in his view, was bound to tarnish the Court's good image in the public eye.

Events of this genre are not peculiar to Canada. Similar debates about the role of the country's highest court and desirable changes in the method of appointments are taking place in Australia, England and New Zealand, and in the Council of Europe with respect to the European Court of Human Rights. At the same time, a vast literature has been spawned in the U.S. about the confirmation procedure for appointments to the U.S. Supreme Court following the Senate's rejection of Robert Bork's nomination in 1988 and the approval of Clarence Thomas by a narrow margin in 1991.

What is surprising about the Canadian scene is that since the rejection by Canadian voters of the Charlottetown Accord, both the Conservative and Liberal governments have evinced no interest in revising the selection method for appointments to the Supreme Court. In the case of the current administration, this may suggest either that Prime Minister Chrétien is quite happy with the existing system or that he feels that any changes must take place in the framework of generally agreed upon constitutional changes – changes, as he has often made clear, that are unlikely to take place in the foreseeable future. Another article, therefore, on appointments to the Supreme Court may seem futile. I do not share this pessimism and this article proceeds from the premise that greater accountability and transparency in the appointments is much overdue although some constitutional hurdles may have to be overcome in order to bring about the necessary changes.

Two alternative or cumulative recommendations are presented below to address the shortcomings of the existing system of appointments:

- The establishment of a nominating committee that would present the Prime Minister with a short list of candidates to fill vacancies as they arise;
- The introduction of a parliamentary confirmation procedure for candidates presented by the Prime Minister for appointment to the Supreme Court.

[*Ed. Note:* Only the second of these two recommendations is reprinted here.]

The Supreme Court's Adjudicative Roles

An appropriate starting point for the discussion is an appreciation of the overarching role played by the Supreme Court in Canada's legal firmament. The Court's position as the final arbiter of the meaning and interpretation of the *Charter of Rights and Freedoms* is its most visible and intrusive role since 1982, but it is only one of several roles. Since the abolition of appeals to the Privy Council in 1949, the Court has also become the court of last resort in appeals concerning the division of powers between the federal and provincial governments and on all other constitutional questions arising under the *Constitution Act*, including being expected to advise the country on the meta-legal rules applying in a post-secessionist Canada!

Thirdly, unlike many other constitutional courts in the Western hemisphere, the Supreme Court discharges the very heavy burden of supervising Canada's criminal justice system and other public law areas, as well as having the last word on judicially crafted doctrines and principles in the private law area applicable at both the provincial and federal levels. It is common to speak of the Supreme Court's role in the non-constitutional arena as being interstitial in character since its decisions can be changed by legislation. This is true in theory but it does not reflect the actual practice since to a large extent the federal and provincial legislatures have been content to let the courts apply and develop private law principles with little interference, especially those applying outside Quebec. Significantly, the Supreme Court's value-laden *Charter* role has also encouraged it to adjudicate much more boldly on non-*Charter* issues than it did before 1982.

Still, it is the Court's decisions on the *Charter* that have engendered the most debate and, it is safe to assume, will continue to do so in the future. It is easy to see why. In a couple of dozen sections the *Charter* entrenches those democratic, legal and egalitarian values regarded as fundamental in regulating relations in a modern liberal state between a government and its citizens. Unavoidably, since the values themselves are open-ended and relative, so are the *Charter* provisions. It is left to the nine members of the Court to give them meaning and content, and equally to determine when the rights-oriented norms can be departed from under section 1 of the *Charter* because of compelling societal needs. Apparently some Canadian judges still believe that this "interpretive" task is no different from the roles played by the Supreme Court before 1982, but clearly this is not so. In giving content to the *Charter* provisions, judges are bound to bring into play their own political philosophies and life experiences and thus to support or disappoint the various interests appearing before them.

This consequence of the entrenchment of a bill of rights is well understood in the U.S. and accounts for the close scrutiny and sometimes fierce debates surrounding new appointments to the U.S. Supreme Court. As Justice Felix Frankfurter wrote in 1930, "It is because the [U.S.] Supreme Court wields the power that it wields, that appointment to the Court is a matter of general public concern and not merely a question for the profession. In truth, the Supreme Court *is* the Constitution". These words are equally apt in describing the role of the Canadian Supreme Court.

...

The Case for a Confirmation Procedure

[This] brings us face to face with what is currently the most contentious issue in Canadian discussions of appropriate selection procedures for the Supreme

Court. This is whether a confirmation procedure is needed and whether it is also required where a nominating committee system has been installed.

Neither the CBA nor the CALT committee recommended the introduction of confirmation procedures for appointments to the Supreme Court, or to any other court whose judges were appointed by the federal government. They did not feel it was needed given the existence of a credible nomination procedure. I was a member of the CALT committee and I concurred with my colleagues' views. I have changed my mind since then, at least so far as the Supreme Court is concerned.

The most important reason for my change of position is this. It is precisely because of the intensely political role (I use the word political in a positive and not pejorative sense) played by the Supreme Court judges in applying and interpreting the *Charter* as well as the rest of the constitution that it is critical to inject a democratic and balancing note in the appointing process. Canadians should be able to learn about, see, and evaluate the candidate before his or her appointment becomes a *fait accompli*. If the federal government has chosen well, with or without the help of a nomination committee, it will have little to fear. The candidate is likely to earn quick approval from the confirming body.

If the candidate is controversial, underqualified or otherwise unacceptable to a significant constituency, all the more reason why his or her merits should be publicly debated while there is still time for it. If candidates for the office of Prime Minister are expected to expose themselves to close public scrutiny, why should we require less of a nominee for the Supreme Court, who is likely to remain in office long after the appointing Prime Minister has disappeared from the public scene and who, in many respects, wields as much power as the Prime Minister and with less accountability?

There is also another reason that justifies the introduction of a separate confirmation procedure. Assuming the confirming body is made up of parliamentarians, it will help to educate our elected representatives on the impact of the *Charter* on traditional concepts of responsible government and give them a better appreciation of where the line should be drawn between their role and the *Charter's* role. Members of Parliament and senators (and likewise their provincial counterparts) have been slow to react to the steady erosion of Parliament's authority, implicit though it may be in the very existence of the *Charter*. As noted at the beginning of this article, the mood of acquiescence is changing and Canadians are beginning to appreciate the important roles of personalities and judicial philosophies in the interpretation and application of the *Charter* norms. The "inconvenience" of a confirmation procedure will be readily forgiven if it provides a regular opportunity for reviewing the work of the Supreme Court and in raising our collective awareness of its norms propounding role.

The notion of a confirmation procedure is no longer radical. It appeared in the report of the Ontario Advisory Committee on the Constitution in 1978 and in Bill C60 introduced by the federal government in the same year. Both provided for confirmation of Supreme Court nominees by a revised Upper

Chamber. In the case of Bill C-60, Upper Chamber approval would have been necessary even though the nominee would have been selected by the co-operative efforts of the Attorney General of Canada and the attorney general of the appointee's province. The Charlottetown Accord saw a confirmation role for the revised Senate in the appointment of members of senior government agencies and boards. It would surely be anomalous if the public were given a greater opportunity to comment on the potential head of the CBC, the CRTC or the Canadian Transportation Agency than is available to them to assess the qualities and suitability of a future member of the Supreme Court or a candidate for the chief justiceship of Canada.

As we have seen, Justice La Forest accepted the legitimacy of confirmation hearings after he retired from the Supreme Court a year ago, whereas Justices Cory and Iacobucci have taken a very different position. We know that other members of the Supreme Court share their misgivings, so they deserve closer analysis. The objections appear to fall under two main headings, though it may be that the second is only a subset of the first.

The first objection is that the existing system works well, so why knock it? The defence of the status quo is coupled with a warning not to be beguiled by foreign models (more particularly the U.S. confirmation procedure) which may work well in their own environment but are alien to Canadian soil. This reasoning is quite unpersuasive and ignores the historical reasons for the adoption of the confirmation procedure in the U.S. constitution.

The American Founding Fathers were divided over which arm of government should have the power to appoint the members of the U.S. Supreme Court; some favoured the President, others the Senate. A compromise was reached by conferring the nomination power on the President but requiring the President's nominations to be confirmed by the Senate. The delegates to the Constitutional Convention of 1789 appreciated that giving the President an untrammelled power of appointment would give rise to abuses or lead to an unrepresentative Court. History has amply confirmed their intuition. Between 1789 and 1992, the Senate refused to confirm 28 of the 142 Supreme Court nominees, or nearly one out of five nominees, whose names were submitted by the President. We may be sure that an even larger number of prospective nominees were never forwarded to the Senate because the President and his advisors anticipated rejection of their choices.

In short, even allowing for political partisanship in the Senate, the U.S. confirmation requirements have on the whole met the Founding Fathers expectations in eliminating clearly unqualified candidates and in ensuring that the nominees enjoyed broad political acceptance. If U.S. confirmation hearings have erred, it is on the side of accommodating the President's choice even where the candidate was not of the first quality, an almost inevitable result where the President's party also dominates the Senate.

Had Canada had an equivalent screening device for appointments to the Supreme Court, the well documented abuses of the appointment power that occurred during the first 75 years of the Court's history might well have been avoided. In what sense then, has Canada been well served by a paternalistic executive power of appointment not subject to public scrutiny? It is true that the quality of appointments has been much better over the past 20 years or so. Even so, there is little room for complacency. There have undoubtedly been weak appointments and a surprising number of Supreme Court judges have taken early retirement for reasons other than ill health. We are also entitled to ask how much *better* the appointments might have been if there had been an independent nominating procedure or if the government's selections had been subject to a confirmation requirement. The warning against the danger of importing foreign innovations must also be viewed with much skepticism, given the fact that Canada has borrowed many legal concepts from the U.S. during its relatively short history, including, not unimportantly, the concept of an entrenched bill of rights!

But what about Justice Cory's complaint that prospective appointees to the Supreme Court should not have to run the gauntlet of public questioning by politicians? The concern is that parliamentarians may be more interested in embarrassing the candidate or in scoring political points than in engaging in serious debate on the meaning of the *Charter* or the role of Supreme Court judges as guardians of *Charter* values. Justice Cory has also argued that it is unfair to expect candidates to justify decisions they may have rendered many years earlier as lower court judges and highly improper to ask them to explain their positions on current legal controversies or to predict how they would decide those issues as members of the Supreme Court.

The horror stories the critics have in mind no doubt are the confirmation hearings of Robert H. Bork and Clarence Thomas before the U.S. Senate. However, they overlook the fact that public questioning of candidates is a relatively recent innovation in proceedings by the Senate Judiciary Committee and that there were exceptional features about the Bork and Thomas cases. The more recent nominees that have appeared before the Judiciary Committee have been approved without difficulty and they have not complained about unfair treatment. The nominees have reserved the right not to answer questions concerning their position on future cases that could come before the Supreme Court, and that right is generally conceded. If it was deemed appropriate or necessary in the Canadian context, rules could also be adopted to delimit the scope of a nominee's examination before the parliamentary committee.

We can also learn from overseas experience. The public hearings before the South African Judicial Service Commission show that they can be conducted with decorum and that the chair can be relied on to prevent improper questioning. According to a perceptive British observer, "The original fear that good candidates would not put themselves forward does not appear to have materialized." Again, to quote the reactions of the Deputy President of the Constitutional Court to his appearance before the JSC:

Speaking as a person who is sitting on this seat now, I must say I would have preferred not to have been interviewed at all, but I realize that the interviewing process is useful and I think it is essential and correct and I am fully in support of having open hearings.

Several other objections to a Canadian confirmation procedure involving the use of parliamentary committees also deserve to be noted. One is that the Senate cannot be expected to supply the federal component in confirmation hearings because its members do not speak for the provinces. Equally the Senate cannot remedy the democratic deficit in the appointment of Supreme Court judges since its members are unelected. Both these points seem to militate against the Senate playing a role in the appointive process of members of the Supreme Court. Nevertheless, the Senate is an integral part of Parliament and it may seem anomalous that it should be denied any role in a confirmation procedure when it continues to play an active role in the enactment of legislation. A case can therefore be made for giving the Senate *some* representation on a confirmation committee, say up to one half the total membership of the committee, even before the long delayed reform of the Senate is finally agreed upon.

There are also difficulties in expecting a House of Commons confirmation committee to remain free of partisan bias. The members of the House of Commons are of course elected, but they are also expected to follow party discipline. In the case of a majority government, this means that the committee's approving vote would be a foregone conclusion unless somehow the government could be persuaded to give its members a free vote. The same difficulty would arise if a full House of Commons vote were required to approve the committee's recommendation with respect to the government's nominee for the Supreme Court.

One solution to these obstacles would be to require supermajority voting in the committee and/or the full House of Commons.... [T]he results of recent parliamentary elections [show] that a two-thirds majority voting requirement would have given the opposition parties an effective voice in voting for confirmation in six of the seven parliamentary elections held between 1972 and 1997.

Nevertheless, the requirement of a supermajority vote runs very much against the grain of our parliamentary tradition and even if voluntarily adopted by the present administration would not be binding on future governments unless the requirement were constitutionally entrenched.

...

Conclusion

In addressing future appointments to the Supreme Court of Canada, there are two key questions. The first is whether we are satisfied with the existing system of appointments which vests complete and unaccountable discretion in the Executive even though the judges of the Supreme Court are the ultimate arbiters of the Canadian constitution and collectively exercise a power as great as that of the federal Cabinet. If this question is answered no, the second question is what changes we deem desirable to bring transparency and accountability to the selection procedure and to ensure that only the best qualified candidates are appointed.

There may be honest differences of opinion about the answer to the second question, but there should be little doubt about the answer to the first. Over the past 15 years there has been a near unanimous chorus of opinion among scholars reinforced by many publicly-sponsored reports that the existing system of appointments is incompatible with a modern federal democratic constitution governed by the rule of law and incorporating one of the most powerful bills of rights in the Western hemisphere. What ought to give cause for concern is that none of these reasoned arguments have had any apparent impact on successive federal governments whose spokespersons continue to insist that there is no need for change and that the federal government is and has been doing an impeccable job. One's best hope is that there will be a rising tide of opinion in favour of change within the major political parties and that more members of the Supreme Court will join Justice La Forest in recognizing the anomaly of owing their appointments to the unrevealed and undebated preferences and partialities of one or more unaccountable members of the federal Cabinet.

4.9

Key Terms

Concepts

group representation
ideological judicial appointments
impartiality
judicial independence
merit nominating commission
merit screening committee
political patronage
politics of rights
regional representation
accountability
transparency
parliamentary confirmation process
V.O. Key's "iron rule of politics"

Institutions, Events, and Documents

National Committee on the Judiciary (1966)
Office of Special Advisor to the Minister of Justice (1973)
Alberta Judicial Council
Saskatchewan Judges Affair (1982)
Commissioner for Federal Judicial Affairs (1977)
Meech Lake Accord (1987)
Judge Bork Affair (1987)
1988 Reforms of Federal Judicial Appointments Procedure
Russell-Ziegel Study (1989)
gender bias seminars for judges
Ontario Judicial Appointments Advisory Committee (1989)

Judicial Independence, Ethics, and Discipline

5

Disputes are a fact of life in political communities. In the course of their personal and commercial interactions, individuals become involved in disputes over what happened (questions of fact) and what the rule is that governs their situation (questions of law). Typically neither party is willing to allow the other to unilaterally answer these questions, for fear that an adversary will exploit any ambiguity of fact or law to his or her own advantage. The self-interest of both parties prevents either from serving as arbiter of the dispute. What is needed is an outside third party who is independent of both disputants and thus can be expected to render an impartial inquiry and resolution of the dispute.

While the need for a mechanism of dispute resolution is common to all societies, different cultures have met this need in different ways. In the Western European tradition, the institutions that have evolved to perform this function are what we know today as courts. Historically speaking, Canada is a very recent part of the Western European tradition, and our legal system (like the rest of our culture) is in large part inherited and adapted from this tradition. The authority of contemporary Canadian courts still rests on the ancient requirement of impartiality. We are willing to submit our disputes to judges and to obey their decisions voluntarily, even if we lose, because we believe that they provide an unbiased and reasoned application of the laws to the facts of our particular dispute. In order to insure impartiality, we expect a judge to be independent of our adversary. In the area of criminal law and other types of disputes between individuals and the state, this means that judicial independence from the Crown is an essential prerequisite for the proper functioning of our legal system.

Canada's legal system did not evolve from the Western European tradition at large, but rather from the distinctive British common law tradition.[1]

---

1 Except for Quebec, whose Civil Law originated in France. However, since criminal law and procedure are matters of federal jurisdiction, the criminal law process in Quebec is based on the same common law practices as the rest of Canada.

This means that Canada has been fortunate enough to inherit the British institutional practices and safeguards of judicial independence that for centuries have made Great Britain an exemplary model for the protection of individual freedom.[2]

While the tradition of judicial independence is much older, it became an official part of Britain's "unwritten constitution" as part of the *Act of Settlement* in 1701. During the seventeenth century, the Stuart kings had flagrantly violated the independence of the British courts. After James II was deposed in the "Glorious Revolution of 1688," Parliament and the English bar were eager to provide more certain guarantees for judicial independence in the future. As part of the *Act of Settlement*, they forced the new king, William III, to agree to legal provisions securing the independence of the judiciary. Judicial tenure of office was established on the principle of *quamdiu se bene gesserint* – "during good behaviour" – and henceforth judges could be removed only by address of both houses of Parliament. In addition, judicial salaries had to be ascertained and established by law and were no longer set by royal decree.

Having established judicial independence at home, the British Parliament was somewhat reluctant to introduce it in British North America. Originally, colonial judges served only "at pleasure." This practice inevitably led to abuses by colonial governors, and these abuses were one of the grievances enumerated in the *Declaration of Independence* by the American revolutionaries in 1776.[3] Significantly, no sooner had the Americans successfully thrown off British political rule than they entrenched the British provisions for judicial independence in their new state and federal constitutions.[4] It was not until the 1830s and 1840s that similar provisions for judicial independence were made for the rest of British North America.

At Confederation in 1867, the now-familiar terms of judicial independence were written into the *Constitution Act*. Section 99 provides that "judges of the superior courts shall hold office during good behaviour, but shall be removable by the Governor General on address of the Senate and House of Commons." In 1960, this was amended to require mandatory retirement at the age of 75. Section 100 requires that the "salaries, allowances and pensions of the judges of the Superior, District, and County Courts ... be fixed and provided by the Parliament of Canada."

---

2 See the admiration of the nineteenth-century French political thinker Alexis de Tocqueville, quoted by A.V. Dicey in Reading 1.4.

3 "He has made judges dependent on his will alone, for the tenure of their offices, and the amount and payment of their salaries.

4 Note that there was no national judiciary under the first American constitution, *The Articles of Confederation*. The more centralist *Constitution* of 1788 created a national Supreme Court and provided for judicial independence in essentially the same terms as the *Act of Settlement*. The practice of electing judges in some American states, referred to in chapter four, dates from a later period in American history.

These tenure provisions apply explicitly only to the superior courts created pursuant to section 96. This has raised the question of whether the judges of the Supreme Court and Federal Court of Canada, County and District Court judges, and the judges of the section 92 provincial courts enjoy less independence than their superior court brethren. Writing in 1976, Professor Lederman argues that, although the independence of these courts is not constitutionally entrenched in explicit, written provisions, it remains part of Canada's "unwritten constitution." While tenure of office in these courts is provided for only by ordinary statute, Lederman declares that these provisions are "'ordinary' in form only, because they are declaratory of basic constitutional principles and traditions" (Reading 5.1). The constitutional reforms of 1982 appear to further reinforce the independence of the Supreme Court of Canada by entrenching its present size and composition. As noted earlier, the unsuccessful 1987 *Meech Lake Accord* would have formally extended the written guarantees of sections 99 and 100 to the Supreme Court of Canada.[5]

Historically, the concept of judicial independence extends beyond these formal, institutional guarantees. It also stands for the convention of non-interference in the judicial process by members of the executive and legislative branches of government, as well as the non-interference of judges in the political process. The former branch of the non-interference doctrine was illustrated in the "1976 Judges Affair," when it came to light that several different members of the Trudeau cabinet had personally telephoned judges to inquire about cases they were in the process of deciding. While none of the cabinet ministers ultimately resigned, the government issued a policy guideline stating that:[6]

> In the future no member of the Cabinet may communicate with members of the judiciary concerning any matter which they have before them in their judicial capacities, except through the Minister of Justice, his duly authorized officials, or counsel acting for him, nor may any member of the Cabinet communicate with quasi-official bodies which are constituted as courts of record concerning any matter which they have before them in their judicial capacities except through the minister responsible, his duly authorized officials, or counsel acting for him.

This policy has been strictly observed. Two years later, when it was discovered that MP John Munroe had telephoned a judge who was hearing a case involving one of Munroe's constituents, Munroe was forced to resign as minister of labour. The change in government in 1984 did not affect the strict

---

5 See Introduction to Chapter 3.

6 A more detailed account of this matter may be found in Peter H. Russell, *The Judiciary in Canada: The Third Branch of Government* (Scarborough, ON: McGraw-Hill Ryerson, 1987), pp. 78–87.

enforcement of this policy. In 1989, the then Conservative minister of fitness and amateur sport, Jean Charest, resigned following revelations that he had telephoned a judge concerning a case then under consideration.

A different but related aspect of judicial independence arose in the wake of the Donald Marshall scandal in the 1980s: Can a duly constituted royal commission compel a judge to testify about the reasons for a decision or the composition of the panel of judges that heard a case? When the case arrived at the Supreme Court, the Court cited precedents and practice dating back to the 1692 case of *Knowles' Trial* that judges cannot be forced to testify about the reasons for decisions that they have rendered. While the Court was unanimous on this issue, they divided on whether judges had the right to refuse to testify as to the composition of a panel, that is, an administrative matter. The majority judgment, written by Justice McLachlin, held that, while judges did not enjoy a general immunity from answering questions about all aspects of judicial administration, there was such immunity on the critical issue of the assignment of judges. Justices Cory and Wilson dissented. While agreeing that judges enjoy a qualified immunity from testifying about administrative decisions, the facts in the Marshall case made it one of those rare exceptions where the judges should be compelled to testify in order "to reaffirm public confidence in the administration of justice."[7]

In recent decades, increased attention has been given to a new dimension of the old issue of judicial independence: the administrative independence of the judges collectively from the executive branch of government. Historically, the departments of justice at both the federal and provincial levels have been responsible for administering their respective judicial systems. This has resulted in multiple roles for the respective Attorneys General and ministers of justice, who are also responsible for arguing the Crown's position in cases before these same courts. An increased sense of the potential for conflict of interest in this situation has resulted in a series of reforms. In 1977, the federal government created the Commissioner for Federal Judicial Affairs to administer federal judicial business independently of the minister of justice. This commissioner has the rank and status of a deputy head of a government department and can be best described as "the personnel office of the federally appointed judiciary." Under the 1977 amendments to the *Judges Act*, the commissioner was made responsible for the administration of the salaries, benefits, and programs of all federally appointed judges. In 1988, the commissioner was given the additional responsibility for most of the judicial recruitment process, which was previously carried out by an advisor within the justice minister's personal office. Several provinces, including British Columbia, Manitoba, New Brunswick, and Ontario, also have created professional court administrators.

In 1981, Justice Jules Deschenes and Professor Carl Barr completed a study commissioned by the Canadian Judicial Council investigating the problem

---

7   See *Hickman v. MacKeigan* [1989] 2 S.C.R. 796.

of the administrative independence of the courts. They concluded that the problem was sufficiently serious to merit complete judicial control of court administration. However, in September, 1982, the Canadian Judicial Council rejected complete administrative autonomy, at least for the present, and called instead for more and better consultation and decision-sharing between court administrators and judges.

The issue of judicial independence re-appeared shortly after the adoption of the *Charter*. Section 11(*d*) of the *Charter* provides that "any person charged with an offence has the right to ... a fair and public hearing by an independent and impartial tribunal." A provincial court judge in Ontario argued that the discretion of the executive branch to set judicial salaries without enactment by the legislature undermined his independence and thus violated the *Charter*. In *Valente* v. *The Queen* (1985), the Supreme Court ruled that the section 11(*d*) requirement of an "independent and impartial tribunal" does include "financial security" (as well as "security of tenure" and "administrative independence") but found that it was not violated in this instance. The following year, the Court rejected a similar claim by a federally appointed judge in *Beauregard* v. *The Queen* (1986).

However, the issue soon returned to the Court. Responding to the public deficit/debt crisis of the 1990s, several provincial governments imposed across-the-board salary reductions on all public servants – including judges. Provincial judges in Alberta, Manitoba and P.E.I. responded by challenging their salary reductions as a violation of section 11(*d*) of the *Charter*. While there were factual differences in each province, the Supreme Court consolidated the three cases and decided them together in its 1997 decision *Reference re Remuneration of Judges of the Provincial Court (PEI)* (Reading 5.6).

This time, the Court accepted the judges' claim. The Court's reasoning and remedy were both novel and controversial. Writing for the majority, Chief Justice Lamer argued that, not only did section 11(*d*) guarantee financial security as part of the independence of provincial (section 92) judges, but that judicial independence is also an "unwritten constitutional principle" implied by the Preamble to the *Constitution Act, 1867*. As for a remedy, Lamer ruled that this "unwritten constitutional principle" requires all provinces to create independent judicial compensation commissions to set judges' salaries. In a scathing dissent, Justice La Forest denounced the majority judgment as contrary to "reason and common sense [and as] subvert[ing] the democratic foundations of judicial review." The reference to judicial independence in the *Charter*, La Forest emphasized, appears in a section intended to benefit those accused of crimes, not judges. In the absence of any credible textual basis for the majority's ruling, Justice La Forest characterized it as "tantamount to enacting a new constitutional provision" and ordering the creation of "what in some respects is a virtual fourth branch of government." Notwithstanding considerable unhappiness in provincial capitals, all ten provinces complied with this ruling by creating new judicial compensation commissions as specified by Chief Justice Lamer. Indeed, even the federal government amended the *Judges Act* to create a new judicial compensation commission for section 96 court judges. Predictably, judicial salaries have increased dramatically in the wake of the *Provincial Judges Reference*.[8]

No matter is more critical to the maintenance of judicial independence than the procedure for removing judges guilty of serious misconduct or gross incompetence. While such exigencies must be provided for, the removal procedure must be structured so as to minimize the potential for political abuse. Section 99 of the *Constitution Act, 1867* puts in writing the British convention of requiring address by both houses of Parliament in order to remove a judge for violating the norm of "good behaviour." Since Confederation, there have been only five petitions filed with Parliament for removal of a judge, four of which were in the nineteenth century, several of which involved alcoholism. For various reasons (including the death of one judge and the resignation of another), Parliament did not vote to remove any of the judges involved. However, in 1967, Parliament was preparing to vote on a motion to remove Ontario Supreme Court Judge Leo Landreville when he resigned instead. Landreville had been the mayor of Sudbury before his appointment to the bench, and it was alleged that as mayor he had accepted bribes in the form of stock. The investigation of the charges against Landreville had been carried out by a one-judge commission authorized by Parliament. This process became the subject of controversy and eventually a successful lawsuit by Landreville.[9]

In 1971, dissatisfaction with the way in which the Landreville investigation had been handled led the Trudeau government to create the Canadian Judicial Council (CJC). The CJC consists of the chief justices and associate chief justices of all the superior courts and is chaired by the Chief Justice of the Supreme Court of Canada. The responsibility to investigate allegations of judicial misconduct was transferred from the justice minister to the new council. If the council discovers sufficiently serious misconduct on the part of a judge, it can direct the removal of county and district court judges and recommend to Parliament the removal of superior court judges. The transfer of the responsibility to investigate allegations of judicial misconduct from the executive branch to the judges themselves was intended to reduce the potential for political abuse and to enhance the independence of the judiciary.

The CJC came close to exercising its new powers in 1982 at the conclusion of its investigation into allegations of misconduct by then Justice Thomas Berger of the British Columbia Court of Appeal. On November 5, 1981, the federal government and all the provinces except Quebec reached a compromise agreement on the proposed constitutional reforms

---

8 For details, see Morton and Knopff, *The Charter Revolution and the Court Party* (2000), pp. 108–9.

9 For a fuller account of these matters, see Martin L. Friedland, *A Place Apart: Judicial Independence and Accountability in Canada* (Canadian Judicial Council, 1995), pp. 82–90.

of the Trudeau government. One of the compromises was the federal government's agreement to delete those sections that dealt with the protection of the "aboriginal rights" of Native peoples. In the weeks following, Justice Berger publicly criticized Canadian political leaders for this action on at least two occasions. These criticisms were reported in the press, and a justice of the Federal Court, upon reading these reports, lodged a complaint of judicial misconduct with the CJC (Reading 5.3). The Judicial Council appointed a committee of investigation and invited Justice Berger to testify in his own defence. He refused but sent two letters defending his actions as a matter of conscience and a question of principle (Reading 5.3). The Committee of Investigation's final report concluded that Justice Berger was guilty of judicial misconduct and stated that they would have recommended removal from office had it not been for the unique circumstances of the incident (Reading 5.3). The Judicial Council modified the Investigation Committee's report. Its final report to the minister of justice declared that Justice Berger's actions had been "indiscrete" but that they did not constitute grounds for removal from office. In the event, Justice Berger announced his intention to resign anyhow and did so several months later.

The Canadian press gave the "Berger affair" considerable publicity, and some editorials criticized the Canadian Judicial Council for trying to censor or punish Justice Berger for exercising his "freedom of speech." The late Chief Justice Bora Laskin was sufficiently upset with what he considered to be a gross misunderstanding of these events to publicly address the issue in a speech to the Canadian Bar Association in September, 1982 (Reading 5.3). The late chief justice's remarks are important because they demonstrate that judicial independence cuts both ways. Not only does it prohibit politicians from interfering in the judicial process, but it also prohibits judges from interfering in the political process. In response to Berger's appeal to individual conscience, Laskin argued that a judge's "abstention from political involvement is one of the guarantees of his impartiality, his integrity, his independence."

The CJC itself has become entangled in the ongoing battle between feminists and conservatives over the role of judges and the courts. As noted earlier, REAL Women filed an unsuccessful complaint with the Judicial Council over a speech by then Justice Bertha Wilson in 1990. This episode was repeated in 1991, when Justice Beverley McLachlin, in a speech to the Elizabeth Fry Society in Calgary, explicitly criticized Canada's traditional laws on abortion and prostitution as denying women equality and reflecting the bias of male legislators. REAL Women again accused a member of the Supreme Court of advancing "a feminist analysis of the law" that was not shared by all women and represented a violation of her judicial oath of impartiality. Again the Judicial Council rejected the complaint outright, replying that Justice McLachlin's remarks were an "informative and thoughtful historical analysis" of the issues she addressed.

This response prompted an angry reply from REAL Women, which compared McLachlin's 1991 speech to Justice Berger's 1981 speech and alleged that the council was not evenly enforcing Chief Justice Laskin's principle that speaking on political issues of the day is "forbidden territory" for judges. The council's refusal to take action against Justice McLachlin, said REAL Women, "indicates that there has either been a very significant change in the role of judges in Canada," or an inconsistent application of the old rule:

> Either Canadian judges are now permitted by the Canadian Judicial Council
> to engage in political debate or, in the alternative, only those judges support-
> ing the feminist ideology and analysis of the law are permitted to do so.

While REAL Women no doubt thought that the council was playing favou-rites, the truth may be closer to the alternative explanation: that with the expanded political involvement of judges under the *Charter of Rights*, the council should adopt (or has adopted) a more lenient policy for off-the-bench speeches by sitting judges. This possibility, however, appears to be contra-dicted by a 1991 publication of the Canadian Judicial Council, *Commentaries on Judicial Conduct*. This work was the product of a two-year study by the council's Judicial Independence Committee to "formulate a statement of practical ethics to help judges and the public alike." On the subject of "When the judge makes a speech," the *Commentaries* state: "We agree that the *Charter* has tended to blur the distinction between political and legal issues. Almost any issue may now become the subject of litigation. We see that as a reason for judges to become more, rather than less, circumspect than in the past."[10]

The 1990s witnessed more not less controversy over allegations of judi-cial misconduct. In 1996, for the first time in its short history, the CJC voted (22–7) to recommend to Parliament to remove a judge: Judge Jean Bienvenue of the Quebec Superior Court. In the process of sentencing a woman who had been convicted of murder for slitting her husband's throat with a razor, Judge Bienvenue made several disparaging comments about women and Jews killed in the Holocaust. The CJC found that "the public can no longer reasonably have confidence" in him. However, the Judge Bienvenue resigned before Parliament was able to vote on the recommendation.[11]

The most publicized incident of the decade was the 1999 "McClung Affair" (Reading 5.4). This incident arose out of a sexual assault case known as *R. v. Ewanchuk* and turned on the issue of "implied consent." The accused, Ewanchuk, admitted that he had sexually touched the complainant but said

---

10 Canadian Judicial Council, *Commentaries on Judicial Conduct* (Cowansville, PQ: Editions Yvon Blaise, 1991), p. 42.

11 For details, see "Quebec judge's conduct under investigation," *Globe and Mail*, March 6, 1996, A4; "Rock may ask Commons, Senate to remove judge from bench," *Globe and Mail*, Sept. 21, 1996, A1.

that he thought she did not object. When she did, on several occasions, he stopped. This defence of "honest but mistaken belief" raises a nest of prickly issues that have been a source of controversy and conflict between feminists and criminal defence lawyers for several decades. When does a sexual advance become a sexual assault? Is any unsolicited advance an assault? Or must woman signal that a sexual advance is or is not welcome? Can this signal be non-verbal and/or implied? How is the partner supposed to know?

The trial judge acquitted Ewanchuk of sexual assault by relying on the defence of implied consent. The Alberta Court of Appeal, in a judgment written by Judge John McClung, upheld that acquittal. The Supreme Court reversed both the trial court and McClung and ruled that there is no defence of "implied consent" in Canadian law. This ruling was warmly praised by feminists but harshly criticized by criminal defence lawyers. The latter claimed that it took away the defence of "honest but mistaken belief" and thus violated the requirement of *mens rea*.

In a concurring opinion, Supreme Court Justice l'Heureux-Dubé undertook a caustic point-by-point repudiation of McClung's judgment from the Alberta Court of Appeal. Angered by what he considered a personal attack, McClung responded in a letter to the *National Post* and a subsequent interview. McClung's public response was immediately and strongly condemned. McClung then apologized privately to l'Heureux-Dubé and publicly via a letter in the *National Post*. The apologies notwithstanding, women's and other rights advocacy groups filed complaints against McClung with the CJC alleging misconduct and demanding his removal. Complaints were also filed against McClung for *obiter dicta* he had written in a 1996 judgment in the widely publicized gay rights case of *Vriend* v. *Alberta*, a ruling that also was subsequently reversed by the Supreme Court. McClung's judgment in *Vriend* had already gained notoriety for its outspoken denunciation of "crusading, ideologically determined judges [and] the creeping barrage of special interest constituencies that now seem to have conscripted the Charter."[12] In this respect, the gauntlet had been thrown down several years earlier. The whole affair was given added poignancy by the fact that Judge McClung is the grandson of one of Canada's best known suffragettes and early advocates of women's rights, Nellie McClung.

For a week straight, national and metropolitan newspapers were filled with editorials, guest columns, and letters to the editor denouncing and defending both the Court's decision and the two feuding judges. There has been nothing quite like this before or since. In the end, the CJC ruled that McClung's public retort to l'Heureux-Dubé and his remarks about homosexuality in *Vriend* were "inappropriate" and "detract from respect for equality rights." However, the Council stopped at this reprimand and did

---

12 See F.L. Morton, "Canada's Judge Bork: Has the Counter-Revolution Begun?" *Constitutional Forum* 7, no. 4 (1976), 121–26.

not recommend removal. The McClung Affair is the subject of the public documents presented in Reading 5.4.

Six months later, the shoe was on the other foot. As a result of a series of lectures she had given during the summer and fall of 1999, Justice l'Heureux-Dubé found herself charged with judicial misconduct. This time, the issue was gay rights and whether the Justice's remarks went beyond fair comment to advocacy. Several newspaper editorialists suggested they did and that she should be recused in any future cases dealing with these kinds of issues. In a column in the *National Post*, F.L. Morton took the charge one step further and said that l'Heureux-Dubé should resign for violating the same norms that Berger had run afoul of in 1981: that a judge must not only be impartial but appear impartial.

A complaint against l'Heureux-Dubé was eventually made, but the CJC rejected it. According to Justice McEachern's report for the CJC, the context of l'Heureux-Dubé's remarks were distinguishable from those of Berger's – there was no constitutional crisis. In addition, McEachern observed that Canadian judges have always participated in judicial education and in discussions with learned societies. McEachern did leave open the possibility that l'Heureux-Dubé might be recused when and if these issues come before her again. These documents are presented in Reading 5.5. Students can decide for themselves which version of these events is more persuasive.

Twelve months later, it was Justice Michel Bastarache's turn to get into hot water for off-the-bench comments. In a candid interview with *Lawyers Weekly* in January, 2001, Bastarache declared that sometimes the Supreme Court has gone "too far" in expanding the rights of the accused in criminal cases. He said the Court's tendency to "automatically" exclude evidence obtained from detained suspects was "an invention of the court, a principle that was created by the court ... [and] inconsistent with the very wording [of the *Charter*]." Bastarache also criticized the Court's expansion of the *Charter* rights against "unreasonable search and seizure" (section 8) and the "right to be informed of the right to counsel" (section 10(*b*)). These decisions, he said, were "result-oriented," driven by the "policy" considerations of the judges and not "principle." Bastarache also said that he did not think that the Supreme Court has "a mandate to ... define a whole social policy for Canada" and that he hoped that he could persuade the Court to revisit some of the decisions with which he disagreed.[13] These comments provoked angry protests and eventually a formal complaint to the CJC by the Ontario Criminal Lawyers' Association.

Bastarache's comments on aboriginal issues provoked still greater controversy. Courts, he said, are "not the right forum" to settle land claims

---

13 "Supreme Court goes 'too far': judge," by Cristin Schmitz. *National Post*, Jan. 13, 2001; "The Bastarache interview: reasoning to results at SCC," by Cristin Schmitz, *The Lawyers Weekly*, Jan. 26, 2001, p. 19.

and other "ill-defined" aboriginal rights. Commenting on the Court's 1999 *Marshall* decision expanding aboriginal fishing rights in Atlantic Canada, Bastarache said, "I myself didn't agree with the majority decision." He said that he was particularly concerned with the public's perception "that the Court was very result-oriented and was inventing rights that weren't even in the treaties that were brought before the court in that case." A second problem, he said, was that "the court was maybe seen as being unduly favourable to the native position in all cases, and that it sort of has an agenda for extending these [aboriginal] rights and that it has no concerns for the rights of others."[14] Again, there were howls of protest against Bastarache. Soon after the interview, the Atlantic Policy Congress of First Nations Chiefs filed a complaint of "apprehension of bias," declaring that "We strongly feel we could never have a fair hearing in front of a court of which he was a member."[15]

Once again, the CJC rejected the complaint. The CJC cautioned Bastarache that judges should "exercise restraint when speaking publicly ... particularly [on] issues that are likely to come before their court in the future." However, it concluded that "no Panel could conclude that your comments so profoundly affect public confidence in your impartiality as to warrant your removal from office." As in the l'Heureux-Dubé incident, the CJC did leave open the possibility of a future recusal.

The growing turmoil over the conduct of Canadian judges may be better understood in light Professor Conor Gearty's widely discussed inaugural lecture as Professor of Human Rights Law, Kings College, London (Reading 5.8). Gearty raises the perennial question – "What are judges for?" – in light of the UK's decision to make the *European Convention of Human Rights* justiciable in British courts.[16] Gearty suggests that as judges take on a greater law-making function, there will inevitably be increased demands for a more "representative judiciary" and greater judicial accountability. In part, Gearty makes a plea for judicial deference to parliamentary policy choices as a way of moderating these new demands. In part, he makes the case for increased accountability over a more "representative judiciary." Representative of what? Gearty asks. Why privilege sex, race, or ethnicity? Why not economic class and occupation? In terms of the latter categories, no occupational group is less representative than British judges. Similarly in Canada, McCormick and Greene reported in 1990 that the overwhelming majority of Canadian judges are of English or French origin, married, in their fifties, of Judeo-Christian faith, middle and upper-middle class.[17] Justice Wilson's 1993 report for the CBA found that "socially judges come

14 "SCC wrong forum for native land claims: Bastarache," by Cristin Schmitz, *The Lawyers Weekly*, Jan. 19, 2001, p. 20.

15 "Judge should be fired for showing bias: native group," *National Post*, Jan. 31, 2001.

16 See the Introduction to Chapter 1 for information about Britain's adoption of the *European Convention on Human Rights*.

disproportionately from upper-class backgrounds."[18] There is no evidence that the significant increase in women judges appointed during the last decade has changed the class character of the Canadian bench. Indeed, the opposite may well be true.

For reasons such as these, Gearty opts for increased judicial accountability as preferable. He notes that in Ireland the main opposition party has proposed a judicial board to oversee judges' decisions and to discipline them for "mistakes." He endorses the adoption of parliamentary confirmation hearings for the appointment of British judges. And he predicts that British judges may soon be asked to come before Parliament to explain or defend judicially inspired policy change. "The revolution brought about by the *Human Rights Act* does not stop at the door of the law courts," Gearty concludes. "'What judges are for?' is set to become one of the liveliest issues in our public culture in the decades that lie ahead."

Gearty's predictions for the U.K. are already becoming reality in Canada. In Ontario, in 2000, the Harris government introduced a bill that would create a public registry that would track the sentencing record of judges and allow for "performance reviews" of judges.[19] This initiative was widely denounced by the Canadian and Ontario bar associations as a threat to judicial independence. The Reform Party of Canada (1988–2000) called for replacing the current system of appointing judges with "a democratic and accountable method." It also called for parliamentary confirmation hearings for all federal judicial nominees. Its successor party, the Canadian Alliance Party, the official opposition in the federal Parliament elected in 2000, is considering a policy initiative calling for the election of all federally appointed judges.

According to Greene et al.'s 1998 study, Canadian judges already are experiencing unprecedented pressures on traditional norms of judicial independence (Reading 5.7). This study interviewed 101 appellate court judges in the early 1990s. Greene reports that two-thirds reported some form of threat to judicial independence. This finding contrasts sharply with a similar study of trial and appellate court judges done a decade earlier in which not a single judge reported experiencing a threat to judicial independence. The most common threat reported was pressure from interest groups and for "politically correct" decisions. Criticism of judicial decisions by politicians and the media were also high on the list of reported threats. Interestingly, seven judges complained that the CJC itself was a threat to their judicial independence because it gave chief justices too much influence over the

---

17 Peter McCormick and Ian Greene, *Judges and Judging: Inside the Canadian Judicial System* (Toronto: James Lorimer, 1990).

18 Madame Justice Bertha Wilson, *Touchstones for Change: Equality, Diversity and Accountability* (Ottawa: Canadian Bar Association, 1993).

19 "Sentencing-registry bill angers legal community," *Globe and Mail*, May 5, 2000, A3.

careers and working conditions of the other judges. Greene concludes that there is no doubt that this upsurge in perceived threats to judicial independence is almost completely *Charter*-driven.

Greene's conclusions are explained – indeed predicted – by Paul Weiler's more theoretical model of the relationship between judicial function and judicial accountability. Weiler reminds us that the reason judges are purposely made "unaccountable," unlike other high-ranking officials of the state, is that the judges' function is perceived as non-political. To the extent that courts openly and explicitly engage in policy-making, the justification of judicial independence is eroded. Weiler argues that a court that actually resembled his hypothetical "policy-making model" could not logically lay claim to judicial independence. The "judges" of such a court would be much more like administrative executives who would serve "at the pleasure" of the executive and could be changed with the change of political party control of the House of Commons.

Note that Weiler's analysis is completely at odds with the view advanced by former Chief Justice Dickson in the *Beauregard* (1986) decision and quoted by then Justice McLachlin in the 1989 *Marshall* case:

> The rationale for this two-pronged modern understanding of judicial independence is recognition that the courts are not charged solely with the adjudication of individual cases. That is, of course, one role. It is also the context for a second, different, and equally important role, namely as protector of the Constitution and the fundamental values embodied in it.... In other words, judicial independence is essential for fair and just dispute-resolution in individual cases. It is also the lifeblood of constitutionalism in democratic societies.[20]

According to a past and the present chief justice of the Supreme Court of Canada, the need for judicial independence becomes even greater when the courts assume the additional role of "protector of the Constitution." According to Weiler's model (and also Gearty's), appellate courts exercising the function of judicial review (with constitutional veto power) will be subject to more not fewer demands for institutional accountability.

Much of the current controversy in Canada over the Supreme Court's role under the *Charter* stems from these two conflicting understandings. For example, when Justice l'Heureux-Dubé reports that "bench-bashing seems to have moved from the fringe to the mainstream.... Attacking judges has become an eminently reputable activity for the political and the legal establishment" – she interprets this as a serious threat to judicial independence (Reading 13.8). Weiler, on the other hand, would interpret this development

---

20 *Hickman* v. *Mackeigan* [1989] 2 S.C.R. 796. Hickman was the Chief Justice of Nova Scotia who refused to testify before the Royal Commission investigating the Donald Marshall affair. Hickman represented the Royal Commission.

as a logical and even desirable form of democratic accountability. Or to repeat V. O. Key's "iron law" of politics: "where power rests, there influence will be brought to bear."[21]

While the Dickson–McLachlin–l'Heureux-Dubé argument is logical as a matter of abstract legal theory, the accuracy of Weiler's political or democratic logic is reflected in the real-world practice of other countries with more experience with a powerful constitutional court. The sporadic periods of "court packing" in American history are only the most dramatic evidence of the generally accepted fact of American politics that "policy views dominant on the Court are never for long out of line with the policy views dominant among the lawmaking majorities of the United States."[22] Keeping the court "in tune with the times" need not take such traumatic and conflictual forms. It can be institutionalized through constitutional procedures such as that used by the state of California, whereby a judge appointed to the state supreme court must, after his or her first nine years of service, undergo a confirmation vote in a general election.[23] France accomplishes the same objective by limiting the term of each judge on its *Conseil Constitutionnel* to a non-renewable nine-year term, staggering the terms so that one-third of its nine-person membership is replaced every three years. This guarantee of a constant flow of "new blood" onto the court means that it is unlikely to stay out of step with the governing majority coalition for long.

These foreign examples may indeed seem repugnant to Canadians long accustomed to Professor Lederman's assumption that judicial independence is a prerequisite of the "rule of law." But they help us to "think the unthinkable," in Weiler's words; that is, the institutional implications of increasing the policy-making role of courts for the tradition of judicial independence. These examples encourage us to assess the potential costs (and not just the potential benefits) of the greater policy-making role for Canadian courts made possible by the *Charter of Rights*.

---

21 V. O. Key, *Politics, Parties and Pressure Groups* (New York: Thomas Y. Crowell, 1958), p. 154.

22 Robert Dahl, "Decision-Making in a Democracy: The Supreme Court as National Policy-Maker," *Journal of Public Law* 6 (1958), pp. 279–95.

23 See Introduction, Chapter 4.

5.1

The Independence of the Judiciary

W.R. Lederman

In A.M. Linden, *The Canadian Judiciary* (Toronto: Osgoode Hall, 1976), 1–12. Reprinted with permission.

Introduction

An independent judiciary has long been an established feature of our Constitution in Canada, coming to us as a primary part of our great inheritance of English public law and governmental institutions. My purpose here is an ambitious one – to explain the essential *positive* functions of an independent judiciary as an integral part of our total constitutional system. This involves examining the relations between the judiciary on the one hand, and parliaments and cabinets on the other, as they play their respective parts in making and applying laws for our country, at both the provincial and the federal levels. Also, of course, this task requires some examination of the institutional arrangements that are the basis of judicial independence, and some assessment of the relevance of such independence to the needs of our time for good government under law…. What I have to say falls under three main headings:

1. Our English Constitutional Inheritance,
2. Essential Operational Elements of Judicial Independence, and
3. Judicial Independence, Democracy, and The Rule of Law.

1. Our English Constitutional Inheritance

Sir Arthur Goodhart has told us, in his distinguished lectures on "English Law and the Moral Law," that the English are not as much without a constitution as they frequently profess to be. He gives four principles which he maintains are equally basic as first or original principles of the English constitution. They are briefly as follows: (1) "That no man is above the law" (among other things, this means that all official persons, the Queen, the judges and members of Parliament included, must look to the law for the definition of their respective positions and powers). (2) "That those who govern Great Britain do so in a representative capacity and are subject to change…. The Free election of the members of the House of Commons is a basic principle of English constitutional law." (3) That there shall be freedom of speech, of thought and of assembly. (4) That there shall be an independent judiciary.

The fourth and final principle which is a basic part of the English constitution is the independence of the judiciary. It would be inconceivable that Parliament should today regard itself as free to abolish the principle which has been accepted as a cornerstone of freedom ever since the Act of Settlement in 1701. It has been recognized as axiomatic that if the judiciary are placed under the authority of either the legislative or the executive branches of the Government then the administration of the law might no longer have that impartiality which is essential if justice is to prevail.

Sir William Holdsworth expressed a very similar view on the status of the judiciary. He said:

The judges hold an office to which is annexed the function of guarding the supremacy of the law. It is because they are the holders of an office to which the guardianship of this fundamental constitutional principle is entrusted, that the judiciary forms one of the three great divisions into which the power of the State is divided. The Judiciary has separate and autonomous powers just as truly as the King or Parliament; and, in the exercise of those powers, its members are no more in the position of servants than the King or Parliament in the exercise of their powers ... it is quite beside the mark to say that modern legislation often bestows undivided executive, legislative and judicial powers on the same person or body of persons. The separation of powers in the British Constitution has never been complete. But some of the powers in the constitution were, and still are, so separated that their holders have autonomous powers, that is, powers which they can exercise independently, subject only to the law enacted or unenacted. The judges have powers of this nature because, being entrusted with the maintenance of the supremacy of the law, they are and always have been regarded as a separate and independent part of the constitution. It is true that this view of the law was contested by the Stuart kings; but the result of the Great Rebellion and the Revolution was to affirm it.

... For present purposes, two things are noteworthy about the Canadian judicial system. First, while it is true that the guarantee of removal from office only by joint address of the Parliament of Canada is explicitly specified by the *B.N.A. Act* just for the Superior courts of the Provinces, this most emphatically does not mean that there is no constitutional protection for the security of tenure in office of other judges in the total judicial system just described. The same point applies concerning the explicit guarantee of salaries in the *B.N.A. Act*, which mentions only the Superior, District and County courts of the Provinces. The position in my view is that the Superior Courts, by virtue of the explicit provisions for them in the *B.N.A. Act* afford the prototype – the model – which should be followed for all other Canadian courts.

In other words, I am saying that security of tenure and salary for judges in Canada, as a matter of basic constitutional law and tradition, is not limited to the strictly literal reach of sections 99 and 100 of the *B.N.A. Act*. I remind you of the words of Goodhart and Holdsworth. They make it clear that essential provision for the independence of the judiciary generally has long been deeply rooted as an original principle in the basic customary law of the constitution. In Britain herself, the explicit provisions about judicial security are in the ordinary statutes – but these ordinary statutes, including the *Act of Settlement* itself, manifest the more fundamental unwritten constitutional principle I have described, as Goodhart and Holdsworth insist. The same point can and should be made about the status of Canadian judges. In Canadian Federal statutes we have provisions ensuring the independence of the County and District Court judges, the judges of the Federal Court of Canada and the judges of the Supreme Court of Canada itself. In various Provincial statutes, security is likewise provided for provincially-appointed judges, for example the Provincial Criminal Court judges in Ontario. My point is that though these are ordinary statutory provisions, they are "ordinary" in form only because they are declaratory of basic constitutional principles and traditions.

Now of course, for the judges who depend on ordinary statute in this respect, there is room for variations in just how their basic constitutional independence is to be implemented. But, provided they are guaranteed security of tenure in office until a reasonable retirement age, subject only to earlier removal for grave misconduct or infirmity, after full due process by way of inquiry, then the basic constitutional mandate for their independence is satisfied. I am not arguing that all judges are, or have to be, under the parliamentary joint address procedure in order to be secure and independent. Adequate due process leading to removal for cause may take several forms. In this respect, we should note the recent advent of the Canadian Judicial Council, under which the federally-appointed judges as a group themselves apply due process and self-discipline concerning any of their own members against whom complaints may have been entered. This is a progressive step in safeguarding the independence of the judiciary that is quite in harmony with the concept of independence....

2. Essential Operational Elements of Judicial Independence

What I have said so far implies that the elements of judicial independence fall into two groups, individual elements and collective ones.

The individual elements may be stated in these terms. A judge is not a civil servant, rather he is a primary autonomous officer of state in the judicial realm, just as cabinet ministers and members of parliament are the primary official persons in the executive and legislative realms respectively. No minister of the Crown, federal or provincial, and no parliament, federal or provincial, has any power to instruct a judge how to decide any one of the cases that comes before him. If a parliamentary body does not like the judicial interpretation of one of its statutes in a particular case, then it can amend the statute, use different words, and hope that this will cause a different judicial interpretation when next the statute is before a court. But that is all a parliamentary body can do or should attempt to do under the constitution. As for ministers of the Crown, when the government is an interested party in litigation or prosecution before the courts, then the minister can instruct counsel to appear and argue in court for the result the executive government would prefer, but that is all a minister can do or should attempt to do under the constitution. The judge remains autonomous, both as to his determinations of fact and his interpretations of the applicable law. As Chief Justice Laskin said recently, the judge must supply his own answers from his own resources, and thus there is something of the loneliness of the long distance runner in every judge. Long term security of tenure in office with the corresponding guarantee of salary ensures that the judge can maintain this position, especially as he is not allowed to hold any other office concurrently with his judicial office.

The reason for this individual independence of judges is best explained in the words of the late Robert MacGregor Dawson, as follows:

> The judge must he made independent of most of the restraints, checks and punishments which are usually called into play against other public officials.... He is thus protected against some of the most potent weapons which a democracy has at its command: he receives almost complete protection against criticism; he is given civil and criminal immunity for acts committed in the discharge of his duties; he cannot be removed from office for any ordinary offence, but only for misbehaviour of a flagrant kind; and he can never be removed simply because his decisions happen to be disliked by the Cabinet, the Parliament, or the people. Such independence is unquestionably dangerous, and if this freedom and power were indiscriminately granted the results would certainly prove to be disastrous. The desired protection is found by picking with especial care the men who are to be entrusted with these responsibilities, and then paradoxically heaping more privileges upon them to stimulate their sense of moral responsibility, which is called in as a substitute for the political responsibility which has been removed. The judge is placed in a position where he has nothing to lose by doing what is right and little to gain by doing what is wrong; and there is therefore every reason to hope that his best efforts will be devoted to the conscientious performance of his duty....

... But, assuming the appointment of able people to judicial office, this is not in itself enough to ensure that the judicial system functions well as a whole and in all its parts. There are problems of the whole system of courts that have an important bearing on the independence of the judiciary....

... First, my outline of the many parts that make up the unitary Canadian judicial system shows that responsibility for necessary appointments and legislation is shared between the federal and provincial levels of government.

Accordingly, for the solution of these system problems, there must be a great deal of federal-provincial consultation and collaboration at the cabinet and parliamentary levels. This applies also to the provision of adequate financial support for the judicial system. Generally speaking, the administration of justice in Canada has been seriously under-financed, and both levels of government are to blame for this.

In the second place, in certain vital respects, collective responsibility for the effective operation of the judicial system should be invested in the judges themselves. Here the role of the Chief Justices and the Chief Judges is very important, as spokesmen for themselves and their brother judges. This refers particularly to the assignment of judges to case lists, and to determination of priorities for the grouping and hearing of cases. In my view, to safeguard the basic independence of the judiciary, the Chief Justices and the Chief Judges should be in operational control of these matters for their respective courts, with adequate administrative staff responding to their directions.

I have now spoken of the individual and the collective elements that go to make up an independent judiciary. But there is a final question that remains to be answered. What, in the end, is the main purpose of maintaining an independent judiciary? Sir William Holdsworth said, "The judges hold an office to which is annexed the function of guarding the supremacy of the law." My third and final topic is an attempt to explain why he said this.

3. Judicial Independence, Democracy, and the Rule of Law

At this point I return with particular emphasis to the special importance of our superior courts of general jurisdiction. We say that we have the rule of laws rather than of men, but this has a special dependence on the men who are the superior court judges. Constitutionally they have the last word on what the laws mean, so, does this not really mean the personal supremacy of superior court judges? I deny this for the following reasons. It is basic to the rule of law that doctrines, ideas and principles are supreme, not persons. The great case of *Roncarelli* v. *Duplessis* confirmed this as the position in Canada. In aid of this supremacy, we find that the superior courts possess under the constitution a final supervisory review function over lesser courts, and over officials, boards and tribunals of all kinds, to ensure that they stay within the limits of the powers respectively given them by the constitution, or by statute, or by common law. The superior courts have power to nullify decisions of other officials and tribunals for excess of jurisdiction or breach of natural justice in procedure. But here we encounter that basic constitutional dilemma – Who watches the watchman? Who checks the superior courts themselves for excess of jurisdiction or breach of natural justice in procedure? The answer is that, at this primary level of constitutional responsibility, the superior court judges must be trusted to obey the laws defining their own functions, and to check themselves. Believing in the supremacy of law, they must themselves scrupulously obey it. They must be all the more careful about this precisely because there is no one to review their powers, as they review the powers of others. Judicial restraint on these terms at the superior court level is the ultimate safeguard of the supremacy of the law, enacted and unenacted, to use Holdsworth's terms. Remember too that at the intermediate and final levels of judicial appeal you have a plural bench, so that a majority of several judges is necessary to reach a decision. Several heads are better than one, and in the process purely personal peculiarities are likely to be cancelled out. It seems to me that this is as close as we can get to the rule of laws rather than of men.

There are further reasons for confidence in the independent judiciary, and I am speaking now of all judges, both provincially-appointed and federally-appointed. The conditions on which they hold office mean that they have a personal career interest to be served by the way they go in deciding cases that come before them. The laws to be interpreted and applied must be expressed in words, and words are not perfect vehicles of meaning. Hence there is frequently room for partisan interpretation, and that is precisely what you would get if one of the interested parties was in a position to make his interpretation prevail. At least the judges have no such personal interest in biased interpretation one way or the other, hence, in the words of Sir Arthur Goodhart, they are able to bring to the administration of the law that impartiality which is essential if justice is to prevail.

Finally, I assert that the power of the independent appointed judiciary is neither undemocratic nor anti-democratic. The statutes of our popularly elected legislatures do have priority, and will be made to prevail by the courts, if the parliamentarians speak plainly enough. [*Ed. note*: This was written in 1976, before the adoption of the *Charter of Rights* in 1982.] But often their statutes speak only in general terms that must be further particularized by someone else, or they speak in ambiguities that must be resolved by someone else. These tasks fall to interpretative tribunals, especially the courts at all levels of the judicial system. Judicial procedure respects the individual by giving him a fair hearing and allowing him and his counsel to argue that the reason of the law is in their favour. This is as much a feature of democracy as it is to give the same citizen a vote, as a means of influencing his own fate. As for judicial law making, the judicial tasks just referred to do involve discretions that are at times legislative in character. But I must stop here, for the judge as lawmaker is another large subject, with its own place later in this book.

5.2

The Berger Affair
Berger Blasts "Mean-Spirited" Ministers

Ottawa Advocate Citizen. November 10, 1981, A4. Reprinted with permission.

Justice Tom Berger said Monday the decision of all Canadian first ministers to abandon native rights as one of the prices for agreement on the constitution was "mean-spirited and unbelievable."

The B.C. Supreme Court justice also said the compromise provincial override clauses on major parts of the charter of rights is a cause for grave concern in the light of the treatment of minorities by all Canadian governments.

Berger was head of the Royal commission on the MacKenzie Valley pipeline, which heard the concerns of native people about industrial development in the North.

"Last week our leaders felt it was in the national interest to sacrifice the rights because they felt they were serving the greater good in reaching an agreement."

"It was mean-spirited. There are a million and more natives in Canada: Indians, Inuit and Métis and for the most part they are poor and powerless. They were the people who were sacrificed in this deal."

"That is the whole point of minority rights, that they should not be taken away for any reason."

Berger said "I can still hardly believe that it has happened. We have had 10 years of increasing consciousness of native rights and land claims."

"It has had an impact on many people but not on Canadian statesmen. It passed right by them."

Berger said the blame lies with all first ministers including René Lévesque since he did not point to the denial of native rights as a reason for his refusal to sign the agreement.

Berger said Canadians, concerned about the protection of unpopular minorities, can take little comfort from the fact that the federal government insisted on a five-year renewal of every action to override the fundamental, legal and equality rights in the *Charter of Rights.*

Berger said the problem is always "the first time when an inflamed majority wants to strike at a defenceless minority, not five years later when it is irrelevant."

Report of the Committee of Investigation to the Canadian Judicial Council

May 31, 1982

From the material annexed it can be seen that Mr. Justice Berger intervened in a matter of serious political concern and division when that division or controversy was at its height. His office and his experience as a Royal Commissioner (appointments made because of his office and his competence), obviously made his comments newsworthy. He described the decision of the first ministers to "abandon" native rights to be "mean-spirited and unbelievable." In his article he criticized the loss of Quebec's veto and argued for one amending formula in preference to another. He again attacked the first ministers for "repudiating" native rights and argued for the restoration of s.34 "for the recognition and confirmation of aboriginal and treaty rights of Indians, Inuit and Métis."

Justice Berger, while agreeing that what he did may be unconventional, argues that the issues he discussed transcended partisan politics. Because the resolution of the issues in his opinion bore directly on how we were to be governed for the next 100 years, he felt obliged to speak out publicly. He refers to the late Mr. Justice Thorson and Chief Justice Freedman speaking on public issues. We do not have the facts with relation to those matters and are not in a position to comment on them.

Justice Berger also notes that no complaint was made to the Judicial Council about his address to the Canadian Bar Association. It is true that it appears that judges, in speaking to legal bodies, are accorded somewhat greater leeway in expressing their views than they are in speaking to the general public. However, it should be noted that a great part of the address seems to be a thoughtful philosophical discussion of the nature of Canada and its parts and the importance of its preservation. It may be, on reflection, that some of the statements made in this address, although not of as strident a nature as the material complained of, were inappropriate for a judge. It may also be that because he was speaking to an audience of lawyers and judges, the media and others took no notice of his remarks.

Justice Berger's views, which he eloquently defends in his letter to Chief Justice Laskin, are not in issue. What is in issue is his use of his office as a platform from which to express those views publicly on a matter of great political sensitivity. It is possible that other members of the judiciary held opposing views, as obviously elected representatives did, with equal conviction. Justice Berger makes reference to the Honourable Mr. Martland's statements with regard to the *Charter of Rights* after he retired from the bench. The analogy is not a helpful one except to underline the principle that judges do not speak out on political issues while holding office. Mr. Martland at the time he gave his interview was no longer a judge. His franchise had been restored and there was no longer any possibility that he would be called on to determine issues as an impartial judge. In our view, Justice Berger completely misses the mark when he says "does it make all the difference that nothing was said until he (Mr. Martland) retired?" It makes the greatest of difference. Politically controversial statements by a citizen who is no longer a judge and who can never again be called on to be a judge, do not destroy the necessary public confidence in the impartiality of judges.

Not only must judges be impartial, the appearance of impartiality, as Lord Devlin pointed out, must be maintained for the fair and proper administration of justice. If a judge feels compelled by his conscience to enter the political arena, he has, of course, the option of removing himself from office. By doing so, he is no longer in a position to abuse that office by using it as a political platform. One would not have expected Justice Berger's views to have been given the media attention they were given if he had not been a judge but merely a politician expressing his views in opposition to other politicians.

Judges, of necessity, must be divorced from all politics. That does not prevent them from holding strong views on matters of great national importance but they are gagged by the very nature of their independent office, difficult as that may seem. It can be argued that the separation of powers is even more emphatic here than in England. In England, High Court judges have the right to vote. Here, federally appointed judges are denied the right to vote in federal elections and in a number of provinces they have been deprived by statute of a right to vote in provincial elections, and in some cases, even in municipal elections.

It is apparent that some of the native peoples are unhappy with s.35 of the Canadian *Charter of Rights and Freedoms*. If Justice Berger should be called on to interpret that section, for example, the meaning to be given to the word "existing" in the phrase "the existing aboriginal and treaty rights of the aboriginal peoples of Canada," would the general public have confidence now in his impartiality? After Justice Berger spoke publicly on the necessity for Quebec retaining a veto, his brother judges in Quebec were called on to determine whether such a right existed.

Conclusion

In our view it was unwise and inappropriate for Justice Berger to embroil himself in a matter of great political controversy in the manner and at the time he did. We are prepared to accept that he had the best interests of Canada in mind when he spoke, but a judge's conscience is not an acceptable excuse for contravening a fundamental rule so important to the existence of a parliamentary democracy and judicial independence. To say that not all judges are cast in the same mould, as does Justice Berger, is only to state the obvious. On every great matter of political concern it would be probable that judges would hold opposing views privately and, if Justice Berger's view is acceptable, it would be possible to have judges speaking out in conflict one with the other because they hold those opposing views from a sense of deep conviction.

We say again if a judge becomes so moved by conscience to speak out on a matter of great importance, on which there are opposing and conflicting political views, then he should not speak with the trappings and from the platform of a judge but rather resign and enter the arena where he, and not the judiciary, becomes not only the exponent of those views but also the target of those who oppose them.

This is not a question, as Mr. Justice Berger suggests, which each judge must decide for himself. That question has been answered for him from the moment he accepts the Queen's Patent as a judge.

So far as the material before us reveals, Justice Berger's impropriety has been an isolated instance. Chief Justice McEachern also advised us in his Submission that Justice Berger had disengaged himself from the constitutional debate as soon as the Chief Justice spoke to him. Nevertheless, we view his conduct seriously and are of the view that it would support a recommendation for removal from office. There are, however, in addition to those already noted, special circumstances which make this case unique. As far as we are aware, this is the first time this issue has arisen for determination in Canada. It is certainly the first time the Council has been called on to deal with it. It is possible that Justice Berger, and other judges too, have been under a misapprehension as to the nature of the constraints imposed upon judges. That should not be so in the future. We do not, however, think it would be fair to set standards *ex post facto* to support a recommendation for removal in this case.

The judicial office is one which confers important privileges, obligations and protections necessary to the carrying out of the duties of one of Her Majesty's judges. A judge must accept the duty to protect that office, his fellow judges and the public from political controversy as the best way of maintaining "the historic personal independence" of judges.

We conclude that the complaint *non se bene gesserit* is well founded but, for the reasons stated, we do not make a recommendation that Justice Berger be removed from office.

A Matter of Conscience

Justice Thomas R. Berger
Letter to Canadian Judicial Council, December 3, 1981.

CONFIDENTIAL   3rd December, 1981.
The Honourable Chief Justice Bora Laskin,
c/o Canadian Judicial Council
130 Albert Street
Ottawa, Ontario, K1A 0W8

Dear Chief Justice:

I understand that you and your colleagues on the Judicial Council are concerned by my intervention in the constitutional debate. I spoke at Guelph
University on November 10th. The following week the *Globe and Mail* published an article of mine on the constitutional accord of November 5th. I
enclose copies of both the speech and the article. The Prime Minister has
accused me of making a foray into politics.

What I have done may be unconventional. But it was not a venture
into politics in any ordinary sense. It is not as if I had discussed the ordinary stuff of political debate – inflation, interest rates, the budget, or the
nationalization of the Asbestos Corporation. The issues which I discussed
transcended partisan politics. In fact, when the vote on the constitutional
resolution was taken this week, there were dissenting votes by members of
all parties in the House.

This was, after all, a moment of constitutional renewal, unique in our
country's history. The First Ministers (except Premier Lévesque) had signed
a constitutional accord. I felt a sense of great dismay about the accord. My
remarks were directed not to the Prime Minister or any one of the premiers,
nor to any political party, but to our leaders collectively.

While these are questions that rise above narrow partisanship, they
are nevertheless political questions in the broad sense. Indeed, they bear
directly on the question of how we are to be governed for the next 100
years. It was for this reason that I felt obliged to speak out publicly.

What I did is not without precedent. Mr. Justice Thorson used to participate in the campaign for nuclear disarmament. Chief Justice Freedman
went on television in October, 1970, to declare his support for the invoking of the *War Measures Act*. On the occasion of his visit to Vancouver to
open the new Court House in September, 1979, Lord Denning told us that
the trade unions in England were a threat to the freedom of that country.
No doubt each of these judges felt compelled to speak out. It may be said
that it would undermine the independence of the judiciary if judges were

constantly engaged in such activity. But they are not. These interventions by judges are infrequent, even rare.

I enclose a copy of the Prime Minister's remarks made here in B.C. He taxes me for not supporting him at an earlier stage of the debate (he had also done this at a press conference a week earlier) and then goes on to urge that my conduct has been offensive. In fact, I did support his Charter before he abandoned it. I enclose a speech I made to the annual meeting of the Canadian Bar Association in Vancouver in September, to an audience of 1,000 or more lawyers and judges, presenting the case for the Charter. (I remind you that Lord Scarman is one of the leading figures in England who has publicly urged the adoption of a *Charter of Rights* in that country.) I was, I am afraid, outspoken. Yet none of the lawyers, judges or politicians there present complained. I do not understand why what was opportune before November 5th became "inopportune" after November 5th. The views I expressed had not changed (though couched, perhaps, in more forceful language after November 5th).

What I did was done after considering carefully what I should do, and with the best interests of my country in mind. I do not believe that anything I have done has impaired the independence of the judiciary.

The Prime Minister has, with respect to my intervention, urged the judges to "do something about it." I believe it is a mistake to think it is possible to place fences around a judge's conscience. These are matters that no tidy scheme of rules and regulations can encompass, for all judges are not cast from the same mould.

Mr. Justice Addy's letters have arrived. I do not think anything that he has said calls for a reply beyond what I have already written in this letter. It is a question of principle. Should the Judicial Council issue edicts on matters of conscience? If you and your colleagues agree with Mr. Justice Addy, there is nothing more to be said. I believe, however, that these are matters that individual judges must decide for themselves.

Yours sincerely,

Thomas R. Berger

cc: The Hon. Chief Justice McEachern

Outspoken B.C. Judge Resigning

Calgary Herald, May 15, 1982.

VANCOUVER (CP) – Justice Thomas Berger, an outspoken champion of minority rights who refused to accept that his judicial robes include a gag, will be stepping down from the B.C. Supreme Court this summer.

And when he departs on August 27, he will leave an imprint that, flouting tradition, endorses the concept of judges defending minorities against parliamentary incursions.

"I believe a judge has the right, a duty, in fact, to speak out on an appropriate occasion on questions of human rights and fundamental freedoms," Berger said last year.

On Wednesday, Berger resigned from the bench, citing differences between himself and Supreme Court of Canada Chief Justice Bora Laskin and the Canadian Judicial Council over constraints imposed on public speaking by judges.

Starting in September, Berger will teach constitutional law and civil liberties at the University of B.C. two days a week and resume a limited law practice....

... In a letter addressed to Justice Minister Mark MacGuigan, he said his differences with Laskin and the Judicial Council are well known.

He said this extended beyond the dispute over his intervention in a constitutional debate in November, 1981, when he said that on rare occasions a judge may have an obligation to speak out on human rights. Berger said his departure also concerns Laskin's views on judicial involvement in royal commissions.

MacGuigan said Thursday he has no qualms about accepting Berger's resignation, but he was unhappy that Berger made public his letter of resignation now when he plans to remain a judge until August 27.

MacGuigan said judges should avoid public controversies.

5.3

The Meaning and Scope of Judicial Independence
Chief Justice Bora Laskin
From an address to the Annual Meeting of the Canadian Bar Association, September 2, 1982. Reprinted with permission.

… I hope I do not abuse this privilege if I strike a serious note in this address. It would please me better if I could banter and amuse, which I may assure you is not beyond my capacity. But special reasons, to which I will come shortly, impel me to speak more soberly on a subject of fundamental importance to the judicial office. That subject is the meaning and scope of judicial independence. I would have thought that its meaning would have been well understood over the years in which the Judges have exercised their judicial roles. I would have thought that there was a clear public understanding that Judges cannot be measured in the same way as other holders of public office or any members of the public. In my understanding, and in that of most of the members of the legal profession and members of the Bench, Judges are expected to abstain from participation in political controversy. Obviously, considering the storm that has brewed early this year on the Berger affair, I was somewhat mistaken. The limited public role of the Judge, one perfectly clear to me, seems to have been misunderstood or forgotten, even by lawyers, let alone by members of the press and of the public.

A fundamental principle has pervaded the judicial role since it took root in the reign of Queen Anne. It was established – not without fits and starts – that Judges would no longer hold office at the pleasure of the Crown, at the pleasure of the government. They would have security of tenure, once assigned to their position, and would hold office during good behaviour to the age of retirement. Their duration in judicial office would no longer depend on governmental whim, and they could be removed only for judicial misbehaviour.

What this imported, as it evolved over the years, was the separation of the executive and the judiciary; no admixture of the one with the other; no mixture of the judiciary in politics or political controversy; correspondingly, no intermeddling of the executive with the judiciary; each branch was to be independent of the other, left alone to carry on its separate duties. For the Judges, they had utmost freedom of speech in the discharge of their judicial functions. Unbelievably, some members of the press and some in public office in this country, seem to think that freedom of speech for the Judges gave them the full scope of participation and comment on current political controversies, on current social and political issues. Was there ever such ignorance of history and of principle?

A Judge, upon appointment – and I am speaking here of appointments which cover all members of our provincial and federal superior courts as well as the Supreme Court of Canada – takes a prescribed oath of office. It is a short oath which is common to all superior court Judges, being as follows:

> I do solemnly and sincerely promise and swear that I will duly and faithfully, and to the best of my skill and knowledge, execute the powers and trust reposed in me as....

> So help me God.

But it is invested with all the authority and surrounded by all the limitations that are imported by the principle of judicial independence and that are spelled out in the *Judges Act*, the federal statute which defines the judicial office.

What does the *Judges Act* say about the judicial office? It says quite clearly that a Judge may not, directly or indirectly, engage in any occupation or business other than his judicial duties. There is a limited exception for him or her to act as commissioner or arbitrator or adjudicator or referee or conciliator or mediator, if so appointed in respect of a federal matter by the federal Government; and similarly, if so appointed by the provincial government in respect of a provincial matter. These are short-term, temporary assignments not intended to give a Judge a regular assignment to carry out a non-judicial role. Two recent illustrations of the distinction may be mentioned. A few years ago, the Government of Canada wished to appoint a Judge as a Deputy Minister of an executive department. He was unwilling to accept the position unless he retained his security as Judge. The Government was prepared to go along. I felt it my duty as Chief Justice to protest and did so vigorously, pointing out that it was either the one position or the other, but not both.

A Judge who wishes to accept an executive appointment could not remain Judge at the same time. In the case I mentioned, the Judge put more store on his judicial position than on the proposed executive position. The matter was accordingly dropped. The same thing happened a little later in Ontario when the provincial government wished to appoint an Ontario Supreme Court Judge as Chairman of the provincial Workmen's Compensation Board. Again, I protested; if the Judge wished to accept the provincial appointment, he should resign from the Bench; he could not be both Judge and non-judicial or executive functionary. The principle was accepted and the matter was abandoned.

These instances concerned permanent appointments to governmental positions. The authorized exceptions to allow governments to appoint Judges to special assignments as, for example, by order-in-council or by a limited inquiry, do not involve Judges in executive government or in governmental operations. They are asked to perform a particular service, with generally a short-term duration, although some inquiries like the MacKenzie Valley Pipeline and the McDonald Inquiry into the RCMP did go on for some years.

I am myself not a great supporter of the use of Judges to carry out short term assignments at the behest of a government, federal or provincial. Apart from anything else, it is not always convenient to spare a particular Judge, given the ever increasing workload of all Courts. Moreover, there is always the likelihood that the Judge will be required to pass on policy, which is not within the scope of the regular judicial function. But I recognize that governments will continue to ask Judges (generally with the consent of their Chief Justice) to perform these limited tasks. The important thing to remember is that these short-term assignments are not intended to establish a career for the Judge in the work he or she carried out. The Judge is expected to make his or her report to the particular government and to regard the assignment as completed without any supplementary comment. Any comment or action is for the government; the Judge himself or herself is *functus*, done with the matter. This has been the general behaviour of Judges who have accepted and carried out special or particular governmental assignments. Whatever has been the value of the inquiry must rest in what it says – the Judge is certainly not intended to be a protagonist, however enamoured he or she may become of the work. Nor is the Judge intended to make a career of the special assignment.

There has been a large increase in the number of federally-appointed Judges in the last decade. Indeed, there are now 466 superior court Judges throughout Canada and 232 county and district court Judges. I do not take account of provincial court Judges who are appointed by provincial governments. The increase in the number of federally-appointed Judges increased the burden of judicial administration, the need to monitor complaints (which are inevitable, even if in most cases misconceived) and the need also to provide outlets for judicial conferences. It was beyond the capacity of Parliament to provide for these matters and they also raised sensitive matters engaging the independent position of the Judges.

In 1971, a new policy was introduced by Parliament to govern supervision of judicial behaviour or, I should say, alleged misbehaviour....

... The Canadian Judicial Council came into being in October, 1971 and has had a considerable amount of business in the past decade. It has exercised its powers of inquiry and investigation with great care, seeking on the one hand to satisfy complaints against alleged judicial misbehaviour and on the other hand to protect the reputation of the Judge against unfounded allegations. The most common type of complaint received against Judges has to do with objections to their judgments. Laymen have misconceived the role of the Council: it is not a court of appeal to rectify decisions alleged to be in error; for that there are established appeal courts, and the Council repeatedly has to tell complainants that the recourse is an appeal, not an invocation of the powers of the Canadian Judicial Council.

Since the Canadian Judicial Council has a statutory mandate to conduct inquiries into alleged judicial misbehaviour, it can hardly ignore a responsible complaint. In the Berger case, the complaint was made by a long-serving superior court Judge. Was the Canadian Judicial Council to ignore it? At least, it had the obligation to consider whether the complaint merited investigation, that it was not merely frivolous. Those members of the press who became engaged with the complaint in Justice Berger's support seemed entirely ignorant of the mandate of the Canadian Judicial Council. They appeared to be of the view that a Judge's behaviour was for him to measure, that it was not open to the Canadian Judicial Council to investigate, let alone admonish a Judge in respect of a complaint against objectionable behaviour. This was clearly wrong and could have been established by some modest inquiry.

My mention of the Berger case is not to reopen an issue which is closed. It is only to set the record straight on the statutory function and duty of the Canadian Judicial Council, whoever be the subject of a complaint to it. In view of the obvious misunderstanding to which the Berger incident gave rise, it seemed important to me that I, as Chairman, should underline the role and duty of the Canadian Judicial Council, however distasteful it may be to assess the behaviour of a fellow Judge. I would have welcomed, as I always do, the balance provided by the media, by the press, and I regret that it was unfortunate that they did not discharge that responsibility on this occasion.

There was one respect in which members of the press, and indeed some public "bodies" and members of Parliament, showed their ignorance of judicial propriety. It was said that pursuit of the complaint against Justice Berger was an interference with his freedom of speech. Plain nonsense! A Judge has no freedom of speech to address political issues which have nothing to do with his judicial duties. His abstention from political involvement is one of the guarantees of his impartiality, his integrity, his independence. Does it matter that his political intervention supports what many, including the press, think is a desirable stance? Would the same support be offered to a Judge who intervenes in a political matter in an opposite way? Surely there must be one standard, and that is absolute abstention, except possibly where the role of a Court is itself brought into question. Otherwise, a Judge who feels so strongly on political issues that he must speak out is best advised to resign from the Bench. He cannot be allowed to speak from the shelter of a Judgeship.

In the Berger case, the Judge's intervention was on critical political and constitutional issues then under examination by the entire Canadian ministerial establishment. No Judge had a warrant to interfere, in a public way, and his conviction, however well intended, could not justify political intervention simply because he felt himself impelled to speak. To a large degree, Judge Berger was reactivating his McKenzie Valley Pipeline inquiry, a matter which was years behind him and should properly be left dormant for a political decision, if any, and not for his initiative in the midst of a sensitive political controversy.

The Canadian Judicial Council – one member of Parliament accused us of being engaged in a witch hunt – was badly served by those who, obviously, did no homework on the Council's role and on its obligation. There was another matter which seemed rather shabby, also the result of failure to do any homework. It was indicated, quite explicitly in some news quarters, that the Canadian Judicial Council acted because the Prime Minister had complained of the Judge's intrusion into the political sphere when the Prime Minister was giving a press interview in Vancouver. The record on this matter is quite clear. The written complaint against Justice Berger was addressed to me under dates of November 18 and 19, 1981 and delivered to me, from Ottawa, on those days. The next day, November 20, 1981, I sent a memorandum to the Executive Secretary of Council asking that the complaints – there were two successive ones – be referred for consideration by the Executive Committee. So far as the Canadian Judicial Council was concerned, the complaint had become part of our agenda. The interview of the Prime Minister did not take place until November 24, 1981. It is therefore mere mischief making to suggest that the Canadian Judicial Council was moved to action by the Prime Minister.

The Berger inquiry, as I have said, is behind us, and I regret that I found it necessary to say as much as I did about it. However, the Canadian Judicial Council, which does not and cannot reach out publicly to the media, deserves to have its record cleared. This would not have been necessary if we had been better served by the press throughout the whole affair. A matter like the Berger case is not likely to recur; the Canadian Judicial Council has signalled the danger of recommended removal from office if it should recur. As it was, the Council took a placating view and administered an admonishment in the following terms:

1. The Judicial Council is of the opinion that it was an indiscretion on the part of Mr. Justice Berger to express his views as to matters of a political nature, when such matters were in controversy.
2. While the Judicial Council is of the opinion that Mr. Justice Berger's actions were indiscreet, they constitute no basis for a recommendation that he be removed from office.
3. The Judicial Council is of the opinion that members of the judiciary should avoid taking part in controversial political discussions except only in respect of matters that directly affect the operation of the Courts.

In view of the obfuscation that surrounded the Berger case, there are a number of propositions that must be plainly stated. First, however personally compelled a Judge may feel to speak on a political issue, however knowledgeable the Judge may be or think he or she may be on such an issue, it is forbidden territory. The Judge must remain and be seen to remain impartial. Compromise which would impair judicial independence and integrity is out, if the Judge is to remain in judicial office. Second, no federally-appointed Judge can claim immunity from the examination by the Canadian Judicial

Council of complaints (unless obviously frivolous) lodged against the Judge; nor against the decision of the Canadian Judicial Council to investigate the complaints through a formal inquiry. Third, the Canadian Judicial Council is not limited to recommending removal or dismissal; it may attach a reprimand or admonishment without either recommending removal or abandoning the complaint. Only if it gets to removal does it become necessary, in the case of a superior court Judge, to engage the Minister of Justice and Parliament, whose approval on a recommended removal must be sought. Fourth, Judges who are objects or subjects of a complaint are entitled to a fair hearing, to appear before the Council or before an appointed committee or to refuse to appear (as Justice Berger did refuse). Refusal to appear does not paralyze the Council, and did not in the Case under discussion....

5.4

The McClung Affair
He Said, She Said

National Post, February 26, 1999, A3.

Justice Claire L'Heureux-Dubé of the Supreme Court issued a point-by-point rebuke yesterday to Justice John McClung of the Alberta Court of Appeal, for comments he made in a sexual-assault ruling last year in which he acquitted Steve Ewanchuk:

Judge McClung said: "It must be pointed out the complainant did not present herself (to the accused) in a bonnet and crinolines."
Judge L'Heureux-Dubé countered: "These comments made by an appellate judge help reinforce the myth that under such circumstances, either the complainant is less worthy of belief, she invited the sexual assault, or her sexual experience signals probable consent to further sexual activity."

Judge McClung said: "She told Ewanchuk that she was the mother of a six-month-old baby and that, along with her boyfriend she shared an apartment with another couple."
Judge L'Heureux-Dubé countered: "One must wonder why he felt necessary to point out these aspects of the trial record. Could it be to express that the complainant is not a virgin?"

Judge McClung said: "There was no room to suggest that Ewanchuk knew, yet disregarded, her underlying state of mind as he furthered his romantic intentions."

Judge L'Heureux-Dubé countered: "These were two strangers, a young 17-year-old woman attracted by a job offer trapped in a trailer with a man approximately twice her age and size. This is hardly a scenario that one would characterize as reflective of romantic 'intentions.' It was nothing more than an effort by Ewanchuk to engage the complainant sexually, not romantically."

Judge McClung said: "During each of these three clumsy passes by Ewanchuk, when she said no, he promptly backed off."

Judge L'Heureux-Dubé countered: "The expressions used by (Justice) McClung to describe the accused's sexual assault, such as 'clumsy passes', are plainly inappropriate in that context as they minimize the importance of the accused's conduct and the reality of sexual aggression against women."

Judge McClung said: "The sum of the evidence indicates that Ewanchuk's advances to the complainant were far less criminal than hormonal."

Judge L'Heureux-Dubé countered: "According to this analysis, a man would be free from criminal responsibility for having non-consensual sexual activity whenever he cannot control his sexual urges."

Judge McClung said: "In a less litigious age, going too far in the boyfriend's car was better dealt with on site, a well chosen explicative, a slap in the face, or, if necessary, a well directed knee."

Judge L'Heureux-Dubé countered: "According to this stereotype, women should use physical force, not resort to the courts to 'deal with' sexual assaults and it is not the perpetrator's responsibility to ascertain consent ... but the women's not only to express an unequivocal 'no' but also to fight her way out of a situation."

McClung's Letter to the *National Post*

Mr. Kenneth Whyte
Editor in Chief
National Post
Don Mills, ON

Dear Sir:

   Madam Justice Claire L'Heureux-Dubé's graceless slide into personal invective in Thursday's judgment in the *Ewanchuk* case allows some response. It is issued with "the added bitterness of an old friend."

   Whether the *Ewanchuk* case will promote the fundamental right of every accused Canadian to a fair trial will have to be left to the academics. Yet there may be one immediate benefit. The personal convictions of the judge, delivered again from her judicial chair, could provide a plausible explanation for the disparate (and growing) number of male suicides being reported in the province of Quebec.

   Yours truly,

   (signed)
   J.W. McClung
   Justice of Appeal

McClung's Public Letter of Apology

Issued on March 1, 1999

For 40 years I have served the Courts of Alberta at four different levels and to the best of my ability. But last week I made an overwhelming error. When I read the Supplementary Reasons for Judgment of Madam Justice L'Heureux-Dubé in the Ewanchuk case, I allowed myself to be provoked into writing to the *National Post*. It was published on Feb 26. The letter has been widely quoted and condemned.

   I wish to acknowledge that there was no justification for my doing so. I regret my reaction and appreciate that no circumstance could justify the media as the avenue for the expression of my disappointment.

   My letter made reference to curtain suicide statistics in the Province of Quebec and was only included as a facetious chide to the judge. I thought it would be so understood. What compounded my indiscretion was the fact, unknown to me, that Justice L'Heureux-Dubé had undergone a suicide bereavement in her own family. I immediately conveyed my explanation and apology to her later the same day. I sincerely regret what happened and have so advised her. It was cruel coincidence to which she ought not have been subjected. But it is a coincidence for which I am answerable.

On Saturday Feb. 27, the *National Post* attributed to me further remarks about the Ewanchuk case. Any remarks were not designed to call into question the authority or finality of the Supreme Court of Canada resolution of the case, nor were they designed to impugn the complainant involved in the Ewanchuk assault. The discussion I had with Mr. Ohler, the reporter, was held as background to the issues in the case. I thought it was an off-the-record discussion, as were discussion the previous day. Obviously Mr. Ohler did not. That, in hindsight, was also my mistake.

To be clear I recognize the overriding authority of the Supreme Court of Canada and any suggestion to the contrary is incorrect. The Canadian system of justice could not function in the absence of a hierarchy of courts. I deeply regret that what has happened has ignited a debate which could place the administration of justice in an unfortunate light. If so, it was unintentional as I have the highest regard for the justice system in which I serve.

(signed)
John W. McClung
Justice of Appeal

The Canadian Judicial Council Ruling

News Release: "Panel expresses strong disapproval of McClung conduct," Ottawa, May 21, 1999.

A three-member Panel of the Canadian Judicial Council has expressed strong disapproval of the conduct of Mr. Justice John W. McClung of the Alberta Court of Appeal following reversal of his court decision in the *Ewanchuk* case.

The Panel was critical of Mr. Justice McClung's letter to *The National Post* published February 26, 1999 and comments subsequently quoted by the newspaper after the Supreme Court of Canada reversed the *Ewanchuk* decision.

The Council released a letter to Mr. Justice McClung signed by the Panel Chairperson, Nova Scotia Chief Justice Constance R. Glube, setting out the Panel's response to 24 complaints from individuals and organizations. Other members of the Panel were the Quebec Chief Justice Pierre Michaud and Ontario Chief Justice R. Roy McMurtry.

The Panel concluded that the file should be closed with an expression of disapproval of the conduct of Mr. Justice McClung, but that there was no requirement for a formal investigation by an Inquiry Committee under ss. 63(2) of the *Judges Act* for the purpose of deciding whether or not to recommend that the judge be removed from office.

The Panel disagreed with Mr. Justice McClung's characterization of Madam Justice Claire L'Heureux-Dubé's reasons for judgment in the *Ewanchuk* appeal as an attack on him or "unfair and unearned" criticism.

The Panel noted Mr. Justice McClung's apology for his letter to the newspaper and his unequivocal recognition that the letter and its tone were entirely inappropriate.

"In the circumstances, the Panel considers it to be an impetuous and isolated incident which does not warrant further consideration by the Council," said the Panel's letter.

But Mr. Justice McClung's comments on the *Ewanchuk* case in the *National Post* interview were entirely inappropriate, and "can only cause distress to the victim and reflect negatively on the judiciary."

The Panel's letter also addressed complaints about passages in Mr. Justice McClung's reasons for judgment in *Ewanchuk* and in the 1996 *Vriend* [gay rights] case.

It was "simply unacceptable conduct for a judge" to imply in the *Ewanchuk* judgment that the complainant was not a "nice girl" or that she could have resolved any difficulties with a "slap in the face" or a "well-placed knee", the Panel said.

Moreover, Mr. Justice McClung's "gratuitous observations" about gays and lesbians in his reasons for judgment in *Vriend* "constitute inappropriate conduct for a judge," the Panel said. The passages could be interpreted as an assertion that gay people are inherently immoral and as categorizing gays and lesbians as sexual deviants who prey on children, said the Panel's letter.

"The Panel has concluded that your comments cross beyond the boundary of even the wide latitude given to judges in expressing their reasons. They have no logical connection to the issues in the case and detract from respect for equality rights. They constitute inappropriate conduct for a judge."

Mr. Justice McClung's comments in both *Vriend* and *Ewanchuk* were "flippant, unnecessary and unfortunate", said the Panel's letter. But the comments in *Vriend* did not demonstrate underlying homophobia and the comments in *Ewanchuk* did not reflect an underlying bias against women. These comments would not preclude Mr. Justice McClung from treating all litigants fairly and impartially in future.

"In reaching its conclusions, the Panel has taken into account that the two judgments in which your inappropriate comments were made were reversed by the Supreme Court of Canada," the letter said. "The Panel also gave consideration to your long and distinguished career as a lawyer and judge in the years preceding these complaints. In sum, the Panel has found your conduct to be inappropriate but not malicious or reflecting oblique motive. The Panel expects that you will learn from this experience in dealing with future cases."

5.5

L'Heureux-Dubé Crosses the Line

F.L. Morton
National Post, December 8, 1999.

In November,1981, the Canadian Judicial Council reprimanded then Judge Thomas Berger for publicly criticizing a First Ministers' decision to delete aboriginal rights from the *Charter of Rights*. (Aboriginal rights were later restored on the condition that they apply only to "existing" rights.) Berger's speaking out on "a matter of serious political concern and division when that ... controversy was at its height," the CJC ruled, violated the age old judicial norm that a judge must not only be impartial but appear impartial.

The CJC concluded that Judge Berger's "impropriety" was serious enough to "support a recommendation for removal from office," but stopped short of recommending this because it was the "first time this issue has arisen in Canada." In the event, Judge Berger chose to resign anyhow.

What was it that Judge Berger had said that brought him within a hair's width of removal from office? He had criticized the First Ministers' decision as "mean spirited and unbelievable." Describing most natives as "poor and powerless," Berger said their well-being had been "sacrificed" in the bargain struck by the First Ministers.

Now compare Judge Berger's infraction with current Supreme Court of Canada Justice L'Heureux-Dubé's recent declarations on the issue of gay rights and homosexual marriage. In October, she told a conference on "domestic partnerships" at Queen's University that, "In failing to recognize and support partnerships, traditional or otherwise, are we not doing violence to the fabric of our community?"

The rhetorical form of L'Heureux-Dubé's question hardly disguises her own position. Or at least it didn't to a national journalist covering the conference, who reported the speech as follows:

> Justice Clair L'Heureux-Dubé ... says its time for the law to look beyond traditional relationships of men and women and start extending equality to partners of all types who choose to live together." According to the same article, "Judge L'Heureux-Dubé ... added her support to the concept of extending benefits to all couples who live in relationships of economic dependency, whether they are gays, lesbians, or even widowed sisters or old army buddies.

These remarks were made in the wake of the Supreme Court's controversial gay rights ruling in *M and H* last May, which struck down the *Ontario Family Act's* definition of spouse as a member of the opposite sex. This ruling affected 67 other Ontario statutes, and similar traditional definitions of spouse in hundreds of other provincial and federal statutes.

Indeed, the Judge made these remarks just four days before the Ontario government announced the legislative amendments that Premier Harris said it was "forced" to make in order to comply with the six month deadline imposed by L'Heureux-Dubé and her colleagues last May.

One might have thought that this might violate the CJC's rule against judges' speaking out on "a matter of serious political concern and division when that ... controversy was at its height." Apparently not L'Heureux-Dubé.

Indeed, the outspoken Judge made even more pointed remarks at an international gay rights conference in London, England in July. Readers may recall that in 1994 the Ray government attempted to amend the *Ontario Family Act* to include same-sex partners. This was defeated in a free-vote, in which a number of Government MPPs joined opposition parties to defend the traditional definition of spouse. L'Heureux-Dubé described this to her audience as an example of "a general failure in the political process to recognize the rights of lesbians and gays without the pressure of court decisions behind them."

Why, we might ask, is the outcome of a free vote described as a "failure" and not just a "loss"? What message did this send to the current Ontario government that was then in the midst of deliberating its own legislative response to *M and H*?

Evidently, L'Heureux-Dubé did not want her message to be veiled. After summarizing gay rights legal victories in Canada, she declared:

> Despite these developments, however, there is much work to be done. Definitions of spouse in many federal laws that exclude same-sex partners are still present in many laws in many provinces [*sic*], and discrimination and prejudice against gays and lesbians in Canadian society is still too prevalent. The day has not yet come when all laws in Canada recognize same-sex partnerships as equally worthy and valuable as those between members of the opposite sex. Amending the many legislative distinctions between same sex and opposite sex couples will require extensive legislative amendments to a variety of statutes, or many court challenges to individual statutes.

Is she saying that if the legislatures won't do it, the courts will?

In her reported oral remarks, L'Heureux-Dubé went even further.

She appeared on the same dais as Justice Michael Kirby of the Australian High Court, a recently out-of-the-closet gay, the Svend Robinson, as it were, of the new international judicial jet set. Kirby encouraged judges to use ambiguity in statutes or common law to advance the cause of gay equality. Not to be outdone, L'Heureux-Dubé announced herself as "an equality person." "I hate discrimination," she exclaimed, "I will do anything I can to achieve it [equality]."

Anything? Again, L'Heureux-Dubé did not leave her audience guessing as to her meaning: "We [judges] have lots of discretion," she told them. "So put yourself in where there is nothing else to go on.... I am not afraid to strike down laws."

Indeed, she is not. No one doubts her moral convictions and readiness to act on them. But this is precisely what the Berger Inquiry said that sitting judges must refrain from doing:

> if a judge becomes so moved by conscience to speak out on a matter of great importance, on which there are opposing and conflicting political views, then he should not speak with the trappings and from the platform of a judge but rather resign and enter the arena where he, and not the judiciary, becomes not only the exponent of those views but also the target of those who oppose them.

The Berger Inquiry was clear on the reasons for this rule:

> Politically controversial statements by a citizen who is no longer a judge and who can never again be called on to be a judge, do not destroy the necessary public confidence in the impartiality of judges.... Not only must judges be impartial, the appearance of impartiality must be maintained for the fair and proper administration of justice.

Judge L'Heureux-Dubé has gone far beyond the permissible limits identified by the Berger Commission. She has staked out clear positions on issues that are under active political debate and will certainly be subject to additional litigation. Indeed, EGALE, the rights advocacy organization that directs most gay rights litigation in Canada, has recently announced that it intends ask the Supreme Court to overturn Ontario's legislative response to *M and H* as inadequate. Egale charges that the Harris government has introduced "a separate and unequal category which reinforces discrimination against lesbians and gay men." This "privileging [of] heterosexual relationships," EGALE argues, "is contrary to the equality guarantee and thus unconstitutional." How can Judge L'Heureux-Dubé appear to be impartial on this issue?

Both the *National Post* and columnist Ian Hunter have already written that Judge L'Heureux-Dubé should be excused from any future gay rights cases before the Supreme Court. No doubt she should. But this hardly goes far enough. The facts in this case demand a sterner sanction. L'Heureux-Dubé's political advocacy from the bench far exceeds that of Berger's. The Canadian Judicial Council made it clear at the time that Berger's infractions "would support a recommendation for removal from office," but they refrained from doing so because it was the first instance of this kind. But as the late Chief Justice Bora Laskin told the Canadian Bar Association several months later, "A matter like the Berger case is not likely to recur; the Canadian

Judicial Council has signalled the danger of recommended removal from office if it should recur."

As a Canadian citizen, Claire L'Heureux-Dubé is free to join the gay rights movement. But not as a sitting Canadian judge.

The usual Court Party partisans have already sprung to the defence of their favourite judge. No doubt more will. And the public will soon be bombarded with a barrage of (intentionally) confusing legalese. But in this case, both the facts and the issue are about as clear as they ever get.

Response of the Canadian Judicial Council to a complaint laid against Justice l'Heureux-Dubé

Addressed to the complainant. March 6, 2000

> I write further to my letter of December 31, 1999 concerning your complaint about Madam Justice Claire L'Heureux-Dubé of the Supreme Court of Canada. I forwarded your complaint to the Honourable Allan McEachern, Chairperson of the Judicial Conduct Committee of the Council and Chief Justice of British Columbia.
>
>   . . .
>
> You say that your complaint is contained in an article written by Mr. Ted Morton that was published in the *National Post* on December 8, 1999. Chief Justice McEachern observes that that article, and therefore your complaint, is based upon a misunderstanding of this Council's 1981 decisions in the case of Mr. Justice Berger, who was then a judge of the Supreme Court of British Colombia. The passages quoted by Mr. Morton came not from the decision of the Council, but rather from the report of a committee, which the Council did not adopt. It should be noted that Mr. Justice Berger's criticisms of political leaders were made in the midst of a constitutional crisis relating to the adoption of a new Constitution. The only decision made by the Council as that Mr. Justice Berger's comments were indiscrete. Thus, there is little profit in making comparisons with Mr. Justice Berger's case.
>
> Chief Justice McEachern recognizes, however, that the real gist of your complaint is not just a comparison with the Berger case but is rather the comments made by Madam Justice L'Heureux-Dubé on the two occasions mentioned in Mr. Morton's article. In that respect, Chief Justice McEachern advises that Canadian judges have always participated in judicial education and in discussions with learned societies. So the attendance of Madam Justice L'Heureux-Dubé and participation at these conferences was not unusual.
>
> Chief Justice McEachern notes that both Conferences were convened after the decision of the Supreme Court of Canada in the *M.v.H.* case, which clearly established some principles relating to the meaning of equality provisions in the *Charter*. Madam Justice L'Heuereux-Dubé was the moderator of a panel of discussion at the London Conference. Her remarks comprise

only four pages. The first two pages reviewed existing jurisprudence including *M.v. H.*; *Mossop* v. *Canada*; *Eagan* v. *Canada*, and *Vriend*. On the third page, she reviewed two decisions of the Ontario courts, *Rosenberg* v. *Canada*, and *Re K.* At the foot of page 3, she commented, correctly, that the changes brought about by these cases have caused "considerable social and political controversy", which is simply a statement of fact. At the top of page 4 she offered some statistical evidence to support the view she then stated that the judgments of the Supreme Court do reflect the values of ordinary Canadians. In her last paragraph, Madam Justice L'Heureux-Dubé comments, correctly, that there has been a "tremendous change in the recognition of the legal status of same-sex relationships" and she invited the participants to "reflect" on the "advantages and disadvantages" of recognizing these changes by court decisions rather than through legislation. Having concluded that these decisions represent "progress" towards the recognition of "equality rights", Madam Justice L'Heuereux-Dubé posed a number of rhetorical questions for consideration by the participants at the Conference.

It should be noted that the major quote attributed by Mr. Morton to Madam Justice L'Heureux-Dubé does not appear in the text of either address. What is quoted may be a summary of what a reporter thought she said. Moreover, Madam Justice L'Heureux-Dubé cannot be faulted for the decision of the conveners to also invite Mr. Justice Kirby of the High Court of Australia to appear on the same program with her, as Mr. Morton suggests. Chief Justice McEachern finds no valid grounds for criticism of Madam Justice L'Heureux-Dubé resulting from her remarks at the London conference.

Turning to the Conference at Queen's University, Chief Justice McEachern observes that this address includes reference to many learned authors, scholars and historical events, including Anatole France, Aristotle, Martin Luther, John Locke, Rousseau, John Stuart Mill, Immanuel Kant, Simone de Beauvoir, The Universal Declaration of Rights, The International Covenant on Civil and Political Rights, the Ontario Law Reform Commission, and several landmark decisions of the Supreme Court of Canada, all for the purpose of tracing the evolution of Canadian law towards the concept of greater equality in Canadian society. Madam Justice L'Heureux-Dubé is jurisprudentially correct when she concludes towards the end of her address that: "The last ten years have seen a tremendous change in recognition of the legal status of non-traditional relationships in Canadian law and, more generally, in the approach taken to equality rights by the courts". She added that: "The next ten years are full of promise." While the meaning of this sentence is not entirely clear, there can be no doubt that there will be further developments in the progress of the law towards the goal of equality, which is hardly a surprising statement to anyone who understands the history Madam Justice L'Heureux-Dubé had already described in her remarks.

Chief Justice McEachern adds that a scholarly attempt by a respected jurist to trace the recent development of the law of equality in post-*Charter* Canada at an academically sponsored Conference could rarely be characterized as misconduct, although he recognizes that there is always a tension between judicial reticence to make public pronouncements on any subject and judicial contributions to legal education and learned discussion about matters of public importance.

Chief Justice McEachern adds that, as with the London Conference, the remarks of Madam Justice L'Heureux-Dubé at Queen's University were largely an historical review of Canadian equality law, interspersed with a few brief comments about what that history suggests for the future. Some judges may have said less, some may have said more, and some may have said nothing at all. The comments of Madam Justice L'Heureux-Dubé in this regard are hardly enough to establish an inference that she would not judge future cases fairly. In this connection, Chief Justice McEachern notes that a copy of your complaint was sent to the Chief Justice of Canada for comments. Chief Justice McLachlin has replied: "My only comment is that over the ten years during which I have sat with Madam Justice L'Heureux-Dubé, I can recall no case in which preconceived bias or views as to the outcome prevented her from impartially considering the evidence and the applicable law. I fully expect that she will continue to do so in the future, regardless of the nature of the issues that present themselves".

Chief Justice McEachern recognizes that some, possibly including yourself, may think judges should take no part in academic dialogue about these matters, while others believe judicial participation is useful and healthy. It is clear that the history and analysis of existing law furnished by Madam Justice L'Heureux-Dubé was perfectly proper. In the ultimate analysis, therefore, the question is whether the balance of her remarks should be characterized either as misconduct, or as conduct incapacitating her from the due execution of the office of judge. Keeping in mind the foregoing comment of the Chief Justice of Canada and the right to any litigant to request Madam Justice L'Heureux-Dubé to recuse herself in any future case, Chief Justice McEachern has concluded that no further action is required in this matter. Accordingly, this file will be closed with this reply.

Yours sincerely,

Jeannie Thomas
Executive Director

5.6

Reference re Remuneration of Judges of the Provincial Court (P.E.I.)
Supreme Court of Canada (1997)

The Chief Justice –

I. Introduction

The four appeals handed down today – *Reference re Remuneration of Judges of the Provincial Court of Prince Edward Island* , *Reference re Independence and Impartiality of Judges of the Provincial Court of Prince Edward Island, R. v. Campbell, R. v. Ekmecic* and *R. v. Wickman,* and *Manitoba Provincial Judges Assn.* v. *Manitoba (Minister of Justice)* – raise a range of issues relating to the independence of provincial courts, but are united by a single issue: whether and how the guarantee of judicial independence in s.11(*d*) of the *Canadian Charter of Rights and Freedoms* restricts the manner by and the extent to which provincial governments and legislatures can reduce the salaries of provincial court judges. Moreover, in my respectful opinion, they implicate the broader question of whether the constitutional home of judicial independence lies in the express provisions of the *Constitution Acts, 1867 to 1982*, or exterior to the sections of those documents. I am cognizant of the length of these reasons. Although it would have been possible to issue a set of separate but interrelated judgments, since many of the parties intervened in each other's cases, I find it convenient to deal with these four appeals in one set of reasons. Given the length and complexity of these reasons, I thought it would be useful and convenient to provide a summary, which is found at para. 287. [*Ed. note:* pp. 227–28 of this book.]

The question of judicial independence, not only under s.11(*d*) of the *Charter*, but also under ss.96–100 of the *Constitution Act, 1867*, has been the subject of previous decisions of this Court. However, the aspect of judicial independence which is engaged by the impugned reductions in salary – financial security – has only been dealt with in any depth by *Valente* v. *The Queen*, [1985], and *Beauregard* v. *Canada*, [1986]. The facts of the current appeals require that we address questions which were left unanswered by those earlier decisions.

Valente was the first decision in which this Court gave meaning to s.11(*d*)'s guarantee of judicial independence and impartiality. In that judgment, this Court held that s.11(*d*) encompassed a guarantee, *inter alia*, of financial security for the courts and tribunals which come within the scope of that provision. This Court, however, only turned its mind to the nature of financial security which is required for *individual* judges to enjoy judicial independence. It held that for individual judges to be independent, their salaries must be secured by law, and not be subject to arbitrary interference by the executive. The question which arises in these appeals, by contrast, is the content of the *collective* or *institutional* dimension of financial security for judges of provincial courts, which was not at issue in *Valente*. In particular, I will address the institutional arrangements which are comprehended by the guarantee of collective financial security.

Almost a year after *Valente* was heard, but before it had been handed down, this Court heard the appeal in *Beauregard*. In that case, the Court rejected a constitutional challenge to federal legislation establishing a contributory pension scheme for superior court judges. It had been argued that the pension scheme amounted to a reduction in the salaries of those judges during their term of office, and for that reason contravened judicial independence and was beyond the powers of Parliament. Although the Court found that there had been no salary reduction on the facts of the case, the judgment has been taken to stand for the proposition that salary reductions which are "non-discriminatory" are not unconstitutional.

There are four questions which arise from *Beauregard*, and which are central to the disposition of these appeals. The first question is what kinds of salary reductions are consistent with judicial independence – only those which apply to all citizens equally, or also those which only apply to persons paid from the public purse, or those which just apply to judges. The second question is whether the same principles which apply to salary *reductions* also govern salary *increases* and salary *freezes*. The third question is whether *Beauregard*, which was decided under s.100 of the *Constitution Act, 1867*, a provision which only guarantees the independence of *superior court* judges, applies to the interpretation of s.11(*d*), which protects a range of courts and tribunals, including *provincial court* judges. The fourth and final question is whether the Constitution – through the vehicle of s. 100 or s.11(*d*) – imposes some *substantive limits* on the extent of permissible salary reductions for the judiciary.

...

II. Facts

[*Summary:* In P.E.I., the province, as part of its budget deficit reduction plan, enacted the *Public Sector Pay Reduction Act* and reduced the salaries of Provincial Court judges and others paid from the public purse in the province. Following the pay reduction, numerous accused challenged the constitutionality of their proceedings in the Provincial Court, alleging that as a result of the salary reductions, the court had lost its status as an independent and impartial tribunal under s.11(*d*) of the *Charter*. The Lieutenant Governor referred a series of questions to the Appeal Division concerning all three elements of the judicial independence of the Provincial Court: financial security, security of tenure, and administrative independence. The Appeal Division answered most of the questions to the effect that the Provincial Court was independent and impartial.

In Alberta, three accused in separate criminal proceedings in Provincial Court challenged the constitutionality of their trials. They each argued that, as a result of the salary reduction of the Provincial Court judges pursuant to the *Payment to Provincial Judges Amendment Regulation* the Provincial Court was not an independent and impartial tribunal for the purposes of s.11(*d*). The superior court judge found that the salary reduction of the Provincial Court judges was unconstitutional because it was not part of an overall economic measure – an exception he narrowly defined. The Appeal Court refused to review this holding.

In Manitoba, the enactment of *The Public Sector Reduced Work Week and Compensation Management Act* ("Bill 22"), as part of a plan to reduce the province's deficit, led to the reduction of the salary of Provincial Court judges and of a large number of public sector employees. The Provincial Court judges through their Association launched a constitutional challenge to the salary cut, alleging that it infringed their judicial independence as protected by s.11(*d*) of the *Charter*. They also argued that the salary reduction was unconstitutional because it effectively suspended the operation of the Judicial Compensation Committee ("JCC"), a body created by *The Provincial Court Act* whose task it is to issue reports on judges' salaries to the legislature. The trial judge held that the salary reduction was unconstitutional because it was not part of an overall economic measure which affects all citizens. The reduction was part of a plan to reduce the provincial deficit solely through a reduction in government expenditures. The Court of Appeal rejected all the constitutional challenges.]

IV. Financial Security
A. Introduction: The Unwritten Basis of Judicial Independence

These appeals were all argued on the basis of s.11(*d*), the *Charter's* guarantee of judicial independence and impartiality. From its express terms, s.11(*d*) is a right of limited application – it only applies to persons accused of offences. Despite s.11(*d*)'s limited scope, there is no doubt that the appeals can and should be resolved on the basis of that provision....

Nevertheless, while the thrust of the submissions was directed at s.11(*d*), the respondent[s] ... addressed the larger question of where the constitutional home of judicial independence lies, to which I now turn. Notwithstanding the presence of s.11(*d*) of the *Charter*, and ss.96-100 of the *Constitution Act, 1867*, I am of the view that judicial independence is at root an *unwritten* constitutional principle, in the sense that it is exterior to the particular sections of the *Constitution Acts*. The existence of that principle, whose origins can be traced to the *Act of Settlement* of 1701, is recognized and affirmed by the preamble to the *Constitution Act, 1867*. The specific provisions of the *Constitution Acts, 1867 to 1982*, merely "elaborate that principle in the institutional apparatus which they create or contemplate": *Switzman v. Elbling*, [1957].

I arrive at this conclusion, in part, by considering the tenability of the opposite position – that the Canadian Constitution already contains explicit provisions which are directed at the protection of judicial independence, and that those provisions are exhaustive of the matter. Section 11(*d*) of the *Charter*, as I have mentioned above, protects the independence of a wide range of courts and tribunals which exercise jurisdiction over offences. Moreover, since well before the enactment of the *Charter*, ss.96-100 of the *Constitution Act, 1867*, separately and in combination, have protected and continue to protect the independence of provincial superior courts. More specifically, s.99 guarantees the security of tenure of superior court judges; s.100 guarantees the financial security of judges of the superior, district, and county courts; and s.96 has come to guarantee the core jurisdiction of superior, district, and county courts against legislative encroachment, which I also take to be a guarantee of judicial independence.

However, upon closer examination, there are serious limitations to the view that the express provisions of the Constitution comprise an exhaustive and definitive code for the protection of judicial independence. The first and most serious problem is that the range of courts whose independence is protected by the written provisions of the Constitution contains large gaps. Sections 96-100, for example, only protect the independence of judges of the superior, district, and county courts, and even then, not in a uniform or consistent manner. Thus, while ss.96 and 100 protect the core jurisdiction and the financial security, respectively, of all three types of courts (superior, district, and county), s.99, on its terms, only protects the security of tenure of superior court judges. Moreover, ss.96-100 do not apply to provincially appointed inferior courts, otherwise known as provincial courts.

To some extent, the gaps in the scope of protection provided by ss.96-100 are offset by the application of s.11(*d*), which applies to a range of tribunals and courts, including provincial courts. However, by its express terms, s.11(*d*) is limited in scope as well – it only extends the envelope of constitutional protection to bodies which exercise *jurisdiction over offences*. As a result, when those courts exercise civil jurisdiction, their independence would not seem to be guaranteed. The independence of provincial courts adjudicating in family law matters, for example, would not be constitutionally protected. The independence of superior courts, by contrast, when hearing exactly the same cases, would be constitutionally guaranteed.

...

The proposition that the Canadian Constitution embraces unwritten norms was recently confirmed by this Court in *New Brunswick Broadcasting Co.* v. *Nova Scotia (Speaker of the House of Assembly)*, [1993]. In that case, the Court found it constitutional for the Nova Scotia House of Assembly to refuse the media the right to record and broadcast legislative proceedings. The media advanced a claim based on s.2(*b*) of the *Charter*, which protects, *inter alia*, "freedom of the press and other media of communication." McLachlin J., speaking for a majority of the Court, found that the refusal of the Assembly was an exercise of that Assembly's unwritten legislative privileges, that the

Constitution of Canada constitutionalized those privileges, and that the constitutional status of those privileges therefore precluded the application of the *Charter*.

...

In my opinion, the existence of many of the unwritten rules of the Canadian Constitution can be explained by reference to the preamble of the *Constitution Act, 1867*. The relevant paragraph states in full:

> Whereas the Provinces of Canada, Nova Scotia, and New Brunswick have expressed their Desire to be federally united into One Dominion under the Crown of the United Kingdom of Great Britain and Ireland, with a Constitution similar in Principle to that of the United Kingdom:

Although the preamble has been cited by this Court on many occasions, its legal effect has never been fully explained. On the one hand, although the preamble is clearly part of the Constitution, it is equally clear that it "has no enacting force": *Reference re Resolution to Amend the Constitution*, [1981]. In other words, strictly speaking, it is not a source of positive law, in contrast to the provisions which follow it.

But the preamble does have important legal effects. Under normal circumstances, preambles can be used to identify the purpose of a statute, and also as an aid to construing ambiguous statutory language. The preamble to the *Constitution Act, 1867*, certainly operates in this fashion. However, in my view, it goes even further. In the words of Rand J., the preamble articulates "the political theory which the Act embodies": *Switzman* [1957]. It recognizes and affirms the basic principles which are the very source of the substantive provisions of the *Constitution Act, 1867*. As I have said above, those provisions merely elaborate those organizing principles in the institutional apparatus they create or contemplate. As such, the preamble is not only a key to construing the express provisions of the *Constitution Act, 1867*, but also invites the use of those organizing principles to fill out gaps in the express terms of the constitutional scheme. It is the means by which the underlying logic of the Act can be given the force of law.

What are the organizing principles of the *Constitution Act, 1867*, as expressed in the preamble? The preamble speaks of the desire of the founding provinces "to be federally united into One Dominion," and thus, addresses the structure of the division of powers. Moreover, by its reference to "a Constitution similar in Principle to that of the United Kingdom," the preamble indicates that the legal and institutional structure of constitutional democracy in Canada should be similar to that of the legal regime out of which the Canadian Constitution emerged. To my mind, both of these aspects of the preamble explain many of the cases in which the Court has, through the normal process of constitutional interpretation, stated some fundamental rules of Canadian constitutional law which are not found in the express terms of the *Constitution Act, 1867*.

I turn first to the jurisprudence under the division of powers, to illustrate how the process of gap-filling has occurred and how it can be understood by reference to the preamble.

...

These examples – the doctrines of full faith and credit and paramountcy, the remedial innovation of suspended declarations of invalidity, the recognition of the constitutional status of the privileges of provincial legislatures, the vesting of the power to regulate political speech within federal jurisdiction, and the inferral of implied limits on legislative sovereignty with respect to political speech – illustrate the special legal effect of the preamble. The preamble identifies the organizing principles of the *Constitution Act, 1867*, and invites the courts to turn those principles into the premises of a constitutional argument that culminates in the filling of gaps in the express terms of the constitutional text.

The same approach applies to the protection of judicial independence. In fact, this point was already decided in *Beauregard*, and, unless and until it is reversed, we are governed by that decision today. In that case (at p. 72), a unanimous Court held that the preamble of the *Constitution Act, 1867*, and in particular, its reference to "a Constitution similar in Principle to that of the United Kingdom", was "textual recognition" of the principle of judicial independence. Although in that case, it fell to us to interpret s.100 of the *Constitution Act, 1867*, the comments I have just reiterated were not limited by reference to that provision, and the courts which it protects.

The historical origins of the protection of judicial independence in the United Kingdom, and thus in the Canadian Constitution, can be traced to the *Act of Settlement* of 1701. As we said in *Valente*, [1985], that Act was the "historical inspiration" for the judicature provisions of the *Constitution Act, 1867*. Admittedly, the Act only extends protection to judges of the English superior courts. However, our Constitution has evolved over time. In the same way that our understanding of rights and freedoms has grown, such that they have now been expressly entrenched through the enactment of the *Constitution Act, 1982*, so too has judicial independence grown into a principle that now extends to all courts, not just the superior courts of this country.

I also support this conclusion on the basis of the presence of s.11(*d*) of the *Charter*, an express provision which protects the independence of provincial court judges only when those courts exercise jurisdiction in relation to offences. As I said earlier, the express provisions of the Constitution should be understood as elaborations of the underlying, unwritten, and organizing principles found in the preamble to the *Constitution Act, 1867*. Even though s.11(*d*) is found in the newer part of our Constitution, the *Charter*, it can be understood in this way, since the Constitution is to be read as a unified whole....

In conclusion, the express provisions of the *Constitution Act, 1867* and the *Charter* are not an exhaustive written code for the protection of judicial independence in Canada. Judicial independence is an unwritten norm, recognized and affirmed by the preamble to the *Constitution Act, 1867*. In fact, it is in that preamble, which serves as the grand entrance hall to the castle of the Constitution, that the true source of our commitment to this foundational principle is located. However, since the parties and interveners have grounded their arguments in s.11(*d*), I will resolve these appeals by reference to that provision.

B. Section 11(d) of the *Charter*

As I mentioned earlier, these appeals were heard together because they all raise the question of whether and how s.11(*d*) of the *Charter* restricts the manner by and extent to which provincial governments and legislatures can reduce the salaries of provincial court judges. Before I can address this specific question, I must make some general comments about the jurisprudence under s.11(*d*).

The starting point for my discussion is *Valente*, where in a unanimous judgment this Court laid down the interpretive framework for s.11(*d*)'s guarantee of judicial independence and impartiality. Le Dain J., speaking for the Court, began by drawing a distinction between impartiality and independence. Later cases have referred to this distinction as "a firm line." Impartiality was defined as "a *state of mind or attitude* of the tribunal in relation to the issues and the parties in a particular case." It was tied to the traditional concern for the "absence of bias, actual or perceived". Independence, by contrast, focussed on the *status* of the court or tribunal. In particular, Le Dain J. emphasized that the independence protected by s.11(*d*) flowed from "the traditional constitutional value of judicial independence," which he defined in terms of the *relationship* of the court or tribunal "to others, particularly the executive branch of government" (p. 685).

...

The three core characteristics identified by Le Dain J. are *security of tenure, financial security,* and *administrative independence*....

...

The three *core characteristics* of judicial independence – security of tenure, financial security, and administrative independence – should be contrasted with what I have termed the two *dimensions* of judicial independence. In *Valente*, Le Dain J. drew a distinction between two dimensions of judicial independence, the *individual independence* of a judge and the *institutional or collective independence* of the court or tribunal of which that judge is a member. In other words, while individual independence attaches to individual judges, institutional or collective independence attaches to the court or tribunal as an institutional entity....

...

What I do propose, however, is that financial security has *both* an individual and an institutional or collective dimension. *Valente* only talked about the individual dimension of financial security, when it stated that salaries must be established by law and not allow for executive interference in a manner which could "affect the independence of the individual judge."

...

However, *Valente* did not preclude a finding that, and did not decide whether, financial security has a collective or institutional dimension as well. That is the issue we must address today. But in order to determine whether financial security has a collective or institutional dimension, and if so, what collective or institutional financial security looks like, we must first understand what the institutional independence of the judiciary is....

C. Institutional Independence

As I have mentioned, the concept of the institutional independence of the judiciary was discussed in *Valente*. However, other than stating that institutional independence is different from individual independence, the concept was left largely undefined. In *Beauregard* this Court expanded the meaning of that term, once again by contrasting it with individual independence. Individual independence was referred to as the "historical core" of judicial independence, and was defined as "the complete liberty of individual judges to hear and decide the cases that come before them." It is necessary for the fair and just adjudication of individual disputes. By contrast, the institutional independence of the judiciary was said to arise out of the position of the courts as organs of and protectors "of the Constitution and the fundamental values embodied in it – rule of law, fundamental justice, equality, preservation of the democratic process, to name perhaps the most important." Institutional independence enables the courts to fulfill that second and distinctly constitutional role.

...

But the institutional independence of the judiciary reflects a deeper commitment to the separation of powers between and amongst the legislative, executive, and judicial organs of government....

What follows as a consequence of the link between institutional independence and the separation of powers I will turn to shortly. The point I want to make first is that the institutional role demanded of the judiciary under our Constitution is a role which we now expect of provincial court judges. I am well aware that provincial courts are creatures of statute, and that their existence is not required by the Constitution. However, there is no doubt that these statutory courts play a critical role in enforcing the provisions and protecting the values of the Constitution. Inasmuch as that role has grown over the last few years, it is clear therefore that provincial courts must be granted some institutional independence.

...

D. Collective or Institutional Financial Security

...

Given the importance of the institutional or collective dimension of judicial independence generally, what is the institutional or collective dimension of financial security? To my mind, financial security for the courts as an institution has three components, which all flow from the constitutional imperative that, to the extent possible, the relationship between the judiciary and the other branches of government be *depoliticized*. As I explain below, in the context of institutional or collective financial security, this imperative demands that the courts both be free and appear to be free from political interference through economic manipulation by the other branches of government, and that they not become entangled in the politics of remuneration from the public purse.

I begin by stating these components in summary fashion.

First, as a general constitutional principle, the salaries of provincial court judges can be reduced, increased, or frozen, either as part of an overall economic measure which affects the salaries of all or some persons who are remunerated from public funds, or as part of a measure which is directed at provincial court judges as a class. However, any changes to or freezes in judicial remuneration require prior recourse to a special process, which is independent, effective, and objective, for determining judicial remuneration, to avoid the possibility of, or the appearance of, political interference through economic manipulation. What judicial independence requires is an independent body, along the lines of the bodies that exist in many provinces and at the federal level to set or recommend the levels of judicial remuneration. Those bodies are often referred to as commissions, and for the sake of convenience, we will refer to the independent body required by s.11(*d*) as a commission as well. Governments are constitutionally bound to go through the commission process. The recommendations of the commission would not be binding on the executive or the legislature. Nevertheless, though those recommendations are non-binding, they should not be set aside lightly, and, if the executive or the legislature chooses to depart from them, it has to justify its decision – if need be, in a court of law. As I explain below, when governments propose to single out judges as a class for a pay reduction, the burden of justification will be heavy.

Second, under no circumstances is it permissible for the judiciary – not only collectively through representative organizations, but also as individuals – to engage in negotiations over remuneration with the executive or representatives of the legislature. Any such negotiations would be fundamentally at odds with judicial independence. As I explain below, salary negotiations are indelibly political, because remuneration from the public purse is an inherently political issue. Moreover, negotiations would undermine the appearance of judicial independence, because the Crown is almost always a party to criminal prosecutions before provincial courts, and because salary negotiations engender a set of expectations about the behaviour of parties to those negotiations which are inimical to judicial independence.

...

Third, and finally, any reductions to judicial remuneration, including *de facto* reductions through the erosion of judicial salaries by inflation, cannot take those salaries below a basic minimum level of remuneration which is required for the office of a judge. Public confidence in the independence of the judiciary would be undermined if judges were paid at such a low rate that they could be perceived as susceptible to political pressure through economic manipulation, as is witnessed in many countries.

...

These different components of the institutional financial security of the courts inhere, in my view, in a fundamental principle of the Canadian Constitution, the separation of powers. As I discussed above, the institutional independence of the courts is inextricably bound up with the separation of powers, because in order to guarantee that the courts can protect the Constitution, they must be protected by a set of objective guarantees against intrusions by the executive and legislative branches of government.

...

What is at issue here is the character of the relationships between the legislature and the executive on the one hand, and the judiciary on the other. These relationships should be *depoliticized*. When I say that those relationships are depoliticized,... I mean ... the legislature and executive cannot, and cannot appear to, exert political pressure on the judiciary, and conversely, that members of the judiciary should exercise reserve in speaking out publicly on issues of general public policy that are or have the potential to come before the courts, that are the subject of political debate, and which do not relate to the proper administration of justice.

...

The depoliticized relationships I have been describing create difficult problems when it comes to judicial remuneration. On the one hand, remuneration from the public purse is an inherently political concern, in the sense that it implicates general public policy....

...

With respect to the judiciary, the determination of the level of remuneration from the public purse is political in another sense, because it raises the spectre of political interference through economic manipulation. An unscrupulous government could utilize its authority to set judges' salaries as a vehicle to influence the course and outcome of adjudication. Admittedly, this would be very different from the kind of political interference with the judiciary by the Stuart Monarchs in England which is the historical source of the constitutional concern for judicial independence in the Anglo-American tradition. However, the threat to judicial independence would be as significant....

...

(2) The Components of Institutional or Collective Financial Security
(a) Judicial Salaries Can Be Reduced, Increased, or Frozen, but not Without Recourse to an Independent, Effective and Objective Commission…

(ii) Independent, Effective and Objective Commissions

Although provincial executives and legislatures, as the case may be, are constitutionally permitted to change or freeze judicial remuneration, those decisions have the potential to jeopardize judicial independence. The imperative of protecting the courts from political interference through economic manipulation is served by *interposing* an independent body – a judicial compensation commission – between the judiciary and the other branches of government. The constitutional function of this body is to depoliticize the process of determining changes or freezes to judicial remuneration. This objective would be achieved by setting that body the specific task of issuing a report on the salaries and benefits of judges to the executive and the legislature, responding to the particular proposals made by the government to increase, reduce, or freeze judges' salaries.

I do not wish to dictate the exact shape and powers of the independent commission here. These questions of detailed institutional design are better left to the executive and the legislature, although it would be helpful if they consulted the provincial judiciary prior to creating these bodies. Moreover, different provinces should be free to choose procedures and arrangements which are suitable to their needs and particular circumstances. Within the parameters of s.11(*d*), there must be scope for local choice, because jurisdiction over provincial courts has been assigned to the provinces by the *Constitution Act, 1867*. This is one reason why we held in *Valente, supra*, at p. 694, that "[t]he standard of judicial independence for purposes of s.11(*d*) cannot be a standard of uniform provisions".

Before proceeding to lay down the general guidelines for these independent commissions, I must briefly comment on *Valente*. There is language in that decision which suggests that s.11(*d*) does not require the existence of independent commissions to deal with the issue of judicial remuneration. In particular, Le Dain J. stated that he did "not consider the existence of such a committee to be essential to security of salary for purposes of s.11(*d*)." However, that question was not before the Court, since Ontario, the province where *Valente* arose, had an independent commission in operation at the time of the decision. As a result, the remarks of Le Dain J. were strictly *obiter dicta*, and do not bind the courts below and need not today be overruled by this Court.

The commissions charged with the responsibility of dealing with the issue of judicial remuneration must meet three general criteria. They must be independent, objective, and effective.

…

First and foremost, these commissions must be *independent*. The rationale for independence flows from the constitutional function performed by these commissions – they serve as an institutional sieve, to prevent the setting or freezing of judicial remuneration from being used as a means to exert political pressure through the economic manipulation of the judiciary. It would undermine that goal if the independent commissions were under the control of the executive or the legislature.

...

What s.11(*d*) requires instead is that the appointments not be entirely controlled by any one of the branches of government. The commission should have members appointed by the judiciary, on the one hand, and the legislature and the executive, on the other. The judiciary's nominees may, for example, be chosen either by the provincial judges' association, as is the case in Ontario, or by the Chief Judge of the Provincial Court in consultation with the provincial judges' association, as in British Columbia. The exact mechanism is for provincial governments to determine. Likewise, the nominees of the executive and the legislature may be chosen by the Lieutenant Governor in Council, although appointments by the Attorney General as in British Columbia (*Provincial Court Act*, s.7.1(2)), or conceivably by the legislature itself, are entirely permissible.

In addition to being independent, the salary commissions must be *objective*. They must make recommendations on judges' remuneration by reference to objective criteria, not political expediencies...

Finally, and most importantly, the commission must also be *effective*. The effectiveness of these bodies must be guaranteed in a number of ways. First, there is a constitutional obligation for governments not to change (either by reducing or increasing) or freeze judicial remuneration until they have received the report of the salary commission. Changes or freezes of this nature secured without going through the commission process are unconstitutional. The commission must convene to consider and report on the proposed change or freeze. Second, in order to guard against the possibility that government inaction might lead to a reduction in judges' real salaries because of inflation, and that inaction could therefore be used as a means of economic manipulation, the commission must convene if a fixed period of time has elapsed since its last report, in order to consider the adequacy of judges' salaries in light of the cost of living and other relevant factors, and issue a recommendation in its report. Although the exact length of the period is for provincial governments to determine, I would suggest a period of three to five years.

Third, the reports of the commission must have a meaningful effect on the determination of judicial salaries. Provinces which have created salary commissions have adopted three different ways of giving such effect to these reports. One is to make a report of the commission binding, so that the government is bound by the commission's decision....

The model mandated as a constitutional minimum by s.11(*d*) is somewhat different from the ones I have just described. My starting point is that s.11(*d*) does not require that the reports of the commission be binding, because decisions about the allocation of public resources are generally within the realm of the legislature, and through it, the executive. The expenditure of public funds, as I said above, is an inherently political matter....

For the same reasons, s.11(*d*) does not require a negative resolution procedure, although it does not preclude it....

However, whereas the binding decision and negative resolution models exceed the standard set by s.11(*d*), the positive resolution model *on its own* does not meet that standard, because it requires no response to the commission's report at all. The fact that the report need not be binding does not mean that the executive and the legislature should be free to ignore it. On the contrary, for collective or institutional financial security to have any meaning at all, and to be taken seriously, the commission process must have a meaningful impact on the decision to set judges' salaries.

What judicial independence requires is that the executive or the legislature, whichever is vested with the authority to set judicial remuneration under provincial legislation, must formally respond to the contents of the commission's report within a specified amount of time. Before it can set judges' salaries, the executive must issue a report in which it outlines its response to the commission's recommendations. If the legislature is involved in the process, the report of the commission must be laid before the legislature, when it is in session, with due diligence. If the legislature is not in session, the government may wait until a new sitting commences. The legislature should deal with the report directly, with due diligence and reasonable dispatch.

Furthermore, if after turning its mind to the report of the commission, the executive or the legislature, as applicable, chooses not to accept one or more of the recommendations in that report, it must be prepared to justify this decision, if necessary in a court of law. The reasons for this decision would be found either in the report of the executive responding to the contents of the commission's report, or in the recitals to the resolution of the legislature on the matter. An unjustified decision could potentially lead to a finding of unconstitutionality. The need for public justification, to my mind, emerges from one of the purposes of s.11(*d*)'s guarantee of judicial independence – to ensure public confidence in the justice system. A decision by the executive or the legislature, to change or freeze judges' salaries, and then to disagree with a recommendation not to act on that decision made by a constitutionally mandated body whose existence is premised on the need to preserve the independence of the judiciary, will only be legitimate and not be viewed as being indifferent or hostile to judicial independence, if it is supported by reasons.

...

I hasten to add that these comments should not be construed as endorsing or establishing a general duty to give reasons, either in the constitutional or in the administrative law context. Moreover, I wish to clarify that the standard of justification required under s.11(*d*) is not the same as that required under s.1 of the *Charter*. Section 1 imposes a very rigorous standard of justification....

The standard of justification here, by contrast, is one of simple *rationality*. It requires that the government articulate a legitimate reason for why it has chosen to depart from the recommendation of the commission, and if applicable, why it has chosen to treat judges differently from other persons paid from the public purse. A reviewing court does not engage in a searching analysis of the relationship between ends and means, which is the hallmark of a s.1 analysis. However, the absence of this analysis does not mean that the standard of justification is ineffectual. On the contrary, it has two aspects. First, it screens out decisions with respect to judicial remuneration which are based on purely political considerations, or which are enacted for discriminatory reasons. Changes to or freezes in remuneration can only be justified for reasons which relate to the public interest, broadly understood. Second, if judicial review is sought, a reviewing court must inquire into the reasonableness of the factual foundation of the claim made by the government, similar to the way that we have evaluated whether there was an economic emergency in Canada in our jurisprudence under the division of powers (*Reference re Anti-Inflation Act*, [1976]. [*Ed Note:* This decision is the subject of Reading 10.4]

Although the test of justification – one of simple rationality – must be met by all measures which affect judicial remuneration and which depart from the recommendation of the salary commission, some will satisfy that test more easily than others, because they pose less of a danger of being used as a means of economic manipulation, and hence of political interference. Across-the-board measures which affect substantially every person who is paid from the public purse, in my opinion, are *prima facie* rational. For example, an across-the-board reduction in salaries that includes judges will typically be designed to effectuate the government's overall fiscal priorities, and hence will usually be aimed at furthering some sort of larger public interest. By contrast, a measure directed at judges alone may require a somewhat fuller explanation, precisely because it is directed at judges alone.

By laying down a set of guidelines to assist provincial legislatures in designing judicial compensation commissions, I do not intend to lay down a particular institutional framework in constitutional stone. What s.11(*d*) requires is an institutional sieve between the judiciary and the other branches of government. Commissions are merely a means to that end. In the future, governments may create new institutional arrangements which can serve the same end, but in a different way. As long as those institutions meet the three cardinal requirements of independence, effectiveness, and objectivity, s.11(*d*) will be complied with.

(b) No Negotiations on Judicial Remuneration Between the Judiciary and the Executive and Legislature

Negotiations over remuneration are a central feature of the landscape of public sector labour relations. The evidence before this Court (anecdotal and otherwise) suggests that salary negotiations have been occurring between provincial court judges and provincial governments in a number of provinces. However, from a constitutional standpoint, this is inappropriate, for two related reasons. First, as I have argued above, negotiations for remuneration from the public purse are indelibly political. For the judiciary to engage in salary negotiations would undermine public confidence in the impartiality and independence of the judiciary, and thereby frustrate a major purpose of s.11(*d*)....

...

Second, negotiations are deeply problematic because the Crown is almost always a party to criminal prosecutions in provincial courts. Negotiations by the judges who try those cases put them in a conflict of interest, because they would be negotiating with a litigant. The appearance of independence would be lost, because salary negotiations bring with them a whole set of expectations about the behaviour of the parties to those negotiations which are inimical to judicial independence. The major expectation is of give and take between the parties. By analogy with *Généreux*, the reasonable person might conclude that judges would alter the manner in which they adjudicate cases in order to curry favour with the executive....

...

(c) Judicial Salaries May Not Fall Below a Minimum Level

Finally, I turn to the question of whether the Constitution – through the vehicle of either s.100 or s.11(*d*) – imposes some substantive limits on the extent of salary reductions for the judiciary. This point was left unanswered by *Beauregard*. I note at the outset that neither the parties nor the interveners submitted that judicial salaries were close to those minimum limits here. However, since I have decided to lay down the parameters of the guarantee of collective or institutional financial security in these reasons, I will address this issue briefly.

I have no doubt that the Constitution protects judicial salaries from falling below an acceptable minimum level. The reason it does is for financial security to protect the judiciary from political interference through economic manipulation, and to thereby ensure public confidence in the administration of justice. If salaries are too low, there is always the danger, however speculative, that members of the judiciary could be tempted to adjudicate cases in a particular way in order to secure a higher salary from the executive or the legislature or to receive benefits from one of the litigants. Perhaps more importantly, in the context of s.11(*d*), there is the perception that this could happen. As Professor Friedland has written:

> We do not want judges put in a position of temptation, hoping to get some possible financial advantage if they favour one side or the other. Nor do we want the public to contemplate this as a possibility.

I want to make it very clear that the guarantee of a minimum salary is not meant for the benefit of the judiciary. Rather, financial security is a means to the end of judicial independence, and is therefore for the benefit of the public....

...

I offer three final observations. First, I do not address the question of what the minimum acceptable level of judicial remuneration is. We shall answer that question if and when the need arises.... Second, although the basic minimum salary provides financial security against reductions in remuneration by the executive or the legislature, it is also a protection against the erosion of judicial salaries by inflation.

Finally, I want to emphasize that the guarantee of a minimum acceptable level of judicial remuneration is not a device to shield the courts from the effects of deficit reduction. Nothing would be more damaging to the reputation of the judiciary and the administration of justice than a perception that judges were not shouldering their share of the burden in difficult economic times. Rather, as I said above, financial security is one of the means whereby the independence of an organ of the Constitution is ensured. Judges are officers of the Constitution, and hence their remuneration must have some constitutional status.

VI. Section 1

[*Ed. note:* The Chief Justice ruled that since neither Alberta nor P.E.I. presented the Court with any Section 1 arguments, their violations of s.11(*d*) cannot be justified. Manitoba did provide a section 1 defence, but the Chief Justice rejected it as inadequate.]

VIII. Summary

Given the length and complexity of these reasons, I summarize the major principles governing the collective or institutional dimension of financial security:

1.   It is obvious to us that governments are free to reduce, increase, or freeze the salaries of provincial court judges, either as part of an overall economic measure which affects the salaries of all or some persons who are remunerated from public funds, or as part of a measure which is directed at provincial court judges as a class.

2.   Provinces are under a constitutional obligation to establish bodies which are independent, effective, and objective, according to the

criteria that I have laid down in these reasons. Any changes to or freezes in judicial remuneration require prior recourse to the independent body, which will review the proposed reduction or increase to, or freeze in, judicial remuneration. Any changes to or freezes in judicial remuneration made without prior recourse to the independent body are unconstitutional.

3.   As well, in order to guard against the possibility that government inaction could be used as a means of economic manipulation, by allowing judges' real wages to fall because of inflation, and in order to protect against the possibility that judicial salaries will fall below the adequate minimum guaranteed by judicial independence, the commission must convene if a fixed period of time (e.g. three to five years) has elapsed since its last report, in order to consider the adequacy of judges' salaries in light of the cost of living and other relevant factors.

4.   The recommendations of the independent body are non-binding. However, if the executive or legislature chooses to depart from those recommendations, it has to justify its decision according to a standard of simple rationality – if need be, in a court of law.

5.   Under no circumstances is it permissible for the judiciary to engage in negotiations over remuneration with the executive or representatives of the legislature. However, that does not preclude chief justices or judges, or bodies representing judges, from expressing concerns or making representations to governments regarding judicial remuneration.

...

La Forest J. (dissenting in part) –

I. Introduction

The primary issue raised in these appeals is a narrow one: has the reduction of the salaries of provincial court judges, in the circumstances of each of these cases, so affected the independence of these judges that persons "charged with an offence" before them are deprived of their right to "an independent and impartial tribunal" within the meaning of s.11(*d*) of the *Canadian Charter of Rights and Freedoms*? I have had the advantage of reading the reasons of the Chief Justice who sets forth the facts and history of the litigation. Although I agree with substantial portions of his reasons, I cannot concur with his conclusion that s.11(*d*) forbids governments from changing judges' salaries without first having recourse to the "judicial compensation commissions" he describes. Furthermore, I do not believe that s.11(*d*) prohibits salary discussions between governments and judges. In my view, reading these requirements into s.11(*d*) represents both an unjustified departure from established precedents and a partial usurpation of the provinces' power to set the salaries of inferior court judges pursuant to ss.92(4) and 92(14) of the *Constitution Act, 1867*. In addition to these issues, the Chief Justice deals with a number of other questions respecting the independence of provincial court judges that were raised by the parties to these appeals. I agree with his disposition of these issues.

But if the Chief Justice and I share a considerable measure of agreement on many of the issues raised by the parties, that cannot be said of his broad assertion concerning the protection provincially appointed judges exercising functions other than criminal jurisdiction are afforded by virtue of the preamble to the *Constitution Act, 1867*. Indeed I have grave reservations about the Court entering into a discussion of the matter in the present appeals. Only minimal reference was made to it by counsel who essentially argued the issues on the basis of s.11(*d*) of the *Charter* which guarantees that anyone charged with an offence is entitled to a fair hearing by "an independent and impartial tribunal." I observe that this protection afforded in relation to criminal proceedings is *expressly* provided by the *Charter*.

...

I am, therefore, deeply concerned that the Court is entering into a debate on this issue without the benefit of substantial argument. I am all the more troubled since the question involves the proper relationship between the political branches of government and the judicial branch, an issue on which judges can hardly be seen to be indifferent, especially as it concerns their own remuneration. In such circumstances, it is absolutely critical for the Court to tread carefully and avoid making far-reaching conclusions that are not necessary to decide the case before it. If the Chief Justice's discussion was of a merely marginal character.... I would abstain from commenting on it. After all, it is technically only *obiter dicta*. Nevertheless, in light of the importance that will necessarily be attached to his lengthy and sustained exegesis, I feel compelled to express my view.

II. The Effect of the Preamble to the *Constitution Act, 1867*

I emphasize at the outset that it is not my position that s.11(*d*) of the *Charter* and ss.96-100 of the *Constitution Act, 1867* comprise an exhaustive code of judicial independence. As I discuss briefly later, additional protection for judicial independence may inhere in other provisions of the Constitution. Nor do I deny that the Constitution embraces unwritten rules, including rules that find expression in the preamble of the *Constitution Act, 1867*.... I hasten to add that these rules really find their origin in specific provisions of the Constitution viewed in light of our constitutional heritage. In other words, what we are concerned with is the meaning to be attached to an expression used in a constitutional provision.

I take issue, however, with the Chief Justice's view that the preamble to the *Constitution Act, 1867* is a source of constitutional limitations on the power of legislatures to interfere with judicial independence. In *New Brunswick Broadcasting, supra*, this Court held that the privileges of the Nova Scotia legislature had constitutional status by virtue of the statement in the preamble expressing the desire to have "a Constitution similar in Principle to that of the United Kingdom." In reaching this conclusion, the Court examined the historical basis for the privileges of the British Parliament. That analysis established that the power of Parliament to exclude strangers was absolute, constitutional and immune from regulation by the courts. The effect of the preamble, the Court held, is to recognize and confirm that this long-standing principle of British constitutional law was continued or established in post-Confederation Canada.

There is no similar historical basis, in contrast, for the idea that Parliament cannot interfere with judicial independence. At the time of Confederation (and indeed to this day), the British Constitution did not contemplate the notion that Parliament was limited in its ability to deal with judges. The principle of judicial independence developed very gradually in Great Britain; see generally W. R. Lederman, "The Independence of the Judiciary." [*Ed. note*: reprinted in this book as Reading 5.1.] In the Norman era, judicial power was concentrated in the hands of the King and his immediate entourage (the *Curia Regis*). Subsequent centuries saw the emergence of specialized courts and a professional judiciary, and the king's participation in the judicial function had by the end of the fifteenth century effectively withered. Thus Blackstone in his *Commentaries* was able to state:

> ... at present, by the long and uniform usage of many ages, our kings have delegated their whole judicial power to the judges of their several courts; which are the grand depository of the fundamental laws of the kingdom, and have gained a known and stated jurisdiction, regulated by certain established rules, which the crown itself cannot now alter but by act of parliament.

Despite these advances, kings retained power to apply pressure on the judiciary to conform to their wishes through the exercise of the royal power of dismissal. Generally speaking, up to the seventeenth century, judges held office during the king's good pleasure (*durante bene placito*). This power to dismiss judges for political ends was wielded most liberally by the Stuart kings in the early seventeenth century as part of their effort to assert the royal prerogative powers over the authority of Parliament and the common law. It was thus natural that protection against this kind of arbitrary, executive interference became a priority in the post-revolution settlement. Efforts to secure such protection in legislation were scuttled in the two decades following 1688, but at the turn of the century William III gave his assent to the *Act of Settlement*, which took effect with the accession of George I in 1714. Section 3, para. 7 of that statute mandated that "Judges Commissions be made *Quandiu se bene gesserint* [during good behaviour], and their Salaries ascertained and established; but upon the Address of both Houses of Parliament it may be lawful to remove them". Further protection was provided by an Act of 1760, which ensured that the commissions of judges continued notwithstanding the demise of the king. Prior to this enactment, the governing rule provided that all royal appointees, including judges, vacated their offices upon the death of the king.

Various jurists have asserted that these statutes and their successors have come to be viewed as "constitutional" guarantees of an independent judiciary. Professor Lederman writes, for example, that it would be "unconstitutional" for the British Parliament to cut the salary of an individual superior court judge during his or her commission or to reduce the salaries of judges as a class to the extent that it threatened their independence. It has thus been suggested that the preamble to the *Constitution Act, 1867*, which expresses a desire to have a Constitution "similar in Principle to that of the United Kingdom" is a source of judicial independence in Canada.

Even if it is accepted that judicial independence had become a "constitutional" principle in Britain by 1867, it is important to understand the precise meaning of that term in British law. Unlike Canada, Great Britain does not have a written constitution. Under accepted British legal theory, Parliament is supreme. By this I mean that there are no limitations upon its legislative competence. As Dicey explains, Parliament has "under the English constitution, the right to make or unmake any law whatever; and, further, that no person or body is recognised by the law of England as having a right to override or set aside the legislation of Parliament." This principle has been modified somewhat in recent decades to take into account the effect of Great Britain's membership in the European Community, but ultimately, the British Parliament remains supreme.

The consequence of parliamentary supremacy is that judicial review of legislation is not possible. The courts have no power to hold an Act of Parliament invalid or unconstitutional. When it is said that a certain principle or convention is "constitutional," this does not mean that a statute violating that principle can be found to be *ultra vires* Parliament. As Lord Reid stated in *Madzimbamuto v. Lardner-Burke*, [1969]:

> It is often said that it would be unconstitutional for the United Kingdom Parliament to do certain things, meaning that the moral, political or other reasons against doing them are so strong that most people would regard it as highly improper if Parliament did these things. But that does not mean that it is beyond the power of Parliament to do such things. If Parliament chose to do any of them the courts could not hold the Act of Parliament invalid.

This fundamental principle is illustrated by the debate that occurred when members of the English judiciary complained to the Prime Minister in the early 1930s about legislation which reduced the salaries of judges, along with those of civil servants, by 20 percent as an emergency response to a financial crisis. Viscount Buckmaster, who vigorously resisted the notion that judges' salaries could be diminished during their term of office, admitted that Parliament was supreme and could repeal the *Act of Settlement* if it chose to do so. He only objected that it was not permissible to effectively repeal the Act by order in council. It seems that the judges themselves also conceded this point.

The idea that there were enforceable limits on the power of the British Parliament to interfere with the judiciary at the time of Confederation, then, is an historical fallacy. By expressing a desire to have a Constitution "similar in Principle to that of the United Kingdom", the framers of the *Constitution Act, 1867* did not give courts the power to strike down legislation violating the principle of judicial independence. The framers *did*, however, entrench the fundamental components of judicial independence set out in the *Act of Settlement* such that violations could be struck down by the courts. This was accomplished, however, by ss.99-100 of the *Constitution Act, 1867*, not the preamble.

It might be asserted that the argument presented above is merely a technical quibble. After all, in Canada the Constitution is supreme, not the legislatures. Courts have had the power to invalidate unconstitutional legislation in this country since 1867. If judicial independence was a "constitutional" principle in the broad sense in nineteenth-century Britain, and that principle was continued or established in Canada as a result of the preamble to the *Constitution Act, 1867*, why should Canadian courts resile from enforcing this principle by striking down incompatible legislation?

. . .

A more general answer to the question lies in the nature of the power of judicial review. The ability to nullify the laws of democratically elected representatives derives its legitimacy from a super-legislative source: the text of the Constitution. This foundational document (in Canada, a series of documents) expresses the desire of the people to limit the power of legislatures in certain specified ways. Because our Constitution is entrenched, those limitations cannot be changed by recourse to the usual democratic process. They are not cast in stone, however, and can be modified in accordance with a further expression of democratic will: constitutional amendment.

Judicial review, therefore, is politically legitimate only insofar as it involves the interpretation of an authoritative constitutional instrument. In this sense, it is akin to statutory interpretation. In each case, the court's role is to divine the intent or purpose of the text as it has been expressed by the people through the mechanism of the democratic process. Of course, many (but not all) constitutional provisions are cast in broad and abstract language. Courts have the often arduous task of explicating the effect of this language in a myriad of factual circumstances, many of which may not have been contemplated by the framers of the Constitution. While there are inevitable disputes about the manner in which courts should perform this duty, for example by according more or less deference to legislative decisions, there is general agreement that the task itself is legitimate.

This legitimacy is imperiled, however, when courts attempt to limit the power of legislatures without recourse to express textual authority. From time to time, members of this Court have suggested that our Constitution comprehends implied rights that circumscribe legislative competence. On the theory that the efficacy of parliamentary democracy requires free political expression, it has been asserted that the curtailment of such expression is *ultra vires* both provincial legislatures and the federal Parliament....

This theory, which is not so much an "implied bill of rights", as it has so often been called, but rather a more limited guarantee of those communicative freedoms necessary for the existence of parliamentary democracy, is not without appeal. An argument can be made that, even under a constitutional structure that deems Parliament to be supreme, certain rights, including freedom of political speech, should be enforced by the courts in order to safeguard the democratic accountability of Parliament. Without this limitation of its powers, the argument runs, Parliament could subvert the very process by which it acquired its legitimacy as a representative, democratic institution.... It should be noted, however, that the idea that the Constitution contemplates implied protection for democratic rights has been rejected by a number of eminent jurists as being incompatible with the structure and history of the Constitution.... [*Ed. note:* For a discussion of the "implied bill of rights" doctrine, see the Introduction to Chapter 11.]

Whatever attraction this theory may hold, and I do not wish to be understood as either endorsing or rejecting it, it is clear in my view that it may not be used to justify the notion that the preamble to the *Constitution Act, 1867* contains implicit protection for judicial independence. Although it has been suggested that guarantees of political freedom flow from the preamble, as I have discussed in relation to judicial independence, this position is untenable. The better view is that if these guarantees exist, they are implicit in s.17 of the *Constitution Act, 1867*, which provides for the establishment of Parliament. More important, the justification for implied political freedoms is that they are supportive, and not subversive, of legislative supremacy. That doctrine holds that democratically constituted legislatures, and not the courts, are the ultimate guarantors of civil liberties, including the right to an independent judiciary. Implying protection for judicial independence from the preambular commitment to a British-style constitution, therefore, entirely misapprehends the fundamental nature of that constitution.

This brings us back to the central point: to the extent that courts in Canada have the power to enforce the principle of judicial independence, this power derives from the structure of *Canadian*, and not British, constitutionalism. Our Constitution expressly contemplates both the power of judicial review (in s.52 of the *Constitution Act, 1982*) and guarantees of judicial independence (in ss.96-100 of the *Constitution Act, 1867* and s.11(*d*) of the *Charter*).

While these provisions have been interpreted to provide guarantees of independence that are not immediately manifest in their language, this has been accomplished through the usual mechanisms of constitutional interpretation, not through recourse to the preamble. The legitimacy of this interpretive exercise stems from its grounding in an expression of democratic will, not from a dubious theory of an implicit constitutional structure. The express provisions of the Constitution are not, as the Chief Justice contends, "elaborations of the underlying, unwritten, and organizing principles found in the preamble to the *Constitution Act, 1867*" (para. 107). On the contrary, they *are* the Constitution. To assert otherwise is to subvert the democratic foundation of judicial review.

In other words, the approach adopted by the Chief Justice, in my view, misapprehends the nature of the *Constitution Act, 1867*. The Act was not intended as an abstract document on the nature of government. The philosophical underpinnings of government in a British colony were a given, and find expression in the preamble. The Act was intended to create governmental and judicial structures for the maintenance of a British system of government in a federation of former British colonies. Insofar as there were limits to legislative power in Canada, they flowed from the terms of the Act (it being a British statute) that created them and *vis-à-vis* Great Britain the condition of dependency that prevailed in 1867. In considering the nature of the structures created, it was relevant to look at the principles underlying their British counterparts as the preamble invites the courts to do.

In considering the nature of the Canadian judicial system in light of its British counterpart, one should observe that only the superior courts' independence and impartiality were regarded as "constitutional"....

This was the judicial organization that was adopted for this country, with adaptations suitable to Canadian conditions, in the judicature provisions of the *Constitution Act, 1867*. In reviewing these provisions, it is worth observing that the courts given constitutional protection are expressly named. The existing provincial inferior courts are not mentioned, and, indeed, the Probate Courts of some provinces were expressly excluded.... As the majority stated in *McVey (Re)*, [1992], "it would seem odd if general words in a preamble were to be given more weight than the specific provisions that deal with the matter."

This is a matter of no little significance for other reasons. If one is to give constitutional protection to courts generally, one must be able to determine with some precision what the term "court" encompasses....

...

These are some of the issues that have persuaded me that this Court should not precipitously, and without the benefit of argument of any real relevance to the case before us, venture forth on this uncharted sea. It is not as if the law as it stands is devoid of devices to ensure independent and impartial courts and tribunals. Quite the contrary, I would emphasize that the express protections for judicial independence set out in the Constitution are broad and powerful. They apply to all superior court and other judges specified in s.96 of the *Constitution Act, 1867* as well as to inferior (provincial) courts exercising criminal jurisdiction. Nothing presented in these appeals suggests that these guarantees are not sufficient to ensure the independence of the judiciary as a whole. The superior courts have significant appellate and supervisory jurisdiction over inferior courts. If the impartiality of decisions from inferior courts is threatened by a lack of independence, any ensuing injustice may be rectified by the superior courts.

...

III. Financial Security

I turn now to the main issue in these appeals: whether the governments of Prince Edward Island, Alberta and Manitoba violated s.11(*d*) of the *Charter* by compromising the financial security of provincial court judges....

...

The Chief Justice also finds, as a general principle, that s.11(*d*) of the *Charter* permits governments to reduce, increase or freeze the salaries of provincial court judges, either as part of an overall economic measure which affects the salaries of all persons paid from the public purse, or as part of a measure directed at judges as a class. I agree. He goes on to hold, however, that before such changes can be made, governments must consider and respond to the recommendations of an independent "judicial compensation commission." He further concludes that s.11(*d*) forbids, under any circumstances, discussions about remuneration between the judiciary and the government.

I am unable to agree with these conclusions. While both salary commissions and a concomitant policy to avoid discussing remuneration other than through the making of representations to commissions may be desirable as matters of legislative policy, they are not mandated by s.11(*d*) of the *Charter*....

...

By its express terms, s.11(*d*) grants the right to an independent tribunal to persons "charged with an offence." The guarantee of judicial independence inhering in s.11(*d*) redounds to the benefit of the judged, not the judges. Section 11(*d*), therefore, does not grant judges a level of independence to which they feel they are entitled. Rather, it guarantees only that degree of independence necessary to ensure that accused persons receive fair trials.

...

From the foregoing, it can be stated that the "essential objective conditions" of judicial independence for the purposes of s.11(*d*) consist of those minimum guarantees that are necessary to ensure that tribunals exercising criminal jurisdiction act, and are perceived to act, in an impartial manner. Section 11(*d*) does not empower this or any other court to compel governments to enact "model" legislation affording the utmost protection for judicial independence. This is a task for the legislatures, not the courts.

With this general principle in mind, I turn to the first question at hand: does s.11(*d*) require governments to establish judicial compensation commissions and consider and respond to their recommendations before changing the salaries of provincial court judges? As noted by the Chief Justice in his reasons, this Court held unanimously in *Valente, supra,* that such commissions were not required for the purposes of s.11(*d*). This holding should be followed, in my opinion, not simply because it is authoritative, but because it is grounded in reason and common sense....

...

In my view, it is abundantly clear that a reasonable, informed person would not perceive that, in the absence of a commission process, all changes to the remuneration of provincial court judges threaten their independence. I reach this conclusion by considering the type of change to judicial salaries that is at issue in the present appeals. It is simply not reasonable to think that a decrease to judicial salaries that is part of an overall economic measure which affects the salaries of substantially all persons paid from public funds imperils the independence of the judiciary. To hold otherwise is to assume that judges could be influenced or manipulated by such a reduction. A reasonable person, I submit, would believe judges are made of sturdier stuff than this.

Indeed, as support for his conclusion that s.11(*d*) does not prohibit non-discriminatory reductions, the Chief Justice cites a number of commentators who argue that such reductions are constitutional.... As stated by Professor Renke, "[w]here economic measures apply equally to clerks, secretaries, managers, public sector workers of all grades and departments, as well as judges, how could judges be manipulated?" If this is the case, why is it necessary to require the intervention of an independent commission before the government imposes such reductions?

...

The threat to judicial independence that arises from the government's power to set salaries consists in the prospect that judges will be influenced by the possibility that the government will punish or reward them financially for their decisions. Protection against this potentiality is the *raison d'être* of the financial security component of judicial independence. There is virtually no possibility that such economic manipulation will arise where the government makes equivalent changes to the remuneration of all persons paid from public funds. The fact that such a procedure might leave *some* members of the public with the impression that provincial court judges are public servants is thus irrelevant. A reasonable, *informed* person would not perceive any infringement of the judges' financial security.

...

... Under the reasonable perception test, however, commissions are not a necessary condition of independence. Of course, the existence of such a process may go a long way toward showing that a given change to judges' salaries does not threaten their independence. Requiring commissions *a priori,* however, is tantamount to enacting a new constitutional provision to extend the protection provided by s.11(*d*). Section 11(*d*) requires only that tribunals exercising criminal jurisdiction be independent and impartial. To that end, it prohibits governments from acting in ways that threaten that independence and impartiality. It does not require legislatures, however, to establish what in some respects is a virtual fourth branch of government to police the interaction between the political branches and the judiciary. Judges, in my opinion, are capable of ensuring their own independence by an appropriate application of the Constitution. By employing the reasonable perception test, judges are able to distinguish between changes to their remuneration effected for a valid public purpose and those designed to influence their decisions.

...

I now turn to the question of discussions between the judiciary and the government over salaries. In the absence of a commission process, the only manner in which judges may have a say in the setting of their salaries is through direct dialogue with the executive. The Chief Justice terms these discussions "negotiations" and would prohibit them, in all circumstances, as violations of the financial security component of judicial independence. According to him, negotiations threaten independence because a "reasonable person might conclude that judges would alter the manner in which they adjudicate cases in order to curry favour with the executive."

In my view, this position seriously mischaracterizes the manner in which judicial salaries are set. *Valente* establishes that the fixing of provincial court judges' remuneration is entirely within the discretion of the government, subject, of course, to the conditions that the right to a salary be established by law and that the government not change salaries in a manner that raises a reasonable apprehension of interference. There is no constitutional requirement that the executive discuss, consult or "negotiate" with provincial court judges.... Provincial judges associations are not unions, and the government and the judges are not involved in a statutorily compelled collective bargaining relationship.... The atmosphere of negotiation the Chief Justice describes, which fosters expectations of "give and take" and encourages "subtle accommodations," does not therefore apply to salary discussions between government and the judiciary. The danger that is alleged to arise from such discussions – that judges will barter their independence for financial gain – is thus illusory.

...

V. Conclusion and Disposition

[*Ed. Note:* La Forest dissents from the Lamer-majority judgment on the central issues of whether the Preamble to the *Constitution Act, 1867* creates a constitutional rule of judicial independence and whether s.11(*d*) of the *Charter of Rights* requires the creation of judicial compensation committees.]

5.7

Judicial Independence: The Views of Appellate Judges

Ian Greene, Carl Baar, Peter McCormick, George Szablowski, and Martin Thomas,
"Judicial Independence," in *Final Appeal: Decision-Making in Canadian Courts of Appeal*
(Toronto: James Lorimer, 1998), 183–91. Reprinted with permission.

Judicial Independence

The rule of law requires that disputes about the application of the law be settled as impartially as possible. Judicial independence is one of the mechanisms developed in rule of law countries to promote judicial impartiality; it refers to procedures that are intended to insulate the outcome of a particular decision or class of decisions from any influence outside of legitimate courtroom activity, including the general public but especially the legislative or executive branches of government. In the *Valente* decision of 1985, the Supreme Court of Canada set out three essential conditions for judicial independence: security of judicial tenure (judges can be removed only for judicial misbehaviour and only after a fair and impartial hearing), financial security for judges (their salaries must be established by general legislation), and the institutional independence of tribunals on all matters directly affecting adjudication.

Of sixty judges who responded to the open-ended question, "What does the principle of judicial independence mean to you?" thirty-nine (65 per cent) understood it to mean that no one may attempt to interfere with impartial adjudication, particularly members of the legislative and executive branches of government. Three other types of responses each received support from about one-eighth of the judges interviewed: no interference from other judges, impartiality, and complete freedom to decide. The idea of autonomy (including administrative autonomy) was mentioned by a tenth of the judges. (Multiple responses were recorded so that the totals to our open-ended questions sometimes exceed 100 per cent.)

The judges were also asked whether they perceived any threats to judicial independence at the present time, and if so, what constituted these threats. Of the eighty judges who responded, more than two-thirds (55) listed one or more threats. This proportion was surprising, especially in comparison to the results of interviews with ninety-one trial court and appellate judges in Alberta and Ontario conducted by McCormick and Greene in the early 1980s. Asked if they could think of any instances when their judicial independence had been tampered with, not a single judge in the earlier study could give any examples of such tampering, although some referred to four well-publicized incidents not involving them personally where a federal cabinet minister had telephoned a judge about a particular case. Although the question in the current study is worded slightly differently, we do not think that the stark contrast between the results of the two studies is merely a result of the difference in wording of the question.

A fifth of the appellate judges who perceived threats to their independence (12 out of 55) were concerned that special interest groups seemed to be attempting to bring pressure to bear on the direction of judicial decisions. Five judges complained about pressure to make decisions which were perceived to be "politically correct," and five complained about the impact of media criticism that they could not respond to without themselves violating judicial independence. As well, a handful of judges were concerned that the inaccurate or sensationalist handling of judicial decisions by the media was in a sense putting pressure on them to make decisions that would result in a "good press." As a result of the *Charter of Rights and Freedoms*, Canadian appellate courts have made controversial decisions regarding subjects such as abortion, rape shield legislation, drunkenness as a defense in sexual assault cases, compulsory retirement, gay rights, Sunday shopping, the rights of refugee claimants, and the spending of union dues for political purposes. These decisions have resulted in an unprecedented level of commentary in the media about judicial decisions, much of it critical. There have even been demonstrations in front of courthouses following controversial decisions – an absolute novelty for Canadians.

Nor has it been only the judges' decisions which have ignited controversy. In 1990 Madam Justice Bertha Wilson, the first woman appointee to the Supreme Court of Canada, gave an address at Osgoode Hall Law School in which she argued that women judges are likely to have different views from male judges on family law, but not criminal law issues. A right-wing women's organization complained to the Canadian Judicial Council that Wilson – the wife of a United Church of Canada minister who had once written a pro-choice opinion – had violated judicial independence. The council exonerated Wilson.

Some appellate judges were also concerned about what they considered to be unwarranted pressure from the executive branch of government. These pressures included criticism of judicial decisions by politicians (9 judges), lack of appropriate administrative support (8 judges), and inappropriate procedures for determining judicial salaries (6 judges). Some judges were particularly concerned about the propensity of some provincial attorneys general publicly to criticize judges' sentencing practices or to take a judge to task for a particular decision which undercut government statements or ran counter to provincial policy priorities. More than one judge reported an impression that provincial governments had cut back on administrative support services to the appellate courts because they were unhappy about the direction of appellate court decisions. One example was the suggestion that judicial secretarial support was being reduced and the provision of personal computers refused in order to force the judges to write briefer decisions. Concerning judicial salaries, several judges were angry that the federal government rejected the advice of the independent commission established to review judicial salaries. Although the government cited the deficit and debt crisis as the reason, some judges were afraid that the real reason was that the appellate judges were making too many decisions that irritated the government.

Seven judges were worried that the Canadian Judicial Council, a body composed of all of the federally appointed chief justices and associate chief justices, had developed inappropriate procedures for disciplining judges. The Judicial Council is empowered to investigate complaints against federally appointed judges, and its annual reports provide a chronicle of how it handles the 150 or so annual complaints it now receives. Many complaints are about a judicial decision, and in these cases complainants are advised of their rights of appeal. Many others do not provide enough facts to make an investigation possible. The few remaining are referred to an investigation panel, which normally results either in the judge providing a satisfactory explanation of his or her actions, or (more rarely) in a judge deciding to retire prior to the completion of the investigation. In only one case since the council was formed in 1971 has it publicly found fault with a judge prior to the judge's retirement. This was the case of Mr. Justice Thomas Berger, who publicly criticized the 1981 constitutional accord for ignoring the rights of native Canadians and women. The council criticized Berger's actions, but did not recommend that he be removed on the grounds that the degree to which judges could make "political" statements had not been clear.

In general, the seven judges who were critical of the council's investigatory procedures felt that it was improper for chief justices to have disciplinary powers through the council. A better approach, they felt, would be to have federally appointed judges elect a judicial disciplinary tribunal. Their argument was that because the puisne judges know that their chief sits on the body that could investigate complaints against them and would likely be involved in deciding whether a complaint warranted a full investigation, the puisne judges would feel pressured to stay on their chief's good side, for example, by supporting his or her point of view in hard cases where the court was split. As well, the chief justices have the reputations of their respective courts to consider, creating an incentive in borderline situations either to exonerate judges who have been complained against or to seize the opportunity to deal with a good but controversial judge. Disciplinary tribunals elected by the judges themselves would be less intimidating, less likely to have a "chilling effect" on the puisne judges. Mr. Justice David Marshall makes a similar point in his book on judicial independence, which suggests that these concerns may be even more widespread than our interviews indicated.

It is clear that the *Charter of Rights* has precipitated most of the concerns of the judges about threats to judicial independence. Pressure group activities towards the courts are frequently the result of a *Charter* decision. Critical remarks by attorneys general and other cabinet ministers are sometimes prompted by *Charter* decisions, but in any case the *Charter* has exposed the judges' policy-making role and therefore has drawn judges into political controversy. The increasing visibility of the judiciary has resulted in an unprecedented level of official complaints about judicial behaviour. For example, the number of complaints received by the Canadian Judicial Council has increased from forty-seven in 1987–88 (the year of the Supreme Court's controversial *Charter* decision striking down Canada's abortion legislation), to 164 in 1993–94 and 200 in 1995–96. However, the number of complaint files opened dropped to 186 in 1996–97.

The Impact of the *Canadian Charter of Rights and Freedoms*

Here we consider how appellate judges feel about the expanded lawmaking role they have been assigned because of the *Charter of Rights*. It should be remembered that this enlarged lawmaking role is both directly and indirectly a result of the *Charter*. For example, one judge told us that his colleagues had been much more prone to altering the common law since the *Charter*. "After the *Charter* gave the judges the right to strike down a statute, altering the common law was a piece of cake." This approach might also explain why Canadian courts have, since the *Charter*, given more weight to the provincial bills of rights and the human rights acts – all legislation not forming part of the official constitution – than they ever did before 1982. It was not until 1987 that Justice Duff's doctrine that freedom of speech is protected by the original Canadian constitution inexplicably gained majority support on the Supreme Court – forty-nine years after it was first enunciated.

We asked eighty-nine judges to what extent they perceived themselves to be lawmakers, as opposed to being merely law interpreters. They were asked to answer on a five-point scale, with 1 representing "lawmaker" and 5 representing "law interpreter." The average response was 3.8, closer to the law-interpreter role, although the average response of seven Supreme Court judges was just 3.1. Twenty-six judges (29 per cent) saw themselves fundamentally as law interpreters, while only two placed themselves squarely on the lawmaking side of the continuum. However, in response to a question about whether the lawmaking role was changing, half of the judges thought that the *Charter* had moved them closer to the lawmaking side of the continuum, while only three-tenths thought that the lawmaking role had not changed significantly. On average, the judges thought they were lawmakers in only about 15 per cent of the cases they heard (but one Supreme Court of Canada judge ventured that as many as 60 per cent of the top court's cases involved lawmaking).

On the other hand, more than one long-serving judge suggested that their court used to make law much more frequently than was the case today. They argued that until recently, the Supreme Court of Canada had not dealt with a wide variety of legal issues, which meant that provincial courts of appeal "made law" by addressing these issues for the first time. Similarly, the first wave of *Charter* cases confronted the appeal courts with "first time" issues that called for imaginative solutions. By contrast, in recent years the Supreme Court has been much more committed to resolving a broad range of legal issues, and the basic elements of *Charter* interpretation have been clearly established. Thus, the role of intermediate appellate courts has changed not only in terms of how judges relate to legislative institutions but also how the judges on one court relate to judges on another.

We asked the judges whether they thought the *Charter* had created a "crisis of legitimacy" for the courts – a phrase which was used by some judges in the mid-1980s to describe their fears about judges becoming involved in lawmaking through high-profile *Charter of Rights* cases. The judges were evenly split on this issue, with thirty-three of seventy-three thinking that such a crisis existed (45 per cent), and thirty-two saying that there was no crisis; the remainder were neutral. The twenty-two judges who described themselves fundamentally as law interpreters were more likely to think that there was a crisis of legitimacy than those who perceived themselves as having a mixed lawmaking and law-interpreting role.

It was most certainly the case prior to the *Charter* that nearly all Canadian judges resisted a lawmaking role for the courts, and many denied its possibility altogether. Instead, they espoused the legal-positivist school of thought that good judges merely interpret the law. It is striking how quickly and completely this traditional view has faded: all but two appellate court judges now admit to having at least some lawmaking role. However, half were clearly uncomfortable with this newly visible role, as reflected by their responses to the "crisis of legitimacy" question.

Worries about the public perception of the lawmaking role of the courts aside, we were curious as to whether appellate judges thought that it was legitimate for Canadians to try to change the law through the courts rather than through the more overtly political process of Parliament and the legislatures. In response to the question, "How appropriate is it for social and public interest groups to use the courts to achieve social change?" thirty of sixty-five judges (45 per cent) thought that these activities were not appropriate, while only twenty-three (35 per cent) thought they were. On a 1 to 5 scale, 5 being "extremely appropriate" and 1 being "not at all appropriate," the average response of the four Supreme Court judges was 3.5, compared with 2.7 for appellate judges as a whole. Two Supreme Court judges mentioned that interest groups can present very useful briefs as intervenors, and one said that the courts are an important part of the democratic process, open for business to those wanting to promote legitimate democratic change. One Supreme Court judge, however, was worried about the consequences of the courts being used as political tools.

Supreme Court of Canada judges are less concerned about the newly expanded lawmaking role of the judges. Four out of five felt that the *Charter of Rights* had changed the role of the court, bringing it closer to a lawmaking function. But of five judges questioned, all disagreed with the proposition that the *Charter* had created a crisis of legitimacy for the court, and one strongly disagreed. The consensus was that through the political process, the Supreme Court had been handed a lawmaking role by the people of Canada, and that this new role was generally accepted. But there was certainly no such consensus among appellate judges as a whole on the question.

Collegial Decision-making on Appellate Courts

One major difference between trial and appellate courts is that trial court decision-making is an individual process, while there is always a collegial process involved in the appellate courts (except when appellate judges act individually to consider matters such as interlocutory motions and motions for intervenor status).

The most common outcome is a unanimous decision. Peter McCormick reports that 60 per cent of reported Supreme Court of Canada decisions on appeals from the lower appellate courts have been unanimous since 1949. The proportion of unanimous decisions in the provincial courts of appeal is much higher, ranging from about 96 per cent in Ontario to 85 per cent in Quebec and Manitoba. Dissenting opinions are more common than separate concurring opinions, which are rare outside of the Supreme Court of Canada.

The issue of how extensive dissenting and separate concurring opinions should be is an important one when considering the role of appellate courts in a democracy, because one of the strengths of democratic government is its ability to respect dissenting voices. As we noted in Chapter 4, we asked the judges whether it was important for a panel to try to avoid dissenting opinions. On the 5-point scale, with 1 representing "not at all important" and 5 representing "extremely important," the average was 2.1, meaning that dissents are considered a perfectly acceptable part of the process. Most judges stressed the importance of dissenting opinions in the development of the law, although a few also talked about the need to try to avoid unnecessary or confusing dissents either for the sake of clarity in the law or to help the losing side to accept its loss. On the other hand, some judges in the provincial appeal courts said they were sometimes tempted to register a dissent just in order to give the appellant an opportunity to appeal to the Supreme Court of Canada, as the Supreme Court must hear appeals in criminal cases where there has been a dissent registered in the provincial appeal court.

Separate concurring decisions were another story. Based on the same scale, the average response was 3.5, but it was only 2.9 for eight Supreme Court of Canada judges. This result means that avoiding separate concurring decisions is an important part of the collegial decision-making process in the penultimate appellate courts, but not as important at the Supreme Court level.

The two most common explanations given to us by the judges for unnecessary separate concurring decisions were that newly appointed judges sometimes consider the finer points of law to be more important than they do later in their careers and that some judges are "prima donnas" whose inability to see the legitimacy of alternative views prevents the kind of col-legial give – and-take necessary for a court and for democratic society gener-ally to work effectively.

For some judges the effort to avoid unnecessary separate decisions was so important that they would be willing to invest hours either redrafting their own opinions or suggesting changes to their colleagues' decisions in order to reach an acceptable compromise. Just over half of the judges had taken at least one judgment-writing course, and nearly all of them found the courses helpful; some mentioned how the courses had helped them to write deci-sions that were more likely to discourage separate opinions from others on a panel. But others were simply willing to let the chips fall where they may and were not concerned at all about multiple opinions.

The Supreme Court has been criticized in recent years for producing too many separate concurring decisions; these multifarious judgments do not help to clarify the law in the minds of lawyers and judges in the courts below. An extreme form of this is the "plurality decision" where no single statement of "outcome plus reasons" is able to draw the signatures of a majority of the panel, and this result usually occurs at least once or twice each year. Not surprisingly, a slight majority of Supreme Court judges do not see the number of separate concurring decisions as a major problem. From their perspective, the law is always in a state of flux, and too much rigidity mitigates against fairness and justice. On the other hand, three Supreme Court judges felt that one way to improve the decision-making process in the Supreme Court would be for the judges to find a way to reduce the number of separate concurring decisions.

There are at least two ways of thinking about attempts to avoid non-unanimous decisions from the perspective of democratic theory, and they roughly parallel the two different views expressed about concurring deci-sions by Supreme Court judges. One view is that in order to respect the rights of minorities, both dissenting opinions and separate concurring opin-ions are important to ensure that losing litigants are treated with equal con-cern and respect and to provide an opportunity for a losing class of litigant to become a winning class in the future – such opinions can become the springboards for the future development of the law. The other view is that dissenting and separate concurring decisions are sometimes the result of "prima donna" judges and that the law is better served by a court whose behaviour is made more predictable by a single clear statement of the law. This is a reflection of a more absolutist approach to the law, and one that is more appropriate to a court that is performing a technical exercise than to one that is engaged in a democratic dialogue with citizens.

5.8

What Are Judges For?

An inaugural lecture delivered by Conor A. Gearty, Professor of Human Rights Law at King's College London, on Monday, 11 December 2000. Reprinted with permission.

Lord Russell did during his judicial career have something very important to say about another kind of matter for which he thought the judges ill-suited. His views are to be found set out in the well-known decision of *Kruse* v. *Johnson* [1898] 2 QB 91, and it has a strong contemporary ring. The case concerned the validity of byelaws promulgated by a local council. For years the Victorian judges had become inured to scrutinising such laws very closely, and to striking them down if they were judged deserving of such a fate. But here what was in issue was a byelaw made by one of the "public representative bodies" that had lately emerged as a consequence of the democratisation of local government.

To Lord Russell this democratic character made them very different from their forbears in the worlds of railway and canal regulation and the like. He considered that they "ought to be supported if possible," or as he also put it, to be "'benevolently' interpreted." In *Kruse* v. *Johnson*, Lord Russell took the opportunity to express as full a theory of judicial restraint – and as resounding an answer to the question what are judges *not* for – as any that has subsequently appeared in more famed, juristic circumstances:

> A byelaw is not unreasonable merely because particular judges may think that it goes further than is prudent or necessary or convenient, or because it is not accompanied by a qualification or an exception which some judges may think ought to be there. Surely it is not too much to say that in matters which directly and mainly concern the people of the county, who have the right to choose those whom they think best fitted to represent them in their local government bodies, such representatives may be trusted to understand their own requirements better than judges. (p. 100)

Now this is a marvellous though implied statement of where judges fit in the modern democratic process, as agents of the expression of the community political will rather than as antagonists of that will. But that life is not simple (and this is what makes *Kruse* v. *Johnson* exceptionally interesting) is demonstrated by looking at what the facts were before Lord Russell and his colleagues. For the byelaw that the local people had enthusiastically enacted was draconian indeed: a ban on all playing of music or singing within fifty yards of a dwelling house after having being asked once to stop. The point was not to stop all music and to return this part of England to a puritan dark age, but rather to facilitate the stopping of one particular source of music, namely that emanating from the Salvation Army. The case was just one of many from this era involving the army, the most famous of which was *Beatty* v. *Gillbanks* ([1882] 10 QBD). In modern terms, the majority had used its power to curb the religious freedom of an unpopular minority. Was Lord Russell right or wrong to stand by, or should he have allowed his respect for the democratic process to have been (to use the well-worn modern phrase) "trumped" by his determination to protect minority rights? This question is at the heart of what it means to be a judge at the start of the 21st century.

If to some extent we now know what judges are not for – to function as figleafs for illiberal executive action and to override legislative intent with their own versions of the public interest –, then we are still frustratingly far away from identifying precisely what it is that it is their primary job to do. My pocket thesaurus – describing the judge as *inter alia* a "doomster," "doomsman" and the "great unpaid – is entertaining but of little direct assistance.

...

If independence were what judges were for, and if that independence were then defined in opposition to other branches of government (as to be meaningful it would have to be), then it would be quite clear that the judges were not what it was their primary function to be, namely independent. But of course independence is not a purpose or a function of anything; it is a condition which makes possible the discharge of function: it is a means to an end, not an end in itself.

What then is that end? Here we are finally close to what judges are primarily for, which is surely as simple – and anticlimactic – as this: to adjudicate fairly by applying the law to disputes between private parties and (when the need arises) to disputes between individuals and the state. Far from making less peculiar the fact that the senior judges sit in the legislature, however, this function once expressly articulated makes it even more obviously wrong that any of them should be in the Lords at all....

The moment we identify the judicial role in our society as primarily adjudicative the deeper do the anachronisms in the British constitution inevitably seem to be. These go far further than the presence of the senior judges in the legislature. If we think about legislation in functional rather than institutional terms, i.e., as the making of general rules for the governance of the community rather than as a place which does things, it becomes quite obvious – so apparent that we don't really notice its implications most of the time – that the judges have been far more deeply involved in legislating than the occasional speech in the House of Lords would suggest.

I am thinking of course about the way in which the judges oversee the "development" of the common law. In theory, such law is not made, merely recognised. But as a great teacher of mine, the Yale professor and now U.S. judge Guido Calabresi once remarked in the context of the equally ludicrous search for fault in negligence, do we not have enough duplicity in our lives without also lying when we don't have to, in our spare time as Monty Python might have put it? Who could read this summer's decisions

on the barristers' immunity and on the liability in negligence of local educational authorities, for example, without seeing that a very direct kind of
law making is going on, with general rules being made which reach well
beyond the confines of the cases which throw them up and which will shape
for years the conduct of those affected by them?

Clearly this is law making. And this common law is also far from "ethi-
cally aimless" as many have argued: I have far more respect for it than that.
Its ideology is and has always been manifestly rooted in respect for property
rights and for the need to ensure the enforceability of contracts. No one could
read Anthony Lester and Geoffrey Bindman's pathbreaking work on *Race
and the Law* – the early chapters of which cover the hostility of the common
law to race discrimination law – and come to any other conclusion.

Not only do we lawyers often simply not see that the common law is legislative in effect; we also have difficulty in seeing that it is driven by a particular and highly political (in the broadest sense) view of the world. Indeed
those academic writers who have made the articulation of such an insight
part of their scholarly project, writers such as Professor John Griffith (to
whom I owe an immense intellectual debt since I first came across his *The
Politics of the Judiciary* at a university where it was (metaphorically speaking) hidden – like pornography – from student view) and Patrick McAuslan
(whose *The Ideologies of Planning Law* first got me to think seriously about
what law was for) – such writers have found themselves exposed on this
account alone to partisan attack. That most scholarly of practitioners Murray
Hunt has perhaps explained it best when he observed in a recent essay that
"it is a defining characteristic of legal cultures that [their] participants often
do not perceive the cultural specificity of their ideas about legal argument."

Of course in truth we have long known that despite their claim to be
merely adjudicators, the judges have been routinely making rules for us all
to live by. If this has not been as obvious as it should be in relation to the
common law, then it has been more publicly to the fore in the context of
the second way in which the judges can affect the general rules by which
we are governed, namely through the process of statutory interpretation –
which to its critics has sometimes looked like an attempt to tame the desires
of the representative branch in order to make them more compatible to the
common law's underlying and ideologically driven assumptions about the
public interest.

The issue of the legitimacy of judicial decision making has therefore been
around for a long time. So too has the debate about what kind of people
should be judges. This latter question has been recently addressed by Sir
Thomas Legg in his Street lecture, which I gather is to be published soon in
Public Law. Of course one is intuitively in favour of a "representative" judiciary or one which "reflects" the sort of people – in terms of gender, race,
ethnicity, social class and so on – that we find living on these islands. But
Thomas Legg's lecture forces us to reflect on why we all feel like this. Why
do we assume that judges should be "representative" in these sorts of ways?

The answer is in my view indelibly linked to function, to the question of what judges are for.

Let us envisage an abstract spectrum of judicial types. On the extreme left (no political point intended) is the strict constructionist whose only job is to work out the meaning of the words deployed by the legislature and then to give effect to them. There is no common law to interpret, only statutes together with a civil and (perhaps) a criminal code. Then in the centre is the judge who engages in statutory interpretation in a rather more creative way and who has full autonomy in a particular legislative field, described as the common law. Finally on the extreme right (again no subliminal message intended) is the judge as overt law maker, whose origins as an adjudicator have long been transcended by his or her overriding responsibility both to make and to oversee the making of general rules for the public good.

Now it will be obvious that as we move along that spectrum, from left to right, the pressure for a more accountable judiciary is bound to grow. Where the judicial function is purely technical all we want are experts who can do the community's bidding most effectively: lawyers are probably the right people to turn to though linguistic philosophers (if there were enough of them) would be better. It is when we see the judge not as a professional virtuoso but as the maker of general rules for the community as a whole that we become uneasy about his or her lack of a democratic base. And when the judge has reached the far right of our spectrum then we end up – as in the United States – trying desperately to get our people on the bench, voting for a presidential candidate who will put our people onto the supreme court, trying to block in Congress those proposed justices who do not fit our political ideology and if all that fails marching past the judge's office shouting our views in the hope that they will be heard and maybe acted on.

It is an odd way to run a democracy. I may be irretrievably nostalgic or a true revolutionary (I am not sure which it is – perhaps both) but I have a strong hankering for a very limited judicial function, somewhere well to the left of the spectrum I have described, in other words a society in which broadly speaking the rules are made by representatives, interpreted by the courts and enforced if needs be by the executive arm.

This is not however where the United Kingdom's judiciary are, just at the moment. Of course they have never been entirely on the left of my spectrum: the existence of the common law has seen to that. Nor however have they been too far to the right. Their "legislative" function has been well camouflaged and in the main (with one or two exceptions of course) timidly deployed.

But what no one could have expected was that the legislative branch itself would invite the judiciary to exercise legislative power of a far more general and pervasive nature than has ever hitherto been countenanced. This is the effect of the *Human Rights Act*, "the most significant formal redistribution of political power in this country since 1911, and perhaps since 1688" as my colleague, friend and writing partner over many years Professor K. D. Ewing has so aptly described it.

This is the real turn up for the books and the stunning answer to those of us who have long argued for a limited judicial function in order to allow our representative legislature to get on with the business of making general rules. What are we to say when that self same legislature decides of its own volition to transfer a huge and open-ended portion of its legislative function to the judiciary? Now I know that the *Human Rights Act* is theoretically repealable, that acts of Parliament may not be struck down and so on, but the fact remains that the *Act* positively mandates the judiciary to transform its function, to move much further along the spectrum I have just outlined and to engage in the formulation of general rules in a far more robust fashion. Section 3 alone would be enough evidence for the general case: it gives the courts the power to roam around all legislation – past and future – transforming it where possible for Convention compatibility. If such a power were given to any other branch or sub-branch of the State, and certainly if it were given to the executive, the legal community would be up in arms, conferences would be held, papers issued, deploring this unprecedented "Henry VIII clause," as the cognoscenti would call it. But because it is the judges we seem to assume it must be all right.

Of course there are aspects of the quasi legal revolution that is being ushered in by the *Human Rights Act* that are salivating to the public interest minded lawyer. The extension of the *Act* to private law through section 6(3)(a) may over time prove to be the most important legislative intervention in the ethical base of the common law since the latter's emergence in medieval times. The duty on all public authorities to respect Convention rights has already begun to frame the public discourse in beneficial ways: local newspapers, radio programmes and many members of the general community are thinking in terms of dignity and rights more than would have been the case without the *Act*. If the measure's clear commitment to three simple principles – those of legality, respect for civil liberties and human dignity – can be kept prominently on centre stage then the *Act* may well do some good, in cultural as well as legal terms.

It is a big "if" however and all judgments must so early in its life be inevitably contingent. The most important civil liberty of them all is the right to vote, and it remains to be seen how much effect the judges will give to the respect for parliamentary democracy that permeates the *Human Rights Act*, often sitting in various corners of the *Act* gazing sulkily across at the noisy human rights subsections which have been getting all the attention and excited praise from the legal community. I do have a great deal of sympathy for the judges on this point. They have been given an impossible task by Parliament: being effectively told: to "please override us where human rights are in issue – but in no circumstances do so where we really do not want you to." Like all of us, Parliament is in favour of human rights in principle, but very much against so many of their concrete manifestations.

Pleasing both parliament and the human rights community – as the *Act* requires the judges simultaneously to do – will be a difficult trick to pull off. Apparently easier for the judges, but I think in fact ultimately more challenging, will be to guide the measure away from the kind of constipated legalism with which the adversarial system invariably seeks to both swamp and destroy all novel laws. Here the signs are not good. There have been some decisions in Scotland which I am bound to say I think have adopted a highly legalistic, and at the same time very narrow, approach to the *Act*. Of course many of the huge number of books on human rights law now squeezing all other subjects from the legal bookshops are very good. But some at least, I think, betray a depressing commitment to the old way of "getting on top of a new statute" – along the lines of "here are twenty commission/court/whatever decisions on substance/admissibility/ whatever which answer the following sixteen narrow questions and leave open the following three points of law in my narrow area of specialisation – upon which I am now a human rights expert."

But the *Human Rights Act* is different and if it is to have any chance of success has to be seen to be different. To use the well-worn cliché, it is not a tax statute – though of course it might apply to one. It requires judges and legal practitioners to think. It requires arguments to be framed in terms of principle – it tries to close the gap between our ethical and our professional selves. Now it was precisely because this goal was thought too ambitious that the idea of the human rights act was considered by some to be an unnecessary or even wrong-headed reform. But that is an old argument, which Parliament has ended – for the time being at least.

So the judges are in for an exciting time. As Lord Hope famously put it in *ex parte Kebilene*, the "entire legal system" is about to be subjected "to a fundamental process of review and, where necessary, reform by the judiciary" (*R v DPP ex parte Kebilene* [1999] 3 WLR 972 at 988).

But as the Home Secretary might have responded to Lord Hope, with such rights come responsibilities. Steering the *Act* away from judicial supremacism and in a direction which respects the public interest as expressed through our representative institutions is one such challenge. So too is the need to protect the *Act* from legal constipation and arid collateral litigation, which I have also discussed above.

But there are further challenges which flow directly from earlier points of tension in the role of the judges in our society, points of tension which we must expect to be hugely exacerbated as a result of the *Human Rights Act*. The first of these relates to the new, strong version of the requirement for judicial independence and impartiality which is to be found in Article 6(1) of the Convention and which is now the right of all persons facing criminal charges or the determination of their civil rights. Of course we have had our own excitements within this jurisdiction already, with the Hoffman complication to the *Pinochet* litigation and the *Lockabail* ruling in the Court of Appeal. But post *Human Rights Act* the presence not just of the Lord Chancellor but of all the law lords in the legislative chamber will no doubt be raised sooner rather than later. And as my colleague at King's Paul Matthews has pointed out in relation to the well-known McGonnell case from Guernsey

(*McGonnell* v. *United Kingdom*), a judge does not have to be an active participant in a legislative process in order to be deemed – as Paul puts it – "a judicial imbecile, incapable of reaching an impartial and independent decision."

On the same principle, too, I feel judges will have to be careful about what
they say in print outside the courtroom. The following remarks are not
those of Professor Gower's embittered academic I assure you, but I wonder
how many judges know – as they contribute so fully to the law reviews –
how valuable such space is to the law lecturer desperately trying to comply
with his or her RAE demands, with the clock ticking relentlessly towards
the end of year cut off point and the difficult interview with the head of
department?...

However the *Human Rights Act* may make judicial interventions in the
academic literature which are more than mere summaries of past cases difficult to justify. Supposing the judge before me on an issue of the application
of section 6(3)(a) of the *Human Rights Act* – the vital "horizontality" point –
has already made clear in a law review article his or her view that the *Act*
does not apply to private parties. What can I do other than ask such a judge
not to hear the case?

The problem here is of a lack of fit between the appearance that what is
going on in the courtroom is a narrow battle between two adversaries on a
point of law, and the reality that huge issues of policy are in fact being
formulated as legal rules of general application. Now as I said earlier, this
lack of fit between the narrow remit of the judicial process and the polycentric consequences of decisions taken in it has been around for a long time.
In the days before the collapse of confidence in our representative democratic structures, it was a subject of a very lively scholarly and public debate.
Important contributions have been made by John Griffith and more recently
by John Allison. We need now to return to this literature and work out what
is the best way of getting the full facts before a court so that when it makes a
ruling on the law under the *Human Rights Act*, it does so explicitly acknowledging its legislative character and with a clear understanding of its widespread implications. This goes further than the occasional *amicus* brief or the
importation, without more, of American ideas drawn from a different constitutional culture.

I think that the Court of Appeal, the appellate committee and the judicial
committee should have appointed to them a "public interest officer" with
a small team of officials, whose job it is to prepare reports on the effects of
possible rulings not just on the law but on the wider public and on society
as a whole. It seems to me that such an officer is absolutely necessitated by
parliament's insistence (in for example ss 3(2) and 6(2)) that the effectiveness and continuing operation of legislation not be irreparably damaged by
judicial interpretation. But how can judges know about such operational
matters. How can the lawyers for the various litigants know? How can the
court be sure that an *amicus* brief that has been filed is authoritative? How
can it choose between *amicus* briefs if there is a conflict? The advantage of

a "public interest statement" filed by a court officer would be that it would take such huge issues out of the narrow and artificial confines of the adversarial process, and it would also – an additional advantage I would say – open up the process to persons other than lawyers.

I end by returning to a point I made earlier about the large pressure that is growing up for a representative judiciary. I said then that the answer to this question is closely linked to function. Well now that we have a judicial branch engaged in quasi-legislative work, is not the case for a "representative" judiciary unanswerable? But if it were, why would we have chosen to locate such power away from the representative branch in the first place? Are those who argued so passionately for such a change now having second thoughts, and seeking to transform the judiciary into a pale reflection of the assembly from which they have so successfully taken so much power? I say "pale" because no one is yet – so far as I know – arguing for an elected judiciary. But if not elected, what does a "representative" judiciary mean? Of course as Phil Thomas' very important new book shows us there are huge questions about equality and race to be addressed in the legal profession as well as in the universities and indeed everywhere else: see *Discriminating Lawyers* (2000). But I remain to be convinced that it is the job of our liberal institutions to paper over the inequality that we have as a society – through underinvestment in the public sector and a lack of egalitarian edge in our community choices – that we have as a society decided to tolerate? At the very least, the action taken by the professions and the universities should be accompanied by a more focused political analysis on how our young people and school leavers have got to such a situation of inequality in the first place. But perhaps human kind cannot bear too much reality?

I prefer not to emphasise judicial representativeness so much as judicial accountability. In the new era of judicial legislation, the judges are I believe going to have to gird themselves to be treated far more politically than in the past. The main opposition party in Ireland has recently published proposals under which the judges would be overseen by a Judicial Board and individual judges subjected to penalties where the Board thought they had got things wrong. I expect the pressure for appointment only after a process of selection involving parliament cannot long be resisted here in the UK, and more to the point should not be resisted. There will soon be in the select committee on human rights an ideal forum for such (let us call them) "confirmation hearings" to be heard. Now everybody recoils from this because of the U.S. experience. But there are not nearly so many controversial candidacies in the U.S. as is widely believed, and the main ones we know about – those involving Robert Bork and Clarence Thomas – were rightly controversial in my view. U.S. federal judges have in the main drawn a degree of comfort from their confirmation hearings, feeling that it has given them at least a degree of democratic legitimacy in relation to their subsequent judicial work.

I also think senior U.K. judges will have to be prepared to meet with Parliament – perhaps with this new human rights committee – to explain in general terms what is happening in the courts under the *Human Rights Act* and to defend – not specific decisions but general policy developments – to that body. The Committee might quite legitimately want to investigate for example what has happened to Parliament's criminal statutes under the *Human Rights Act*. Or it might want to assess the cost of particular decisions, or the rationale behind some particularly controversial declaration of incompatibility.

Of course all this will be very new for the judges. But it surely flows from the enactment of the *Human Rights Act* in what is still a highly democratic culture. Far from being antagonistic about such developments, the judges should welcome them, as part of that dialogue with the other branches of government for which many have so long argued. The revolution brought about by the *Human Rights Act* does not stop at the door of the law courts. "What judges are for" is set to become one of the liveliest issues in our public culture in the decades that lie ahead.

5.9

Key Terms

Concepts

administrative independence
impartiality
judicial accountability
judicial compensation commissions
judicial independence
Key's "iron law of politics"
"representative judiciary"
"tenure for good behaviour"
administrative independence

Institutions, Events, and Documents

Act of Settlement (1701)
Bastarache interview (2001)
Beauregard v. *The Queen* (1986)
Berger Affair (1981)
Canadian Judicial Council (1971)
Charter of Rights and Freedoms, s.11(d)
Constitution Act, 1867, ss.96-100
Judges Affair (1976)
Knowles Trial (1692)
L'Heureux-Dubé Complaint (1999)
McClung Affair (1999)
Meech Lake Accord (1987)
Provincial Judges Reference (1997)
R. v. *Ewanchuk* (1999)
Valente v. *The Queen* (1985)

Access to Judicial Power

6

Traditionally, access to the courts has been strictly limited to individuals who meet the threshold requirements of "standing," the right to bring a case before a court. In order to establish standing, a would-be litigant must usually prove the existence of a *lis*, or legal dispute. Not all disputes raise legal issues, and not all legal issues arise in the context of real life disputes. In the realm of constitutional law, mere distaste for or opposition to a particular statute or government policy does not constitute a dispute. A legally recognizable dispute requires the existence of a specific legal interest and an injury or a demonstrable threat of injury to that interest. Finally, a case must not become "moot" during the course of litigation. If the original dispute that gave rise to the case ceases to exist, a judge will normally refuse to answer the legal issues raised and terminate the judicial hearing.

Like other aspects of the judicial process, these restrictions on access to the courts can be traced back to the original purpose of common law courts as adjudicators of real life disputes between individuals. As the celebrated American jurist Felix Frankfurter once observed, "the mechanisms of the law – what courts are to deal with which causes and subject to what conditions – cannot be dissociated from the ends that the law serves."[1] As with other human tools and institutions, the ends influence the means, the "what" shapes the "how."

These traditional restrictions on access to the courts ably serve their original adjudicatory purposes but are subject to criticism in modern public law cases, which often have a policy dimension that transcends the immediate dispute. As Weiler has pointed out, other policy-making institutions are not restricted in these ways. If final appeal courts are essentially policy-makers, why should an interest group have to wait for a dispute involving one of its members in order to bring its policy issue into court? These rules not only frustrate the ability of groups to get their issues before a court; they also restrict the ability of judges to act in a timely fashion.

---

1 Felix Frankfurter and James Landis, *The Business of the Supreme Court* (New York, 1928), p. 2.

Given the historical attachment of Canadian judges to the more British, adjudicatory view of the judicial process, it was not surprising that until quite recently the rules governing standing and mootness in Canadian constitutional law were stricter than their American counterparts. For example, in 1953 in the celebrated *Saumur* case, the Supreme Court struck down the Quebec City bylaw used to prosecute Jehovah's Witnesses for distributing their pamphlets. The fifth and deciding vote for the Supreme Court majority ruled that the bylaw violated Quebec's own *Freedom of Worship Act*. The government of Quebec Premier Maurice Duplessis promptly responded to this decision by amending the *Act* to exclude the Jehovah's Witnesses' pamphleteering from its protection. When Saumur initiated a new legal action to have this amendment declared invalid, the Supreme Court (affirming the judgment of the Quebec courts) ruled that, since the amended legislation had not actually been applied against any Witnesses, there was no real *lis* (dispute). Thus, the Court refused to rule on the validity of the amended *Act*.

The rules on standing remained restrictive until the mid-1970s. The governing precedent was the 1924 ruling in *Smith* that, "An individual ... has no status to maintain an action restraining a wrongful violation of a public right unless he is exceptionally prejudiced by the wrongful act."[2] In 1975, the Supreme Court overruled this precedent by granting standing to Thorson, a federal civil servant seeking a declaratory judgment that the Trudeau government's new bilingualism legislation was invalid even though he was not personally affected by it. Three judges, led by Justice Judson dissented, arguing that, "the action was an attempt to get an opinion which the Court had no right to give."[3] But the other six judges granted Thorson standing, based on what Chief Justice Laskin declared was "the right of the citizenry to constitutional behaviour by Parliament."[4] Justice Judson's dissent shows that Laskin's decision to eliminate the requirement of a *lis* served not just to broaden access for litigants, but also expanded the Court's jurisdiction and thus its ability to intervene in the policy process.

The rules governing standing were further relaxed the following year in *Nova Scotia Board of Censors* v. *McNeil*.[5] Even though the Censor Board's ruling applied only to theatre owners, not the viewing public, the Court granted standing to a reporter to challenge the board's ruling to ban the film, *Last Tango in Paris*. This trend reached its peak in the Court's 1981 ruling in *Minister of Justice of Canada* v. *Borowski* (Reading 6.2).[6] The Court ruled that, even though pro-life crusader Joe Borowski was not personally harmed or even affected by the abortion law, he could still challenge its constitutional validity. The majority ignored Chief Justice Laskin's dissent, which warned

---

2 *Smith* v. *Attorney-General of Ontario*, [1924] S.C.R. 331, at pp. 337–38.

3 *Thorson* v. *Attorney-General of Canada*, [1975] 1 S.C.R. 138.

4 Ibid., p. 163.

5 [1976] 2 S.C.R. 265.

6 [1981] 2 S.C.R. 575.

that "the result would be to set up a battle between parties who do not have a direct interest [and] to wage it in a judicial arena." The *Borowski* decision seems to remove the traditional requirement that a would-be litigant demonstrate a concrete personal interest that is affected by the legal issue raised and created instead a very broad right for all citizens to go to the courts and demand that the judges force the government to "behave constitutionally."

In 1992, the Court placed some restrictions on standing when it ruled that an interest group (the Canadian Council of Churches) did not have standing to challenge new amendments to the *Immigration Act* because the same challenge could have been brought by a private individual.[7] But while the Court was saying "no" to the Canadian Council of Churches, it reaffirmed its very broad discretion to grant standing in *Charter* cases:

> By its terms the *Charter* indicates that a generous and liberal approach should be taken to the issue of standing. If that were not done, *Charter* rights might be unenforced and *Charter* freedoms shackled. The *Constitution Act, 1982* does not of course affect the discretion the Court possesses to grant standing to public litigants. What it does is entrench the fundamental right of the public to government in accordance with the law.

The Supreme Court has also weakened the doctrine of mootness as a barrier to engaging the courts in constitutional politics. In October, 1988, Borowski returned to the Supreme Court, this time to challenge the abortion law on its merits. However, eight months earlier in its second *Morgentaler* decision, the Supreme Court had struck down the abortion law, although for the very opposite reasons argued by Borowski. The Court now ruled that, with no law left to challenge, Borowski's case had become moot and dismissed it, again without ruling on the merits. But even as it dismissed Borowski's claim as moot, the Supreme Court elaborated a new mootness doctrine that allows otherwise moot cases to be decided if they can meet certain criteria (Reading 6.3).

Borowski has turned out to be the exception, not the rule, and is an example of a *Charter* "loss" that has actually broadened access for subsequent *Charter* litigants. In other *Charter* cases that became moot, the Court still proceeded to rule on the merits, even though its judgments held no practical meaning to the actual litigants. For example, in the Court's most far-reaching gay rights decision to date, *M v. H* (1999),[8] the dispute over property division between the two lesbian partners had already been resolved in an out-of-court settlement. In *Mercure* v. *Saskatchewan*, a French-language rights case involving a challenge to Saskatchewan's English-only legal system, the original plaintiff had already died before his appeal reached the Supreme

---

7 *Canadian Council of Churches* v. *Minister of Employment and Immigration*, [1992] 1 S.C.R. 236.
8 *M* v. *H.*, [1999] 2 S.C.R. 3.

Court.[9] This did not stop the Court from hearing the case and ruling in his favour. In short, mootness is no longer a meaningful barrier to hearing a case that the Court wants to decide for legal or policy reasons.

In its 1985 decision in *Operation Dismantle*, the Supreme Court rejected a "political questions" doctrine from precluding judicial review of government decisions involving foreign policy or national defence.[10] Operation Dismantle, a coalition of anti-nuclear "peace groups," had petitioned the courts to declare illegal the government's decision to allow the American testing of unarmed cruise missiles over western Canada. They alleged that the development of the cruise missile would make nuclear war more likely by stimulating the arms race. This was said to infringe on section 7 of the *Charter*, which protects the rights to life and security of the person. The government responded by arguing that the courts lacked jurisdiction to even hear the case because the *Charter* did not apply to foreign-policy decisions based on "crown prerogative" and because the case presented a "political question."

The political questions doctrine is a convention developed by the American Supreme Court that prevents courts from hearing constitutional challenges to foreign policy or national defence decisions of the government. It is based on the judges' view of the proper role of the court: that responsibility for such decisions is explicitly allocated to other branches of government (i.e., separation of powers); that judges lack the expertise and facts necessary to make such decisions; and that foreign-policy decisions are based on practical judgment and thus are not susceptible to judicial decision based on "neutral principles." While foreign precedents have only "persuasive" value for Canadian courts, there was reason to believe that the Supreme Court would be reluctant to involve itself in reviewing foreign-policy and defence decisions for the same reasons as its American counterpart. There were also Canadian precedents suggesting that judicial deference was the appropriate policy in these circumstances.[11]

The Supreme Court of Canada, in a decision written by Chief Justice Dickson, avoided dealing with the political questions doctrine and dismissed Operation Dismantle's claim because it was based on alleged facts that could not be proven. In a concurring opinion, however, Justice Wilson boldly stated that crown prerogative did not shield the government's foreign-policy decisions from *Charter* challenges nor did any political-questions doctrine. The issue, declared Wilson, was "whether the courts *should* or *must*

---

9 *Mercure v. Saskatchewan*, [1988] 1 S.C.R. 234.

10 *Operation Dismantle v. The Queen*, [1985] 1 S.C.R. 441.

11 Cf. The JCPC's discussion of whether a wartime emergency still existed in *Fort Frances Pulp and Power Co. v. Manitoba Free Press*, [1923] A.C. 695: "The question of the extent to which provisions for circumstances such as these may have to be maintained is one of which a Court of law is loath to enter. No authority other than the central Government is in a position to deal a problem which is essentially one of statesmanship."

rather than ... whether they can deal with such matters." For her, the answer was clear: "The question before us is not whether the government's defence policy is sound but whether or not it violates the appellants' rights under s.7 of the *Charter*. This is a totally different question."

Justice Wilson's reasoning has been greeted skeptically. Professor Monahan identified the problem when he wrote that Justice Wilson's

> statement is only meaningful if the issue of legality can be determined without recourse to questions of "wisdom." Madame Justice Wilson's confident assertion that the issues are 'totally different' seems based on the fact that the Court is being called on to interpret and to apply a specific "legal" standard, in this case s.7. But the mere fact that the statutory language is involved does not, in itself, provide a distinction between legal and political questions. The issue is whether it is possible to apply the statutory language without an inquiry into the "wisdom" of the legislation under review.[12]

Many agree with Monahan that *Operation Dismantle* is a good example of a case where the legal question is inseparable from the policy question. These criticisms notwithstanding, *Operation Dismantle* appears to have pre-empted the development of a political-questions doctrine that would restrict the scope of the *Charter*'s applicability.

The *Thorson, McNeil, Operation Dismantle* and the two *Borowski* decisions, combined with the *Charter of Rights*, have had the net effect of significantly increasing the potential for judicial policy-making. There would appear to be few remaining legal barriers to prevent the litigation of the constitutionality of most government decisions or policies. If American practice is any guide, interest groups that "lose" in the legislative arenas are inclined to take advantage of this new forum to challenge government policy that they oppose. If a majority of the judges on the Supreme Court decide they want to become involved, they are no longer restrained by the doctrines of mootness, standing, or political questions.

Getting into court is one thing; getting to the Supreme Court of Canada is another. As noted above (Reading 3.0), Parliament amended the *Supreme Court Act* in 1975 to abolish most "appeals by right." Since then, the Court only grants "leave to appeal" in those cases that it deems to raise legal issues of "public importance." Since "public importance" is not defined in the *Supreme Court Act*, the Court has virtually complete discretion in deciding which appeals to hear and which not to. Professor Roy Flemming's recent study of Supreme Court "agenda setting" found that the Court rejects four out of every five leave applications that it receives (Reading 6.6).

How does the Supreme Court decide if a case raises an issue of sufficient "public importance"? The late Justice John Sopinka identified five important

12 Patrick Monahan, *Politics and the Constitution: The Charter, Federalism, and the Supreme Court of Canada* (Toronto: Carswell-Metheun, 1987), pp. 52–53.

considerations: a novel constitutional issue; a significant federal statute of general application; a provincial statute similar to legislation in other provinces; conflicting decisions in the provincial courts of appeal; and the need to revisit an important question of law. Applying these legal criteria, however, is "an art not a science," and they do not impose any significant restrictions on the judges' discretion to hear only those cases they want to hear.

Flemming's study attempts to provide an empirical explanation of what factors influence how the Supreme Court decides which appeals to hear (Reading 6.6). He finds that the most important legal factors influencing the Court's selection are the novelty of the issue, conflicting lower court decisions, dissenting votes in the lower court decision, invitations to revisit an earlier decision, and a demonstrable effect on the interests of either the federal or provincial governments. Asking the Court to correct an alleged lower court mistake, however, did not have a positive effect. These findings confirm Justice Sopinka's advice to lawyers that the Supreme Court is "not a court of error and the fact that a court of appeal reached the wrong result is in itself insufficient" to grant leave to appeal.

Flemming also tested for what extra-legal factors play a role in the judges' choices. He found that the Court was more likely to grant leave to appeal to cases in which applicants have greater resources (or "status") than the respondent. Thus, governments are more likely to succeed than non-government organizations, and organized interests are more likely to succeed than individuals. "Repeat players" (defined as lawyers with more experience before the Court) do not appear to have an advantage over "one-shotters" (lawyers with less experience). Nor does hiring a Queen's Counsel to argue your case appear to be an advantage.

Gaining control of its docket has been one of the most important factors in the Supreme Court's rise in political prominence over the past two decades. It has allowed the Supreme Court to "set its own agenda" rather than having to take whatever appeals happen to come along. This new ability to control its docket, combined with the weakening of the rules on standing and mootness, constitute a significant new strategic asset for Supreme Court justices who want to influence the outcome of leading political controversies of the day.

An important exception to the traditional requirement of a *lis* is the reference procedure (Reading 6.1). Starting with the original *Supreme Court Act* of 1875, the federal government has given itself the authority to "refer" questions of law to the Supreme Court of Canada for answering. A reference procedure is not really a case in the true sense, as there is no real dispute and no real litigants, but only a request for an advisory opinion on a hypothetical legal issue. This distinctive characteristic of the Canadian judicial process is not found in American jurisprudence. Article III of the American Constitution spells out the requirement of a *lis* by limiting the federal courts to hearing only "cases or controversies." At a very early stage, this "case or controversy" requirement was interpreted as preventing the Supreme Court from providing "advisory opinions" to the federal government.

The fact that reference cases are technically "advisory opinions" on hypothetical questions of law should not lead one to underestimate their importance. Approximately one quarter of all final appellate court decisions involving constitutional law have been references. Since 1949, this figure has declined to sixteen per cent. Among these are many of Canada's most important constitutional law decisions. Predictably, governments almost never refer questions to the courts in a political vacuum. References tend to be timely politically, either anticipating a political problem that is on the horizon or, in some cases, already being litigated in a lower court. The 1977 *Anti-Inflation Reference* (Reading 10.4), the 1981 *Patriation Reference* (Reading 2.3), the 1997 *Provincial Judges Reference* (Reading 5.6) and the 1998 *Quebec Secession Reference* (Reading 2.4) all illustrate the political potential of the reference procedure. Finally, even though judicial decisions in references are not technically binding on anyone (since there are no real parties), they are still regarded as authoritative.

The reference procedure has generated ongoing controversy in Canadian jurisprudence. In the original *Supreme Court Act* of 1875, some provincial leaders perceived it as suspiciously resembling the much disliked disallowance power of the federal government and opposed the entire *Supreme Court Act* for this reason (Reading 10.1). This suspicion was nurtured by the rather non-judicial characteristics of the original reference procedure. Only the federal government could refer questions of law to the Supreme Court, but these could be questions concerning the validity of provincial laws. Once the question was referred, there was no opportunity for affected parties – including provinces – to present oral or written arguments in defence of their interests. When the Supreme Court decided a reference, it did not provide any written opinion to support or explain its decision.

In response to continued provincial criticism of the reference procedure, it was substantially reformed in 1891 to make it more closely resemble a normal judicial proceeding. The 1891 amendments require that interested parties be given the opportunity to submit oral and written arguments to the Court and that the Court hand down a written opinion with its final decision. While the federal government did not give provinces the authority to refer questions to the Supreme Court, during the next decade, most provinces gave themselves a reference power to their own courts of appeal. Even after these reforms, the question remained whether answering reference questions from the executive branch was a proper judicial function. This question was put to rest in 1912, when the Judicial Committee of the Privy Council decided a provincial challenge to the constitutionality of the federal government's reference procedure. The JCPC ruled that, although answering references was a "non-judicial function," it could nonetheless be imposed on the courts by statute. It also noted in passing that similar provincial practices implicitly supported the legitimacy of the federal reference procedure.

The advantages and disadvantages of the reference procedure are ably discussed by Justice Barry Strayer in Reading 6.1. One of the alleged advantages, however, deserves further comment. The reference procedure, Strayer and others have argued, is a practical device for each level of government to police the constitutional excesses of the other. While no doubt true in theory, in practice, there has been a tendency for both levels of government to abuse the reference device as a political weapon to attack policies of the other. The federal government's *Off-Shore Mineral Rights Reference* in 1967 is commonly cited as an example of a bad-faith effort of the federal government to seize through the reference procedure what it could not get through political negotiation. The Supreme Court's decision in favour of the federal government in this case seriously harmed the Court's image as an impartial arbiter of federal-provincial disputes, and thus its long-term authority.

Another example was Newfoundland Premier Brian Peckford's use of the reference procedure to improve his bargaining position on the issue of who had the legal authority to control the development of the offshore Hibernia oil reserves. Although Peckford's gamble backfired miserably,[13] he had made it clear from the start that he would not accept the "moral authority" of a Supreme Court decision that went against him. This type of political manoeuvring often places the Supreme Court in a no-win situation, where the justices are "damned if they do, and damned if they don't." This sort of political abuse of the reference procedure threatens to erode the authority of the courts.

In 1997, the Court found itself in just this position when the Liberal government in Ottawa used a reference to ask the Court to rule on the constitutionality of a "unilateral declaration of independence" by Quebec separatists. As William Thorsell pointed out at the time, Ottawa's use of the reference was purely political – to influence public opinion in Quebec (Reading 4.7). Thorsell (and others, including the Quebec government) argued that the Court should refuse to allow itself to be used by the Chrétien government for political purposes. The Court can and has in the past refused to answer reference questions it deems too speculative or ill-defined. In this instance, it chose to hear and answer the reference questions (Reading 2.4). To protect its authority in Quebec, it again tried to craft a compromise that gave something to both parties. To do this, the Court relied on – some would say invented – some unorthodox reasoning based on "unwritten constitutional principles." The problematic nature of the Court's ruling in the *Quebec Secession Reference* is discussed in the introductions to chapters 2 and 10.

For both governments and interest groups, there is an alternative to participating directly as a party in public law litigation: the legal device of the intervenor or *amicus curiae* ("friend of the court"). Under this form of "third-party" participation, a court may grant permission to an individual, group, or

---

13   *Reference re Newfoundland Shelf*, [1984] 1 S.C.R. 86. The federal government referred the same issue to the Supreme Court of Canada before the Newfoundland Court of Appeal made a decision, and the Supreme Court ruled in favour of the federal government. The decision effectively destroyed any legal support for Newfoundland's position on Hibernia development.

government to present a written factum, participate in oral argument, or both. Historically, there was considerable reluctance to allow such third-party participation because it violates the logic of the adversarial process. If the principal function of the court is to resolve the dispute before it, the judges can and should rely on the self-interests of the disputants to develop the legal arguments and facts. If one party fails to do this adequately, only the individual litigant suffers the consequences. However, this argument is less persuasive in public law cases, where the policy dimension of the dispute means that parties beyond the disputants will also be affected. If a constitutional ruling is going to affect other governments or groups, why should they not be allowed to present legal arguments and facts to the court?

Accordingly, the practice of allowing governments to intervene in federalism cases developed early (1880s). In a federal state, a loss or gain of jurisdiction for one government has implications for all governments. Currently, when a constitutional issue (division of powers or *Charter*) is before the Supreme Court, all governments are notified and requests to participate as intervenors are automatically accepted. Intervenors are especially common in constitutional references, both because of their long-term jurisdictional implications and the absence of any concrete factual context within which to judge the issues. For example, in the 1976 *Anti-Inflation Reference*, the Supreme Court granted intervenor status to five provincial governments and five labour unions (Reading 10.4). In 158 federalism cases between 1970 and 1989, there were only twenty-eight without any governmental intervenors.[14]

With the exception of references, Canadian courts have not been receptive to allowing non-government parties to intervene. This reflected the traditional British adjudicatory view of the judicial function and the desire not to encourage interest groups to look to the courts as agents of social change.[15] This policy seemed to be changing in the 1970s, when, under the leadership of Chief Justice Laskin, non-government parties were allowed to participate as intervenors in cases involving the controversial issues of sex discrimination against Indian women and abortion.[16] With the adoption of the *Constitution Act, 1982*, there was a widespread expectation amongst the advocacy groups that had lobbied for the *Charter* that the Court would continue to welcome non-government intervenors. To their chagrin, this did not happen. From 1983 to 1986, the Supreme Court rejected more than half the interest group requests for intervenor status.

The Supreme Court's "closed-door" policy provoked a chorus of protests from interest groups counting on participating in the judicial development of "their" new constitutional rights by intervening in *Charter* litigation. One of

---

14 See Katherine E. Swinton, *The Supreme Court and Canadian Federalism: The Laskin-Dickson Years* (Toronto: Carswell, 1990), pp. 68–75.

15 See the discussion of Kenneth McNaught's thesis in the introduction to chapter 7.

16 Swinton, *The Supreme Court and Canadian Federalism*, p. 70.

the most influential actors in the campaign to persuade the Court to change its ways was Alan Borovoy, General Counsel of the Canadian Civil Liberties Association (CCLA). In an unusual "open letter" to the Supreme Court of Canada (Reading 6.4), Borovoy forcefully argued that it was both unfair and unwise to allow governments but not rights-advocacy groups to intervene in the scores of *Charter* appeals that were beginning to filter their way up to the Court. In such a novel document as the *Charter*, the Court was essentially working on a "blank slate." The Court's first interpretation of each right would become an instant "landmark" precedent, shaping the course of subsequent development. Borovoy predicted (correctly) that most governments would instinctively oppose broad interpretations of rights because these would result in more limitations on governments' choice of policy goals and means. It was important for the country, Borovoy argued, for the Court to hear "countervailing long-term theories for interpreting the *Charter*." Allowing non-government intervenors would mean a better informed Court, which in turn would produce a better *Charter* jurisprudence.

The protest worked. In 1987, the Supreme Court issued new rules for intervenors (factums limited to twenty pages; no oral argument except for special circumstances) and also began a new "open-door" policy. Brodie's study (Reading 6.5) found that, since 1987, the Court has accepted more than eighty per cent of requests to intervene. Encouraged by the Court's new policy, the number of interest-group requests to participate as intervenors also soared. Between 1983 and 1986, there were an average of nineteen requests per year to intervene. This average climbed to twenty-nine per year between 1987 and 1990; and to seventy-four per year between 1991 and 1999. Brodie found that the Supreme Court now hears intervenors in more than sixty per cent of its *Charter* decisions. The routine presence of non-government interest groups in the Court's proceedings marks a radical departure from the pre-*Charter* era and is another indicator of its increased policy-making role.

While there are persuasive legal reasons for allowing non-government intervenors, the policy also encourages and supports interest group litigation as a political tactic. What Borovoy did not state in his open letter to the Court was that the CCLA and other *Charter* groups also have a vested interest in "theories for interpreting the *Charter*." Most *Charter*-oriented groups want to encourage judges to give a broad judicial reading of the rights that most directly concern them. This is what Alan Cairns has described as the process of "constitutional imperialism," a process in which political actors – a group previously limited to governments but that now includes the various "*Charter*-Canadian" groups – "work the constitution" to advance their short- and long-term jurisdictional/jurisprudential objectives. This process of "influencing the influencers" can take different forms, such as writing law review articles that support a preferred interpretation or influencing the appointment of judges. But the most direct way to "lobby the Court" is to participate in constitutional litigation, if not as a litigant then as an intervenor. Their presence as intervenors allows interest groups to provide appellate judges with legal arguments and favourable social facts to support preferred interpretations of the rights in question. It also serves as a political "cue" to signal interest-group support or opposition to the policy issues before the Court. For a court whose decisions are based purely on law and legal principle, such "cueing" would be irrelevant. However, if, as some critics charge and even some judges admit,[17] the Court's decisions are sometimes "result-oriented," then the presence of interest groups before the Court takes on new significance. Interest-group use of litigation is the subject of the next chapter.[18]

6.1

Constitutional References
Barry Strayer
The Canadian Constitution and the Courts: The Function and Scope of Judicial Review. 2nd ed. (Toronto: Butterworths, 1988), 311–34. Reprinted with permission.

One of the most distinctive features of Canadian judicial review is its frequent resort to the constitutional reference. This frequency can be demonstrated by a survey of the leading cases: those reaching the Privy Council up to 1949, the Supreme Court of Canada thereafter, decided from 1867 to 1981. Of 282 cases involving the constitutional issues, 77 had their origins in a constitutional reference while 205 involved concrete cases. Nor does the fact that over a quarter of the leading decisions were given in such proceedings reveal the full significance of constitutional references. In terms of impact on the political, social, and economic affairs of the country the decisions in these cases have had an effect far beyond their numerical proportion. It is therefore essential in any study of judicial review of legislation in Canada to give some particular attention to this device.

...

Advantages

To the extent that problems of standing can still prevent judicial review on constitutional grounds, references provide a means whereby constitutional issues may be placed before the courts.

... Rules of standing in constitutional cases have largely depended in the past on the requirements of particular remedies and ... as a result certain

---

17 See discussion of the "Bastarache Interview" in Readings 5.0 and 9.0.

18 For the most recent and comprehensive treatment of interveners, see Ian Brodie, *Friends of the Court: The Privileging of Interest Group Litigants in Canada* (Albany: State University of New York Press, 2002).

remedies were available for judicial review only to persons with an "interest" distinct from that of the general public. At best the applicant for a declaration, injunction, *certiorari* or prohibition, who does not have such a specific interest, will be subject to the discretionary power of the court to grant or withhold standing, and in the case of *mandamus* he will not be able to proceed. There may be certain constitutional norms, such as the requirements for distribution of constituencies or of periodic elections, in which no individual would be regarded as having a sufficient interest in such judicial review. There may be issues, such as the validity of the federal spending power when used in areas of provincial legislative jurisdiction, or the propriety of constitutional amending procedures, where no individual could persuade a court to grant him standing.

It must be recognized, however, that if the recent trend continues with respect to the discretionary grant of standing in declaratory actions for judicial review, the resort to references to overcome standing problems in constitutional cases may be of marginal importance.

As well as permitting initial judicial review where it would not otherwise be available, a reference may be used to obtain the opinion of a higher court where an appeal would not lie. It is improbable that this precise type of situation would arise now with respect to an appeal from the highest court of a province to the Supreme Court of Canada. Since 1949 the *Supreme Court Act* has permitted appeals without limitation in any matter where either the provincial appellate court or the Supreme Court gives leave. In a constitutional case leave would no doubt be forthcoming from either court. Yet the reference will still be a good substitute for an appeal in some cases. In some provinces there may be situations where an appeal to the highest court is not available, and a reference may be used. Or the parties to the original litigation may not wish to carry a case to the Court of Appeal or the Supreme Court and the provincial or federal Attorney General may be powerless to do so. There is also the possibility that the courts may refuse leave to appeal a case which the Government feels should be appealed. While the Government's power should not be used lightly in such circumstances, the court could be forced by a reference to deal with the issue on which they had refused leave to appeal. Or a reference could be used instead of an appeal to raise related issues not involved in the lower court.

In cases where judicial review will be ultimately possible through private litigation, a reference may nevertheless be desirable to hasten the process. To facilitate public or private planning it may be very valuable to have a judicial opinion in advance with respect to the legality of a particular course of action. For example, the Government may wish to have clarified the constitutionality of a nation-wide unemployment insurance scheme or a marketing scheme before establishing elaborate machinery for its operation. A vivid example of this kind of situation may be found in *Reference re Anti-Inflation Act*. In order to move swiftly to combat a high rate of inflation Parliament had passed this *Act* on December 15, 1975, effective October 14, 1975 directly imposing wage and price controls in the federal public and private sectors, and providing for the imposition of similar controls in the provincial sector where any province entered into an agreement to have those controls apply along with federal administration thereof. All provinces except Quebec entered into such agreements and Quebec established parallel controls. Questions were soon raised as to the validity of the federal law, and its application by agreement to the Ontario provincial domain was being challenged in an action commenced in the courts of that province. Other cases were contemplated elsewhere in Canada. Since the application of the law would disrupt a myriad of transactions throughout the country it was urgent that the constitutional position be clarified. It was referred to the Supreme Court on March 11, 1976, argued on May 31-June 4, 1976, and judgment was given on July 12, 1976, generally upholding the validity of these arrangements. Thus within seven months of the passage of the Act a definitive ruling of the highest court had been obtained as to its validity. The disruptive effect of continuing uncertainty, and the probability of much longer delays before all the issues would otherwise have reached the Supreme Court by ordinary appeal, made the reference device a valuable means of clarifying the situation.

It may be important to businessmen to know under which level of Government they are to operate, and speed of clarification of this issue may be useful in encouraging economic development. This justification has been used, for example, in connection with references to the courts to seek judicial opinions on questions of jurisdiction and ownership over offshore resources.

There will also be situations where speedy determination is more of a necessity than a convenience. Emergency conditions such as war make it imperative that the Government be assured at once of the validity of proposed action. For example, if it wishes to create a regulatory system to ensure the maintenance of vital supplies and the prevention of waste, it cannot afford the luxury of waiting for chance litigation to uphold or strike down the scheme.

A reference may also provide relief where a private citizen would not find it convenient to take a constitutional case to the higher courts. A litigant may have grave doubts about the validity of a statute applied against him, but it may be less expensive for him to drop his objection than to carry the case to an appeal. Yet such a statute applied similarly to dozens or hundreds of people may collectively cause great expense or injustice. In addition, various lower courts may hold conflicting views as to the validity of the law, some upholding it and others deeming it invalid. If no affected individual is prepared to undertake the expense and trouble of appeal, the enforcement of the statute will fall into chaos and the law itself into discredit. A reference to an appellate court may provide the authoritative decision required to restore order. If the statute is held invalid, numerous citizens will be relieved from compliance with legislation which it was not practical for them to contest individually.

With respect to issues which the courts usually regard as non-justiciable a reference might be used to permit judicial determination. There are obviously many non-justiciable issues where the decision ought not to be made by the judiciary, in any form of procedure, because a policy determination is required and there are no objective criteria for guidance. But there are other areas, such as the propriety of parliamentary procedure, where pre-established norms are available for application. It is not certain that a court would review a federal statute on the basis that it was passed by a procedure not in accordance with the *Constitution Act*. Yet the directions of the Act in this regard are as clear as those of sections 91 and 92 which the courts constantly apply.

Finally, references provide a flexible means for each level of Government to challenge the constitutional authority of the other level of Government. The federal Government was given this power in another form through the disallowance procedure. But federal disallowance of provincial legislation on the sole grounds that it was *ultra vires* fell into disfavour and by 1935 was expressly abandoned. Even where the power was exercised on this ground, it was common for the Federal Government first to refer the question of validity to the Supreme Court and be guided by its advice. The reference is now the principal means for the Government of Canada to challenge the validity of provincial legislation. It may of course refer such legislation on its own initiative or at the request of the province concerned. Equally, the provinces may challenge the validity of federal legislation or even a parliamentary resolution by referring it to a provincial court, in this way ensuring that it will ultimately reach the highest tribunals. In Ontario the Attorney General may, in the alternative, seek a declaration that an Act of Parliament is invalid, but presumably the reference procedure would be speedier.

The essential advantage of the reference system thus appears to be facilitation of judicial review. In some cases it makes the impossible possible, in others it speeds the process where time is of the essence. To those for whom enforced judicial activism poses no threat, the constitutional reference may appear as an unmixed benefit. But it is also essential to consider some of the problems which arise out of its use.

Disadvantages

Two principal disadvantages of references can be identified: they may foster abstract jurisprudence because they require an opinion from the court without the benefit of an adequate factual context; and they may cause the court to decide issues which are not really justiciable because Governments are seemingly unlimited in the questions they can refer. These difficulties flow from the very nature of references: that is, they do not arise out of a specific controversy between parties where legal rights are in issue.

The first problem mentioned, the lack of an adequate factual basis, has been thought not only to hinder sound characterization of laws, but also to lead more frequently to a finding of invalidity.

The suspicion that they favour findings of invalidity cannot be clearly confirmed on a statistical basis. A survey of leading constitutional cases from 1867 through 1981, those reaching the highest tribunal available, either the Privy Council or the Supreme Court, shows that the results in the courts for each level of Government were not dramatically different as between references and ordinary litigation. Of cases involving provincial competence, in 42 references provincial authority was upheld in 22 cases and found lacking in 20 cases – a failure rate of about 50%. In ordinary litigation, in 138 cases the provinces succeeded in 82 and lost in 55, a failure rate of about 40%. For the federal authority, in 38 references there was a finding of invalidity in 11 cases, a loss rate of about 29% whereas the loss rate in ordinary litigation was 13 of 68 cases, or about 20%. So the contrasts are far from marked as between results achieved in references and ordinary litigation. The statistical results are unreliable because of the relatively small numbers and the probable existence of other factors involved as between references and litigation and as between federal and provincial results.

It is interesting, however, to look at some of the most abstract and influential reference decisions in our constitutional history to understand the nature of this problem. One need only look at a few examples. In the 1916 *Reference re Insurance Act* the Supreme Court was asked for an opinion as to the validity of certain sections of the federal *Insurance Act*, 1910. This legislation required the federal registration of insurance companies before they could carry on business. It was broad enough to cover provincially incorporated companies carrying on business in Canada outside the province of incorporation. A majority of the Supreme Court confined itself to an exercise in semantics, holding that the federal power to regulate "trade and commerce" could not include "a trade." The insurance business was regarded as "a trade," hence not susceptible to federal control. One of the dissenting judges, Davies J., took a more functional approach. He took judicial notice of the national significance of the insurance business, the mobility of insured persons, and the possible national repercussions of the failure of a major company. This enabled him to find that the business of insurance was clearly a matter of national trade and commerce. But the Privy Council on appeal sided with the majority below, Viscount Haldane at his dogmatic best holding that

> ... it must now be taken that the authority to legislate for the regulation of trade and commerce does not extend to the regulation by a licensing system of a particular trade in which Canadians would otherwise be free to engage in the provinces.

Here was a reference involving the bare question, "Are sections 40 and 70 of the 'Insurance Act, 1910,' or any or what part or parts of the said sections, *ultra vires* of the Parliament of Canada?" No factual information was included with the reference, nor apparently was any otherwise presented to the court. Without consideration of the factual context in which the legislation would operate, the majority of the Supreme Court and the Privy Council set aside the legislation on a conceptual analysis of the word "trade." The net result was to bar the Parliament of Canada from regulating businesses which were interprovincial in scope, because their operations could be analytically dismembered into a collection of "particular trades" carried on in particular provinces....

... This examination of a few major reference decisions of historic importance illustrates their potential for creating abstract jurisprudence. There are, however, several mitigating factors which should be recognized in assessing the merits of the reference system in this respect.

First it should be recognized that while such decisions were conceptual rather than functional, this was also true of contemporary decisions in normal litigation. There were many concrete cases where facts were probably available but not relied on. In defence of the Privy Council decisions of this period, whether on references or in litigation, it has been argued that, whatever their economic validity, they were politically realistic.

Secondly, there are situations where there is no need for a factual study of legislative effect or administrative action. This arises where the issue is solely that of an interpretation of a section of the constitution where no legislation is involved and no official action is being questioned. These cases will be rare, and the decision therein may be of limited use. But occasionally they will be valuable, where the issue in question is sufficiently narrow. For example in *Edwards* v. *A.G. Can.* the question was whether the word "persons" in section 24 of the B.N.A. Act included women, thus making the latter eligible for appointment to the Senate. The answer turned completely on internal evidence in the Act. The effect of each possible interpretation was readily apparent....

... Thirdly the remedy for abstract reference decisions should not be total abandonment of this sometimes useful device, but rather a more selective use of it accompanied by adequate fact-introduction.... It has been demonstrated that the Supreme Court has led the way in emphasizing the importance of facts in references and the trend appears to be for counsel to meet these judicial expectations. What we are seeing in reality is a rather unsteady movement from the conceptual jurisprudence so beloved by the Judicial Committee and its followers to a more functional jurisprudence in which facts are all important. Therefore much of this particular problem traditionally associated with the reference process may disappear, although the inherent nature of the device is a reminder that constant care must be exercised in its use. There should be a careful framing of questions so that issues may be raised as precisely as possible. Courts should refuse to answer questions which are too general or which require a factual context if none is provided. They should also avoid answering questions not clearly included in the reference order. If these principles are faithfully applied in reference cases, there will be far less complaint of abstractness.

The second major problem with references noted above is that they may call upon a court to answer questions that are not justiciable. Reference statutes at both the federal and provincial level allow Governments to refer any "matter" to the courts. This would appear on its face to include any question not only of law, but also of politics, science, or taste. It has recently been held, however, by a majority of seven in the Supreme Court in the *Re Resolution to Amend the Constitution* that such a provincial statute

> ... is wide enough to saddle the respective courts with the determination of questions which may not be justiciable and there is no doubt that those courts, and this Court on appeal, have a discretion to refuse to answer such questions.

Given the lack of a clear separation of powers in our system it is perhaps not surprising that the court did not deny itself the right to decide non-justiciable questions but only asserted a power to decline to do so at its discretion. It is encouraging to know that the courts will not feel obliged to decide questions which functionally belong elsewhere. But at the same time it must be noted that, having asserted the right to refuse to answer, the court in this same case proceeded to answer questions posed by provincial Governments to their courts and appealed to the Supreme Court as to the existence and nature of a political convention concerning the use of legal powers.

While Legislatures have thus authorized Government to refer non-justiciable questions to the courts, normally they do not do so nor, it is submitted, should they do so if they wish to protect the court from undue political controversy and resulting hazards to their legitimacy. The federal Government has in fact articulated such a principle in the course of resisting pressures for references to the Supreme Court.

When governments do not exercise self-restraint in this respect, it is open to the courts to do so and to decline to decide such issues. When these safeguards are not employed, the reference system does thrust the courts into the decision of non-justiciable issues that may in the long term impair their effectiveness.

Lesser criticisms of the reference system include that of possible interference with private rights. Judges have occasionally hesitated to answer a referred question because, though worded generally, it may include issues on which the rights of specific individuals may turn. It is thought unfair to render such decisions where individuals who may be seriously affected are not represented before the court. As previously noted, this criticism appears specious for the same may be said of almost any decision....

... The real fault lies, not in the initial reference decision having possible implications for private individuals, but rather in the misplaced fidelity with which such decisions are subsequently followed. This is part of the broader complaint that reference decisions have generally been given undue precedential value. In other words, what were originally intended to be opinions only have been treated as judgments.

When the *Supreme Court Act* was amended in 1891 reference opinions were described as "advisory only." This was soon ignored and the Privy Council and Supreme Court expressly followed the decisions in earlier federal references with undiscriminating zeal. Not until 1957, after the "advisory only" provision had actually been dropped from the *Supreme Court Act* did the Supreme Court suggest the possibility that it would ignore earlier reference decisions, even those of the Judicial Committee. It then stated that it was not bound by a decision of the Judicial Committee rendered in a reference involving some of the same issues and parties now before it in a concrete case. It may be noted, however, that this was *obiter dicta*, for the Supreme Court accepted the opinion of the Privy Council.

It is to be hoped that this judicial declaration of independence will not be forgotten by its authors. Uncritical following of reference decisions brings discredit on the whole reference system. The rendering of opinions on hypothetical questions or on issues affecting private rights would create few problems if they were not subsequently treated as conclusive. An opinion on an abstract question should be regarded as of limited value, valid only in relation to the assumptions and facts on which it was rendered....

... Combined with the abandonment of *stare decisis* with respect to reference opinions, there should be a more discriminating use of such opinions when invoked for persuasive purposes. In analyzing what a reference actually "decided," the opinion should be carefully examined in relation to the precise hypotheses put to the court and the facts, if any, before it. Such analysis may reveal that the opinion decided very little, in which case it ought not to be an embarrassment in subsequent cases.

In sum, it is suggested that if references have created premature or overly broad precedents the fault lies more in judicial practice than in the reference system. Judicial reform would remove the substance of this complaint.

Conclusion

The controversy over references is really an aspect of the larger controversy with respect to the role of the judiciary in interpreting and applying the constitution. Judicial activists will generally approve of a system which overcomes obstacles to judicial review. Those who take a more restricted view of the role of the judiciary will see it as a hazardous procedure, burdening the courts with hypothetical questions and producing premature decisions with mischievous consequences.

On balance the case for the use of references seems more supportable. If one accepts the courts as the best arbiters of constitutional rules, one should favour a system which facilitates judicial review. There are some situations where a reference will be justified in the interests of speed, clarification for the benefit of many individuals who would not readily be able to seek judicial review, or the elimination of technical barriers to bringing actions or taking appeals.

Several caveats must be entered, however. In the first place, some of the justifications for the use of references have been attenuated by developments of the last decade. The obstacles to standing for individuals to seek declarations on constitutional issues, the nearest substitute for a reference, have largely disappeared. With almost universal legal aid for the individual and numerous special interest groups able to undertake or support litigation, Government initiatives by way of a constitutional reference are now not as necessary to ensure judicial review. At the same time the development of a more functional jurisprudence with greater emphasis on the factual context tends to militate against the use of the reference which often lacks factual substance. So although there is still a role for the reference it has been somewhat reduced by events.

Where there are reasons for resorting to a reference, Governments should still avoid doing so if the issue to be referred is not justiciable in the sense that it is one better left to another branch of Government or one which lacks objective criteria for its determination. The principal danger to be avoided here is the reference of essentially a political issue to the courts: where there are few, if any, genuinely legal criteria to which courts can resort for a rationale for their decision, they may be perceived as making a political judgment which may impair their long-term credibility.

Once the decision is taken to refer a constitutional question, then care should be taken in its framing so that the issues are precisely defined. The referring Government and counsel on all sides should make every effort to ensure that all relevant facts are placed before the court.

As for the courts, they should be astute enough to refuse answers to questions that are non-justiciable, or too vague to be effectively answered. They should have regard to gleaning all relevant evidence, including an active resort to judicial notice. They should also examine critically earlier opinions and be prepared to disregard or distinguish those which were too general, too vague, or too abstract.

Even a carefully constructed reference system must play a secondary role in judicial review, however. A decision based on complete facts and real issues is to be preferred to one based on incomplete facts, or hypothetical problems, and a binding authority is likely to be more reliable than an advisory opinion. Thus, if other circumstances are equal and judicial review through a concrete case is feasible, it should be preferred. The reference should be seen as a useful supplement to our judicial review system, but one to be resorted to with caution and perhaps, in the future, with diminishing frequency. The second century of Confederation has so far seen a sharply reduced rate of references in comparison to the volume of ordinary constitutional litigation, and this trend is likely to continue.

6.2

Minister of Justice of Canada v. Borowski
Supreme Court of Canada (1981)

Laskin C.J.C. (dissenting): This appeal, which is here by leave of this Court given on terms as to costs, arises out of a taxpayer's action brought in the Court of Queen's Bench of Saskatchewan. The purpose of the action was to obtain a declaration against the appellants, the Minister of Justice of Canada and the Minister of Finance of Canada, that the so-called abortion provisions of *Criminal Code*, s.251(4), (5) and (6) are inoperative as offending ss.1(a) and 2(e) and (g) of the *Canadian Bill of Rights* and that any expenditure of public money to support therapeutic abortions under the aforesaid provisions of the *Criminal Code* is consequently illegal. Issue was taken by the defendants appellants as to the jurisdiction of the Court of Queen's Bench to entertain the action.... In their statement of defence, the defendants also challenged the standing of the plaintiff to maintain the action, regardless, apparently, of the appropriateness of the forum.

I start with the proposition that, as a general rule, it is not open to a person, simply because he is a citizen and a taxpayer or is either the one or the other, to invoke the jurisdiction of a competent Court to obtain a ruling on the interpretation or application of legislation or on its validity, when that person is not either directly affected by the legislation or is not threatened by sanction for an alleged violation of the legislation. Mere distaste has never been a ground upon which to seek the assistance of a Court. Unless the legislation itself provides for a challenge to its meaning or application or validity by any citizen or taxpayer, the prevailing policy is that a challenger must show some special interest in the operation of the legislation beyond the general interest that is common to all members of the relevant society. This is especially true of the criminal law. For example, however passionately a person may believe that it is wrong to provide for compulsory breathalyzer tests or wrong to make mere possession of marijuana an offence against the criminal law, the Courts are not open to such a believer, not himself or herself charged or even threatened with a charge, to seek a declaration against the enforcement of such criminal laws.

The *rationale* of this policy is based on the purpose served by Courts. They are dispute-resolving tribunals, established to determine contested rights or claims between or against persons or to determine their penal or criminal liability when charged with offences prosecuted by agents of the Crown. Courts do not normally deal with purely hypothetical matters where no concrete legal issues are involved, where there is no *lis* that engages their processes or where they are asked to answer questions in the abstract merely to satisfy a person's curiosity or perhaps his or her obsessiveness with a perceived injustice in the existing law. Special legislative provisions for references to the Courts to answer particular questions (which may be of a hypothetical nature) give that authority to Governments alone and not to citizens or taxpayers. Merely because a Government may refuse a citizen's or taxpayer's request to refer to the Courts a question of interest to the taxpayer does not *per se* create a right in the citizen or taxpayer to invoke the Court's process on his or her own, or by way of a class action on behalf of all citizens or taxpayers with the same interest.

There are exceptions to the general rule and to the policy. One of the earliest recognized has been a municipal taxpayer action to restrain an allegedly illegal municipal expenditure.... An explanation of this exception is that it involved a public right to see that municipal expenditures were lawfully made, being expenditures which were limited by considerations that do not apply to a Province or to Canada. No municipal taxpayer could raise a *lis* in the ordinary sense or court a penalty or other sanction in respect of an allegedly illegal municipal expenditure and, hence, unless a taxpayer action was permitted, the illegality would go unchallenged and unchallengeable.

In the provincial and federal field, the issue of an illegal, or perhaps unconstitutional, expenditure would not likely arise *per se* but, in the main, only (as is alleged in this case) in connection with the operation of challenged legislation: the challenge to the expenditure would thus depend on the outcome of the challenge to the legislation.

Another exception (but a more limited one in view of the discretion associated with it) is shown in the judgment of this Court in *Thorson* v. *A.G. Can. et al. (No. 2)* (1974).... That case involved a taxpayer's class action to obtain a declaration of the invalidity of the *Official Languages Act*, now R.S.C. 1970, c. 0-2, and of the illegality of the appropriation of money to administer it. It was clear that a justiciable question was raised to the claim of invalidity, namely, whether Parliament had respected the limits of its legislative authority under the *British North America Act, 1867*. Again, the *Official Languages Act* was not a regulatory type of statute nor a penal one but rather, uniquely, a declaratory and directory statute, a statute which created no offences and imposed no penalties. Unless, therefore, a citizen or taxpayer action was permitted to question its validity, there would be no way in which its validity could be tested unless the federal Attorney-General did so through a reference and a request to this end had been denied....

... There is, in this respect, in the permissive provisions of s.251(4), (5) and (6), some similarity perhaps to the directory features of the legislation in the *Thorson* case. However, these provisions are part of a scheme which embraces sanctions as well, and I do not find the similarity to be sufficient to put the legislation here on the same level as the statute involved in the *Thorson* case. Indeed, to borrow from the words of this Court in the *Thorson* case, the present case is not one where all members of the public are affected alike. This, in my view, is a central consideration in the exercise of the Court's discretion against giving standing here to the plaintiff respondent.

It is contended on the plaintiff's behalf that if he cannot bring himself within the *Thorson* case, his position as to standing is as strong as that of the respondent in this Court's follow-up decision to *Thorson* in *Nova Scotia Board of Censors* v. *McNeil* (1975).… That was also a case where a taxpayer action challenging the validity of legislation, provincial legislation in that case, was held to be maintainable.… The *Theatres and Amusements Act* of Nova Scotia, whose validity was challenged in the *McNeil* case, was a regulatory statute directed to film exchanges, theatre owners and cinematograph operators and apprentices. It also provided for the appointment of a Board, empowered to permit or prohibit the use or exhibition in Nova Scotia, for public entertainment, of any film or any performance in any theatre. Licensing regulations were provided for in respect of theatres and film exchanges, in respect of cinematograph operators and apprentices and in respect of theatre performances. Unfettered discretion to suspend or revoke any licence was vested in the Board. It had, to put it shortly, complete control over the exhibition of films and over theatres in the Province. Although there was a statutory right of appeal to the Lieutenant-Governor in Council, it was not open to a member of the public.

The Nova Scotia Courts, before whom the question of standing came, and this Court on appeal construed the challenged statute as involving members of the public in so far as the Board had the power to determine what members of the public were entitled to view in theatres and other places of public entertainment. This Court assessed the matter as follows:

> Since the issue of validity does not fall for determination here and, indeed, has not even been argued in relation to the question of standing I would not, in this case, go beyond the tentative conclusion that there is an arguable case under the terms of the challenged legislation that members of the Nova Scotia public are directly affected in what they may view in a Nova Scotia theatre, albeit there is a more direct effect on the business enterprises which are regulated by the legislation. The challenged legislation does not appear to me to be legislation directed only to the regulation of operators and film distributors. It strikes at the members of the public in one of its central aspects.

> In my view, this is enough, in the light of the fact that there appears to be no other way, practically speaking, to subject the challenged Act to judicial review, to support the claim of the respondent to have the discretion of the Court exercised in his favour to give him standing.

This passage underlines at least one important difference between the situation in *McNeil* and the present case. In *McNeil*, the plaintiff could legitimately complain (on this Court's construction of the challenged statute) that he was a person within its terms who was being deprived of a right to view a film because of an allegedly unconstitutional exercise of legislative and administrative power. In the present case, there is no deprivation under or by reason of the challenged legislation of which the plaintiff can complain. In short, the plaintiff here is not in the same position under the legislation which he challenges as was McNeil in his case. There he was a person within the compass of the enactment that he was challenging; the plaintiff is outside the *Criminal Code* provisions that he is attacking.

I am of the opinion that the plaintiff in this case cannot bring himself within the *McNeil* case nor within the *Thorson* case, so far as concerns the character of the legislation involved here as compared with the legislation in those cases.... My reason for distinguishing the legislative situation is that here there are persons with an interest in the operation of s.251(4), (5) and (6) who might challenge it as offending the *Canadian Bill of Rights*. I refer to doctors and to hospitals, both having a clearer interest in the operation of s.251(4), (5) and (6) than does the plaintiff. Husbands who might object to their pregnant wives seeking therapeutic abortions also have a clearer interest. It may be that in their case there would be a dilemma, having regard to the inexorable progress of a pregnancy.... In principle, however, this should not be preclusive; the point will have been decided at the instance of a person having an interest and not at that of a person having no interest other than as a citizen and taxpayer.

... The present case lacks concreteness despite the fact that it raises a highly charged issue. Moreover, it appears to me that to permit the issue to be litigated in as abstract a manner as would be the case in having the plaintiff alone carry it against two Ministers of the Crown would hardly do justice to it, absent even any intervenors who might, with the same obsessiveness on the opposite side of the issue, argue for the valid operation of the challenged provisions. Even accepting, as is probable, that if standing was accorded to the plaintiff, other persons with an opposite point of view might seek to intervene and would be allowed to do so, the result would be to set up a battle between parties who do not have a direct interest, [and] to wage it in a judicial arena.

I would hold, therefore, that not only has the plaintiff failed to establish any judicially cognizable interest in the matter he raises but, on any view of this case, the discretion of the Court should be exercised to deny him standing. It follows that his action should be dismissed....

MARTLAND, J. (for the Court):

... The issue raised is a difficult and important one, involving the question as to whether the human rights declared in the *Canadian Bill of Rights* protect a human foetus.

In his statement of claim, the respondent states that he is a citizen of Canada and a taxpayer to the Government of Canada. He goes on to state in the following paragraphs of the statement of claim:

3. On February 20, 1969 the Plaintiff was elected by the voters of the provincial constituency of Thompson, Manitoba to represent them in the Legislative Assembly of Manitoba, a position

he maintained until June 28, 1973. In his capacity as taxpayer, elected representative of the people in the Legislative Assembly, a member of the governing party in the legislative Assembly of Manitoba and Minister of and adviser to Her Majesty the Queen in Right of the Province of Manitoba, the Plaintiff has continuously promoted and defended the rights of individual human foetuses, including their right to life.

4.   The Plaintiff has canvassed all practicable means to invoke action on the part of both Provincial and Federal Governments to repeal or to impugn the validity of the abortion sections of the *Criminal Law Amendment Act*, Statutes of Canada, 1968-69, chapter 38, section 18, (now section 251, subsections (4), (5) and (6), of the *Criminal Code of Canada*, hereinafter referred to as "the abortion section of the *Criminal Code*") and to cease and desist from spending public funds to abort and destroy individual human foetuses.

5.   The steps taken by the Plaintiff included:

    (a) His resignation, on or about September 5, 1971, *inter alia,* because as Minister of and adviser to Her Majesty the Queen, he "could not be a party to, or accept, child-destroying legislation in which we (are) involved";

    (b) His address in the Legislative Assembly of Manitoba, on May 4, 1973, opposing adoption of the budget presented by the Provincial Treasurer that proposed to finance the abortion and destruction of individual human foetuses by the expenditure of public funds;

    (c) His continuous objection over a term of years to payment of his personal income tax to the Federal Government to protest its expenditures of public moneys collected by personal income taxes, to finance and to promote the abortion and destruction of individual human foetuses, and his conviction and sentence to terms in jail for his stand;

    (d) His personal correspondence with the Premier and Cabinet of the Province of Manitoba, with the Prime Minister of Canada and with Members of his Cabinet including the Minister of Justice, the Minister of Finance, and the Solicitor-General of Canada requesting that they take appropriate legal action to protect the rights of individual human foetuses;

    (e) His request addressed to the Official Guardian of Manitoba in the year 1977, to take legal proceedings on behalf of individual human foetuses to prevent their abortion and destruction, and to protect their right to life.

In every instance, the efforts of the Plaintiff to move public officials to impugn the validity of the abortion provisions referred to in paragraph 4 hereof by judicial proceedings met with negative response. No one undertook to subject these provisions, of great public importance, to judicial review.

For the purpose of these proceedings, all of these statements must be accepted as being true....

In both the *Thorson* and *McNeil* cases, the challenge to the legislation in question was founded upon their alleged constitutional invalidity. In the present case, the challenge is based upon the operation of the *Canadian Bill of Rights*. I agree with the view expressed by the Chief Justice that no distinction should be made between a declaratory action to obtain a decision on validity under the *British North America Act, 1867* and a declaratory action to obtain a decision on the operative effect in the face of the *Canadian Bill of Rights*.

The legislation under attack here is not declaratory or directory as in the case of the *Official Languages Act* nor is it regulatory as in the case of the *Theatres and Amusements Act*. It is exculpatory in nature. It provides that in certain specified circumstances conduct which otherwise would be criminal is permissible. It does not impose duties, but instead provides exemption from criminal liability. That being so, it is difficult to find any class of person directly affected or exceptionally prejudiced by it who would have cause to attack the legislation.

Doctors who perform therapeutic abortions are protected by the legislation and would have no reason to attack it. Doctors who do not perform therapeutic abortions have no direct interest to protect by attacking it, and, consequently, an attack by a doctor in that category would be no different from that made by any other concerned citizen. The same thing applies to hospitals. A hospital which appoints a therapeutic abortion committee has no reason to attack the legislation. A hospital which does not appoint such a committee has no direct reason to attack the legislation.

There is no reason why a pregnant woman desirous of obtaining an abortion should challenge the legislation which is for her benefit. The husband of a pregnant wife who desires to prevent an abortion which she desires may be said to be directly affected by the legislation in issue in the sense that by reason of the legislation she might obtain a certificate permitting the abortion if her continued pregnancy would be likely to endanger her life or health and thus prevent the abortion from constituting a crime. However, the possibility of the husband bringing proceedings to attack the legislation is illusory. The progress of the pregnancy would not await the inevitable lengthy lapse of time involved in Court proceedings leading to a final judgment. The abortion would have occurred, or a child would have been born long before the case had been finally terminated, perhaps in this Court.

The legislation proposed to be attacked has direct impact upon the unborn human foetuses whose existences may be terminated by legalized abortions. They obviously cannot be parties to proceedings in Court and yet the issue as to the scope of the *Canadian Bill of Rights* in the protection of the human right to life is a matter of considerable importance. There is no reasonable way in which that issue can be brought into Court unless proceedings are launched by some interested citizen.

In the light of the *Thorson* and *McNeil* cases, it is my opinion that the respondent should be recognized as having legal standing to continue with his action. In the *Thorson* case, the plaintiff, as an interested citizen, challenged the constitutional validity of the *Official Languages Act*. The legislation did not directly affect him, save in his position as a taxpayer. He had sought, without avail, to have the constitutional issue raised by other means. He was recognized to have status. The position is the same in the present case. The respondent is a concerned citizen and a taxpayer. He has sought unsuccessfully to have the issue determined by other means.

In the *McNeil* case, the plaintiff was concerned about censorship of films in Nova Scotia. He had sought by other means to have the validity of the *Theatres and Amusements Act* tested, but without success. In that case there were other classes of persons directly affected by the legislation who might have challenged it. None the less, he was recognized as having legal standing because it also affected the rights of the public. The position of the respondent in this case is at least as strong. There are in this case no persons directly affected who could effectively challenge the legislation.

I interpret these cases as deciding that to establish status as a plaintiff in a suit seeking a declaration that legislation is invalid, if there is a serious issue as to its invalidity, a person need only to show that he is affected by it directly or that he has a genuine interest as a citizen in the validity of the legislation and that there is no other reasonable and effective manner in which the issue may be brought before the Court. In my opinion, the respondent has met this test and should be permitted to proceed with his action.

6.3

Borowski v. *Attorney-General of Canada*
Supreme Court of Canada (1989)
[Intervenors: Interfaith Coalition on the Rights and Wellbeing of Women and Children, REAL Women of Canada, and Women's Legal Education and Action Fund (LEAF)]

The judgment of the Court was delivered by SOPINKA J.: This appeal by leave of this Court is from the Saskatchewan Court of Appeal, [1987] which affirmed the judgment at trial of Matheson J. of the Saskatchewan Court of Queen's Bench, [1984] dismissing the action of the plaintiff (appellant in this Court). In the courts below, the plaintiff attacked the validity of subss.(4), (5) and (6) of s.251 of the *Criminal Code*, relating to abortion, on the ground that they contravened protected rights of the foetus. Subsequent to the decision of the Saskatchewan Court of Appeal but by the time the appeal reached this

Court, s.251, including the subsections under attack in this action, had been struck down in *R. v. Morgentaler* [1988].

From this state of the proceedings it was apparent at the commencement of this appeal that a serious issue existed as to whether the appeal was moot. As well, it appeared questionable whether the appellant had lost his standing and, indeed, whether the matter was justiciable. The Court therefore called upon counsel to address these issues as a preliminary matter. Upon completion of these submissions, we reserved decision on these issues and heard the argument of the merits of the appeal so that we could dispose of the whole appeal without recalling the parties for argument should we decide that, notwithstanding the preliminary issues, the appeal should proceed.

In view of the conclusion that I have reached, it is necessary to deal with the issues of mootness and standing only. Since it is a change in the nature of these proceedings which gives rise to these issues, a review of the history of the action is necessary....

[*Ed. note*: Justice Sopinka recounts Borowski's first trip to the Supreme Court, culminating in the 1981 decision granting standing [Reading 6.2]. Sopinka notes that Borowski's claim was amended in 1983 to include claims based on the 1982 *Charter of Rights*. Borowski's *Charter* challenge to section 251 was rejected by the Saskatchewan Court of Queen's Bench (1983) and the Saskatchewan Court of Appeal (1987).]

On January 28, 1988, after leave to appeal was granted, this Court decided *R. v. Morgentaler (No. 2), supra*, in which all of s.251 was found to violate s.7 of the *Charter*. Accordingly, s.251 in its entirety was struck down.

In July of 1988 in light of this Court's judgment in *R. v. Morgentaler (No. 2), supra*, counsel on behalf of the Attorney General of Canada applied to adjourn the hearing of the appeal. The respondent argued that the issue was now moot as s.251 of the *Criminal Code* had been nullified and that the two remaining constitutional questions (numbers 1 and 3) which simply ask whether a child *en ventre sa mère* is entitled to the protection of ss.7 and 15 of the *Charter* respectively are not severable from the other, now moot constitutional questions. Although the respondent claimed the matter was moot, no application to quash the appeal was made. The application to adjourn the hearing of the appeal was denied by Chief Justice Dickson on July 19, 1988, leaving it to the Court to address the mootness issue.

I am of the opinion that the appeal should be dismissed on the grounds that: (1) Mr. Borowski's case has been rendered moot and (2) he has lost his standing. When s.251 was struck down, the basis of the action disappeared. The initial prayer for relief was no longer applicable. The foundation for standing upon which the previous decision of this Court was based also disappeared.

Mootness

The doctrine of mootness is an aspect of a general policy or practice that a court may decline to decide a case which raises merely a hypothetical or abstract question. The general principle applies when the decision of the court will not have the effect of resolving some controversy which affects or may affect the rights of the parties. If the decision of the court will have no practical effect on such rights, the court will decline to decide the case. This essential ingredient must be present not only when the action or proceeding is commenced but at the time when the court is called upon to reach a decision. Accordingly if, subsequent to the initiation of the action or proceeding, events occur which affect the relationship of the parties so that no present live controversy exists which affects the rights of the parties, the case is said to be moot. The general policy or practice is enforced in moot cases unless the court exercises its discretion to depart from its policy or practice. The relevant factors relating to the exercise of the court's discretion are discussed hereinafter.

The approach in recent cases involves a two-step analysis. First it is necessary to determine whether the required tangible and concrete dispute has disappeared and the issues have become academic. Second, if the response to the first question is affirmative, it is necessary to decide if the court should exercise its discretion to hear the case. The cases do not always make it clear whether the term "moot" applies to cases that do not present a concrete controversy or whether the term applies only to such of those cases as the court declines to hear. In the interest of clarity, I consider that a case is moot if it fails to meet the "live controversy" test. A court may nonetheless elect to address a moot issue if the circumstances warrant.

When is an Appeal Moot? – The Authorities

The first stage in the analysis requires a consideration of whether there remains a live controversy. The controversy may disappear rendering an issue moot due to a variety of reasons, some of which are discussed below.

In *The King ex rel. Tolfree* v. *Clark*, [1944] this Court refused to grant leave to appeal to applicants seeking a judgment excluding the respondents from sitting and exercising their functions as Members of the Ontario Legislative Assembly. However, the Legislative Assembly had been dissolved prior to the hearing before this Court. As a result, Duff C.J., on behalf of the Court, held at p. 72:

> It is one of those cases where, the state of facts to which the proceedings in the lower Courts related and upon which they were founded having ceased to exist, the sub-stratum of the litigation has disappeared. In accordance with well-settled principle, therefore, the appeal could not properly be entertained.

A challenged municipal by-law was repealed prior to a hearing in *Moir* v. *The Corporation of the Village of Huntingdon* (1891), leading to a conclusion that the appealing party had no actual interest and that a decision could have no effect on the parties except as to costs. Similarly, in a fact situation analogous to this appeal, the Privy Council refused to address the constitutionality of challenged legislation where two statutes in question were repealed prior to the hearing: *Attorney-General for Alberta* v. *Attorney-General for Canada*, [1939] A.C. 117 (P.C.)....

The particular circumstances of the parties to an action may also eliminate the tangible nature of a dispute. The death of parties challenging the validity of a parole revocation hearing (*Re Cadeddu and The Queen* (1983)) and a speeding ticket (*Saskatchewan* v. *Mercure*, [1988]) ended any concrete controversy between the parties.

As well, the inapplicability of a statute to the party challenging the legislation renders a dispute moot: *Law Society of Upper Canada* v. *Skapinker*, [1984]. This is similar to those situations in which an appeal from a criminal conviction is seen as moot where the accused has fulfilled his sentence prior to an appeal: *Re Maltby* v. *Attorney-General of Saskatchewan* (1984).

The issue of mootness has arisen more frequently in American jurisprudence, and there, the doctrine is more fully developed. This may be due in part to the constitutional requirement, contained in s.2(1) of Article III of the American Constitution, that there exist a "case or controversy."...

However, despite the constitutional enshrinement of the principle, the mootness doctrine has its roots in common law principles similar to those in Canada....

The American jurisprudence indicates a similar willingness to consider the merits of an action in some circumstances even when the controversy is no longer concrete and tangible. The rule that abstract, hypothetical or contingent questions will not be heard is not absolute....

Is This Appeal Moot?

In my opinion, there is no longer a live controversy or concrete dispute as the substratum of Mr. Borowski's appeal has disappeared. The basis for the action was a challenge relating to the constitutionality of subss.(4), (5) and (6) of s.251. That section of the *Criminal Code* having been struck down in *R.* v. *Morgentaler (No. 2)*, the *raison d'être* of the action has disappeared. None of the relief claimed in the statement of claim is relevant. Three of the five constitutional questions that were set explicitly concern s.251 and are no longer applicable. The remaining two questions addressing the scope of ss.7 and 15 *Charter* rights are not severable from the context of the original challenge to s.251. These questions were only ancillary to the central issue of the alleged unconstitutionality of the abortion provisions of the *Criminal Code*. They were a mere step in the process of measuring the impugned provision against the *Charter*.

In any event, this Court is not bound by the wording of any constitutional question which is stated. Nor may the question be used to transform an appeal into a reference....

By reason of the foregoing, I conclude that this appeal is moot. It is necessary, therefore, to move to the second stage of the analysis by examining the basis upon which this Court should exercise its discretion either to hear or to decline to hear this appeal.

The Exercise of Discretion: Relevant Criteria

Since the discretion which is exercised relates to the enforcement of a policy or practice of the Court, it is not surprising that a neat set of criteria does not emerge from an examination of the cases. This same problem in the United States led commentators there to remark that "the law is a morass of inconsistent or unrelated theories, and cogent judicial generalization is sorely needed." I would add that more than a cogent generalization is probably undesirable because an exhaustive list would unduly fetter the court's discretion in future cases. It is, however, a discretion to be judicially exercised with due regard for established principles.

In formulating guidelines for the exercise of discretion in departing from a usual practice, it is instructive to examine its underlying rationalia. To the extent that a particular foundation for the practice is either absent or its presence tenuous, the reason for its enforcement disappears or diminishes.

The first rationale for the policy and practice referred to above is that a court's competence to resolve legal disputes is rooted in the adversary system. The requirement of an adversarial context is a fundamental tenet of our legal system and helps guarantee that issues are well and fully argued by parties who have a stake in the outcome. It is apparent that this requirement may be satisfied if, despite the cessation of a live controversy, the necessary adversarial relationships will nevertheless prevail. For example, although the litigant bringing the proceeding may no longer have a direct interest in the outcome, there may be collateral consequences of the outcome that will provide the necessary adversarial context....

In the United States, the role of collateral consequences in the exercise of discretion to hear a case is well recognized.... The principle that collateral consequences of an already completed cause of action warrant appellate review was most clearly stated in *Sibron* v. *New York*. The appellant in that case appealed his conviction although his sentence had already been completed. At p. 55, Warren C.J. stated:

> ... most criminal convictions do in fact entail adverse collateral legal consequences. The mere "possibility" that this will be the case is enough to preserve a criminal case from ending "ignominiously in the limbo of mootness."

In Canada, the cases of *Law Society of Upper Canada* v. *Skapinker, supra,* and *Saskatchewan* v. *Mercure, supra,* illustrate the workings of this principle. In those cases, the presence of interveners who had a stake in the outcome supplied the necessary adversarial context to enable the Court to hear the cases.

The second broad rationale on which the mootness doctrine is based is the concern for judicial economy. It is an unfortunate reality that there is a need to ration scarce judicial resources among competing claimants. The fact that in this Court the number of live controversies in respect of which leave is granted is a small percentage of those that are refused is sufficient to highlight this observation. The concern for judicial economy as a factor in the decision not to hear moot cases will be answered if the special circumstances of the case make it worthwhile to apply scarce judicial resources to resolve it.

The concern for conserving judicial resources is partially answered in cases that have become moot if the court's decision will have some practical effect on the rights of the parties notwithstanding that it will not have the effect of determining the controversy which gave rise to the action....

Similarly an expenditure of judicial resources is considered warranted in cases which although moot are of a recurring nature but brief duration. In order to ensure that an important question which might independently evade review be heard by the court, the mootness doctrine is not applied strictly. This was the situation in *International Brotherhood of Electrical Workers, Local Union 2085* v. *Winnipeg Builders' Exchange, supra.* The issue was the validity of an interlocutory injunction prohibiting certain strike action. By the time the case reached this Court the strike had been settled. This is the usual result of the operation of a temporary injunction in labour cases. If the point was ever to be tested, it almost had to be in a case that was moot. Accordingly, this Court exercised its discretion to hear the case....

There also exists a rather ill-defined basis for justifying the deployment of judicial resources in cases which raise an issue of public importance of which a resolution is in the public interest. The economics of judicial involvement are weighed against the social cost of continued uncertainty in the law. See *Minister of Manpower and Immigration* v. *Hardayal* [1978]. Locke J. alluded to this in *Vic Restaurants Inc.* v. *City of Montreal, supra,* at p. 91: "The question, as I have said, is one of general public interest to municipal institutions throughout Canada."

This was the basis for the exercise of this Court's discretion in the *Re Opposition by Quebec to a Resolution to amend the Constitution,* [1982] 2 S.C.R. 793. The question of the constitutionality of the patriation of the Constitution had, in effect, been rendered moot by the occurrence of the event. The Court stated at p. 806:

> While this Court retains its discretion to entertain or not to entertain an appeal as of right where the issue has become moot, it may, in the exercise of its discretion, take into consideration the importance of the constitutional issue determined by a court of appeal judgment which would remain unreviewed by this Court.
>
> In the circumstances of this case, it appears desirable that the constitutional question be answered in order to dispel any doubt over it and it accordingly will be answered.

Patently, the mere presence of an issue of national importance in an appeal which is otherwise moot is insufficient. National importance is a requirement for all cases before this Court except with respect to appeals as of right; the latter, Parliament has apparently deemed to be in a category of sufficient importance to be heard here. There must, therefore, be the additional ingredient of social cost in leaving the matter undecided. This factor appears to have weighed heavily in the decision of the majority of this Court in *Forget v. Quebec (Attorney-General)* [1988].

The third underlying rationale of the mootness doctrine is the need for the Court to demonstrate a measure of awareness of its proper law-making function. The Court must be sensitive to its role as the adjudicative branch in our political framework. Pronouncing judgments in the absence of a dispute affecting the rights of the parties may be viewed as intruding into the role of the legislative branch. This need to maintain some flexibility in this regard has been more clearly identified in the United States where mootness is one aspect of a larger concept of justiciability....

In my opinion, it is also one of the three basic purposes of the mootness doctrine in Canada and a most important factor in this case. I generally agree with the following statement in P. Macklem and E. Gertner: "Re Skapinker and Mootness Doctrine" (1984), 6 *Supreme Court L. Rev.* 369, at p. 373:

> The latter function of the mootness doctrine – political flexibility – can be understood as the added degree of flexibility, in an allegedly moot dispute, in the law-making function of the Court. The mootness doctrine permits the Court not to hear a case on the ground that there no longer exists a dispute between the parties, notwithstanding the fact that it is of the opinion that it is a matter of public importance. Though related to the factor of judicial economy, insofar as it implies a determination of whether deciding the case will lead to unnecessary precedent, political flexibility enables the Court to be sensitive to its role within the Canadian constitutional framework, and at the same time reflects the degree to which the Court can control the development of the law.

I prefer, however, not to use the term "political flexibility" in order to avoid confusion with the political questions doctrine. In considering the exercise of its discretion to hear a moot case, the Court should be sensitive to the extent that it may be departing from its traditional role.

In exercising its discretion in an appeal which is moot, the Court should consider the extent to which each of the three basic rationalia for enforcement of the mootness doctrine is present. This is not to suggest that it is a mechanical process. The principles identified above may not all support the same conclusion. The presence of one or two of the factors may be overborne by the absence of the third, and vice versa.

Exercise of Discretion: Application of Criteria

Applying these criteria to this appeal, I have little or no concern about the absence of an adversarial relationship. The appeal was fully argued with as much zeal and dedication on both sides as if the matter were not moot.

The second factor to be considered is the need to promote judicial economy. Counsel for the appellant argued that an extensive record had been developed in the courts below which would be wasted if the case were not decided on the merits. Although there is some merit in this position, the same can be said for most cases that come to this Court....

None of the other factors that I have canvassed which justify the application of judicial resources is applicable. This is not a case where a decision will have practical side effects on the rights of the parties. Nor is it a case that is capable of repetition, yet evasive of review. It will almost certainly be possible to bring the case before the Court within a specific legislative context or possibly in review of specific governmental action. In addition, an abstract pronouncement on foetal rights in this case would not necessarily promote judicial economy as it is very conceivable that the courts will be asked to examine specific legislation or governmental action in any event. Therefore, while I express no opinion as to foetal rights, it is far from clear that a decision on the merits will obviate the necessity for future repetitious litigation.

Moreover, while it raises a question of great public importance, this is not a case in which it is in the public interest to address the merits in order to settle the state of the law. The appellant is asking for an interpretation of ss.7 and 15 of the *Canadian Charter of Rights and Freedoms* at large. In a legislative context any rights of the foetus could be considered or at least balanced against the rights of women guaranteed by s.7. See *R. v. Morgentaler (No. 2), supra, per* Dickson C.J.C., at p. 75; *per* Beetz J. at pp. 122-23; *per* Wilson J. at pp. 181-82. A pronouncement in favour of the appellant's position that a foetus is protected by s.7 from the date of conception would decide the issue out of its proper context. Doctors and hospitals would be left to speculate as to how to apply such a ruling consistently with a woman's rights under s.7. During argument the question was posed to counsel for REAL Women as to what a hospital would do with a pregnant woman who required an abortion to save her life in the face of a ruling in favour of the appellant's position. The answer was that doctors and legislators would have to stay up at night to decide how to deal with the situation. This state of uncertainty would clearly not be in the public interest. Instead of rendering the law certain, a decision favourable to the appellant would have the opposite effect.

Even if I were disposed in favour of the appellant in respect to the first two factors which I have canvassed, I would decline to exercise a discretion in favour of deciding this appeal on the basis of the third. One element of this third factor is the need to demonstrate some sensitivity to the effectiveness or efficacy of judicial intervention. The need for courts to exercise some flexibility in the application of the mootness doctrine requires more than a consideration of the importance of the subject matter. The appellant is requesting a legal opinion on the interpretation of the *Canadian Charter of Rights and Freedoms* in the absence of legislation or other governmental action which would otherwise bring the *Charter* into play. This is something only the government may do. What the appellant seeks is to turn this appeal into a private reference. Indeed, he is not seeking to have decided the same question that was the subject of his action. That question related to the validity of s.251 of the *Criminal Code*. He now wishes to ask a question that relates to the *Canadian Charter of Rights and Freedoms* alone. This is not a request to decide a moot question but to decide a different, abstract question. To accede to this request would intrude on the right of the executive to order a reference and pre-empt a possible decision of Parliament by dictating the form of legislation it should enact. To do so would be a marked departure from the traditional role of the Court.

Having decided that this appeal is moot, I would decline to exercise the Court's discretion to decide it on the merits.

Standing

… There have been two significant changes in the nature of this action since this Court granted Mr. Borowski standing in 1981. The claim is now premised primarily upon an alleged right of a foetus to life and equality pursuant to ss.7 and 15 of the *Canadian Charter of Rights and Freedoms*. Secondly, by holding s.251 to be of no force and effect in *R. v. Morgentaler (No. 2), supra*, the legislative context of this claim has disappeared.

By virtue of ss.24(1) of the *Charter* and 52(1) of the *Constitution Act, 1982*, there are two possible means of gaining standing under the *Charter*. Section 24(1) provides:

> 24. (1) Anyone whose rights or freedoms as guaranteed by this *Charter*, have been infringed or denied may apply to a court of competent jurisdiction to obtain such remedy as the court considers appropriate and just in the circumstances.

In my opinion s.24(1) cannot be relied upon here as a basis for standing. Section 24(1) clearly requires an infringement or denial of a *Charter*-based right. The appellant's claim does not meet this requirement as he alleges that the rights of a foetus, not his own rights, have been violated.

Nor can s.52(1) of the *Constitution Act, 1982* be invoked to extend standing to Mr. Borowski. Section 52(1) reads:

> 52. (1) The Constitution of Canada is the supreme law of Canada, and any law that is inconsistent with the provisions of the Constitution is, to the extent of the inconsistency, of no force or effect.

This section offers an alternative means of securing standing based on the *Thorson, McNeil, Borowski* trilogy expansion of the doctrine.

Nevertheless, in the same manner that the "standing trilogy" referred to above was based on a challenge to specific legislation, so too a challenge based on s.52(1) of the *Constitution Act, 1982* is restricted to litigants who challenge a law or governmental action pursuant to power granted by law. The appellant in this appeal challenges neither "a law" nor any governmental action so as to engage the provisions of the *Charter*. What the appellant now seeks is a naked interpretation of two provisions of the *Charter*. This would require the Court to answer a purely abstract question which would in effect sanction a private reference. In my opinion, the original basis for the appellant's standing is gone and the appellant lacks standing to pursue this appeal.

Accordingly, the appeal is dismissed on both the grounds that it is moot and that the appellant lacks standing to continue the appeal....

6.4

Interventions and the Public Interest
Alan Borovoy
Reprinted with permission.

July 17, 1984

    TO: Supreme Court of Canada
    RE: Interventions in Public Interest Litigation
    FROM: Canadian Civil Liberties Association
             per A. Alan Borovoy (General Counsel)

In the era of the *Charter of Rights and Freedoms*, the issue of participation in the cases before the Supreme Court of Canada has acquired a new significance. It is likely that a great many *Charter* cases will be determining issues of fundamental principle affecting the very nature of Canadian democracy. Moreover, the impact of the Court's judgments will be far less vulnerable than ever to abridgement or amendment at the hands of the political authorities. It is significant that in the more than 200 years of American history, the political authorities in that country have enacted fewer than 25 amendments to their Constitution. In many ways, the new Canadian Constitution will be even harder than its American counterpart to amend at the political level.

While it is possible, of course, for Parliament and the provincial legislatures to invoke the override in section 33 against the application of key *Charter* provisions, that is likely to be a relatively rare event outside the Province of Quebec. As a result of the widespread public participation in the Joint Parliamentary hearings and their aftermath, the *Charter* has acquired enormous prestige throughout much of the country. In every jurisdiction apart from Quebec, the ousting of *Charter* protections will entail a substantial political price. During all the years that such overrides have existed in both the federal *Bill of Rights* and a number of its provincial counterparts, they have been invoked in a relatively infinitesimal number of cases – and, so far, not once to overcome the impact of a judicial decision.

The effective transfer of so much power to the judiciary raises issues of fundamental fairness. Since the entire community will be increasingly affected for substantially longer periods by the decisions of the Court, larger sectors of the community should be able to participate in the process which produces those decisions. It is simply not fair to limit such participation on the basis of the coincidence of which parties litigate first. Public respect for both the *Charter* and the Court will require a more inclusive process.

The peculiar position of government serves to strengthen these considerations. In many cases, government will be a party. In criminal matters, for example, the federal or a provincial government will be prosecuting. But, even when they have not been parties, governments seeking to intervene have usually been allowed to do so. The frequency of such involvement in *Charter* cases will enable governments in a systematic way to put before the Court their various theories of what the *Charter* provisions mean. This gives the governments a special advantage over every other interest in the community. The party against which a government is litigating in any particular case might well not have any interest in addressing the long-term implications of whatever interpretation may be at issue. Indeed, the limited interest of a particular party might be better served by making certain tactical concessions to the government's long-term point of view. If no one else but the immediate parties regularly participate, the Court and the community will likely be deprived of countervailing long-term theories for interpreting the *Charter*.

Suppose, for example, section 7 were to become an issue in the context of a criminal case. It may well be in the interest of the prosecuting government to argue for the narrowest interpretation possible. The accused, on the other hand, might wish to argue that the concluding words in the section must have a substantive as well as a procedural impact. He might consider it tactically wise, therefore, to concede to the government that the word "liberty" is restricted to *physical* freedom. But there may be a number of free enterprise groups which would agree with the substantive interpretation of the concluding words but would argue that 'liberty' includes freedom of contract. There may also be some social democratic groups which would argue that "liberty" means something more than physical freedom and something less than contractual freedom but would urge nevertheless that the concluding words should receive a procedural construction only.

Or, suppose the leaders of a pressure group were charged with a breach of the *Election Expenses Act*. The accused might believe that it is in their interest to argue that no such restriction on interest group advocacy is compatible with the *Charter*'s protections for "freedom of expression." On the other hand, it might be in the interests of the prosecuting government to argue that its goal of financial equity during election campaigns constitutes a reasonable limit on *Charter* freedoms and the restriction at issue is the only way to achieve such a goal. But there may be other groups in the community which differ with both litigants. They may believe that the government's goal is legitimate but not its means. They may wish to demonstrate to the Court how a less restrictive means could adequately achieve the same goal.

The examples go on and on. Suffice it, for present purposes, to acknowledge how both the quality of jurisprudence and the appearance of fairness can be undermined by restricting participation in court to the principal litigants.

In this regard, it would be helpful to consult the experience of the common law democracy which has developed the most sophisticated adjudication in the area of constitutional rights – the United States. Both at the appellate level and in the U.S. Supreme Court, there has been a growing receptivity to the participation of third parties. While *amicus* counsel are rarely heard during the course of oral argument, they are frequently permitted to file written briefs. In the Supreme Court, the inclusion of an amicus brief is virtually automatic on the written consent of the principal parties. And, if such consent is not forthcoming, there are special provisions for obtaining leave directly from the Court itself.

What is most significant about the American situation, however, is not simply the rules but also the actual experience. With the passage of time, the rules have been applied in an increasingly liberal fashion. Indeed, in cases of crucial public importance, the principal parties rarely object to amicus participation. There is reason to believe that the attitude of the Court itself paved the way for this development.

As long ago as 1952, the late Mr. Justice Felix Frankfurter criticized the U.S. Solicitor-General for refusing too often to grant such consent.

> For the Solicitor-General to withhold consent automatically in order to enable this Court to determine for itself the propriety of each application is to throw upon the Court a responsibility that the Court has put upon all litigants, including the government....

Two years later, a similar observation was made by the late Mr. Justice Hugo Black.

> Most of the cases before this Court involve matters that affect far more people than the immediate record parties. I think the public interest and judicial administration would be better served by relaxing rather than tightening the rule against *amicus curiae* briefs.

A recent survey illustrates the growing liberalism of the American practice. During the period from 1941 until 1952, fewer than 19 percent of the cases in the U.S. Supreme Court involved the participation of *amicus curiae*. From 1953 until 1966, this participation rose to 23.8 percent. And, during the period 1970 until 1980, *amicus* involvement had increased to more than 53 percent of all cases in the U.S. Supreme Court. These statistics produced the following remark in a journal of legal scholarship.

> It seems fair enough to conclude.... that *amicus curiae* participation by private groups is now the norm rather than the exception.

When the kinds of cases are examined, the statistics acquire an even greater significance. During the period between 1970 and 1980, there was *amicus* participation in more than 62 percent of the cases involving church-state issues. The free press cases recorded more than 66 percent *amicus* participation and in race discrimination matters, such involvement had climbed to more than 67 percent. Union cases revealed a remarkable 87.2 percent participation by *amicus curiae*. Moreover, there is also a growing number of cases in which there is *multiple amicus* participation. In those cases during the 1970–1980 period which featured the involvement of at least one *amicus* brief, as many as 26.7 percent included the participation of four or more such interventions. In the famous *Bakke* case involving affirmative action for Blacks in university enrollment, there were more than 50 *amicus* briefs.

The American experience suggests also that these *amicus* briefs have played a vital role in a number of important cases. Consider, for example, the brief of the American Civil Liberties Union in the famous case of *Miranda* v. *Arizona*. Samuel Dash, counsel to the Senate Watergate Committee and Director of the Institute of Criminal Law and Procedure at Georgetown University Law Centre, made the following comment.

> Perhaps the most striking lesson to learn from these materials is the role an *amicus* brief can play in shaping a majority opinion, even without oral argument. Undoubtedly, the most effective presentation to the Court was the *amicus* brief of the American Civil Liberties Union.... It is clear that it presented a conceptual legal and structural formulation that is practically identical to the majority opinion – even as to use of language in various passages of the opinion. Also, it is from this brief and its appendix that the Court apparently draws its lengthy discussion of the contents of leading and popular police interrogation manuals. Both the ACLU brief and the Court explain that resort to the manuals is necessary because of the absence of information on what actually goes on in the privacy of police interrogation rooms.

In the case of *Mapp* v. *Ohio*, the issue was whether unlawfully seized evidence could be introduced against an accused in a state trial. Although such evidence had for some years been rendered inadmissible in federal prosecutions, the 1949 case of *Wolf* v. *Colorado* had held that this principle did not extend to state prosecutions. Although counsel for the accused in *Mapp* attempted to distinguish the Wolf case, an *amicus* brief filed by the ACLU urged the court to over-rule the earlier case. The majority of the court accepted the ACLU argument and over-ruled *Wolf*. As lawyer Ernest Angel commented in a subsequent law journal article, "the *amicu* scored an important victory."

In *Poe* v. *Ullmann*, a majority of the U.S. Supreme Court held that a prohibition on the distribution of birth control information was not justiciable. But the dissent of Mr. Justice Douglas argued that the law was unconstitutional on a ground raised by the *amicus* brief of the ACLU – the right to privacy. Four years later, in *Griswold* v. *Connecticut*, the Court majority adopted a position closer to that of Justice Douglas and the ACLU. According to Ernest Angel,

> The case is noteworthy for the .... invalidation of of the statute ... *for the part played by the amicus* and for the formulation of a right of privacy doctrine. (emphasis ours)

There is some suggestion that the *amicus* brief of the National Association for Advancement of Coloured People played an important role in the case of *Furman* v. *Georgia* where the U.S. Supreme Court held that the death penalty constituted "cruel and unusual punishment" in the circumstances at issue. In the famous *Bakke* case, the Court included as an appendix to its judgment the joint *amicus* brief which had been filed by Columbia, Harvard, Standford, and Pennsylvania Universities.

While such non-party interventions have not arisen often in Canada, they are nevertheless rooted in our legal history. Apart from those few cases where it may have been considered equitable to accommodate certain private interests, most of the interventions in recent Canadian history have been prompted by broad and fundamental issues of public policy. As far back as 1945, for example, in the case of *Re Drummond Wren*, the Supreme Court of Ontario permitted the Canadian Jewish Congress to argue, *amicus curiae*, that racially restrictive covenants were not legally enforceable. During the last decade, however, the number of such interventions has increased significantly. On at least a dozen occasions during this period, Canadian tribunals have permitted the involvement of strangers to the litigation. In a good number of these cases, the matter at issue concerned an interpretation of our quasi-constitutional statute, the *Canadian Bill of Rights*. Whatever considerations have motivated this and other courts to permit such interventions in cases involving the *Bill of Rights*, the argument will be even stronger when the document at issue is the new *Canadian Charter*.

It is our view, therefore, that the Supreme Court of Canada should develop a rule on interventions which broadens the effective right of constituencies other than the immediate parties to participate in important public interest litigation. We recognize, of course, that these considerations must be balanced against the concerns of efficiency. Among the consequences accompanying the advent of the *Charter* is an increased workload for the

Supreme Court of Canada. Understandably, therefore, the Court will feel obliged to avoid, where possible, the prospect of unduly long and repetitive hearings. We believe, however, that the valid interests of efficiency can coexist with an expanded role for intervenors.

This objective can be accomplished by permitting a wide latitude for partial interventions, i.e., interventions primarily through written briefs rather than oral argument. A liberal rule for the inclusion of such briefs would broaden the right to participate and permit the judges to obtain an ever expanding amount of assistance without in any way increasing the amount of time allocated for the Court's hearings.

While the practice in the U.S. Supreme Court is a possible model, we believe that some reasonable modifications are in order. Instead of foreclosing almost automatically on the oral participation of intervenors, our Court might adopt the practice of selectively inviting their counsel to appear for the purpose of speaking to whatever limited issues would assist in the disposition of the cases at Bar. From their advance reading of the briefs and factums, the judges could decide which, if any, of the intervenors' counsel they may wish to hear and on what issues. Such invitations to counsel could range from involvement on one or more limited points to virtually full-scale participation in certain special cases. Even at that, the presentations of such counsel could be subject to abridgement at the hearing itself to whatever extent it became evident that they were not contributing significantly beyond what had already been advanced on behalf of the parties. In all of these ways, the Court could still control its processes and prevent any undue prolongation of the oral hearings.

The adoption of this approach should also help to overcome some of the concerns that have been expressed about interventions in criminal cases. To whatever extent there were several interventions on the side of the Crown, it has been said that the situation might look like a "ganging up" on the accused. It will be appreciated, however, that such an appearance is rendered far less likely when the interventions are handled primarily through written briefs rather than oral argument. In any event, such interventions would be addressed, not to the guilt or innocence of a particular accused, but rather to the resolution of a question of law or the interpretation of a section of the *Charter*. All of these considerations should militate against prohibiting interventions in criminal cases.

Moreover, there is no reason why this approach should not apply equally to the proposed interventions of the various attorneys general. Governmental intervenors are no more likely (and may well be less likely) than non-government intervenors to adopt arguments which are significantly different from those of the immediate parties. Upon meeting whatever liberal threshold test is adopted, government intervenors, like their non-government counterparts, should be able to participate. But they too should do so subject to the rules applying to everyone – usually through partial rather than full intervention.

In the submission of the Canadian Civil Liberties Association, it is essential to continue and expand the role of intervenors before the Supreme Court of Canada. The *Charter of Rights and Freedoms* has launched a new era in the relationship between the judicial and political processes of this country. Ever since the Joint Parliamentary hearings on the Constitution, there has been a heightened public awareness and concern about *Charter* developments in particular and public interest law in general. Indeed, one of the consequences of the constitutional deliberations has been a raised public consciousness with respect to a wide spectrum of public law issues. Many of the processes of the Court, therefore, will be the subject of increased scrutiny. Thus, it is more important than ever that those processes conform to public perceptions and expectations of fairness. On the basis of all these considerations, the Canadian Civil Liberties Association respectfully urges the adoption of an approach which is hospitable to non-party interventions in public interest litigation.

6.5

Intervenors and the *Charter*
Ian Brodie
Revised for third edition of this book.

An intervenor is a person, organization or government department that is not a direct party to a case but receives a court's permission to present its own arguments in that case. Intervenors can only discuss the legal issue at stake in the case and cannot ordinarily introduce new evidence to the record. Nonetheless, they can present legal arguments that the direct parties would not have made before the court. Sometimes an intervenor is called an *amicus curiae*, the Latin phrase for "friend of the court". Since the late 1980s, some Canadian interest groups have become frequent intervenors before the Supreme Court. Although the Court was reluctant to hear from intervenors in the early years after the *Charter* was adopted, it has since become quire receptive toward "public interest" intervenors.

Until the 1970s, interest groups rarely intervened in Canadian court cases, and even in the 1970s, intervenors were not common. Interest groups sometimes intervened in reference cases, but few groups bothered intervening in other cases. Nor were the courts enthusiastic about hearing their arguments. The first generally recognized instance of an interest group intervention in a Canadian court case was in 1945. In that year, the Canadian Jewish Congress intervened in an Ontario case about racially restrictive housing agreement. Not until 1963 was there a notable interest group intervention in the Supreme Court of Canada, when the Court agreed to hear the Lord's Day Alliance of Canada in the Bill of Rights Sunday-closing case, *Roberts and Rosetanni* v. *The*

Queen. In that case, the Lord's Day Alliance feared that governments would not try hard enough to defend their Sunday-closing laws.

By contrast, interest groups have frequently participated in U.S. Supreme Court cases as *amici curiae* in recent years. Interest group *amici* played prominent roles in leading U.S. Supreme Court controversies since the famous 1954 school desegregation case, *Brown* v. *Board of Education*. In fact, groups like the National Association for the Advancement of Colored People (NAACP) and the American Civil Liberties Union (ACLU) became famous in the 1950s and 1960s because of their *amicus* appearances before the U.S. Supreme Court. By the 1970s, interest groups were intervening in over half of the U.S. Supreme Court's cases and almost two-thirds of its non-criminal cases. *Amicus* activity reached a record in 1978 when 57 *amici* appeared in the "reverse discrimination" case of *Regents of the University of California* v. *Bakke*. The Court even appended one of the *amicus curiae* briefs to its decision in that case.

After the *Charter* was adopted in 1982, some interest groups and lawyers expected the Supreme Court of Canada to follow the U.S. pattern and open its doors to more interest group intervenors. The Court had started to allow some interest groups to intervene in its cases during the 1970s. In 1976, for example, the first time Henry Morgentaler challenged Canada's abortion laws before the Supreme Court, the case attracted interventions from both pro-choice and pro-life groups. After 1982, both legal commentators and interest group activists thought that the broader policy impact of *Charter* cases would push the courts toward hearing from the groups that could be affected by their decisions.

Instead, the Supreme Court turned away many would-be interest group intervenors. The Court was struggling with its new *Charter* workload, and was temporarily short of judges, so it began to limit the number of groups it heard. It was also trying to come to terms with its new place in Canada's system of government, and was not sure it wanted to hear from interest groups. In 1983, the Court's Registrar asked Chief Justice Laskin whether he might be interested in allowing the noted judicial administration expert, Carl Baar, to intervene in the judicial independence case of *Valente*. Laskin fired back a curt memorandum declaring that, "I am not going to let this kind of thing [intervenors] get out of hand. The answer is plainly 'no'." Soon after, the Canadian Civil Liberties Association (CCLA) was denied permission to intervene in the high-profile case of *Oakes*, in which the Supreme Court first laid out a comprehensive approach to interpreting the *Charter's* critical Section 1 "reasonable limits" clause. In 1984, the Court decided not to hear the Seventh-day Adventist Church in the Sunday-closing case, *Big M Drug Mart*. In 1986, the Court also refused to let the Canadian Labour Congress and other unions intervene in three major *Charter* cases involved labour law.

The Court's refusal to hear from so many interest groups provoked vigorous protests from the groups planning to intervene in *Charter* cases to influence the development of *Charter* law. In 1984, Alan Borovoy, longtime general counsel of the CCLA, kicked off this campaign by writing an open brief to the Court that demanded it hear from more interest group intervenors. [Ed. note: See Reading 6.4] In 1986, one CCLA Vice-President publicly complained that, by refusing to hear from interest groups, the Court was losing a valuable help with its new *Charter* cases. Other legal commentators and interest group litigators also criticized the Court's coolness toward intervenors. The Supreme Court responded by asking the Canadian Bar Association (CBA) to investigate the entire issue and recommend a new policy to the Court. A CBA committee heard presentations from the CCLA, the Women's Legal Education and Action Fund (LEAF) and other public interest litigators before meeting with three of the Court's judges to recommend that the Court adopt a more open-door policy on intervenors.

In the wake of the CBA's work, the Court reversed its approach to intervenors. Since 1987, it has rarely refused interest group requests to intervene. From 1983 through 1986, the Court accepted fewer than half of interest group requests to intervene. From 1987 through 1990, the success rate soared to over 85 per cent and has remained well over 80% since then. This change in approach encouraged more groups to intervene. From 1983 through 1986, the Supreme Court received an average of 19 applications for leave to intervene per year. From 1987 through 1990, the average rose to 29. From 1991 through 1999, the average climbed again to 74. Some groups have been especially successful. Between 1985 and 1999, LEAF applied to intervene in 29 cases and was successful every time. The CCLA made 20 applications and succeeded 19 times. The Criminal Lawyers' Association made twelve applications and succeeded only seven times.

The Court has recently considered cutting back the number of intervenors it hears. In the spring of 2000, Justice Iacobucci publicly questioned whether there are too many intervenors at the Court. He speculated that the Court might have needed intervenors more in the early years of its *Charter* interpretation. "Looking back, those intervenors played a highly significant role. But it's now getting on to be 18 years or so later. Should we be looking at the question in different ways?" A few weeks later, Chief Justice McLachlin said it was "only just and fair" to allow intervenors in cases that would affect "not only the parties but a wide range of other people." Justice Bastarache suggested, in the same interview, that "we have lived with the *Charter* for 18 years ... There isn't the same need there was in 1982 to obtain help from intervenors."

It is too early to say whether these comments indicate another change in the Court's approach. In the meantime, the Supreme Court now hears almost as many intervenors in its *Charter* cases (almost 60% of *Charter* cases since 1984 attracted intervenors) as the U.S. Supreme Court hears in its cases (three-quarters of its cases since 1986). This willingness to accept interest group intervenors testifies to the new political role of the Court under the *Charter*.

6.6

Agenda Setting:

The Selection of Cases for Judicial Review in the Supreme Court of Canada

Roy B. Flemming

This article is reprinted as Reading 12.2.

6.7

Key Terms

Concepts

Amicus curiae
standing
lis
case or controversy requirement
taxpayer's suit
declaratory judgment
intervenor
moot case
constitutional reference
advisory opinion
political questions doctrine
justiciable
"agenda setting"
jurisprudential choice hypothesis
litigant resources hypothesis
strategic choice hypothesis
"repeat player"
"one-shotter"

Institutions, Events, and Documents

The Supreme Court Act (1875)
Minister of Justice of Canada v. *Borowski* (1981)
Operation Dismantle v. *The Queen* (1985)
Borowski v. *A.-G. Canada* (1989)
Canadian Civil Liberties Association (CCLA)
American Civil Liberties Union (ACLU)
Smith v. *Attorney-General of Ontario* (1924)

Interest Groups and Litigation

7

The difference between traditional litigation and "litigation designed to elicit policy-making" is that the latter "is designed primarily to promote the interests of a class of persons rather than to correct the wrongs done to a particular litigant."[1] Politically motivated litigation also usually involves interest groups, either as litigants, financial sponsors, or intervenors (*amicus curiae* in U.S.). Prior to the adoption of the *Charter*, there was a sharp contrast between Canadian and American attitudes and practice with regard to interest-group litigation.

In the United States, this kind of litigation has become commonplace and accepted. One of the important developments in American law and politics since World War II has been the strategic use of constitutional litigation by organized interest groups to achieve public policy objectives. This new form of political action was successfully pioneered by the National Association for the Advancement of Colored People (NAACP), the leading Black civil rights group, in its fight against racial segregation in the American South. Politically stymied in both the national Congress and in the Southern state legislatures, the NAACP turned to the federal courts for help. The success of the NAACP inspired other interest groups to adopt similar strategies to change existing public policies on such issues as electoral distribution ("re-apportionment"), criminal process, capital punishment, abortion, censorship of pornography, and women's rights. Most of the politically important decisions of the American Supreme Court since 1954 have been litigated directly or indirectly by organized interest groups.

In Canada, by contrast, strategic, pro-active use of litigation by interest groups was rare, a tactic of last resort. This pattern reflected a social consensus that discouraged judicial activism and viewed interest-group litigation as illegitimate. In 1975, Kenneth McNaught, one of Canada's leading historians, concluded that his study of Canadian political trials

---

1 Jeremy Rabkin, "The Charismatic Constitution," *The Public Interest* 73 (Fall, 1983), p. 42. Quoting Aryeh Neier, *Only Judgment: The Limits of Litigation in Social Change* (Middletown, CT: Wesleyan University Press, 1983).

... strongly suggests that our judges and lawyers, supported by the press and public opinion, reject any concept of the courts as positive instruments in the political process. In Canada the positive aspects of politics seems more clearly to belong to the political parties, the legislatures, and the press. A corollary of this is that political action outside the party-parliamentary structure tends automatically to be suspect – and not the least because it smacks of Americanism.[2]

As if to underscore the accuracy of Professor McNaught's assessment, later that same year, the Supreme Court of Canada sent Dr. Henry Morgentaler to jail for performing illegal abortions.[3]

Seven years later, the *Charter of Rights* was adopted. One of the important questions at that time was whether the *Charter* would act as a catalyst for litigation as an interest-group activity in Canada. After twenty years in "*Charter*land," the answer to this question is clearly "yes." There has been a veritable surge in interest group litigation since 1982. There were two related but distinct factors that accounted for this change. One was the issue of access, and it depended on the Supreme Court. Would the Court adapt the rules governing standing, mootness, political questions, and intervenors to allow interest groups access to the judicial process? The readings in Chapter 6 show that the Court did precisely this. The other factor was the response of the interest groups. The Supreme Court could open the courthouse door, but it could not force interest groups to come in.

In fact, organized interests have flocked to the courts since the adoption of the *Charter* and the Supreme Court's relaxing of judicial rules controlling access. Epp identified the rapid growth of "rights advocacy organizations" as one of the three critical elements in the development of the "support structure for legal mobilization" that has stimulated a "rights revolution" in Canada (Reading 11.7). Advocacy groups have been involved, either as parties or as intervenors, in most of the Court's important or controversial *Charter* decisions.[4] Brodie (Reading 6.5) found that intervenors have participated in sixty per cent of all *Charter* cases decided by the Supreme Court.

Greg Hein's research (Reading 7.5) has uncovered even wider interest-group participation. In a study of over 2,500 Supreme Court and Federal

---

2 Kenneth McNaught, "Political Trials and the Canadian Political Tradition," in M. L. Friedland, *Courts and Trials: A Multidisciplinary Approach* (Toronto: University of Toronto Press, 1975), p. 137.

3 See F. L. Morton, *Morgentaler v. Borowski: Abortion, the Charter and the Courts* (Toronto: McClelland & Stewart, 1992).

4 Advocacy groups have participated in cases involving abortion, aboriginal rights and land claims, Bill 101, equality of voters, euthanasia, capital punishment, gay rights, hate speech, judicial salaries, language rights, political action committees (PACs), pornography, prisoner voting rights, sexual assault, Sunday closing, tobacco advertising, and many legal rights/criminal law issues.

Court decisions (1988–98), Hein found 819 organizations involved as litigants or intervenors. These organizations came from across the political spectrum: aboriginal groups, civil libertarians, corporate interests, labour interests, professionals, social conservatives, victims of crime, *Charter* Canadians, and New Left activists (Table 1). By far the most frequent participants before these courts were corporate interests – representing fifty-six per cent (*n*=468) of the total (Figure 1). Hein argues that such diversity plus the heavy corporate involvement disproves the criticism that interest-group litigation is primarily a tool of interests on the political left. To the contrary, Hein claims that his data show the *Charter* has had a democratizing effect on the Canadian political system by opening up the courts to interests that in the past were typically excluded.

While corporate interests were the most frequent participants, most of their involvement was in civil cases against other corporations or private parties and not challenges to government laws and policies. They thus had less direct effect on public policy. Also, Hein found that corporate propensity to litigate was lower than that of the various social justice groups (Table 3).

Hein also presents a theory why such diverse groups end up in courts. Sometimes, they are "pushed" by the necessity of responding to adverse new laws or a new legal challenge to a policy or legal precedent they support. Sometimes, they are "pulled" by organizational characteristics such as strong legal resources, rights-based identities, and "normative visions that demand judicial activism." These are the "judicial democrats" who believe that judicial activism in defence of the rights of minorities is good because it remedies a structural defect in Canada's parliamentary democracy – its tendency to under-represent the politically disadvantaged. In response to *Charter* critics, Hein responds that, "We now have a judicial system that responds to a diverse range of interests."

Hein's "judicial democrats" thesis is challenged by Brodie, who points out that judges are even less "representative" of Canadian society than legislatures. Brodie claims that, if these groups were truly "disadvantaged," they could not afford to use systematic litigation strategies. Rather than being the "grass-roots, bottom-up" movement described by Hein, Brodie points to substantial government funding (such as the Court Challenges Program) as the real explanation for judicial democrats' extensive and successful litigation efforts (Reading 7.6).

The largest, best organized, and best financed use of *Charter* litigation has been mounted by Canadian feminists. Feminists gained a head-start on other interest groups by successfully lobbying Parliament for favourable wording of section 15 equality rights while the *Charter* was still in draft stage. Soon after the *Charter* was proclaimed, the Canadian Advisory Council on the Status of Women (CACSW) commissioned a study of the "precedents, resources, and strategies" for feminist use of the *Charter* (Reading 7.1). The study surveyed the experience of feminist and minority-group use of constitutional litigation in the United States and concluded that, with the adoption of the *Charter*, "we find ourselves at the opportune moment to stress litigation as a vehicle for social change." The study recommended the creation of a single, nationwide "legal action fund" to coordinate and pay for a policy of "systematic litigation" of strategic "test cases." During the three-year moratorium before the equality rights provisions took effect, feminist lawyers conducted a massive "statutory audit" to identify potential violations of section 15. The primary purpose of this study was to assist legislatures to purge their statutes of discriminatory laws. But if legislatures failed to take the initiative, the study also provided a list of targets for future section 15 litigation. On April 13, 1985, only days before the equality rights section of the *Charter* came into effect, the Women's Legal and Education Action Fund (LEAF) was launched. Its purpose was "to assist women with important test cases and to ensure that equality rights litigation for women is undertaken in a planned, responsible, and expert manner."

Sherene Razack's account of LEAF's activities and strategies since 1985 discloses some of the subterranean aspects of *Charter* politics (Reading 7.2). In addition to taking test cases to court as part of a plan of systematic litigation, LEAF has also conducted a behind-the-scenes campaign of "influencing the influencers." This campaign was based on the belief that "Rights on paper mean nothing unless the courts correctly interpret their scope and application." By "correct interpretation," LEAF meant a theory of equality that stressed equality of results or "adverse impact," not just equal application of equal laws. To ensure that the theory of equality adopted by the courts was the right one, LEAF undertook a broad range of activities in addition to the traditional techniques of lobbying legislators and top bureaucrats. These included encouraging and even sponsoring legal scholarship that supported an "adverse impact" interpretation of section 15, participating in judicial training programs, participating in the relevant committees of the Canadian Bar Association and provincial legal societies, encouraging the appointment of feminist judges, and cultivating contacts in the media (Reading 7.2). This effort went so far as to include a three-hour, one-on-one lobbying effort on Peter Hogg, author of a very influential constitutional law textbook, to try to persuade him of the "correct" interpretation of section 28 of the *Charter*. The feminist lawyer later ruefully recounted that, even after three hours, Professor Hogg "Still got it wrong" (i.e., he disagreed).[5]

These out-of-court activities are designed to complement and support the litigation campaign. When LEAF lawyers go into court, they can cite law review articles and books that support their arguments for theories of "adverse impact" on "historically disadvantaged groups." They might even be fortunate enough to appear before judges who have attended one of their judicial education seminars. Razack recounts how much of LEAF's original pro-active strategy of systematic litigation and "occupying the field" has

---

5 Michael Mandel, *The Charter of Rights and the Legalization of Politics in Canada* (Toronto: Wall-Thompson, 1989), p. 40.

been frustrated by a large number of section 15 cases brought by men. This has sometimes forced LEAF into a reactive mode and explains its frequent appearance as an intervenor, a strategy that at the outset it hoped to avoid.

These setbacks notwithstanding, a recent study of feminist litigation suggests that LEAF's organizational efforts have been rewarded.[6] In a study of forty-seven appeal court decisions between 1982 and 1996, the feminist party or interest won seventy-two per cent of the disputes and changed public policy in a desired direction in seventeen of those cases. Since ten of the thirteen "losses" were *Charter* challenges to existing policies, feminists lost policy ground in only three cases. Success rates were actually higher in the twenty-six non-*Charter* cases (77%) than in the twenty-one *Charter* cases (67%), supporting the legal realist view that the "judicial mind" is more important than the law in explaining how judges decide. Feminist litigation efforts were most successful in the areas of abortion, private sector discrimination, and pornography, and least successful in sexual assault and tax cases. The study noted that, in addition to the immediate legal outcomes, interest-group litigation can serve a number of other valuable political purposes: agenda setting, mobilization of public support, problem-definition, legitimating, and consolidating earlier legal victories.[7]

Another set of interest groups that has successfully mobilized *Charter* litigation to achieve their policy objectives are Canada's official minority language groups (MLGs) – the anglophone minority in Quebec and various francophone minorities in the other nine provinces. Professor Ian Brodie explains how the federal government initially created the Court Challenges Program to assist the beleaguered anglophone minority in Montreal to bring legal challenges against the restrictive policies of Bill 101, the centrepiece of the separatist Parti Québécois' language policies (Reading 7.3). Professor Christopher Manfredi's study of how francophone communities have used their new rights under section 23 of the *Charter* to "litigate education reform" is the subject of Reading 7.4.

Manfredi's study also traces the historical evolution of theories of interest-group litigation. These theories originated in the United States, since that is where systematic litigation strategies were first developed. The first was known as the "political disadvantage theory" and reflected the experience of the National Association for the Advancement of Colored People's (NAACP) use of litigation to challenge racial segregation laws in the South – especially in public education. The political disadvantage theory postulated that "political outsiders" such as the Black minority in the United States could turn to the courts for protection of basic rights. Because judges are independent of majority opinion and electoral accountability, courts can defend the rights of

---

6 F. L. Morton and Avril Allen, "Feminists and the Courts: Measuring Success in Interest Group Litigation in Canada," *Canadian Journal of Political Science* 29, no. 1 (March, 2001), pp. 55–84.

7 Ibid.

unpopular minorities when they are threatened by majority-rule democracy.

The political disadvantage theory was soon challenged because it failed to explain why some disadvantaged groups lose in court while many advantaged groups still win. Prior to the 1950s, for example, Black Americans suffered many serious political losses because of U.S. Supreme Court decisions, while powerful corporate interests often won victories. In 1974, Mark Galanter offered a competing explanation, known as the "repeat-player" theory. Galanter divided litigants into two categories: repeat players (RP) and one-shotters (OS). RP litigants have greater resources and experience and use litigation pro-actively to protect or expand long-term institutional interests by achieving favourable new precedents. Governments and interest groups that pursue systematic litigation strategies – such as the NAACP in the United States or LEAF in Canada – are examples of RP litigants. OS litigants focus on the short-term outcome of a specific case. OS litigants go to court in response to new legislation that harms them. Because they are reactive not pro-active, OS litigants tend to have fewer resources and experience. An example is the unsuccessful challenge to the Liberals' long-gun registration law, C-68, by sporting and gun clubs.

Susan Olson further refined the critique of the political disadvantage theory by challenging its assumption that litigation is a fall-back strategy for groups with such low political resources that they cannot win in the electoral-legislative arena. Olson rejects the either/or assumption and argues that litigation and traditional forms of interest-group lobbying are complementary strategies that can be pursued simultaneously. Which option a group chooses in any instance is a function not of its "absolute" resources but of its "relative" resources – relative to its political adversary. Olson postulates that if the group's ratio of political to legal resources is smaller than its opponent's ratio, then it chooses litigation.[8]

Manfredi illustrates these theories through his case study of LMG litigation in Canada. He shows how LMGs have successfully used *Charter* (section 23) litigation to expand the size and scope of francophone education services outside of Quebec. These cases illustrate both modes of interest-group litigation involvement – as direct sponsors and intervenors – as well as strategic issues such as case selection and "sequencing." Case selection means choosing favourable fact situations – where the evidence supporting a rights violation is strong – for test cases. Sequencing means selecting legal arguments that only change constitutional rules incrementally – but in the desired direction. Tactically, this translates into choosing "easy" or more winnable cases first, based on incremental changes to existing law/precedent; but building, through a series of more ambitious cases, toward a new constitutional doctrine/rule that advances or protects a group's policy

---

8 See "The Political Disadvantage Theory," in Ian Brodie, *Friends of the Court: The Privileging of Interest Group Litigants in Canada* (Albany: State University of New York Press, 2002), chapter 1.

objectives.

Interest in using litigation to elicit the judicial creation of favourable new legal rules (precedents) distinguishes RPs from one-shotters. RPs are typically more interested in shaping the judicial creation of favourable new constitutional rules that enhance their influence. For government RPs, such legal victories serve to protect their legislated policies and freedom of action from future court challenges. Non-governmental RPs can use favourable new constitutional precedents/rules to extract future policy concessions from governments – either through more litigation or just the threat of litigation. Note how in the latter instance a legal resource – a favourable precedent – can become a political resource – a bargaining chip when lobbying government for policy change. Conversely, political resources can translate into legal resources. The Trudeau government's political support for national bilingualism and MLGs led to the creation of the Court Challenges Program in 1977 to provide MLGs funding for court challenges to Bill 101 – i.e., new legal resources.

Interest-group use of *Charter* litigation has been further encouraged by the Court Challenges Program initiated in September 1985 by the federal government (Reading 7.3). The government allocated $9 million over five years to fund litigation arising under the equality rights, language rights, and multiculturalism provisions of the *Charter*. Applications for financial support were screened according to the criteria of "substantial importance … legal merit [and] consequences for a number of people." The administrators of the program stated that they would "emphasize the setting of social justice priorities." Selected cases were eligible for $35,000 at each stage of litigation – trial, provincial appeal court, and the Supreme Court of Canada. The Court Challenges Program was renewed in 1990 for another five-year term but was then abruptly cancelled in February, 1992. The Mulroney government explained the cancellation as part of its program of financial restraint. Critics complained that it was because some feminists opposed the 1992 Charlottetown Accord, the last of the Mulroney government's failed constitutional initiatives.

In 1994, the newly elected Liberal government fulfilled its campaign promise to revive the CCP. The CCP was reinstated as an independently incorporated body, was moved to Winnipeg, and was given a budget of several million dollars annually. Critics complain that the CCP's directors are mostly drawn from the membership of the same rights-advocacy groups that receive moneys from the CCP. The CCP has never released the names of rejected applicants, and, in 2001, announced that it would no longer publish an annual list of grant recipients because of lawyer-client confidentiality. Critics scoffed at this explanation, alleging that it is yet another way that the CCP shields its operations from public scrutiny.

The fact that governments fund *Charter* litigants also suggests that it is no longer accurate to conceive of all *Charter* litigation as a contest between the individual and the state. In many cases, it may be a contest between different components of the state (i.e., federal versus provincial governments), or certain social interests versus others, with different governments lining up on different sides. Manfredi's study of MLG litigation clearly illustrates this pattern.

The significance of interest groups' use of the *Charter* does not rest only on their success in particular cases. Organized interest groups have significantly influenced the Court's agenda during this critical formative period of *Charter* interpretation. The Supreme Court, like all courts, is essentially a passive institution: it must wait for litigants to come to it with cases. Although it is now free to choose which cases it will hear, it still must choose from cases initiated by others. What Cairns wrote of the JCPC in 1971 is equally true of the *Charter*: "A comprehensive explanation of judicial decisions ... must include the actors who employed the courts for their own purposes."[8]

Indeed, Cairns has extended this analysis to interest group use of the *Charter. Charter* politics, Cairns suggests, is a new variation of the old game of constitutional imperialism.[9]

> The *Charter* is imperialistic. Its various clientele groups seek to extend its jurisdiction. In a general way, the attitude of Charterphiles to their instrument is analogous to the attitudes of Oliver Mowat, W.A.C. Bennett, and Peter Lougheed to section 92 of the *BNA Act*, or for Lougheed to section 109. These premiers sought, at a minimum, to protect, and more ambitiously, to extend the scope of the powers crucial to their governing capacities. Thus LEAF is to section 28 of the *Charter*, and the Canadian Ethno-Cultural Council to section 27, what Oliver Mowat was to section 92 of the *BNA Act*. The efforts of Charter supporters to eliminate the notwithstanding clause precisely parallels the efforts of provincial premiers to get rid of the federal power of disallowance.

While Cairns refers primarily to constitutional negotiations and constitutional litigation, the concept of protecting and expanding one's "constitutional turf" extends to the less visible but equally important aspects of interest groups' *Charter* activities. Successful litigation depends on sympathetic judges, and judicial sympathy can be cultivated in a variety of indirect ways: advocacy scholarship (Reading 9.5), judicial education seminars (Reading 7.2), influencing judicial appointments (Reading 4.6), and even influencing the selection of Supreme Court clerks (Reading 12.2). These various ways of "influencing the influencers" have become an important if less visible part of interest-group litigation under the *Charter*.

---

8 Alan C. Cairns, "The Judicial Committee and its Critics," *Canadian Journal of Political Science* 3 (1971), p. 301.

9 "The *Charter*: An Academic (Political Science) Perspective," paper presented at "Rountable Conference on the Impact of the *Charter* on Public Policy Process," Osgoode Hall Law School, Toronto, November 15-16, 1991, p. 2.

7.1

Equality Rights and Legal Action
M. Elizabeth Atcheson, Mary Eberts, and Beth Symes (with Jennifer Stoddart),
Women and Legal Action: Precedents, Resources and Strategies for the Future (Ottawa:
Canadian Advisory Council on the Status of Women, 1984), 163–72.
Reprinted with permission.
[*Ed. note*: all emphasis is from the original document.]

After looking carefully at some of the landmark legal cases involving matters of crucial interest to women in Canada, and after studying how American women's groups have chosen to play a role in their legal system, we can now outline a course of action. *We have come to the conclusion that a legal action fund to concentrate on issues of sex-based discrimination is an essential component of an effective strategy to promote the interests of women in the Canadian legal system.*

First of all, we find ourselves at the opportune moment to stress litigation as a vehicle for social change. The *Canadian Charter of Rights and Freedoms* has brought about a significant change in our legal system, moving us further from a system where the legislatures are the supreme lawmakers to a system where the courts may be asked to review the activities of legislatures and governments in accordance with the rights established in the *Charter*.

Unlike American women who have fought with mixed results for a constitutional guarantee of equality through the interpretation of the Fourteenth Amendment and the proposed Equal Rights Amendment, we have achieved a constitutional guarantee of equality through nation-wide lobbying. Section 28 of the *Charter* came into force on April 17, 1982, and section 15 comes into force on April 17, 1985. The challenge is to make the application of these equality guarantees meaningful and to ensure that the equality theory which our courts will develop and apply on a case-by-case basis is in the best interests of women. Accepting the challenge will necessitate a change in the way Canadian women approach law reform because the role of courts has been enhanced by the *Charter*. Litigation, more than ever, has been opened up as a strategy to achieve equality.

As we saw in our review of the legal efforts of Canadian women to improve their lives, in the past women have had to take action as individuals and they have had to stand alone. Their cases were isolated ones, not part of an overall scheme to advance equality for Canadian women. The successful cases, such as the *Persons Case*, advanced rights for women and added momentum to subsequent cases and lobbying activities. The losses, such as *Bliss* and *Murdoch*, were devastating to the individual women and also had serious adverse effects on the case law affecting all women in the years immediately following the decisions. However, as symbols of women's inequality those losses triggered persistent and effective lobbying for legislative change. When we see our rich legacy, we also see how much more powerful a unified approach to change can be.

There can be no doubt that women and men will invoke section 28 of the *Charter* and section 15 when it comes into force, and that many decisions will be made which will influence how quickly, and by what means, Canadian women achieve equality. It makes sense, then, to find ways to increase the number of successful cases, to pursue the development of legal precedents of real value to the greatest number of Canadian women and to distribute the costs of such activity.

A. Why a Fund at All?

In our view, Canadian women should not assume that the existing legal system or existing groups will fill the current vacuum and devote sufficient resources to establishing organizations which will pursue *Charter* litigation in women's interests. It is difficult, if not impossible, for individual lawyers working in relative isolation to do systematic litigation. Furthermore, although lawyers often do provide some legal services at little or no charge, the reality is that they must bill for most of their services in the same way that any business would. They are not motivated, nor should they be expected, to bear the full cost of taking cases which are in the public's interest.

In addition, legal aid schemes do not fit in with the theory of systematic litigation. Generally, legal aid exists to assist people in paying for regular legal services which are important to the conduct of their day-to-day lives. So while economic support is provided, it is provided only where the person is involved in certain types of legal matters and is unable to pay. The worthwhile goals of legal aid do not always mesh with the need to select strategic cases.

Of the Canadian groups organized to undertake legal advocacy, none has selected women's issues as a priority for activity. In addition, none of the Canadian women's groups organized to focus on various women's issues has undertaken legal advocacy as a priority for activity.

B. One Fund or More?

On the one hand, it would seem better to have one large fund because that fund would have the opportunity to achieve greater control over the development of the law of equality than if a variety of funds were pursuing separate legal actions. A single fund would make better use of scarce financial resources whereas a variety of funds would compete for limited public and private monies. A single fund could speak on behalf of a large number of Canadian women with one voice whereas a variety of funds might be perceived as sectarian, divisive and fragmented. One such fund could more easily coordinate its efforts with groups bringing or sponsoring cases on behalf of those in other categories, like race or handicap, which are protected by section 15.

On the other hand, it would be complicated to organize one national legal action fund because lawyers are admitted to practice on a province-by-province basis and very few lawyers are qualified to practise law in more than one province or in both of Canada's two legal systems. One law fund may have difficulty accommodating the variety of legal issues which women in various regions of the country feel are important. As well, differences in political orientation may militate against a single law fund. In fact, a law fund might have to spend so much time and energy keeping itself together in these circumstances that its capacity to undertake litigation may be diminished.

Similarly, there are arguments for and against a variety of funds. The advantages of multiple funds are: the task facing women is enormous and should be shared; the expertise that is developed can be enriched by co-operation and communication amongst funds; funds have a ripple effect in that they provide a valuable service to a community, whether defined by geography or issue; and they enhance the public profile of women's issues and solutions for those issues.

The clear risks are that funds may operate at cross purposes or waste limited resources. Solving these problems, if they occur, will also detract from litigation activity.

The American experience cautions us that when there are several funds it is crucial that they work cooperatively. Resources can be squandered and efforts duplicated or what is worse, cancelled out, if individual funds do not establish "issue focuses" – in other words, priorities or goals – which mesh and contribute to the overall goal of equality.

Over and above the foregoing considerations, however, is the pending implementation of section 15. It seems to us that some fund with substantial resources is essential to ensure that cases are found and prepared in time to establish a responsible presence in the field of equality after April 1985. Furthermore, cases invoking equality will begin to enter the courts at that time and women will wish to become involved in cases brought by other parties under sections 15 and 28 to protect their interests and to contribute to the clarification of the law. One fund will have a better opportunity of doing this than would a number of funds in their formative stages.

After weighing all of those arguments, we believe that one national fund is the most attractive option for now.

C. What Will the Fund Do?

In our view, a legal action fund concentrating on the litigation of equality under the Charter *should take, as the basis of its method of operation, the systematic approach to litigation developed in the United States.* As described in this report, that approach would require taking the following four basic steps:

(1) defining a goal in terms of the desired principle of law to be established;

(2) plotting how the principle of law can be established from case to case in incremental, logical and clear steps;

(3) selecting winnable cases suitable for each stage taken to achieve the goal;

(4) consolidating wins at each stage by bringing similar cases to create a cluster of cases in support of the principle established.

Implicit in this theory are two fundamental organizational principles: first, *success is dependent upon direct sponsorship of cases;* second, *cases which will frustrate or complicate the development of the principle should be avoided if possible.*

The importance of these two principles cannot be underestimated. The success or failure of the American women's law funds can be measured, in large part, by the extent to which direct sponsorship of all cases in a given area has been possible. The ACLU Women's Rights Project, which uses direct sponsorship more than most of the other women's groups, has had more impact in achieving equality in areas such as employment than have the NOW Legal Defense and Education Fund and Women's Equity Action League which have relied primarily on an *amicus* strategy. Drawing upon the historical development of public interest litigation in the United States, the specific experience of the women's law funds and the Canadian groups discussed earlier, *we conclude that the direct sponsorship of litigation is the most productive strategy and therefore the strategy of first choice for any Canadian fund.* It is the most expensive option, but it is potentially the most productive. Moreover, in Canada, there may not be another option. It is becoming increasingly difficult for non-parties to intervene in ordinary court proceedings and it is difficult to predict how receptive courts will be to such interventions in *Charter* cases. [*Ed. note:* This was written before the Supreme Court's policy reversal in 1987, as described in Reading 6.5.] In any case, it would not be advisable to use the scarce resources and time of a women's fund to wage a campaign to broaden the law on interventions when the preferred course of action is direct sponsorship of cases either by being the plaintiff itself or by providing the legal services for the individual woman plaintiff. As well, even in direct sponsorship, there may be one more hurdle to face in Canadian law. Unlike the American law of public interest litigation, the right of a fund to sponsor cases is not necessarily assured in Canada.

The merit of systematic litigation is that it is premised on an appreciation of how law develops in the judicial system. Left to its own devices, the development of law on a case-by-case basis tends to be uneven and unpredictable because judges can only decide on the case that is before them and no one plans the order in which the cases arise or the issues they will deal with. The systematic approach to litigation attempts to impose some order on this process by following the four basic steps outlined above. Implicit in this process is the commitment to the development of law in a steady, predictable manner over a long period of time.

There can be no better time than the present for Canadian women to contemplate undertaking such systematic litigation. Largely as a result of energetic lobbying pursued by Canadian women, the wording of the equality rights provision of the *Charter* makes a clear break with the restrictive interpretation of the equality rights provision of the *Canadian Bill of Rights* developed in the *Lavell* and *Bliss* cases discussed in Chapter 1. The time is right to begin to develop a theory of equality that will meet the expectations of Canadian women.

D. How Will the Fund Be Structured?

The next consideration is: what should be the structure of the fund? Ideally, a fund should have a membership base. It will take time and effort to establish a large base but our review of the American funds showed us that a large national membership provides the organization with a source of funds, longevity and impact both in lobbying efforts and in the courts.

A fund should start off with *a small working board of directors*; some directors can be chosen for their legal expertise so that they can provide information and assistance to the staff on a regular basis. Directors with stature in the community can attract funds to the undertaking.

A successful fund needs adequate staff. There must be a commitment to a large enough staff to ensure the ongoing existence of the organization. A skilled fund raiser is essential. An administrator is necessary to perform the functions of accounting, personnel, office maintenance, budgets, planning, and reporting to the funding sources and the membership. The fund should have lawyers on staff: they will work with the board to establish legal priorities, to review and select cases and to conduct litigation through trial. As well, the fund should plan to retain more senior lawyers to give advice from time to time and to take charge of the difficult and important cases. Staff members must also have a commitment to the ongoing education of women with respect to their legal rights and be prepared to lobby for legislative change.

E. Where Will the Money Come From?

Once the important decision is made to establish a fund, the next question to deal with is: where will the money come from? Our review of American funds showed us that finding adequate funding is a perennial time-consuming concern. When we look at the prospects for fundraising in Canada, it is clear that there are differences from the American situation. First, there is simply not as much private foundation money available in Canada for any kind of public interest work. Second, foundations in Canada do not appear to have a history of commitment to funding civil rights or human rights projects. This lack of involvement may be because the foundations have not been approached or it may be because the foundations have not perceived these issues to be important. In any event, the foundations may not be as rich a source of seed money as in the United States.

Third, the Canadian women's groups have accepted considerable funds from governments over the past number of years. However, it must be recognized that the principal defendant in *Charter* cases will be the provincial or federal government. Canadian organizations such as the Consumers' Association of Canada and the Public Interest Advocacy Centre have not faced this problem because they participate in regulatory settings where their target is most often the regulated party, for example, Bell Canada, and not the government itself. The Canadian Civil Liberties Association, whose adversary is often the government, makes it a policy never to accept government funding.

Fourth, there are real benefits in securing money from a broad membership base. The contributors feel that they have a stake in the process and will assist the organization to flourish. With a widespread membership base, the fund can speak with greater authority.

As well, in the United States the normal rule is that each party pays its own legal costs win or lose. In Canada, on the other hand, the normal rule is that the losing party must pay the costs of the winner. Thus, Canadian funds face the possibility of a real financial drain due to the structure of our court system. In litigation under the *Charter*, this will mean that an individual who loses may have to pay the costs of the government which has successfully opposed her case. She, in turn, will look to the fund for indemnification (compensation) of the costs awarded against her as well as for her own legal costs. These expenses must be built into any litigation scheme.

Several valuable lessons are apparent from the American experience. *Every attempt should be made to obtain funding from a variety of sources – from individuals and corporations as well as foundations – so that failure to have one grant renewed will not jeopardize the life of the organization. The amount of tied funds should be controlled,* or the organization will begin to replace its priorities with those of its funders. Sufficient funds must be raised in order to ensure that staff members are not required to work for insufficient compensation and so that an adequate staff can be hired for the workload; expertise is developed over time and a high staff turnover or rate of burn-out can significantly hinder a fund's effectiveness. This is particularly important in Canada because very few lawyers have experience in equality litigation. Finally, *legal action funds should give high priority to developing permanent fundraising skill* and allocate sufficient staff resources to that task.

F. Beyond Litigation

Even though we strongly believe in the necessity to create a women's legal action fund, we also believe that *litigation should not be seen as a replacement for the varied activities of the women's movement.* The long-term goal of equality for women will best be furthered by a strategy which combines public education, lobbying, use of the media, law reform, education of lawyers and the judiciary, as well as litigation. Litigation is time-consuming, expensive, and a risky route for change. A win may be interpreted to affect only the parties who are before the court while the interpretation of a loss may act to limit the progress of all women for years. Litigation is a blunt instrument, with large downside costs and generally does not provide for accommodation or compromise. On the other had, litigation may be the most effective means of achieving change on an issue. The American and Canadian experience has shown that as a strategy for change, litigation should be used in conjunction with other tools.

A legal action fund or funds would strengthen the general aim of the organized women's movement in Canada – equality. The optimum situation would be to have an overall strategy combining a number of elements.

First, efforts must continue to ensure that the *public is educated to raise its awareness of equality and discrimination issues*. The staff of a fund can contribute to this by establishing and building contacts with the media, by creating media events around issues, by public speaking, and by being a resource for information and materials for other lawyers concerning the issues. It is critical to the long-term success and existence of a fund that it build links to the publics so that the fund is seen as a respected and necessary institution for the community. Judges, too, live in the real world and are not immune to public perceptions.

Second, as have many other women's groups, *the fund must establish a presence at all levels of government* so that it can lobby for legislative change, ensure that new laws do not discriminate against women and monitor the government's enforcement of legislation. It is important that a fund have visibility and credibility in the community so that when it appears before public bodies seeking changes, politicians and government officials will listen, not only because of the content of the presentation, but also because of the constituency or interest group that the fund is seen to represent. Over time, the fund staff will be seen by governments, politicians and civil servants as a valuable information resource and will be consulted before laws are drafted. It must be realized that essential cases will be lost in the courts. It is important then to have built contacts with legislators so that laws can be enacted to reverse such losses.

Third, *it is critical to build a theory of equality which is accepted by academics, lawyers and the judiciary*. Legal writing in respected law journals, presentation of papers at legal seminars or "educationals," and participation in judges' training sessions are all means of disseminating and legitimizing such theories of equality. It will be important to coordinate these endeavours with other organizations such as lawyers' professional groups, or with those who seek equality on the basis of race, age, or mental or physical handicap. An exchange of ideas and resources will benefit all such groups and further the definition of equality.

Finally, *the fund can be a resource centre for other litigants and women's groups*. For example, fund staff might assist in drafting pleadings and act as a clearinghouse for the most recent cases and legal writings in an area of law. The staff might also collect economic and statistical data on the effects of discrimination, including retaining experts who will give evidence in court, and who can predict future trends in society to assist in planning a long-term litigation strategy.

How an organization undertakes these activities, and the extent to which it undertakes these activities, will determine its structure, its size, and its effectiveness. We have learned from the American experience that these combined activities, although expensive and time-consuming, are effective in achieving the goal of equality. We have learned from our own experience that Canadian women can sustain a commitment to litigation, both financially and with other resources, and we suspect that with an organized long-term approach the gains of Canadian women made through litigation could parallel and strengthen those made through legislative lobbying.

The challenge is ours.

7.2

The Women's Legal Education and Action Fund
Sherene Razack

Canadian Feminism and the Law: The Women's Legal Education and Action Fund and the Pursuit of Equality (Toronto: Second Story Press, 1991), 36–63. Reprinted with permission.

Rights on paper mean nothing unless the courts correctly interpret their scope and application. *Charter* activists began trying to influence judicial interpretation through charterwatching, an all-consuming activity. It entailed having national consultations, planning conferences, writing books and articles, making speeches, doing audits of statutes, offering workshops; in short, attempting to inform the decision-makers, women, and the Canadian public (in that order) exactly what the new equality guarantees should mean in law.

The frenzy of activities began, as though by a starter's gun, when the government included in its constitution bill a three-year moratorium on section 15's equality rights. Ostensibly giving governments sufficient time to bring their legislation into conformity with the law, the delay inspired women to plan for the day when they could take their unresolved equality claims to court, armed with the hard-won guarantees of sections 15 and 28.

Not surprisingly, the women most compelled to plan for litigation and to charterwatch were those legally-trained or connected to the women's organizations active on the lobby. As early as March 1981, Marilou McPhedran recorded in her diary her awareness of the experience of American women's legal defence funds and their possible relevance to the Canadian context. In May 1981, when the long-delayed Canadian Advisory Council on the Status of Women (CACSW) conference on Women and the Constitution took place in Ottawa, Beth Atcheson, later a founder of LEAF, mentioned the idea of a

Canadian women's litigation fund in her speech, which she had prepared in collaboration with Beth Symes and Marilou McPhedran. Mary Eberts, the chair of the conference, Beth Symes, and Beth Atcheson were then commissioned by the CACSW to work with the researcher Jennifer Stoddart on a feasibility study of a women's litigation fund. Although the study, *Women and Legal Action*, [See Reading 7.1] was not available until the fall of 1984, its authors relied on its findings to start organizing support for the idea in 1982 … In May, 1982, … several of the women connected to the issue applied for funding and organized a national think tank which was held in Toronto. They invited well-known constitutional experts Peter Hogg and Walter Tarnopolsky because, not only were they trying to secure answers to their questions about what the constitutional equality guarantees meant, they were beginning to adopt what they described as a process of "influencing the influencers," an approach fuelled by their increasing awareness that "things were being written that we didn't exactly agree with." A number of ideas surfaced at this time about how best to promote women's interests in law: the idea of a defence fund was already on the table and to this was added the idea of a legal text book and a symposium, all based on the belief that "it was very important to get in at the academic level."

In their own educational session, billed as a workshop on the *Charter* and held in the same month as the think tank, the women proceeded to determine what their position was on the new law…. Again, the rationale was the same: if women could convey their point of view to those in "responsible positions," they could influence how equality rights were ultimately understood in the courts.

Energetic in their efforts to promote women's constitutional interests, a core of women in Toronto, who were active on constitutional issues, created a trust fund known as the Charter of Rights Educational Fund (CREF), a Charter of Rights Coalition (CORC), and called together 30 women in the area who launched several educational activities. The minutes of the meeting held on November 25, 1982, at the large and prestigious law firm of Tory, Tory (where Mary Eberts worked) indicated a general consensus on the need to publicize the issues and further educate women on the specifics of the equality guarantees. Under the auspices of CREF, two study days were planned and, at a later meeting, a committee was struck to coordinate the massive undertaking of an audit of federal and provincial statutes not in compliance with the *Charter*. The idea of a legal defence fund, supported very strongly by the group's only independently wealthy member, Nancy Jackman, is described in the minutes as the "least formalized" of all the projects.

The study days, held on January 15 and February 19, 1983, attracted over 170 persons, largely women from the legal community. The papers presented, and which were later published, made clear that the group saw their task as one of shaping the legal community's views, and the judiciary's in particular, on the meaning of equality….

The statute audit project, born "out of the nasty suspicion that their [the government's] idea of equality and ours was not going to be the same," intended to pinpoint for Canadian legislatures exactly what had to be done to avoid subsequent legal battles over equality; but, it was also meant to provide women with a "catalogue" of changes which they might launch a litigation effort. The Americans, with whom the CACSW'S *Women and Legal Action* team had spoken, had generally concurred that litigation had to be staged and to do so required a clear knowledge of the range of laws that discriminated against women. The 70 women who worked on the audit were organized into teams and coordinated by a CREF member. They began on the premise that equality means "more to women than the equal opportunity to participate in a male-defined world." They then examined 10 areas of women's lives, suggesting where and how the law had contributed to a situation of inequality. Key to their approach was the notion that "the aim is not to sex-neutralize all laws and pretend that one has thereby created equality: the aim is to positively accommodate sex specific situations."

While both the audit and the study days dealt with the complexities of using the equality guarantees in litigation, the activities of the Charter of Rights Coalition were more broad-based in appeal. A key figure behind CORC'S creation was Pat Hacker who, during her lobbying for section 28 and later when she served as chair of NAC'S constitution committee, was concerned that Canadian women had to be made aware of the three-year moratorium and of the need to push governments into action before this time was up. As a result, NAC created CORC as a subcommittee of its constitutional committee....

The CORC group received government funding to plan a national conference on *Charter* issues that would complement the symposium then being planned "for legal types." Nancy Jackman, who led the CORC team, remembered that they then began to build a series of "mini-coalitions" across the country, using the institutionalized women's groups as a base. The function of these coalitions was to "bug" their governments about the moratorium and educate women about the *Charter*. CORC prepared a slide tape show and an educational kit which optimistically declared:

> There is potential in the *Charter of Rights* to support whatever change women want. It's like a magic wand one could wave to bring about things like fair labour legislation, better protection for women in areas such as sexual assault and enactment of affirmative action programs. *Women can get what we want if we lobby now and do our research and help judges understand what equality means.* [Emphasis in original]

The idea of a national conference, however, proved unworkable given the difficulties of Quebec women's groups with the charter issue. The CORC group settled for a series of regional task forces and conferences, thereby facilitating the development of regional bases – in B.C., for example, where CORC women later formed the West Coast LEAF – and providing an opportunity for women from Toronto and Ottawa to travel the country and organize a litigation fund....

***

In August of 1984, nine months before section 15 of the *Charter of Rights and Freedoms* came into effect, specific planning began for the birth of the Women's Legal Education and Action Fund. The small group that met at 21 McGill, a private Toronto women's club, on August 9, 1984, began the organizing of the fund with characteristic energy and a shared sense of what needed to be done. Besides the authors of the forthcoming *Women and Legal Action*, the planning group for LEAF initially included Marilou McPhedran, two well-known professional women Shelagh Day and Kathleen O'Neil, and Nancy Jackman whose importance as a potential financial contributor to the fund would become evident over the next few months.

Events moved quickly. In September the group considered who might form the board of LEAF, which was scheduled for birth immediately after section 15 came into force; by October, they had received for their use $100,000 from the Jackman Foundation. The release of *Women and Legal Action* that month made it clear that a litigation fund could not succeed without a great deal of money, a requirement that made funding for LEAF the greatest priority. High profile professional women, typically lawyers and human rights professionals, were drawn into the organizing, and fund-raising began in earnest. Kathleen O'Neil was asked to go to her organization, the Federation of Women Teachers of Ontario; endorsements were sought from the YWCA; and every conceivable network was activated in the interest of finding the financial support for LEAF.

Kasia Seydegart was hired to plan the fundraising and suggested that the group cultivate well-known human rights advocates such as the Canadian Human Rights Commission's Gordon Fairweather ... and Judge Rosalie Abella, who wrote the *Report of the Royal Commission on Equality in Employment* published in October 1984. By November, animated by "the dream ... to make the promise of equality contained in section 15 a reality for all Canadian women," the group could record in the minutes their finances to date: $117,000 from the Federation of Women Teachers of Ontario ($70,000 in funds and the rest in services); an initial $50,000 from the Jackman Foundation; and $700 in smaller donations. Appeals to wealthy women and grant applications consumed the rest of 1984.

In the frenzy of organizing, LEAF women relied heavily on their traditional networks. Thus, although the minutes of January 11, 1985, contained a passing reference to the need to involve immigrant women and women of colour, and Magda Seydegart recalled pressing for community involvement, the composition of both the working committee and the board remained homogeneous in character. Seventeen professional white women made up the working committee struck on December 18, 1984; eleven of them were either lawyers or human rights professionals. On April 13 and 14, 1984, when LEAF officially came into being with an elected board and an executive committee, the composition did not change.

LEAF embodied the three main features recommended in *Women and Legal Action*: the establishment of a single national fund, the direct sponsorship of (preferably winnable) cases, and a complementary strategy of education and lobbying. As the epicentre of this strategy LEAF, Mary Eberts wrote, had a good chance of occupying the field of equality rights in the courtroom, but

> expertise can be applied in ways other than this case-by-case approach. Counsel and volunteers from the organization can become involved in legal writing, legal education, and continuing education of bench and bar. In this fashion, they may come to influence how decision-makers view the legal issues involved. Just as important, however, they may influence how lawyers prepare and present cases they bring forward.

"Occupying the field" on equality issues in court, doing proactive litigation, influencing the influencers, were components of LEAF's vision. The criteria for selecting cases, as adopted at the founding meeting, reflected their ambitious intent. Cases taken had to concern equality rights; arise under the *Charter of Rights and Freedoms* or under Quebec's *Charter*; present strong facts; and be of importance to women. Finally, LEAF declared itself particularly interested in cases in which women were doubly disadvantaged, that is, subjected to sex discrimination as well discrimination on the basis of race, disability, etc.

A decision was made early on to begin immediately in the courtroom. On April 17, 1985, in a blaze of publicity, LEAF announced its first two cases – one concerned the right of married women to keep their own names, and the other attacked the requirement that welfare recipients, the majority of whom are women, live as single persons in order to qualify for assistance. Beth Symes described the day:

> [Counsel] Eloise Spitzer's name change case involved the Yukon, a Francophone [Suzanne Bertrand, a French Canadian living in the Yukon who wished to retain her maiden name because it reflected her French-Canadian ancestry] and a blatant case we could win. The second case, the spouse-in-the-house case, was chosen [because] it was for disadvantaged women and because it was a symbol of the state oppressiveness [toward] women. April 17 was a wonderful spectacle on the hill. We raised $20,000 that day in Ottawa and $25,000 in Toronto.

It was an auspicious beginning, full of hope and confidence and undeterred by the enormity [*sic*] of the task at hand....

***

Equality of results was clearly the prevailing rhetoric of the 1980s. Federal government reports, while they did little to concretely achieve it, did not quarrel with its major premises: that inequality was a group phenomenon, that white men could no longer be the norm against which everyone was measured, and that equality meant the recognition of both biological and social differences. Even the courts had begun to accept some of these perceptions. In the *O'Malley* case, involving the demotion of a woman whose newly-acquired religious beliefs prevented her from working on Saturdays, the Honourable Mr. Justice McIntyre ruled that "it is the result or the effect of the action complained of which is significant. If it does, in fact, cause discrimination, if its effect is to impose on one person or group of persons obligations, penalties or restrictive conditions not imposed on other members of the community, then it is discriminatory." Thus when Lynn Smith declared, in an article first presented at the symposium on equality rights, that equality is measured by whether it means "equal results for women in light of their reality, as it does for men in light of their reality," she was expressing a results-oriented view of equality advanced by some members of the judiciary, the legal profession, human rights professionals, women's groups, and groups representing Native people, disabled people, and visible minorities....

***

When the Women's Legal Education and Action Fund officially came into being on April 17, 1985, its founders intended its structure to replicate the best features of American litigation funds and to avoid their worst shortcomings. Impressed by the record of the American organization the National Association for the Advancement of Colored People (NAACP), in particular their strategy of pursuing incremental gains in specific areas, LEAF's founders concluded that Canadian women would best secure their legal rights in a similar way. In American terminology, the NAACP approach was to "occupy" a particular area of law and become known as the expert litigators in that field, and by selecting winnable issues and controlling the development of case law, judges could be asked to take small steps at any one time. Such a long-term strategy of staged litigation requires considerable funding, preferably from a broad, non-governmental base. The intention is for the litigating organization to act as the sponsor of a party to the case, financially a more onerous role than that of intervenor where an organization acts as a "friend of the court" and limits its participation to offering a written and oral opinion on how the case affects the interests it promotes. In the United States, the vision of a proactive legal fund usually involves lobbying and public education, activities that mandate a close relationship with feminist communities.

LEAF's founders intended to pursue a proactive strategy involving the building of test cases. Accordingly, they developed five criteria for case selection, and, following Karen O'Connor's recommendations in her book on American women's legal organizations, they erected a structure to complement the strategy of seeking out important cases nationally, researching them, and having the financial resources to shepherd cases through the lengthy and costly court process. O'Connor also emphasized the importance of strong national headquarters and highly-skilled legal volunteers, the value of publicity both for funders and for credibility in the legal community, the value of local affiliates in keeping the organization in touch with its constituency, and the importance of both legal and public education. Conspicuously absent was any mechanism for ensuring the legal fund's accountability to feminist communities.

LEAF's structure acknowledged the importance of the factors O'Connor outlined. Its board of directors included a national chair and vice-chair, a national legal committee made up of representatives from across the country, finance and fundraising chairs, a chair of public education and research, and local affiliates on the prairies, in the Yukon, and on the west and east coasts....

LEAF's first litigation report recognized that "selecting the right test cases for litigation involves a careful process of winnowing, investigation and research." Typically (and LEAF, as I show below, has not been typical in this respect), someone brings a possible test case or, more commonly, a legal problem women have experienced to the organization's attention. The staff then proceeds to research the issue involved, meeting with a variety of legal consultants before it reaches the legal committee for consideration. Unless one or more of the consultants contacted have a strong community orientation, and unless there are sufficient time and a resources to seek consultation further afield, only the legal aspects of the issue are considered. For LEAF, then, as a feminist organization seeking to protect and improve women's legal rights essentially through the telling of women's stories in court, the first challenge is to accommodate a variety of women's voices to a process that fundamentally negates consultation and difference....

Attracting the large sums of money that litigation requires also places a women's legal defence fund under greater than usual pressure to respond to funders' desires. LEAF's founders knew from the beginning that a broad funding base was desirable, but in actively pursuing it those involved in funding gained a keen appreciation of the compromises in image that would be required. To Marilou McPhedran, the group's chief fundraiser at several points in its history, fundraising meant "breaking into those echelons where feminists have never been very comfortable" and presenting an appropriate image for corporate and government funders that spoke of LEAF women's credibility as members of the legal, not the feminist, community. To another LEAF founder, Beth Atcheson, LEAF had to appear to be an elite corps because this was the only way to garner sufficient financial support from those most able to give it. This left LEAF, however, in the position of being attractive to its funders but alienated from the feminist communities it served and needed. When LEAF hosted a $100-a-plate dinner, it raised funds from the middle and upper classes but strengthened its image as an organization with few ties to women in the community. Moreover, as the beneficiaries of relatively large government grants, LEAF was vulnerable to the rancour of some segments of the community who felt that litigation activities attracted more governmental support than grass-roots activities – rape crisis centres, for example.

Perhaps because of who in Canadian society are legally trained and the necessity of attracting large sums of money (and therefore being "credible" to potential corporate and government funders), LEAF's founders and its main activists, as we have seen, were a remarkably homogeneous group who for the most part chose to remain professionally anchored in the corporate legal world. LEAF women themselves have noted that one way of coming to terms with the contradiction of a feminist challenge from within the corporate world is to capitalize on this insider status. LEAF certainly reflected this approach: it used the resources of large law firms, the status of well-known litigators, and its own credibility as a legal organization with elite connections (when lobbying governments, for example) to contribute to its success. In both its internal and external activities, however, an organization that operates in this fashion runs the risk of losing the self-critical edge that comes with diversity of races, classes, and occupations. It might also be argued, as Andrea Nye has argued of women who must work within the language of patriarchal discourse, that "respectability is inevitably self-defeating" because challenge is unlikely to be sustained from within. Those who felt at odds with the style and approach of LEAF women found it hard to participate. Indeed, for many would-be supporters of LEAF it was LEAF's image as an "intellectual, trail-blazing organization" with a stellar legal cast that was attractive, while others mentioned their early sense of discomfort with the organization's "corporatist–feminist" approach and the priority litigation had, at least in the first two years of LEAF's operation, over the building of a strong community base....

In what was to become a trend of disturbing significance, men began to use the *Charter* soon after its promulgation to protest against the few protections women enjoyed in law. In one of these cases, *Seaboyer/Gayme*, two men accused of rape protested that their right to a fair trial as guaranteed in the *Charter* was infringed upon because of provisions in the Criminal Code that prohibited using as evidence a victim's previous sexual history (except in three specific instances). LEAF applied for and was granted intervenor status whereupon it had 30 days to submit its legal argument concerning why these "rape shield" provisions should continue to stand. In what was intended to be a strategic move, LEAF hired a well-known male criminal lawyer who prepared a somewhat scant brief for the court; it included some examples of possible infringements on the right to a fair trial that might result from the rape shield provisions of the Criminal Code. Further, the approach taken was a rather conservative one where no mention was made of the relationship between these provisions in the Code and women's right to equality under section 15 of the *Charter*. A group of feminists working on the possibility of civil remedies for women harmed by pornography were highly critical of the LEAF brief, pointing out the lack of equality arguments and noting particularly the ill-advised examples that conceded there may be times when a women's previous sexual history may be relevant to a determination of whether or not she was raped.

For LEAF, the *Seaboyer/Gayme* case was its first reminder of the perils of not seeking consultation within the wider feminist community. To its credit, the organization then responded constructively to criticism and developed a process of "workshopping" cases with working groups of feminists who had specific expertise on the issues under consideration. Indeed, the working group formed to discuss what had gone wrong in *Seaboyer/Gayme* remained active for subsequent cases, and workshopping has continued to be the approach taken, the cost of such consultation notwithstanding. According to Mary Eberts, a working group is formed for cases where there is enough lead time, consisting of a member of the national legal committee and/or LEAF's executive director, volunteer lawyers, and representatives from the local LEAF chapter. Each working group develops its own links with the women's community. As the report on the second year of LEAF litigation commented: "Developing case strategy requires a sure vision about the meaning of equality and how that theory should be made concrete in this particular instance, a vision that cannot be arrived at in isolation." ...

***

While the progress made in winning acceptance of the principle of adverse impact was heartening, LEAF had no sooner begun its litigation activities when it became clear that, the favourable judicial climate of the 1980s notwithstanding, it would not be able to maintain the type of control over equality litigation it had originally anticipated. More was at stake than judicial recognition of unintentional discrimination. As Beth Symes ruefully reflected at the round table discussion in 1988, in which LEAF's founders discussed their achievements and common history:

> If you're going to build law with respect to equality, you want to build it your way. So therefore, you flood the courts with your cases and your issues in the order in which you want the court to hear them. We have not occupied the field. Men have. We have been involved in damage control ... men have been popping up all over Canada in various courts challenging things that we as women fought to get, such as maternity benefits, such as the rape shield provisions. Resources have gone into these interventions.

LEAF's careful building of feminist jurisprudence based on precedent and their planning the court's progress toward acceptance of key concepts fell by the wayside when proactive quickly turned to reactive and LEAF found itself acting as a third party, as an intervenor in cases brought by men. They were thereby forced to abandon their agenda and respond to one set by men's claims for equality. The intervention process poses two major constraints: first, it involves extreme time pressures (only 30 days remain from the time an appeal is filed to the time an intervenor must file its request for intervention); once granted the status to intervene, an intervenor then has a further 30 days from the time the last party's factum (written argument) is filed to file her own. Second, as one American legal advocate has observed, the lawyer representing the (male) party bringing the case to court has a considerable advantage in characterizing the issue. Canadian intervenors are required to speak to the specific interests they claim to defend and are seldom empowered to bring evidence, cross-examine, or expand upon the issue in any way. LEAF women entered the legal fray under these constraints, factors that influenced their success more than the benefits of an otherwise favourable judicial climate.

***

In its first three years of litigation, LEAF opened over 300 files. Of these, it adopted 64 cases for consideration by the legal committee, pursuing over 30 in some detail. Its caseload far exceeded capacity, and in 1989 LEAF had to limit its acceptance of intake calls to one day of the week. While there were cases where LEAF took a proactive approach, initiating court action and seeking to build on acceptance of such concepts as adverse impact (and these naturally had a longer gestation time than others), most of its cases to date were those in which LEAF acted as an intervenor, defending women's interests in cases brought by men. Thus, at the board's annual meeting in June of 1986, decisions were made to concentrate on proactive work in the two major areas of employment law and income assistance for low-income women (areas where routine policies or practices had an adverse impact on certain groups of women), and to establish a strategy to cope with the epidemic of cases brought by men. As the board concluded, "the strong *Charter* attacks brought by men against legislative protection for victims of sexual assault were thought to require an appropriate response." ...

7.3

The Court Challenges Program
Ian Brodie
Revised for third edition of this book.

Court cases are always expensive enterprise, but taking a case all the way to the Supreme Court of Canada can cost hundreds of thousands of dollars. Since 1985, the federal government's Court Challenges Program (CCP) has helped certain interest groups launch *Charter of Rights* and language rights cases against both the federal and provincial governments. The CCP has even helped to create some of the groups it has funded.

Many Canadian interest groups became involved in the process of drafting the *Charter* in 1981. They hoped that they would be able to use the *Charter* later to protect or advance their policy objectives in the courts. After the *Charter* was adopted, they realized how costly *Charter* cases would be. Some would-be *Charter* litigators lobbied the federal government to help pay for this expensive litigation. In response, in 1985, Justice Minister John Crosbie and Secretary of State Benoit Bouchard announced a new federal program to help pay for court cases launched under the *Charter*'s equality rights provisions and the various constitutional language rights guarantees. The federal government gave this Court Challenges Program a budget of $9 million for its first five years. The CCP would be allowed to give each case up to $35,000 at each level of the court system the case reached. A single case could therefore receive up to $105,000 if it went all the way to the Supreme Court.

This new Court Challenges Program was, in fact, an extension of an earlier Court Challenges Program. The Trudeau government had established the first CCP in 1977 as part of its battle against Quebec's language law, *Bill 101*. When the separatist Parti Québécois government was elected in 1976, it passed a wide-ranging language law, known as *Bill 101*, to promote the French language in Quebec, in many cases by restricting the use of English. *Bill 101* contradicted Trudeau's own policy of promoting bilingualism as a means of achieving national unity. The Trudeau government was so outraged by *Bill 101* that it briefly considered using the reference procedure to ask the Supreme Court to declare it unconstitutional. However, Trudeau's cabinet decided that a reference case would look too much like the federal government was "ganging up" on Quebec. Instead, the government decided to wait for private individuals to challenge *Bill 101* in the courts. When no challenges were mounted, the government created a small Court Challenges Program to pay the legal costs of interest groups and individuals that used the constitution to challenge *Bill 101* and other provincial language laws. This money went to anglophone groups in Quebec and francophone groups outside Quebec that had been sponsored by the federal government since the 1960s.

The old Court Challenges Program was run "in-house" by the federal Justice Department because the federal government wanted to keep a close eye on the cases that it was funding. When the Mulroney government expanded the CCP in 1985, it agreed to give the CCP a bit more independence, so it hired the Canadian Council on Social Development (CCSD) to run the CCP and to operate at "arms length" from the government.

Under the contract, CCSD had to create two panels of experts to determine which cases would get CCP funding – one panel for language rights cases and another for equality rights cases. The two panels operated quite differently. The language rights panel could fund any case that involved constitutional language guarantees, even if the case challenged a provincial law. Indeed, the language rights sections of the *Charter* had been specifically written to "target" restrictive provincial laws. Most of the cases funded by the language panel were launched by groups that the federal Secretary of State's department also funded. For example, L'Association canadienne-française de l'Ontario received $8.7 million between 1983 and 1990 from the Secretary of State and also received a grant to intervene in the language rights case of *Mahé* v. *Alberta* at the Supreme Court from the CCP.

The equality rights panel, on the other hand, was only authorized to fund cases that challenged federal laws, and then only cases that involved sections 15, 27, and 28 of the *Charter*. The Mulroney government had been elected on a promise to bring harmony to federal-provincial relations and thought that it would be too controversial to fund challenges to provincial laws generally. Despite these restrictions, the equality rights side of the CCP spent much more money than the language rights panel. Even so, as with the language rights panel, much of the equality rights funding went to groups that also received operating grants from the federal Secretary of State.

For example, the Supreme Court's first case to interpret the equality rights provisions of the *Charter* (section 15) involved a provincial law. Despite the restrictions on the CCP, the Court Challenges Program paid the research costs for two of the interest group intervenors in the case – $15,400 to the Women's Legal Education and Action Fund (LEAF) and $35,000 to the Coalition of Provincial Organizations of the Handicapped (COPOH). Both of these groups used CCP money to argue that section 15 was intended to improve the position of historically disadvantaged groups, the position that the Supreme Court eventually adopted. Both LEAF and COPOH also received regular grants from the Secretary of State in the years leading up to the case.

The CCP also had a long-standing involvement in *Mahé* v. *Alberta,* a case about minority language schooling in Alberta and the leading precedent under the *Charter*'s guarantee of minority-language education rights, section 23. The old Court Challenges Program had funded some of the litigants in *Mahé* to help launch the case, and subsequently also funded several of the intervenors in the case like the Quebec Association of Protestant School Boards and L'Association canadienne-française de l'Ontario when it reached Court. In *Mahé,* the Supreme Court confirmed that the *Charter* allowed French-language parents outside Quebec access to French-language schools, but it also began the process of giving these parents control over their schools as well. The *Mahé* precedent, of course, applies equally to all ten provinces.

Some of the CCP's funding decisions brought political controversy. The saga of the abortion cases in the courts provides one example. When anti-abortion crusader Joe Borowski appeared before the Supreme Court to argue that Canada's abortion law violated the *Charter*'s section 7 right to life for the unborn, the CCP provided $35,000 to LEAF to oppose Borowski's claims. When LEAF's conservative counterparts, REAL Women, applied for money to enable it to support Borowski's side, it was turned down. The equality rights panel claimed that REAL Women's arguments would reduce the control that women exercised over their own lives and were therefore inimical to the equality rights of women. This decision was strongly criticized by REAL Women, who charged the CCP was being run by and for radical feminists. As a result, the CCP was charged with taking sides in the abortion debate, at the very time when the Mulroney government was drafting a new abortion law in response to the *Morgentaler* decision.

The CCP also appeared to be pursuing a partisan agenda when it encouraged the creation of new groups that would in turn qualify for CCP funding. For example, the CCP organized a meeting of prisoners' rights advocates in 1989 that led to the creation of the Canadian Prisoners' Rights Network. Similar meetings sponsored by the CCP led to a Working Group on Aboriginal and Treaty Rights and the Canadian Ethnocultural Council's Equality Rights Committee. Most of these groups in turn received CCP funding to launch court cases. By taking an active role in creating groups who were in turn given funding, the CCP has invited criticism that it has used public money to promote a particular policy agenda.

The CCP was renewed for five years in 1990 and transferred from CCSD to the University of Ottawa's Human Rights Centre. However, in its February 1992 budget, part way through that five-year period, the Mulroney government unexpectedly cancelled the CCP. The decision was part of a broader cost-cutting program that saw other federal programs wound-up. The government also defended the decision by saying that by bringing the first-generation of landmark *Charter* cases to court, the CCP's objectives had been achieved. The groups that had received money from the CCP greeted the cancellation with universal condemnation. CCP staff and its clientele groups immediately launched a campaign to have its funding restored. This campaign was soon endorsed by a House of Commons Committee, the Canadian Human Rights Commission, and retired Supreme Court Justice Bertha Wilson.

During the 1993 election, both the Progressive Conservative and Liberal parties promised to re-create the CCP in some form. When the Liberals won the election, they hired a private consulting firm to meet with some of the groups that had received CCP funding and involve them in efforts to re-establish it. In 1994, the federal government incorporated an independent Court Challenges Program in Winnipeg and placed it under the control of the main groups that had received CCP funding before. The renewed CCP continues to operate with the close involvement of the groups it funds, and in 1999/2000 received almost $3.5 million from the federal government.

7.4

Constitutional Rights and Interest Advocacy:
Litigating Educational Reform in Canada and the United States

Christopher P. Manfredi
Adapted from Leslie Seidle, ed.; *Equity and Community* (Montreal: IRPP), 91–117.
Reprinted with permission.

Although constitutional litigation has long been a weapon in the arsenal of Canadian interest groups, there can be little doubt that the *Charter of Rights and Freedoms* has had a profound impact on both the theory and practice of interest group litigation in Canada. One consequence of the *Charter* is that interest groups now articulate their legal claims in the language of rights rather than of federalism. Unlike judicial review on federalism grounds, in which interest groups derive secondary benefits from a redistribution of legislative power, *Charter* review provides groups with a primary benefit that has future value in political negotiations and additional legal battles. Consequently, interest groups are now better able to use litigation as a pro-active reform strategy rather than simply as a tactical response to adverse legislation. A second consequence of the *Charter* is that interest group litigation now invites continuous judicial management of social policy by providing remedial powers previously unavailable to Canadian courts.

...

The purpose of this [study] is to analyze the issues raised by this post-*Charter* transformation of Canadian interest group litigation by examining its use to enforce minority language educational rights in cases that involve three different provinces and each level of the Canadian court system. In order to accomplish this purpose, the [study] is divided into three parts. The first surveys a number of theoretical perspectives on interest group litigation. The use of litigation by African-Americans to achieve educational reform in the United States is next examined. [*Ed. Note:* This section has been deleted.] Finally, the [study] explores three cases in which minority language groups employed litigation to pursue their policy agendas.

The selection of education policy as the subject of this study is driven by two considerations. First, since education is a policy field under provincial jurisdiction, the involvement of federally appointed judges in the design and management of education policy reveals the extent to which the application of new rights overlaps with traditional issues of federalism. That this should be the case is not surprising, since the *Charter*'s political supporters continue to perceive it as a nationalizing instrument. The second reason for selecting education policy as the focus for this study is that federal judicial management of state education policy – with race rather than language constituting the key issue – has been a principal objective of interest groups in the U.S. Consequently, an emphasis on education policy facilitates a natural comparison between Canada and the U.S. which should enhance our understanding of interest group litigation.

Interest Group Litigation: Theoretical Perspectives

The literature on systematic interest group litigation encompasses two broad theoretical concerns. The first is with the general conditions under which interest groups choose litigation, rather than another form of political activity, to pursue their policy objectives. Until recently, conventional wisdom held that the decision to litigate stems from the political disadvantage experienced by certain groups and the tremendous benefits that accrue from the transformation of interests into rights. The second concern is with the factors that influence how interest groups select their specific litigation strategies and tactics. Interest group litigators must choose strategies that ensure centralized control over litigation while taking advantage of favourable venues. Tactically, it is important to select cases that do not require unusual departures from established constitutional doctrine to achieve the desired outcome.

Deciding to Litigate

The most common explanation for interest group litigation is that it occurs when other avenues of political action are closed. Litigation, in other words, is the ultimate weapon of political outsiders. Termed the "political disadvantage" theory, this explanation is closely associated with the experiences of the National Association for the Advancement of Colored People (NAACP). Until the 1960s, restrictive election laws and voting requirements in a significant portion of the U.S. ensured that African-Americans remained unable to defend or advance their interests through normal democratic political participation. Thus, as early as 1915, the NAACP entered the judicial arena to defend the legal rights of African-Americans, and, in 1939, it established an independent Legal Defense and Education Fund (LDEF) to undertake a systematic program of social reform through constitutional litigation. Among the targets of this program, three stand out as particularly important: segregated education, covenants restricting property ownership and discriminatory voting and election laws. These legal struggles culminated respectively in 1948 (restrictive covenants), 1954 (segregated education), and 1964 (voting rights). To be sure, each of these victories required further legal and political action to become effective, but the LDEF's success provided a model for other groups to follow. The NAACP's experience provided both a theoretical and practical guide to interest group litigation in the U.S.

In the 1970s, however, this experience began to appear increasingly anomalous. First, scholars noted that not every interest group litigator suffered from the same political disadvantages experienced by the NAACP. Second, politically *advantaged* interest group litigators were often more successful in court than their disadvantaged counterparts. In an important 1974 article, Marc Galanter attempted to explain these departures from the model of interest group litigation based on the NAACP experience. According to Galanter, participants in the legal process can be divided into one-shot (OS) and repeat player (RP) litigants. RP litigants, which include governments and interest groups engaged in systematic reform litigation, are less interested in the outcome of specific cases than in pursuing their long-term institutional interests. Consequently, they will expend resources on litigation only in cases where there is a high probability of affecting the development of fundamental legal and political rules. Moreover, regardless of their political status, RP litigants enjoy an advantage in the judicial process because of their accumulated expertise and more extensive legal resources. These characteristics assist in explaining why repeat players like the NAACP might be successful where other politically disadvantaged litigants would fail. In addition, Galanter's observations provide an explanation for litigation by politically advantaged groups: they will litigate whenever fundamental rules affecting their long-term institutional interests are at stake.

The political disadvantage theory has been challenged even more recently by Susan Olson. What Olson finds particularly inadequate about the theory is its assumption that interest group litigants would prefer to pursue their objectives through the majoritarian political process, but are forced into the legal arena because of their status as political outsiders. Olson argues instead that litigation and other forms of interest advocacy are complementary political activities that interest groups pursue simultaneously. The choice between these two alternatives in specific instances, according to Olson, depends on the distribution of legal and political resources among interest groups and their adversaries. More precisely, groups initiate litigation when their ratio of political to legal resources is smaller than their opponents' ratio of these two sets of resources. Consequently, since the absolute level of political resources is not the key variable, Olson's theory explains why politically strong groups would choose litigation. Indeed, as Kim Scheppele and Jack Walker point out, one might expect politically advantaged groups to litigate even more frequently, since they are more likely to possess extensive organizational resources such as large staffs, diffuse financial support and longer time horizons, all of which facilitate litigation. Litigation activity will become even more frequent if these groups are sensitive to changes in the political landscape and engaged in structured and intense conflict with regular opponents, since under these circumstances the benefits of litigation will outweigh the costs of engaging in the inherently conflictual process of adversarial confrontation that characterizes judicial dispute resolution.

These theories underscore the interdependence of legal and political resources. Legal victories can provide political resources, and political resources can increase the probability of legal victory. This observation is particularly salient when considering the litigation activity of minority language groups (MLGs) in Canada, since these groups possess an interesting array of legal and political resources. The most obvious legal resource that MLGs possess is section 23 of the *Canadian Charter of Rights and Freedoms*, which provides explicit constitutional protection for minority language educational rights. In addition, section 24(1) of the *Charter* provides a constitutional basis for the broad, prospective remedies necessary to enforce those rights. These legal resources also constitute a political resource, since they provide MLGs with a credible litigation threat when their political demands are ignored. This political resource is limited, however, because of the contingent nature of both sections 23 and 24(1). Consequently, given the uncertain scope of these provisions, litigation concerning them is inevitable.

In addition to these legal resources, MLGs possess several important political resources. First, the federal government and some provincial governments are politically committed to the extension of minority language rights generally, and of minority language educational rights in particular. This political resource also adds to the legal resources of MLGs, since these governments can financially support the litigation activities of MLGs, as well as provide direct legal support by intervening in cases on their behalf. Second, there are important political alliances among MLGs that provide additional legal support through participation in litigation as interveners. In terms of Galanter's classification of litigants, this array of legal and political resources can provide local minority language groups, who possess the limited resources of one-shot litigators, with the additional resources necessary to make them competitive with repeat players like provincial governments.

Strategies and Tactics

The success or failure of interest group litigation depends on a number of strategic and tactical choices. The basic strategic choice that interest groups must make is between direct sponsorship of test cases designed to alter legal rules, and participation as interveners in cases brought by others. Direct sponsorship of test cases maximizes interest group control of litigation, but is very expensive; intervener participation is less costly, but affords far less control over the development of legal rules. In general, a complete litigation strategy will encompass both types of activities. However, choosing to litigate test cases imposes additional strategic constraints. First, since social change through litigation is the quintessential example of incremental policy-making, it is important that cases be brought in the proper sequence. Second, cases must be brought in favourable venues in order to increase the probability of success. Finally, a systematic reform litigation strategy requires centralized control in order to ensure that other strategic constraints are met and that counterproductive litigation does not occur in the target policy field.

...

For minority language groups asserting section 23 rights, both venue selection and strategic coordination are important considerations because of the incremental nature of judicial policy-making. Indeed, the most effective litigation strategy will involve venues in which there are obvious constitutional violations that can easily be remedied, and in which there exists a political environment sympathetic to the claims of minority language groups. This requires some form of coordination among the various MLGs in each province.

The strategic choices that interest groups make are closely related to the principal tactical choice they face: selecting specific cases and determining what arguments to make in those cases. The incremental character of judicial policy making means that the ultimate constitutional objectives of a litigation campaign can only be achieved through the gradual development of discrete rules that eventually form the basis for a new, over-arching, constitutional doctrine. In practical terms, this means that cases raising the easiest constitutional questions must be identified and litigated first, before moving on to cases raising more problematic constitutional issues. The NAACP's experience is again instructive on this point. Its ultimate objective was to establish the constitutional doctrine that segregation in public education violates the equal protection clause of the Fourteenth Amendment. In order to establish this doctrine, the NAACP attacked three cornerstones of educational segregation: differential teaching salaries based on race; segregation of public graduate and professional schools; and inequalities in the physical facilities of African-American and white elementary and secondary schools. Both the nature and sequencing of these attacks were important, because at each step the NAACP broadened the legal concept of educational equality and applied it to progressively more difficult cases. These cases rendered the final step to the constitutional doctrine that separate public education facilities are inherently unequal less drastic than it might otherwise have been.

The theory and practice of interest group litigation in the U.S. provide a useful framework for analyzing the litigation activity of minority language groups in Canada. This framework suggests that the starting point for any analysis of minority language rights litigation is the particular alignment of legal and political resources on each side of language policy disputes both generally and in specific cases. The next step is to determine whether choices concerning modes of participation, sequencing of cases and venue selection are consistent with an effective strategy of systematic reform litigation. Finally, the framework suggests that tactical choices concerning plaintiffs and specific doctrinal arguments are crucial. In the case of litigation involving section 23 of the *Charter*, the easiest cases would be those in which there is a blatant denial of basic instructional services to a large number of minority language students. Doctrines established in these cases could then be applied to situations where the denial of basic services is less evident, or where MLGs seek to expand the services available to them....

...

Litigation and Minority Language Educational Rights

There are parallels between the quest for racial justice in American education and the contemporary demands of minority language groups in Canada. Many of these parallels stem from the similar roles that language and race have played in Canadian and American constitutional development. In historical terms, linguistic divisions produced important compromises in Canada's original constitutional design, as did racial tensions in the U.S. Canada has a federal constitution largely because of its sizeable and geographically concentrated French-speaking minority. Moreover, to the extent that the original constitution protected any substantive rights, it protected certain language rights and the rights of denominational schools (since religious and linguistic divisions were closely linked, especially in Quebec). In contemporary politics, language (again like race in the U.S.) is the source of continuing constitutional conflict, which is evident in the fact that almost one-quarter of the *Charter of Rights and Freedoms* concerns the rights of official language minorities. Indeed, section 23 of the *Charter* is the direct product of one of those conflicts.

Shortly after gaining power in 1976, the Parti Québécois (PQ) government enacted *Bill 101* (*Charte de la langue française*), which affirmed that French is the official language of Quebec and placed restrictions on the public use of English in the province. In particular, sections 72 and 73 of *Bill 101* limited access to English-language education in Quebec to the children of parents who had received their own education in English in the province. The federal government responded to these regulations by including section 23 in the *Charter*, which contains specific provisions designed to override the restrictive education provisions of the PQ's legislation, as well as to protect the educational rights of francophones living outside Quebec. Not surprisingly, the PQ government never accepted the legitimacy of section 23, because of both its specific provisions and its association with a constitutional settlement to which the province never consented.

The Supreme Court recognized the direct conflict between the "Canada Clause" of section 23 and the "Quebec Clause" of *Bill 101* in its judgment in *A.-G. Quebec v. Association of Quebec Protestant School Boards* (1984). Given the obvious purpose and clear language of section 23, Quebec had to concede that its legislation infringed the rights guaranteed to the province's English-speaking minority, and then attempt to defend that infringement as a reasonable limit under section 1 of the *Charter*. The Supreme Court refused to entertain Quebec's section 1 argument, however. It found instead that the "Quebec Clause" constituted a total abrogation, rather than a mere limitation, of the *Charter* rights in question. This allowed the Court to invalidate Quebec's legislation without considering any section 1 justification for the "Quebec Clause." Although issued in the midst of a political conflict between Quebec and the federal government, the *Protestant School Boards* judgment was less controversial than one might expect because it did not create any new rights, but simply restored rights that English-speaking Quebecers had enjoyed prior to *Bill 101*. Moreover, the Court was able to restore those rights through the relatively straightforward remedy of judicial nullification. The same cannot be said for the implementation of section 23 outside Quebec, since it permits the francophone minority in other provinces to make novel claims against provincial governments.

The major difference between the NAACP's litigation campaign and the activities of MLGs in Canada is found in the role of the federal state. Indeed, if any single factor can account for the litigation activities of MLGs, it is the financial, political and legal support of the federal government. This support began prior to the *Charter*'s entrenchment, with the Secretary of State encouraging both the creation and litigation activities of minority language groups such as Alliance Quebec (1982) and the Fédération des francophones hors Québec (FFHQ) (1976). The emergence of the FFHQ is particularly interesting, since the federal government encouraged its creation to serve as an umbrella organization to coordinate provincial MLGs and articulate their interests to the federal government. These federally sponsored groups were the beneficiaries of another federal program: the Secretary of State's Court Challenges Program, which funded six language rights cases (three each in Quebec and Manitoba) between 1978 and 1982. The inclusion of section 23 in the *Charter* added strength to the existing litigation campaign, with federal assistance not surprisingly expanding after 1982. For example, the six most active MLG litigators received more than $36 million in federal financial support for their general activities between 1982 and 1991. In addition, they received funding for their litigation activities from a revamped Court Challenges Program, which, by 1988, was providing $300,000 annually for this purpose. What is apparent from this pattern is that MLGs became instrumental agents through which the federal state could indirectly pursue policy objectives that it could not achieve through direct political action. To put this another way, the federal government mobilized these interests and supported their activities in pursuit of its own constitutional agenda.

The federal government's role in minority language rights litigation illustrates two political aspects of interest advocacy through the *Charter*. First, it supports the argument made as early as 1983 that the genesis of the *Charter* can be found not only in a concern with protecting rights, but also (and perhaps principally) in the politics of national unity. Not only did the *Charter* target specific provincial policies considered anathema to national unity through provisions like section 23, but the very process of subjecting provincial legislation to final constitutional review by a predominantly national institution (the Supreme Court) serves to establish a "unifying counter to decentralizing provincial demands in the Canadian constitutional debate." Second, the federal involvement demonstrates the interdependent relationship between macro-constitutional politics, which involves bargaining over formal constitutional amendments among governments and institutionalized societal actors, and micro-constitutional politics, which involves institutional design through litigation. Macro-constitutional politics sets the framework within which micro-level institutional design occurs, while micro-constitutional politics allows governments and other actors to bypass the constraints of formal bargaining when pursuing their constitutional policy agendas....

Although the political origins and nature of minority language education rights have raised questions about how far courts can go in enforcing them, commentators generally agree that section 23 encourages new forms of litigation and remedial action. This became apparent in *Marchand* v. *Simcoe Board of Education* (1986), in which an Ontario court declared that the plaintiffs had been denied their right under section 23 to receive an appropriate, publicly funded secondary education in French. In this instance, francophone parents had begun lobbying for a French-language secondary school in 1968, and by 1982 had succeeded in persuading the provincial education department and the local school board to provide such a facility. This success was only partial, however, since the school was located in temporary structures that did not contain a cafeteria or industrial arts shops. Consequently, francophone students who wished vocational training had to be bused to an English-speaking school.

The enactment of the *Charter* in 1982 provided parents with a new weapon with which to attack these inequities in their children's education, and, in January 1984, they brought suit against the board of education under section 23. The commencement of the lawsuit coincided with the introduction of amendments to Ontario's *Education Act*, which provided even greater protection for minority language education rights than those guaranteed by section 23. Indeed, the provincial government intervened in the case to ask the court to delay its decision until after the passage of these amendments, which had received second reading in the Ontario legislature and been referred to committee. The *Education Act* amendments would have created a French-language section of the board of education within three years to govern all matters concerning the board's French-language instructional units.

Although affirming that "[l]egislative action in the complex and important field of education is much to be preferred to judicial intervention," the trial court felt compelled to intervene in the absence of any attempt by either provincial or local authorities to comply expeditiously with section 23. After determining that the number of minority language students was sufficient to trigger review of the education provided to francophone students, the court held that section 23 guarantees linguistic minorities a level of education equal to that available to the majority. In the court's view, the qualitative differences in the secondary education provided to francophone and anglophone students constituted a denial of the section 23 rights guaranteed to francophones.

In one sense, the court placed primary responsibility for remedying this infringement of section 23 with the provincial legislature, declaring that it had been obligated since 1982 to enact legislation to ensure that the plaintiffs and similarly situated francophone parents could exercise their *Charter* rights. However, in the absence of legislative action, the court determined that it was "appropriate and just" under section 24(1) to issue a mandatory injunction against the local board of education ordering it to provide the facilities and funding necessary to make the level of education in its French-language secondary school equal to that available in its English schools. In addition, the court issued a mandatory order requiring that proper facilities be established at the francophone secondary school to provide industrial arts and shop programs equal to those provided in the English schools. The court thus combined traditional (declaration of rights) and novel (mandatory injunction) constitutional remedies to vindicate minority language educational rights.

Marchand can be compared to the somewhat more complicated proceedings in *Lavoie v. Nova Scotia*, decided by the trial division of the Nova Scotia Supreme Court in 1988 and reviewed by that court's appellate division in 1989....

... [T]he section 23 claim ... foundered at the trial level on the "where numbers warrant" qualification to minority language educational rights. Although the plaintiffs advanced evidence that approximately 300–400 students would take advantage of a French-language education, the trial judge did not find this convincing because it was unclear where the French school would be located or what type of education would be provided there. Consequently, the court feared that there might be such a significant gap between potential and actual enrolments in the school that vindication of the plaintiffs' section 23 rights would be enormously impractical. Instead of denying the plaintiffs' claim altogether, however, the court ordered the local school board to design a program of French-language instruction, "designate a suitable education facility reasonably accessible to the students eligible for minority-language instruction," and conduct a registration to determine the number of students who would enrol in the facility. When the registration produced only fifty students for the French-language program, the school board refused to provide either minority language instruction or a minority language educational facility. In subsequent proceedings the trial judge agreed that the board's inaction was reasonable, and denied the plaintiffs' section 23 claims.

The appellate proceedings in *Lavoie* thus concerned the ability of courts to substitute their judgment for that of local and provincial education officials about whether the number of students in a geographic area warrants the provision of minority language instruction or educational facilities. Resolving this issue depended in turn on the answer to certain interpretive questions concerning the scope of section 23. Some courts had relied on the Supreme Court's judgment in *Société des Acadiens v. Association of Parents for Fairness in Education* (1986) to hold that, since they were the product of political compromise, the *Charter*'s language rights should be interpreted more narrowly and with greater judicial deference than other *Charter* rights. The appellate court in *Lavoie* noted, however, that the *Société des Acadiens* decision pertained exclusively to sections 16 to 22 of the *Charter*, and that it therefore did not necessarily apply to the interpretation of section 23. The court held instead that section 23 is a "new remedial provision" the purpose of which "is to give education rights to specified linguistic minorities." This justified a "large and liberal interpretation" in which judicial deference to ministerial decisions is inappropriate. Consequently, the appellate court held that fifty students was indeed a sufficient number to warrant the provision of minority language instruction, although not yet sufficient to warrant separate minority language educational facilities.

The *Marchand* and *Lavoie* cases illustrate two facets of the judiciary's combined task under sections 23 and 24(1) of the *Charter*. In *Marchand*, minority language students were receiving a secondary education in their own language, but the quality of that education was questionable. In *Lavoie*, minority language students did not have access to an education in their language, and the principal issue was whether they even had a constitutional right to that education. As in *Marchand*, this determination partially rested on the answer to certain qualitative questions. Section 23 clearly requires that courts do more than simply decide discrete questions about whether minority language instruction or educational facilities must be provided. It also involves courts in qualitative issues such as the type of instruction or facilities available, educational programs, and siting of facilities. Section 24(1) becomes the instrument through which remedial decrees containing specific orders about these matters are issued.

The policy impact of judicial enforcement of section 23 became more apparent with the Supreme Court's decision in *Mahé* v. *Alberta* (1990). At issue was whether the school system in Edmonton, Alberta, and the legislation under which it operated, satisfied the requirements of section 23. The plaintiffs in *Mahé* were francophone parents who, despite the provision of minority language elementary and secondary education in exclusively French-speaking facilities, found fault with two aspects of their children's education. First, they attacked as excessive a provincial regulation requiring francophone students to devote 20 percent of each school day to instruction in English. Second, they claimed that section 23 granted them the right to control minority language education through an autonomous French school board rather than through a less powerful parents' advisory board.

At the trial level, these issues were presented in the context of a relatively narrow dispute between a particular set of parents and the Alberta government. The only non-party participants were the Association canadienne-française de l'Alberta (which supported the parents) and the Alberta School Trustees Association (which supported the government). All pretensions of bipolarity were abandoned at the Supreme Court level, however, as eleven sets of interveners presented arguments in the case. These interveners included four provincial governments; three MLGs from Alberta, Quebec, and Ontario; representatives of two denominational school boards; the Attorney General of Canada and the Commissioner of Official Languages.

These interveners overwhelmingly (although not unanimously) supported a broad interpretation of section 23.

The Court focussed most of its attention on the degree of "management and control" over instructional matters and educational facilities to which section 23 entitles minority-language parents. In deciding this issue, the Court commented on both the general interpretive approach to section 23 and the particular meaning of the phrase "minority language educational facility." Writing for a unanimous Court, Chief Justice Dickson rejected the argument that section 23 should be interpreted narrowly because it reflected a political compromise rather than a universal moral principle. Instead, he agreed with the appellants that section 23 deserves a broad interpretation because its purpose is to prevent the assimilation of minority official language groups. The Court then turned to whether the text of section 23(3)(b) provides minority language parents with a right to manage and control educational facilities. The argument on this point centered on the difference in meaning of the English ("minority language educational facilities") and French ("*établissements d'enseignment de la minorité linguistique*") versions of section 23(3)(b). While the English text merely suggests a right to separate physical resources (e.g., school buildings), the equally authoritative French text, which employs the possessive form and translates literally as "the linguistic minority's educational facilities," suggests a right to facilities belonging to and controlled by the linguistic minority. Wishing to avoid the English text's ambiguity, as well as to ensure that minority language educational services would not be completely at the mercy of the majority, the Court agreed that section 23(3)(b) guarantees some degree of management and control over that education. This forced the Court to address the obvious question: How much management and control?

According to Dickson, the explicitly remedial character of section 23 imposes special obligations on both legislatures and courts. Section 23, he asserted, "confers upon a group a right which places positive obligations on government to alter or develop major institutional structures." Moreover, the Chief Justice stressed that courts have an obligation to "breathe life" into section 23 by implementing "the possibly novel remedies needed to achieve that purpose." That the remedial design of new institutional structures envisioned by Dickson requires extensive judicial involvement became apparent in the test he developed for determining the precise nature of a government's liability under section 23. According to Dickson, the rights "where numbers warrant" to "minority language instruction" or to "minority language educational facilities" do not constitute two distinct rights separated by a specific numerical threshold. Instead, he declared that the specific terms of sections 23(3)(a) and (b) represent the end points of a spectrum of minority language educational services, ranging from mere instruction in the minority language to management and control of facilities through separate boards of education with independent taxing powers. Liability under section 23, therefore, is not measured against a fixed standard, but according to an indeterminate "sliding scale." Section 23, in other words, "simply mandates that governments do whatever is practical in the situation to preserve and promote minority language education." What the "sliding scale" mandates, however, cannot be known without judicial assistance, making necessary a significant degree of judicial management of education policy through remedial decrees.

Although the Court determined that francophone parents in Edmonton did not have a right to an independent school board with full powers of taxation, it did find that they have a right to guaranteed representation on local school boards in proportion to the number of minority language students within the board's jurisdiction. In addition, the Court declared that these minority language representatives should have exclusive authority to make decisions about various matters pertaining to minority language education, including expenditures of funds, appointment of administrators and teachers responsible for minority language education, design and implementation of instructional programs, and the making of agreements for education and services for minority language students.

The remedy developed by the Court in *Mahé* was process oriented, since it established an institutional structure designed to safeguard minority language educational rights in Edmonton. There are at least two explanations for why the Court chose this remedial strategy. First, prior to the litigation, there was a relatively high level of cooperation from education officials in providing minority language educational services; the dispute in *Mahé* was largely over questions of degree rather than over the principle of whether such services should be provided. Second, the process remedy allowed the Court to avoid the judicial management and control of minority language education that its interpretation of section 23 made possible by transferring that responsibility to the parents involved.

The *Mahé* remedy can be contrasted with the remedies granted in *Marchand* and *Lavoie*. In *Marchand*, the actions of the local school board led the court to formulate a remedy containing both performance standards (i.e., francophone education must be qualitatively equal to anglophone education) and specific direct actions (i.e., improvements in the industrial arts and shop programs available to francophone students). In *Lavoie*, the trial court granted a process remedy for determining whether the specific circumstances warranted the provision of section 23 rights; and when education officials answered this question negatively, the appellate court ordered a more intrusive performance standards remedy accompanied by the threat that refusal to comply would lead to court-ordered specified direct actions. Thus, the failure of a process remedy to resolve the dispute caused the appellate court to broaden the trial court's liability finding and to take further remedial steps. In both cases, lack of cooperation by local and provincial education officials led to more intrusive remedies. The degree of judicial intervention varied in all three cases according to the extent of the constitutional violations and to the apparent willingness of officials and the broader political culture to support and implement the necessary institutional changes.

Marchand, Lavoie, and *Mahé* are examples of how the adjudicative process can be utilized to achieve policy reform. Consequently, they illustrate the external political forces which shape the structure and outcome of remedial decree litigation. As the one case of the three which progressed to the Supreme Court, these forces were most apparent in *Mahé*. The case created two apparently odd political alliances: one between the plaintiff francophone parents and Alliance Quebec, an English language rights group in Quebec; and another between the provinces of Alberta and Quebec. The origins of these alliances are relatively easy to explain, however, since they were forged out of common interests. Like francophones in Alberta, Alliance Quebec had an interest in a broad judicial interpretation of minority language educational rights in order to strengthen its position with respect to the Quebec government. Similarly, Quebec shared with Alberta an interest in maintaining maximum provincial control over education policy. Two other provinces (Manitoba and Saskatchewan) joined Alberta and Quebec in defending provincial policy autonomy in this area.

However, two provinces (New Brunswick and Ontario), as well as the federal government and the Commissioner of Official Languages, supported the extension of minority language educational rights. The actions of New Brunswick and Ontario are particularly puzzling, since their interventions, in effect, invited judicial interference in a policy area traditionally within exclusive provincial control. The solution to this puzzle lies in the fact that both provinces were facing political opposition to policies extending minority language educational rights and other rights of their francophone minorities. New Brunswick, which enacted its own *Official Languages Act* in 1969, had periodically been forced to navigate rough political seas in implementing these legislative guarantees for its large francophone minority. This opposition reached a peak in 1991, when the Confederation of Regions Party elected eight members to the provincial assembly on the basis of anti-bilingualism sentiment. Similarly, although Ontario had resisted attempts to declare itself officially bilingual, various administrations enhanced the status of French in the province during the 1980s. Opposition to these efforts increased in the aftermath of Quebec's use of the notwithstanding clause to implement Bill 178. A positive Court decision in *Mahé* could be mobilized by both provinces to dilute this opposition by allowing them to argue that their new policies were required by their constitutional obligations. New Brunswick would take this strategy a step further in 1993 by negotiating a constitutional amendment with the federal government to guarantee certain rights of its francophone minority. The two provinces' apparently suboptimal behaviour (i.e., the expenditure of resources to encourage federal judicial interference in a policy area within provincial jurisdiction) resulted from their simultaneous engagement in political conflict in electoral arenas where their francophone minorities were significant factors.

It is apparent from the circumstances surrounding these three examples of minority language educational rights litigation that the federal government and its provincial allies encouraged particularized interest advocacy in order to advance their own generalized policy agendas. Indeed, it is not by accident that the same coalition of provincial governments that initially supported Prime Minister Trudeau's 1980 constitutional proposals also supported the MLG claims in *Mahé*. Their efforts to entrench minority language educational rights in the *Charter* ensured that the policy debate on this issue would eventually acquire the structured and intensely conflictual character that leads interest groups to litigate. The federal government's actions further ensured that local MLGs and individual parents would have access to the legal resources generally available only to repeat player litigants. Finally, by securing a constitutional right to management and control of minority language education, the litigation activities of MLGs could immunize them from changes in the political landscape, as well as from demographic changes.

Conclusion

Like their racially persecuted counterparts in the U.S., MLGs (especially those outside Quebec) had found provincial legislatures and the federal government largely unresponsive to their interests for most of Canadian history. MLGs had sought to redress this problem through litigation even prior to 1982, but without concrete success. The *Charter* provided an important legal resource for continuing the litigation effort, which was matched by political resources conferred on MLGs by the federal government. The existence of umbrella minority language organizations created and funded by the federal government facilitated the communication necessary to optimize the sequencing and location of cases. As the Supreme Court's recent decision on section 23 in Manitoba illustrates, these efforts have been successful, at least at the level of constitutional law.

Although similar in form to the NAACP's litigation campaign, there are two uniquely Canadian features of minority language educational rights litigation, both of which are related to the federal government's involvement. First, the litigation campaign for minority language educational rights reflects a familiar phenomenon in Canadian history: the use of an outside advocacy strategy by political or socio-economic insiders. Litigation, in other words, is not always a strategy employed by politically disadvantaged groups that lack the resources necessary to advance their cause through ordinary political activity. Although MLGs may be outsiders with respect to provincial governments, their association with the federal government makes them political insiders at another level. Indeed, when MLGs act as proxies for the political and constitutional interests of the federal government, litigation becomes an obvious tool in the hands of political insider.

The second unique feature is related to the first, and involves a peculiar structure of constitutional politics in Canada. As macro-constitutional politics has become increasingly difficult to manage, micro-constitutional politics has emerged as the principal means by which governments and society-based actors can undertake institutional design. The irony is that success at the micro-level further complicates and enervates macro-level constitutional politics. In particular, the increasing importance of micro-constitutional politics places a premium on procedural and structural changes that affect the process of constitutional litigation. This became evident as governments and interest groups fought over the precise wording of interpretive provisions like Meech Lake's "distinct society" clause and Charlottetown's "Canada clause." Indeed, the last two rounds of constitutional negotiation suggest that designing the rules governing micro-constitutional politics has become one of the principal preoccupations of macro-level constitutional bargaining. Since the participants in this bargaining process now understand that litigation is necessary to operationalize abstract constitutional agreements, each of them has an incentive to obtain the most favourable interpretive rules possible. The impact of interest advocacy through litigation thus extends beyond specific policy issues to affect the larger constitutional life of the nation.

7.5

Interest Group Litigation and Canadian Democracy
Gregory Hein

Adapted from *Choices: Courts and Legislatures* (Montreal: IRPP 6:2 (2000)). Reprinted with permission.

Anyone who wants to understand judicial politics in Canada has to consider the efforts of organized interests. Groups are at the centre of most policy debates, trying to persuade an audience of elected officials, bureaucrats, editorialists and ordinary citizens to accept rival positions. The stakes are higher when they enter the courtroom.

Canadians can no longer ignore interest group litigation because it affects the style and substance of our political life. It has become an important strategy for interests trying to shape public policy. Stories about court challenges are reported in the media every week and interest groups participate in most of the cases: civil libertarians guard free expression with vigilance, even if their efforts help men who produce and consume child pornography; disabled people refuse to accept laws that ignore their needs; feminists take on defence lawyers who attack Criminal Code measures designed to counter sexual assault; pro-choice activists and pro-life groups return to court to argue about the presence or absence of fetal rights; gays and lesbians pursue an ambitious campaign to stop discrimination based on sexual orientation; First Nations assert Aboriginal treaty rights; hunters enter the courtroom to oppose measures that restrict the use of guns; groups that promote law and order denounce judges for paying too much attention to the rights of the criminally accused and too little attention to the victims of violent crimes. Unions enter the judicial system to help workers and corporations challenge regulations that frustrate their ability to maximize profits. Their adversaries also litigate. Environmentalists and economic nationalists try to enforce laws that discipline the free market.

Canadians who find these efforts unsettling identify several concerns. Organizations raise difficult moral, economic and political questions, but courts are not designed to sustain public discussions on complex issues. The most controversial claims pit courts against legislatures by asking judges to reject choices made by elected officials. Political life is pulled into our judicial system by groups that generate a steady stream of cases, but without confirmation hearings we know little about the men and women elevated to the Supreme Court. We know even less about superior court judges who also exercise broad powers. These fears are expressed by those who think that litigation can undermine the struggle for a better society and by those who insist that democracy is threatened by organizations that encourage judicial activism.

The debate in the 1980s was initiated by critical legal scholars and neo-Marxists who refused to believe that courts would be transformed into brash agencies of social change. The debate in the 1990s has been dominated by scholars and politicians on the right. According to their account, activists on the left have been wildly successful because so many judges are "removed from reality." These interests flood the courts because they cannot win the support of legislative majorities: most voters find their demands radical and dogmatic. We are told that gays and lesbians want to impose values that will undermine the traditional family. Aboriginal Peoples are determined to establish title over huge tracts of land and secure access to lucrative resources just by presenting flimsy oral histories. Feminists promote an interpretation of equality that leads to "reverse discrimination." Civil libertarians, by guarding the rights of alleged criminals, make it more difficult for police and prosecutors to secure law and order. For critics on the right, these "special interests" belong to a coalition which could be called the "court party." They bring the claims that fuel the growth of judicial power. Instead of trying to build public support for their ideas, these activists urge the Supreme Court to expand social services and benefits, alter the meaning of Aboriginal treaties written centuries ago, bolster regulatory regimes or repair legislative omissions. This use of litigation diminishes Canadian democracy, we are told, because it allows members of the court party to circumvent the legislative process.

This study offers an alternative argument by marshalling a large body of empirical data. The account advanced by conservative critics is incomplete and misleading. While warning us about "zealous" activists who invite judicial activism, they never tell us that courts are filled with a broad range of interests that express a wide array of values. Litigants talk to judges about child custody, labour disputes, income tax policy, advertising laws, medical procedures that cause harm, and the dangers of hazardous substances. This diversity exists because successive generations of Canadians have asked courts and governments to create new opportunities to participate in the judicial system and the legislative arena. We will see that critics on the right are correct when they argue that social activists are eager to pursue legal strategies. However, their interpretation ignores the economic interests that also appreciate the benefits of litigation. Corporations exert a surprising degree of pressure by asking judges to scrutinize the work of elected officials.

The evidence suggests that Aboriginal Peoples, *Charter* Canadians, civil libertarians, and new left activists have the greatest potential to influence public policy through litigation because they are pulled and pushed into the courtroom by the stable characteristics and the changing circumstances. These interests can be called *judicial democrats* because a provocative idea is embedded in their legal arguments and political appeals – judicial review can enhance democracy. Finding deficiencies that weaken our system of government, they believe that the courts should listen to groups that lack political power, protect vulnerable minorities and guard fundamental values, from basic civil liberties forged by the common law tradition to ecological principles that have emerged in the past century.

This study also reveals that corporations do not have the stable characteristics that elevate the propensity to litigate. However, they do confront the changing circumstances that make legal action a compelling strategic manoeuvre. Businesses counter hostile actions, to block investigating government agencies and to go to court when their political resources have been depleted.

The Study

In vibrant liberal democracies, we find a dizzying array of interests that take different shapes. Nine categories were identified that are both coherent and salient. Examples appear in Table 1.

1. Aboriginal Peoples have a unique claim to land and resources as the first inhabitants of the continent now called North America. They are nations struggling to win recognition of land, treaty and self-government rights.
2. Civil libertarians are determined to stop the state from undermining traditional guarantees that many individuals prize. Students, journalists, writers, church activists and defence lawyers challenge laws that violate freedom of expression, freedom of religion and rights that protect the criminally accused.
3. Corporate interests are businesses that compete in a range of

sectors: financial, retail, manufacturing, construction, pharma-ceutical, agricultural, communications and natural resources. Their advocacy groups demand low levels of taxation, flexible regulatory regimes and trade liberalization.

4. Labour interests are organized into unions and advocacy groups that represent miners, loggers, civil servants, teachers, nurses, police officers, auto-makers and technicians. Eager to improve the lives of workers, they defend the welfare state and oppose trade policies that produce unemployment.

5. Professionals have the credentials to practice as lawyers, judges, accountants, academics, pharmacists, doctors, architects and engineers. Most work in the private sector as entrepreneurs, but some are employed by large public institutions. They pursue collective action to promote their interests and to protect the integrity of their respective professions.

6. Social conservatives want to preserve traditional values sustained for centuries by church and family. They oppose open access to abortion services, homosexuals who demand "special rights," gun regulations that punish citizens without reducing crime, feminists who want to marginalize fathers, and a popular culture that encourages promiscuity.

7. Groups that represent victims want to help individuals hurt by cancer, AIDS, drug addiction, smoking, intoxicated drivers, violent crimes, mining tragedies, silicone breast implants, the transmission of infected blood and sexual abuse in schools.

8. *Charter* Canadians believe that state intervention is required to solve pressing social problems. They derive inspiration and impressive legal resources from the 1982 Constitution. Groups representing ethnic, religious and linguistic minorities, women and the disabled can base their claims on guarantees designed to protect their interests.

9. New left activists also believe that state intervention is needed to address grave social problems, but they do not enjoy constitutional rights that were explicitly designed to protect their interests. Environmentalists, gays and lesbians, anti-poverty advocates and economic nationalists can invoke the *Charter* to stop military tests, fight discrimination, preserve wild spaces and stop governments from dismantling the welfare state, but they have to hope that judges will use their discretion to extend the scope of existing guarantees.

To understand the legal strategies that groups pursue every decision appearing in the Federal Court Reports (1,259) and the Supreme Court Reports (1,329) from 1988 to 1998 was reviewed. Organizations appear as *parties* when they have a direct stake in a case. If groups are allowed to participate

Table 1
Categories of Organized Interests

Aboriginal Peoples

Assembly of First Nations
Assembly of Manitoba Chiefs
Congress of Aboriginal Peoples
Dene Nation
Native Council of Canada
Union of New Brunswick Indians

Civil Libertarians

Amnesty International
Canadian Civil Liberties Association
Canadian Council of Churches
Canadian Federation of Students
Centre for Investigative Journalism
Criminal Lawyers' Association

Corporate Interests

Canadian Bankers' Association
Canadian Manufacturers' Association
Canadian Telecommunications Alliance
Merck Frosst Canada
Thomson Newspapers
R.J.R. MacDonald

Labour Interests

Canadian Labour Congress
International Longshoremen's and
   Warehousemen's Union
National Federation of Nurses' Unions
Public Service Alliance of Canada
Union des employés de service
United Fishermen and Allied Worker's Union

Professionals

Association provinciale des assureurs-vie du
   Québec
Association québécoise des pharmaciens
   propriétaires
Canadian Association of University Teachers
Canadian Bar Association
Canadian Institute of Chartered Accountants
Canadian Medical Association

Social Conservatives

Alliance for Life
Evangelical Fellowship of Canada
Human Life International
Inter-Faith Coalition on Marriage and the Family
National Firearms Association
REAL Women

Victims

Canadian Cancer Society
Canadian Council on Smoking and Health
Canadian HIV/AIDS Legal Network
Canadian Resource Centre for Victims of Crime
Central Ontario Hemophilia Society
Westray Families

Charter Canadians

Canadian Council of Refugees
Canadian Disability Rights Council
Canadian Jewish Congress Fédération
des francophones hors Québec
Native Women's Association of Canada
Women's Legal Education and Action Fund

New Left Activists

Canadian Peace Alliance
Council of Canadians
Equality for Gays and Lesbians Everywhere
National Anti-Poverty Association
Sierra Legal Defence Fund
Société pour vaincre la pollution

as *intervenors*, they can present oral arguments and written submissions to address issues raised in a dispute. To understand the purpose of litigation, six possible targets were identified.

1. Groups can achieve their objectives by confronting *private parties*. They counter individuals, unions, professional associations and corporations.
2. Litigants also take aim at *constrained officials* who exercise limited statutory powers. Some work for line departments, but most have positions on boards, tribunals, commissions and inquiries.
3. Organizations can bring claims against *Cabinet ministers* to block unfavourable decisions or to make governments act. By seeking writs of mandamus, they can ask courts to enforce mandatory duties.
4. The stakes are higher when groups mobilize the law to overturn the *statutes and regulations* that are introduced by governments.
5. To improve their chances of winning future contests, litigants can try to shape *judicial interpretations*. The primary goal of this strategy is to direct judges when they define the meaning, purpose and scope of common law rules, ordinary statutes and constitutional guarantees.
6. Groups also enter the courtroom to defend favourable policies when their adversaries launch *hostile actions*.

Interest Group Litigation Before the *Charter*

Courts played an important role before the *Charter* was entrenched by protecting property, hearing administrative actions, enforcing the criminal law and resolving disputes between both levels of government. Courts were also asked to defend civil liberties, even in the nineteenth century. Most cases were initiated by individuals facing charges or governments fighting jurisdictional battles, but organizations supported some challenges at a distance.

These efforts were exceptional. For more than a century, few organizations entered the courtroom to affect public policy and it was possible to have a complete understanding of Canadian politics without ever thinking about interest group litigation. The labour movement concentrated on the party system because courts did little to help workers. Activists who wanted to solve social problems pressured legislators and devised novel strategies in order to change public attitudes. While achieving some of their objectives in court, corporations lobbied Cabinet ministers and senior officials because they appreciated the importance of elite accommodation and the power of bureaucracies.

Interest Group Litigation after the *Charter*

This study reveals that a transformation has occurred. Interest group litigation is now an established form of collective action. Organizations present 819 claims between 1988 and 1998. They appear as parties or intervenors in 30 percent of the disputes considered by the Federal Court and the Supreme Court. Figure 1 records the frequency of participation.

Groups from every category pursue legal strategies. This single finding is remarkable – we now find the same mix of political players trying to influence courts and governments. We find elements of continuity and change. Court dockets are still laden with corporations. They bring 468 legal actions, far more than the other interests. Companies engage in civil litigation against private parties, and challenge regulations governing banking, federal elections, international trade, environmental protection and the pharmaceutical industry. Groups representing professionals participate in 32 cases. As employees, they try to win higher salaries and as experts, they talk to judges about a range of issues, including the principles that guide child custody disputes and criminal investigations. Very few of their challenges try to alter major public policies. The unions and advocacy groups that represent labour interests bring 58 claims. They back members alleging gender discrimination, fight for higher salaries, counter measures that undermine collective bargaining, try to escape criminal contempt charges and assert the right to strike.

The big change is that courts now hear from interests that struggled for decades to win access. For more than a century, courts and governments in Canada maintained barriers that discouraged or even prevented litigation.

Graph 1 reveals that litigation is now an important strategy for groups that once confronted these obstacles:

- Aboriginal Peoples launch 77 claims between 1988–98. First Nations take on the federal government when it fails to act in their best interests; they secure title to lands by asserting Aboriginal rights and challenge laws that fail to respect treaty rights.
- *Charter* Canadians are just as active: 80 legal arguments are presented to oppose measures restricting abortion services, to chastise provincial governments for breaching language rights, to reveal racism in the criminal justice system, and to overturn election laws that discriminate against the mentally ill.
- Civil libertarians participate in 40 cases that attack policies impairing democratic rights, fundamental freedoms and guarantees that protect the criminally accused.
- New left activists bring 37 claims. The activists enter the courtroom in order to protect delicate ecosystems, help poor people facing arrest, overturn policies that exclude homosexuals, and counter measures that limit demonstrations.

Figure 1
Organized Interests in Court, 1988–98

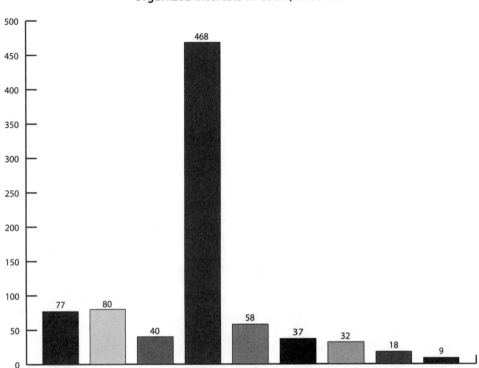

- Social conservatives bring fewer claims, only 18. The most controversial claims try to persuade courts to recognize fetal rights. Unlike their American allies and their Canadian adversaries, social conservatives have not formed any legal advocacy groups; these are specialized organizations designed to fight legal campaigns. In the early 1990s, the Canadian Rights Coalition was established to take on doctors who dared to perform abortions, but it soon disappeared.
- Organizations that represent victims bring even fewer court challenges, only nine. They usually participate outside the courtroom. Most legal claims are brought by individuals who allege negligence or breach of trust to win compensation. Class actions are also orchestrated to counter threats that harm hundreds of victims.

We find this diverse range of interests because governments and courts have created new opportunities to participate. The *Charter* was entrenched by federal politicians who wanted to strengthen the national community and weaken regional identities. Since the patriation round in 1982, governments have introduced funding programs and statutory rights to make administrative regimes, the regulatory process and the judicial system more accessible.

The Supreme Court has also introduced changes that have encouraged interest group litigation. The law of standing has been liberalized in stages. The old common law rule favoured property owners and corporations trying to protect private rights and filtered out citizens who wanted to address public problems. Under the new rule, applicants who ask a serious legal question and demonstrate a "genuine interest" can win access if certain conditions are satisfied. The Supreme Court has also relaxed the requirements for intervening. Groups with a record of advocacy displaying expertise in a particular area usually receive permission to appear as friends of the court.

The Legal Status of Participants

[*Ed. note:* Hein's database indicates that groups seeking "private" benefits (e.g., corporations, unions, professionals) usually participate as actual parties, while groups seeking "public goods" (e.g., *Charter* Canadians, civil libertarians, new left activists) typically participate as interveners.]

Confronting Private Parties and Constrained Officials

The debate over judicial activism gives us a distorted picture of interest group litigation because it *focusses* on the contentious cases that pit courts against legislatures. This study reveals that organizations achieve some of their objectives without asking judges to review the work of elected officials. Half of the actions initiated by corporations are civil claims against private parties and are driven by one of the great engines of capitalism – the desire to accumulate profits. Businesses enter the courtroom to stop trademark, copyright and patent infringement. They also seek damages for negligence and breach of contract. It is important to acknowledge this body of litigation to understand why companies enter the courtroom, but these cases rarely affect public policy.

Groups from every category target constrained officials exercising statutory powers. Some of these claims are ignored because they lack the drama of constitutional challenges. However, organized interests know that bureaucracies, boards, tribunals, commissions and inquiries make thousands of decisions that implicate major public policies.

Shaping the Interpretive Process

Courts define the meaning, purpose and scope of common law rules, ordinary statutes and constitutional guarantees. Organizations aware of this central fact know that precedents are building blocks. Over time they can persuade judges to jettison old standards, reject threatening arguments advanced by adversaries and improve their chances of winning future contests.

Charter Canadians and civil libertarians pursue this strategy more than other interests. A full quarter of their claims target judicial interpretations.

Challenging Elected Officials

The other claims are more captivating because the stakes are higher. When litigants target Cabinet decisions and public policies they ask appointed judges to reject choices made by politicians who have won the support of citizens in general elections. Decisions can rearrange legislative agendas that reflect public concerns, strain regulatory regimes already burdened by onerous responsibilities, alter spending priorities when governments are striving to trim deficits and spark violent reactions that divide communities. The evidence presented in Table 2 cuts to the very heart of the debate over judicial activism. It demonstrates which interests exert pressure on the federal state by challenging laws and political executives.

Table 2
Targeting Elected Officials, 1988-1998

Organized Interests	Cabinet Ministers		Statutes and Regulations		Total	
	No of Claims	(%)	No of Claims	(%)	No. of Claims	(%)
Corporate Interests	48	42	45	34	93	38
Aboriginal Peoples	33	29	18	14	51	21
Charter Canadians	10	9	19	14	29	12
New Left Activists	15	13	9	7	24	10
Civil Libertarians	2	2	20	15	22	9
Labour Interests	3	3	9	7	12	5
Social Conservatives	1	1	6	5	7	3
Professionals	1	1	5	4	6	2
Victims	0	0	0	0	0	0
Totals	**113**	**100**	**131**	**100**	**244**	**100**

Source: Court Challenges Database

Professionals oppose mandatory retirement, social conservatives attack laws that fail to protect the fetus, and unions question measures that restrict collective bargaining and the right to strike, but these are the exceptions. Overall, these groups bring only 10 percent of the claims that target elected officials and most cases try to knock down minor provisions. Groups supporting victims never pursue this strategy.

Far more pressure is generated by the interests that worry critics on the right. Aboriginal Peoples, *Charter* Canadians, civil libertarians and new left activists bring 52 percent of the claims that attack Cabinet decisions and public policies. To win, these litigants have to persuade judges to accept controversial roles – they have to be full partners in the legislative process. Aboriginal Peoples and new left activists question laws passed by both levels of government, but they often target Cabinet ministers.

Charter Canadians and civil libertarians also pursue this strategy, but they tend to target statutes and regulations.

The big surprise is that corporate interests are so active. Table 2 reveals that they present 38 percent of the claims that challenge laws and Cabinet decisions. Requesting writs of mandamus, businesses try to enforce rules governing international trade. Invoking the federal division of powers, they attack laws that address competition, new drugs, environmental protection and tax policy. The *Charter* is also mobilized by corporate litigants.

Propensity to Litigate

This study demonstrates that hundreds of businesses enter the judicial system to advance their interests and a significant proportion ask courts to confront governments. However, the evidence does not suggest that they are inclined to litigate. To understand strategic preferences, we have to consider the entire universe of associations – those that choose legal action and those that stay outside the judicial system. A ratio indicating litigation propensity can be formulated if we estimate the number of associations and the number of court challenges they mount.

What do we find? On the one hand, there are at least 180,000 businesses generating more than 500,000 dollars in revenue annually. They bring 468 claims. On the other hand, Aboriginal Peoples, *Charter* Canadians, civil libertarians and new left activists are represented by only 1,600 organizations. They participate in 234 cases. This comparison suggests that corporations do not display a propensity to litigate. Table 3 confirms what many already suspect. The interests that conservative critics blame for the expansion of judicial power are far more inclined to litigate.

Table 3
Propensity to Litigate

Organized Interests	Population	No. of Claims	Ratio
Corporations	180,000	468	1:385
Aboriginal Peoples, Charter Canadians Civil Libertarians, New Left Activists	1,600	234	1:7

Source: Court Challenges Database

[*Ed. note:* The section "Understanding Interest Group Litigation" has been deleted for space reasons except for the subsection on "judicial democrats."]

Entering the Courtroom to Enhance Democracy

Aboriginal peoples, *Charter* Canadians, civil libertarians and new left activists believe that litigation has the potential to make our public institutions more accessible, transparent and responsive, if courts hear from a diverse range of interests, guard fundamental social values and protect disadvantaged minorities. We know that some activists agree with the neo-Marxists and critical legal scholars who warned social movements to resist the lure of constitutional litigation. They doubt that lawyers and judges are the real champions of democracy. We also know that Aboriginal Peoples, *Charter* Canadians, civil libertarians and new left activists make shrewd strategic calculations to improve their chances of success. However, the normative assertion that is embedded in their legal claims and political appeals is a crucial distinguishing feature. These interests display a greater propensity to litigate because the architects who design campaigns and the allies who work outside the courtroom believe that judicial review can enhance democracy. They are moved by this conviction.

Judicial democrats emphasize a structural defect that all liberal democracies confront. Without courts enforcing constitutional guarantees, governments can make choices that harm minorities, especially if they are vulnerable or unpopular. This threat is serious, they argue, because our representative institutions do not reflect the diversity of Canadian society. For example, a growing number of women sit in Parliament and the provincial legislatures, but men still dominate these chambers; we see few visible minorities and even fewer Aboriginal Peoples. This deficiency raises the possibility that policies will not reflect the interests of "weaker voices" that struggle for recognition. Moved by public sentiments, ideological preoccupations or financial pressures, governments might be tempted to impose limits on the rights that minorities assert. This problem exists, we are told, even when politicians do not intend to discriminate. The men who dominate our representative institutions often fail to appreciate the deleterious effects of laws that appear to be fair.

Judicial democrats who believe that courts should protect minorities suggest that majorities are more apparent than real. They identify faults acknowledged by political scientists and disenchanted voters. Elections are blunt instruments for registering preferences. During campaigns, personality is more important than policy and debates lack substance. Parties usually win control of the state by securing the support of pluralities not majorities. After taking office, a new government with only a general mandate can decide to pursue a disruptive legislative agenda that most citizens oppose. Because party discipline is so strong, it is difficult to know how many representatives actually support a proposed policy.

The activists who offer this critical assessment also tell us that democracy is weakened by a persistent bias. Interests trying to shape public policy do not enjoy the same opportunities. Some have access to the Cabinet ministers and bureaucrats who exercise real power. Others are excluded or ignored because they question deeply held attitudes and practices that have been accepted for generations. Corporations are privileged because of their role in the economy. Worse, their influence has been bolstered by the pressures of globalization. Groups concerned about public problems are often dismissed when they demand expensive social programs and strict regulations that penalize important industries. The judicial democrats who see this bias do not believe that our institutions are open and transparent. Elite accommodation leaves little room for public deliberation and bureaucrats draft thousands of regulations away from the scrutiny that shapes the legislative process – they write "secret laws."

Aboriginal Peoples, *Charter* Canadians, civil libertarians and new left activists who want courts to enforce fundamental values find cautionary narratives in our past. They tell us that federal officials undermined Aboriginal culture and suspended basic human rights. Adults did not enjoy the privileges of citizenship and children were sent away to residential schools, wrenched from their families and communities. Voters could have objected to these practices in general elections, but they did not. In Manitoba, the Protestant Anglophone majority failed for more than a century to respect rights designed to protect the Catholic Francophone minority. During the 1940s, Japanese Canadians were taken to detention camps. Civil libertarians also remember the 1950s, when religious minorities in Quebec were subjected to a campaign of harassment, orchestrated by the Premier and carried out by the police. In several provinces, mentally disabled women were forced into sterilization programs. During the 1960s, the RCMP investigated thousands of civil servants to root out homosexuals. Feminists were still fighting blatant forms of discrimination in the 1970s, opposing social policies that stopped pregnant women from receiving unemployment benefits, provisions in the Indian Act that stripped Aboriginal women of their status and a family law regime that hurt women by discounting their contributions.

Judicial democrats display a propensity to litigate because still believe that courts have to counter grave threats. Civil libertarians have to be vigilant because police officers who resent the *Charter* and politicians who promise law and order are tempted to limit fundamental guarantees. Aboriginal women who want to advance their interests have to litigate to win access to constitutional conferences. Legal action is still an essential strategy for environmental groups; provincial officials eager to promote economic growth still leave pollution laws unenforced; federal officials are still tempted to circumvent the requirements for environmental assessments, especially when lucrative projects could be jeopardized. Disabled men and women have to fight for services they deem to be essential. Coalitions of anti-poverty activists feel compelled to litigate when governments pass laws that stigmatize and harass homeless people. Francophones in English Canada and Anglophones in Quebec have to invoke education rights to secure good facilities and autonomous school boards; they have to ask judges to supervise provincial officials who are reluctant to redistribute revenue and authority. Feminists must go to court to help women who are victims of sexual violence. Governments are willing to draft comprehensive agreements, Aboriginal leaders tell us, because courts continue to enforce Aboriginal rights.

Unlike these judicial democrats, the executives and lobbyists who represent corporations and entire industries do not believe that active courts should try to enhance democracy. In certain contexts, they say the very opposite. When litigation has hampered their ability to generate profits, businesses espouse an argument that is also made by conservative critics. They admire the virtues of majoritarian democracy and lament the loss of legislative supremacy. This defence becomes apparent when governments try to improve access to legal remedies. In Ontario, coalitions organized to stop the Class Proceedings Act during the late 1980s and the Environmental Bill of Rights during the early 1990s. To oppose these threatening measures, businesses questioned the legitimacy of judicial review, criticized the institutional capacity of courts and emphasized the disruptive effects of litigation. What did they fear? Mischievous activists would "flood" the judicial system with "frivolous" claims. Because courts would become partners in the regulatory process, it would become less flexible and more cumbersome. Favourable decisions made by politicians who appreciate the central role that corporations play would be overturned by judges who are shielded from the realities of a competitive global economy.

Countering Immediate Threats

Judicial democrats and corporate interests are also pushed into the courtroom by immediate threats that can only be stopped through litigation. Table 4 reveals an inescapable strategic problem. Organizations have to target hostile actions to defend public policies, Criminal Code provisions, common law standards, judicial interpretations and administrative orders that favour their interests. It is startling to see that 34 percent of the claims brought by *Charter* Canadians are intended to counter these threatening claims. Critical legal scholars and neo-Marxists predicted this trend. After the patriation round, they warned social reformers who were dazzled by the possibilities of constitutional litigation that time and money would have to be spent reacting to claims brought by their enemies. Feminists intervene to protect Criminal Code provisions governing sexual assault, hate speech and pornography. Groups representing the disabled support policies that mandate special education. A growing number of issues pull competing organizations into the courtroom: cases that implicate the fetus attract pro-choice activists and pro-life groups; fishing companies and Aboriginal peoples fight over valuable natural resources; some Aboriginal bands oppose Aboriginal women who challenge residency requirements; rival drug manufacturers try to secure and block the notices that allow companies to produce pharmaceuticals; and new left activists and businesses defend or attack measures designed to protect the natural environment.

Table 4
Hostile Actions

Organized Interests	No. of Claims	Percentage of Total Claims Brought by Groups in Each Category
Charter Canadians	27	34
New Left Activists	7	19
Civil Libertarians	6	15
Aboriginal Peoples	10	13
Corporate Interests	25	5

Source: Court Challenges Database

Corporations face another threat that can only be countered through litigation. Governments conduct inspections, initiate civil actions and bring criminal charges to enforce a range of laws. We already know that businesses raise the Constitution as a sword to cut away policies that constrain their activities. Corporate litigants also hold up the Constitution as a shield to block the state from scrutinizing their affairs. Businesses can devise a wide array of legal arguments because the Supreme Court has decided that any *Charter* guarantee can be invoked as a defence. To advance their interests, businesses attack procedures allowing authorities to conduct searches and seizures, general inquiry powers, regulatory offences and measures that restrict the right to counsel in the old Combines Investigation Act, the new Competition Act, the Income Tax Act and laws governing the banking industry. This desire to obstruct scrutiny will always be an important source of litigation.

Diminished Political Resources

Organizations also enter the courtroom when contextual changes diminish the level or value of their political resources. Their fortunes can be affected by the rate of economic growth, unemployment, environmental disasters, the appointment of new Cabinet ministers and international conflicts. Because influence is not a fixed characteristic, all interests can be placed at a disadvantage – even huge industries that employ thousands of workers and generate billions of dollars in revenue. We know that tobacco companies have been hurt by compelling scientific evidence and adverse public opinion for more than a decade. Governments have introduced a number of measures to restrict the use of their product. Jurisdictions in Canada and the United States have initiated civil claims to recover health-care costs. This hostility makes litigation an attractive strategy. For example, R.J.R. Macdonald won an impressive victory in a decision that has been denounced by health-care advocates, groups representing victims and new left activists who feel that corporations wield too much power. Invoking the guarantee of free expression, it persuaded the Supreme Court to remove an advertising ban. The other cases are less dramatic. Fishing companies on both coasts have been hit hard because federal officials have taken remedial steps that restrict commercial enterprises to halt the decline of stocks. Businesses unable to secure favourable policies have responded by pressing their claims in court.

Only ideologues believe that corporations are invincible. Still, in a world shaped by the pressures of globalization, businesses that can survive in the international economy enjoy an advantage. Governments determined to eliminate annual deficits and tackle accumulated debts now support policies that favour competitive corporations. They are promoting the benefits of trade liberalization, deregulation, and tax reduction. This shift has undermined other interests. Politicians trying reduce the size of the state are less willing to agree with activists who demand expensive national programs and onerous regulatory regimes. In this climate, judicial democrats find litigation even more compelling, especially when they encounter indifference and hostility. After failing to win in the legislative arena, *Charter* Canadians can mount legal challenges to reform the *Income Tax Act* and expand the scope of social services. When federal officials fail to implement the core recommendations of a royal commission that examines the plight of Aboriginal Peoples, First Nations can ask judges to hear their concerns. New left activists ignored by political elites can knock down policies that exclude homosexuals and demand the strict enforcement of environmental laws. Governments that have achieved a budget surplus have more room to consider policy options, but judicial democrats have learned an important lesson during the past decade: litigation is indispensable when the country is toiling through tough times.

Interest Group Litigation and Canadian Democracy

This study tells us what we need to know to contemplate the effects and implications of interest group litigation.

- The central insight is that Aboriginal Peoples, *Charter* Canadians, civil libertarians, and new left activists are drawn into court by the stable characteristics that elevate the propensity to litigate and by the changing circumstances that make legal strategies seem compelling. These are the judicial democrats. They will continue to generate a steady stream of controversial claims because they believe that democracy can be enhanced by judicial review.
- Judicial democrats are not in court alone. The judicial system is filled with a wide array of groups that express a broad range of

values. This diversity is a triumph for citizens who struggled for decades to win new opportunities to participate in our public institutions.

- Some organized interests are reluctant litigants. Professionals, social conservatives and victims mobilize the law sporadically. Although groups that represent workers are more willing to bring legal claims, they usually attack constrained officials, leaving major public policies unscathed.

- Corporations do not display a propensity to litigate, but they do encounter the changing circumstances that push interests into the courtroom. They ask judges to overturn cabinet decisions and laws passed by both levels of government, often to resist state intervention.

The purpose of this study is to understand a controversial form of collective action, but it can also help us assess the current relationship between citizens, legislators, and judges. In the current debate over judicial activism, most commentators exaggerate the hazards and underestimate the rewards.

Courts interpreting cryptic constitutional declarations and treaties signed centuries ago do make decisions that cause turmoil. They can disrupt legislative agendas, strain regulatory regimes already burdened by arduous responsibilities and force governments to adjust the allocation of resources. Our political life might be less tranquil and more uncertain today. However, we now have a judicial system that responds to a diverse range of interests. This is an accomplishment that Canadians should celebrate. Judges hear from professionals advancing pecuniary claims, Aboriginal Peoples who want their treaty rights respected, and environmentalists who monitor the erosion of important. Courts enforcing the *Charter* help businesses trying to protect commercial expression, homosexuals who want the family law remedies that heterosexuals expect and linguistic minorities struggling to preserve their culture.

Critics troubled by active courts want to restore the relative calm we once enjoyed by resurrecting "traditional judicial review." What do they propose? The Supreme Court has to bring back the old standing requirements, discourage interests from intervening, consider only narrow legal questions raised by live controversies and question the value of extrinsic evidence. They resent judges who allow political adversaries to clutter the courtroom, evaluate policy alternatives with misplaced confidence and try to settle future disputes in a single decision. Conservative critics believe that prudence should replace arrogance. It is too easy for judges to advance their personal preferences, they insist, if the "living tree metaphor" can be invoked as a *licence* to alter the meaning and scope of enumerated guarantees. The Supreme Court has to remember the primary purpose of a liberal democratic constitution: to protect individuals by placing limits on the state. Legal remedies should not increase the presence of the state. Judges should never punish governments for failing to act by filling perceived omissions. They should also resist the temptation to expand services, benefits, regulatory regimes and Aboriginal treaties.

This argument can sound appealing, especially when the Supreme Court delivers a decision that divides the country. Still, the measures that conservative critics propose have a distinct bias that Canadians should know about. Resurrecting traditional judicial review would filter out certain interests and values. Returning to the old rules governing standing and intervenor status would hurt public interests unable to demonstrate a direct stake in a dispute. Excluding extrinsic evidence would make it more difficult for litigants who want to trace the adverse effects of a law. Freezing the meaning and scope of constitutional guarantees would leave judges unable to address new social problems that create discrimination. If courts only placed limits on the state, litigation would be a poor strategy for citizens who want to bolster regulatory regimes or expand social services. Taken together, these obstacles would hinder interests concerned about racism, homophobia, gender inequality, environmental degradation, poverty, the lives of the disabled and the plight of Aboriginal Peoples. Traditional judicial review would not, however, frustrate litigants advancing conventional pecuniary claims and legal action would still be an effective strategy for interests that want to resist state intervention.

Although constrained courts would cause fewer disruptions, we would pay a price. Litigation would help corporations but not groups trying to address public problems. Critics of judicial activism stumble here. They want to stop social reformers from seeking the legal remedies that businesses have always requested. Seen from this perspective, the current relationship between citizens, legislators, and judges is attractive because it meets a basic requirement of democracy that many Canadians embrace. Nations composed of diverse interests should not have institutions that respond to some and ignore others.

7.6

Response to Gregory Hein
Ian Brodie

Gregory Hein writes that interest group litigation is now an established part of Canadian political life, and he is right. His defence of interest group litigation's influence on Canadian politics is a bit harder to accept.

Many people criticize the judicialization of politics. Hein acknowledges the most common criticisms. It undermines the influence of elected officials. It brings political issues to courts, and courts are poorly equipped to deal with these issues. It turns important decisions over to judges who are appointed through a secretive process. In response, he argues that the courts attract the same kinds of interests as other political institutions. Both "progressive" groups and corporations use litigation to achieve their goals. He also argues that for years Canadians have demanded more ways to participate in the judicial and political processes.

Up to this point, Hein is arguing that interest group litigation does little to change the overall thrust of Canadian politics. The same kinds of interests are being pursued in the political process as in the courts. More interest group litigation is all about increasing participation in politics, and the more participation the better.

Hein then goes on to look at the views of "judicial democrats." These groups (and, I suspect, Hein himself) think the judicialization of politics improves Canadian politics. How? Because Canada's elected institutions do not represent the full diversity of Canadian society. They often overlook the weaker voices in society and tend to favour corporations over public interest groups. According to this argument, interest groups use the courts to protect disadvantaged minorities and even the political score.

These arguments are not persuasive. First, the argument that Canada's elected institutions do not represent all the diversity of Canadian society. Which groups are underrepresented? Does parliament need more women? More poor people? More farmers? More factory workers? More transgendered persons? The alternative the judicial democrats propose is to have more decisions by judges. Judges are all lawyers. They are also wealthier, whiter, and older than the rest of the population. The courts are much less diverse than parliament or most provincial legislatures. Do judicial democrats think that having judges make more political decisions will improve the "representativeness" of Canadian government?

Second, Hein's judicial democrats say that interest group litigation protects disadvantaged minorities. The political process is biased against interests that lack the resources to be heard in parliament, cabinet, or the bureaucracy. Certainly, groups with money, a stable staff, solid political strategies, and expertise tend to get access to political decision-makers. However, the judicial process also has biases, as Hein points out. Groups must have money, experienced lawyers, and expertise to win in court. Do these kinds of groups have trouble getting a meeting with a senior bureaucrat, a cabinet minister, or a political aide? Would a group that was truly shut out of the political process be able to mount a single court case, let alone long-term litigation campaigns?

This point hints at a deeper problem in Hein's argument. He portrays interest group litigation as a grassroots phenomenon, a ground-up process. He writes as if groups of Canadians band together spontaneously to challenge government actions in court. However, this is hardly accurate. Governments often support the "judicial democrats" through programs like the Court Challenges Program (see Reading 7.3). If a group has government support for its litigation, is it really "disadvantaged"?

7.7

Key Terms

Concepts

litigation as a form of interest group activity
"influencing the influencers"
constitutional imperialism
Charter imperialism
political disadvantage theory
"judicial democrats"
systematic litigation
test case
direct sponsorship vs. intervenor
amicus curiae
political trial
"support structure for legal mobilization" (SSLM)
rights advocacy organizations
minority language groups (MLGs)
repeat player (RP)
one-shotter (OS)
favourable case selection
sequencing
macro-constitutional politics
micro-constitutional politics

Institutions, Events, and Documents

Court Challenges Program (CCP)
Quebec Bill 101
Alliance Quebec
Quebec Protestant School Boards v. *Quebec* (1984)
Mahé v. *Alberta* (1990)
National Citizens' Coalition v. *A.-G. Canada* (1984)
Women's Legal Education and Action Fund (LEAF)
National Association for the Advancement of Colored People (NAACP)

Fact Finding in the Courts

All informed decisions must be based on an adequate knowledge of relevant facts, and different kinds of decisions require different kinds of facts. Accordingly, decision-making institutions have developed different fact-finding procedures designed to suit their distinctive needs.

The original adjudicatory function of courts has strongly influenced the procedures and rules governing judicial fact-finding. In order to determine guilt or innocence – "what really happened" (or "historical facts") – common law courts developed special rules to guard against biased or false evidence. The judge assumed a neutral and passive role. The parties to the dispute were responsible for developing all the relevant facts and legal arguments. Hearsay evidence was excluded altogether, and first-hand testimony had to be given under oath, subject to cross-examination and the introduction of contradictory evidence by one's adversary. The giving of false information under these circumstances, perjury, was itself made criminal. These rules and procedures are known collectively as the adversary process, and they constitute the core of the judicial process in all common law countries.

Precisely because it is well suited to its original purpose, the adversary process is much less adept at collecting the kind of facts relevant to public policy-making decisions. Policy-makers want to know about general patterns of human behaviour – what Horowitz calls "social facts" – in order to formulate public policy. (See Reading 8.1) To get these facts, legislators and administrators may consult past studies of the problem, commission new studies to provide current socio-economic information, and conduct extensive hearings to gather additional information, including indications of political support and opposition. Under the traditional rules of the adversary process, judges can do none of this.

The advent of written constitutional law and judicial review placed serious strains on the common law courts' fact-finding procedures. While the inevitable policy impact of constitutional law decisions created a felt need among judges for additional factual information, their procedures were inadequate and even hostile toward such information. There was also a strong sense that it was inconsistent with the adjudicatory function of courts to base a decision on "social facts." This was perceived as more a legislative than a judicial activity. As Weiler points out, this perception was not, and is not, simply an old-fashioned attachment to traditional ways. If a judge makes unanticipated use of non-traditional factual materials, is this fair to unsuspecting litigants who presented facts and arguments along traditional lines? In some cases the relevant "historical facts" and the "social facts" may actually suggest conflicting solutions. Should judges ignore the plight of the individual plaintiff in the name of making policy for the many? In short, when it comes to collecting and using facts, there are serious and real tensions between the adjudicatory and policy-making functions of courts.

Horowitz describes this tension as the problem of institutional capacity, as distinct from the problem of institutional legitimacy. The latter questions the legitimacy of un-elected, unaccountable judges making policy in a democracy. The question of institutional capacity is whether courts are institutionally equipped to make informed and effective policy choices.

Historically, Canadian judges have used "extrinsic evidence" (the Canadian legal term for social facts) very sparingly. The adjudicatory view of the judicial function, the influence of the decisions and style of the British Privy Council, and a deference to the tradition of parliamentary supremacy all led Canadian judges to use a textually oriented form of judicial reasoning. The written opinions accompanying the Court's decisions have tended to be highly conceptual and not grounded in the socio-economic contexts that gave rise to the cases. This problem is further aggravated in reference procedures, where there are not even any "historical facts" to guide the judges' reasoning.[1]

This textual approach has been especially criticized in the area of constitutional law as too legalistic. There have been calls for a more sociological jurisprudence, a kind of judicial reasoning "which insists that constitutional words and statutory words must be carefully linked by judicially noticed knowledge and by evidence to the ongoing life of society."[2] This type of jurisprudence requires a more extensive use of extrinsic evidence than Canadian judges have been willing to accept until quite recently.

For similar reasons, American judges also refused to allow social facts into court until 1908. In that year a young lawyer (later to become a Supreme Court justice) named Louis Brandeis successfully defended the state of Oregon's maximum hour labour laws by submitting studies showing a higher incidence of serious maternal health problems for women working

---

1 See Paul Weiler's discussion on the *Chicken and Egg Reference* for a notorious example of what can happen in these circumstances: *In the Last Resort: A Critical Study of the Supreme Court of Canada* (Toronto: Carswell-Metheun, 1974), pp. 156–64. Reprinted in the first edition of this book.

2 W.R. Lederman, "Thoughts on Reform to the Supreme Court of Canada," *The Confederation Challenge*, Ontario Advisory Committee on Confederation, Vol. II (Toronto: Queen's Printer, 1970), p. 295.

long hours in certain occupations. He asked the judges to accept these studies as proof that the legislators had a "reasonable basis" for enacting the mandatory restrictions on freedom of contract. The Supreme Court agreed, and thus began the American practice of the "Brandeis brief," or judicial use of pertinent socio-economic facts.[3] This practice is consistent with the greater policy-making role of the American Supreme Court, and distinguishes it from other final appellate courts.[4]

The Canadian Supreme Court's 1976 decision in the *Anti-Inflation Reference* suggested that the Canadian aversion to extrinsic evidence was waning, and has since come to be recognized as a turning point in Canadian practice.[5] (See Reading 8.3) The question of the validity of the federal government's wage and price control legislation was referred to the Supreme Court. The mandatory restraint policies clearly were being applied to sectors of the economy that were normally under provincial jurisdiction, and could not be supported by the federal government's normal section 91 power to regulate "trade and commerce." Based on existing precedents, the mandatory wage and price controls could only be justified as an exercise of the federal residual power to make laws for the "peace, order, and good government" of Canada. There were, however, only two possible legal justifications for the exercise of the POGG power: the "national emergency" test or the "inherent national importance" test. Both of these tests seemed to pose an essentially empirical question: had inflation become so serious in Canada by the mid-1970's as to constitute a "national emergency" or an issue of "inherent national importance"?

Recognizing the inadequacy of the traditional factum and oral argument procedures to deal with this dimension of the case, then Chief Justice Bora Laskin summoned the counsel for the various governments and private intervenors involved in the case. After several private meetings, the late Chief Justice announced a two-stage procedure for the submission of factual evidence and an opportunity to rebut evidence prior to oral argument. The result was a new chapter in Canadian judicial process.

The federal government submitted its "white paper" on inflation, the documentary basis of its legislative policy, and also a Statistics Canada bulletin showing changes in the monthly consumer price index. The Canadian Labour Congress, one of the intervenors opposed to the wage and price controls, submitted a 64-page economic study of inflation in Canada, which had

---

3 *Muller* v. *Oregon*, 2O8 U.S. 412 (1908).

4 The High Court of Australia does not even receive a written factum or brief before oral argument, thus precluding any "Brandeis brief" presentation of "social facts." The same is true of courts in Great Britain and New Zealand. The refusal to use written factums in these countries is an implicit commentary on their self-perception as adjudicators not policy-makers.

5 See Katherine E. Swinton, *The Supreme Court and Canadian Federalism: The Laskin-Dickson Years* (Toronto: Carswell, 1990), pp. 75–85.

been especially commissioned for the occasion. It was later supported by telegrams from 38 Canadian economists. On the "rebuttal date," the federal government and Ontario made additional submissions responding to the economic arguments advanced in the CLC's original submission.

In the end the Supreme Court made minimal use of the extrinsic evidence that had been submitted. Laskin's opinion noted that the extrinsic material supported the contention that the government had a "rational basis for the legislation," while Ritchie's opinion cited the "white paper" as proof of the existence of an "emergency." More importantly, the *Anti-Inflation Reference* set a new precedent for the use of "social science" briefs in Canadian constitutional law. Henceforth, the Supreme Court may resurrect the procedures elaborated by Laskin whenever it deems it appropriate.

There are other less dramatic devices that judges can use to import social facts into a judicial proceeding. One is the traditional practice of "judicial notice," which is a technique through which a judge may unilaterally take notice of factual matters that he or she deems relevant to the legal questions that must be answered. A good example was the late Chief Justice Laskin's opinion for the majority in a 1972 "breathalyzer" case brought under the 1960 *Bill of Rights*. In finding that the breathalyzer requirement did not violate "due process of law," Laskin declared,

> I am, moreover, of the opinion that it is within the scope of judicial notice to recognize that Parliament has acted in a matter that is of great social concern, that is the human and economic costs of highway accidents arising from drunk driving, in enacting s. 223 and related provisions of the Criminal Code.[6]

A judge may not "take notice" of extrinsic facts that are highly technical or not well-known. As the preceding example illustrates, "judicial notice" is limited to facts that are generally known and accepted, or at least easily demonstrated. While it is thus an effective vehicle for introducing common sense into judicial proceedings, it has much more limited value in cases involving complex policy issues.

Yet another device for the introduction of social facts into judicial proceedings is the use of the "expert witness." Under the *Canada Evidence Act* each party can call up to five "expert witnesses" to testify on a subject at issue before the court. One restriction is that the subject must be sufficiently complex that specialized study is required to become an "expert" on it. For this reason an Ontario judge refused to allow Father Philip Berrigan, an American "peace activist," to testify at the trial of the 63 persons charged with trespassing during an anti-nuclear demonstration at a Litton Systems Canada plant in November, 1983. The judge ruled that Berrigan's testimony was not relevant to the trespassing charge.

---

6 *Curr v. the Queen*, (1972) S.C.R. 889.

By contrast, several months later a *Charter of Rights* case in Calgary saw a total of four expert witnesses called to testify on the issue of whether Canada's election law violates the "freedom of speech" provision of the *Charter*. These included a Canadian and an American political scientist, a Canadian constitutional historian, and Canada's Chief Electoral Officer.[7] The use of such "experts," both as *viva voce* witnesses and as authors of specially commissioned studies, has since become quite common in politically important *Charter* cases. The use of experts, however, has the disadvantages pointed out by Horowitz. They are hired and paid by the parties to the case, so they are inevitably partisan. Nor is there any guarantee that the "experts'" definition of the relevant facts and issues is adequate.

A related matter is the judicial use of "legislative history" in determining the constitutional validity of a statute. While legislative history is not the same as social facts, it can serve a similar purpose of situating a case in the real-world context from which it comes. Historically common law courts did not go beyond the actual text of a statute in interpreting its meaning. With the advent of ever increasing government social and economic regulation, courts have felt the need to go beyond the texts of statutes to discover their legislative purposes. American courts began to use legislative history in constitutional cases during the 1920s, and now do so extensively. Legislative history has usually been held inadmissible in Canada, but again the 1976 *Anti-Inflation Reference*, and the use of the government "white paper," marks a departure from past practice. Since then, the Supreme Court has made more frequent use of Hansard and other historical sources in constitutional cases.

While historically Canadian courts were reluctant to admit, much less use social facts, the changes that began in the 1970s have accelerated since 1982 under *the Charter of Rights*. As noted by Justice Bertha Wilson in 1986, several *Charter* sections seem to require some presentation of social facts. Section 1, for example, declares that the subsequently enumerated rights are not absolute, but subject to "such reasonable limitations prescribed by law as can be demonstrably justified in a free and democratic society." The last element of this test suggests comparisons between challenged Canadian practices and practices of other "free and democratic societies." This occurred in the series of "one person, one vote" cases decided in B.C., Saskatchewan, the Supreme Court, and Alberta between 1988 and 1991. Both litigants and judges made extensive comparisons of Canadian electoral distribution practices with those of England, Australia and the United States.[8]

The Supreme Court further encouraged the presentation of social facts by embracing the so-called "*Charter* two-step" approach to interpreting

---

7 See Janet Hiebert, "Fair Elections and Freedom of Expression under the Charter," *Journal of Canadian Studies*, 25:4 1989-90), pp. 72–86.

8 See chapter 12, "Fair and Effective Representation," in Rainer Knopff and F.L. Morton, *Charter Politics* (Toronto: Nelson Canada, 1992), pp. 332–73.

section 1.[9] In its landmark 1986 decision in *R.* v. *Oakes*, the Court ruled that once a violation of a *Charter* right has been identified, the burden then shifts to the government to prove that the challenged statute or policy serves a "pressing and substantial objective;" that the means used are "rationally connected" to that objective; that the law impairs the rights involved as little as is reasonably possible (i.e. there is no "alternative means" of achieving the same end with less impairment of rights); and that on balance the public good achieved outweighs the private harm to individual rights. Needless to say, government lawyers cannot meet this burden of proof by assertion alone. They need social facts to document their claims. Perhaps this also explains Chief Justice Lamer's remark that when judges interpret section 1, they are making "essentially what used to be a political call."[9]

A similar need for social facts seems implicit in the section 15 right to "equal benefit of the law" and the section 23 right to minority language education "where numbers merit." In its leading section 15 decision, *Andrews* v. *Law Society of British Columbia* (1988), the Supreme Court emphasized that section 15 requires laws not just to provide "equal treatment" but to have "equal effects," especially for historically disadvantaged groups. The effect or impact of a public policy can only be determined by reference to social science studies. There is thus increasing pressure on Canadian judges to allow and to use extrinsic evidence and social facts more than in the past.

Former Justice Bertha Wilson has expressed optimism that the courts, with the help of interveners, will be up to this challenge and will not fall victim to the problems of institutional capacity described by Horowitz. Weiler points out, however, that getting relevant social facts into the courts does not guarantee that they will be understood or properly used. He argues that there is a qualitative difference between the judicial use of social facts to determine whether there is a "reasonable basis" for government legislation (the original purpose of the Brandeis brief and also the role played by social facts in the *Anti-Inflation Reference*), and the judges' use of social science data to craft a new judicially created policy.[11]

Carl Baar's account (See Reading 8.2) of the Supreme Court's attempt to craft a policy implementing the section 11(b) right to trial within a reasonable time bears out Weiler's skepticism. In trying to determine how much delay is too much, the Supreme Court erred not once but twice in its use of social facts. In its 1990 decision in *R.* v. *Askov*, the Court laid down a maximum permissible delay of six to eight months for "institutional delay," delay caused by overcrowded court calendars and facilities. To the dismay of the Court, law-enforcement agencies and many in the general public, this new policy led to the dismissal of tens of thousands of criminal cases for

---

9 For a fuller exposition of the section 1 "*Charter* two-step," see Knopff and Morton, *Charter Politics*, pp. 38–57.

10 "How the *Charter* changes Justice, " *The Globe and Mail*, April 17, 1992, A17.

11 "Two Models of Judicial Decision-Making," *Canadian Bar Review* 46 (1968), pp. 406–71.

failure to meet the new limit. The source of the problem was subsequently traced to Justice Corey's erroneous use of data from Montreal, data that the Court had obtained on its own initiative *after* oral argument; and his failure to carefully read (or understand) the statistics on court delay submitted by Askov's lawyer. These statistics, taken from a study by Professor Baar, indicated that a six to eight month rule would negatively affect about 25% of the criminal cases studied in the Toronto area.

In response to the negative impact of *Askov* and the criticism it generated, the Supreme Court moved quickly to "fix" its alleged mistake. In March, 1992, with Justice Corey conspicuously absent from the panel of seven judges who heard the appeal, the Supreme Court issued an opinion in *R. v. Morin*, which was intended to clarify the "*Askov* rule." Justice Sopinka's majority opinion blamed the "large number of stays and withdrawals" on the "interpretation and administration" of the *Askov* rule by lower court judges. *Askov* was intended as "an administrative guideline," wrote Sopinka, and was "not intended to be applied in a purely mechanical fashion." It was "neither a limitation period nor a fixed ceiling," and should be reasonably interpreted in light of the different facts of each case. Sopinka recognized the relevance of statistical evidence from other jurisdictions, but cautioned "care must be taken that a comparison of jurisdictions is indeed a comparative analysis." He then acknowledged that the use of the Montreal data in *Askov* had been inappropriate, but blamed Professor Baar – incorrectly – for providing the Court with the Quebec data!

The *Morin* case, unlike *Askov*, dealt with delay in a section 92 provincial court hearing a summary conviction offence. Sopinka went on to propose a longer period of permissible delay for trials conducted in provincial courts – eight to ten months – on the grounds that the section 92 courts are busier than the superior courts and that statistics show that on average it takes longer to dispose of cases in provincial courts than in superior courts. Once again, the source of the Court's data was Professor Baar's affidavit in *Askov*, and once again the Court got it wrong. Indeed, the Court misinterpreted Baar's data not once but twice: first, by confusing "median total time" for the trial of indictable offences (in s. 92 and s.96 courts combined), with the median delay for provincial court stage of the same cases; and second, by treating the latter as if it were the median delay for provincial court disposal of summary conviction offences (trials that start and finish in section 92 courts).

Such problems should not come as a surprise for a judiciary that has plunged so quickly into a greater policy-making role. Horowitz, Weiler and others have shown there is an inherent tension between the fact-finding procedures and judicial expertise associated with adjudicating disputes and the data-gathering and analysis required by a policy-making role. At a minimum, the public embarrassment of *Askov* and *Morin* should stimulate both the justices and their clerks to circulate draft opinions more widely and proof read more critically. Perhaps it will also induce more caution in judges who are inclined to use social facts to craft new policies.

The Court can also continue to "re-tool" its procedures to allow for the introduction of more extrinsic evidence – through intervenors, judicial notice, expert witnesses, and so forth. In the British context, Professor Gearty, anticipating these types of problems, has called for the appointment of a "'public interest officer' with a small team of officials, whose job it is to prepare reports on the effects of possible rulings, not just on the law, but on the wider public and on society as a whole." "How," Gearty asks, "can judges know about such operational matters? The advantage of a public interest statement filed by a court officer would be that it would take such huge issues out of the narrow and artificial confines of the adversarial process, and it would also open up the process to persons other than lawyers." (Reading 5.8).

This may be all be true, but, as Horowitz and Manfredi have pointed out, after all the institutional re-tooling is done, how do the re-designed courts differ from the institutions whose decisions they are supposed to be reviewing? And if they do not differ, why should they be given the power of judicial review? Clearly, there is no perfect solution to the challenge of judicial fact-finding as courts increase their role in the policy-making process.

8.1

Fact Finding in Adjudication
Donald C. Horowitz
The Courts and Social Policy (Washington: The Brookings Institute, 1977), 45–51. Reprinted with permission.

The fact that judges function at some distance from the social milieu from which their cases spring puts them at an initial disadvantage in understanding the dimensions of social policy problems. The focused, piecemeal quality of adjudication implies that judicial decisions tend to be abstracted from social contexts broader than the immediate setting in which the litigation arises, and, as already indicated, the potentially unrepresentative character of the litigants makes it hazardous to generalize from their situation to the wider context.

The judicial fact-finding process carries forward this abstraction of the case from its more general social context. To make this clear, it is necessary to distinguish between two kinds of facts: historical facts and social facts. Historical facts are the events that have transpired between the parties to a lawsuit. Social facts are the recurrent patterns of behavior on which policy must be based. Historical facts, as I use the term, have occasionally been called "adjudicative facts" by lawyers, and social facts have also been called "legislative facts." I avoid these terms because of the preconceptions they carry and the division of labor they imply. Nonetheless, by whatever designation they are known, these are two distinct kinds of facts, and a process set up to establish the one is not necessarily adequate to ascertain the other.

Social facts are nothing new in litigation. Courts have always had to make assumptions or inferences about general conditions that would guide their decisions. The broader the issue, the more such imponderables there are. The breadth of the issues in constitutional law has always made it a fertile field for empirical speculation. Does a civil service law barring alleged subversives from public employment have a "chilling effect" on free speech? Is the use of third-degree methods by the police sufficiently widespread to justify a prophylactic rule that would exclude from evidence even some confessions that are not coerced? Does pornography stimulate the commission of sex crimes, or does it provide cathartic release for those who might otherwise commit such crimes?

Constitutional law is a fertile field, but it is not the only field in which such questions arise. If a court refuses to enforce against a bankrupt corporation an "unconscionable contract" for the repayment of borrowed money, will that make it more difficult for firms needing credit to obtain it and perhaps precipitate more such bankruptcies? Does it encourage carelessness and thus undercut a prime purpose of the law of negligence if an automobile driver, a shopkeeper, or a theater owner is permitted to insure himself against liability inflicted as a result of his own fault?

These are, all of them, behavioral questions. They share an important characteristic: no amount of proof about the conduct of the individual litigants involved in a civil service, confession, obscenity, bankruptcy, or negligence case can provide answers to these probabilistic questions about the behavior of whole categories of people. As a matter of fact, proof of one kind of fact can be misleading about the other. What is true in the individual case may be false in the generality of cases, and vice versa. The judicial process, however, makes it much easier to learn reliably about the individual case than about the run of cases.

The increasing involvement of the courts in social policy questions has increased the number and importance of social fact questions in litigation. As the courts move into new, specialized, unfamiliar policy areas, they are confronted by a plethora of questions about human behavior that are beyond their ability to answer on the basis of common experience or the usual modicum of expert testimony. A few examples, drawn from a social science manual for lawyers, will make the point:

> Do the attrition rates for different racial groups applying for admission to a union apprenticeship program suggest a pattern of racial discrimination?

> How would the elimination of a local bus system through bankruptcy affect low income people and the elderly poor in particular?

> How are different income groups and communities of varying sizes differentially affected by the formula allocation of General Revenue Sharing funds?

Obtaining answers to such behavioral questions has become exigent, and not only because the interstices in which courts make fresh policy keep expanding. If a judge or a jury makes a mistake of fact relating only to the case before it, "the effects of the mistake are quarantined." But if the factual materials form the foundation for a general policy, the consequences cannot be so confined.

Traditionally, the courts have been modest about their competence to ascertain social facts and have tried to leave this function primarily to other agencies. They have shielded themselves by applying doctrines that have the effect of deferring to the fact-finding abilities of legislatures and administrative bodies, to avoid having to establish social facts in the course of litigation.

The reasons for this general modesty are well grounded. There is tension between two different judicial responsibilities: deciding the particular case and formulating a general policy. Two different kinds of fact-finding processes are required for these two different functions. The adversary system of presentation and the rules of evidence were both developed for the former, and they leave much to be desired for the latter.

In general, the parties can be depended upon to elicit all of the relevant historical facts, through the ordinary use of testimony and documentary evidence, and the judge or jury can be presumed competent to evaluate that evidence. Social facts, on the other hand, may not be elicited at all by the parties, almost surely not fully, and the competence of the decision-maker in this field cannot be taken for granted.

These deficiencies of the adversary process have led to proposals for the employment of outside experts as consultants to the courts. So far, relatively few impartial experts have been appointed, and the proof of social facts has largely been left to the traditional adversary method.

Expert testimony is the conventional way for the litigants to prove social facts, but its deficiencies are considerable. The experts are usually partisans, employed by the parties, and their conclusions tend to reflect that status. If the parties provide a skewed picture of the problem they purport to represent, their expert witness may do the same. Finally, reliance on expert witnesses hired by the parties makes the judge the prisoner of the parties' definition of the issues of social facts that are involved.

The rules of evidence are equally inapt for the verification of social facts. They are geared to the search for truth between the parties, not to the search for truth in general. Understandably, there is a prohibition on the introduction of hearsay evidence. Courts must act on what happened, not on what someone said happened. The emphasis in judicial fact-finding on choosing between conflicting versions of events by assessing the credibility of witnesses also places a premium on requiring witness to have firsthand knowledge of the events about which they testify. Sensible though the hearsay rule may be, however, it makes the ascertainment of scientific facts of all kinds including social science, very difficult. Books and articles constitute inadmissible hearsay; they are not alive and cannot be cross-examined. Consequently, when behavioral materials are introduced into evidence, it is usually pursuant to some exception to the hearsay rule....

... The use of expert testimony involves another kind of exception. Duly qualified experts, unlike ordinary witnesses, need not confine themselves to testifying about facts. They may also state their opinion, which may be nothing more than a guess or a bias. Yet the studies on which their opinion may be based remain inadmissible as hearsay (though they may be introduced to impeach an expert's opinion).

All of these cumbersome devices tend to make the judge dependent on secondary interpretations of the relevant empirical material and to discourage him from going directly to the material itself. As we shall see in later chapters, filtered knowledge has its problems.

If new rules and mechanisms do develop to aid in informing the courts about social facts, further problems will arise. The courts may have to administer a dual system of evidence – one part for historical facts, another for social facts – and there is the problem of what might be called contamination. Evidence introduced for one purpose may, as it often does, spill over to infect the other set of issues. Compartmentalization to prevent contamination is one of the hardest jobs a judge must perform. This particular problem suggests again the underlying tension between deciding the litigants' case and making general policy.

How have social fact issues been handled by the courts in practice? They have been handled in much the same way that the rules of evidence and the adversary system have been adapted to accommodate social facts: by neglect or by improvisation.

A first, quite common way is to ignore them or to assume, sometimes rightly, sometimes wrongly, that the litigants' case is representative. This is patently inadequate....

... A third way of dealing with social facts is to go outside the record of the case in search of information. This is what Mr. Justice Murphy did when he sent questionnaires to police forces in thirty-eight cities in order to determine the relationship between the admissibility of illegally obtained evidence and police training in the law of search and seizure. The same impulse has sometimes moved other judges, restless in their ignorance of behavioral fact, to consult experts of their acquaintance, as Judge Charles Clark, then former Dean of the Yale Law School, consulted the Yale University organist about a music copyright case that was pending before him. These attempts, primitive as they are, show the existence of a deeply felt need rather than a method of satisfying it.

What these examples also suggest is that the need for empirical data is often not even sensed until the case is on appeal. The traditional formulation of causes of action rarely incorporates social facts as an element of proof. When behavioral facts are implicitly incorporated (for example, "reasonable care of a prudent man under the circumstances"), these standards are often not met by evidence but left to the decision-maker to judge from his own experience.

The law thus tends to slight the need for behavioral material in a number of ways. In practice, this means that the option of utilizing such material falls on counsel. Generally, public-interest lawyers have been much more assiduous about introducing evidence of social facts than have other lawyers, and it is they who have often compiled voluminous records of expert testimony and memoranda....

That the process of adjudication places the emphasis heavily on the accurate ascertainment of historical facts, while it neglects and renders it difficult to prove social facts, is, of course, exactly what might be expected from its traditional responsibilities. This is to say, the fact-finding capability of the courts is likely to lag behind the functions they are increasingly required to perform.

To argue that this problem of capability exists is still to say nothing of the materials on which proof of social facts might be based. The problems here are considerable. There may be no studies that cast light on the issue in litigation. If there are, the behavioral issue may be framed in a way quite inappropriate for litigation. Studies may, of course, be specially commissioned for the purposes of the lawsuit. Even if the potential bias of such studies is overcome, the constraints of time and resources may dictate research methods much less than satisfying. On large issues, existing data are likely to be fragmentary. Then the question becomes one of generalization from partial or tentative findings, or one of drawing inferences from proxies. This is no place for a full-scale consideration of the imperfect fit between law and social science. It is enough to say here that the problems of social science do not disappear in litigation, but are instead compounded by the litigation setting, the different ways in which lawyers and social scientists ask questions, and the time constraint.

This last point needs to be underscored. As I have said earlier, litigation is, for the most part, a mandatory decision process. Courts do not choose their cases; cases choose their courts. With certain exceptions, a case properly brought must be decided. Whereas a legislator or administrator has some freedom to shy away from issues on which his quantum of ignorance is too great to give him confidence that he can act sensibly, courts are not afforded quite the same latitude. Courts have difficulty finding and absorbing social facts in the context of a largely mandatory decision process that puts them at a comparative disadvantage in social policymaking.

8.2

Social Facts, Court Delay and the *Charter*
Carl Baar
Written for the second edition of this book.

The case of *Regina* v. *Askov*, decided by the Supreme Court of Canada on October 18, 1990, became one of the most important and controversial Supreme Court judgments interpreting legal rights under the Canadian *Charter of Rights and Freedoms*. It was the Supreme Court's fifth judgment on section 11(b) of the *Charter*, guaranteeing accused persons a "trial within a reasonable time." It was, however, the Court's first section 11(b) case to address the question of whether excessive "institutional delay" violates the *Charter*. Institutional delay is the time that elapses not because the crown is proceeding too slowly or a particular case is very complex, but because resources and practices make it impossible for a court to deliver an earlier trial date.

As a direct result of the decision in *Askov*, more than 40,000 criminal charges, largely but not exclusively within the province of Ontario, were dismissed for failure to bring accused persons to trial within a reasonable time. Yet the reasons given by the majority in *Askov* concluded by saying that there would be little difficulty complying with the decision in "most regions" of the country. The surprising result was acknowledged publicly in July 1991, by Justice Cory, the author of the majority judgment, and by March, 1992, the Supreme Court used its next section 11(b) case, *Regina* v. *Morin*, to limit the possibility for accused persons to cite *Askov* to gain dismissal of pending criminal charges.

What made the *Askov* controversy both frustrating and ironic was that the Supreme Court had in fact made social science data – "social facts" in Donald Horowitz's terms – more central to its judgment than in any previous constitutional case. For many years, Canadian court watchers had urged the Court to consider social facts, following the American practice of the "Brandeis brief." In *Askov*, the Court accepted and used an affidavit reporting systematic data on elapsed time of criminal cases in 10 Canadian cities in three provinces, but still failed to anticipate the results of its judgment.

This failure can be attributed to a number of characteristics of the judicial process in Canada which, taken together, make it difficult for the courts to deal effectively with social facts. *Askov* itself shows in key respects a fundamentally sound understanding of section 11(b) of the *Charter*, and is likely to be beneficial in its long-term impact on Canadian criminal justice. But its immediate shortcomings illustrated one of the most troubling aspects of *Charter* adjudication.

The Historical Facts

The particular facts of the *Askov* case are straightforward. Askov and three co-accused were charged with a number of offences arising from the use of threats and violence to corner the market on exotic dancers in the Metropolitan Toronto area. Following their arrests in November, 1983, they were brought to Provincial Court, the starting point for any criminal court proceeding in Canada. They elected to be tried by a judge and jury, which required that their case be moved to a section 96 court (one staffed by federally appointed judges), because only federally appointed judges can preside over jury trials in Canada. Before the accused could proceed to trial in the section 96 court, they had to be committed to trial by a Provincial Court judge, and were entitled to a preliminary hearing before committal.

The preliminary hearing for Askov and his co-accused began on July 4, 1984, in the Provincial Court in Brampton, Ontario. Following a postponement, the preliminary hearing was completed on September 21 and the accused were committed to trial in the District Court, which had jurisdiction over most criminal jury cases in Ontario at that time (it was replaced in 1990 following a province-wide reorganization). The ten-month period from arrest to committal, while longer than most cases, was not unusual, and was not challenged by the accused, since it was a result in part of an effort to find a convenient time for the lawyers for all four accused to be present together in court.

However, when the accused appeared in the District Court on October 1, 1984, to set a date for trial, the earliest available date was October 15, 1985. When the accuseds' trial date arrived a year later, and their place on the list was still not reached by October 25, the case was put over for trial on September 2, 1986. When that date arrived, more than 23 months after the case left Provincial Court, the accused successfully argued that the delay in District Court violated their right to be tried within a reasonable time.

Askov's case was different from cases that arose before the *Charter*. Prior to 1982, accused persons could only contest excessive delays if they could show that the delay resulted from the crown abusing its discretion in prosecuting the case (for example, by refusing to bring a case to trial for a long period of time while pursuing related charges against another person). In *Askov*, no allegations were made about the crown's conduct of the case. Both sides agreed that the delay was entirely a result of the unavailability of any earlier trial date. But prior to the *Charter*, the unavailability of a trial date was not grounds for dismissal of charges.

The Supreme Court was thus faced in *Askov* with a new and important question. Should delay not attributable to the crown or the accused be covered by section 11(b)? If the lack of a trial date counts against the crown, an accused could go free through no fault of the prosecution. If, on the other hand, the lack of a trial date does not count against the crown, an accused could wait years for trial and have no remedy.

The Court ruled unanimously that these "institutional delays" must count against the crown. The Court declared that to do otherwise would be to negate section 11(b). The Court further reasoned that the provincial government, which was responsible for prosecuting criminal cases, was also responsible for providing the institutional resources that would allow trial courts to offer trial dates within a reasonable time.

Defining Reasonable Time

Once the Supreme Court agreed on the principle that institutional delay could count as a factor in determining whether section 11(b) had been violated, the next question was the practical and more difficult one: how long is too long?

The first task of Askov's counsel was to argue that 23 months from committal to the beginning of trial was too long. But no standard existed in Canadian law to draw that conclusion. Unlike a number of jurisdictions outside Canada, we have no statutes or court rules that indicate the number of days or months within which a criminal case must be completed. The federal government introduced Criminal Code amendments in 1984 that would have set a standard of six months from first appearance to trial or committal in the Provincial Court, and an additional six months from committal to trial in the section 96 court, with certain important exceptions as well. The proposal died when the Liberal government called the election in 1984, and no other proposal to set a time standard has been introduced by subsequent Conservative governments.

Earlier decisions under section 11(b) provided some clues about how Askov's counsel could approach the task of enunciating a standard in the absence of legislation. Particularly relevant was the extensive set of reasons presented by the then-Justice Lamer (speaking for himself but not for the Court) in *Regina* v. *Mills*, the first section 11(b) case decided by the Supreme Court of Canada. Lamer argued that allowable time should be based on comparative jurisdictional analysis, so that the "appropriate models" are those courts with "greater degrees of promptness" or "lesser amounts of systemic delay."

Quite apart from the *Askov* case, in 1988 political scientist Carl Baar had obtained funding from the Social Sciences and Humanities Research Council to conduct empirical research on the Canadian judicial system. One of his chief objectives was to obtain data on the pace of litigation in Canadian trial courts that would allow comparison with the pace of litigation in the United States. He adapted measuring instruments first used in an influential study of 21 American state trial courts (Thomas Church's *Justice Delayed*, 1978), and focused on Ontario criminal cases that had their final dispositions in section 96 trial courts. By the time data gathering was completed in 1989, a sample of close to 3,000 criminal cases, primarily from 1987, had been collected from five Ontario court centres, as well as three in New Brunswick and two in British Columbia. Among the five Ontario courts was Brampton, chosen because of its reputation as one of the province's slowest courts, and London, chosen because of its reputation as one of the most expeditious. New Brunswick was also chosen because it was usually considered very expeditious.

While the data were being gathered during 1988–89, a casual conversation between Baar and University of Toronto law professor Lorraine Weinrib prompted her to mention the then pending *Askov* appeal. As it turned out, one of her students was working on the case as a class project with Askov's lawyer, Michael Code. Baar met with the student and provided background literature and studies on court delay. When Code realized that Baar's data base included over 400 criminal cases from the Brampton District Court (all 1987 dispositions), as well as data from other urban centres comparable to Brampton (London and Ottawa in Ontario, as well as Vancouver and the Vancouver suburbs covered by the New Westminster court), he sought an affidavit from Baar presenting a summary of the data and relevant findings on court delay that could be presented to the Supreme Court of Canada.

By the spring and fall of 1989, analysis of the elapsed time in the various court centres confirmed the informed judgment of those familiar with criminal litigation in Ontario. Brampton was indeed the slowest of five Ontario courts, both in terms of the total time from first appearance in Provincial Court until disposition in the section 96 court, and in terms of the "upper court time" alone, counting only from the time the indictment was lodged in the section 96 court (following committal) until disposition in that court. London was the most expeditious of the other four Ontario courts, and the two British Columbia courts had a pace comparable to or faster than those Ontario courts. In turn, New Brunswick's Court of Queen's Bench was faster than any of the B.C. and Ontario courts.

What was more revealing was that when compared with courts in the United States, no Canadian court was particularly fast. The pace of criminal litigation in Toronto and Ottawa, for example, was well behind large American urban centres like Detroit, Oakland and New Orleans. By this comparison, in the much-quoted words of Justice Cory in *Askov*, Brampton was the slowest court "anywhere north of the Rio Grande."

Baar's affidavit summarizing these findings was submitted to the Supreme Court early in 1990. The findings were accepted by the crown, and incorporated in Code's oral argument in March. The affidavit focused on where the elapsed time in *Askov* fit into the overall pattern of criminal litigation in Canada, concluding that the *Askov* case took longer than over 90 percent of the criminal cases concluded in Brampton in 1987, while Brampton itself was slower than all other locations for which data were available. By any analysis of comparable jurisdictions, Code could conclude, delay in Askov's case was unusually long.

Going Beyond the Facts of *Askov*

How then could a decision in an apparently exceptional case lead to the dismissal of thousands of cases, not only those facing trial in section 96 courts, but also those pending in Provincial Courts? Stated most simply, this happened because the Supreme Court not only held that 23 months from committal to trial was too long, but also suggested that six to eight months from committal to trial (i.e., "upper court time") "might be deemed to be the outside limit of what is reasonable" for normal and uncomplicated cases. This stricter standard was then applied by Ontario judges and crown attorneys to Provincial Court cases as well, since the principles underlying the Court's recommendation of a six to eight month standard appeared to apply with equally persuasive force to the period from first appearance to trial or preliminary hearing in the Provincial Court.

The Supreme Court arrived at the six to eight month standard by doubling the amount of time it took an average case to proceed from committal to trial in the Montreal area, which the Court chose as a comparable jurisdiction that was performing well. Unfortunately, this reasoning had two fundamental flaws:

First, there was no evidence before the court on the pace of criminal cases in Montreal. Baar gathered no data from Quebec in his 1988–89 study, and the crown submitted no data from Quebec. In an appendix to his affidavit, Baar even indicated that Quebec data might not be comparable because the division of criminal jurisdiction between the Quebec Superior Court and the Cour du Québec (that province's equivalent to the Provincial and Territorial Courts elsewhere in Canada) was unique.

In fact, the Supreme Court of Canada had obtained the Montreal data on its own initiative after oral argument, without the knowledge of either party to the appeal. Also, it is not clear whether the Montreal times cited by the court were median times, as used by Baar, or mean times, or some other measure of expected time to trial.

Thus the "social facts" most important to the Supreme Court's reasoning were not subject to examination and assessment through the adversary process. While critics of the judicial process, including Horowitz, see the adversary process as preventing courts from considering social facts, the Supreme Court in *Askov* ran into difficulties when it made insufficient use of the adversary process, doing its own research that led to a constitutional standard based on information not reviewed or questioned by counsel.

Second, there was no empirical basis for the Supreme Court to conclude that multiplying the average time in a good jurisdiction (i.e., Montreal) by two would yield a constitutionally reasonable maximum in a normal and uncomplicated case. In fact, a more careful reading of the empirical data submitted to the Court should have engendered great caution. The median time in various Canadian courts (the time it takes 50 percent of the cases to be completed) is, by definition, faster than the time it takes for 75 percent or 90 percent of the cases to be completed. Exhibit E to Baar's affidavit, a collection of tables derived from his data, showed how much longer those cases take. The first table in Exhibit E indicated that while it took 133 days for the median case in the Toronto District Court to go from committal to disposition ("upper court time"), it took 251 days for 75 percent of the Toronto cases to proceed from committal to disposition. Since 251 days is over eight months, this means that over 25 percent of the cases disposed of in Toronto in 1987 could have potentially been in jeopardy under the *Askov* standard. Since Justice Cory indicated his belief that Toronto was operating within an acceptable time period, one can conclude either that the six to eight month standard was more flexible than lawyers and judges realized, or that the standard was established without an adequate understanding of available empirical evidence on the pace of criminal litigation.

The possibility that the Supreme Court of Canada did not fully understand a dense set of tables and explanatory notes should not be seen as a criticism of a lack of statistical knowledge on the part of any individual justice. We demand exceptional backgrounds and abilities of the nine men and women who serve on our highest court, and they have developed their skills through many years of law practice and experience on the bench. Where the difficulties arose in *Askov* was in the process by which the Court obtained and applied empirical data. Yet there are at least three alternatives the Court could have pursued, in keeping with existing procedures, that would have facilitated more effective consideration of social facts.

The Court could have held, as it did, that the 23-month delay in *Askov* violated the *Charter*, and that institutional delay must count against the crown. At that point, rather than state how much delay is too much, it could have waited for later cases with shorter delays and evolved a standard incrementally, in keeping with the case-by-case approach associated with traditional common law decision making.

Alternatively, if the Court wished to avoid an incremental approach that would have created uncertainty over a period of years, it could have scheduled the *Askov* case for reargument, informing counsel that it wished to hear further argument on the length and nature of a standard for reasonable time. Counsel could have focused their submissions on that issue, other provinces might have chosen to intervene and present additional data, and the Court could have sought clarification of its interpretation of previously submitted social facts. The most famous use of this two-step approach in American constitutional law was in the school desegregation cases, *Brown* v. *Board of Education*. The United States Supreme Court decided in 1954 that *de jure* school segregation was unconstitutional, but set for reargument the question of what remedy and standard it would prescribe for ending segregation. [*Ed. note*: In the 1976 AIB Reference, Chief Justice Laskin created special procedures for the introduction of extrinsic evidence. See Reading 10.4.]

A third possibility would have been for the Court to render the same judgment that it made in *Askov*, but then state that its six to eight month standard would be phased in. For example, the Court could have given the provinces a period of time to implement the standard, as it did in 1985 when it gave the province of Manitoba five years to translate its statutes into the French language even after holding that English-only statutes were invalid. At the very least, the Court could have applied the standard only to new cases, not those already in the courts, since provincial governments and crown attorneys had no inkling that a numerical standard was likely to emerge from *Askov*.

From *Askov* to *Morin*

Since the decision in *Askov* was applied retroactively, the six to eight month time standard led to tens of thousands of charges being dismissed. While the impact of the case was felt largely in Ontario, by August, 1991, even normally reticent members of the judiciary were describing *Askov* as a "public relations disaster."[1]

In an effort to clarify and if appropriate modify its holding in *Askov*, the Supreme Court of Canada scheduled oral argument in two pending section 11(b) cases arising out of pre-*Askov* dismissals in the Provincial Court in Ontario. The two cases, *Morin* and *Sharma*, involved impaired driving charges that awaited trial in Provincial Court for periods of 14 and 12 months. Both cases were uncomplicated, and impaired driving is the most frequent charge in Ontario's Provincial Court. Nonetheless, in March, 1992, the Supreme Court of Canada ruled in favour of the crown and held that no violation of section 11(b) had taken place.

Speaking for the Court, Mr. Justice Sopinka declared that the six to eight month standard should be enforced flexibly, and that an eight to ten month guideline was more appropriate for the high-volume Provincial Courts. Sopinka's reasons made less reference to empirical data than Cory's in *Askov*, although the affidavits submitted by defence and crown in *Askov* were both resubmitted in *Morin* along with supplementary information. However, on the two occasions in which Sopinka referred to social facts, his references were erroneous.

First, Sopinka correctly noted that elapsed times in Montreal were not necessarily comparable to those in Ontario or other provinces, a point that had been stressed by the crown in oral argument (and in the public criticism of *Askov*). But in so doing, he incorrectly attributed the Montreal data to Baar's affidavit, rather than to the subsequent data gathering efforts of the Supreme Court itself.

The second error was more serious, as it lies at the core of the Court's decision. Part of Sopinka's justification for the additional time allowed in the Provincial Courts was his conclusion that the elapsed times in Provincial

---

1 *The Lawyers Weekly*, September 6, 1991, p. 1.

Courts are longer than elapsed times in section 96 courts. He supported this statement by reference to data derived originally from a paragraph in Baar's *Askov* affidavit. Unfortunately, he misinterpreted Baar's data, confusing the total times that elapsed in both the Provincial Courts and section 96 courts combined (Baar's *Askov* data) with the elapsed times for Provincial Courts alone.

This error may have derived from the use of the same numbers by Justice Cory in his judgment in *Askov*. Cory's language suggests the possibility of a misinterpretation, but neither the "total time" nor the Provincial Court elapsed time were relevant to that case, so Cory's paragraph went unnoticed at the time. The crown in *Morin* was never asked during oral argument to discuss those figures. Thus the Supreme Court of Canada, while using the *Morin* case in an effort to clarify the constitutional rule and reasoning in *Askov*, compounded its difficulties in interpreting the relevant social facts. In theory, the use of social facts should have enhanced the Supreme Court's ability to implement an important *Charter* right. In practice, the gains were mitigated by the criticism that resulted from the Court's intervention.

The Lessons of *Askov* and *Morin*

In *Askov*, the Supreme Court of Canada showed justifiable impatience with the failure of governments to act to ensure that *Charter* guarantees of trial within a reasonable time were respected. Cory's judgment also showed an understanding of criminal court delay as a condition that not only jeopardizes rights under the *Charter*, but also harms the public and the victims of crime. In the process, the Court enunciated a standard where Parliament had not acted.

When courts set general policy, however, they need the background information necessary to assess the impact of their action. *Askov* was a rare case in that directly relevant empirical data were available to the Court. But questions inevitably arise about whether and how the available data apply. The Supreme Court must develop a process to identify and answer those questions and test the social facts before it, or risk the kinds of misunderstandings that found their way into the *Askov* and *Morin* decisions.

* * *

[*Ed. note*: A comparison on the two relevant paragraphs may reveal more clearly Justice Sopinka's error:]

Affidavit of Carl Baar in the case of *Askov* v. *The Queen*:[2]

---

2 Supreme Court of Canada, sworn 16 January, 1990, pp. 6–7.

The tables found in Exhibit "E" show that New Brunswick is more expeditious than either British Columbia or Ontario, measuring both total time from first appearance in Provincial Court to final disposition in s.96 Court, as well as measuring total time in s.96 Court after the lodging of the indictment in the court. *The median total time in New Brunswick was 152 days and the median upper court time was 72 days.* (emphasis added) Within Ontario, London was consistently the most expeditious of the five locations studied. It had a median total time of 239 days and median upper court time of 105 days. Toronto, Ottawa and St. Catharines were clustered close together with median total times between 315 and 349 days and median upper court times between 133 and 144 days. Median times in Vancouver, British Columbia, were somewhat faster than London, Ontario, while New Westminster, British Columbia, was comparable to Toronto, Ottawa and St. Catharines. By all measures used in the study, Brampton District Court was significantly slower than any other location studied: median total time was 607 days and median upper court time was 423 days....

Judgment of Justice Sopinka in *R. v. Morin* (March 26, 1992):

A longer period of institutional delay for Provincial Courts is justified on the basis that not only do these courts dispose of the vast majority of cases, but that on average it takes more time to dispose of cases by reason of the demands placed on these courts. *Statistics for 1987 submitted by the respondent show a median delay in New Brunswick of 152 days for Provincial Court and 72 days for upper courts.* (emphasis added) Delay in London, Ontario was shown to be 239 days in Provincial Court and 105 in upper courts; Toronto, St. Catharines and Ottawa showed delays of 315 to 349 days in Provincial Court and 133 to 144 days in upper courts; median delays in Brampton were 607 days for Provincial Court and 423 for upper courts. Figures for Vancouver were similar to London and for New Westminster comparable to Toronto, St. Catharines and Ottawa.

[*Ed. note*: Sopinka's error was in fact two-fold. First, he mistook figures involving the preliminary hearing, provincial court stage of indictable offences (such as *Askov*, which are eventually "disposed of" in section 96 "upper courts") for figures about summary conviction proceedings (cases such as *Morin*, which are "disposed of" entirely in provincial courts). Secondly, Sopinka did not even correctly identify the figures for the provincial court stage of indictable offences. He mistook figures for total elapsed time in indictable offence cases (the italicized figures in Baar's affidavit, above) for figures about total provincial court time for the same cases. Exhibit E of Baar's *Askov* affidavit showed that median times for lower courts (from first appearance to committal) were usually about the same, and in some instances much lower, than median upper court time. But no lower court time was anywhere near twice as long as upper court time, the ratio suggested by Sopinka's figures. Thus, even if the time spent at the provincial court stage of an indictable offence proceeding was relevant to the question of how long it takes to dispose of summary offences in provincial courts (which it is not), the figure is nowhere as high as Sopinka suggests and would not support the longer periods of institutional delay that he allows. The data in Professor Baar's affidavit simply did not address the issue before the Court in *Morin*: how long it takes provincial courts to schedule and decide cases involving summary conviction offences.]

8.3

The *Anti-Inflation* Case:

The Anatomy of a Constitutional Decision

Peter H. Russell

This article is reprinted as reading 10.4.

8.4

Key Terms

Concepts

historical / adjudicative facts
social / legislative facts
adversary process
rule of hearsay evidence
perjury
extrinsic evidence
"Brandeis brief"
judicial notice
expert witness
legislative history
institutional capacity
institutional legitimacy

Institutions, Events, and Documents

The *Anti-Inflation Reference* (1976)
R. v. *Askov* (1990)
R. v. *Morin* (1992)

Precedents, Statutes, and Legal Reasoning

9

One of the most distinctive characteristics of the judicial process is its formalized method of reasoning. Because their authority flows from the public perception that they are "merely" applying pre-existing rules to resolve new disputes, judges are not permitted the broad prerogative enjoyed by the legislative and the executive branches. Unlike the latter, courts are not supposed to create new policies to deal with new problems. In their oral or written judgments, judges must explain where and how they derived the "rule" used to settle a case. There are three principal sources for these "rules": a written constitution, legislative statutes (including administrative regulations), and prior judicial decisions, known as precedents. Constitutional interpretation is the subject of the following two chapters. This chapter is concerned with the role of precedent and statutory interpretation in judicial reasoning.

Until the middle of the nineteenth century, most internal or domestic law in English-speaking societies was common law. Common law originated in the judicial recognition and enforcement of traditional usages and customs of the Anglo-Saxon and later Norman peoples in the British Isles. As these judicial decisions were made, they in turn became part of the common law. The common law in contemporary Canadian society consists of all previous judicial decisions by Canadian and British courts, as they are recorded in the case reports of these nations. The common law system is distinguished from the Civil Law system by its basis in precedent rather than legislative enactment. The Civil Law system originated in ancient Roman law, developed on the European continent, and was imported into Quebec by the French. It is based on a single, comprehensive code, enacted by the legislature.

The law of precedent, or *stare decisis*, is a self-imposed judicial rule that "like cases be decided alike." As Gordon Post explains, the law of precedent is essentially a formalization of the common-sense use of past experience as a guide to present conduct (Reading 9.1). The value of judicial adherence to *stare decisis* is two-fold. First, continuity and certainty in the law is a prerequisite of civilized human activity. If there is no reasonable guarantee that what is valid law today will still be valid law tomorrow, personal, economic, and political intercourse would grind to a halt. In each of these spheres of human activity, present-day decisions and activities are predicated on expectations about the future. Ensuring a high degree of predictability and continuity between the present and the future is one of the primary purposes of a political regime. As the institutions charged with interpreting and adapting the laws over time, the courts are responsible for maintaining continuity and certainty. As Dicey said, "a law which was not certain would in reality be no law at all" (see Reading 9.2). Adherence to the rule of precedent – "deciding like cases alike" – is the mechanism that provides this certainty.

The rule of precedent also contributes to guaranteeing the "rule of law, not of men." One of the ideals of the Western tradition's conception of justice is that the laws be applied equally and impartially to all persons. This ideal precludes any *ad hoc* application of the laws and demands instead that laws be applied uniformly or that any deviation from the rule be justified on principle, that is, by another rule. The idiosyncracies or personal preferences of a judge are not permissible grounds for judicial decisions. This would reintroduce the "rule of men" rather than the "rule of law." By minimizing the discretion or freedom of individual judges, *stare decisis* preserves the "rule of law."

Stare decisis minimizes but does not eliminate the element of judicial discretion or creativity. While legal reasoning presents itself as a deductive process, the reality is a more subtle blend of both inductive and deductive reasoning. Legal reasoning is accurately described as "reasoning by example."[1] The judges are essentially asking, "Whether the present case resembles the plain case 'sufficiently' and in the 'relevant' aspects."[2] In determining what is "sufficient" and what is "relevant," the judge must ultimately make certain choices. Because of this element of choice, a judge is responsible for striking the balance between continuity and innovation. The central thrust of the theory of legal realism (discussed in chapter two) has been to emphasize this element of choice and judicial discretion and the ensuing responsibility of the judge for his choice.

Weiler's analysis of the Supreme Court's responsibility for the development of tort law is based on this legal realist perspective (see Reading 9.3). Weiler argues that judges can no longer claim that precedent "dictates" nonsensical or patently unfair legal conclusions. Judges must be critical in their use of precedent and go beyond the surface "rule" to discover the animating "principle." The proper function of the common-law judge, according to Weiler, is to derive specific rules from more general principles, as the situation demands. Since situations change, rules must change also. While the "cattle trespass" exemption to normal tort law responsibility may have been appropriate to the rural, agricultural society of eighteenth-century England,

---

1 Edward H. Levi, *An Introduction to Legal Reasoning* (Chicago: University of Chicago Press, 1949), p. 1.

2 H.L.A. Hart, *The Concept of Law* (Oxford: Oxford University Press, 1961), p. 124.

it had become a dangerous anachronism in twentieth-century Canada (see Reading 9.3). Similarly in *Boucher* v. *the King*, the Court was faced with a conflict between the definition of "seditious libel" developed in nineteenth-century, homogeneous, protestant Britain and the norms of freedom of religion and speech in twentieth-century, pluralistic Canada (see Reading 9.4). Appeal court judges have a duty, says Weiler, to adapt the common law to the changing needs and circumstances of contemporary society.

Strict adherence to *stare decisis* is yet another aspect of the "adjudication of disputes" function of courts that poses problems for judicial policy-making. Refusal to disavow or change past decisions plays no constructive role in a policy-making institution, as the examples of legislative and executive practice make clear. While certainty and continuity are legal virtues, adaptability and innovation are more important in the policy-making process. The case for abandoning a strict adherence to precedent is especially strong in constitutional law. Not only is policy-impact more probable, but constitutional law lacks the flexibility of common law and statutes. If the courts make a "mistake" in the latter areas, it can be corrected by remedial legislation. But if the Supreme Court makes a constitutional decision with undesirable policy consequences, the only direct way to correct the damage is through formal constitutional amendment, an extremely cumbersome and difficult process.[3] Predictably, the U.S. Supreme Court was the first court of appeal in a common-law nation to abandon *stare decisis* as an absolute requirement. The demotion of *stare decisis* from a binding rule to a guiding principle is another index of a court's evolution toward a greater policy-making role.

The recent advent of judicial realism in Canadian jurisprudence has brought with it a decline in the status of the rule of *stare decisis*. Long after the American Supreme Court had abandoned absolute adherence to precedent, the Canadian Supreme Court continued to perceive itself as bound to adhere not only to its own previous decisions but to those of the British House of Lords as well. (Ironically, the Judicial Committee of the Privy Council, which served as Canada's final court of appeal until 1949, did not consider itself bound by its previous decisions, since, technically, it was not a court of law but an advisory board to the Imperial Crown.) Ten years after the abolition of that role, the Supreme Court declared its independence from British precedents as well (see Reading 9.3). In 1966, the British House of Lords officially declared that, when appropriate, it would no longer follow its own prior decisions. However, the Supreme Court of Canada continued to profess strict adherence to its prior decisions until the 1970s. Under the leadership of Bora Laskin, the Canadian Supreme Court began to move in the same direction. In 1972, before his appointment as chief justice, Laskin had written that *stare decisis* was "no longer an article of faith in the Supreme Court of

---

3 This is not true of judicial decisions based on sections 2 and 7 through 15 of the *Charter of Rights*, which are subject to the section 33 "legislative override" provision.

Canada, but it still remains a cogent principle."[4] Speaking as the new Chief Justice at the Centennial Symposium of the Supreme Court in 1975, Laskin repeated that *stare decisis* was no longer "an inexorable rule," but rather,

> simply an important element of the judicial process, a necessary consideration which should give pause to any but the most sober conclusion that a previous decision or line of authority is wrong and ought to be changed.[5]

Practising what he preached, Laskin led the Supreme Court to overturn three precedents during the next three years, including an old Privy Council decision dealing with the federal division of powers.[6] This abandoning of strict adherence to *stare decisis* is yet another indicator of the Supreme Court's institutional evolution toward more of a policy-making court.

The second principal source of law is legislative statutes. Beginning in the nineteenth century, legislatures in Great Britain, Canada, and the United States began to codify large portions of the common law. In large part, this was a democratic reaction against the perceived elitism of the "judge-made" character of the common law. By reducing the confusing maze of common-law precedent to clearly worded, legislative statutes, it was thought that the law would be made easier for "the people" to understand, and that the democratic authority of "government by consent" would be enhanced.

The influential nineteenth-century British philosopher Jeremy Bentham was a leading critic of the common law ("customary law") and an advocate of codification. According to Bentham, common law was uncertain and unpredictable:

> The customary law, you say, punishes theft with hanging: be it so. But by what law is this done? Who made it? When was it made? Where is it to be found? What are the parts that it contains? By what words is it expressed? Theft, you say, is taking under certain circumstances: but taking by whom? Taking of what? Under what circumstances? Taking by a person of such a sort, taking a thing of such a sort, taking under such and such circumstances. But how know you this? Because so it has been adjudged. What then? Not if it be a taking by any other person, nor if of any other thing, nor if under any other circumstances. O yes, in many other cases....
>
> It appears then, that the customary law is a fiction from beginning to end.

Bentham also criticized the common law because it gave too much political power to lawyers and judges. Of lawyers, he said:

---

4 "The Institutional Character of the Judge," *Israel Law Review*, 7 (1972), p. 341.

5 Bora Laskin, "The Role and Functions of Final Appellate Courts: The Supreme Court of Canada," *Canadian Bar Review*, 53 (1975), p. 478. See Reading 3.1.

6 *R. v. Paquette*, [1977] 2 S.C.R. 189; *McNamara Const. Western Ltd.* v. *The Queen*, [1977] 2 S.C.R. 654; and *Reference re Agricultural Products Marketing Act*, [1978] 2 S.C.R. 1198.

"By this means two monopolies establish themselves, one within another: a monopoly by the profession itself against the rest of the people; and a monopoly of the illustrious in the profession itself against the obscure."

Bentham's view of judges was even less charitable:

"Caligula published his laws in small characters: but still he published them: he hung them up high, but still he hung them up. English judges neither hang up their laws, nor publish them."[7]

The codification reform movement became widely influential by the end of the century. In Canada in 1892, the Canadian Parliament abolished all criminal offences at common law and replaced them with a comprehensive statute, the *Criminal Code*. In so doing, Parliament hoped to reap the alleged advantages of codification mentioned above, including restricting judicial discretion in the criminal law. Since crimes were now clearly and authoritatively defined, judges would simply apply the law as Parliament had written it. It would no longer be necessary to refer to a vast and confusing system of precedent to apply the criminal law, or so it was hoped.

In fact, precedent and *stare decisis* quickly found their way back into the criminal law. Perhaps, as Parker has suggested, it was (and still is) impossible for judges and lawyers trained in the common-law tradition to properly construe a code of law.[8] More likely the common law "habit" simply compounds a more serious problem – the ultimate ambiguity of statutory terminology itself. Try as they might, legislators will never be able to draft statutes that anticipate and encompass all possible future situations. This is due in part to the inherent tension between the generality of words and the specificity of reality, and in part to human ignorance of the future. As new situations inevitably arise, the applicability of the original wording of statutes becomes increasingly questionable. The only practical way to bridge this gap is through judicial discretion; and the traditional (if not the only) way to discipline the exercise of judicial discretion is through adherence to *stare decisis* – to decide like cases alike. In the final analysis, judicial interpretation of statutes is similar to the "reasoning by example" method of the common law.

The preceding argument notwithstanding, judicial discretion in interpreting statutes, including the *Criminal Code*, is much more circumscribed than in interpreting the common law. As Weiler says, judges can develop new torts, but not new crimes, and there are sound reasons for preferring this arrangement. As issues of tort law are rarely the subject of partisan

---

7 Excerpts are from Chapter 15, "No Customary Law Complete," in *The Collected Works of Jeremy Bentham: Of Laws in General*. Edited by H.L.A. Hart (London: Athlone Press, 1970), pp. 184–95.

8 Graham Parker, *An Introduction to Criminal Law*, 2nd ed. (Toronto: Metheun, 1983), p. 43.

political controversy, an innovative court cannot be accused of usurping the legislative function. The controversies over capital punishment and abortion show that the same is not true of the criminal law. In the area of tort law, judicial expertise is very high, relative to other policy-making institutions. Finally, judicial initiatives in substantive criminal law would pose the threat of punishing innocent persons. No comparable problem of "due process" arises in tort law.

A secondary but important influence on judicial reasoning is legal scholarship – commentary on judicial decisions and legal problems that is published in law reviews and academic books. Legal commentaries summarize, clarify, and critique individual judicial decisions or a series of related precedents related to a particular issue of law. A lawyer arguing a point of law before a court may cite a law review article to support the interpretation he is trying to persuade the judges to adopt. Likewise, judges may cite legal commentary to bolster the authority of their interpretive choice on a given point of law.

Today most of this commentary is written by university law professors, and most law reviews are published by university-based law schools. Legal commentaries have a long history in the English common law. Some of the most respected jurists of the common law – William Blackstone (1723-1780), for example – are famous precisely because of their published commentaries.

Notwithstanding such longevity, the practice in the Supreme Court of Canada until quite recently was not to consider or cite commentaries by *living* authors. At the end of the 1960s, the Supreme Court Reports contained "barely a dozen references a year to academic texts, and virtually none to legal journals."[9] In the 1990s, by contrast, the Supreme Court cites hundreds of books and articles a year, most written by living authors. Although most references are to Canadian authors, U.S. writers now account for about one half as many citations as Canadians. This new judicial reliance on contemporary legal scholarship is most prominent in three categories of cases – *Charter*, family law, and tort.[10]

Legal commentary has taken on added significance in the case of the *Charter*. In 1982, the *Charter* represented something of a fresh start in Canadian law. There were few past precedents that were unambiguously applicable to *Charter* interpretation. As the deputy minister of justice told a conference in 1991, "Imagine the difficulty of advising the government what the *Charter* means when there have been no decisions."[11] This left a legal vacuum that was quickly filled by an avalanche of *Charter* scholarship.

Of the 136 law-related Canadian journals and reporters, 48 – or 35 per cent

---

9 Greene et al., *Final Appeal*, 150.

10 Greene et al., *Final Appeal*, 150.

11 Mary Dawson, Justice Department, Human Rights Division. "Oral remarks," (*Roundtable Conference on the Impact of the Charter on the Public Policy Process*, Centre for Public Law and Policy: York University, 15–16 Nov. 1991.) [unpublished]

– have been started since 1980. The avalanche of academic commentary that followed the adoption of the *Charter* was not simply spontaneous. It was in part a calculated component of the strategy of rights-advocacy groups to maximize the political utility of *Charter* litigation. The 1984 report that led to the creation of the Women's Legal Education and Action Fund (LEAF) declared that "a critical component of this [systematic litigation] strategy [is] to build a theory of equality which is accepted by academics, lawyers and the judiciary. Legal writing in respected law journals, presentations of papers at legal seminars, and participation in judges' training sessions are all means of disseminating and legitimating such theories of equality" (See Reading 7.1). Once LEAF was established, it adopted a self-styled campaign of "influencing the influencers" that included fostering supportive legal scholarship (See Reading 7.2).

Professor Martin Shapiro's observation about American legal scholarship is even truer in the post-1982 Canadian context: "[T]he study of law and courts [is] part of the process of making the [law]; that is, [part of] the public discourse that continuously constitutes and reconstitutes constitutional and other law."[12] Legal scholars follow and comment on what the courts are saying, and the judges take note of what the law professors write. The authors of legal commentary have become important partners in the development of Canadian law.

In Reading 9.6, Professor Troy Riddell presents a systematic study of English-language law review articles on the section 1 "reasonable limitations" clause of the *Charter*. Former Chief Justice Brian Dickson aptly described section one as "the most important section of the *Charter*," since its interpretation usually makes or breaks a *Charter* claim against a statute. Canadian rights-advocacy groups had a strong incentive to try to shape the scope of section 1, first at the framing stage in 1980-81, and subsequently through judicial interpretation. A narrow interpretation of what constitutes a "reasonable limitation" of a right invites strict judicial scrutiny of legislative policy decisions, enhancing the odds of winning a *Charter* claim. Conversely, a broad interpretation invites judicial deference, minimizing judicial intervention in the policy process and reducing the potential for successful interest-group litigation.

In his study of twenty pieces of English-language legal scholarship dealing with section 1, Riddell found that they overwhelmingly endorsed interpretive choices that would make it easier for rights claimants to win their cases. By favouring interpretive choices that maximized the scope of judicial scrutiny of public policy, these commentators encouraged the kind of judicial activism that rights-advocacy groups would need to succeed in their *Charter* test cases. In its 1987 landmark section 1 ruling of *R. v. Oakes*,[13] the Supreme Court adopted all of these recommendations.

12　Martin Shapiro, "Public Law and Judicial Politics," A.W. Finifter ed., *The State of the Discipline II* (Washington, D.C.: APSA, 1993): 365–81 at 373.

13　*R. v. Oakes* [1986] 1 S.C.R. 103.

Advocacy literature has played a similarly important role in gay rights litigation. Gay advocates view law as an important formative and pedagogical force. Just as the traditional family has been "constructed" by the law, so changing the law can deconstruct it. Didi Herman, Canada's most published gay rights lawyer/professor, has stated: "law reform is part of an ideological battle, and fighting over the meanings of marriage and family constitutes resistance to heterosexual hegemony."[14]

To use the *Charter* as part of such an ideological battle, gay and lesbian activists first had to overcome the framers' intentional omission of sexual orientation from the list of prohibited grounds of discrimination in section 15 of the *Charter*. They thus began publishing articles advocating that it be added by way of judicial interpretation. According to Herman, this publishing strategy aimed to supply "the appropriate argument for lesbian and gay litigants to make."[15]

In Reading 9.5, David Greener elaborates the role of law as an instrument for social reform. Law is not just "shaped by" society, it also shapes society. Law influences how individuals in a society "imagine the real." If social reformers can persuade judges to change the language of law, this may in turn influence how people perceive what is right and wrong. Greener's study focuses on twenty-two law review articles that discuss the definition of "the family" (all published since 1982). While the broader social science literature on the family revealed a lively debate about the merits of the family, including defences of the traditional family, the law journal articles were "uniformly critical of 'familial ideology'... [especially] the 'traditional family'," which was portrayed as "the ideological centrepiece of heterosexual supremacy." This strategy appears to have achieved most of its objectives. The Supreme Court has used its power of interpretation to add "sexual orientation" to section 15 of the *Charter* and has begun redefining "spouse" so as to include homosexual relationships.

The growth of advocacy research in the field legal scholarship is a predictable consequence of the *Charter*'s empowerment of judges. One of the iron rules of politics is that "where power rests, there influence will be brought to bear."[16] Patrick Monahan has correctly identified the incentives that encourage advocacy scholarship: "Because of the political potency of *Charter* arguments, there is a tremendous incentive to try to shape perceptions of the *Charter*'s meaning so as to advance one's political goals."[17]

14 From Didi Herman. "Are We Family?: Lesbian Rights and Women's Liberation," *Osgoode Hall Law Journal* 28, no. 4 (Winter, 1990): 803 as cited by Greener, p. 54.

15 Herman, "The Good, the Bad, and the Smugly," p. 203.

16 V.O. Key, *Politics, Parties and Pressure Groups* (New York: Thomas Y. Crowell, 1958), 154.

17 Monahan and Finkelstein, "The *Charter* and Public Policy," p. 46.

American political scientist Martin Shapiro has more bluntly described constitutional scholarship in his own country as a form of "lobbying the courts."[18] "The distinction between scholarship and advocacy," Shapiro writes,

> "has always been uncertain or nonexistent in most of the legal scholarship produced in law schools. Much of that scholarship consists of doctrinal analysis that purports to yield the correct or a good, better or best statement of the law. The central strategy is a massive and deliberate confusion of is and ought. The previous cases are examined to show that, properly interpreted, the body of existing law really adds up to the law as the author thinks it ought to be. In short, most such writing consists of expanded and embroidered legal briefs. The key question in understanding such work is, "'Who's the client?'"[19]

The studies by Riddell and Greener highlight the growing influence of legal commentators and advocacy scholarship on legal reasoning in contemporary Canadian law.

9.1

Stare Decisis:

The Use of Precedents

G. Gordon Post

Introduction to Law (Englewood Cliffs: Prentice Hall, 1963), 80–83. Reprinted with permission.

In the resolution of conflicts a court invokes and applies rules of law to proven facts. A question arises: Just where does a court find these rules?

There are two *chief* sources of law: *statutes* and *precedents*. The former, of course, come from the legislature which consists of the elected representatives of the people. The latter come from the courts; precedents are the products of earlier decisions. To the latter, we should add the decisions of an increasing number of administrative bodies and the precedents established thereby, but of this matter we shall speak later.

Most everybody knows what a statute is, but what is a precedent? In a general, non-legal way, precedent plays an important role in our lives. Often, we do things as our parents did them and cite their experience as precedent for what we do now; out of some continuing or repetitive situation there comes a rough rule of thumb. When a father is questioned as to

---

18 Shapiro "Public Law and Judicial Politics," p. 374.
19 Ibid.

why he spanked his son for some infraction of the household rules, he might reply that as a boy in like circumstances he had been spanked as had his father before him. He might go on to explain that such treatment was an application of the rule of experience, "Spare the rod and spoil the child."...

... In all of these instances, there is the application of a rule of experience to a given situation. These are homely examples. Clubs, business organizations, boards of trustees, student groups all have their rules, some written, some unwritten, which are often invoked as precedent for doing, or not doing, one thing or another. And a precedent here is defined by Webster as "something done or said that may serve as an example or rule to authorize or justify a subsequent act of the same or analogous kind."

Judicial Precedent

A judicial precedent is defined in the same dictionary as "a judicial decision, a form of proceeding, or course of action that serves as a rule for future determinations in similar or analogous cases."

The driver of a wagon loaded with buckskin goods stopped for the night at a certain inn. He was received as a guest and the innkeeper took charge of his property. During the night a fire broke out which resulted in the destruction of horses, wagon and goods. The owner of the property thus destroyed sued the innkeeper for damages.

Let us suppose that this was a case of first impression, that is, a situation which is before a [Canadian] court for the first time. After hearing the evidence from both sides, the judge does not simply say "I decide for the plaintiff," or "I decide for the defendant." He decides for one or the other and gives his reasons. He will speak as follows: "An innkeeper is responsible for the safe keeping of property committed to his custody by a guest. He is an insurer against loss, unless caused by the negligence or fraud of the guest, or by the act of God or the public enemy." The judge looks to the English common law and finds that the liability of innkeepers was expressed tersely in *Cross* v. *Andrews*: "The defendant, if he will keep an inn, ought, *at his peril*, to keep safely his guests' goods," and at greater length by Coke in *Calye's Case*: "If one brings a bag or chest, etc., of evidences into the inn as obligations, deeds, or other specialties, and by default of the innkeeper they are taken away, the innkeeper shall answer for them."

The judge will go on to explain the reason for the rule. He will say that the rule has its origins in public policy.

> Every facility should be furnished for secure and convenient intercourse between different portions of the kingdom. The safeguards, of which the law gave assurance to the wayfarer, were akin to those which invested each English home with the legal security of a castle. The traveller was peculiarly exposed to depredation and fraud....

Stare Decisis

Let us suppose that a year or so later, another driver with a wagon load of hides spends the night at an inn. Again, the horses, the wagon, and the hides, are turned over to the innkeeper; and again, a fire occurs during the night and the property of the guest is burned up. The owner of the property then sues the innkeeper for damages. The situation here is exactly the same as in the earlier case.

The judge in the second case, according to the theory, will apply the rule or principle (which is the precedent) and decide in favour of the plaintiff. The precedent or authority of the first case is precise and fits the facts of the second case very nicely. This application by courts of rules announced in earlier decisions is spoken of as *stare decisis,* which means "let the decision stand." This has been, and is, a fundamental characteristic of the common law, although … it is the practice upon occasion for a high court to overrule its own precedents.

Obviously, a legal system in which judges could decide cases any which way, manifesting prejudice, whimsy, ignorance and venality, each decision being a entity in itself unconnected with the theory, practices and precedents of the whole, would be a sorry system, or, one might say, no system at all, and a source of little comfort either to attorneys or litigants. Speaking of *stare decisis* many years ago, Judge Maxwell said: "In the application of the principles of the common law, where the precedents are unanimous in the support of a proposition, there is no safety but in a strict adherence to such precedents. If the court will not follow established rules, rights are sacrificed, and lawyers and litigants are left in doubt and uncertainty, while there is no certainty in regard to what, upon a given state of facts, the decision of the court will be."

One concludes, after a little thought, that *stare decisis* is "the instrument of *stability* in a legal system," that it "furnishes a legal system with *certainty* and *predictability*," and "clothes a legal system with reliability"; in addition, it "assures all persons of *equality and uniformity of treatment*" and judges with "an instrument of *convenience and expediency*." In short, "*Stare decisis* preserves the judicial experience of the past."

After a little more thought, however, one also sees that stare decisis is an instrument of conservatism, of immobility, of eyes-in-the-back-of-the-head, of stultification. The application of the same rule, decade after decade, long after changed conditions have robbed the rule of its validity, makes the rule a troublesome fiction.

But, American high courts do not hesitate to overrule their own precedents when social, economic, or political change demand a corresponding change in the law. Cardozo has said that,

> If we figure stability and progress as opposite poles, then at one pole we have the maxim of *stare decisis* and the method of decision by the tool of

a deductive logic; at the other we have the method which subordinates origins to ends. The one emphasizes considerations of uniformity and symmetry, and follows fundamental conceptions to ultimate conclusions. The other gives freer play to considerations of equity and justice, and the value to society of the interests affected. The one searches for the analogy that is nearest in point of similarity, and adheres to it inflexibly. The other, in its choice of the analogy that shall govern, finds community of spirit more significant than resemblance in externals.

"Much of the administration of justice," says Pound, "is a compromise between the tendency to treat each case as one of a generalized type of case, and the tendency to treat each case as unique." "Each method," concludes Cardozo, "has its value, and for each in the changes of litigation there will come the hour for use. A wise eclecticism employs them both."

9.2

The Duty of a Court
A.V.C. Dicey
Lectures on the Relation between Law and Public Opinion in England during the Nineteenth Century. 2nd ed. (London: MacMillan, 1914), 365, 367. Reprinted with permission.

The duty of the court … is not to remedy a particular grievance but to determine whether an alleged grievance is one for which the law supplies a remedy…. If Parliament changes the law, the action of Parliament is known to every man and Parliament tries in general to respect acquired rights. If the Courts were to apply to the decision of substantially the same case, one principle today and another principle tomorrow, men would lose rights which they already possessed; a law which was not certain would in reality be no law at all.

9.3

Architect of the Common Law
Paul Weiler
In the Last Resort: A Critical Study of the Supreme Court of Canada. (Toronto: Carswell-Methuen, 1974), 57–65. Reprinted with permission.

I shall begin my analysis of the role and performance of the Supreme Court of Canada by reviewing some of its decisions in the area of tort liability for personal injuries. Perhaps some students of the judicial process will ask why bother with these rather insignificant cases? Let's get on to the attention-getting constitutional or civil liberties decisions. However, there are several reasons why I think tort law is a good starting point. First, we can fully understand much of the contemporary character of the judicial process only if we see how it is directed at the adjudication of private law disputes between one individual and another. Moreover, most of this area of law is almost totally judge-made, the *common law*. Our Supreme Court is a useful vehicle for reflecting on the true range and complexity of the judicial function precisely because of the breadth of its jurisdiction. The Court regularly handles the garden variety tort case as well as the newsworthy public law dispute. We must not miss the opportunity to appraise the exercise of judicial creativity in a private law area where the Court is not distracted by the involvement of other institutions, whether legislative or administrative. Finally, as I shall try to demonstrate, these attitudes concerning the private law role of the Supreme Court of Canada are wrong. Tort cases do raise important issues of public policy, and it is critical that they be settled intelligently. Let us start with a typical motor vehicles action which reached the Court, and produced a not-so-typical response.

The Curious Doctrine of Cattle Trespass

One sunny summer afternoon, Floyd Atkinson was driving a jeep along a gravelled country road in a farming district in Ontario. Suddenly, upon reaching the brow of a hill, he was confronted with a herd of cows belonging to a farmer named Leo Fleming. Although he applied his brakes and steered past some of the cows, Atkinson's jeep eventually struck three of the animals, killing two, and causing serious injuries to his own knee. The driver sued the farmer for his personal injuries and the latter responded with a claim for his two dead cows. Apparently Fleming took the attitude that he could let his cows wander where they wanted and they customarily pastured on the highway, strolling back and forth across the road. The trial judge found this to be negligence on his part and, given a certain lack of due care on the driver's part also, apportioned the relative responsibility 60 percent to the farmer and 40 percent to Atkinson.

This would seem to be a relatively straightforward case and easy to resolve in terms of the ordinary doctrines of negligence law. Unfortunately, hidden away in the nooks and crannies of the common law was a legal rule which absolved the farmer of any duty to prevent his cattle from straying on the highway and endangering its users. This rule owed its origin to two factors: (1) when highways were first created at the end of the medieval period in England, land was dedicated by the adjoining landowners subject to their own right of passage for their animals; (2) for a very long time this created no risk of danger from domestic animals such as cattle because traffic was so slow moving that the animals could easily be avoided. With the advent of automobiles, this factual situation was radically changed. However, the

House of Lords, in its 1947 decision in *Searle* v. *Wallbank*, declined an invitation to revise the legal duties of the farmer to bring them into line with modern needs, and the Ontario Court of Appeal felt compelled to respect the authority of this common law precedent in its 1952 decision in *Noble* v. *Calder*. The true wishes of the Ontario judges were expressed in these concluding passages from their own opinion in *Fleming* v. *Atkinson*.

> I do not want to part with this case without expressing the hope that it may draw attention to the present unsatisfactory state of the law in this province as to civil liability for injuries sustained due to the presence on our public highways of straying domestic animals. *The Courts cannot change the law; the legislation can.* The common law as applied by the House of Lords in England to the highways there is not adequate here, and yet the Courts of this province must follow those decisions.... [emphasis added].

... When the case reached the Supreme Court of Canada, one judge, Mr. Justice Cartwright, agreed that the English common law, as reflected in *Searle*, defined the duties of the cattle owner until and unless they were changed by legislation. In his view it was not the function of the judges to alter a legal doctrine when it no longer reflected reasonable social policies. Fortunately for Canadian law, and for Floyd Atkinson, Mr. Justice Judson for the majority took a wider view of the judicial mission. He did not consider himself bound by an English doctrine which originated in features which are not part of Canadian society and which was reiterated in a heavily-criticized House of Lords decision. The decision of the Supreme Court in *Fleming* v. *Atkinson* is important because it clearly expressed our judicial independence of the House of Lords, especially when that body adheres to such an irrational legal anomaly. It is even more important as an example of the style of legal reasoning which a truly independent Supreme Court, at the top of our judicial hierarchy, must exhibit.

> A rule of law has, therefore been stated in *Searle* v. *Wallbank* and followed in *Noble* v. *Calder* which has little or no relation to the facts or needs of the situation and which ignores any theory of responsibility to the public for conduct which involves foreseeable consequences of harm. I can think of no logical basis for this immunity and it can only be based upon a rigid determination to adhere to the rules of the past in spite of changed conditions which call for the application of rules of responsibility which have been worked out to meet modern needs. It has always been assumed that one of the virtues of the common law system is its flexibility, that it is capable of changing with the times and adapting its principles to new conditions. There has been conspicuous failure to do this in this branch of the law and the failure has not passed unnoticed. It has been criticized in judicial decisions (including the one under appeal), in the texts and by the commentators.... My conclusion is that it is open to this Court to apply the ordinary

rules of negligence to the case of straying animals and that principles enunciated in *Searle* v. *Wallbank*, dependent as they are upon historical reasons, which have no relevancy here, and upon a refusal to recognize a duty now because there had been previously no need of one, offer no obstacle.

Judson's opinion is almost a textbook illustration of the conception of legal reasoning I proposed in the preceding chapter. Judges should not just blindly follow a legal rule because it has been recognized in the law for a long time. If the rule appears to require unjust results in the immediate situation, the judge must ask why. He should have a sense of unease when asked to use a rule that does not fit comfortably into the basic principles of tort responsibility which condition a lawyer's perception of the area. Perhaps there will be good reasons for this exceptional doctrine: on investigation of the cattle trespass rule, its only support turns out to be ancient history. In such a situation the legal obligation of a judge is clearly the forthright elimination of the legal anomaly which produces that kind of injustice.

The Need for Judicial Renovation

What are the lessons we can draw from *Fleming* v. *Atkinson* about when and how the Court should respond in the common law? The case is certainly an unprepossessing factual situation with which to lead off a detailed assessment of the work of the Supreme Court across the spectrum of Canadian law. The question of whether the farmer or the motorist should bear the losses caused by a cow does seem to be of a somewhat lesser order of importance than constitutional disputes, issues of civil liberties and due process, problems of administrative regulation of the economy, and other such issues which regularly appear before the Supreme Court. The legal situation in the *Fleming* case is typical of the private law disputes which still constitute the bulk of the Court's work and which many now advocate deleting from its jurisdiction. [*Ed. note*: This is no longer true, as right of appeal in civil cases was abolished in 1975.] I will leave my assessment of these proposals for later when we have a more detailed view of the kinds of problems involved in these cases. For the moment we must recognize that there was an issue of general law to be resolved in the case and that the Supreme Court of Canada still has final judicial authority in this area. As is typical of a great many private law doctrines, tort liability for escaping cattle will not affect very many people but when it does arise, the question of whether damages can be collected will be of vital importance to the person involved. There are many legal doctrines with precisely this impact and the cumulative quality of their policies tells a lot about the justice afforded to the individual in our society. Up to now, the judiciary has been primarily responsible for their development in Canada. It behooves us then to enquire into the Court's performance in this area and to suggest the standards by which it should govern itself.

As Mr. Justice Judson stated in *Fleming* v. *Atkinson*, there is a general *principle* of law firmly established in this area. A person is required to take reasonable care in his behaviour when it creates the risk of physical injuries to another. If he does not take care and his faulty behaviour causes losses to another, the law requires that he assume responsibility for payment of damages to make whole the innocent victim. This legal principle had been clearly and authoritatively established in the general law of torts in the case of *Donoghue* v. *Stevenson*, but had become embedded in the motor vehicle area some time earlier. Appraised in the light of this theory of liability, the special immunity for "cattle trespass" was an historical anomaly. As Judson J. showed in his opinion, there may have been some rationale for its original adoption in England several hundred years ago but there certainly was no valid argument which could be made for its retention in contemporary Canada.

Mr. Justice Cartwright's dissent did raise some doubt whether the Court should leave it to the legislature to administer the *coup de grace* to the doctrine. To adopt the framework of analysis I sketched earlier, assuming there are good policy reasons for tort liability in this situation, are there countervailing legal values which should make a court wary of itself abolishing the immunity? In my view, the *Fleming* case is significant because when we assess in a realistic way the arguments against judicial innovation, they seem largely inapplicable here. In this respect *Fleming* is typical of tort law and, indeed, of much of the private law area.

What about the argument of predictability in the law and the possibility that judicial elimination of the immunity will defeat the expectations of those who relied on it being the law? Did the farmer rely on his immunity from tort liability when he failed to take reasonable care to control his cattle? If he did, is this the kind of expectation the legal system should be concerned to satisfy? Simply to ask these questions is to answer them. In tort law, at least as regards accidental injuries, the reliance on interest of possible defendants enters primarily at the point of insurance planning against liability for the risk. Studies have indicated that special rules of tort immunity such as this one, especially when they are hedged in by equally anomalous exceptions, are irrelevant to insurance decisions. Indeed, if there are any reasonable expectations which will be frustrated in a situation similar to that of the *Fleming* case they will be those of the injured motorist when he consults his lawyer and finds that the farmer is protected by a special rule dating back to medieval England. If the farmer's lawyer (or that of his insurer) has any understanding of this whole area of tort law and the rationale for its evolution, he can estimate the shakiness of the farmer's immunity and anticipate its probable removal. For these reasons, the Supreme Court in *Fleming* v. *Atkinson* could quite confidently ignore the argument about the damage to the predictability of the law.

What about the competence of the Court to make an intelligent change in the law? The possible defects in judicial law reform seem irrelevant to this actual problem. There is no need for lengthy investigations, social science research, expert testimony, and so on, to decide about change. The issue is basically one of esoteric "lawyer's law" which can be resolved by careful analysis of the implications of the basic legal principles underlying the area. If the legislature were moved to reform in this area, it would have to rely on the same sort of appraisal and it would find it in the textbooks and law review articles which are equally available to the courts.

In fact, the "cattle trespass" rule is one in which the resources of the judicial forum are especially valuable. The issue is narrow in compass, occurs infrequently, and is only one of a very large number of such relatively independent tort problems. Yet there are a lot of judges in a lot of courts hearing such cases all the time. Each judge sees the human implications of the issue vividly portrayed in the concrete dispute before him. On the basis of the research and arguments prepared for him by opposing counsel, he can work out the solution which seems most rational in the light of the basic policies in the area. This proposed rule, when reported, can become a piecemeal addition to the evolving common law of torts. The legislature seems much too bulky and unwieldy an instrument to solve the problem of cattle trespass. It operates at the wholesale level while so much of our private law requires retail treatment.

But at least the legislature is elected, one may suggest. Should not changes in the law be made by a representative body, rather than the appointed and tenured court? We must turn to the reasons for our qualms about judicial innovation and take a realistic view of their relevance to particular cases. The problem in *Fleming* v. *Atkinson* is not one which will figure in an election campaign. It is inconsistent with democratic values (though not always illegitimate for this reason) for a court to intervene and impose its own policies in an area where the popular will has been expressed in the political arena. If the legislature were moved to reform in this esoteric problem area, it would merely be ratifying a proposal worked out by an equally unrepresentative Law Reform Commission at as invisible a level as would be a judicial innovation.

Once more we find that not only is there no real argument against a judicial initiative, but there are positive reasons in favour of such an active role. Private law doctrines such as this often lead to a distortion of the legislative process. Pressure for reform is very diffuse and unorganized. There is no lobby of accident victims petitioning the government. Instead, there is usually only an academic who has shown how some legal relic is working a real injustice on the very few people who run afoul of it. However, there is often a narrow interest group which might be somewhat harmed by the change. The farmer's insurance premiums will go up a bit and he may have to answer for his negligence in a lawsuit. A politician might be a little worried about the farmers' votes if their organizations object, especially if there is no countervailing lobby pressing for the reform. It is extremely unlikely he would be moved to *create* the cattle trespass immunity, but he might be loath to come out in the open and remove it entirely. The safest course in his eyes is to "let sleeping dogs lie," allow the proposal to die on the legislative order paper, and rationalize this inaction on the grounds (often valid) that he is busy on too many other problems.

By contrast, the Supreme Court was duty-bound to reach a positive conclusion about this legal problem in order to resolve the concrete dispute between Fleming and Atkinson. It had to hear the arguments from both sides, decide which position was most persuasive, and justify its conclusion in a written opinion which is reported for others to see and criticize. If judges within such an institution are willing to exercise their power to develop our law in a rational way, then we can provide the individual litigant who has been hurt with a forum to which he can come as a one-man lobby looking for legal justice. There is something to be said in a democracy of an institution which will resolve such disputes on the basis of the quality of the arguments presented, rather than the number of votes represented.

On just about every dimension then, these legal or institutional values seem to favour *judicial* initiative in this area, and they certainly do not warn against it. In order to complete this picture, let me give an example of a tort law reform I do not think a court is entitled to make, even though the judges may be convinced of its substantive desirability. The basic principle underlying our current law of torts, the one appealed to in *Fleming* v. *Atkinson*, is that negligent fault is the basis of liability. More and more voices contend that this is too narrow a criterion. Especially in the motor vehicle accident area, we hear proposals for a market deterrence, etc. I think we are going to see some such doctrine adopted in Canada shortly but this reform should be the work of the legislature, not the court. Why is this so?

In the first place, this will introduce a very substantial change in the incidence of legal liability and it may require substantial increases in the premium level. To the extent that insurance companies have charged lower premiums in reliance on the fault doctrine, they can claim that this justifiable expectation should not be frustrated by retrospective judicial alteration of the law. I am not sure myself how compelling this argument is. It depends on the degree of increased recovery in the new system and the ability of the insurance industry to finance the extra payments for past losses out of future premiums.

The real point is that the court could not likely estimate this either, which brings us to a second and major objection against judicial adoption of strict liability. The court simply is not competent to set up a complete new scheme for compensating automobile accident victims. This is not a simple matter of eliminating an irrational anomaly like the cattle trespass doctrine and applying the established principle of fault. The objectives of a strict liability scheme require a complex series of adjustments in the kinds and level of damages recoverable, the relationship of tort liability to various other forms of liability compensation, the nature of the insurance which is to be used, and even the forum in which claims are to be made. To perform this job, we want royal commissions, legislative committees and research by a battery of experts. We cannot rely on the efforts of a few Supreme Court judges sitting in their chambers in Ottawa.

Finally, the Court does not have the authority to adopt such a scheme into law. Let us suppose that a Royal Commission had been appointed, had laboured for several years examining the issues and the various alternatives, and then worked out a detailed scheme. The expert work has been done but the legislature, for various reasons, has not gotten around to acting on it. Should the Court decide to implement this new scheme in substitution for the common law of fault-based tort liability on the assumption that it is indeed a better system? In my view, the answer is still no! As anyone who reads Canadian newspapers will realize, the desirability of compensation without fault is a matter of sharp political controversy in several Canadian provinces. It has figured prominently in several election campaigns and governments have teetered on the edge of defeat in trying to get schemes enacted. The various plans present important and ambiguous value judgments about such matters as social welfare, compulsory government insurance, administrative agencies, and the responsibility of the dangerous driver. The place where these controversial issues should be aired and inevitable compromises worked out is the public legislative arena where the participants can be held responsible for their judgments. The last place in which we would want the decision made is the sheltered, closed world of the judges who are in the process of resolving a private lawsuit....

9.4

Boucher v. The King
Supreme Court of Canada (1951)

Rand J.: For the reasons given by me following the first argument, I would allow the appeal, set aside the verdict and conviction and enter judgment of not guilty.

[*Ed. note*: The reasons given by Mr. Justice Rand, following the first argument, read as follows.]

This appeal arises out of features of what, in substance, is religious controversy, and it is necessary that the facts be clearly appreciated. The appellant, a farmer, living near the town of St. Joseph de Beauce, Quebec, was convicted of uttering a seditious libel. The libel was contained in a four page document published apparently at Toronto by the Watch Tower Bible & Tract Society, which I take to be the name of the official publishers of the religious group known as The Witnesses of Jehovah. The document was headed "Quebec's Burning Hate for God and Christ and Freedom Is the Shame of all Canada": it consisted first of an invocation to calmness and reason in appraising the matters to be dealt with in support of the heading; then of general references to vindictive persecution accorded in Quebec to the Witnesses as brethren in Christ; a detailed narrative of specific incidents of persecution; and a concluding appeal to the people of the province, in protest against mob rule and Gestapo tactics, that through the study of God's Word and obedience to its commands, there might be brought about a "bounteous crop of the good fruits of love for Him and Christ and human freedom." At the foot of the document is an advertisement of two books entitled "Let God be True" and "Be Glad, Ye Nations," the former revealing, in the light of God's Word, the truth concerning the Trinity, Sabbath, prayer, etc., and the latter, the facts of the endurance of Witnesses in the crucible of "fiery persecution."

The incidents, as described, are of peaceable Canadians who seem not to be lacking in meekness, but who, for distributing apparently without permits, bibles and tracts on Christian doctrine; for conducting religious services in private homes or on private lands in Christian fellowship; for holding public lecture meetings to teach religious truth as they believe it of the Christian religion; who, for this exercise of what has been taken for granted to be the unchallengeable rights of Canadians, have been assaulted and beaten and their bibles and publications torn up and destroyed, by individuals and by mobs; who have had their homes invaded and their property taken; and in hundreds have been charged with public offences and held to exorbitant bail. The police are declared to have exhibited an attitude of animosity toward them and to have treated them as criminals in provoking, by their action of Christian profession and teaching, the violence to which they have been subjected; and public officials and members of the Roman Catholic clergy are said not only to have witnessed these outrages but to have been privy to some of the prosecutions. The document charged that the Roman Catholic Church in Quebec was in some objectionable relation to the administration of justice and that the force behind the prosecutions was that of the priests of that Church.

The conduct of the accused appears to have been unexceptionable; so far as disclosed, he is an exemplary citizen who is at least sympathetic to doctrines of the Christian religion which are, evidently, different from either the Protestant or the Roman Catholic versions: but the foundation in all is the same, Christ and his relation to God and humanity.

The crime of seditious libel is well known to the Common Law. Its history has been thoroughly examined and traced by Stephen, Holdsworth and other eminent legal scholars and they are in agreement both in what it originally consisted and in the social assumptions underlying it. Up to the end of the 18th century it was, in essence, a contempt in words of political authority or the action of authority. If we conceive of the governors of society as superior beings, exercising a divine mandate, by whom laws, institutions and administrations are given to men to be obeyed, who are, in short, beyond criticism, reflection or censor upon them or what they do implies either an equality with them or an accountability by them, both equally offensive. In that lay sedition by words and the libel was its written form.

But constitutional conceptions of a different order making rapid progress in the 19th century have necessitated a modification of the legal view of

public criticism; and the administrators of what we call democratic government have come to be looked upon as servants, bound to carry out their
duties accountably to the public. The basic nature of the Common Law lies
in its flexible process of traditional reasoning upon significant social and
political matter; and just as in the 17th century the crime of seditious libel
was a deduction from fundamental conceptions of government, the substitution of new conceptions, under the same principle of reasoning, called for
new jural conclusions....

... The definition of seditious intention as formulated by Stephen, summarized, is, (1) to bring into hatred or contempt, or to excite disaffection against,
the King or the Government and Constitution of the United Kingdom,
or either House of Parliament, or the administration of justice; or (2) to
excite the King's subjects to attempt, otherwise than by lawful means, the
alteration of any matter in Church or State by law established; or (3) to incite
persons to commit any crime in general disturbance of the peace; or (4) to
raise discontent or disaffection amongst His Majesty's subjects; or (5) to promote feelings of ill-will and hostility between different classes of such subjects. The only items of this definition that could be drawn into question here
are that relating to the administration of justice in (1) and those of (4) and
(5). It was the latter which were brought most prominently to the notice of
the jury, and it is with an examination of what in these days their language
must be taken to mean that I will chiefly concern myself.

There is no modern authority which holds that the mere effect of tending
to create discontent or disaffection among His Majesty's subjects or ill-will
or hostility between groups of them but not tending to issue in illegal conduct, constitutes the crime, and this for obvious reasons. Freedom in thought
and speech and disagreement in ideas and beliefs, on every conceivable subject, are of the essence of our life. The clash of critical discussion on political, social and religious subjects has too deeply become the stuff of daily
experience to suggest that mere ill-will as a product of controversy can strike
down the latter with illegality. A superficial examination of the word shows
its insufficiency: what is the degree necessary to criminality? Can it ever, as
mere subjective condition, be so? Controversial fury is aroused constantly
by differences in abstract conceptions; heresy in some fields is again a mortal
sin; there can be fanatical puritanism in ideas as well as in mortals; but our
compact of free society accepts and absorbs these differences and they are
exercised at large within the framework of freedom and order on broader
and deeper uniformities as bases of social stability. Similarly in discontent,
affection and hostility: as subjective incidents of controversy, they and the
ideas which arouse them are part of our living which ultimately serve us in
stimulation, in the clarification of thought and, as we believe, in the search
for the constitution and truth of things generally.

Although Stephen's definition was adopted substantially as it is by the
Criminal Code Commission of England in 1880, the latter's report, in this
respect, was not acted on by the Imperial Parliament, and the *Criminal Code*

of this country, enacted in 1891, did not incorporate its provisions. The latter omits any reference to definition except in section 133 to declare that the intention includes the advocacy of the use of force as a means of bringing about a change of government and by section 133A, that certain actions are not included. What the words in (4) and (5) must in the present day be taken to signify is the use of language which, by inflaming the minds of people into hatred, ill-will, discontent, disaffection, is intended, or is so likely to do so as to be deemed to be intended, to disorder community life, but directly or indirectly in relation to government in the broadest sense: Phillimore, J. in *R. v. Antonelli* "seditious libels are such as tend to disturb the government of this country...." That may be through tumult or violence, in resistance to public authority, in defiance of law. The conception lies behind the association which the word is given in section 1 of chapter 10, C.S. Lower Canada (1860) dealing with illegal oaths:

"To engage in any seditious, rebellious or treasonable purpose;" and the corresponding section 130 of the *Criminal Code*: "To engage in any mutinous or seditious purpose."

The baiting or denouncing of one group by another or others without an aim directly or indirectly at government, is in the nature of public mischief: *R. v. Leese & Whitehead*; and incitement to unlawful acts is itself an offence.

This result must be distinguished from an undesired reaction provoked by the exercise of common rights, such as the violent opposition to the early services of the Salvation Army. In that situation it was the hoodlums who were held to be the lawless and not the members of the Army: *Beatty v. Gillbanks*. On the allegations in the document here, had the Salvationists been arrested for bringing about by unlawful assembly a breach of the peace and fined, had they then made an impassioned protest against such treatment of law abiding citizens, and had they thereupon been charged with seditious words, their plight would have been that of the accused in this case.

These considerations are confirmed by section 133A of the *Code*, which is as follows:

WHAT IS NOT SEDITION – No one shall be deemed to have a seditious intention only because he intends in good faith, –

(a) to show that His Majesty has been misled or mistaken in his measures; or

(b) to point out errors or defects in the government or constitution of the United Kingdom, or of any part of it, or of Canada or any province thereof, or in either House of Parliament of the United Kingdom or of Canada, or in any legislature, or in the administration of justice; or to excite His Majesty's subjects to attempt to procure, by lawful means, the alteration of any matters in the state; or,

(c) to point out, in order to their removal, matters which are producing or have a tendency to produce feelings of hatred and ill-will between different classes of His Majesty's subjects.

This, as is seen, is a fundamental provision which, with its background of free criticism as a constituent of modern democratic government, protects the widest range of public discussion and controversy, so long as it is done in good faith and for the purposes mentioned. Its effect is to eviscerate the older concept of its anachronistic elements. But a motive or ultimate purpose, whether good or believed to be good, is unavailing if the means employed is bad; disturbance or corrosion may be ends in themselves, but whether means or ends, their character stamps them and intention behind them as illegal.

The condemned intention lies then in a residue of criticism of government, the negative touchstone of which is the test of good faith by legitimate means toward legitimate ends. That claim was the real defence in the proceedings here but it was virtually ignored by the trial judge. On that failure, as well as others, the Chief Justice of the King's Bench and Galipeault, J. have rested their dissent, and with them I am in agreement.

9.5

The Transformative Power of the Legal Narrative
David Greener
Excerpted from David Greener's M.A. thesis, "Deconstructing Family: A Case Study of Legal Advocacy Scholarship" (University of Calgary, 1997)

If one wants to transform society, why not man the political barricades rather than write in law journals? Why go to the courts to transform society? Obviously, legal activists perceive the law to be a significant transformational force, one that can reconstruct basic social structures, and perhaps one that offers less resistance than traditional political activism. Now, law can obviously transform social relations in the immediate instrumental sense of prohibiting or requiring certain behaviours. But legal advocacy scholarship rests on a much broader view of legal agency, namely that law has an educative or pedagogic function, that it shapes society by forming consciousness and thus identity.

In this view, law presents narrative visions of reality to society. The purpose of these legal narratives is to help make sense of or give meaning to our experience of the social world and thereby affect how we act in the world. In Mary Ann Glendon's formulation, the law "tells us stories about the culture that helped shape it and which it in turn helps to shape." Similarly, James Boyd White writes that we should regard "the law as a sort of social literature, as a way of talking about people and their relationships." Like Glendon, White thinks that in talking about social life, the 'literature' of the law does not merely describe it but 'in turn helps to shape' it. In defining, organizing and interpreting the experiences of those engaged in social life, the law constructs imaginative visions of reality (stories) which may or may not cohere with current societal sensibilities but are certain to have an impact upon them. The way law describes our lives, White insists, influences "the constitution of the social world." Similarly, Glendon contends that law is not merely "interpretive" but, more importantly, "constitutive." Its 'constitutive' impact, she writes, is evident when the law "affects[s] ordinary language" thereby influenc[ing] the manner in which we perceive reality" and thus act toward it. In Clifford Geertz's terms, law is one of the most powerful ways in which we 'imagine the real'; and reality is partly constituted by how we imagine it. Advocacy scholarship represents an attempt to influence how the law imagines reality and thus the stories that the law will tell us. It thus has the eventual goal of influencing societal perceptions of reality.

As an example of the constitutive impact of law, consider the issues of domestic violence or drinking and driving. The law's hardening stance on these crimes can be seen as influencing societal attitudes. While social activists concerned with these issues campaign to have the law address these areas more effectively, the law has done more than simply respond to the public will. It has listened to the arguments for a new approach to these problems and has produced legal narratives that go beyond enforcement to have an educative and even constitutive impact. So it is that activists speak of a heightened awareness of domestic violence or drinking and driving. The law has been part of a strategy to attach greater stigma to these offenses. Using authoritative legal stories in this way represents an attempt to act in the world in a way that affects our understanding of it. Thus the motive to produce narratives that are sanctioned by the law can be understood as arising from a desire to use law to influence our perceptions of social reality, to create and shape meanings, indeed to 'constitute' social identity. This *use* of law is especially of consequence if both law and society are 'communities' dependent on language and thus open to narrative (re)visions of the real.

For both Glendon and White, legal stories 'constitute' reality mainly by establishing the categories or labels into which we fit social experience, and through which we make sense of that experience. To categorize something is to 'name' it, and for Glendon "the way we name things is very important for the way we analyze them, feel about them and act towards them." For example, to call someone 'mother' is important to how that person will be perceived. Societal expectations lead to the categorization of a mother as a nurturing person, as one who is intimately involved in child rearing. 'Mother,' moreover, is a label that goes with 'father,' another category of significance. When the law told the story of 'mother and father,' it invoked and confirmed a host of expectations about appropriate sex roles in family life. As the law replaces the gender-specific categories of 'mother' and 'father' with the single gender-neutral category of 'parent,' it subtly tells a different story, one that is less rooted in sex-role differentiation. At the extreme, for example, the category of 'parent' can be made available to homosexual couples in a way that the labels 'mother' and 'father' cannot. Similarly, to evoke the story of 'husband' is to set up a category of significance and perception that helps us to distinguish between husbands and non-husbands. As in the case of mother/father, 'husband' exists because of the binary of husband/wife. A legal narrative using these categories tends to reproduce such traditional roles as husband/father, so that, for example, non-husbands are not readily associated as fathers; that is, fatherhood, in its 'proper' expression, is linked exclusively to the category of husband.

Categories of perception (names or labels) influence reality in part by setting up hierarchies of relationships. For example, legally recognizing the category of 'husband' elevates this identity above non-husband. The category of husband/father becomes the norm (the expected role for adult males) and non-husband a somewhat marginalized social identity. Likewise, the story of family brings with it the binary of family/non-family, and this binary leads to a hierarchy of family over non-family. The boundaries created by the story of family tend to set up certain role-expectations and 'marginalize' as non-family those who are unable or unwilling to fulfill these role-requirements. Family becomes the norm. The identities, norms and experiences fostered by the story of family are in a sense 'given' to us by the narrative. That is, by telling this story of family, law takes part in the formation of consciousness and identity.

To the extent that legal labels or categories constitute reality, one can change reality (at least gradually) by changing the labels or 'names.' Thus one way to undermine and transform the social expectations and identities entailed by the story of husband/father-wife/mother is to replace that story in law with the story of spouse/parent. To be sure, a shift in legal categories is likely to be resisted by those who were formed by, and remain attached to, the old categories. But even if one resists, one will nevertheless be engaged in a social world that has accepted or at least acknowledged the reconstituted narrative. The official entrenchment of new conceptions of reality cannot be ignored; only their impact can be resisted. For example, if the Court were to authoritatively rename the family to include homosexual unions, the shift in meaning could not be ignored nor could the existence of homosexual marriages be overlooked. Immediately, the process of educating the public to accept the Court's story of family would begin. At this point, the new distribution of meaning could be resisted and argued against, but the consequences of the story's symbolic and material impact would engage all in society; none could ignore it. White doubts that such resistance is forever possible if one finds oneself in a hostile culture speaking an alternative language and appealing to alternative stories. He writes, "One cannot maintain forever one's language and judgment and feelings against the pressures of a world that works in different ways, for one is in some measure the product of that world."

Indeed, some argue that the transformative impact of new legal categories is likely to be much greater today than at any time in the past. In the past, the law had powerful competitors as a source of 'official' stories (e.g., religion, history, literature). What is special about modern legal discourse is that it seems to authoritatively name concepts in a way that now private centres of power (e.g., the Church) no longer can. In Glendon's words, "it has become quite difficult to convincingly articulate common values by reference to shared history, religion, or cultural tradition." This, she maintains, is "both cause and consequence of our increasing tendency to look to law as an expression and carrier of" social values. As other sources of norms decline, in other words, "law has a tendency to move into [the] vacuum." It "has assumed an increasingly prominent position in relation to other social norms." Moreover, because many increasingly take their "*moral* bearings to some extent from the law" any change in the law will carry "a moral charge," and will affect the understandings and actions of citizens.

Glendon is a moderate social conservative on such issues as the family, and she thus worries about the increased constitutive power of law. Because law is constitutive, she writes, "we need to be especially careful" in how we employ and deploy it, lest we damage important institutions of civil society such as the family. Given law's power, in other words, "it is incumbent on us to be attentive, intelligent, reasonable, and responsible in the 'stories we tell', the 'symbols we deploy', and the 'visions we project'."

The same understanding of law that is a source of concern and caution for Glendon is a cause for celebration for social activists who wish to transform reality by altering the way in which the law induces us to 'imagine the real.' It is a radical version of this view of law that makes legal advocacy scholarship an attractive form of political action. Certainly, it is the view of law that underpins the advocacy scholarship on the family that is the subject of this thesis. For example, Jody Freeman, a contributor to that scholarship, writes, "The symbolic power of law is potentially too enormous, and its influence on culture too profound, to abandon it as a site of dialogue, confrontation, and resistance." And while she does not believe "that a single legal decision, even from the Supreme Court, would change social attitudes and lead to the acceptance of non-conforming families," Freeman does write that "who is family and who is not is a product of legal among other, discourses; it is not a product of nature." Because the family, in Freeman's account, is socially constructed (by 'discourses') and not based on biological considerations (e.g., begetting children), it follows that it can be radically deconstructed and reshaped by new legal discourses....

Advocacy scholarship, in its attempt to affect the story of family, represents an attempt to constitute an alternative vision of family. The presumption is that law can transform basic social structures (e.g., family) through storytelling. This position seems dependent on the idea that *current* ways of describing family in law are best thought of as 'stories.' The argument is then made that present stories are inadequate given the needs of modern families. Advocacy scholars propose to develop and then present alternative stories of family to society via the law. These stories are meant to foster particular social meanings and identities, and accordingly influence the way one describes and experiences family. Central to this reorganization of the story of family is the removal of the distinction between heterosexual (family) relations and homosexual (non-family) relations.

The law (i.e., the Court) considers the merits of differing accounts of what the proper definition of family should be. It thus encourages the production of narrative descriptions of family (i.e., advocacy scholarship on the family). Law is, or should be, open to such arguments and agreeable to change if a particular narrative is persuasive. White argues that this process "makes our choice of language conscious rather than habitual and creates a moment at which controlled change of language and culture becomes possible." Because of its openness to arguments regarding what narrative of family the law should embrace, "[l]egal argument is an organized and systematic process of conversation by which our words get and change their meaning." It is a way that the present meaning of family can be solidified or altered. During this process of claiming meaning the legal storyteller creates a narrative about the family. This narrative, in turn, aims to influence the "creation of social identity and meaning" by using the transformative power of a law that tells stories.

This is what Clifford Geertz means when he writes that law "is part of a distinctive manner of imagining the real." In the process of explaining the social world, we in society, and those in the legal community in particular, must choose how to contextualize incident. For example, how do we choose to describe single-motherhood, the marriage bond, or what we expect the roles of family members to be? Signifying or giving meaning to that which we observe in society requires an account of reality, yet a narrative cannot be a pure reflection of reality in the social world. This is in part because there are competing conceptions of social reality from which to choose, each interpretation coming with its own way of imagining itself and its environment. Choosing one conception involves imagining reality to be a certain way and accepting the stories distinct organization of meaning. Moreover, the law will often present an idealized representation of reality. In the past the traditional family was idealized in law. The law did not confine itself to stating what the family was, it presented a vision to which people should aspire. More recently, the legal community has adopted a more fluid (and many argue a more representative) concept of family, free from 'oppressive' family ties, as the ideal version of family. And, the argument goes, such constitutive narratives participate in the formation of consciousness and thus identity.

To be sure, the legal understanding of the social world is not formed without reference to the current actualization of social reality. This does not mean, however, that the law is necessarily captured by the reality it seeks to represent. Instead, the law can be seen as both a conforming and reforming force in society, alternatively describing social phenomena in ways that reinforce or alter that which is described. This occurs because in representing social reality in a certain way, the narrative of the law invariably supports or even adopts one version of reality, and in so doing, commits itself to normalizing alternative accounts of the social world....

9.6

The Influence of Legal Commentary on Judicial Interpretation of the *Charter*

Troy Riddell

Adapted for this book by Troy Riddell from his M.A. thesis, *The Development of Section 1 of the Charter of Rights: A Study in Constitutional Politics* (University of Calgary, 1994).

Decisions made by judges, especially Supreme Court justices, often have important policy consequences; therefore, students of Canadian judicial politics should be interested in what factors influence how judges make decisions. This essay investigates the potential influence that legal scholarship played in the interpretation given to section 1 of the *Charter of Rights* by the Supreme Court. Section 1 of the *Charter* states that the rights set out in the *Charter* are subject "to such reasonable limitations as can be demonstrably justified in a free and democratic society." Section 1 plays a pivotal role in determining whether a law challenged under the *Charter* is upheld or struck down. Therefore, how section 1 was interpreted by the Supreme Court had important consequences for the policy-making role of the Court and helped determine who won and lost cases involving abortion, homosexual rights, immigration, welfare, tobacco advertising, French-only signs, euthanasia, Sunday closing and other important policy matters. The study links the interpretation given to section 1 by the Supreme Court to the interpretations of section 1 favoured by legal commentators, thus revealing that factors within a judicial institution's legal, social and political environment can influence how judges make decisions. In turn, this means that judges do not just apply the "law" when making a decision (as suggested by the "legal" model of judicial decision-making), nor do they necessarily decide cases according to their own personal ideology (as suggested by the "behavioral" model of judicial decision-making).

There would have been no potential for the influence of legal scholarship on the interpretation of section 1 if it were obvious from the beginning how section 1 should be interpreted. However, the Supreme Court faced a number of interpretive choices when deciding how to apply section 1. How the Court chose to operationalize section 1 – put it into effect – would make it easier or more difficult for *Charter* claimants to win their case, since the section 1 test would act as a prism through which rights claims would be filtered. Four questions surrounding the interpretation of section 1 were particularly important. One, should it be easy for *Charter* claimants to show that their rights were violated and then make governments justify their rights limitations under section 1, or should rights be internally limited, thereby making it harder for *Charter* claimants to show that their rights were violated and making resort to section 1 less likely? Two, should governments be made to prove that a limitation of a right was "reasonable" or should *Charter* claimants be forced to prove that a limitation of a right was "unreasonable"? Three, how strictly should the Court look at whether the government has a "valid objective" behind the passage of the legislation in question? Four, how difficult or easy should it be for governments to defend the means used to achieve the legislative objective? A section 1 test that broadly defined rights, placed the burden of proof on the government, made it difficult for a government to justify its legislative objective, and also made it difficult for a government to justify the means used to meet the legislative objective would make it easier for a rights claimant to successfully challenge government legislation under the *Charter*. Conversely, a section 1 test that made the opposite interpretive choices would be more deferential, thereby making it easier for governments to justify their legislation under section 1 and making it more difficult for rights claimants to challenge government legislation under the *Charter*.

It turns out that in the 1986 *R. v. Oakes* case the Supreme Court operationalized section 1 in such a way as to make it difficult for governments to justify their legislation under section 1. In other words, rights claims would be filtered through a prism that favoured the *Charter* claimant. Was this interpretation given to section 1 a coincidence or by design? Did legal commentary play a role in how the *Oakes* test was fashioned? To help answer these questions, I coded twenty pieces of legal commentary written before the Supreme Court's interpretation of section 1 in the 1986 *Oakes* case according to how they answered five interpretive questions, including the four described above. If a commentator advocated an interpretive choice that increased the chances that a law would be struck down by the courts, he or she was coded as "activist." Conversely, a commentator who recommended an interpretive choice that would more likely result in a piece of legislation being upheld was coded as promoting "restraint." Authors who advocated a middle position were coded as "both" and those who did not address a particular issue were coded as "not applicable." The results described below show that legal commentators heavily favoured the interpretive choices adopted by the Court in *Oakes*. Following the description of results is a brief discussion about how it is likely that this convergence between the Court's interpretation of section 1 and the interpretation favoured by legal commentators was *not* coincidental. That discussion is followed by a brief review of how the findings fit with theories of judicial decision-making and what the political implications of the results are.

The first interpretive choice that the legal commentary was coded for was whether the Court should broadly define rights and then analyze limitations under section 1 or whether the Court should limit rights by definition, thereby making resort to section 1 less frequent. Legal commentators who advocated the former approach were coded as favouring a more activist, policy-making role for the Court. This is because a broad reading of what constitutes a right – "free speech," "equality," "fair trial," etc. – would make it easier on the rights claimant to show that a right was violated and more difficult for the government to argue that a right was not violated. This would usually result in a "two-step" process whereby a right (broadly defined) is found to have been limited and then, under section 1, a determination is made as to whether the limitation is reasonable and justified. Making such determinations under section 1 would often involve judges in making decisions about complex policy tradeoffs, including the need to balance individual and/or groups rights against the rights of others and society as a whole. The results for question 1 are shown below in Table 1.

Table 1

Question 1: Should the Court adopt a "two-step" approach by broadly defining rights and then analyzing limitations under Section 1?

Possible Responses	Raw Score	Adj. Score
'1' = yes (activist)	9/20 (45%)	9/13 (69%)
'2' = no (restraint)	4/20 (20%)	4/13 (31%)
'3' = both	0/20 (0%)	0/13 (0%)
'4' = not applicable	7/20 (35%)	———

A "two-step" approach does not necessarily entail shifting the burden of proof to the government to prove the reasonableness of its restriction. It would have been just as plausible, and more consistent with constitutional tradition, to require the rights claimant to prove the unreasonableness of the restriction. Of course, this latter option would have reduced the probability of success for *Charter*-based interest groups (and their ideological allies in the legal academy) when challenging government policy. Therefore, authors who favoured placing the burden of proof on the government under section 1 were coded as advocating the "activist" approach. The results are shown in Table 2.

Table 2

Question 2: Should the burden of proof be on the government under Section 1?

Possible Responses	Raw Score	Adj. Score
'1' = yes (activist)	18/20 (90%)	18/19 (95%)
'2' = no (restraint)	0/20 (0%)	0/19 (0%)
'3' = both	1/20 (5%)	1/19 (5%)
'4' = not applicable	1/20 (5%)	———

Whether or not the government or rights claimant has the initial burden to prove limitations were reasonable or not, the next question becomes what would be required for a government to "demonstrably justify" that its limitation on a right was required to meet a necessary objective. The old test, used under the 1960 *Bill of Rights*, was that the government had to show that it was meeting a "valid objective" – a fairly easy rule to meet. A stricter test, such as making the government show that it was meeting a "pressing social need," would make it more difficult for a government to justify its limitations on rights. The results of the coding on this interpretive choice are shown in Table 3.

Table 3

Question 3: Should the government have to pass a more rigorous test than the "valid objective" test to justify why it was limiting rights under section 1?

Possible Responses	Raw Score	Adj. Score
'1' = yes (activist)	13/20 (65%)	13/16 (81%)
'2' = no (restraint)	2/20 (10%)	2/16 (13%)
'3' = both	1/20 (5%)	1/16 (6%)
'4' = not applicable	4/20 (20%)	———

Again the legal commentary supported the "activist" interpretive choice for section 1. Not only did a majority of authors want a stricter test under section 1 than the "valid objective" test, they also wanted the courts to force governments to provide concrete evidence to back up their claim. Bender, for instance, declared that the test ought to require governments to require "factual (rather than speculative) support for a substantial or compelling (rather than merely legitimate [or valid]) governmental or social interest."

The second and potentially more difficult aspect of justifying a government restriction on rights is the reasonableness of the means used to achieve the government's objective. A relatively easy test for a government to pass is showing that there is a "reasonable or rational connection" between the means and the objective. A harder test involves having the government show that the means used are the "least restrictive" ways of limiting rights in order to meet an objective. It would be more difficult, for example, for a government to prove that restricting tobacco advertising was the "least restrictive means" by which to reduce tobacco consumption (the objective) than it would be for a government to prove that restricting tobacco advertising had a "reasonable or rational connection" to the objective of reducing tobacco consumption. Table 4 shows that most of the legal commenators advocated the more difficult test for governments to pass.

Table 4

Question 4: Should the means test go beyond looking for a "reasonable or rational connection"?

Possible Responses	Raw Score	Adj. Score
'1' = yes (activist)	10/20 (50%)	10/14 (71%)
'2' = no (restraint)	1/20 (5%)	1/14 (7%)
'3' = both	3/20 (15%)	3/14 (21%)
'4' = not applicable	6/20 (30%)	———

Although the interpretive choices favoured by the majority of legal commentators on section 1 would tend to make it easier for *Charter* claimants to have legislation struck down, question five is designed to discover whether legal commentators wanted the courts to be more aggressive in scrutinizing government policy under the *Charter*. More specifically, Table 5 examines whether the legal commentary explicitly criticized the courts for being too cautious and deferential when interpreting the 1960 *Bill of Rights*.

Table 5

Question 5: Was the "self-restrained" jurisprudence of the Bill of Rights criticized?

Possible Responses	Raw Score	Adj. Score
'1' = yes (activist)	9/20 45%)	9/10 (90%)
'2' = no (restraint)	0/20 (0%)	0/10 (0%)
'3' = both	1/20 (5%)	1/10 (10%)
'4' = not applicable	10/20 (50%)	———

Although only ten authors specifically mentioned the *Bill of Rights*, nine of those that did criticized the *Bill of Rights* and asked for a more active jurisprudence under the *Charter*. Whitley predicted that section 1 would be used as a "sword" against restrictive government action. The interpretive choices for section 1 favoured by the most of the legal commentators were designed to encourage the judiciary, especially the Supreme Court, to make it difficult for governments to justify that their limitations on rights (broadly defined) were reasonable.

These findings are not surprising. Many law professors are intimately associated with *Charter*-based groups, such as the feminist Legal Education and Action Fund (LEAF), which try to use litigation and the courts to pursue their preferred policies. Part of the litigation strategy involves "influencing the influencers" to adopt favourable interpretations of constitutional text, since *Charter* groups recognized that "rights on paper mean nothing unless they are properly interpreted." [*Ed. note:* See Reading 7.2.) The writing of legal commentary was part of this "influencing the influencers" campaign. While legal commentators and *Charter*-based interest group activists are not always one and the same (even though in many instances they are), *Charter*-based activists and many legal scholars share similar ideological commitments to particular definitions of "equality" and "freedom" and the use of courts to achieve policy goals. Moreover, legal scholars are not hesitant to advance their claims through their commentary. The "extensive intermingling of the academic and political spheres" remarked Alan Cairns, has produced a *Charter* commentary that is increasingly "purpose driven and laced with advocacy."

In its 1986 *Oakes* decision, the Supreme Court adopted the interpretive choices favoured by a majority of the legal commentary, while ignoring government arguments that the Court be deferential and restrained when applying section 1. The section 1 *"Oakes"* test stipulates that judges adopt a two-step approach by first broadly defining rights and then, if rights were found to be violated, looking to section 1 to see if limitations on the right were demonstrably justified by the government to be reasonable. Under *Oakes*, to prove a limit is reasonable, the government must show that the legislation in question has a "pressing and substantial" objective and that it uses the "least restrictive means" to meet the objective.

Was it just coincidental that the interpretation given to section 1 in *Oakes* paralleled the majority of legal commentary on section 1? While no "smoking gun" exists that definitively links the legal commentary to the Oakes test, there is circumstantial evidence to suggest that legal commentary influences how judges, especially on the Supreme Court, interpret the *Charter*. For instance, Walter Tarnopolsky maintained that "the support of the academic community for an 'effective' *Charter*" was one of the keys to understanding the activism of the Supreme Court in interpreting the *Charter*. The connection between "activist" constitutional decisions and legal commentary advocating such outcomes has also been made in the U.S., France, and Germany.

More specifically, in 1983, Justice Dickson, who wrote the majority judgment in *Oakes*, pointed out that there is a "growing recognition of the importance of academic writing to the judicial process." A former Excutive Legal Officer of the Supreme Court (1985-1987) observed that "[t]here was, throughout his entire judicial career, a very special relationship between Chief Justice Dickson and the Canadian academic community.... [H]e devoured much of the literature produced by the Canadian legal academic community and drew upon it as he decided cases and wrote judgments ... [T]he Chief Justice's ... law clerks ... were under instruction to watch the law reviews and bring good articles to his attention." Justice Dickson referred to a piece of section 1 legal commentary in his *Oakes* decision though no reference was made to that work in the legal briefs to the Court, and he interpreted section 1 in a manner that fit with the interpretive choices favoured by the majority of section 1 legal commentators. It appears that section 1 legal commentators successfully encouraged and legitimated an interpretation of section 1 that allowed for a more active policy-making role by the Supreme Court under the *Charter*.

Although not conclusive, this research suggests that outcomes are influenced by forces in the social, legal, and political environment that surrounds the judiciary as an institutional branch of government. These are factors that are not identified by the two dominant theories about how judges make decisions – the "behaviouralist" model and the "legal" model. To oversimplify, the former proposes that a judge's own personal characteristics and political ideology most influence the decision a judge reaches while the latter asserts that outcomes are derived by judges neutrally applying established legal principles to the facts of the case. The "legal" model would have predicted that the Supreme Court would have followed the judicial self-restraint found in 1960 *Bill of Rights* precedents, which was what various government factums prior to *Oakes* urged the Court to do with section 1. The "behavioural" model would predict that judges would apply section 1 in such a way as to arrive at their predetermined conclusions based on their personal beliefs and ideologies. However, this pattern does not always hold. For example, in his 1975 *Morgentaler* decision, Justice Dickson argued that the Supreme Court under the *Bill of Rights* had no business examining the federal government's policy on abortion, but in 1988 then Chief Justice Dickson struck down Canada's abortion law after claiming that the law did not pass the section 1 *Oakes* test under the *Charter*. Assuming that Dickson's personal attitudes toward abortion had stayed the same over that period, it seems plausible based on the evidence presented above that legal commentary advocating a more activist Court under the *Charter* and section 1 contributed to changes in Chief Justice Dickson's decision-making.

Of course, neither the legal model of judicial decision-making nor the behaviouralist model of decision-making should be dismissed out of hand. Although the stringent version of the *Oakes* test was later modified in certain situations, the general *Oakes* model remains a central element in *Charter* arguments and Supreme Court decisions. In other words, as predicted by the legal model, it remains a crucial *Charter* precedent. Importantly, it is a precedent that brings the Court into the policy-making process and, all other things being equal, tilts the balance towards making it more difficult for governments to defend legislation, particularly when compared to 1960 *Bill of Rights* jurisprudence. Nevertheless, according to statistics, different judges had quite different records on whether governments won or lost the section 1 *Oakes* test (see Reading 12.3). Some judges display a pattern of deference to governments, while others are more activist and tend to strike legislation down, which reveals that there is an element of subjectivity in the application of the *Oakes* test. Therefore, it appears that the "behavioral" model of judicial decision-making has explanatory power as well. This, in turn, means that how the Court is composed influences the fate of important policy areas under section 1 and has led to calls for changes to the Supreme Court appointment process.

However, this essay highlights that the environment in which judges operate can also influence how they make decisions. Others have argued also that judges are influenced by elements in their environment, such as the public, the media, and governments. Yet, the influence of legal academics is potentially stronger than other factors that shape the decisions of appellate courts because they have a more direct link to appellate judges than do other elements within the social, legal, and political environment. Marc Gold, for example, has observed that it sometimes "appears as if the [Canadian Supreme] Court is writing for the [legal] academy." Similarly, Justice Kleinfeld of the U.S. Court of Appeals explains: "To the extent that we have an audience other than our law clerks, that responds in a way that we can see or hear, it consists mostly of legal academics and legal periodicals. That audience shares the politicized culture of the university."

Arguably, many legal academics not only share this politicized culture but also promote it in teaching and writing that advocates particular visions of civil liberties, equality rights, and judicial power. Perhaps this explains why the U.S. and Canadian Supreme Courts have overturned legislation passed by elected politicians and supported by the public in a number of controversial policy areas, including those involving abortion and education. Whether one agrees with the outcomes of such decisions or not, this study illuminates how rights advocacy groups are aided by legal scholarship in their quest to achieve policy change through the courts.

9.7

Key Terms

Concepts

common law system
stare decisis
ratio decidendi
obiter dicta
precedent
predictability
"distinguishing a precedent"
"limiting a precedent"
"ignoring a precedent"
"overruling a precedent"
statute
administrative rules and regulations
civil law system
codification
policy-making by exegesis
legal commentary
advocacy scholarship

Institutions, Events, and Documents

Jeremy Bentham
James Fitzjames Stephen, Draft Code of 1879
Criminal Code (1892)
Fleming v. *Atkinson* (Cattle Trespass Case) (1959)
Boucher v. *The King* (Seditious Libel Case) (1951)
R. v. *Oakes* (1986)

Judicial Review and Federalism

10

Constitutional Origins

The *Constitution Act, 1867*, united on a federal basis the separate colonies that had until that time constituted British North America. The federal form was essential to the act of union. None of the provinces, particularly Quebec, was willing to relinquish the degree of political autonomy and self-government to which they aspired and to be subsumed under a single unitary state. At the same time, the most influential leaders of the confederation movement, men like John A. Macdonald and George Brown, desired a strong central government based on "legislative union," in order to avoid what they considered to have been the near fatal weakness of the central government in American federalism.[1]

The *Constitution Act, 1867*, represented an uneasy compromise between these conflicting goals. Provincial demands for preserving local autonomy and self-government were accommodated through a distribution of legislative powers between the newly created federal government and the provinces, primarily in sections 91 and 92 of the *Act*. The centralists' goals were recognized by a very broad wording of the federal government's section 91 law-making powers, and by the unilateral power to strike down provincial laws through the devices of disallowance (s.56) and reservation (s.90). The result was a written constitutional document establishing a highly centralized form of federalism. As it turned out, this original design was modified considerably by subsequent political developments in which judicial review played a major role.

It is now accepted that judicial review is a corollary to a federal form of government based on a written distribution of powers between two levels of government. For a federal division of legislative powers to be effective,

---

1 This skepticism toward federalism appeared quite justified at the time. The Confederation process took place during and after the bloody American Civil War, which had pitted the "states' rights" advocates of the Southern slave-holding states against the national government.

there must be a mutually acceptable process for settling the inevitable disputes over where one government's jurisdiction ends and the other's begins. Neither level of government can be permitted to define unilaterally (and thus to redefine) the boundaries of federal-provincial jurisdiction, as this would violate the equal status of both levels of government, a central principle of federalism.[2] In practice, the need for a "neutral umpire" of federal systems has been met through judicial review by a final court of appeal. Of the six federal democracies studied by Lijphart in 1984, only one – Switzerland – did not have judicial review. Those federations with judicial review included Australia, Canada, Germany, Austria, and the United States.[3]

Historical Origins

Originally, judicial review of the constitution came easily and without controversy in Canada. The *Constitution Act* took the form of an Imperial statute, and section 129 mandated the continuation of the existing legal regime. This meant that the *Constitution Act* was subject to the already existing *Colonial Laws Validity Act*, which required consistency of colonial law with British Imperial statutes. The Judicial Committee of the Privy Council was charged with the responsibility of enforcing this policy. The Judicial Committee had served as the final court of appeal for British North America prior to Confederation, and simply continued in this capacity after 1867. Any alleged violation of the federal division of powers set out in the *Constitution Act* could be challenged in the existing superior courts of the provinces and appealed from a provincial court of appeal directly to the Judicial Committee in London.

This explained the founders' lack of urgency in creating a Supreme Court of Canada. The absence of a national court of appeal also made the introduction of judicial review in Canada easier. When the federal government

---

2 The disallowance and reservation powers violate the principle of parity, and for that reason it has been argued that Canada is not a "true" federal state. However, neither power has been exercised by Ottawa for over forty years. Although both powers still exist *legally*, it is generally accepted that a convention of non-use has been established, and that it is politically unacceptable for the federal government to re-activate either of these powers. For example, in 1989, when the Quebec government invoked the section 33 legislative override to reinstate its "French-only" public signs law (which had been struck down by the Supreme Court a month earlier), some MPs called on Prime Minister Mulroney to use disallowance to protect the rights of the Anglophone minority in Quebec. With much of his Cabinet from Quebec and Alberta, two of the most vocal advocates of provincial rights, it was not surprising that the Prime Minister did not consider disallowance a viable option.

3 Arend Lijphart, *Democracies: Patterns of Majoritarian and Consensus Government in Twenty-One Countries* (New Haven, CT: Yale University Press, 1984), p. 195.

moved to exercise its section 101 authority to create such a court, controversy quickly erupted. As Professor Smith explains, the attempt to create the Supreme Court of Canada became entangled in the already robust politics of federal-provincial competition (Reading 10.1). This controversy was engendered in large part by the inclusion of the reference procedure as part of the *Supreme Court Act*. Some "provincial rights" advocates perceived the creation of a "federal" court of appeal and the simultaneous creation of a reference authority vested exclusively with the federal government as an ill-disguised attempt to refurbish the already controversial disallowance power by cloaking it with judicial legitimacy. This suspicion of "disallowance in disguise" was supported by the original form of the reference procedure and the comments of centralists such as John A. MacDonald.

Provincial fears of a centralizing Supreme Court notwithstanding, the *Supreme Court Act* was finally adopted in 1875. The newly created Supreme Court of Canada immediately began to exercise the power of judicial review and did so without controversy. However, its decisions could be appealed to the Privy Council, and it could be avoided altogether by *per saltum* appeals directly from a provincial court of appeal to the Privy Council. Both of these routes of appeal were abolished by amendments to the *Supreme Court Act* in 1949, which established the Supreme Court of Canada as the final and exclusive court of appeal for Canada. Until 1949, however, the Supreme Court was decidedly the junior partner in overseeing the judicial aspects of Canada's constitutional development. Its early decisions were frequently overturned by the Privy Council, and the doctrine of *stare decisis* meant that it was bound to follow the Privy Council's lead. This meant that the Supreme Court of Canada was functionally more like a middle-tier British appeal court until 1949. The habits and procedures associated with such a court – such as trying to follow the "right" precedent rather than creating a new precedent – lingered on for almost another generation.

Students should note the shifting basis of authority for the Canadian courts' exercise of judicial review. Initially, the authority for the judicial enforcement of the *Constitution Act, 1867*, was the *Colonial Laws Validity Act*. This remained true until 1931, when federalism replaced imperialism as the basis for judicial review. After Word War I, mounting discontent with the inferior status implied by the *Colonial Laws Validity Act* led to demands for its abolition by Canada and other British dominions. Canada, however, requested and received an exemption for the *Constitution Act, 1867*. Canadian leaders feared that, without the *Colonial Laws Valdity Act*, the federal division of powers could be altered unilaterally by either level of government. The preservation of Canadian federalism, they believed, required the continuation of the legal paramountcy of the *Constitution Act, 1867*. Unable to agree upon an amending formula of their own, Canadian leaders request that the *Constitution Act, 1867*, remain under the legal regime of the *Colonial Laws Validity Act*. This anomalous condition was finally brought to a close in 1982 with the patriation of the constitution. Sections

38-42 of the *Constitution Act, 1982*, set out a "made in Canada" amending formula and section 52 clearly established constitutional supremacy as the new legal basis for judicial review.

Constitutional Interpretation

Constitutional interpretation raises problems that do not occur in common law or statutory interpretation. Because constitutional law regulates the powers of governments (rather than the private rights of individuals or corporations), it inevitably affects the making of public policy. Judicial review thus injects into the judicial process a political dimension that previously did not exist. Common law judges have been reluctant to acknowledge the policy-making function conferred on them by judicial review, as it seems to contradict and undermine so many of the traditional aspects of the judicial process. As a result, Canadian, British, and Australian judges have tended simply to transfer the techniques of statutory interpretation to constitutional interpretation.

This was especially true of the Privy Council's approach to the *Constitution Act*. While this is easily explained by the unfamiliarity of British judges with the practice of a "written constitution" (indeed, to them it was just another Imperial statute), it had the unfortunate effect of establishing this mode of constitutional interpretation as the standard for Canadian judges to follow. Discontent with the substance of the Privy Council's constitutional decisions (discussed below) led in turn to criticisms of its technique of interpretation. These critics called for an approach to constitutional interpretation that acknowledged the inherent policy dimensions of constitutional law and reflected the need to adapt a written constitution to the changing needs and circumstances of the society it governs. The late Professor William Lederman summarized this issue as follows:

> There are principally two types of interpretation – literal or grammatical emphasizing of the words found in statutes and constitutional documents; and sociological, which insists that constitutional words and statutory words must be carefully linked by judicially noticed knowledge and by evidence to the ongoing life of society.[4]

Examples of these two different approaches to constitutional interpretation are found in the excerpts from the Privy Council opinions of Lord Sankey (Reading 10.2) and Lord Atkin (Reading 10.3). Lord Sankey articulated his now famous "living tree" approach in his opinion in the well-known

---

4 W.R. Lederman, "Thoughts on Reform of the Supreme Court of Canada," *The Confederation Challenge*, Ontario Advisory Committee on Confederation, Vol. II (Toronto: Queen's Printer, 1970), p. 295.

"Persons Case."[5] Henrietta Muir Edwards, a leader of the women's suffrage movement in the West, had been proposed for an appointment to the Senate from Alberta. At issue was whether any woman could be appointed to the Senate. Legally, the case boiled down to whether the term used in section 24 of the *Constitution Act*, "qualified persons," included women. The Supreme Court of Canada ruled that it did not, basing its decision on internal evidence of the *Constitution Act* itself and the indisputable fact that, at the time of Confederation, women did not have the right to vote, much less to hold public office. While this decision was arguably correct in a narrowly technical sense, it was overturned on appeal by the Privy Council. Lord Sankey stressed the necessity of interpreting constitutional language in light of society's changing beliefs and needs and not just internal grammatical constructions and original intent of the framers.

Lord Atkin's very different approach to constitutional interpretation occurred in the 1937 *Labour Conventions Case*.[6] This case raised the issue of Parliament's authority to enact legislation implementing Canada's treaty obligations when the legislation involved matters that would normally have fallen under the provinces' section 92 jurisdiction. Despite the recent *Statute of Westminster* (1931), which had affirmed the sovereignty of Canada in the conduct of her foreign affairs, Lord Atkin ruled that the federal government's treaty-making power did not allow it to trench upon matters of provincial jurisdiction when implementing a treaty. This decision was widely perceived as a serious blow to the effective conduct of Canadian foreign policy and was blamed on Lord Atkin's "watertight compartments" view of Canadian federalism. This view was widely condemned as being out of touch with the economic and political realities of twentieth-century Canada.

Constitutional Politics

The Privy Council's decision in the *Labour Conventions Case* is only one in a long series of constitutional cases that progressively narrowed the scope of the federal government's section 91 powers while expanding the section 92 jurisdiction of the provinces. The federal government's broad residual power to make laws for the "Peace, Order, and good Government of Canada" was whittled away to almost nothing by the Privy Council's "emergency doctrine" test. The unrestricted power to make laws for the "Regulation of Trade and Commerce" was soon reduced to the narrow ambit of "interprovincial trade" by judicial interpretation. At the same time, the Privy Council's decisions expanded what originally appeared to be the rather meagre provincial powers to make laws in relation to "Property and Civil Rights in the Province" and "all matters of a merely local or private Nature in the

---

5 *Re Meaning of the Word "Persons" in Section 24 of the B.N.A. Act* [1928], S.C.R. 276.
6 [1937] A.C. 327; III Olmstead 180.

Province." Throughout all of these decisions, the Privy Council adhered to the textually oriented, legalistic method of interpretation described above.

Mounting dissatisfaction with the Privy Council's performance as final constitutional arbiter for Canada manifested itself in the "judicial nationalism" discussed in Chapter One. Following the recommendations of the 1939 O'Connor Report, Parliament abolished all appeals to the Privy Council in 1949. While Canadian critics of the Judicial Committee were unanimous in condemning the provincial bias of its decisions, they were far from agreed upon a diagnosis of the problem or a prescription for an acceptable "made in Canada" jurisprudence after 1949. One school of thought criticized the Judicial Committee of the Privy Council for being too textual and literal in its interpretation of the constitution, and thereby failing to make it a "living constitution," in accord with the changing times. The other principal group of critics accused the Judicial Committee of not following the centralist orientation of the text closely enough.[7] The inability of Canadian scholars, judges, and political leaders to agree on an appropriate constitutional jurisprudence has carried over into the post-1949 era. The latent pro-Ottawa attitudes of the old J.C.P.C. critics have not been acceptable to Quebec leaders or other "provincial rights" advocates. The result has been a continuing credibility problem for the Supreme Court whenever it acts as final arbiter in jurisdictional disputes between Ottawa and the provinces.

The most important post-1949 federalism case has been the 1976 *Anti-inflation Reference*[8] (Reading 10.4). As Peter Russell recounts, this case seemed to present a perfect opportunity for the Supreme Court, led by its new chief justice, Bora Laskin, a known centralist, to repudiate once and for all the moribund "emergency doctrine" of the Privy Council. Several post-1949 decisions of the Supreme Court had silently ignored the old "emergency doctrine," and spoke instead of an "inherent national importance" test. Centralists anticipated that the time was ripe to institute this new and much broader basis for the exercise of the federal government's residual power. The public policy significance of the case was underscored by the large number of intervenors, consisting of both provincial governments and private groups. The Supreme Court itself tacitly acknowledged the policy dimensions of the case by devising new procedures to allow for the introduction of very untraditional, socio-economic evidence by both sides.[9] While the Supreme Court's final decision modestly increased the "Peace, Order, and Good Government" authority of the federal government, it did not repudiate the work of the Privy Council. The "emergency doctrine" was preserved and even extended to peace-time situations. This compromise result may appear somewhat anticlimactic, but it illustrates the Supreme

---

7   See Alan C. Cairns, "The Judicial Committee and its Critics," *Canadian Journal of Political Science*, 4 (September, 1971), p. 301.

8   [1976] 2 S.C.R. 373.

9   See Introduction to Chapter Eight.

Court's sensitivity to conflicting elite views of federalism and its instinct for the middle ground when this occurs.

As it turned out, the *Anti-Inflation Reference* was the first in a series of Supreme Court decisions during the late seventies that dealt with federalism issues – all of which were won by Ottawa.[10] These decisions contributed to federal-provincial tensions on other fronts and led to growing provincial suspicions about the dependence of the Supreme Court on the Liberal government in Ottawa. Shortly following several of these cases, an article appeared in the press suggesting that "the image of Chief Justice Laskin and his eight 'sober, grey men' acting as spear-carriers for the federal prime minister fails to add anything to one's hopes for improved national unity."[11]

The implications of these remarks so upset Chief Justice Laskin that he purposely went out of his way to respond publicly. At a hastily arranged "Seminar for Journalists" the same month, the late Chief Justice declared:

> I have to be more sad than angry to read of an insinuation that we are "acting as spear carriers for the federal prime minister" or to read of a statement attributed to a highly respected member of the academic community that "the provinces must have a role in the appointment of members of the Supreme Court in order to ensure that they have confidence that it can fairly represent the interests of the provincial governments as well as of any federal government."

> ... The allegation is reckless in its implication that we have considerable freedom to give voice to our personal predilections, and thus to political preferences.... We have no such freedom, and it is a disservice to this Court and to the work of those who have gone before us to suggest a federal bias because of federal appointment.[12]

There is no doubting the sincerity of the late Chief Justice's remarks, and he was subsequently supported by Professor Peter Hogg in an article that argued persuasively against a federal bias in recent Supreme Court decisions.[13]

---

10 The principal cases were two cases dealing with provincial regulation of broadcasting, *Capital Cities Communications* v. *C.R.T.C.* [1978] 2 S.C.R. 141, and *Public Service Board* v. *Dionne*. [1978] 2 S.C.R. 191; and two cases dealing with provincial authority to tax and regulate the production of natural resources, *CIGOL* v. *Government of Saskatchewan* [1978] 2 S.C.R. 545, and *Central Canada Potash* v. *Government of Saskatchewan*, [1979] 1 S.C.R.42.

11 Edwin R. Black, "Supreme Court Judges as Spear-Carriers for Ottawa: They need watching," *Report on Confederation* (Feb. l978), p. 12.

12 Bora Laskin, "Judicial Integrity and the Supreme Court of Canada," *Law Society Gazette* (1978), pp. 118, 120.

13 P.W. Hogg, "Is the Supreme Court of Canada Biased in Constitutional Cases?" *The Canadian Bar Review* (1979), p. 722.

But in politics, perceptions, not facts, often carry the day, and the Supreme Court has a public image problem. This 1978 incident betrayed a continuing lack of confidence in the Supreme Court among provincial elites.[14] This problem took on heightened significance in the 1980s, as the Supreme Court began to interpret and enforce the 1982 *Charter of Rights and Freedoms*. It was not a coincidence that less than a decade after the clash between former Chief Justice Laskin and Professor Black, the Meech Lake Accord (1987) proposed to amend the constitution to transfer the power of nominating Supreme Court judges to provincial governments. While the Meech Lake Accord was eventually defeated, the judicial nominations provision demonstrated continuing tensions between the Court and defenders of provincial rights.

Professor Peter Russell has argued that the Supreme Court is so sensitive to maintaining its image as a "neutral umpire" that it is willing to sacrifice the consistent application of legal principle and precedent in order to achieve "politically balanced" results.[15]

The *Anti-Inflation Reference* (Reading 10.4) and the *Patriation Reference* (Reading 2.3) both illustrate Russell's thesis. In the former, the Court escaped an apparent "no win" situation by upholding the wage and price restraint legislation but on the very novel – and narrower – grounds of a "peace time emergency." Similarly, the Court's ruling in the *Patriation Reference* has been described as "bold statecraft ... questionable jurisprudence." The Court's ruling that federal unilateralism was "legal but unconstitutional" represented a political compromise designed to induce both sides to resume negotiating (which they did). As Mandel and others have noted, however, it took an unprecedented legal ruling on constitutional conventions to reach this result.

A similar pattern is evident in the more recent 1998 *Quebec Secession Reference* (Reading 10.7). This decision was the most recent round in the ongoing struggle between Ottawa and Quebec separatists. Following the near victory of the separatist option in the 1995 Quebec referendum (the "No" side won by less than one percent), there was concern that the Liberal government of Prime Minister Jean Chrétien had been too passive in responding to the Parti Québécois' claim that Quebec has a right to secede unilaterally from Canada if it can win a "fifty-percent-plus one" majority in a secession referendum. There were collateral concerns that the closeness of the 1995 vote was due in part to the intentionally misleading wording of the referendum question that had been cleverly designed by the PQ gov-

---

14 A telling example of Western Canadian skepticism toward the Supreme Court was the front cover of an *Alberta Report*, an influential regional weekly news magazine. Referring to the federal Cabinet's decision to refer the legal issues of the French language dispute in Manitoba to the Supreme Court, the cover headlines read: "FRENCH ROULETTE – Manitoba is hauled into Ottawa's court over provincial language rights" (April 23, 1984).

15 Peter H. Russell, "The Supreme Court and Federal-Provincial Relations: The Political Use of Legal Resources," *Canadian Public Policy* 11 (1985), pp. 161–70.

ernment. In an attempt to pre-empt a repetition of the 1995 near defeat, the Chrétien government decided to challenge this assumption by referring these issues to the Supreme Court for determination.

The Supreme Court's decision (Reading 10.7) once again conformed to Russell's prediction. It gave something to both sides, but at the expense of legal clarity. The Court ruled that a "unilateral declaration of independence" (UDI) by Quebec would be unconstitutional. However, the Court went on to say that if the separatist option were to win a "clear majority on a clear question," then there would be a constitutional duty for Ottawa and the rest of Canada to negotiate the terms of separation with the Quebec government. If the governments of English Canada failed to negotiate "in good faith," then Quebec would be justified in proceeding alone. As in the 1981 *Patriation Reference*, both sides claimed victory. In this respect, the Court's strategy seemed to achieve its goal of being accepted by both sides.

However, the legal reasoning behind this "split decision" broke new constitutional ground and raised more legal questions than it answered.[16] The key to the Supreme Court's decision was its "discovery" of four "foundational constitutional principles" – democracy, federalism, the rule of law, and the protection of minorities – that it said underlie written constitutional rules and practice. This was not the first time that the Supreme Court had "discovered" such a foundational constitutional principle. The year before, in the *Provincial Judges Reference* (Reading 5.6), the Court appealed to the unwritten constitutional principle of "judicial independence" to bolster its finding that provincial governments have a constitutional duty to create independent judicial compensation commissions. These principles are like constitutional conventions (the focus of the 1981 *Patriation Reference*) in that they are unwritten. But these principles are "superior" to constitutional conventions in that they create "legal duties" for the governments bound by the constitution. The Court relied on the "rule of law" principle to rule against the constitutionality of UDI, and then grounded Ottawa's "duty to negotiate" in the principles of federalism and democracy.

Despite affirming primacy of written rules, the Court wrote over seventy paragraphs without any reference to the written rules of constitutional amendment in Part V of the *Constitution Act, 1982*. Instead, it wrote about balancing the competing demands of the foundational underlying principles of the constitution. This has led some commentators to conclude that these newly discovered "constitutional principles" are more important than the written rules found in the actual text of the Constitution.[17] This possibility is troubling to many (see Justice La Forest's sharp dissent in the *Provincial Judges Reference*,

---

16 For a full range of assessments of this decision, see David Schniderman, ed., *The Quebec Decision: Perspectives on the Supreme Court Ruling on Secession* (Toronto: James Lorimer, 1999).

17 See Donna Greschner, "Goodbye to the Amending Formulas," in Schneiderman, ed. *The Quebec Decision*, pp. 155–57.

Reading 5.6) because it confers broad discretion on the judges to ignore or override explicit constitutional rules, such as the amending formulas.

The Court's decision in the *Quebec Secession Reference* re-ignited the debate over the "impartiality" of the Supreme Court in federal-provincial relations. Critics of the decision in Quebec and the West charged that the Court had acted in a partisan manner both in agreeing to hear the Liberal government's reference and in the specifics of its ruling.[18] While these criticisms are themselves partisan (to varying degrees), they connect with a broader theoretical literature that judicial review has an intrinsic centralist bias. Drawing upon a comparative perspective, André Bzdera has marshalled persuasive evidence that judicial review has had a centralizing effect in each of the nine federal states studied.[19] Bzdera explains the "net centralist/nationalist bias of federal high courts" by their institutional linkages to the central government: creation, administration, budget, internal procedures, and especially the appointment of judges. Bzdera's findings are supported by American political scientist Martin Shapiro. Shapiro's comparative study of centralized court systems – those with a final national court of appeal – found that they tend to "serve upper class and nationalizing interests rather than dominant local interests and thus are more satisfactory to persons trying to break through the web of local interests."[20] The Bzdera-Shapiro thesis helps to explain the provincial governments' persistent attempts to gain an agency in the appointment of judges to the Supreme Court of Canada, as witnessed most recently in the 1987 Meech Lake Accord.

The debate over the neutrality or centralist bias of the Supreme Court must also be placed in the real world of Canadian politics. Patrick Monahan's contribution (see Reading 10.5) demonstrates that, in Canada's ongoing federal-provincial tug-of-war, a loss in court does not necessarily mean a policy loss. His two case studies show how the availability of alternative policy instruments often permit a government to achieve indirectly what the courts have forbidden it from doing so directly. These alternative means include the enactment of the same policy by the other level of government; delegation of the disputed jurisdiction from the "winner" to the "loser;" substitution of an alternative regulatory instrument; and even constitutional amendment. As in the realm of civil liberties, the end of the legal battle does not necessarily mean the end of the "policy war." A judicial ruling becomes one more factor in the battle for elite and/or public opinion. Consensus between governments or sustained determination by one level of government can both lead to alternative means to the same policy objective.

---

18 See the essays by Josée Legault, Jacques Yvan Morin, Ted Morton, and Alan Cairns in Schneiderman, ed. *The Quebec Decision*.

19 André Bzdera, "Comparative Analysis of Federal High Courts: A Political Theory of Judicial Review," *Canadian Journal of Political Science* 25:1 (1993), pp. 3–30.

20 Martin Shapiro, *Courts: A Comparative and Political Analysis* (Chicago: University of Chicago Press, 1981), p. 24.

10.1

The Origins of Judicial Review in Canada
Jennifer Smith
Canadian Journal of Political Science, 16 (1983), 115–34. Reprinted with permission.

For many years students have been taught that the practice of judicial review in Canada is less important than it is in the United States. This is because it has had less scope, and it has had less scope because until recently Canada's written constitution, unlike the American Constitution, included no bill of rights. Whereas in both countries the courts, acting as "umpires" of their respective federal forms of government, have had the power to declare laws beyond the competence of the jurisdiction enacting them, the American courts have had the additional and, to many, fascinating power to enforce against governments the guarantees of the rights of citizens contained in the *Bill of Rights*. Obviously this line of comparison is outmoded now. After a prolonged and at times bitter debate, the federal government and nine of the ten provincial governments reached agreement last year on a set of amendments to the *British North America Act*, among them a *Charter of Rights and Freedoms*. As a result, the breadth of the courts' power of judicial review more closely approximates that possessed by their American counterparts. Is this development consistent with the nature of Canada's constitutional arrangements? Does the *Charter* provide the basis of the completion of an initially limited power?…

… One of the most thorough studies available is B.L. Strayer's *Judicial Review of Legislation in Canada*. Strayer argues that the *BNA Act, 1867* and related acts did not vest explicitly in the courts the power of judicial review. Nor can our common law inheritance be held responsible for it. Instead, judicial review is a product of the British colonial system, "implicit in the royal instructions, charters, or Imperial statutes creating the colonial legislatures." Since these legislatures were bodies of limited power, the colonial charters establishing them typically included clauses prohibiting them from passing laws repugnant to Imperial statutes.…

… As early as the fifteenth century, it was customary for the King's Privy Council rather than English domestic courts to hear appeals arising out of colonial matters. This practice was regulated by the *Privy Council Acts* of 1833 and 1844, which established the Judicial Committee of the Privy Council, specified its membership and authorized it to hear appeals from colonial courts. Thus the Judicial Committee acted as the highest appellate court for the colonies. As Strayer points out, it showed no inclination to question its authority to review the validity of colonial legislation, undoubtedly because the colonies themselves possessed only limited or subordinate legislative powers. He attributes considerable importance to the precedent it set throughout the Empire for the exercise of a similar power by colonial courts. According to Strayer, we must look to the British colonial system, and especially its doctrine of judicial review of colonial legislation, for the origin of judicial review in Canada: "The constitutional law of the Empire in 1867 apparently embraced the convention that where legislative powers were granted subject to limitations the courts would enforce those limitations. The *BNA Act* was drafted and enacted in this context."…

… Thus he [Strayer] is faced with the fact that following Confederation, the Canadian courts took up the power of judicial review, and concludes that this was the result of both pre-Confederation practice and the federal character of the new constitution: "There was a continuity of judicial practice because the Imperial structure had not changed basically.… Colonial legislatures, whether Dominion or provincial, were limited legislatures, and courts could enforce the limitations." The inner logic of federalism with its distribution of legislative powers pointed to the need for something like the kind of judicial enforcement that pre-Confederation practice had established.

Strayer's search for an explanation of judicial review arises out of his insistence that it is not "absolute," that is, not fully guaranteed in the *BNA Act*. In his opinion, the relevant clauses of the *Act* gave Parliament and the local legislatures too much regulatory power over the courts to support such a view, power more in keeping with the principle of parliamentary as opposed to judicial supremacy. Indeed, according to W.R. Lederman, Strayer implies that an "element of judicial usurpation" figures in its establishment, an implication Lederman cannot accept. By contrast, Lederman reads into sections 96 to 100 of the *Act* an "intention to reproduce superior courts in the image of the English central royal courts." If he can demonstrate that these English courts had acquired a "basic independence" enabling them to withstand even the undoubted supremacy of the British Parliament, then courts deliberately modelled after them in Canada would assume a similar status. In "The Independence of the Judiciary," Lederman undertakes such a demonstration.…

… Strayer takes note of this argument and dismisses it by observing that the jurisdiction of Lederman's royal courts was subject to the British Parliament's control and that in any event it never included the power to review the validity of Parliament's acts "in spite of the pretensions of Coke and others." Canadian superior courts can hardly claim by inheritance an inviolable right of judicial review their English forebears never possessed. Lederman's rejoinder is that Canadian courts, both before and after 1867, have never faced legislatures equipped with the full supremacy of the British Parliament. Indeed, until 1931 they dealt with subordinate colonial legislatures, and while the *Statute of Westminster* substituted equality in the place of subordination, the constitution itself remained a British statute. Thus the power to review acts of subordinate bodies undertaken by Canadian courts before 1931 was well established by "history, custom, precedent and the need of federalism" and after 1931 merely continued as a matter of course.… Yet a closer examination of the framers' views may throw some light on this debate.

According to the records of the Quebec Conference edited by Joseph Pope, Macdonald alluded to the need for some form of judicial review in his initial argument on the desirability of federal union. Having put the case for a strong central government, he warned the delegates not so much of the importance of provincial governments per se but of the need of the people in each "section" to feel protected, that is, secure from the reach of an overweening central authority. One way of encouraging this feeling was to provide a guarantee of the test of legality against which centralist incursions on sectional matters might be measured. Since the new construction would take the form of a British statute, he continued, British courts could supply an answer to the question, "Is it legal or not?" The availability of some form of judicial arbitration might satisfy local partisans fearful of abandoning local autonomy to the mercies of a strong central power.

The issue was raised once more towards the end of the Quebec Conference, again in connection with the extent of jurisdiction appropriate to local governments. R.B. Dickey of Nova Scotia, expressing some sympathy for the opinion of E.B. Chandler of New Brunswick that the delegates were in danger of establishing a legislative rather than a federal union by insisting on reserving all unspecified subject matters to the central government, proposed a "Supreme Court of Appeal to decide any conflict between general and state rights." He was supported by George Brown, leader of the "Grits" in Upper Canada, who suggested that provincial courts determine jurisdictional disputes, with provision for appeal to a superior court. Both men appeared to contemplate a Canadian court of last resort on constitutional questions. Jonathan McCully of Nova Scotia, however, disputed this proposal. Throughout the Conference, he had made no bones about his preference for a legislative over a federal union, although he was prepared to accept a highly centralized form of federalism. From this perspective, he succinctly stated the difficulty posed by a constitutional court: "Mr. Brown will land us in [the] position of [the] United States by referring [the] matter of conflict of jurisdiction to [the] courts. You thus set them over the General Legislature."...

... In the Maritime provinces, even less attention was paid to the issue despite the fact that a number of anti-Confederates were sorely exercised by what they deemed the insufficiently federal character of the proposed scheme.... Their major concern was the lack of any provision for the scheme's amendment, but in an aside they observed that the "wise framers" of the American Constitution had given the Supreme Court the "power to decide all questions of jurisdiction and authority, between the general Government and those of the several States." The Quebec scheme, by contrast, did not require the establishment of any such court. Indeed, in their view, it contained no safeguards at all for the provinces in the event of conflict between their legislatures and the central Parliament. Guided by the American example, they recommended establishment of a tribunal authorized to decide disputes arising out of the division of powers. In New

Brunswick A.J. Smith, recently defeated by Tilley's pro-union party in a second election over the Confederation issue, similarly advocated "a court for the determination of questions and disputes that may arise between the Federal and Local governments as to the meaning of the Act of Union."

Such clearly worded statements indicated a view of federalism rather more in line with the American example than that set out in the Quebec scheme. Taken together with the views expressed at the Quebec Conference and in the debate in the Parliament of Canada, they also suggest that no one had any illusions about the significance of judicial review, particularly as it related to the distribution of legislative powers between Parliament and the local legislatures. The point at issue was whether the type of federalism set out in the Quebec Resolutions required it. Under the Resolutions, the central government possessed the power to disallow local laws just as the British government retained the power to disallow Parliament's enactments, a parallel feature not unnoticed by critics of the scheme like Christopher Dunkin. Disallowance not only undermined the need for judicial arbitration, whether by the Judicial Committee or a national court, it also suited partisans of parliamentary supremacy like Jonathan McCully, who clearly understood the threat to this supremacy posed by a tribunal patterned after the American Supreme Court.

The question of whether to establish a final appellate court was settled eight years after Confederation when Parliament finally used the power it possessed under section 101 of the *BNA Act*. The debate at the time is illuminating, since in picking up the threads of the earlier arguments it does so in the light of some years experience of union. It also reveals an attitude towards the new court and its power of judicial review somewhat at variance with that held today....

... While the constitutionality of the bill was generally accepted, there remained the question of members' understanding of the Court's position in relation to the central government. Here opinions varied. In introducing the bill, Fournier stressed the need for a court to settle disputes arising out of conflicting jurisdictional claims, particularly when the extent of provincial powers was in question. In this sense he portrayed the proposed court as the completion of the "young construction" established at Confederation, citing earlier remarks by Cartier and Macdonald in support of this view. Along side the notion of the court as an impartial arbiter, however, there is present in his speech the rather different view of it as a substitute for the failing remedy of disallowance. As he explained, the government was required daily to "interfere" with provincial legislation considered *ultra vires* the provinces' jurisdiction, and it was falling behind in the task. The result was that the statute books were filled with an "enormous mass of legislation" of dubious constitutionality, leaving citizens uncertain about what was and was not law. In light of this definition of the problem, namely, the excesses of provincial legislatures, the suggestion that the new court could resolve it more speedily than the central government's power of disallowance must have struck his listeners as doubtful. Indeed, it quickly became clear he was seeking legitimacy, not speed. The Governor-General, he pointed out, could disallow provincial laws only on the advice of the federal cabinet, in turn advised by law officers of the Department of Justice, and this state of affairs, predictably, was "not satisfactory." What was needed was a tribunal whose decisions – especially those adverse to the provinces – were acceptable to all parties. Apparently Fournier viewed his "independent, neutral and impartial court" as an instrument of the central government. He contended that Ottawa needed "an institution of its own" in order to ensure proper execution of its laws because, however contrary to the spirit of Confederation, the time might come when "it would not be very safe for the Federal Government to be at the mercy of the tribunals of the provinces."

Some members feared that the powers conferred on the court would conflict with the principle of parliamentary supremacy. An Ontario member, Moss, excused the length of his speech by emphasizing the gravity of establishing a tribunal whose power to determine jurisdictional disputes finally rendered it "paramount" to Parliament itself. Rejecting this view, Macdonald interpreted the Court's role under the "Special Jurisdiction" clauses as one of informing the "conscience" of the government. It would function simply as an adviser to the government in much the same way as the Judicial Committee did when asked for advice by the British Crown. Macdonald's view was consistent with Fournier's exposition of these clauses for, as noted earlier, the Minister of Justice had stated that the Court's decisions in such instances were to have the same effect as its decisions in reference questions, namely, a kind of "moral weight." Since moral weight undoubtedly influences but does not command, it would appear that for both men the supremacy of Parliament remained unimpaired. Their position seemed well grounded for neither the reference case provision nor the special jurisdiction clauses gave the new court's opinions the status of legal judgments. Yet many of their colleagues assumed that it did, especially Robert Haythorne, a Liberal senator from Prince Edward Island, who warned members that "their power of interpretation [on constitutional matters] ceased when the bill passed."

Concern over the precise nature of the Court's advisory function on constitutional questions surfaced again in discussion of the reference case clause. Moss thought it "extreme" that the Governor-General in Council might ask the court for an opinion on any matter, since this would result in the Governor-General relying on others for the advice "he ought under our system of Government to obtain from his responsible advisers." However, he was persuaded that the practice was not incompatible with responsible government on the ground that the British, the greatest authorities on responsible government, used the Judicial Committee in the same manner. Others were not so easily persuaded. Senator Haythorne argued that a ministry under pressure to exercise its power of disallowance might be tempted to refer a provincial act to the court for an opinion on its constitutionality, thus relieving itself of the burden of taking a decision and defending it before Parliament. He also thought it unwisely mixed law and politics because it substituted judicial review for disallowance, that is, a judicial ruling in the place of a political decision. From this flowed his third objection, namely, that judicial review was a greater threat to the small provinces' legislative programme than the power of disallowance since any ministry advising the Crown to exercise the latter power was required to defend publicly its advice in the Commons and, more important, the Senate, the very institution in which the provinces could expect support. The Court's opinion faced no such political test....

... Yet while both the constitution and practical necessity apparently pointed in the same direction, members of parliament clearly entertained two different views of the role of the proposed court in the very area that was thought to stand most in need of its services, namely, jurisdictional conflicts. As is evident from the above, some saw in the court an instrument of the federal government that would enable it to deal more satisfactorily with provincial pretensions. How else to interpret Senator Scott's contention?: "The fact that so many of the Acts in the different Provinces were *ultra vires* showed that a bill of this kind was necessary." The raft of suspect provincial statutes, for Scott, posed a problem for which the central government was inadequately equipped. But why was it ill equipped when it possessed the power of disallowance? As noted earlier, for Fournier the central government's problem was its inescapable partisanship. Only a court and its long-standing reputation of nonpartisanship could tame the aggression of the provinces without provoking bitter controversy. Left unstated was the assumption that the central government, by contrast, was unlikely to experience the embarrassment of an adverse ruling in its exercise of legislative power. Thus the view of the court as a tribunal whose very impartiality would serve the federal cause ignored the obvious tension between that impartiality and the central government's partisanship. The opinion of men like Macdonald that the proposed bill must not and, indeed, did not affect the principle of parliamentary supremacy simply overlooked it in favour of the central government. Had he not said that the special jurisdiction clauses were "principally for the purpose of informing the conscience of the Government"? Despite his interest in setting up the court, he was obviously unwilling to relinquish ultimate determination of the constitution to it.

At the same time, as we have seen, many supposed that the new court did signal a shift from the central government's control over the distribution of legislative powers to judicial determination of disputes arising out of it. It might be objected that this view was as incorrect as Macdonald's on the grounds that the executive's control in this respect was only partial to begin with, limited to supervision of provincial enactments through its power of disallowance, and that Parliament's own enactments in turn were subject to disallowance by the British government. Moreover, the Judicial Committee, representing the judicial mode of constitutional arbitration, had retained its position as the highest court of appeal for the new colony at the outset of Confederation. Nevertheless, it is clear that for many participants in the debate, the Court's institution spelled a retreat from the executive fiat of disallowance in favour of the judicial remedy. And they assumed, contrary to Macdonald's supposition, that its jurisdiction would extend to impugned federal as well as provincial enactments. Indeed, opponents of the court, such as Senator Kaulbach of Nova Scotia, criticized it precisely because it would "take from this Parliament the right to decide constitutional questions."…

… In the event it appears that those who subscribed to the second view were closer to the mark. Certainly the new Supreme Court agreed with them. As Strayer points out, in its first reported constitutional decision, *Severn* v. *the Queen* (1878), the court, "without showing any hesitation concerning its right to do so," found an Ontario licensing statute invalid on the ground that it interfered with Parliament's jurisdiction over trade and commerce. The following year, in *Valin* v. *Langlois*, it reviewed and upheld the *Dominion Controverted Elections Act, 1874* as a valid exercise of Parliament's legislative power. In the latter case, Chief Justice Ritchie set out the Court's power of judicial review with unmistakable clarity:

> In view of the great diversity of judicial opinion that has characterized the decisions of the provincial tribunals in some provinces, and the judges in all, while it would seem to justify the wisdom of the Dominion Parliament, in providing for the establishment of a Court of Appeal such as this, where such diversity shall be considered and an authoritative declaration of the law be enunciated, so it enhances the responsibility of those called on in the midst of such conflict of opinion to declare authoritatively the principles by which both federal and local legislation are governed.

Commenting on Ritchie's declaration, Strayer states: "And so the Canadian courts were launched on a course from which they have never swerved. The ease with which they could take up judicial review of legislation after Confederation must have been the result of the situation existing prior to 1867." He nowhere suggests that the Chief Justice might have based his understanding of the Court's role on the terms of the *Supreme Court Act* or the expectations of many of those who participated in its passage four years earlier. But then, as indicated earlier, Strayer pays little attention to the debate surrounding its passage. Thus he is open to Lederman's charge, namely, that his argument implies an assumption of judicial review on the part of the court, an assumption possibly unwarranted. Yet Lederman too ignores the very debate in the light of which Ritchie's view is surely intelligible. The Chief Justice clearly favoured the side of those who, like Moss, thought that the proposed court would be able "to determine the [constitutional] controversy finally, virtually therefore, the Supreme Court could overrule the decisions of this legislature."

Although the Chief Justice's generous conception of the court's role in constitutional matters reaffirmed both the hopes and fears of those who supposed its decisions would be as authoritative as he claimed they were, the notion of the court as an instrument of the central government was not wholly eliminated. There remained the reference case provision of the *Supreme Court Act* which obliged the court to advise the executive on any question referred to it. To the extent that this obligation is understood as an executive advisory function as opposed to a judicial one, it recalls Macdonald's view of the court as an aid to the government, or the "conscience" of the government. If so, it is hardly surprising that the provinces were uncomfortable with the comprehensiveness of the reference case provision, especially since it enabled the government to refer provincial laws to the courts for a ruling on their validity. In the event, Parliament's competence to enact it was tested before the Judicial Committee in *Attorney-General for Ontario* v. *Attorney-General for Canada* (1912). The provinces choosing to intervene argued that it imposed an executive function on the court and thereby violated section 101 of the *BNA Act* which permitted Parliament to establish a tribunal possessed of judicial powers only. In his judgment delivered on behalf of the Judicial Committee, Earl Loreburn, L.C., appeared to accept their contention that the Court's task in the reference case was in essence merely advisory and therefore nonjudicial, but he did not consider this fatal to its judicial character as a whole.

The competing views of the court apparent at its inception have left their mark on it. For example, those who approve its role as umpire of the federal system are critical of the fact that its establishment was permitted rather than required under the terms of the *BNA Act*, that its members are appointed formally by one level of government rather than both, and that the reference case procedure remains. On the other hand, partisans of parliamentary supremacy, understandably less enamoured of the American Supreme Court whose example inspired the criticisms just mentioned, prize these very features as symbols of the Court's ultimate dependence on the will of Parliament. This tension between the court's judicial independence and the claims of the executive figures in the debate between Lederman and Strayer. Lederman, seeking to strengthen and reaffirm its independence, prefers to locate the origins of its power of judicial review in both the tradition of the old English royal courts and the logic of federalism, that is, beyond the reach of Parliament. Thus the intentions of legislators who founded the Court are of little interest to him. By ignoring them, he avoids confronting not only the view of those who supposed they were withholding the full power of judicial review but, more important, the opinion of those who assumed that Parliament could confer it. As a result, he overlooks the possibility that judicial review was deliberately, if tentatively, advanced as a remedy for the failing power of disallowance. In short, since Lederman wishes to secure judicial review, he cannot derive it from anything so precarious as legislators' intentions. This leaves him open to the criticism implied in Strayer's thesis. Strayer, much more sensitive to the claims of the executive, highlights the limitations on the Court's power to review legislative enactments. Yet he is left with the new Court's easy assumption of the power, and since he too disregards the debate surrounding its establishment he looks beyond Parliament to past colonial practice. Thus he does not see the tension between judicial review and executive claims which he ably expands as a reflection of clashing legislative intentions.

Viewed in the light of the older controversy about the Court, the debate culminating in the recent set of amendments contained in the *Constitution Act, 1982* took a familiar turn. In the earlier contest, both opponents and partisans of judicial review focussed attention on its implications for the distribution of legislative powers so critical to the shape of the country's federalism. While some saw in it a solution to conflicts arising out of competing jurisdictional claims, others interpreted it as a direct challenge to their presumption in favour of Parliament's control of the constitution. Over a century later, the issue of judicial versus parliamentary supremacy surfaced again in connection with the proposed *Charter of Rights and Freedoms*. Prime Minister Pierre Trudeau, a determined champion of the notion of a charter, often defended his cause without even referring to the task it necessarily imposes on the courts. Instead, he claimed that it would "confer power on the people of Canada, power to protect themselves from abuses by public authorities." A charter would liberate people by preventing governments from denying specified freedoms. On the other hand, opponents of the idea, like the then Premier of Saskatchewan, Allan Blakeney, attempted to counter the undeniable appeal of this claim by drawing attention to the role of the courts that it implied. According to Blakeney, including rights in a written constitution means transferring responsibility for them from duly elected legislatures, the democratic seat of governments, to nonelected tribunals. It amounts to requiring the courts to make "social judgments" in the course of interpreting a charter's clauses, judgments which, in his view, properly belong to "the voters and their representatives." In the event, a *Charter of Rights and Freedoms* now forms part of Canada's newly amended constitution. Are we entitled to conclude, then, that acceptance of the *Charter*, and the increased scope for judicial review that it entails, signals a resolution of the issue of parliamentary versus judicial supremacy in favour of the latter? The answer is not quite.

It is true, as Peter Russell points out, that section 52 of the *Constitution Act, 1982*, by declaring the Constitution of Canada to be the "supreme law" and any law inconsistent with its provisions to be of "no force or effect," gives the courts' power to invalidate unconstitutional laws an explicit constitutional footing for the first time. Further, under the provisions of the new amending formula, the composition of the Supreme Court is protected from easy change by the stringent requirement of unanimity on the part of the Senate, the House of Commons and provincial legislative assemblies. The Court is also listed under section 42(1) as an item that can be amended only in accordance with the general formula set out in section 38(1). Thus the court is constitutionally entrenched. However, neither the federal government's power to appoint Supreme Court justices nor the nonjudicial advisory task required by the reference mechanism is affected. More important still is the fact that the *Charter* itself, to the disappointment of its partisans, contains a provision enabling the legislative bodies of both levels of government to override some of its guarantees, namely, those dealing with fundamental freedoms, legal rights and equality rights. The provision is qualified to the extent that legislatures choosing to avail themselves of it are required to declare expressly their intention and reconsider the matter every five years, and there has been speculation about the likely effect of these qualifications on politicians' willingness to resort to the "override." Nevertheless, its very appearance in the the context of the *Charter* strikes an incongruous note and is testimony to the strength of the lingering tradition of parliamentary supremacy. Finally, there is the first clause of the *Charter* which subjects its guarantees to "such reasonable limits prescribed by law as can be demonstrably justified in a free and democratic society." Ultimately it is up to the Supreme Court to stake out the "reasonable limits." In the meantime, we do know that they are held to exist, that there is thought to be something higher than, or beyond the *Charter*'s guarantees to which appeal can be made in order to justify their denial or restriction. And the initiative in this regard is secured to governments. While the courts' power of judicial review has undoubtedly surmounted the rather narrow, partisan function envisaged for the new Supreme Court in 1875 by Macdonald, the principle of parliamentary supremacy persists.

10.2

The "Living Tree" Approach to Interpreting the *BNA Act*
Lord Sankey, *The "Persons" Case*, Judicial Committee of the Privy Council, (1928).

... The *British North America Act* planted in Canada a living tree capable of growth and expansion within its natural limits. The object of the *Act* was to grant a Constitution to Canada. "Like all written constitutions it has been subject to development through usage and convention."

Their Lordships do not conceive it to be the duty of this Board – it is certainly not their desire – to cut down the provisions of the *Act* by a narrow and technical construction, but rather to give it a large and liberal interpretation so that the Dominion to a great extent, but within certain fixed limits, may be mistress in her own house, as the Provinces to a great extent, but within certain fixed limits, are mistresses in theirs.

10.3

The "Watertight Compartments" Approach
to Interpreting the *BNA Act*

Lord Atkin, *Labour Conventions Case*, Judicial Committee of the Privy Council (1937).

… It must not be thought that the result of this decision is that Canada is incompetent to legislate in performance of treaty obligations. In totality of legislative powers, Dominion and Provincial together, she is fully equipped. But the legislative powers remain distributed, and if in the exercise of her new functions derived from her new international status Canada incurs obligations they must, so far as legislation be concerned, when they deal with Provincial classes of subjects, be dealt with by the totality of powers, in other words by cooperation between the Dominion and the Provinces. While the ship of state now sails on larger ventures and into foreign waters she still retains the watertight compartments which are an essential part of her original structure. The Supreme Court was equally divided and therefore the formal judgment could only state the opinions of the three judges on either side. Their Lordships are of opinion that the answer to the three questions should be that the *Act* in each case is *ultra vires* of the Parliament of Canada, and they will humbly advise His Majesty accordingly.

10.4

The *Anti-Inflation* Case:
The Anatomy of a Constitutional Decision

Peter H. Russell

Canadian Public Administration, 20 (1977), 632–65. Reprinted with permission.

The Supreme Court of Canada's decision in July, 1976 on the constitutional validity of the federal *Anti-Inflation Act* was probably the Court's most heralded decision since it became Canada's final court of appeal in 1949. For the first time since 1949 a major national policy, upon which the federal government placed the highest priority, was challenged before the Court. Also, this was the first clear test of whether the Supreme Court would "liberate" the federal Parliament's general power to make laws for the "peace, order and good government of Canada" from the shackles placed upon it by the Privy Council's jurisprudence and thereby provide the constitutional underpinning for a revolutionary readjustment of the balance of power in Canadian federalism. And it was the first major constitutional case for a Supreme Court headed by Chief Justice Bora Laskin, who during his academic career had earned a reputation as Canada's leading authority on constitutional law and as an articulate critic of the Privy Council. All in all, the case appeared to be a showdown.

The outcome may seem rather anti-climactic. The federal government's wage and price control policy escaped a judicial veto. But the Court's decision gave it only a temporary and conditional constitutional mandate. More importantly, the Court did not endorse the expansive interpretation of Parliament's general power which a generation of central-minded commentators had hoped for as much as a generation of provincially-minded Canadians had feared.

Instead, the Court as a whole could agree only on the Judicial Committee of the Privy Council's "emergency doctrine," while its majority appeared to endorse a novel and unLaskin-like way of interpreting the peace, order and good government clause.

To understand the significance of these results, the case must be placed in both its legal and political settings. By so doing we may learn something about the nature of judicial review in Canada. Among other things, the case demonstrates the limited importance of judicial review in the politics of Canadian federalism. The Court's decision may signal that a constitutional revolution is not about to occur, but the decision itself is far from being the major factor in preventing such a centralizing shift in the balance of power. The case also reveals how paradoxically political the process of judicial review can be in Canada even though the end product – the opinions of the judges – is cast in a relatively legalistic style. Above all, the case teaches us a good deal about the interaction of law and politics. The main lesson is clear: politicians and interest groups will risk losses in terms of long-run constitutional doctrine in order to secure important short-run policy objectives, although in the process they may try their best to minimize or obscure their constitutional losses.

The Constitutional Stakes

On October 14, 1975 the federal government unveiled the new anti-inflation program. The program had four main prongs, only one of which was highly controversial and required new legislation. This was a scheme to control prices and wages in certain key sectors of the economy. The Liberal party had vigorously opposed a Conservative party proposal for wage and price controls in the federal election fifteen months earlier. But now Mr. Trudeau's government was apparently convinced that this was a policy whose time had come. Legal authority for the wage and price control policy was contained in the *Anti-Inflation Act* which became law December 15, 1975 (with retroactive effect to October 14, 1975) and in the detailed regulations or "guidelines" promulgated on December 22, 1975.

It was clear from the start that there was a good deal at stake constitutionally in the enactment of this legislation. The *Anti-Inflation Act* purported to give the federal government regulatory authority over prices, profit margins and wages in selected areas of the private sector: construction firms with twenty or more employees, other firms with five hundred or more employees, and professionals. The *Act* applied directly to the federal public sector, and it authorized the government to enter into agreements with the provinces to apply the program to the provincial public sectors. Normally most of the economic relations which the federal *Act* purported to regulate in the private sector are under exclusive provincial jurisdiction. Since the *Snider* case in 1925, labour relations has been treated as a field of divided jurisdiction, with federal authority confined to the limited number of activities which can be brought under specific heads of federal power. A long series of judicial decisions, beginning with the *Parsons* case in 1881, gave the provinces the lion's share of regulatory power over business and commercial transactions in the province. The only earlier peacetime attempt to control prices and profit levels on a national basis had been ruled unconstitutional by the Judicial Committee of the Privy Council of the *Board of Commerce* case [1922].

On what constitutional basis then could the federal government hope to rest the *Anti-Inflation Act*? The federal trade and commerce power which would be the basis of federal authority for such legislation in the United States was not a very likely possibility in Canada. "Interprovincial or international" as the main criterion of the trade and commerce which the federal Parliament can regulate has been narrowly interpreted in Canada, and the *Act* made no gestures toward focusing its impact primarily on activities of an interprovincial or international character. Thus, it was the federal Parliament's general power "to make laws for the peace, order and good government of Canada" which appeared to be the only constitutional basis for the *Act*, and it was in the possibility of successfully invoking the general power for this purpose that a revolution in constitutional doctrine was in the making.

Constitutional case-law had produced two rival conceptions of what could sufficiently magnify legislative matter normally subject to provincial jurisdiction to bring them under the general or residual power of the national Parliament: the emergency doctrine and the test of inherent national importance. The emergency doctrine was authored by Viscount Haldane of the Judicial Committee of the Privy Council in the 1920s, and, with but one clear exception, consistently followed by that tribunal until the end of its regime as Canada's highest court. The doctrine's only positive application was to justify the virtually unlimited scope of national power in time of war and postwar transition. Beyond war, the Judicial Committee's vision of emergencies serious enough to set aside the normal distribution of powers and invoke the general power had been limited to such possibilities as "famines," "epidemics of pestilence" or a drastic outbreak of the "evil of intemperance." Economic crisis – even the need for a national scheme of unemployment insurance during the Depression – failed to meet the Judicial Committee's standard of necessity. Further, it appeared that the presumption of constitutionality which attached to war-related legislation did not apply to *permanent* peacetime measures. With the former, the onus of proof rested with the opponents of the legislation who would have to adduce "… very clear evidence that an emergency has not arisen, or that the emergency no longer exists…," whereas, with the latter, the supporters of the legislation would have to provide "evidence that the standard of necessity … has been reached."

In 1946 Viscount Simon in the *Canada Temperance Federation* case wrote an opinion which offered a much wider conception of peace, order and good government than Haldane's emergency test. In dismissing Ontario's attempt to have the Privy Council overrule *Russell* v. *The Queen* (the Privy Council's earliest decision finding federal legislation constitutional on the basis of peace, order and good government), Viscount Simon held that the Dominion Parliament could not legislate in matters which are exclusively within the competence of the provincial legislature "merely because of the existence of an emergency." The "true test" for determining whether the national legislature may assume jurisdiction over matters which are normally provincial "… must be found in the real subject matter of the legislation: if it is such that it goes beyond local or provincial concern or interest and must from its inherent nature be the concern of the Dominion as a whole … then it will fall within the competence of the Dominion Parliament as a matter affecting the peace, order and good government of Canada.…" This holding seemed to return the interpretation of peace, order and good government to the pre-Haldane formula of national dimensions of concern enunciated by Lord Watson in 1896, namely "… that some matters, in their origin local and provincial, might attain such dimensions as to affect the body politic of the Dominion, and to justify the Canadian Parliament in passing laws for their regulation or abolition in the interest of the Dominion." On its face this inherent national importance or national dimensions conception of peace, order and good government appeared to offer the federal government a much wider opportunity to exercise regulatory power in peacetime on more than a temporary basis in areas normally reserved to the provinces.

Court decisions after 1946 were not conclusive as to whether the Haldane emergency doctrine had been superseded by the wider notion of national dimensions. On the two occasions after 1946 when the Privy Council dealt with peace, order and good government it ignored Simon's opinion. The Supreme Court's decision in the *Johannesson* case in 1952 provided the only strong endorsement of Viscount Simon's national importance test. On two subsequent occasions in the 1960s, the Supreme Court employed the vocabulary of "national importance" in upholding federal jurisdiction over the national capital and offshore mineral rights. But in neither case was the Court reviewing a major scheme of federal regulation in an area normally under provincial jurisdiction. Even in *Johannesson*, though the Court sustained the paramountcy of federal control over aeronautics in part on national importance grounds, it was dealing with a regulatory scheme which had been in place for several decades and which could find a large measure of constitutional support in other heads of federal power.

So, coming down to the *Anti-Inflation* case, a large question mark still hung over the peace, order and good government power. That for three decades there had been so little Court action on this issue had much to do with the fact that even during the most centralist years of this period the federal government had relied primarily on its spending power rather than regulatory schemes for carrying out policy initiatives in areas normally under provincial jurisdiction. But inflationary pressures in the 1970s might force the federal government to shift from spending programs to regulatory schemes. Such a shift, as several political scientists have suggested, would increase the occasions for judicial review. Thus, as the federal government in the fall of 1975 moved toward the implementation of a fairly comprehensive scheme of price and wage controls, the question in constitutional law of whether the peace, order and good government clause would provide a basis for national regulation of broad areas of economic and social activity took on more than academic importance.

Political and Legal Strategies of the Parties

With these constitutional stakes in the background, it is interesting to examine the approach taken by the federal and provincial governments and the major interest groups to the constitutional implications of the anti-inflation program. Turning first to the federal government, we find a significant difference between the political and legal aspects of its behaviour. Politically, Prime Minister Trudeau endeavoured to present the program as an exercise in cooperative federalism. The day before the program was presented to Parliament, the ten provincial premiers came to Ottawa to discuss the program. That night, in his address to the nation on radio and television, Mr. Trudeau said that he had asked the premiers "to join as full partners in the attack upon inflation." During this period Mr. Trudeau tended to be somewhat on the optimistic side in referring to the extent to which the provinces supported federal wage and price controls. Following the first ministers meeting on 13 October, a number of premiers reserved any commitment of support for the program until they had reviewed the matter with their provincial cabinets. Ten days later federal and provincial finance and labour ministers met in Ottawa and following their meeting, Mr. Macdonald, the federal Minister of Finance, announced that "No province declared that it is opposed to the programme or will refuse to cooperate." The next day Mr. Macdonald reported in a more positive vein to the House of Commons: apparently all of the provincial governments were now "prepared to support the program and cooperate."

While, on the political front, the federal government proceeded on the assumption that provincial cooperation was a political imperative, the *Anti-Inflation Act* was drafted as if the federal Parliament had full legislative power to proceed with such a program on its own. Section 3 of the *Act* authorizing the federal government to establish guidelines for the restraint of prices and wages in the private and public sectors made no concessions to any constitutional limitations on the scope of Parliament's regulatory power. It is true that the next section of the *Act* exempted a province's public sector unless the provincial government entered into an agreement to apply the *Act* to its public sector. But the implication was that this "opting in" device was entirely dependent on the will of the federal Parliament, and that Parliament, if it had preferred, could have applied the program directly to the provincial public sectors. This implication became explicit later on when the federal government came to defend Ontario's "opting in" Agreement before the Supreme Court. In the absence of any provincial legislation authorizing this Agreement, the only legislative authority for the Agreement was provided by the federal *Act* and, indeed, federal lawyers asserted the power of the federal Parliament to bind the provincial Crown and regulate the provincial public service.

More important than this is the evidence that the *Anti-Inflation Act* was drafted so as to preserve the possibility of basing the legislation on a constitutional foundation wider than the emergency doctrine. Nowhere did the *Act* speak the language of national emergency. Instead, the preamble referred to inflation as "a matter of serious national concern," language clearly suggesting Viscount Simon's approach to peace, order and good government in the *Canada Temperance Federation* case. The only mark of emergency or crisis legislation on the face of the *Act* was its penultimate section limiting its duration to three years unless Parliament agreed to an extension. Statements by government spokesmen in Parliament made it clear that the omission of any reference to a state of emergency was deliberate. Both Mr. Diefenbaker for the Conservatives and Mr. Brewin for the NDP questioned the government on the constitutional propriety of proceeding without a declaration of an emergency. Mr. Trudeau answered this question with rather vague references to alternative constitutional bases for the *Act* such as "the banking power" and "the commerce power." Mr. Macdonald gave a much clearer picture of the government's constitutional assumptions in his evidence to the Standing Committee on Finance, Trade and Economic Affairs:

> The opinion of the government on constitutionality is based on some cases that were pleaded before the Judicial Committee on [sic] the Privy Council in 1946, for instance *The Canada Temperance Federation* case, and, since then before the Supreme Court, *Thamieson and St. Paul*, and *Munro* and the *National Capital Commission*. Accordingly, when we have a scheme that goes beyond reasons that are strictly local, provincial or private, when you have a national scheme like this one, there can be a federal jurisdiction under which to legislate on these matters.

Of course, by the *"Thamieson case"* Mr. Macdonald meant *Johannesson* v. *West*

St. Paul in which the Supreme Court had made its most significant application of the "inherent national importance" test of peace, order and good government.

Now, with the federal government playing something of a double game, how did the provinces respond to the constitutional issue? Briefly, because they saw that it was not in their political interests at the time to oppose the federal program, they agreed not to raise the constitutional issue. However, because they wished to avoid conceding constitutional power to Ottawa, they were careful not to commit themselves to any particular view of the *Act's* constitutional validity. At this stage it was in the interests of both levels of government to suppress the constitutional issue. Apparently the constitutional issue was discussed at the federal-provincial meetings concerning the anti-inflation program, and the federal leaders felt free to declare after these meetings that the provinces would not challenge Parliament's jurisdiction to enact the *Anti-Inflation Bill*. But, as with so much that happens at meetings of this kind, we do not know in what terms the constitutional issue was discussed. My own guess is that the constitutional discussion was kept at a pretty vague level and that there was just enough reference to the temporary nature of the legislation and the provision of an opting in mechanism for the provinces to set aside, at least for the time being, any reservations of a constitutional nature.

The provinces kept their word. They did not exercise the right which all of them have to refer the question of the *Act's* constitutionality directly to the courts. All, in varying ways, took steps to bring their public sectors into the program. But, nonetheless, they kept their constitutional options open and, as we shall see, when the constitutional issue was forced before the Supreme Court, a number of them attacked the broad grounds upon which the federal government tried to defend this legislation. In the legal instrument authorizing provincial participation, it is notable that Quebec, of all the provinces, was most careful to concede as little as possible to federal legislative authority. Thus, Quebec's Agreement not only established the province's own Inflation Control Commission to administer guidelines for the public sector "in consultation with" the federal Anti-Inflation Board, but further gave the province's consent to have the guidelines apply to the private sector. Quebec's submission to the Supreme Court subsequently made it clear that in the province's view, even in the context of an emergency, federal regulation of the provincial private sector of the economy could not take effect without provincial consent.

If the federal and provincial governments were the only agencies for initiating judicial review, there would probably not have been an *Anti-Inflation* case. In Canada, only the federal and provincial governments have access to the most direct means of bringing questions before the courts – the reference procedure. Private litigants can raise constitutional issues in the courts only when they are plaintiff or defendant in normal litigation, and Canadian courts have tended to be relatively stringent in granting "standing" to raise such issues. [*Ed.Note:* This is no longer accurate. See Reading 6.2.]One of the interesting features of the *Anti-Inflation* case is that it was the persistence of private interest groups, namely a number of trade unions, in trying to challenge the constitutional validity of the anti-inflation program through normal litigation which eventually persuaded the federal government to resort to the reference device and bring the issue directly before the Supreme Court.

It is particularly interesting that organized labour rather than business interests were responsible for initiating the constitutional challenge to the anti-inflation program. Traditionally, organized labour has favoured strengthening rather than weakening the capacity of the federal government to deal with national and international economic forces. But once labour representatives perceived what in their view was the unjust character of the federal program, they began to oppose it vigorously, and soon after its introduction officials of the Canadian Labour Congress announced their intention to challenge the program in the courts. There is no indication that union leaders had any qualms about the long-run constitutional consequences if their court action was successful. The attack through the courts was adopted as simply one of the means for conducting the anti-control campaign. However, it should be noted that the grounds upon which the CLC initially proposed to base its challenge were that the controls program was too selective to meet the national dimensions test and that provinces could not turn over their legislative jurisdiction to the federal authority by order-in-council. While these arguments did not so clearly threaten the scope of federal authority, those which union counsel subsequently used before the Supreme Court were much more anti-centralist.

It was not easy for those labour groups who wished to challenge the constitutional validity of the anti-inflation program to gain access to the courts. The most direct means of appealing an order of the Anti-Inflation Administrator to the Appeal Tribunal (and from there to the Federal Court of Canada) was available only to employers. This deficiency in the *Act* was eventually remedied but not until after the federal government had made the reference to the Supreme Court. The legal actions which eventually provoked the reference all involved unions in Ontario resisting the application of the controls to collective agreements they were in the process of negotiating. The most significant of these, in terms of bringing the constitutional issue before the courts, was that of the Renfrew County branch of the Ontario Secondary School Teachers Federation. In November, 1975, the Renfrew teachers had signed a collective agreement with the Renfrew County Board of Education for an amount considerably in excess of the anti-inflation guidelines. This settlement was made pursuant to the result of binding arbitration under Ontario legislation. The arbitration award had been made two weeks after the introduction of the anti-inflation program. On February 10, 1976, the Anti-Inflation Board notified the teachers and the Board that the settlement should be reduced. Six days later the teachers' federation applied to the Divisional Court of the Supreme Court of Ontario for a declaration that Ontario's Agreement with the federal government bringing its public sector under the anti-inflation program was invalid on the ground that the Order-in-Council authorizing the Agreement had been made without the necessary legislation by the province. It is doubtful whether this legal strategy would have worked because the Federal Court of Canada has exclusive jurisdiction to grant declaratory relief. On the same day that the Renfrew teachers submitted their application to Ontario's Supreme Court, a Board of Arbitration in another Ontario labour dispute (this time involving the University of Toronto and a local of the Canadian Union of Public Employees representing the University's library technicians) ruled that it was not bound by actions of the Anti-Inflation Board.

Apparently it was these two developments which convinced the Attorney-General of Ontario, Mr. Roy McMurtry, that in order to avoid a lengthy and uncertain period of litigation he should ask the federal Minister of Justice to refer the issue to the Supreme Court. There were possibly other factors which influenced Mr. McMurtry. The Ontario government had entered into its Agreement with the federal government without any approval from the provincial legislature. The Agreements of all the other provinces except Newfoundland's had some legislative sanction. The Davis government wished to avoid the legislature because it was in a minority there and both opposition parties indicated they would oppose the government on the controls issue. But by February of 1976, the Ontario Liberals under Mr. Stuart Smith's leadership had shown that they did not want an election in the near future and so for the time being they would not use their balance of power in the legislature to defeat the government. Thus, Mr. McMurtry had some assurance that if the Ontario Agreement was ruled invalid by the Supreme Court he could go back to the legislature and with support from a compliant Mr. Smith obtain the necessary approval for the Agreement. This assurance was important, as the validity of the Ontario Agreement was a much more dubious proposition than was the validity of the federal *Act*.

On March 12, the federal Minister of Justice, Mr. Basford, announced that the federal cabinet had approved an order-in-council referring the question of the federal *Act*'s constitutional validity and of the Ontario Agreement's validity to the Supreme Court of Canada. It was, he said, the Renfrew teachers' action which prompted this decision,

> Because the whole thing (the anti-inflation programme) is vulnerable to such challenges and because the work of the nation must go on we have decided to avoid time-consuming litigation over issues like this which ultimately would have to be decided by the Supreme Court anyway.

We might also speculate that Mr. Basford's government, with its program well in place and having secured the cooperation of all the provinces, could now contemplate judicial review of the *Anti-Inflation Act* with a fair degree of confidence.

The Reference: The Parties and their Submissions

The use of Canada's extraordinary reference procedure in the circumstances outlined above illustrates one of the advantages of this device. Once it was reasonably certain that judicial review would occur through private litigation, it was in the government's interest to remove as quickly as possible the legal clouds surrounding the program – especially a program which was encountering considerable resistance from those whose behaviour it was supposed to regulate. In the alternative, if the unions had found their access to the courts completely blocked, the reference would compensate for the relative disadvantage which citizens or private groups are under in obtaining judicial review in Canada and give the unions an opportunity to establish their constitutional rights before the country's highest tribunal.

But the disadvantages of the reference procedure have been advertised just as much as its advantages. The primary criticism has been that the procedure forces judges to make decisions about the constitutional validity of government policies in a highly abstract and hypothetical manner divorced from any consideration of the factual context which gave rise to the legislation and in which the real effect of the legislation may be revealed. Added to this is the fear that such a procedure, by bringing statutes to court "… in the very flush of enactment, while the feelings that produced them were at their highest pitch …" may unduly politicize the process of judicial review and force the judges to participate in a political controversy in a way which will ultimately weaken their authority. It is instructive to review the conduct of the *Anti-inflation Reference* in the light of these criticism and concerns.

Certainly, the questions submitted to the court by the Reference Order were presented in the barest possible way:

1.   Is the *Anti-Inflation Act ultra vires* the Parliament of Canada either in whole or in part, and, if so, in what particulars and to what extent?
2.   If the *Anti-Inflation Act* is in *ultra vires* the Parliament of Canada, is the Agreement entitled "Between the Government of Canada and the Government of the Province of Ontario," entered into on January 13, 1976 effective under the *Anti-Inflation Act* to render that *Act* binding on, and the Anti-Inflation Guidelines made thereunder applicable to, the provincial public sector in Ontario as defined in the Agreement?

The reference itself was not accompanied by any factual material describing the situation which gave rise to the legislation or details concerning the implementation of the Anti-Inflation program. However, procedures were soon set in motion to provide the basic ingredients of a law case – adversaries and their submissions – and make the decision-making process less like an academic seminar and more like the adjudication of a concrete dispute.

There was no difficulty in obtaining parties to argue all sides of both questions. The federal government, of course, would appear in support of the legislation. All the provinces were notified of the hearing but only five decided to participate: Ontario, Quebec, British Columbia and Saskatchewan in support of the legislation (although for the latter three this "support" turned out to be qualified indeed) and Alberta in direct opposition. Alberta would be joined by five unions (or groups of unions) who were considered to have distinct interests at stake in the proceedings. This labour representation included the Ontario teachers and public service unions which had been attempting to litigate the constitutional issues in Ontario courts, the Canadian Labour Congress which had been pressing for judicial review since the introduction of the *Act* and one major international union, the United Steel Workers of America. Thus, the reference procedure, compensating for the relatively cautious policy of Canadian courts in granting access to the judicial process, enabled the major political contestants to do battle in the judicial arena. But the Supreme Court was not prepared to go all the way in the "politicization" of its process and drew the line at political parties, declining to give permission to the Ontario NDP to appear as an interested party.

The material submitted by these parties compensated, in part, for the bareness of the reference questions. Some of it also posed a severe challenge to the Supreme Court's jurisprudential style. Non-legal material such as the "Brandeis brief" prepared by social scientists and designed to support propositions about the social or economic background and implications of legislation has not played an important role in the Canadian Supreme Court's decision-making. This is not because there is any rule formally proscribing such material. It has stemmed primarily from the character of jurisprudence favoured by Canadian judges and lawyers. In constitutional interpretation, as in other areas, Canadian jurists have been most comfortable with a highly conceptual approach in which the focus is on applying definitions of legal categories to the words of the statute with little or no reference to the empirical meaning of this exercise. But in the *Anti-Inflation* case some of the counsel came from a younger generation of lawyers imbued with the example of modern American constitutional jurisprudence which has been far more receptive to social science material. The Chief Justice of the Court both as an academic and a judge had stressed the importance of empirical evidence in constitutional interpretation. Also, one of the basic questions in the case – whether inflation in Canada had become a matter of inherent national importance or a national emergency – seemed to be essentially an empirical issue. Thus, it is not surprising that the Court's reception and use of socio-economic material as an "extrinsic aid" to constitutional interpretation became one of the most significant features of the case.

About a month after the Reference Order was issued, Chief Justice Laskin met with counsel for the various parties to consider some of the procedural issues. On April 6, at the conclusion of this hearing, the Chief Justice made a number of rulings: application to join the proceedings as an interested party would be accepted up until April 15; the Attorney-General of Canada was to prepare the "case" (the material submitted by the appellant in an appeal which would normally include full documentation of the proceedings in the lower courts), which here was to include the federal government's White Paper and any other materials the Attorney-General considered appropriate; the parties were to file their factums (the written briefs setting out each party's arguments on the various issues) by May 10, and could "annex supplementary material" to their factums; parties would have a short period (until May 21) in which to submit additional material in reply to material filed by other parties; the oral hearing of the case would begin on May 31, 1976. These rulings gave an opportunity to all the parties to submit whatever empirical argumentation they wished and met one of the traditional complaints against this type of material by giving the parties an opportunity to prepare written replies to their adversaries' submissions. However, the Chief Justice could not make any commitment as to weight which the Court would give any of this material in reaching its final conclusion.

It is interesting to see how the various parties responded to this opportunity. Only the Canadian Labour Congress annexed supplementary material to its factum. This took the form of a 64-page brief written by Richard G. Lipsey, professor of economics at Queen's University. A group of 38 economists who had been attacking the controls program outside of the judicial arena supported the Lipsey brief. Their telegrams of support were added to the CLC material. Professor Lipsey's study advanced the argument that it was very far-fetched to regard the state of the Canadian economy when controls were introduced as an "economic crisis." This argument was supported both by absolute considerations (inflation is primarily redistributive in its effects so that *average* living standards are not lowered) and, perhaps more impressively, by comparative data showing, for instance, that compared both with other periods in Canadian history and with the economic situation of Canada's major trading partners the level of inflation in the fall of 1975 was not extraordinary. Professor Lipsey concluded that:

> It seems hard to believe that the inflation-unemployment problem is unique in its degree of seriousness.... If it is held that this problem constitutes an economic crisis, then it is hard to avoid the conclusion that economies are nearly always in states of "economic crises." If this kind of "economic crisis" justified the use of extraordinary measures, these extraordinary measures may be nearly always justified.

In the light of the Supreme Court's final holding, this is a very significant conclusion. Professor Lipsey's study also attacked the efficacy of the controls program in reducing inflation. Given the strict taboo in our legal tradition against courts reviewing the wisdom of legislation, this, I believe, was a serious tactical mistake and made it easier for the judges to discount the Lipsey brief.

The only other material of this kind was submitted by the federal government and the Province of Ontario. The "case" material prepared by the Attorney-General of Canada included, in addition to the White Paper requested by the Chief Justice (which nowhere referred to the existence of a "crisis" or "emergency"), the monthly bulletin of Statistics Canada showing fluctuations in the consumer price index up to September, 1975. In reply to the Lipsey brief, the Attorneys-General of Canada and Ontario both submitted additional material. The federal submission was a copy of an after-dinner speech delivered by the Governor of the Bank of Canada, Gerald K. Bouey, a month before controls were introduced. The speech stressed the seriousness of inflation but was in no sense a counter-analysis to Professor Lipsey's brief. But Ontario's additional material, prepared by the province's Office of Economic Analysis, did attempt a direct rebuttal of Lipsey's main argument. It challenged neither the accuracy of his data nor his technical economics, but (on Galbraithian grounds) it questioned his judgment that the severity of Canada's existing economic problems could be expected nearly always to prevail from now on. Perhaps most significantly, it argued that the question of whether or not a "crisis" exists cannot be answered by technical economics but by public opinion polls (although it cited no actual poll results on this question).

While empirical considerations were more prominent than is usually the case in constitutional references, the arguments which predominated in both the written factums and the oral hearing were still essentially legal in character. These arguments were put to the Court by as impressive an array of legal talent as has ever been assembled for a constitutional case. Among the group of participating lawyers were the federal government's counsel, Mr. J.J. Robinette, whom many regard as the outstanding advocate currently practising in Canada, a number of constitutional scholars including a dean, an ex-dean, and a dean elect of law, some of the country's ablest labour and civil rights lawyers, perhaps the most dynamic Attorney-General and Deputy Attorney-General in Canada, as well as some of the leading members of the youngest generation of Canadian lawyers. Certainly it would be difficult to contend that the outcome of this case was influenced by the fact that one or the other side was badly argued. This is important because the strictly adversarial dimension of the proceedings is probably more significant in the Canadian Supreme Court than it is, for instance, in the United States Supreme Court, where the time allowed for oral argument is very limited. In typical Canadian fashion our Supreme Court procedure combines the written American brief (called factums in Canada) with the English emphasis on virtually unlimited time for oral argument. In this case the oral hearing ran for a full week and it is likely that the way in which the adversarial exchange in the courtroom structured the issues had more to do with the Court's final decision than would be the case in the United States.

The Ontario Agreement was defended only by counsel for Ontario and the federal government. The other provinces did not make submission on this question. The unions all vigorously attacked the Agreement's validity. The Ontario unions were able to use the concrete situations which had been the original basis for their litigation as illustrations of the extent to which the Agreement altered the basic law regulating collective bargaining in Ontario. This added considerable strength to their proposition that an executive Agreement without any legislative sanction which purported to set aside existing legislation was a clear violation of the principle of responsible government. The main defence of the Agreement did not contend that the federal *Act* had actually provided the legislative sanction for the Ontario Agreement. Instead it relied primarily on precedents of executive agreements and contracts for which there had been no specific legislative authorization. Nonetheless one of the Canadian Labour Congress counsel, P.W. Hogg, argued that in a federal system of dual sovereignty there must be a basic immunity of the Provincial Crown which would set some limit on federal authority to regulate the remuneration of the provincial civil service directly under ministers of the Crown – even in an emergency, and yes, even during a war. This contention clearly shocked a number of judges, and one was heard to exclaim that "if the argument had any validity it would ultimately deny the existence of a Canadian Nation."

On the issues associated with the first question concerning the *Anti-Inflation Act*'s constitutional validity, the alignment of the parties was revealing. The federal position before the Court was the most predictable. It reflected the double game which the federal government had been playing from the start on the peace, order and good government issue. Ottawa was fairly confident that the *Act* could at the very least be sustained as emergency legislation and its counsel now put forward the emergency use of the general power as a basis for the legislation – *but only as a fall back position.* The primary argument advanced by federal counsel was that "because inflation is a subject matter going beyond local or provincial concern or interests and is from its inherent nature the concern of Canada as a whole," the *Anti-Inflation Act* should be upheld as a proper exercise of the peace, order and good government power. To this was added reference to several specific heads of federal power – trade and commerce, taxation, the power to borrow, currency, banking, interest, legal tender – all of which were closely related to the aims and effects of the anti-inflation program and hence, it was argued, provided evidence of the inherently national character of the legislation. Obviously, the primary federal argument was designed to do more than save the *Act*: if it were accepted by the Court it would consolidate the gains in constitutional law which the federal government hoped would flow from Viscount Simon's decision in the *Canada Temperance Federation* case. Surprisingly, Ontario endorsed the federal position. In fact, Mr. McMurtry in one respect went further in that he did not advance the emergency doctrine even as an alternative argument. For Ontario, Viscount Simon's test of inherent national importance was the only test for invoking peace, order and good government.

But the other provinces and the unions all argued that the only possible way of supporting such legislation was on emergency grounds. The constitutional issue which it had been convenient to suppress in October now came out in the open. The most important constitutional arguments were advanced by Mr. Lysyk, the Deputy Attorney-General of Saskatchewan and Professor Lederman for the Renfrew teachers. They put forward a new thesis on the meaning of previous decisions dealing with peace, order and good government. The gist of this thesis was that outside of emergencies, peace, order and good government can be used only in a residual sense to support federal legislation in discrete, narrowly defined areas of legislation which clearly fall outside provincial jurisdiction. Legislation in an area defined as broadly as "inflation" and clearly intruding on matters which are normally subject to exclusive provincial jurisdiction fails to meet this test. This interpretation of peace, order and good government was a clear alternative to the views expressed by Chief Justice Laskin in his academic writings – views which his frequent interventions from the bench indicated he might still hold.

Even on emergency grounds the federal position received meager support from the provinces. Alberta along with the unions went all the way and argued (in the CLC's submission on the basis of the Lipsey brief) that the *Act* should be found unconstitutional as there was no economic emergency. Quebec, British Columbia and Saskatchewan remained on the federal government's side of the courtroom nominally in support of the legislation. But their support, at times, must have reminded federal counsel of the old saying, "With friends like that, who needs enemies?" In their factums, they were at best agnostic as to whether an emergency existed sufficient to justify the use of the general power. Mr. Vickers, the Deputy Attorney-General for British Columbia, concluded his oral presentation by submitting that the burden of proof (on the existence of an emergency) lay with the federal government, and that "on the evidence now before the court I do not feel one could conclude that there was a national emergency." Counsel for the federal government did not try to meet this burden of proof nor parry the economic arguments of the Lipsey brief. Mr. Robinette's position was that the Court had only to find that it was not unreasonable for Parliament to believe that there was an emergency or "a generally apprehended crisis."

The submissions of the parties in the *Anti-Inflation* case contrast in some important ways with those of counsel in the New Deal references of the 1930s – the last occasion on which there was a serious challenge to federal power through judicial review. In those cases a foreign tribunal witnessed a strong provincial attack on federal legislation rather weakly defended by a government whose political opponents had actually introduced the legislation. Here, a Canadian court in the national capital was considering the constitutional validity of what at the time was the federal government's most important domestic policy initiative. The judges knew that all of the provinces had in fact agreed to cooperate with the federal program. In the courtroom they *saw* on the federal side four provinces (including the three largest) with governments covering the entire Canadian political spectrum supporting the legislation. But they also heard that the only common denominator of constitutional support was the emergency doctrine. In these circumstances it would have taken an exceptionally bold court either to have found the federal *Act ultra vires* or to have based its constitutional validity on a wider footing than the emergency use of peace, order and good government.

The Court's Decision

Five weeks after the conclusion of the hearing the Supreme Court pronounced its judgment. The Court unanimously found that the Ontario Agreement did not render the Anti-Inflation program binding on the provincial public sector. On the question of the *Anti-Inflation Act*'s constitutional validity, the Court split seven to two: seven judges found that it was constitutional on emergency grounds, but Justices Beetz and de Grandpré, both from Quebec and the most recently appointed judges, dissented. That is the bare bones of the decision, but, as is always the case with appellate decisions, the reasons of the judges are more important than their votes.

First, the Court's decision on the validity of the Ontario Agreement, while constituting a small portion of the judgment quantitatively, is not without its constitutional significance. Chief Justice Laskin wrote the Court's opinion on this question. Because the federal *Act* did not spell out precisely how the guidelines should apply to the provincial public sector, the Chief Justice found that the *Act* itself did not provide the necessary legislative sanction for the Ontario Agreement. The Agreement could not be regarded as sanctioned by conditional legislation for which action by the provincial government was merely a "triggering device." However, it is significant that in reaching this conclusion he went out of his way to indicate that he did not accept the view that it would have been beyond federal power to regulate the provincial public service. Assertions of immunity for the provincial public service, he wrote, "misconceive the paramount authority of federal legislative power ... and the all-embracing legislative authority of the Parliament of Canada when validly exercised for the peace, order and good government of Canada." But, in the absence of federal or provincial legislation *clearly* authorizing the Agreement, he ruled that the executive agreement could not make new labour legislation binding on the citizens of the province. The Chief Justice seemed bent on de-emphasizing the constitutional significance of this holding: the issue, he said, did *not* engage "any concern with responsible Government and the political answerability of the Ministers to the Legislative Assembly." Nonetheless, by holding that:

> There is no principle in this country, as there is not in Great Britain, that the Crown may legislate by proclamation or Order in Council to bind citizens where it so acts without the support of a statute of the Legislature; see Dicey, *Law of the Constitution*,

he at least confirms an essential element of our "unwritten constitution." Those concerned about the increasing erosion of the role of the legislature and the trend in Canada toward policy-making within the closed confines of federal-provincial negotiations, should welcome this judicial recognition of an important constitutional principle.

The Court's decision on the primary question concerning the constitutional validity of the *Anti-Inflation Act* can be analyzed by breaking the question into two components: (1) the interpretation of the peace, order and good government clause and (2) the judgment as to whether the *Anti-Inflation Act* could be upheld as emergency legislation. The court split in quite different ways on these two aspects of the question. Three opinions were written: Chief Justice Laskin's reasons were supported by three Justices, Judson, Spence and Dickson; Mr. Justice Ritchie's were concurred in by Justices Martland and Pigeon; Mr. Justice de Grandpré concurred in Mr. Justice Beetz's opinion. On the second aspect of the question, Chief Justice Laskin's group of four and Justice Ritchie's group of three formed the majority which found the *Act intra vires*. But on the first issue – the fundamental question of constitutional doctrine – the reasoning of Mr. Justice Beetz's dissenting opinion was adopted by the Ritchie threesome and so became, in effect, the majority position of the Court.

The short five-page opinion of Mr. Justice Ritchie at least has the merit of highlighting the Court's division on the meaning of peace, order and good government. Ritchie rejects broad considerations of national concern or inherent national importance as the framework within which to test whether Parliament can exercise its peace, order and good government power in areas normally under provincial jurisdiction. For him the relevant precedent is not Viscount Simon's judgment in the *Canada Temperance Federation* case, but the decisions following it, especially the *Japanese Canadians* case, in which the Privy Council returned to the emergency doctrine. Since then, Justice Ritchie takes it to be established "that unless such concern [i.e., national concern] is made manifest by circumstances amounting to a national emergency, Parliament is not endowed under the cloak of the 'peace, order and good government' clause with the authority to legislate in relation to matters reserved to the Provinces under s.92." For more elaborate jurisprudential reasons he refers to Mr. Justice Beetz with whose reasons he is "in full agreement."

Justice Beetz provided a re-interpretation of previous judicial decisions on this constitutional issue. This re-interpretation followed the mainline of argument submitted to the Court by Mr. Lysyk and Professor Lederman. The essence of this approach is to draw a radical distinction between the "normal" and the "abnormal" uses of peace, order and good government. The normal use of the clause is as a national residual power to cover "… clear instances of distinct subject-matters which do not fall within any of the enumerated heads of s.92 and which, by nature, are of national concern."

Thus, it has been invoked successfully in the past to support such fields as radio, aeronautics, the incorporation of Dominion companies and the national capital, all of which in Justice Beetz's view display the requisite "degree of unity," "distinct identity" or "specificity" But the containment and reduction of inflation fails to meet this test of specificity: "It is so pervasive that it knows no bounds. Its recognition as a federal head of power would render most provincial powers nugatory." The normal application of peace, order and good government has the effect of adding, by judicial process, new subject matters of legislation to the list of exclusive federal powers in Section 91 of the *BNA Act*. National concern, national dimensions are still relevant in determining whether such unforeseen, discrete, new subject matters should be brought under the federal residual power or under its counterpart on the provincial side, Section 92(16) – "Matters of a merely local or private nature in the province." But the only constitutional basis for federal legislation cast in such broad terms as the *Anti-Inflation Act* is the abnormal use of peace, order and good government – the emergency doctrine. It is abnormal precisely because it "operates as a partial and temporary alteration of the distribution of power between Parliament and the provincial Legislatures." Once the Court agrees to apply this doctrine no longer is the power of Parliament limited by the identity of subject matters but solely "by the nature of the crisis."

This then was the new constitutional doctrine fashioned by Justice Beetz and supported by a bare majority of the Court. Against it – but by no means in total opposition to it – was Chief Justice Laskin's opinion supported by three other judges. The Chief Justice wrote a long review of all the major cases bearing upon peace, order and good government. While it is not always clear just where this review is going, it contains one basic point of contrast with the majority position. Instead of driving a wedge between the normal and abnormal use of the general power, Chief Justice Laskin tries to weave a single piece of cloth out of all the strands to be found in previous decisions. The key to this approach, the central idea which gives the multi-coloured fabric some shape and pattern, is Lord Watson's proposition in the *Local Prohibition* case that "... matters in origin local or provincial ... might attain national dimensions." Since then Laskin sees the jurisprudence moving in two directions – under Viscount Haldane narrowing to the hint of "studiously ignoring" Lord Watson's "national dimensions," but then returning to it, at first cautiously in judgments written by Lord Atkin and Chief Justice Duff followed by the more expansive views of Viscount Simon. The Chief Justice's response to this legacy of competing emphases is not to pick his own favourite strand and discard the others but to identify the extremes which clearly lie beyond the main body of jurisprudence. Thus, at one extreme, basing the use of peace, order and good government on the mere desirability or convenience of national regulation (a possible interpretation of the first Privy Council decision on this issue, *Russell v. The Queen*) is ruled out. But at the other extreme, a pure Haldane approach which ignores "national dimensions" and confines the use of peace, order and good government to war-related emergencies is equally beyond the pale. In between these extremes there are many possibilities, and the Chief Justice warns against fixing constitutional doctrine so tightly as to prevent the constitution from serving "… as a resilient instrument capable of adaptation to changing circumstances."

In the case at hand, because all of the parties accepted as constitutional doctrine the use of peace, order and good government to deal with a national emergency, "… it becomes unnecessary to consider the broader ground advanced in its support …" So the Chief Justice was willing to rest his decision on the narrow ground of emergency (semantically softened to "crisis"). But unlike the majority he did not rule out the broader ground advanced by the federal government.

For those who have admired the Chief Justice's contribution to Canada's constitutional jurisprudence, the opaque, open-ended quality of his reasoning in this case may be a disappointment. But it is reasonable, I think, to regard his opinion as that of a Chief Justice endeavouring to build a majority around the widest common denominator on his Court without foreclosing jurisprudential possibilities which he personally favoured. That he failed is not too surprising. Since joining the Court in 1970 he has been its most frequent dissenter. The available statistical data (based on the *Supreme Court Reports* from 1970 to 1974 inclusive) reveal that of the 196 dissents recorded during this period more than half (109) were attributed to three justices: Laskin (45), Spence (34) and Hall (30). The relative isolation of these justices is not tied to issues of federalism. Between the time the present Chief Justice joined the Court and the *Anti-Inflation Reference*, the Court rendered 20 decisions on the division of powers in the *BNA Act*. Fifteen of them were unanimous, and although the Chief Justice was on the dissenting side in three of the split decisions, an examination of these cases does not suggest a division on provincial rights/centralist lines. Chief Justice Laskin's differences with a majority of his colleagues more likely stem from general questions of judicial philosophy and style. If there is a consistent pattern of division on matters of substance, it is more likely to be found in cases dealing with criminal law and the *Bill of Rights*.

Given the clear consensus both on the Court and among the litigants concerning the power of Parliament in a national emergency (or crisis) to override the normal division of powers, the second dimension of the constitutional question – whether in fact the *Anti-Inflation Act* was emergency legislation – may become more important than the general doctrinal issue of the meaning of peace, order and good government. The Supreme Court's handling of this issue indicates a significant shift to a more deferential attitude to the exercise of emergency powers in peacetime by the national government.

The Court's split on the issue – Chief Justice Laskin's group of four plus Justice Ritchie's group of three versus Justices Beetz and de Grandpré in dissent – did not turn on the empirical question of whether in fact there was an emergency. It concerned the prior question of whether emergency legislation must be clearly identified as such by Parliament. The dissenters took the position that a necessary but by no means sufficient test of valid emergency legislation is a clear, unambiguous indication by Parliament that it is enacting the legislation on an emergency basis. Justice Beetz emphasized that responsibility for declaring an emergency must lie with the "politically responsible body," not the courts. The court's responsibility begins after the affirmation by Parliament that an emergency exists. In this case not only was there no acknowledgment on the face of the federal *Act* (as there had been with other recent exercises of the emergency power), but there was clear evidence to show that this was no accidental oversight. Breaking the convention which precludes Canadian judges from considering parliamentary history, Justice Beetz referred to the numerous passages in Hansard where government spokesmen refused to be pinned down on the constitutional basis of the legislation and refused to preface the Bill with a declaration of an emergency. Further, the large gaps in the *Act*'s coverage – the omission of farmers and small businesses, the optional nature of the provincial public sector's inclusion – were, in Justice Beetz's view, not easily reconciled with an emergency characterization of the *Act*. He was also impressed by the lack of provincial support for the view that it was emergency legislation.

For the majority, Parliament's failure to declare an emergency or stamp "emergency" on the face of the *Act* was not fatal. The reference in the *Act*'s preamble to a level of inflation "contrary to the interests of all Canadians" which had become "a matter of serious national concern," combined with similar statements in the government's White Paper, were enough to indicate how serious the situation must have appeared to Parliament. The omissions from the Act's coverage and the opting-in approach to the provincial public sector, in Chief Justice Laskin's view, could be accounted for in terms of administrative convenience and need not be regarded as indicating a lack of any sense of crisis. Since there were no formal deficiencies in the federal *Act*, the only grounds upon which its validity as emergency or crisis legislation could be impugned was the factual question: did an emergency exist? Here, for a least three of the justices, the onus of proof was placed squarely on the *Act*'s opponents. The peacetime exercise of the federal emergency power was put on the same footing as its use in time of war. Justice Ritchie cited Lord Wright's statement in the *Japanese Canadians* case.

> But very clear evidence that an emergency has not arisen, or that the emergency no longer exists, is required to justify the judiciary, even though the question is one of *ultra vires*, in overruling the decision of the Parliament of the Dominion that exceptional measures were required or were still required.

In Justice Ritchie's opinion the evidence presented by the opponents of the legislation failed to meet Lord Wright's test.

Chief Justice Laskin approached the issue in terms of assessing the rationality of Parliament's judgment. The Court would be justified in overruling the *Act* as emergency legislation only if it found that:

> ... The Parliament of Canada did not have a rational basis for regarding the *Anti-Inflation Act* as a measure which, in its judgment, was temporarily necessary to meet a situation of economic crisis imperilling the well-being of the people of Canada as a whole and requiring Parliament's stern intervention in the interests of the country as a whole.

In assessing rationality the Chief Justice did not place the burden of proof solely on the *Act*'s opponents. He took into consideration statistics showing the rise in the Consumer Price Index submitted by the federal government as well as the arguments advanced in Professor Lipsey's brief. He noted Professor Lipsey's candid admission that whether "a problem is serious enough to be described as a crisis must be partly a matter of judgment," and added that the Court cannot be governed by the judgment of an economist however distinguished he may be in the opinion of his peers. Positive evidence of the rationality of Parliament' s judgment could be found in the connection between rising inflation and Parliament' s clear constitutional responsibilities in monetary policy...

Thus, the Chief Justice concluded that the Court would be unjustified in finding Parliament lacked a rational basis for its judgment that the legislation was needed to meet an urgent crisis. But we should note how in this part of his opinion he attempted to retain as close a link as possible between the emergency use of peace, order and good government and broad consideration of national dimensions or national aspects. With severe inflation impinging so heavily on areas of federal responsibility, the subject matter of the *Anti-Inflation Act* – the regulation of prices and wages – loses its ordinary parochial or local character and becomes a matter sufficiently urgent for the well-being of all Canadians as to require national action.

The Significance of the Decision

Normally a judicial decision in our system of government "settles" one aspect – the justiciable aspect – of what is usually a larger dispute. In the context of this larger dispute a Court's role is perhaps better described as "dispute processing" rather than "dispute settlement." In assessing the political importance of a judicial decision it is important to see how it affects the political interests involved in the larger area of conflict. The political impact of a constitutional decision by the national court of appeal will usually be felt much more in terms of the long-run significance of the new rules of law it produces than in terms of the immediate outcome of the adjudication.

This is certainly true of the Supreme Court's decision in the *Anti-Inflation* case. For the labour organizations which provoked the case as part of a general anti-controls campaign the immediate outcome was a loss. The controls would continue. Even that part of the decision which invalidated the Ontario Agreement was quickly overcome. The ink was scarcely dry on the Court's judgment when the Ontario government went back to the legislature and obtained retroactive legislative sanction for its participation in the anti-inflation program. The government's minority position in the legislature proved to be no problem, as Mr. Smith, the Liberal leader, was as compliant as predicted. But the "loss" for labour was probably not a very serious one. Labour opposition to the controls program, if anything, intensified rather than diminished after the decision. It is doubtful that the Supreme Court's validation of the *Anti-Inflation Act* added to the program's political legitimacy. In fact, a judicial veto of the *Anti-Inflation Act* might have provided the immediate benefit to the Trudeau government of a politically safe exit from a potentially unpopular program. Besides, the ground of the Court's decision meant that the door was far from closed on future constitutional challenges to the program. If the inflationary situation significantly eased, it would always be possible to argue that the circumstances which made it reasonable to regard the *Act* as an emergency measure no longer existed. Indeed, shortly after the Parti Québécois took over in Quebec City, Mr. Parizeau, Quebec's Finance Minister, announced that he was considering a challenge on precisely those grounds.

The rules of law and the constitutional doctrine which emerge from the decision bear more directly on the interests of the two levels of government in the Canadian federation than upon the labour-capital axis. Indeed, one of the interesting features of the case is the apparent indifference of organized labour to the division of powers question. The federal and provincial governments cannot be indifferent because Supreme Court rulings on the constitution directly increase or diminish their political resources. From this perspective, the Court's judgment on the Ontario Agreement entails a slight decrease in the resources of both levels of government. The decision reduces the freedom of provincial and federal governments to collaborate in making policy through the mechanisms of cooperative federalism without obtaining support from their respective legislatures. This modest restraint on "executive federalism" is a boon for citizens and interest groups (like labour unions), not to mention old-fashioned democrats who believe that major changes in the law should be approved by the legislature. But its significance must not be over-rated. Chief Justice Laskin's decision clearly implies that federal legislation upheld on emergency grounds could, if properly worded, regulate all aspects of a field normally under provincial jurisdiction and eliminate any need for provincial legislative sanction.

As for the meaning of the peace, order and good government clause in the *BNA Act*, the decision did not yield the particular benefit sought by federal legal strategists. The legislation was not sustained on broad grounds of inherent national importance or concern. Viscount Haldane was not put away in mothballs. The jurisprudence of Viscount Simon and the *Johannesson* case, which Mr. Macdonald said his government was counting upon, was not accepted by the Court's majority as the key to interpreting peace, order and good government. But the federal government did not come away from the decision empty-handed. To begin with, what I shall call the "Lederman doctrine" on peace, order and good government, adopted by Justice Beetz and supported by a majority of the judges, means that when new matters of legislation are considered distinct and specific enough to justify the residual or "normal" use of the peace, order and good government, they are added to the list of *exclusive* federal powers. The exclusiveness of federal jurisdiction in areas such as aeronautics and radio communications, which are cited as instances of this normal use, was not clear in the past. The Lederman doctrine, while apparently not as favourable to federal power as Viscount Simon's dictum, still is not necessarily unfavourable. While it may have seemed relatively easy to Justice Beetz and his colleagues to apply the criterion of "specificity" retrospectively, I would contend that it is not an easy test to apply prospectively. In the hands of a nationally-minded court it may be surprising what turns out to be specific enough to come under the federal residual power. Besides, it should be noted that considerations of national concern and importance have not been discarded by the Court. Under the Lederman doctrine, national concern is the test for determining whether a new subject with the requisite degree of specificity should be brought under the federal rather than the provincial residual power. Also, as I have tried to explain above, Chief Justice Laskin's opinion, which after all spoke for four of the Court's nine judges, kept Viscount Simon's jurisprudence alive and, in deciding whether the legislation was valid on emergency grounds, made the national dimensions of the economic crisis a prime consideration.

But the Court's handling of the emergency question constitutes a more distinct gain for the federal authorities. The majority's ruling that Parliament does not have to proclaim an emergency or crisis in order to be able to defend legislation successfully in court as emergency legislation increases the maneuverability of federal government leaders. This is especially important with regard to crisis situations related to peacetime economic management when the open admission in Parliament that an emergency or urgent crisis exists might be politically embarrassing to the government. The majority's position means that the federal government does not have to pay the price of that embarrassment in order to secure the emergency argument as the basis for an Act's constitutional validity. To put the matter bluntly, temporary federal legislation may be upheld on emergency grounds if federal lawyers can persuade the Court that there is not enough evidence to conclude that it would have been unreasonable for Parliament to have regarded a matter as an urgent national crisis at the time it passed the legislation. Given the probable deference of most Supreme Court Justices to the judgment of Parliament, this is at least a small gain for federal authority.

It may, however, be a significant loss to those Canadians who care about maintaining parliamentary democracy and constitutionalism. For it must be remembered that all of the judicial decisions upholding federal legislation on emergency grounds (as well as those denying it on these grounds) indicate that "the rule of law as to the distribution of powers" is set aside for the duration of the emergency. One can understand the need for an overriding emergency power to protect the state against threats to its very survival, as well as the reluctance of judges to question a clear determination by Parliament that such an emergency exists. But the constitution as a limit on governmental authority will come to mean very little if it is set aside too easily. At the very least, the better constitutional policy might be to insist, with Justice Beetz, that it should be the responsibility of Parliament rather than the courts to proclaim an emergency.

Finally, what does the *Anti-Inflation* case indicate about the future of judicial review in Canada? First, I think it is likely that the frequency with which constitutional issues are brought before the court will increase rather than decrease. The Supreme Court's almost perfect record in upholding federal laws will not be a serious deterrent to those who wish to challenge federal legislation. For provincial governments, and even more, for private interest groups, constitutional litigation is just one weapon that can be used to fight a larger campaign. Even the Parti Québécois, for instance, although it has no respect for the Supreme Court as an institution of national government, contemplates constitutional litigation as a tactic in its larger constitutional warfare. If it loses, it can portray the decision as yet further evidence of the hostility of federal institutions to Quebec's interests; if it wins this would vindicate the charge that the federal government is encroaching on areas of provincial jurisdiction. But private individuals and groups may be even more likely to provoke constitutional litigation. The rapid growth of the legal profession, more generous rules of standing, the influence of the American example and the new jurisdictional rules under which the Supreme Court's docket is shaped primarily by judicial selection of nationally important cases, all of these factors are likely to generate more privately-initiated constitutional cases. And, as labour's approach to the *Anti-Inflation* case indicates, when these pressure groups litigate constitutional issues they may be inclined to let the constitutional chips fall where they may for the sake of pursuing some short-run advantage on an immediate policy issue.

So the Supreme Court's decision in this case will not deter resort to judicial review in the future. Nor, despite the scant attention given Professor Lipsey's brief, should future litigants in constitutional cases be deterred from supporting their arguments with this kind of social science evidence. None of the judges denied that Professor Lipsey's brief was admissible evidence, and the Chief Justice explicitly acknowledged its relevancy even though he did not find it completely persuasive. Further, where the question of constitutionality turns on the reasonableness of regarding a situation as an urgent national crisis requiring national legislation, what other than empirical arguments can lawyers who wish to challenge the legislation use? I am not suggesting that there will be a sudden revolution in the

Supreme Court's style of jurisprudence, but that we will likely see more lawyers using this type of material in future constitutional cases. One leading constitution scholar has suggested that "… the admission of social science briefs in constitutional cases where legislative facts are in issue … may prove in the long run to be the most influential point of the case."

On a more fundamental plane, the Court's majority in subscribing to Professor Lederman's approach to peace, order and good government, rather than Professor Laskin's (as he once was), have opted to maintain a more traditional style of opinion-writing. The central concern apparent in this style of reasoning is "distilling the essences" of legal categories and characterizing the subject matter of legislation. It is basically the old game of sticking the legislation in the right pigeon-hole. Most of our judges (and probably, still most of our lawyers) find this a more congenial exercise than reasoning about legislative schemes in terms of the necessary requirements of effective national policy-making.

Judicial decisions based on the majority's approach have the *appearance* of being based on narrow, technical, purely legal considerations. But the preference for this style of jurisprudence is based on larger considerations of constitutional policy. Only Justice Beetz gave a clear expression of the underlying policy reason for rejecting the federal government's first submission that the *Anti-Inflation Act* should be sustained under peace, order and good government as a matter of inherent national importance. "It is not difficult to speculate," he wrote "as to where this line of reasoning would lead: a fundamental feature of the Constitution, its federal nature, the distribution of powers between Parliament and the provincial legislatures, would disappear not gradually but rapidly." So, for policy reasons, a jurisprudential style which would make policy reasons more transparent, is rejected. As a result, Canadians cannot expect judicial reasoning to add very much to the country's stock of constitutional wisdom. The question remains whether this masking of judicial power is in itself a kind of constitutional wisdom.

10.5

Does Federalism Review Matter?
Patrick Monahan
Politics and the Constitution: The Charter, Federalism and the Supreme Court of Canada (Toronto: Carswell, 1987), 224–40. Reprinted with permission.

… [T]here appear to be a variety of ways in which governments or individuals can avoid or modify the effect of constraints associated with federalism. Federalism is premised on a theory of the exhaustion of powers; if one government is denied jurisdiction over a particular matter, then the other level of government must necessarily possess such jurisdiction. Accordingly, if the Supreme Court finds that legislation enacted by one level of government is *ultra vires* on federalism grounds, there are a variety of regulatory alternatives still available. First, the other level of government may choose to enact the legislation in substantially the same form. Alternatively, the results of the litigation may be reversed by intergovernmental agreement, in which the "winning" level of government delegates to the "loser" part or all of the disputed jurisdiction. Finally, the "losing" level of government may simply reassert regulation over the activity in question through substituting an alternative policy instrument in place of the one struck down by the Court.

This leads to the following fundamental maxim of Canadian federalism: contrary to repeated judicial pronouncements to the contrary, it is *always* possible to do indirectly what you cannot do directly. The only relevant question is whether the costs of indirection are so high that they outweigh the benefits.

Yet this "fundamental maxim" is less of a final conclusion than an invitation to further inquiry. Specifically, having noted the theoretical availability of regulatory substitutes, to what extent do governments actually employ such substitutes in order to avoid the constraining effects of judicial interpretations? The remainder of this chapter is an attempt to offer a general and tentative answer to that important question. I begin by setting out a series of principles which must underpin analysis of this issue. I then apply and test these principles through two case studies of the interaction of government and the judiciary. The focus of these case studies is the series of trade and commerce cases decided by the Supreme Court in the late 1970s and analyzed in Chapter 9. As we observed in Chapter 9, the reasoning in many of these decisions was weak; the Court seemed to have a rather poor understanding of the actual purpose and effect of the legislation being considered. Yet, what we will discover in this chapter is that these decisions appear to have had a very modest impact on the formulation of public policy. Governments have been able to overcome the effects of these adverse judicial rulings through intergovernmental agreement or by enacting alternative legislation. Based on the analysis developed in these case studies, I attempt to draw out a series of more general conclusions regarding the instrumental impact of federalism adjudication....

2. Federal Product Regulation: The Aftermath of Dominion Stores and Labatt Breweries of Canada Ltd.

In *R. v. Dominion Stores Ltd. (1980)* and *Labatt Breweries of Canada Ltd.* v. *A.-G. Canada (1980)* the Supreme Court had limited federal power to provide for national product standards. In *Dominion Stores*, the Court had ruled that a scheme prescribing grade names and standards associated with those names could not be applied to intraprovincial traders. In *Labatt*, the Court had struck down s.6 of the *Food and Drugs Act*, ruling that s.6 was an impermissible attempt to regulate local trade. Both of these decisions were widely criticized by commentators at the time, who saw the rulings as threatening national product standards and thus as promoting increased consumer ignorance and confusion in the market.

Today, close to a decade after the rulings in these cases, the chaos and confusion which these commentators feared has failed to materialize. This is not to suggest that consumers are now able to obtain accurate and full information on all the products they buy. The point is simply that the feared balkanization of the Canadian market, in which individual provinces would prescribe different standards and specifications for goods sold there, has not developed. There has been little complaint from federal policy-makers about the deterioration of national product standards or calls for urgent legislative or constitutional reform. Neither of the statutes which was the subject of litigation has been amended. In short, the cases appear to have had little or no impact on the manner in which goods are packaged and sold in Canada or on the agenda of public policy-makers. How can we account for the negligible impact of the cases, particularly in light of the predictions of dire consequences which were heard in the months immediately following the release of the decisions?

Consider first the aftermath of the *Dominion Stores* case. The key to understanding the limited impact of this case is the long history of constitutional litigation dealing with the regulation of farm products. Federal-provincial attempts to regulate the marketing of farm products date back to the mid-1930s. The Privy Council had determined that the regulation of intraprovincial trade in natural products was a provincial responsibility, while only Parliament could regulate interprovincial and international trade. The two levels of government had overcome this division of responsibility through interprovincial bargaining and agreement. The relevant standards would be set through federal-provincial agreement; each province would then implement the agreement for products traded locally, while the federal government would enact legislation covering interprovincial and international trade. In this way a common set of product standards would apply across the country, notwithstanding the constitutional division of responsibility.

This system of dovetailing legislation was in place long before the litigation involving *Dominion Stores*. Part II of the *Canada Agricultural Products Standards Act* established a compulsory scheme of grade names and standards for products moving in interprovincial and export trade. The same set of grade names and standards applied to local traders in Ontario pursuant to the [Ontario] *Farm Products Grades and Sales Act*. The validity of these provisions was not at issue in the appeal. What was challenged was Part I of the federal legislation, which sought to establish a voluntary system of grade names and standards for products traded locally. It was this voluntary system of grade names which was ruled unconstitutional by the Court.

This legislative background makes it easy to understand why the decision in *Dominion Stores* has had minimal impact on the regulation of natural products. Notwithstanding the Court's ruling, the same set of natural product standards remains validly in force. The only difference is that prosecutions must be brought under Part II of the federal *Act* or the relevant provincial legislation, depending upon the origin of the product in question. The consequence is that it will be necessary for investigators to obtain information on the origin of the product before laying a charge. But there is no reason in principle why such information could not be obtained.

Perhaps the greatest irony of the case is that there was evidence that the apples which were the subject of the charge in *Dominion Stores* had been traded interprovincially. Thus, although the charge was laid under Part I of the federal *Act*, the investigators could have proceeded under Part II, which contained compulsory standards for interprovincial traders. Had this latter option been chosen, there would have been no constitutional defence to the charge and the only issue would have been whether the apples complied with the relevant standard. Thus, the constitutional issue was manufactured by a discretionary decision to proceed under Part I of the legislation.

In short, the *Dominion Stores* case was little more than a footnote to the long history of constitutional litigation involving the marketing of farm products. The federal and provincial governments had previously agreed on a package of dovetailing legislation establishing a common set of regulatory standards. The *Dominion Stores* case did not call into question the validity of that federal-provincial arrangement. The only effect of the case was to prevent the federal government from applying a "voluntary" scheme of regulation to products traded locally. Given the continued consensus between federal and provincial governments over the relevant standards to be applied in this area, the impact of the decision has been minimal.

There was no similar set of dovetailing federal-provincial legislation in the *Labatt Breweries* case. Section 6 of the federal *Food and Drugs Act* purported to set down national standards for all food products, without distinguishing whether they were traded locally or interprovincially. There was no comparable provincial legislation in place. Thus, one might have expected that the Court's ruling that s.6 was *ultra vires* to have had a fairly significant impact on food products standards. Yet this impact has yet to materialize. In general, food products sold in Canada continue to meet the standards set down in the federal legislation. Federal officials responsible for compliance with the so-called "food recipe" standards report very few violations in the wake of the *Labatt Breweries* case.

What is the explanation for this continued compliance with standards which are apparently unenforceable? An explanation which appears initially plausible is based on the observation that the food industry has an interest in a common set of food standards. A common set of standards enables the industry to signal to consumers the varying nature and quality of products which may otherwise appear indistinguishable. Consider the sale of "ground beef" as an illustration of this signalling function. The quality of ground beef varies according to the fat content of the meat, yet fat content cannot be determined through visual inspection. The solution is to establish different grades of ground beef according to the fat content of the meat (i.e., "lean," "medium" or "regular") and to package and sell the meat accordingly. The industry has a clear interest in establishing such standards since they can then differentiate between and charge appropriate prices for products which appear indistinguishable through visual inspection. Consumers also have an interest in such standards since they obtain accurate information about the quality of the product they are buying and (in the example above) they are given a choice between three grades of ground beef rather than one.

Given the clear consumer and industry interest in establishing labelling standards, one might expect such standards to arise spontaneously in a market. The reason why this does not occur is because of the difficulty in policing compliance with the standards. Once a product standard is established, there is an immediate incentive to attempt to substitute a lower quality product in place of one of higher quality. To return to the ground beef example, once three grades of ground beef have been established, there is an incentive to market "regular" ground beef as either "medium" or "lean" beef and charge a higher price for the product. This incentive to cheat is all the more powerful because consumers are unable to distinguish the quality of the product through visual inspection. The way out of this dilemma is to establish the product standards through legislation. If the product standards are established and enforced by the state, cheaters can be identified and prosecuted. State intervention makes possible the efficiency gains associated with product standards.

This analysis, far from explaining the continued voluntary compliance with the food standards, makes such compliance all the more curious. Given the inability of the federal government to enforce compliance with the standards, why has there not been a dramatic increase in the numbers of sellers seeking to substitute lower quality products in place of higher quality ones?

There are undoubtedly a number of factors which have contributed to the absence of widespread violations of the *Act*. First, the product standards were already in place and had become widely accepted by the industry as being in its own best interest. Thus, it is hardly surprising that the bulk of the industry would continue to support the product standards even after the result in *Labatt Breweries*. Second, the federal government still possesses considerable authority to enforce the product standards. Since the *Labatt Breweries* litigation, federal officials have sought to enforce the product standards through prosecutions under s.5 of the *Food and Drugs Act*, which provides:

> 5. (1) No person shall label, package, treat, process, sell or advertise any food in a manner that is false, misleading or deceptive or is likely to create an erroneous impression regarding its character, value, quantity, composition, merit or safety.

It is arguable that prosecutions under s.5 are somewhat more difficult than prosecutions under s.6. Under s.6, the relevant test was whether an article was "likely to be mistaken" for food for which a standard had been prescribed under the regulations. If it was likely to be mistaken for such food, then it had to comply with the applicable standard. In contrast, s.5(1) makes it an offence to package food in a manner that is "false, misleading or deceptive or is likely to create an erroneous impression regarding its character"... It is arguable that the standard under s.5 is somewhat higher, since there is an obligation to demonstrate that the labelling of the food is "misleading": it may be, for example, that food has not ben labelled in accordance with the regulations, but that it cannot be demonstrated that this improper labelling was "false, misleading or deceptive."

Yet, on further examination, it is apparent that there are also certain broad similarities between the standards established under ss.5 and 6. Section 6 itself did not directly require compliance with the food standards in the regulations. It was also necessary to demonstrate a "misleading" of the public in order to prosecute under s.6; the offence in s.6 was one of packaging, selling or advertising food "in such a manner that it is likely to be mistaken" for food subject to the regulations. Nor was this "misleading" element of the offence a mere *pro forma* requirement. It should be recalled that the trial judge in the *Labatt Breweries* case had found that "the plaintiff's Special Lite beverage ("food") has not been labelled, packaged or advertised in such a manner that it is likely to be mistaken for the beverage "light beer" ("food"). Thus, even though Labatt's Special Lite did not comply with the standard for "light beer," the trial judge was prepared to grant a declaration that there had not been a violation of s.6 of the *Act*. In short, while s.5 of the *Act* does not permit direct enforcement of the standards in the regulations, neither did s.6. Instead, both sections depend on some demonstration that there has been a misleading of the public.

This leads to the obvious question: is s.5 of the *Act* also vulnerable to a constitutional challenge? While the answer is not altogether free from doubt, it would appear that s.5 of the *Act* could be defended as an exercise of Parliament's jurisdiction over "criminal law." The criminal law power has always included the authority to proscribe trade practices contrary to the interest of the community such as misleading, false or deceptive advertising. There is a strong argument to the effect that s.5 is a valid exercise of that power.

In short, while the federal government can no longer utilize s.6 in order to enforce the food product standards, it has a relatively close regulatory substitute in s.5. Moreover, there is an alternative basis for directly and conclusively enforcing the standards set out in the *Food and Drugs Act*. This alternative is to seek the cooperation of the provinces and to establish a framework similar to that already in place for natural products. Under such a scheme, Parliament could enact food product standards for goods moving in interprovincial and export trade. The provinces would enact parallel standards for goods produced and traded locally. In this way, a common set of food product standards would be binding and enforceable throughout Canada. Federal-provincial negotiations aimed at establishing such a scheme are underway and the federal government expects to introduce legislation setting standards for interprovincial and export trade before the next election.

In summary, neither *Dominion Stores* nor *Labatt Breweries* has had any significant impact on the manner in which goods are marketed or on government policy. The impact of the *Dominion Stores* litigation was minimal due to the existence of dovetailing federal and provincial legislation regulating natural products. As for *Labatt Breweries*, the industry has continued to voluntarily comply with the food recipe standards, notwithstanding the outcome of the litigation. Over the longer term, there are a number of alternative regulatory instruments which can be utilized in order to ensure appropriate compliance with the standards. Neither case seems to have made a great deal of difference for the politics of Canadian federalism.

3. Natural Resource Regulation: The Aftermath of *CIGOL* and *Central Canada*

In the late 1970s, the Supreme Court appeared to have dealt a body blow to provincial attempts to regulate the natural resource industry. In *CIGOL* (1979), the Court struck down a provincial tax designed to capture the dramatic increase in oil prices resulting from the 1973 Middle East war. In *Central Canada Potash* (1979), the Court ruled invalid a provincial scheme establishing quotas and minimum prices for the production of potash in Saskatchewan. There were howls of protest from the western provinces following these decisions. The provinces complained that fundamental issues of federal-provincial politics were being resolved by an institution "not in the mainstream of the political process." Various premiers claimed that the Supreme Court was "biased" in favour of the federal government and that the method of appointment to the Court had to be changed to allow for provincial participation.

A decade after these controversial decisions, constitutional questions no longer seem to feature in discussions of the energy issue. The public policy agenda has become preoccupied with the global over-supply of oil and the resultant drop in world oil prices. The constraints facing contemporary Canadian governments in the energy field are constraints arising from market forces, rather than from the constitutional jurisprudence of the Supreme Court. Indeed, Quebec, rather than the West, has become the principal advocate of Supreme Court reform. Once again, the obvious question: how did provincial governments, particularly those in the West, manage to overcome the constitutional obstacles which seemed so pressing and problematic less than a decade ago?

Consider first the aftermath and provincial response to the *CIGOL* case. The immediate priority of the province of Saskatchewan was to ensure that it would not have to refund the $500 million collected under the invalid production tax. The government achieved this result by levying an income tax on the oil industry, retroactive to December 31, 1973. This alternative form of tax was constitutionally valid, since income taxes are direct taxes and within the provincial taxing power under s.92(2) of the *BNA Act*. The $500 million previously collected by the government under the invalid production tax was to be set off against the liability arising from the income tax. The legislation also imposed limits on the deductibility of expenses for the purpose of calculating liability for tax.

This income tax allowed the government to achieve its main goal, which was to ensure that the increase in energy rents resulting from the oil crisis remained in Saskatchewan. But income taxes are more complex and costly to administer than production taxes. In order to levy an income tax there must be a calculation of the "profit" that is subject to tax; a production tax can be levied on the more straightforward basis of the bare number of units produced or sold. Moreover, an income tax presents opportunities and incentive for tax avoidance behaviour by those subject to the tax. Tax avoidance is a marginal consideration in the administration of a production tax. This means that, although the income tax was an adequate regulatory substitute for the production tax struck down in *CIGOL*, it was not a perfect substitute. The income tax was more costly to the government, in terms of the additional resources which had to be committed to enforcement. The income tax also carried with it a social cost – the cost of the resources invested in socially unproductive tax avoidance behaviour by the industry.

Having imposed an income tax as an interim measure, the province continued to press for some form of constitutional amendment to remedy fully its difficulty. Fortuitously for Saskatchewan, by 1981 the federal government badly needed western support for its constitutional reform package. In an attempt to gather support, the federal government agreed to amend s.92 of the *BNA. Act* so as to broaden provincial powers over the natural resource sector. The new s.92(a) of the *Act*, enacted as part of the constitutional reform package by Westminster in 1982, granted provinces power to make "laws in relation to the raising of money by any mode or system of taxation in respect of … non-renewable natural resources…." This amendment eliminated the requirement that a provincial tax be "direct" rather than "indirect."

The constitutional amendment has enabled the province of Saskatchewan to enact the *Freehold Oil and Gas Production Tax Act*, 1982 as well as the *Mineral Taxation Act*, 1983. The first *Act* provides for a production tax on the freehold oil and gas produced in the province; the second *Act* levies a production tax on the production of specified minerals. In short, the province has now fully regained the constitutional ground it lost in *CIGOL*.

What assessment can be offered of the instrumental impact of the Court's decision? First, it is clear that the decision was not nearly as crippling to provincial regulatory power as had been suggested initially. The province was able to replace immediately the invalid production tax with an income tax, thereby avoiding any significant revenue loss. At the same time, there were nontrivial costs associated with the imposition of an income tax in place of a production tax. In short, while the decision was not the disaster which some had feared, neither was it wholly irrelevant to the formulation of provincial energy policy.

Second, the fact that the result in the case was later reversed by constitutional amendment does not mean that the litigation was thereby rendered meaningless. Because the rule announced by the Court had to some extent limited provincial power, the federal government had been provided with an important constitutional bargaining chip. The federal government was able to play that chip when it was faced with widespread opposition to its constitutional proposals. Had the *CIGOL* litigation been decided the other way, the federal government would have had to have offered some other constitutional concession in order to achieve the same result.

There is a final point that needs to be emphasized, relating to the nature of the federal–provincial bargaining surrounding this issue. The energy issue in the late 1970s and early 1980s was framed and understood in explicitly regional terms, with the resource-rich provinces being pitted against consuming provinces. Federal–provincial bargaining on such a regionally-sensitive issue requires the active involvement of the highest political levels of the respective governments. Further, agreement is impossible without each side being seen to offer significant political concessions to the other. In contrast, the issues arising from the *Dominion Stores* and *Labatt Breweries* litigation have not been perceived as explicitly regional issues. Federal–provincial bargaining on food product standards, for example, is understood as an issue which seems to affect all regions of the country in roughly equal fashion. There are a number of consequences which flow from this difference. First, it is possible to achieve federal–provincial consensus on such "technical" issues without the active involvement of the highest political levels. Second, because the negotiations can be framed in technical rather than political terms, there is no necessity for each side to be seen to be offering "concessions" to the other. These distinctions are important in terms of predicting those cases in which federal-provincial bargaining is likely to be successful; I will return to them in the final section of this chapter.

What of the response to the Supreme Court's decision in the *Central Canada* case? As with *CIGOL*, the ultimate impact on provincial regulatory power was much less severe than had been feared initially. In this case, however, the circumstances which produced this result were largely fortuitous. The provincial regulatory scheme had been enacted in the late 1960s, in response to a serious excess of supply and a drop in the world price of potash. By the time the Supreme Court decision in the case was handed down in 1978, the market for potash had changed. Due in part to the success of the provincial scheme limiting production and fixing prices, the market had stabilized. The industry no longer needed production quotas or price-fixing in order to survive. Thus, the Court's ruling that the provincial scheme was unconstitutional had no appreciable impact on the market or the provincial economy.

Potash producers in Saskatchewan during this period had also been contemplating a constitutional challenge to potash "prorationing fees," levied under the *Potash Proration Fees Regulations, 1972*. The potash producers had laid the groundwork for this challenge by successfully arguing that a province had to refund money collected under an unconstitutional law. However, in 1979 the producers abandoned their constitutional challenge against the prorationing fees by entering into the *Potash Resource Payment Agreement, 1979*. Under this agreement, the producers agreed to abandon their constitutional challenges and to render payments to the province in accordance with a fixed schedule. In return, the province agreed not to levy any further proration fees.

It is easy to identify the gains each party obtained from this agreement. The province obtained a guaranteed series of payments from the industry, thus avoiding the uncertainty associated with the pending constitutional challenges. The industry gained the certainty of knowing in advance what rate of tax it would have to pay to the province, avoiding the possibility of sudden, unexpected increases in their tax liability. By entering into this agreement, both parties purchased certainty about the intentions and future behaviour of the other.

In short, by the late 1970s, constitutional constraints had faded in significance in the relationship between the province of Saskatchewan and the potash industry. This situation was in part a product of the market conditions prevailing at the time, which made strict provincial regulation unnecessary. It was also due to the fact that the province and the industry had purchased constitutional peace through the *Potash Resource Payment Agreement*. The enactment of s.92(a) of the *Constitution Act, 1867* served to confirm provincial power to regulate the potash industry. Section 92(a) grants the province power to enact laws in relation to the management and conservation of non-renewable natural resources. This suggests that, should the market for potash collapse in the future, the province will have ample constitutional authority to restore stability to the market.

4. Conclusion: The Impact of Constitutional Constraint

What general conclusions can be drawn from these case studies of the impact of constitutional adjudication on Canadian government? The first conclusion is obvious: the outcomes of constitutional cases are much less determinative of public policy than is often supposed by lawyers and legal scholars. In each of the cases examined, the constitutional result was initially seen as a significant setback to the losing government. Yet in each instance, the governments concerned have been able to achieve the same regulatory goals through alternative instruments. It must be conceded that in certain instances this conclusion had resulted largely from market forces rather than from the conscious intervention of government. The point remains that there was no instance in which the constitutional rule announced by the Court determined the eventual behaviour of the parties.

This does not mean that constitutional constraints are wholly illusory. As I have emphasized throughout this chapter, often the only means of overcoming a constitutional constraint is through intergovernmental agreement: in such instances, the constitutional decision fixes the initial bargaining position of the parties. In other instances, the alternative regulatory instrument is an imperfect substitute for the device struck down by the Court. The point is simply that constitutional reasons will rarely constitute conclusive reasons against undertaking particular public policies. Federalism does not create regulatory vacuums. There will inevitably be a variety of regulatory instruments or legal arrangements which could be utilized in order to achieve a given policy goal. Constitutional reasons may operate so as to rule out the use of some of those regulatory instruments or legal arrangements. But constitutional constraints will rarely make all of the possible instruments off limits. In this sense, constitutional constraints must be seen in relativistic terms. They operate so as to increase the costs associated with achieving policy goals, forcing government to employ alternative regulatory instruments or else to coordinate efforts with those of other levels of government. Policy-makers are then faced with a choice: either bear the increased costs associated with the alternative instrument or abandon the goal. Constitutional constraints help to shape the legislative demand curve.

10.6

Re Constitution of Canada, 1981: The Patriation Reference

Michael Mandel

This excerpt is reprinted as Reading 2.3.

10.7

Reference re the Secession of Quebec
The Supreme Court of Canada (1998)

This article is reprinted as Reading 2.4.

10.8

Key Terms

Concepts

federalism
judicial review
disallowance (s.56)
reservation (s.90)
Peace, Order and good Government
residual power
emergency doctrine
inherent national importance test
delegation via intergovernmental agreement
regulatory substitute
dovetailing federal-provincial legislation
interpretivist (or textual) approach to constitutional interpretation
non-interpretivist (or "living tree") approach to constitutional interpretation

Institutions, Events, and Documents

Judicial Committee of the Privy Council (1833)
Colonial Laws Validity Act (1865)
Constitution Act, ss. 91 and 92 (1867)
Supreme Court Act (1875)
The Persons Case (1928)
Statute of Westminster (1931)
The Labour Conventions Case (1937)
O'Connor Report (1939)
Amendments to *Supreme Court Act* (1949)
Anti-Inflation Reference (1976)
R. v. Dominion Stores Ltd. (1980)
Labatt Breweries v. *A.-G. Canada* (1980)
CIGOL v. *Saskatchewan* (1977)
Central Canada Potash Co. v. *Saskatchewan* (1979)

Judicial Review and Civil Liberties

11

The practice of judicial review is unique to liberal democratic nations. The grounding principles of liberal democracy posit that good government is "limited government," and a written constitution enforced by judicial review is a means to that end. While all instances of judicial review are found in liberal democracies, not all liberal democracies use judicial review. Historically, Great Britain has always been a liberal democracy, but it did not have a "written constitution," and consequently English judges did not exercise judicial review. (The adoption of the *European Convention of Human Rights* has changed this, but the "final say" still rests with Parliament. See Reading 1.0.) Even some democracies with a written constitution – Belgium, Finland, Luxembourg, the Netherlands, and Switzerland – deny the power of judicial review to their high courts.[1]

The absence of a written constitution and judicial review did not mean that the government of Great Britain was "unlimited." Professor Cheffins reminds us that the starting point of the British and thus the Canadian constitution is that "an individual is free except to the extent restrained by law." The converse is also true: "a governmental official or government agency only has such power as is vested in it or him by law," as illustrated by the *Roncarelli* v. *Duplessis* case (Reading 1.1).[2]

The doctrine of parliamentary sovereignty notwithstanding, Dicey makes it clear that political conventions of self-restraint and fair play, reinforced by public opinion, have operated to protect the same fundamental freedoms of Englishmen as judicial review of the U.S. *Bill of Rights* does for Americans. Dicey clearly preferred the flexibility of an "unwritten constitution" and vesting primary responsibility for the preservation of liberty in an elected, accountable, representative legislature such as Parliament. But he did not rule out the possibility of codifying the fundamental freedoms of the English

---

1 Arend Lijphart, *Democracies: Patterns of Majoritarian and Consensus Government in Twenty-One Countries* (New Haven, CT: Yale University Press, 1984), p. 193.

2 R. I. Cheffins and P. A. Johnson, *The Revised Canadian Constitution: Politics as Law* (Toronto: McGraw-Hill-Ryerson, 1986), p. 132.

people. After enumerating the fundamental components of the "rule of law" – "the right to personal freedom; the right to freedom of discussion; the right of public meeting; the use of martial law; the rights and duties of the army; the collection and expenditure of the public revenue; and the responsibility of ministers" – Dicey concludes:

> If at some future day the law of the constitution should be codified, each of the topics I have mentioned would be dealt with by the sections of the code.

In adopting the *Charter of Rights and Freedoms* in 1982, Canada did what Dicey merely speculated about some one hundred years earlier – to entrench in a written constitution the rights and freedoms that had previously been preserved through the British-style tradition of an "unwritten constitution." The preamble of the *Constitution Act, 1867*, declares that Canada shall have "a Constitution similar in Principle to that of the United Kingdom." This declaration meant not just the Westminster system of parliamentary democracy, but also the entire "unwritten constitution" that accompanied it. During its first ninety-three years Canada indeed had such a constitution, with the important exception of federalism. In 1960, the Diefenbaker government enacted the Canadian *Bill of Rights*, thus beginning the transition away from the British approach to the protection of civil liberties toward the American approach. Twenty-two years later, the Trudeau government's enactment of the *Charter of Rights* completed this transition. Parliamentary supremacy was replaced by constitutional supremacy, enforced by judicial review – or nearly replaced. The last-minute compromise leading to the section 33 "legislative override" power preserved a qualified form of parliamentary supremacy.

Civil Liberties and the Courts prior to 1960

From Confederation until 1960, judicial protection of civil liberties was limited to two techniques. The first was the "interpretive avoidance" approach inherited from British judges. When interpreting a statute of Parliament or one of the provinces, the courts assumed that the legislature intended to respect traditional rights and liberties. If a statute was open to two interpretations, one of which infringed a right or freedom, judges would exercise their discretion to choose the other interpretation. This approach is consistent with parliamentary supremacy, in that the courts do not overrule the legislature by declaring statutes "of no force or effect." "Interpretive avoidance" simply sends a message to parliamentary lawmakers that, until they indicate otherwise, by redrafting the statute in more explicit language, the courts will interpret it as indicated. While a determined majority in Parliament could easily override such judicial attempts at protecting civil liberties, in practice this was rare. The *Roncarelli* case (Reading 11.3) and the *Boucher* case (Reading 11.4) are examples of the Canadian judiciary's use of the "interpretive avoidance" technique to protect traditional freedoms of individual Canadians.

The second method of judicial protection of civil liberties – the use of federalism limitations – was distinctly Canadian. Using this "power allocation" method, Canadian appeal court judges ruled reckless or discriminatory provincial policies *ultra vires* on section 91–92 grounds, even though the real issue was one of civil liberties. For example, in 1938, the Supreme Court struck down the euphemistically titled *Accurate News and Information Act*, which was an attempt by the Alberta Social Credit government to muzzle newspaper criticism of its economic policies. The Supreme Court ruled that this was legislation in relation to criminal law, and therefore beyond the legislative jurisdiction of any province.[3]

A second well-known example of this technique was the 1953 case of *Saumur* v. *Quebec*.[4] This was one of a series of Jehovah's Witnesses' cases from Quebec. In this instance, Quebec City had passed a bylaw prohibiting the distribution of pamphlets in the streets without permission of the Chief of Police. Saumur and other Jehovah's Witnesses were arrested for violating this bylaw. While normally this type of legislation is within the section 92 powers of the provinces, the punitive intentions behind it were clear. In striking down the Quebec bylaw, a number of Supreme Court judges argued that it was legislation in relation to religious freedom and that this was denied to the provinces either by section 91 (criminal law) or section 93 (denominational rights) of the *Constitution Act, 1867*.

While the "power allocation" approach was successfully used to protect civil liberties on several occasions, there were drawbacks to this approach. First, whatever powers were denied to provincial governments were logically conceded to the federal government. While this technique had the disturbing implication that the federal government was free to enact the same, illiberal policy as the province, this never proved to be a practical problem. A more serious objection to this approach was that it forced the judges to use the language of federalism when dealing with the logic of civil liberties. This surreptitious method of reasoning tended to confuse the jurisprudence of both federalism and civil liberties.

There is a third strand of pre-*Bill of Rights* civil liberties jurisprudence that deserves mention, even though it has never been accepted by a Supreme Court majority. Known as the "implied Bill of Rights" approach, it argues that the provisions of the preamble of the *Constitution Act* – that Canada shall have "a Constitution similar in Principle to that of the United Kingdom" – imported into Canada the traditional rights and freedoms protected by Britain's "unwritten constitution." The previously cited passages from Dicey show the plausibility of this argument. In the *Alberta Press Case*, Justice Duff argued that "the right of public debate" was inherent in a parliamentary system and that the preamble provided sufficient grounds to declare the

---

3 *Reference re Alberta Statutes*, [1938] S.C.R. 100, more commonly known as the *Alberta Press Case*.

4 [1953] 2 S.C.R. 299.

Alberta Press Act inoperative. Similarly, in the *Saumur* case, Justices Rand, Kellock, and Locke said that the preamble implicitly protected "freedom of religion" from both levels of government. The strength of this approach lies in its correct recognition of the civil liberties dimension of the "unwritten constitution" inherited from Great Britain. This is also its weakness, since British judges never pretended to have the authority to enforce these freedoms directly against Parliament. It is widely accepted that constitutional custom and convention are not judicially enforceable, and the strength of this tradition prevented the "implied Bill of Rights" approach from ever gaining general acceptance.[5]

Civil Liberties and the Courts under the 1960 *Bill of Rights*

In the aftermath of the Second World War, growing awareness of the Stalinist and Nazi atrocities of the preceding decades alarmed Western democracies about the fragile nature of human rights and civil liberties in the mass societies of the twentieth century. This concern was shared by Canadian leaders, who were also troubled by their own harsh treatment of Japanese Canadians during the war years and the government's harassment of the Jehovah's Witnesses in Quebec. After a decade of committee hearings and public discussion, the Diefenbaker government adopted the Canadian *Bill of Rights* in 1960 (See Appendix B).

The 1960 *Bill of Rights* took the form of a statute of Parliament, not an amendment to the *Constitution Act*. It also applied only to the federal government. The provinces would not consent to additional restrictions on their legislative powers, and Ottawa lacked the authority to impose them unilaterally.

From the start, the *Bill of Rights* was plagued by problems of interpretation. These problems stemmed principally from its legal status as an ordinary statute and the ambiguous wording of its second section. Canadian judges, including those on the Supreme Court, could not agree on what function the *Bill of Rights* assigned to the courts. Some argued that the *Bill of Rights*

---

5 The adoption of the *Charter* in 1982 was thought to terminate the idea of an "implied bill of rights," and the Supreme Court actually said so in an early *Charter* decision. However, its more recent rulings in the *Provincial Judges Reference* (Reading 5.6) and the *Quebec Secession Reference* (Reading 2.4) have resuscitated the notion of judicially enforceable "implied constitutional principles" such as "judicial independence," "democracy," and "protection for minorities." What future courts will do with these new "principles" is difficult to predict, but their potential scope is stunning. See *Lalonde* v. *Ontario*, Ontario Court of Appeal, Dec. 7, 2001 (unreported), for an example of how the Ontario Court of Appeal has used these new "unwritten principles" to overrule the Ontario government's decision to close the French-language Montfort Hospital in Ottawa.

conferred new authority on the courts to declare parliamentary statutes "of no force or effect," if they conflicted with enumerated rights. According to this interpretation, the *Bill of Rights* armed the Canadian courts with an American-style "power denial" function. Others thought that the *Bill of Rights* was essentially a canon of statutory interpretation, a codification of the traditional "interpretive avoidance" method. They pointed to the ambiguous wording of section 2 and the statutory, as opposed to constitutional, status of the Bill.

The Supreme Court's landmark decision in the 1969 *Drybones* case put an end to this particular problem.[6] A majority of the Court took the position that the *Bill of Rights* did confer authority on the judges to declare offending statutes inoperative. The Court ruled that section 94(*b*) of the *Indian Act* denied Drybones his rights to "equality before the law" because it treated him more harshly for public intoxication than other Canadians would have been treated for the same offence, simply because he was an Indian. The *Drybones* decision was hailed as a major development in Canadian constitutional evolution. It seemed to signify an important new restraint on the tradition of parliamentary supremacy and an important new role for the Canadian judiciary in policing *Bill of Rights* violations.

The high expectations created by *Drybones* were short-lived. Subsequent Supreme Court decisions indicated that the judges were still inclined to defer to Parliament's judgment on substantive issues of criminal procedure. This trend culminated in the Supreme Court's 1974 decision of the *Lavell* and *Bedard* cases.[7] Lavell and Bedard were Indian women who had lost their Indian status pursuant to section 12(1)(*b*) of the *Indian Act*. This section provides that Indian women who marry non-Indians lose their status, but no similar disability is imposed on Indian men who marry non-Indians. Lavell and Bedard argued that this violated their right to "equality before the law," since it discriminated against them on the basis of their sex. Based on the *Drybones* precedent, which appeared to prohibit discrimination in the laws based on explicitly prohibited categories such as race and sex, their case seemed strong. The Supreme Court surprised everyone by finding otherwise. A majority of the Court ruled that the right to "equality before the law" meant "equality in the application and administration of the laws." Since there was no question that section 12(1)(*b*) was being applied to Lavell and Bedard the same as it was applied to all other Indian women, there was no violation of the *Bill of Rights*. The dissenting justices protested the apparent inconsistency of this interpretation with the *Drybones* precedent, but to no avail.

In subsequent cases, Chief Justice Laskin described the *Bill of Rights* as a "quasi-constitutional document" and exhorted his colleagues to return to the spirit of *Drybones*, but to no avail. Laskin's arguments were plausible but they fell on deaf ears. The fact of the matter was that a majority of the judges did not want the power of judicial review because they viewed it as

---

6 *The Queen* v. *Drybones*, [1970] S.C.R. 282.

7 *Attorney-General of Canada* v. *Lavell and Bedard*, [1974] 1 S.C.R. 1349.

inconsistent with Canada's political and legal inheritance. Justice Pigeon's opinion in *Drybones*, even though written in dissent, captured the spirit of the Court and of that generation of Canadian lawyers:[8]

> The meaning of such expressions as "due process of law," "equality before the law," "freedom of religion," "freedom of speech," is in truth largely unlimited and undefined. According to individual views and the evolution of current ideas, the actual content of such legal concepts is apt to expand and to vary as is strikingly apparent in other countries. In the traditional British system that is our own by virtue of the *B.N.A. Act*, the responsibility for updating statutes in this changing world rests exclusively with Parliament. If the Parliament of Canada intended to depart from that principle in enacting the Bill, one would expect to find clear language expressing that intention.

Civil Liberties and the Courts under the 1982 *Charter of Rights*

By the late 1970s, Prime Minister Trudeau and his Liberal Party were increasingly interested in a constitutionally entrenched bill of rights as a potential "nation-building" device to counter the increasing intensity of conflict in federal-provincial relations. Trudeau had endorsed the idea of a constitutionally entrenched bill of rights as early as 1967. He argued that a constitutional bill of rights would enhance national unity by emphasizing what Canadians hold in common – citizenship – now to be defined by a common set of rights against both levels of government.[9] Initially there was no market for Trudeau's idea. The attachment of Canadian political and legal elites to the tradition of parliamentary supremacy and provincial suspicions of a centralist court were too strong. (Trudeau tried to allay provincial fears by suggesting that Ottawa would be willing to abolish the federal powers of disallowance and reservation in return for provincial support of a bill of rights.) In the years following the *Lavell and Bedard* (1974) and *Morgentaler* (1975) decisions, feminists and civil libertarian groups became disillusioned with the 1960 *Bill of Rights* as an effective legal instrument to achieve the kinds of judge-led policy reforms that they observed in the United States and wanted to emulate in Canada. They were attracted to Trudeau's proposals for a new, stronger, and broader rights document. Out of these seemingly diverse interests was born the political coalition responsible for the adoption of the *Charter of Rights and Freedoms* in 1982 (Appendix C).

The *Charter* was a central part of the package of constitutional reforms adopted in 1982 and was the product of an extended process of intergovernmental

---

8 Jusice Pigeon, dissenting, *The Queen v. Drybones*, [1970] S.C.R. 282.
9 See Pierre Elliot Trudeau, "A Constitutional Declaration of Rights," *Federalism and the French Canadians* (Toronto: MacMillan, 1968), p. 52.

and interest-group politics. The *Charter* is best understood as a compromise between the advocates and opponents of a greater role for the courts in Canadian politics and policy-making. Trudeau's initiative succeeded in strengthening the role of the courts under the *Charter* in three specific ways, relative to the 1960 *Bill of Rights*. First and foremost, the *Charter* applies to both levels of government, provincial and federal. Second, the *Charter* is constitutionally entrenched, not just a statute as the *Bill of Rights* was. Third, the *Charter* explicitly authorizes the judges to review legislation for violations of enumerated rights (s.24(1)) and to declare "any law that is inconsistent with the provisions of the Constitution ... of no force or effect" (s.52).

The opponents of too great a role for the judges extracted two concessions from the government in return for their support. The first is the "reasonable limitations" clause of section 1, which made explicit what was already understood to be implicit – that none of the enumerated rights are absolute. (Note that this objective was largely defeated when the Supreme Court operationalized section 1 in the "*Oakes* test." See Reading 9.6.) The second, more important concession was the section 33 "notwithstanding clause." Section 33 allows either level of government to "veto" or override a judicial decision to which it objects, if the decision is based on the fundamental freedoms (s.2), legal rights (ss.7–14), or equality rights (s.15) sections of the *Charter*. This "legislative review of judicial review" is important because it preserves the principle of parliamentary sovereignty, albeit in a modified form. (See the debate over section 33 in Readings 13.2, 13.3, and 13.4.)

With three important exceptions, the *Charter* basically amplifies the rights that were already protected by the 1960 *Bill of Rights*, and the latter only codified the rights and freedoms that already existed as common law and as constitutional conventions. The exceptions – language rights (sections 16–23), aboriginal rights (sections 25 and 35) and the exclusionary rule (section 24(2)) – did not exist before. What was new about both the *Bill of Rights* and the *Charter* was the growing transfer of the decision-making process from legislative assemblies to courts. As Russell pointed out when the *Charter* was adopted, "[A] charter of rights guarantees not rights but a particular way of making decisions about rights, in which the judicial branch of government has a much more systematic and authoritative role."[10] The net effect of this evolution, Russell observed, is "its tendency to judicialize politics and to politicize the judiciary." (The latter is discussed in chapter 4.)

Whether the addition of the *Charter* to Canada's written constitution would be an evolutionary or revolutionary development ultimately depended on the interpretation given to it by the Supreme Court. The Court's self-restrained and deferential interpretation of the 1960 *Bill of Rights* effectively prevented that document from having any significant legal or political impact. Would a similar fate meet the *Charter*? Some legal experts predicted so.

---

10 Peter H. Russell, "The Effect of the Charter of Rights on the Policy-Making Role of Canadian Courts," *Canadian Public Administration* 25 (1982), p. 1.

Professor James Kelly's statistical overview of the Supreme Court's first 390 *Charter* decisions (1982–99) reveals that the answer to this question is a resounding "no" (Reading 11.5). [*Ed. note*: Kelly has organized his data into two time periods (1982–92 and 1993–99) in order to identify trends or changes in the Court's treatment of *Charter* cases.] In these 390 *Charter* decisions, the Supreme Court upheld the rights claimant in one out of every three cases. After an initial "honeymoon" (1984–86) when *Charter* claimants won sixty-four per cent (9/15) of the cases decided by the Supreme Court, the success rate has remained steady at thirty-three per cent. By contrast, rights-claimants won only five of thirty-four (15%) of *Bill of Rights* cases in the Supreme Court between 1960 and 1982.

Just as the Court's unreceptive attitude toward the 1960 *Bill of Rights* had the effect of discouraging litigation, the Court's activist jurisprudence under the *Charter* has stimulated litigation. The Court heard only thirty-five *Bill of Rights* cases over a twenty-two year period but has decided 395 *Charter* cases over seventeen years. Since 1993, *Charter* decisions have accounted for twenty-six per cent of the Court's annual caseload, making the Court very much a "public law" court. Another indication of the Court's new activism is the number of statutes that it has declared invalid (in whole or in part): sixty-five by the end of 1999, compared to just one (in *Drybones*) under the 1960 *Bill of Rights*. Note that the breakdown of these sixty-five nullifications is roughly equal between federal (31) and provincial (32) laws.

Kelly argues that these trends show that the Court has abandoned the "highly activist" period of the first ten years (1982–92) in favour of a "moderate activism" and a more "balanced" approach toward provincial laws in particular. While some of Kelly's data supports this claim – for example, the Court's growing reluctance to exclude evidence under section 24(2) (Table 8) – there is also evidence to the contrary. Kelly shows that, since 1993, there has been a surge in judicial activism in the area of aboriginal rights – decisions that have impacted disproportionately on provincial governments.

The same could be said of the Court's two leading gay rights rulings – *Vriend* and *M* v. *H.* – that struck down statutes in Alberta and Ontario, respectively. In what turned out to be one of its most controversial Charter decisions, the Court in *Vriend*, rather than strike down the *Alberta Human Rights Act*, chose as a remedy to "read in" sexual orientation. Amending legislation by judicial fiat as in *Vriend* is even more activist that striking down an offending act.[11] Similarly in *M* v. *H*, the Court overruled a legislative decision that had been made by way of an all-party free vote in the Ontario Legislature.

---

11 Writing as recently as 1985, Professor Peter Hogg, in discussing the incapacities of judges to act as policy-makers, commented that, "of course [courts] have no power to enact a law in substitution for one declared invalid," *Constitutional Law of Canada*, 2d ed. (Toronto: Carswell, 1985), p. 98). The Supreme Court abandoned this "obvious" doctrine seven years later in *Schachter* v. *Canada*, in which it gave itself the

M v. *H* had a "ripple effect" of invalidating hundreds of similar provisions in the family law acts of the other nine provinces.

Kelly emphasizes the declining number of language rights and LMG education claims in the Supreme Court and also their declining success rates. However, as Manfredi's study of LMG litigation points out, many of the most important LMG decisions – *Lavoie* (N.S.) and *Marchand* (Ontario) – have been made at the provincial appeal court level (Reading 7.4). These decisions do not appear in Supreme Court data, but they have still had a serious negative impact on provincial policy autonomy. After Kelly had completed his study, Ontario courts reversed the Harris government's decision to close the French-speaking Montfort Hospital in Ottawa as part of a broader restructuring of health care in the region.[12] The decision was characterized as "a major defeat for the Ontario government."[13] The legal basis of this decision was the "implicit constitutional principle" of "protection of minority rights" announced by the Supreme Court in its 1998 *Quebec Secession Reference* (Reading 2.4). Given the open-ended nature of this "right," its effect on other provinces could be significant.

Two weeks after the *Montfort Hospital* ruling, the Supreme Court reversed another Harris government initiative – not allowing agriculture workers to bargain collectively. The Court ruled that this violated the workers' *Charter* right to freedom of association.[14] To be fair, these decisions were handed down after Kelly had finished his research, but they are hardly supportive of his general claim that, "The Court has generally been supportive of provincial policy since 1990." Students will have to weigh the conflicting evidence for themselves.

The use of the Court's new "veto power" over federal and provincial governments is the most visible effect of the *Charter*, but perhaps not its most significant. Writing about the similar growth in influence of constitutional courts in Europe, Shapiro and Stone have observed that, "Less dramatic, but perhaps of greater long-run systemic significance than big judicial vetoes, is the emergence of a politics of constitutional dialogue ... the change in the discourse that legislators employ in their own internal drafting and debate in anticipation of subsequent constitutional review."[15]

Peter Russell has observed the same phenomenon in post-*Charter* Canada: that the *Charter* is changing Canadians' political discourse; that is, how we

---

new remedial power of "reading in" ([1992] 2 S.C.R. 679). Salvaging an otherwise invalid law by judges' "reading in" new requirements is what the Court did in *Vriend*.

12 *Lalonde* v. *Ontario*, Ontario Court of Appeal, Dec. 7, 2001 (unreported).

13 "Landmark decision preserves French-language hospital," *National Post*, Dec. 8, 2001, A8.

14 *Dunmore* v. *Ontario*, [2001] SCC 94.

15 Martin Shapiro and Alec Stone, "The New Constitutional Politics of Europe," *Comparative Political Studies* 26, no. 4 (1994), 397-420, at 417, 404.

talk about, and thus think about, politics. "Rights talk," Russell claims, has taken issues like abortion and Quebec's *Bill 101* and "recast [them] in less compromising and more strident terms – making consensual resolution of the issues more difficult than before."[16]

"Rights talk" is also evident in Canadian legislatures. In the fall, 2001, when Parliament debated the anti-terrorism legislation brought in after the September 11 attacks, much of the debate focused on whether Bill C-36 violated the *Charter of Rights*. This parliamentary preoccupation with the legality of Bill C-36 replicated Shapiro and Stone's observation about European legislatures: "Legislators begin to debate not only what is good or bad policy, but precisely what has the best chance of surviving scrutiny [by the courts]. In this way, the vocabulary of constitutional law comes to infect the vocabulary of policy-making, and the language of the constitutional lawyer becomes the language of the policy-maker."[17]

This trend towards "rights talk" is known as the "juridicalization of politics," as distinct from the more obvious "judicialization of politics," which denotes the judges' new power to shape public policies and interest-group activities designed to persuade judges to exercise that power . While both Russell and Shapiro suggest that "rights talk" has some negative effects on the policy-process, Shapiro claims that it is good for the courts. "The penetration and absorption of constitutional discourse into day-to-day political discourse has had the effect of enhancing the legitimacy of both the constitution, and thus the regime, and of the constitutional court, and thus constitutional review." [18] Shapiro was writing about European democracies, but his theory may explain why both the *Charter* and the courts continue to enjoy high levels of approval in Canadian public opinion polls, despite criticism of specific *Charter* decisions.

In trying to assess the impact of the *Charter* on the political process more generally, *Charter* litigation can be helpfully divided into two broad categories: attempts to turn cases into causes, and the opposite situation where an interest group attempts to turn its cause into a case. As Hein documents in Reading 11.8, the latter is the truly novel dimension that the *Charter* has brought to Canadian politics.

The first category involves mostly criminal cases raising legal rights claims. These account for two-thirds of the Supreme Court's *Charter* decisions and four-fifths of *Charter* litigation in general. These are typically garden-variety criminal cases that occur spontaneously and whose success depends initially on the ingenuity of the accused's lawyer. An

---

16 "Canadian Constraints on Judicialization from Without," *International Political Science Review* 15, no. 2 (1994), 165–75, at 173.

17 Martin Shapiro and Alec Stone, "The New Constitutional Politics of Europe," *Comparative Political Studies* 26 no. 4 (1994), 397–420, at 417, 404.

18 Martin Shapiro and Alec Stone, "The New Constitutional Politics of Europe," *Comparative Political Studies* 26 no. 4 (1994), 397–420, at 417.

entrepreneurial lawyer argues that amongst the otherwise routine facts of a client's case is an important principle of procedural fairness that is protected by a *Charter* right. Interest groups are rarely involved at the beginning of these cases, and, with the exception of the Canadian Civil Liberties Association, are less likely to become involved at appeal stages. These cases are usually not overtly political and would have arisen even in the absence of a charter.

To say that these cases are not overtly political does not mean that they have not had an important policy impact. Cumulatively, they have reshaped the Canadian criminal process. Prior to the *Charter*, comparative studies of the criminal process regarded Canada as placing effective crime control ahead of maximizing "due process" rights of the accused. Since the *Charter*, the Court's decisions in right to counsel, search and seizure, and exclusion of evidence have moved Canada in the direction of a "due process" model of criminal procedure. A 1990 study found that, in four areas – waiver of right to counsel, roadside detention for breathalyzer tests, police lineups, and involuntary blood samples – the Canadian Court's decisions favoured the accused more than comparable decisions by the American Supreme Court.[19]

Initially, the Court's legal rights/criminal law decisions did not draw attention outside the bar, but this is changing. The *Askov* ruling – resulting in the dismissal of charges against 40,000 accused awaiting trial – was widely publicized (Reading 8.2). The same was true of the Court's 1997 *Feeney* ruling, in which it excluded reliable and incriminating evidence in a murder trial. Opinion surveys indicate that the public disagrees with the Court on the exclusion-of-evidence issue, and the new Reform Party made "law and order" an effective issue in its rise to become the Official Opposition during the 1990s. In the interview that resulted in a complaint to the Canadian Judicial Council, Justice Bastarache criticized some of the Court's legal rights decisions (See Reading 5.0). This incident illustrates that both the CCLA and criminal defence lawyers are developing the same kind of proprietary interests in legal rights that other groups have in other sections of the *Charter*.

The second category of cases involves interest groups trying to turn their cause into a case. This group is numerically smaller but politically more significant. Some have not arisen spontaneously but represent a conscious effort of an interest group (LEAF or the NCC) or an individual (Dr. Henry Morgentaler or Joe Borowski) to get a policy issue into the courts for judicial determination. Many would not have occurred without the *Charter*. Most involve *Charter* rights that do have political constituencies – the section 15 equality-seeking groups such as LEAF and EGALE; the LMGs that litigate under section 23 of the *Charter*; and aboriginal groups pursuing section 35 claims. Some of these cases are part of systematic litigation strategies

---

19 Robert Harvie and Hamar Foster, "Ties That Bind? The Supreme Court of Canada, American Jurisprudence, and the Revision of Canadian Criminal Law Under the Charter," *Osgoode Hall Law Journal* 28, no. 4 (1990), pp. 729–88.

pursued by rights-advocacy groups. These organizations may be involved directly as litigants or indirectly as intervenors or financial sponsors. In many of these cases, the groups/litigants have benefited from the Court's own liberalized rules of standing, mootness, and intervenor participation as well as government funding. Collectively, it is this group of cases, with their associated interest-group activities, that constitute the "judicialization of politics" predicted by Russell in 1982.

The role of organized interests is central to Charles Epp's widely cited theory of the causes of Canada's "rights revolution" (Reading 11.7). Epp rejects as too legalistic the explanation that the adoption of the *Charter* in 1982 was the cause. Citing examples of nations with rights document without much judicial enforcement of those rights, Epp writes that, "The fate of a bill of rights depends on forces outside of it." In response to the question, "Do Bills of Rights Matter?" Epp replies: yes, but only if there is a "support structure for legal mobilization" (SSLM). The three key elements of an SSLM are: (1) "rights advocacy organizations" (2) that enjoy substantial support among skilled lawyers, and (3) that have non-member funding – private foundations (U.S.) or governments (Canada). Epp provides empirical evidence that many of the effects attributed to the *Charter of Rights* actually precede its adoption in 1982, but coincide with the growth of an SSLM in Canada during the 1970s.

Assessment of the impact of "*Charter* politics" has been mixed. Public support for both the *Charter* and the courts appears to be wide. What is less clear is how deep that support is. A survey of elite and mass opinion conducted in 1987 found strong support for the *Charter* in every political party and every province in Canada.[20] A follow-up survey confirmed continuing high levels of support – in the eighty per cent range – for the proposition that the *Charter of Rights* "is a good thing."[21] Similarly, both the 1987 and 1999 polls reported that just over sixty per cent of Canadians responded that courts, not legislatures, should have "the final say" when there is a conflict between a law and the *Charter*. This was true for all regions but not all political parties. Reform Party supporters were evenly divided by this question.

---

20 See Paul Sniderman, Joseph F. Fletcher, Peter H. Russell, and Phillip Tetlock, *The Clash of Rights* (New Haven, CT: Yale University Press, 1996). The authors' claim to have disproven the theory of "democratic elitism" was subsequently challenged. See Richard Vengroff and F. L. Morton, "Regional Perspectives on Canada's Charter of Rights and Freedoms: A Re-Examination of Democratic Elitism," *Canadian Journal of Political Science* 33 (2000), pp. 359–82; and also Sniderman, Fletcher, Russell, Tetlock and Prior, "The Theory of Democratic Elitism Revisited: A Response to Vengroff and Morton," *Canadian Journal of Political Science* 33 (2000), pp. 569–96; and Vengroff and Morton, "The Theory of Democratic Elitism Revisited Again," *Canadian Journal of Political Science* 34 (2001), pp. 169–73.

21 Joseph F. Fletcher and Paul Howe, "Public Opinion and the Courts," in Paul Howe and Peter H. Russell, eds., *Judicial Power and Canadian Democracy* (McGill-Queen's University Press, 2001), pp. 255–96.

Support dropped somewhat when more specific questions were asked. Respondents were evenly divided (43%–42%) on the proposition that "the right of the Supreme Court to decide certain controversial issues should be reduced." Interestingly, fifty-one per cent of Quebeckers agreed. In response to a related question – "Who should choose Supreme Court judges?" – only thirteen per cent said the prime minister. Forty-seven per cent said the provinces, and thirty-seven per cent said Parliament. With respect to specific *Charter* decisions, the 1999 survey found that a majority (high sixty per cent range) opposed Supreme Court decisions excluding improperly obtained but reliable evidence from criminal trials but supported (seventy per cent range) the Court's decision in the gay rights case, *Vriend* v. *Alberta*. In the latter case, Reform Party supporters were again outliers, with less than fifty per cent support. Perhaps as significant was the public's low level of awareness. Despite the fact that *Vriend* had been decided less than twelve months earlier and had been the subject of intense media coverage, fewer than ten per cent of the respondents reported "hearing a lot" about the case and sixty per cent reported "hearing nothing." Similarly, only thirteen per cent of respondents knew that the prime minister appoints Supreme Court justices. Statistical linkages between specific support (or opposition) for a decision and diffuse support for the Court itself were varied.[22] In sum, the surveys suggest that, while the Canadian public likes the *Charter* and the Supreme Court, they do not know much about either, thus leaving in doubt the depth of support.

While the public has been supportive of the *Charter* and the courts, there has been an energetic attack on "*Charter* worship" within the academic community. In the first decade, most of the critics were drawn from old-school social democrats and neo-Marxists. These left-wing *Charter* critics argued that the "judicialized politics" encouraged by the *Charter* primarily benefits the middle and upper classes by legitimizing the status quo and sapping the energy and resources from a class-based politics whose object is the redistribution of wealth. They also argue that the liberal, individualistic nature of the *Charter* threatens the communitarian tradition in Canadian politics and de-legitimates state intervention to protect community and promote equality.[23]

Recently, conservative critics have been more visible. Their primary criticism is that the Supreme Court has not been faithful to the text and original understanding of certain *Charter* rights. Instead, they claim, the justices are simply

---

22 Ibid.

23 The leading lights of the left school of *Charter* critics are Michael Mandel, *The Charter of Rights and the Legalization of Politics in Canada* , revised ed. (Thomson Educational Publishing, 1994); Andrew Petter, "Immaculate Deception: The Charter's Hidden Agenda," *The Advocate* 45 (1987), p. 857; and Allan Hutchinson, *Waiting for Coraf: A Critique of Law and Rights* (Toronto: University of Toronto Press, 1995).

reading in their own notions of social justice and reform. These critics also argue that "rights talk" and the moral hubris it breeds are undermining the practice and the habits of representative democracy – in particular, the willingness to accept the outcomes of elections even when – especially when – one's party loses. They deny that the *Charter* movement is a grassroots or "bottom up" movement. They point to the elitist socio-economic characteristics (high income, high education professionals) of many of the groups and institutions involved and their heavy reliance on state funding. These critics also argue that courts lack the democratic legitimacy and the institutional capacity to fashion public policies designed to promote "equality of results." The neo-liberal agenda of group equality is seen as fostering an oppressive, expensive, and inefficient "rights bureaucracy" that benefits primarily itself.[24] The common denominator of both left- and right-wing *Charter* critics is the flight from democratic politics that it encourages. Behind the rhetoric of rights, both see a reality of an unaccountable government of judges.

To be sure, the *Charter* also has its academic defenders. Greg Hein (Reading 7.5) and James Kelly (Reading 11.5) both present the Supreme Court's *Charter* decisions as a positive force in Canadian political life. David Beatty has written prolifically and enthusiastically about the *Charter*, chastising the Supreme Court for being too restrained and deferential in its interpretation of the *Charter*.[25] The "Court Party" thesis of Morton and Knopff has been challenged by a several leading *Charter* scholars.[26] Richard Sigurdson has presented a critique of "left-wing and right-wing Charterphobia" and his own defence of the *Charter*. Sigurdson points to a substantial list of policy changes achieved through *Charter* litigation and claims that:

24 See F. L. Morton and Rainer Knopff, *The Charter Revolution and the Court Party* (Peterborough, ON: Broadview Press, 2000); Christopher Manfredi, *Judicial Power and the Charter: Canada and the Paradox of Liberal Constitutionalism* (Oxford: Oxford University Press, 2001); Rainer Knopff and F. L. Morton, *Charter Politics* (Scarborough, ON: Nelson Canada, 1992); and Anthony Peacock, ed., *Rethinking the Constitution: Perspectives on Canadian Constitutional Reform, Interpretation and Theory* (Oxford University Press, 1996); Ian Brodie, "The Political Disadvantage Theory," *Friends of the Court: The Privileging of Interest Group Litigants in Canada* (Albany: State University of New York Press, 2002), chapter 1.

25 See David Beatty, *Talking Heads and the Supremes: The Canadian Production of Constitutional Review* (Toronto: Carswell, 1990).

26 See Lorne Sossin, "Courting the Right: Review of *The Charter Revolution and the Court Party*," *Osgoode Hall Law Journal* 38:3 (2000), pp. 531–41; Kent Roach, "The People versus the Supreme Court," *Literary Review of Canada* (June 2001), pp. 13–16; Miriam Smith, "Ghosts of the JCPC: Group Politics and Charter Litigation in Canadian Political Science," *Canadian Journal of Political Science* 35, no. 1 (2002), pp. 3–30; also, Rainer Knopff and F.L. Morton, "Ghosts and Straw Men: A Comment on Miriam Smith's 'Ghosts of the Judicial Committee of the Privy Council," *Canadian Journal of Political Science* 35, no. 1 (2002), pp. 31–42.

All of these victories for underprivileged individuals and groups enhance, rather than undermine, the democratic character of our society. The fact that they were won in the courts rather than in the legislative arena does not make them less democratic."[27]

Some of these same defences have been echoed by the judges, who in recent years have increasingly taken to defending themselves (see Readings 13.8 and 13.9).

As Canada enters its third decade in "*Charter*land," the debate over the *Charter* and the courts is in full bloom. Canadians have lost the instinctive confidence in parliamentary democracy that characterized their political life from Confederation until the 1970s and that contributed to the non-development of the 1960 *Bill of Rights*. The adoption of the *Charter*, its activist interpretation by the Supreme Court, and the spirited defence of both all testify to new support for an increased judicial role in the governing process. Today. there is a perception that constitutional questions are too important to be left with politicians. Contrast this attitude with the opposition to the *Supreme Court Act* in the 1870s on the grounds that constitutional questions were too important to be decided by un-elected judges (see Reading 10.1). This change reflects Canadians' growing disillusion with Parliament and democratic politics.[28] The *Charter* is clearly here to stay. Further debate will focus not on the existence of the *Charter*, but on corollary issues such as the appointment of judges, public funding of interest-group litigation, the use of the section 33 legislative override, and proper modes of interpretation.

Interpretivism and non-interpretivism – the two competing approaches to constitutional interpretation – have different consequences for judicial oversight of the law-making process.[29] Both recognize that constitutional meaning must be flexible enough to keep up with social change, but they draw opposing conclusions about the permissible scope of judicial updating. The interpretivists stress judicial fidelity to the text and the original understanding of that text as illuminated by the framers' intent. New circumstances may require novel applications of that original meaning, but the new meaning may not contradict or overrule the original meaning.

The non-interpretivists do not accept this limitation. They minimize the importance of judicial fidelity to original meaning. For the non-interpretivist, the judge's ultimate responsibility is to keep the constitution in tune with the times, not to keep the times in tune with the constitution. In the law of federalism, this approach usually supports judicial deference to legislative

27 Richard Sigurdson, "Left- and Right-Wing Charterphobia in Canada: A Critique of the Critics," *International Journal of Canadian Studies* 7–8 (1993), pp. 95–115.

28 This trend is not limited to Canada. See Kenneth M. Holland, *Judicial Activism in Comparative Perspective* (London: MacMillan, 1991), Introduction.

29 For a fuller discussion, see Rainer Knopff and F. L. Morton, *Charter Politics* (Nelson Canada, 1992), pp. 108–110.

decisions, but in *Charter* cases it is used to encourage the judicial expansion of rights and the corollary overruling of legislative choices.

The two approaches have their respective strengths and weaknesses. The strength of the interpretivist approach is that it is more principled. This enhances a judicial decision's legal authority (i.e., acceptance by the losing side) because it appears that the decision is "required" by law and deductive logic, not the personal policy preferences of the judge. Judicial decisions that are firmly grounded in principle and/or original understanding allow the judge to say to critics, "Don't shoot the messenger just because you don't like the message." In constitutional cases, the implication is that it is up to the political branches of government to amend a constitutional rule if they do not like it. The liability of the interpretivist approach is that it may result in the enforcement of archaic, out-of-touch constitutional limitations on government action, resulting in a political backlash and loss of political authority. This problem becomes more acute the older the constitutional rule is. The negative connotations of this problem are captured by the "frozen concepts" metaphor.

The advantage of the non-interpretivist approach is that it avoids this liability. If a constitutional rule is clearly out of touch with society's contemporary needs or beliefs, then the judge can use discretion to "update" the rule by adding new meaning. The positive connotations of this approach are captured by the "living tree" metaphor. The downside of the non-interpretivist approach is that it loses in legal authority (for the losing side) what it gains in political acceptance (on the winning side). Critics of decisions based on a non-interpretivist approach can claim that the decision is based not on law but the judges' own policy preferences. Since judges are unaccountable, this raises the problem of democratic legitimacy.

The debate between the interpretivists and non-interprevists is not simply an academic debate. It is at the heart of much of the current debate over the Supreme Court's *Charter* decisions. It is what Justice Bastarache was concerned about in his 2001 interview with *The Lawyers Weekly*. In response to a general question about why he was dissenting so often, Bastarache replied:[30]

> If we don't have a very principled, consistent approach to statutory interpretation we are easily going to be accused of being too subjective in our approach to legislation in order to justify a result that we want. And I don't think that that is good for the legitimacy of the court and its decisions.

When asked if "too subjective" meant the Court was being "result-oriented," Bastarache replied: "Well, yes. I think so. It's when your own values and your own personal convictions become the predominant factor in deciding the issue. The result being, of course, what you think the law should be,

---

30 "The Bastarache interview: reasoning from results at the SCC," by Cristin Schmitz, *The Lawyers Weekly*, Jan. 26, 2001, p. 19.

rather than what you think the law actually is right now as written." Schmitz then asked if it was not "almost the worst accusation you can make against a judge to say that he or she is "result-oriented"? Again, Bastarache did not mince his words:

> Yes. Because it means they are unprincipled, and because they favour a result they would, of course, choose to sort of create reasons according to the result already reached, instead of applying the rules and then coming to a result. So like you say, it is a very serious accusation.

Justice Bastarache's frank remarks boldly highlight one of the central issues in the current debate over the Court's development of the *Charter*. He is not alone. In their interviews with Canadian appellate court judges in the mid-1990s, Greene et al. found that fully half thought the *Charter* had created a "crisis of legitimacy" for the courts. Interestingly, while four of the five Supreme Court judges agreed that the *Charter* had given them more of a law-making than a law-interpreting role, not one of the Supremes thought there was a crisis of legitimacy.[31] Clearly, this debate is far from over.

11.1

Of the Extent of the Legislative Power
John Locke
The Second Treatise (1690)

This excerpt is reprinted as Reading 1.2.

11.2

The Rule of Law
A.V. C. Dicey

This excerpt is reprinted as Reading 1.4.

---

31 Ian Greene, Caarl Baar, Peter McCormick, George Szablowski, and Martin Thomas, *Final Appeal: Decision-Making in Canadian Courts of Appeal* (Toronto: Lorimer, 1998), pp. 187–88.

11.3

Roncarelli v. *Duplessis*
Supreme Court of Canada (1959)

This case is reprinted as Reading 1.1.

11.4

Boucher v. *The King*
Supreme Court of Canada (1951)

This case is reprinted as Reading 9.4.

11.5

The Supreme Court of Canada's *Charter of Rights* Decisions, 1982–1999:

A Statistical Analysis
James B. Kelly

Adapted for this book by James B. Kelly from his Ph.D. dissertation, *The Supreme Court of Canada and the Rebalancing of Liberal Constitutionalism: A Statistical Analysis of 390* Charter *Decisions, 1982-1999.*

Introduction

This study surveys the contours of the judicialization of politics in Canada by means of a statistical analysis of the Supreme Court of Canada's *Charter* decisions from 1982 to 1999. In an earlier study, F. L. Morton, Peter Russell and Troy Riddell provided a statistical analysis of the Supreme Court of Canada's 195 *Charter* decisions between 1982 and 1992. [*Ed. note:* This study is hereafter referred to as the "Morton et al" study and the years covered as "Period I"] The authors acknowledged that descriptive analyses of the Court's use of the *Charter* were not a substitute for jurisprudential analysis. However, such an exercise was considered useful because it could "generate hypotheses about the impact the Court is having on the legal system and about the orientation of its judges." This chapter builds on work of Morton et al. and includes data for the 1993 to 1999 period. [*Ed. note:* This study is hereafter referred to as "Period II."] . For analytical purposes, this subset of cases for Period II is compared to the trends identified by Morton et al. The total number of cases in the data set is 390. By coincidence, there are 195 cases in each of the two time periods surveyed.

The *Charter's* Impact on the Supreme Court's Caseload

The study for Period II found that the *Charter's* impact on the Supreme Court's caseload was consistent with the findings for Period I, with one important exception. The *Charter* still constitutes nearly a quarter of the Court's work load for the entire period surveyed, but the proportion of *Charter* cases decided by the Supreme Court has increased as a proportion of the Court's case load in recent years. The Period I study found that the *Charter* represented 18 per cent of the Court's caseload, but this increased to 26 per cent of the Court's docket for Period II. Indeed, the *Charter* represented 31 per cent of all Court decisions in 1993 and 34 per cent in 1996. This trend suggests that the Supreme Court is increasingly becoming a public law court under the *Charter of Rights and Freedoms*.

Table 1

Charter Decisions by All Supreme Court Decisions

	All Decisions	Charter Decisions	Percent of total
1993	140	43	31%
1994	110	25	23%
1995	110	26	24%
1996	117	40	34%
1997	102	23	23%
1998	91	20	22%
1999	79	18	23%
1982-1999	1859	390	21%
1982-1992	1110	195	18%
1993-1999	749	195	26%

Outcomes of Supreme Court *Charter* Decisions

In the first two years in which the Court heard *Charter* appeals, the rights claimant was successful 64 per cent of the time (9/14). By 1992, this figure had declined to 33 per cent for the first 195 *Charter* decisions. Morton et al argued that the Court's early activism accounted for the increased use of *Charter* arguments in lower court cases. As well, this activism was said to facilitate a form of interest group politics that saw groups increasingly adopt litigation strategies. This judicial support for right claimants represented a sharp break with the Court's approach to rights and freedoms before 1982. The rights claimant was successful only 15 per cent of the time under the *1960 Bill of Rights* (5/34).

Table 2

Outcome of Supreme Court *Charter* Decisions

	Claimant loses	Claimant wins	Inconclusive	Total
1993	33	10 (23%)	0	43
1994	14	11 (44%)	0	25
1995	18	8 (31%)	0	26
1996	26	11 (28%)	3	40
1997	10	13 (57%)	0	23
1998	14	5 (25%)	1	20
1999	11	7 (39%)	0	18
1982-1999	242	130 (33%)	18	390
1982-1992	116	65 (33%)	14	195
1993-1999	126	65 (33%)	4	195

The Court's support rate for *Charter* claimants has remained stable at 33 per cent, exactly the level of support reported by the Period I study. The net effect of the *Charter*'s success rate stabilizing at 33 per cent is the consolidation of the Court's "grey middle." The Period I study concluded that the movement from a Trudeau to a Mulroney court did not substitute an activist voting bloc for a conservative bloc, as David Beatty suggested, but resulted in the emergence of a centre-dominant Court in Canada. Indeed, all current justices except one (Bastarache) would fall within a relatively narrow radius of the Court average of 33 per cent over the first 390 decisions. This narrow radius is important because it represents a growing consensus between the justices regarding the Court's use of the *Charter* and the appropriate scope of judicial review under the *Charter*. More importantly, the stable success rates and the convergence of judicial opinion around the Court average between 1993 and 1999 suggest an important development in *Charter* politics: the Court's growing attempt to accord democratic actors enough deference to ensure that the *Charter* does not overwhelm either federalism or the effective functioning of parliamentary democracy.

Treatment of Different Rights and Freedoms

There is significant variation in success rates for different *Charter* rights. More importantly, different *Charter* rights impact federalism and liberal constitutionalism to varying degrees. In the case of federalism, the *Charter* is largely viewed as a document that limits pluralism, and thus, federal diversity in Canada. But not all *Charter* sections have implications for federalism, and more to the point, the sections that pose the greatest threat to federal diversity have not been the focus of the Supreme Court's *Charter* jurisprudence. This is a point that has not been properly addressed by commentators that decry the *Charter's* nation building imperatives. In many respects, *Charter* critics such as Guy Laforest equate the nation-building potential of the *Charter* with the reality of the *Charter's* effect on Canadian federalism. In simple terms, the *Charter* has not had the enduring effect on federalism that is claimed by *Charter* critics. Indeed, in those areas where the *Charter* was expected to limit provincial autonomy, such as language and education policy, the Court initially proved the critics to be correct. But this has not been a sustaining feature of the Court's jurisprudence, and since the initial activism, the Court has addressed very few language and education policy cases. As such, the Supreme Court has demonstrated a renewed sensitivity to federalism in the 1993 to 1999 period and a greater appreciation of policy variation among the provinces. This is a significant development because the provinces grew increasingly critical of the Supreme Court's interpretation of the *Charter* in the first decade.

There are a number of trends in Table 3 that are consistent with the analogous data for Period I. Legal rights continue to dominate the Supreme Court's *Charter* case load and account for nearly two-thirds of rights cases decided between 1982 and 1999. This is a significant trend that has important implications for both the legitimacy of *Charter* review and the effect of the *Charter* on Canadian federalism. Specifically, legal rights represent a policy area where arguably judges have as much or more policy expertise as legislators. Also, legal rights arise primarily in criminal law cases, a federal jurisdiction. Thirdly, the Court has interpreted legal rights in manner that advances federal diversity. In a series of cases involving challenges to the *Criminal Code* on the basis that the different application of the *Criminal Code* by the provinces violated *Charter* rights, the Supreme Court ruled that variation between the provinces was a natural development in a federal system, and thus, did not violate entrenched rights and freedoms. This formed the basis of the Court's rulings in *Turpin, Lyons* and *Sheldon*. In sum, the Court has selected a docket that arguably enhances the legitimacy of judicial review on *Charter* grounds by minimizing the *Charter's* implications for federalism and focusing on a policy area where the Court has the institutional capacity to be an effective actor.

Table 3

Different Categories of Rights Cases by Result

	Wins	Losses	Unclear	Total
Fundamental Freedoms	16(28%)	38	3	57
Democratic Rights	1(20%)	4	0	5
Mobility Rights	1(15%)	6	0	7
Legal Rights (a)	90(31%)	189	14	293
Equality Rights	10(23%)	29	4	43
Language and Education Rights (b)	7(41%)	8	2	17
Aboriginal Rights (c)	8(53%)	6	1	15
Multicultural Rights	0(0%)	1	0	1
Gender Equality Rights	0(0%)	1	0	1
Totals	133(30%)	282	24	439(d)

(a) includes s.24(2) of *Charter*

(b) includes ss.16-23 of *Charter*, ss.93 and 133 of *Constitution Act*, s.23 of the *Manitoba Act* and s.16 of the *Saskatchewan Act*

(c) includes s.25 of *Charter* and s.35 of *Constitution Act*, 1982.

(d) The total is higher than 390 because several cases contain multiple *Charter* issues and are counted in more than one category.

Fundamental freedoms remain the second largest number of cases addressed during the Court's *Charter* jurisprudence. They remain a distant second to legal rights, accounting for 57 decisions, or 13 per cent of the *Charter* cases decided by the Supreme Court of Canada. There has been a decrease in support rates for fundamental freedoms before the Court, confirming Morton et al.'s conclusion that the Court has not been "activist in cases dealing with the traditional political freedoms of a liberal society." The support rate for fundamental freedoms was 28 per cent for the first 390 *Charter* decisions (16/57), lower than the overall support rate of 33 per cent. This represents a one percentage point decrease from Period I, where the Court supported fundamental freedoms in 29 per cent of the cases decided. In fact, the support levels for all *Charter* rights decreased from the 1994 findings, with the exception of equality rights and democratic rights. In the case of democratic rights, the first successful use of this *Charter* section occurred in 1993 in *Sauvé* v. *Canada*. In this case, the Court ruled that s.51(e) of the *Canada Election Act* which denied prisoners the right to vote was drawn too broadly, and could not be saved under section 1 of the *Charter*.

The *Charter* sections identified with Pierre Elliot Trudeau's nation building project deserve special attention, because they are uniquely Canadian and they impact federalism to a higher degree than other sections of the *Charter*. Mobility rights have not generated a large body of cases before the Supreme Court. To date, the Court has heard 7 cases involving mobility rights and there has been only one victory in *Black* v. *Law Society (Alberta)*, where the Court removed Alberta's restrictions on nonresident lawyers from practicing in the province. Language and education rights continue to exhibit the second highest support rate at 41 per cent, but the support for this *Charter* section has steadily declined. This trend suggests that the loss of policy autonomy for the provinces in education policy was not an enduring feature of the *Charter's* effect on Canadian federalism, but a characteristic of the Court's initial judicial activism. Finally, Aboriginal rights represent the largest growth area in rights-based litigation heard before the Supreme Court. Only one Aboriginal rights case was heard during Period I, and this increased to 15 cases for the first 390 *Charter* decisions. As well, Aboriginal rights have the highest success rates before the Supreme Court at 53 per cent. Many of the victories in cases like *Gladestone, Badger, Nikal, Cote* and *Marshall* have resulted in stronger protections for Aboriginal fishing and hunting rights. Perhaps what is more important is that the Court continues to demonstrate higher support levels for cases which protect linguistic and ethnic minorities against provincial majorities.

A basic consistency characterizes the Court's first 390 *Charter* decisions in the distribution of cases and success rates for different *Charter* rights that was first identified in the Morton et al. study. However, within this consistency a series of developments have emerged in the 1993 to 1999 period which limit the tension been the *Charter* and the politics of federalism in Canada. The Supreme Court's handling of language and education rights cases during the first 100 *Charter* decisions was said to have contributed to the demise of the Meech Lake Accord and the alienation of Quebec within Canadian federalism. In particular, the Court's nullification of important sections of the *Charter of the French Language* in *R. v. Ford* and Quebec's use of the notwithstanding clause shortly afterwards, undermined support for the Meech Lake Accord. In Quebec, the Supreme Court's use of the *Charter* to limit the policy autonomy of the province in *Protestant School Board* increased Quebec's sense of isolation in Canada. However, an examination of trends in support levels for language and education rights show a significant transformation between 1982 and 1999 that reduces an important source of conflict between Quebec and the *Charter* and should reduce Quebec's sense of isolation in Canadian federalism.

The success rate for language and education policy cases for the first 390 *Charter* cases has been significantly higher than the overall level of 33 per cent. The Supreme Court has decided a total of 17 language and education policy cases. There were seven language and education cases in the first 100 *Charter* cases; six in cases 101-195; and only four in cases 196 to 390. What is more important is the consistent downward trend in support levels for language and education policy cases over these three periods. For instance, during the first 100 *Charter* cases the Court supported the language and education rights claimant 57 per cent of the time (4/7), 33 per cent during the next 95 *Charter* cases (2/6) and 25 per cent during the last 195 *Charter* cases (1/4). This trend suggests declining judicial/*Charter* entanglement with the politics of language. This is a trend that usually escapes notice in the *Charter* debate, as many of the examples used to illustrate the Court's insensitivity to federalism and the place of Quebec in Confederation continue to be drawn from the activism of the first 100 *Charter* decisions. This is misleading because the activism of the first 100 *Charter* cases does not accurately characterize the overall effect of the *Charter* on Canadian federalism.

A notable feature of the Court's *Charter* jurisprudence since the constitutional crisis of 1990-1992 is the sharp reduction in cases which involve language and education rights decided by the Supreme Court. Between 1982 and 1992, language and education rights accounted for 6 per cent of the *Charter* cases decided by the Supreme Court (13/213). In the period immediately following the constitutional crisis of 1992, this figure declined to less than 2 per cent (4/226). An examination of the four language and education rights cases decided by the Supreme Court between 1993 and 1999 illustrates the Court's growing reluctance to become involved in the politics of language. Three of the four cases involved denominational school rights under the *Constitution Act, 1867*. In *Reference Re Education Act* (Quebec), *Ontario Home Builders' Association* v. *York Regional Board of Education* and *Adler* v. *Ontario*, the rights claimant was unsuccessful in demonstrating that section 93 of the *Constitution Act, 1867* had been infringed. The Court also rejected that freedom of religion and equality protections were violated in *Adler* and *York*. More importantly, two of the four cases came as references from Manitoba and Quebec with no lower court decision for the Supreme Court to review. Thus, the Supreme Court granted leave to hear only two language and education rights cases between 1993 and 1999, or 1 per cent of the cases heard. In *Reference re Public Schools Act* (Manitoba) the Court ruled that the Public Schools Act did not "provide for the implementation of the rights of the linguistic minority in respect of their educational facilities, including appropriate mechanisms for management and control." This decision reconfirmed the Court's early jurisprudence in *Mahé* v. *Alberta*, and thus, expanded educational services for the Francophone minority outside of Quebec.

In sum, there are important trends in the overall statistics that suggest the Court's moderate activism has demonstrated a renewed sensitivity to federalism, and ensured that *Charter* review has not created a hostile relationship between the legislative and judicial branches of government. Indeed, when the *Charter* is viewed as a layered document with rights and freedoms which effect federalism differently, a more nuanced relationship between the *Charter* and Canadian federalism is revealed. Far from being a document with multiple sections that impact provincial autonomy, the nation-building sections of the *Charter* account for a limited part of the document. The sections of the *Charter* that pose the greatest threat to federal diversity, such as equality rights, language and education rights and mobility rights, constitute a small number of cases decided by the Supreme Court. Further, the nation-building sections of the *Charter* exhibit the sharpest downward trends in success rates for *Charter* rights during the first 390 *Charter* decisions, a development that is reducing the *Charter*'s effect on federalism over time.

The Object of *Charter* Challenges and the Nullification of Statutes

The *Charter* potentially places the judicial and the legislative branches of government in a confrontational relationship that has important implications for the legitimacy of judicial review in Canada. Morton et al. suggested that the Court's use of the *Charter* during the first 195 *Charter* decisions might undermine the legitimacy of judicial review because the Court was more willing to hear cases which challenged the substantive policy choices of democratic actors. In Period I *Charter* decisions, the object of *Charter* cases was largely concerned with challenges to statutes and regulations, and this accounted for 54 per cent of the cases decided by the Supreme Court (122/227). The importance of this development for liberal constitutionalism should be readily apparent. By focusing on statutes and regulations the Court placed itself in a confrontational relationship with democratic actors for control of the policy process in Canada, and this shift in focus intensified the judicialization of politics in a parliamentary democracy.

Table 4

Object of a *Charter* Challenge, 1982-1999

	Wins	Losses	Both	Total
Statute	56	117	12	185
Conduct	79	140	8	227
Regulation	11	7	1	19
Total	146	264	21	431 (a)

(a)   Total is higher than 390 because some *Charter* Challenges involve challenges to both statute and conduct, statute and regulation, etc.

The trends that emerge during the first 390 *Charter* cases have important implications for the relationship between the judiciary and legislative actors in Canada. A trend that clearly demonstrates the rebalancing of liberal constitutionalism in Canada is the transformation in the object of *Charter* challenges before the Supreme Court of Canada since 1992. In a reversal of the trend of Period I, the Court now focuses more on cases that challenge the conduct of public officials rather than statutes and regulations. For Period I, 54 percent of the Supreme Court's *Charter* decisions involved challenges to statutes and regulations. For Period II, 60 per cent of *Charter* cases involved the conduct of public officials (122/204). Not only is the Supreme Court hearing fewer *Charter* challenges to statutes, it is also becoming less supportive of such challenges. The success rate for *Charter* claims against statutes has dropped from 39 percent (20/52) during the Court's first one hundred rulings to 32 percent (26/82) in Period II.

This development is important for several reasons. The Court has curbed its earlier tendency to review the substantive policy choices of Parliament and the provincial legislatures. This shift in focus by the Supreme Court reduces the salience of the anti-democratic critique of judicial review under the *Charter*. Secondly, judicial review that focuses on the conduct of public officials works to the Court's advantage because it tends to focus on the procedural rights of individuals, and this is a role in which the Court arguably has the institutional capacity to perform effectively. The Court appears to have recognized the risk to its authority when it directly challenges the substantive policy choices of government and has retreated to a mode of judicial review that attempts to limit an overly competitive relationship with legislative actors.

The legitimacy of judicial review in Canada extends beyond the judiciary's relationship to democratic actors within liberal constitutionalism. It is also dependent on the *Charter's* effect on the federal character of Canada. The Supreme Court has used the *Charter* to nullify 65 statutes during the first 390 *Charter* decisions. In Period I, the Supreme Court nullified more federal statutes (23) than provincial statutes (18). The number of federal statutes nullified (32) continues to exceed provincial statutes (31) under the *Charter* for the first 390 *Charter* decisions. Morton et al. argued that the higher number of federal statutes nullified misrepresented the *Charter's* impact on federalism because the *Charter* actually had a larger impact on the provinces, despite fewer provincial statutes being nullified. Specifically, federal statutes nullified tended to involve legal rights and be procedural in nature, whereas provincial nullifications tended to be more recently enacted and involve important substantive issues. These qualitative differences between federal and provincial statutes nullified were said to limit the policy autonomy of the provinces and advance policy uniformity in Canada. This conclusion is more pronounced in the case of Quebec, where the Court nullified important sections of the province's language and education policy between 1982 and 1992.

Table 5

Nullification of Statutes and Regulations

	Nullified	Upheld	Total
Federal	32	89	121
Provincial	31	41	72
Territorial	0	1	1
Municipal	2	0	2
1982-1999	65	131	196 (a)
1982-1992	41	78	119
1993-1999	24	53	77

(a)   There are seven instances where the same federal statute is nullified in different cases, and one instance where the same Quebec regulation is nullified in different cases. These cases are counted as one nullification. This is why the total is 196 and not 204 (185 statutes and 19 regulations).

In Period II, there are important qualitative changes that suggest that the *Charter's* disproportionate effect on the provinces is declining, and that the Court is acting in a more balanced fashion toward both levels of government. This trend is evident in Table 6. The trends identified in Period I continued but with much less force. In Period I seventy-four per cent (17) of the 23 federal statutes nullified involved legal rights. In Period II, only thirty-three per cent (3) of the 9 federal statutes nullified were procedural and involved the *Charter's* legal rights. This suggests that the Court has moved beyond a narrow review of federal policies and turned its attention to more substantive federal policies. A corresponding decline was evident in federal statutes nullified which involved aspects of criminal law. In Period I, sixty-five per cent (15) of federal statutes nullified were concerned with criminal law. This figure declined to 33 per cent (3/9) in Period II.

Also important is the increase in federal statutes nullified that were substantive in character. During Period I, twenty-six per cent (6/23) of the federal statutes nullified were substantive in character. For Period II, this value increased to fifty-six per cent (5/9). Morton et al. suggested that "judicial nullification of criminal law serves a law reform function but not a centralizing function." Thus, the *Charter* had a reforming effect on an important area of federal jurisdiction in Period I. While there were some notable federal policies nullified in this period, such as the sections of the *Criminal Code* dealing with abortion services in *Morgentaler*, and the Court's striking procedures for determining refugee status in *Singh*, most federal statutes nullified involved procedural aspects of the *Criminal Code*.

By contrast during Period II, the Supreme Court nullified sections of the *Canada Elections Act* that denied prisoners the right to vote in *Sauvé*. Further, the Court nullified sections of the *Tobacco Products Control Act* that prescribed advertising restrictions on tobacco products in *RJR-Macdonald*. Finally, the Court nullified the retroactive citizenship criteria in *Benner* that required persons born abroad of Canadian mothers to undergo a security clearance as a violation of section 15(1) of the *Charter* and could not be justified as a reasonable limitation. In the overall statistics, the type of federal statute nullified continues to be concerned with criminal law and be procedural in character. However, this aggregate figure masks a departure from this trend in Period II. In this subset of cases, the *Charter* has had a greater impact on federal statutes, and Ottawa has been the *Charter* "loser."

Provincial statutes nullified continue to be overwhelmingly substantive in character. In Period I, seventy-two per cent (13) of the 18 provincial statutes nullified were substantive. This increased to ninety-two per cent (12) of the 13 provincial statutes nullified in Period II. At first glance, this trend suggests that the qualitative differences in statutes nullified continue to have the greatest impact on provincial jurisdiction, and that the *Charter* has reduced the federal character of Canada. However, a closer examination of the statutes nullified in Period II demonstrates that the *Charter* has had a stronger impact on the federal government.

Table 6

Statutes Nullified 1993 to 1999

Statute	Subject Matter	Charter Section	Substantive/ Procedure	Case Name
FEDERAL				
Income Tax Act, S.C. 1970-71-72, c.63, s.231.3 (a.d. S.C. 1986, c.6, s.121	Search and Seizure	s.7 s.8	Procedure	*Baron v. Canada, [1993] 1 S.C.R. 416 Kourtessi v. M.N.R., [1993] 2 S.C.R. 53*
Canada Elections Act, R.S.C. 1985, c. E-2, s.51 (e)	Prisoner voting rights	s.3	Procedure	*Sauvé v. Canada (A.G.), [1993] 2 S.C.R. 438*
Leary Rule (common law)	defence of voluntary intoxication	s.7 s.11(d)	Substantive	*R. v. Daviault, [1994] 3 S.C.R. 63*
Criminal Code, R.S.C., 1985, c.C-46, s.179 (1)(b)	Definition of Public Loitering	s.7	Procedure	*R. v. Heywood,[1994] 3 S.C.R. 761*
Criminal Code, R.S.C., 1985 c.C-46, s.394(1)(b)	Reverse Onus #	s.11(d)	Procedure	*R. v.Laba, [1994] 3 S.C.R. 965*
Tobacco Products Control Act, S.C. 1988, c.20, ss. 4-6, 8,9	Advertising & Promotion restrictions on tobacco products	s.2(b)	Substantive	*RJR-Macdonald Inc. v. Canada, [1995] 3 S.C.R. 199*
Citizenship Act, R.S.C., 1985 c. C-29, ss.3(1), 5 (2)(b), 22(1)(b)	Retroactive Citizenship Criteria	s.15(1)	Substantive	*Benner v. Canada, [1997] 1 S.C.R. 358*
Canada Elections Act, R.S.C., 1985, c. E-2, s.322.1	Publication ban 1 S.C.R. 877.	s.2(b)	Substantive	*Thompson Newspapers Co. v. Canada, [1998]*
Indian Act, R.S.C., 1985, c.I-5, s.77(1)	Voting Restrictions	s.15(1)	Substantive	*Corbiere v. Canada, [1999] 2 S.C.R. 203.*

PROVINCIAL

Statute	Subject Matter	Charter Section	Substantive/ Procedure	Case Name
The Public Schools Act, R.S.M. 1987, c. P250, s. 79(3), (4), (7) (Manitoba)	Minority Language Education Rights	s.23	Substantive	Reference Re Public Schools Act (Man.), [1993] 1 S.C.R. 839
Insurance Act, R.S.O. 1980 ss. 231, 233 (Ontario)	Definition of spouse	s.15(1)	Substantive	Miron v. Trudel, [1995] 2 S.C.R. 418
Wildlife Act S.A. 1984, c. W-9.1, s.26(1), 7 (Alberta)	Aboriginal Hunting and Fishing Rights	s.35(1)	Substantive	R. v. Badger, [1996] 1 S.C.R.771
British Columbia Fishery (General) Regulations SOR/84-248, s.4(1) (British Columbia)	Aboriginal Fishing Rights	s.35(1)	Substantive	R. v. Nikal, [1996] 1 S.C.R. 1013
Quebec Fishery Regulations C.R.C., c.852, ss. 4(1), 5(9) (Quebec)	Aboriginal Fishing Rights	s.35(1)	Substantive	R. v. Adams, [1996] 3 S.C.R.101 R. v. Cote, [1996] 3 S.C.R. 139
Referendum Act, R.S.Q., C. C-64.1, ss.402-404, 406 para. 3, 413, 414, 416, 417 of Appendix Two (Quebec)	Third Party Spending 3 S.C.R. 569	s.2(b)(d)	Procedure	Libman v. Quebec, (A.G.) [1997]
Provincial Court Judges Act, S.A., 1981, s.13(1)(a)(b), 17(1) (Alberta)	Judical Salaries	s.11(d)	Substantive	R. v. Campbell, [1997] 3 S.C.R. 4
Provincial Court Act, R.S.P.E.I, 1988, C-P.24, s.3(3) (P.E.I)	Judicial Salaries	s.11(d)	Substantive	Reference Re Renumeration of the Judges of the Provincial Court of P.E.I., [1997] 3 S.C.R. 4
Individual Rights Protection	Non-inclusion	s.15(1)	Substantive	Vriend v. Alberta, [1998] 1 S.C.R. 493

Statute	Subject Matter	Charter Section	Substantive/ Procedure	Case Name
Act, R.S.A., 1980, c.I-2, preamble, ss.2(1),3,4,7(1),8(1),10,16(1) (Alberta)				
Parks Regulations, 1991, R.R.S., c.P-1.1, Reg.6, s.41(2)(j) (Saskatchewan)	Aboriginal Hunting and Fishing Rights	s.35(1)	Substantive	R. v. Sundown, [1999] 1 S.C.R. 393
Family Law Act, R.S.O., 1990, c.F.3, s.29 (Ontario)	Definition of Spouse	s.15(1)	Substantive	M. v. H., [1999] 2 S.C.R. 3

Statute	Subject Matter	Charter Section	Substantive/ Procedure	Case Name
Maritime Provinces Fishery Regulations, SOR/93-55, ss.4(1), 20 (Nova Scotia)	Aboriginal Hunting and Fishing Rights	s.15(1) s.35(1)	Substantive	R. v. Marshall, [1999]
Labour Relations Code, S.B.C., 1992, c.82, ss.1(1),65,67 (British Columbia)	Definition of Picketing [1999]	s.2(b)	Substantive	U.F.C.W., Local 1518 v.Kmart Canada, [1999]

#only the part of section 394(1)(b) that imposes a legal burden of proving ownership, agency or lawful authority was declared unconstitutional

The increase in substantive nullifications of provincial statutes is the result of the dramatic rise in Aboriginal rights cases decided by the Supreme Court in Period II. Aboriginal rights are largely substantive in character and thirty-nine per cent (5) of the 13 provincial nullifications in this period involved statutes and regulations that affected Aboriginal fishing and hunting rights. More importantly, none of the provincial laws nullified were considered as important to the legislative agendas of provincial governments, though the *Marshall* decision created conflict between the aboriginal and non-aboriginal communities in Atlantic Canada.

The number of provinces to have legislation nullified under the *Charter* increased from six to eight for the first 390 *Charter* decisions. Only Newfoundland and New Brunswick have not lost a statute to *Charter* review. While Quebec remains the province most affected by judicial nullifications, the force of this trend is lessening over time. During the first 100 *Charter* cases decided by the Supreme Court, Quebec had eight statutes nullified and 5 occurred in policy areas important to the Quebec government. In 1984 Quebec suffered two judicial nullifications of education policy in *Protestant School Boards* and *Quebec* v. *Greater Hull School Board*. In 1988 the Supreme Court nullified sections of the *Charter of the French Language* that restricted the use of English on public signs in *Ford* and *Devine*. This use of the *Charter* antagonized Quebec and contributed to the constitutional crisis associated with the demise of the Meech Lake Accord. However, since the defeat of the Meech Lake and the Charlottetown Accords, the *Charter* has not been used to successfully challenge Quebec's autonomy in language and education policy. In particular, the Court has not used the *Charter* to nullify Quebec's language and education policy since Ford in 1988. In the one case involving Quebec's education policy in Period II, the Court supported Quebec in *Reference Re Education Act*.

Even in *Libman*, in which the Court nullified sections of Quebec's referendum law that limited third party spending as a violation of freedom of expression, the Court struck down the Quebec act on narrow procedural grounds. In response to *Libman* the National Assembly introduced amendments to the *Referendum Act* that dealt with the Court's concern that the spending limitation for third party participants was too low. While the Court's decision to strike down sections of the referendum law created a powerful symbolic statement that the *Charter* treats Quebec unfairly, the reality of the *Charter*'s effect on Quebec is markedly different from political rhetoric. The Court has generally been supportive of provincial policy since 1990. More importantly, it has steered clear from the politics of language in Quebec. In cases where the Court has supported minority language rights, such as *Mahé* v. *Alberta*, the *Charter* may have antagonized other provincial governments, but sent an important message to Quebec. The *Charter* will not be used to interfere with provincial autonomy over language policy in Quebec, but will be used to protect the French language outside of Quebec by requiring other provincial governments to provide minority language education services.

510 Judicial Review and Civil Liberties

In sum, there are multiple developments in Period II that should strengthen the legitimacy of *Charter* review and the federal character of Canada. The Court has become more balanced in its treatment of federal and provincial statutes, both quantitatively and qualitatively. The centralizing effect of the *Charter* on provincial policy, emphasized by Morton et al in their study of Period I, declined dramatically in Period II.

Judicial Discretion and Liberal Constitutionalism:
The Court's Use of Sections 1 and 24(2)

The *Charter of Rights and Freedoms* provides two highly discretionary powers that allow courts to engage in a two-stage review of cases that infringe entrenched rights or freedoms. Section 1 of the *Charter* allows courts to determine whether restrictions on rights constitute reasonable limitations in a free and democratic society. Section 24(2) of the *Charter* authorizes courts to exclude evidence in criminal cases if the court determines that admitting such evidence would bring the administration of justice into disrepute. Because of the discretionary nature of sections 1 and 24(2), they are an accurate indication of judicial activism under the *Charter*.

Table 7 summarizes the Supreme Court's use of section 1 between 1982 and 1999. The trends identified in Period I continue. The Court is more likely to reject government attempts to justify public policy as a reasonable limitation (29) than to accept them (49): an acceptance rate of only 37 percent. However, within this overall trends is a series of volatile patterns.. During the Court's initial activist approach to the *Charter*, it accepted only two of the first 10 section 1 defences (1982 to 1987). In the three-year period from 1988 to 1990, the Court's acceptance rate climbed to 55 per cent (16/29). During Period II, the Court's acceptance rate dropped back to thirty-three per cent (8/24) of section one defences. The Court's greater willingness to accept section 1 defences is taken as evidence of the breakdown of the initial 'honeymoon' consensus on the *Charter*.

Table 8 summarizes the Court's use of section 24(2) between 1982 and 1999. Section 24(2) instructs justices to exclude evidence that would bring the administration of justice into disrepute. There have been dramatic changes in the Court's approach to section 24(2) that suggest that the Court is moving back towards the crime control model that characterized Canada's criminal law processes before the introduction of the *Charter*. F.L. Morton and Christopher Manfredi conclude that one effect of the *Charter* is a restructuring of the Canadian process of criminal law from the crime control model of British legal system to the due process of the American legal system. This conclusion is based on the Court's use of section 24(2) in Period I when the Court was more willing to exclude evidence (20) than to allow it (14). This trend was sharply reversed in Period II, when the Court admitted evidence in sixty-nine per cent (25) of the 36 cases in which section 24(2) arguments were raised.

With the stabilization of the Court's use of section 1 and the sharp decline in

Table 7

The Section One Reasonable Limits Defence by Year

	1984	1985	1986	1987	1988	1989	1990	1991	1992	1993	1994	1995	1996	1997	1998	1999	Total
Accepted (gov't wins)	0	0	2	0	5	4	7	1	2	1	1	2	3	0	1	0	29
Rejected (claimant wins)	1	3	2	2	4	3	6	8	4	2	3	2	1	3	2	3	49
Both	0	0	0	0	1	0	0	1	1	0	0	0	1	0	0	0	4

Table 8

Motions to Exclude Evidence

	1984	1985	1986	1987	1988	1989	1990	1991	1992	1993	1994	1995	1996	1997	1998	1999	Total
Rejected (Crown wins)	0	0	0	3	3	1	2	2	3	7	3	5	7	2	1	0	39
Accepted claimant wins)	0	1	1	4	3	3	4	3	1	1	5	1	1	2	1	0	31
Issue not addressed	0	0	0	2	2	2	0	1	0	0	1	0	0	0	1	0	9

the exclusion of evidence in criminal cases, the Court's use of these highly discretionary instruments since 1993 suggests that, compared to the first decade of the *Charter*, the judicialization of politics is being reduced in Canada.

Conclusion

The overall trends in the first 390 *Charter* decisions suggest that the Court has settled into a moderately activist approach to *Charter* review. While the Court continues to nullify both provincial and federal statutes under the *Charter*, the number of statutes challenged is declining, as is the success rate of rights claims against statutes. By reducing this source of conflict with Parliament and provincial legislatures, the Court has enhanced the legitimacy of *Charter* review and the role of the Court. This and other trends are reducing the *Charter's* effect on Canadian federalism, and lessening the Court's contribution to intergovernmental conflict. In effect, the emerging approach to *Charter* review has led to a rebalancing of liberal constitutionalism that stands in stark contrast to the Court's highly activist *Charter* jurisprudence in their first 100 *Charter* decisions.

11.6

Liberal versus Post-liberal Constitutionalism:
Applying the *Charter* to Civil Society

Thomas M.J. Bateman
Political Studies, Augustana University College

This article is reprinted as Reading 1.6.

11.7

Do Bills of Rights Matter?
Charles Epp
American Political Science Review 90, no. 4 (1996), 765–79. Reprinted with permission of author.

Constitutionalism, the attempt to protect liberty through the design of political institutions, is currently enjoying a revival of interest as numerous countries, ranging from former members of the East Bloc to Canada, have engaged in fundamental constitutional reform. Nearly every new constitution or constitutional revision adopted since 1945 (almost 60) contains a bill of rights.

To what extent, and under what conditions, will a bill of rights fulfill its promise to protect liberty? My empirical analysis consists of a quasi-experiment of the effects of the *Canadian Charter of Rights and Freedoms*. The *Charter*, a constitutional bill of rights adopted in 1982, is a leading example of the recent revival of constitutionalism, and it offers a nearly ideal opportunity to test for the effects of constitutional change. When the *Charter* was adopted, Canada's political regime continued much as before; nevertheless, observers of Canadian politics have attributed to the *Charter* remarkably profound effects, particularly a growing emphasis on individual rights; and those claimed effects are relatively easily isolated and tested because they were expected to appear in a single institution, the Canadian Supreme Court. In short, Canada should be an easy case for the hypothesis that a bill of rights independently affects politics.

I shall argue, however, based on data from the agenda of the Canadian Supreme Court, that the effects of a bill of rights are not as direct as constitutional engineers and scholars commonly assume, because those effects depend on structural conditions, in particular the presence of what I shall call a *support structure for legal mobilization*, that vary greatly among countries, across time, and among issue-areas. The support structure consists of resources – sympathetic and competent lawyers, finances, and organizations – that make possible sustained, strategic appellate litigation. The contours of such resources condition access to the higher courts and, therefore, condition the nature of the issues decided by those courts. Bills of rights matter, but only to the extent that individuals can mobilize the resources necessary to invoke them through strategic litigation.

To demonstrate the importance of the support structure, I consider and test several alternative explanations of variations in judicial attention to civil liberties and civil rights. They are a) the presence or absence of a bill of rights; and b) the justices' policy preferences, conditioned by c) the extent of judicial discretion over the docket.

Constitutionalism and the Conditions for Application of a Bill of Rights

Constitutions, the most basic of political institutions, affect ordinary politics by prescribing the rules of the political game. Liberal constitutions typically employ two very different kinds of rules to constrain arbitrary power: a) some rules structure governing institutions in such a way that decision making is channeled and thereby limited (this is the purpose of the separation of powers and federalism), and b) other rules define particular issues as outside the authority of the ordinary democratic process (this is the purpose of bills of rights). Both types of rules, it may appear, produce similarly profound and direct effects on politics. But not all rules are created equal: *federalism and the separation of powers are self-activating; bills of rights are not.*

Bills of rights are not self-activating because, unlike the separation of powers, they provide individuals with no direct control over institutional resources. In other words, although bills of rights create legal interests (rights), they create no corresponding institutional resources to actualize those interests. Thus, in Madison's evocative metaphor, constitutional rights guarantees are mere "parchment barriers." Nonetheless, remarkably profound effects are often attributed to bills of rights. I survey those hypothesized effects and then turn to the conditions – judicial attitudes, discretionary docket control, and external support for legal mobilization – that are likely to influence the application of bills of rights in practice.

Bills of Rights

Bills of rights are often thought to affect politics in several ways. First, observers commonly suggest that they promote an emphasis on rights in political culture. Similarly, some scholars argue that rights guarantees shape the development of political and social movements. Second, observers commonly suggest that bills of rights increase the level of intervention by courts in the policy-making processes of other governmental institutions. Similarly, contemporary scholars often trace the extraordinary vibrancy of judicial review, judicial attention to rights, and judicial policy-making on rights in the United States to the presence of a bill of rights in the U.S. Constitution. Third, contemporary writers have suggested that the presence of a bill of rights, by encouraging a broader policy-making role for the judiciary, opens the political opportunity structure and thereby encourages a fragmentation of broad coalitions and parties into numerous competing interest groups as groups abandon collective solutions in the legislature for more individualized solutions in the courts.

There are reasons to be skeptical, however, that the mere presence of a bill of rights will have much effect. Madison, for instance, wrote to Jefferson that "experience proves the inefficacy of a bill of rights on those occasions when its controul is most needed.... I have seen the bill of rights violated in every instance where it has been opposed to a popular current."

The Support Structure for Legal Mobilization

The most important weakness of a bill of rights, as I previewed above, is that, unlike the self-enforcing structure embodied in federalism and the separation of powers, a bill of rights creates no automatic institutional resources for its own enforcement. Although bills of rights commonly empower at least some courts to redress violations of rights, there remain several weaknesses to the machinery of enforcement. Some scholars emphasize what they believe to be courts' relatively weak enforcement powers. Perhaps as important, however, is that rights-guarantees rarely provide potential litigants with the resources necessary to mobilize the law. The legal system functions as an entrepreneurial market in which development of law is affected by individuals' decisions to mobilize the law; and decisions to mobilize the law depend on individuals' capacity to do so, which depends partly on their access to resources. At the level of national supreme courts, in particular, cost is an important barrier to access. The cost of taking any particular case to a supreme court is substantial. The total cost of getting an issue onto such a court's agenda is not limited only to the cost of the particular case that eventually reaches that agenda, but includes also the cost of the various lower court cases that create the legal conditions that encourage a supreme court to resolve the issue. Those who hope to place a particular issue on the Supreme Court's agenda must have sufficient financial resources to support extensive litigation in lower courts, or must be able to rely on the resources of a broader class of litigants.

Issues are not equally endowed with support, and so the resource prerequisite likely affects the nature of the judicial agenda. Access to resources is likely to be especially important for shaping the application of constitutional rights, because the monetary stakes for the affected parties typically are relatively low. Thus Linda Brown, the named party in *Brown* v. *Board of Education* (1954), could never hope to recoup from a court victory the funds necessary to cover her legal expenses. Therefore, decisions to mobilize the law on public law rights plausibly depend to a great extent on access to resources. For these reasons, we should expect that the presence of civil liberties and rights on the agendas of supreme courts will depend on the existence of support for such cases beyond that provided by the immediate plaintiff in the case.

Three types of resources – organized group support, financing, and the structure of the legal profession – appear to be important conditions shaping access to the judiciary. Together these resources constitute the support structure for legal mobilization. First, a wide range of scholarship identifies organized group litigants as important influences on judicial agendas. Galanter suggested that "repeat players," typically organizations, fare significantly better in court, and influence legal change and agenda-setting significantly more, than do "one shot" litigants. In recent decades, the number and diversity of organized groups providing support for rights litigation has grown significantly in a number of countries. In the United States, organized support for civil liberties and civil rights grew after about 1910 with the development of a number of rights-advocacy organizations. The organizations contributed significantly to the judicial rights agenda. The NAACP-Legal Defense Fund, for example, organized, financed, and provided legal counsel for many of the most important civil rights cases to reach the U.S. Supreme Court.

Another factor contributing to access to the higher judiciary is financing, particularly governmental sources of financing. Governmental sources of financing appear to be necessary conditions for the presence on the agenda of claims by criminal defendants and the poor. In the United States, legal aid in civil cases and the most important forms of aid for criminal defendants are relatively new developments, growing only in the last sixty years.

Finally, access to lawyers and the structure of the legal profession influence access to the judicial agenda. With some exceptions, the assistance of a lawyer is necessary to take a case to a supreme court. Lawyers contribute to legal strategy and they provide much of the network through which information about rights litigation travels. Additionally, the degree of diversity of the legal profession appears to influence access to the judicial agenda. The more racially and ethnically diverse and open to women is a legal profession, the more likely it provides access to the courts to women and members of racial and ethnic minorities. In some countries, and increasingly in the last few decades, the legal profession has become ethnically diverse and contains a growing number of women. The structure of practice in the legal profession also appears to influence access to the judicial agenda. Law firms gain the benefits of economies of scale, which they may use to support litigation campaigns that are not immediately financially productive. Conducting legal practice within firms, however, is a relatively recent development, beginning in the United States in the last hundred years and spreading to some other countries after the early 1970s.

If the existence of a support structure is necessary for rights-advocates to have access to the judicial agenda, we should expect developments in the support structure to be matters of political strategy and controversy. Indeed, this is the case. Much of the support structure's development in the United States and, as I shall discuss shortly, in Canada reflected the political strategies of liberals and egalitarians to use the courts for political change.

Judicial Attitudes

The application of a bill of rights is likely to be influenced also by the policy preferences of judges. It is widely recognized that U.S. Supreme Court justices greatly vary among themselves in their votes on civil rights and civil liberties cases. Moreover, justices vote strategically in setting their agenda, preferring to place on the agenda only those cases in which their preferred position is likely to prevail. Thus the extent of agenda space devoted to rights claims, and the nature of those claims, is conditioned by judicial attitudes. For instance, the U.S. Supreme Court's agenda shifted toward civil liberties and civil rights after the 1930s as judicial liberals gained dominance on the Court. Based on the U.S. experience, we may expect that the extent of liberal control of a court will influence directly its agenda on civil liberties and civil rights. Indeed, the importance of judicial attitudes may be so great as to influence the judicial agenda entirely independently of the presence or absence of a bill of rights.

Discretionary Docket

Although a court's attitudinal composition likely influences its agenda, that influence appears to be conditioned by the extent of discretionary control that judges have over their docket. There is substantial evidence that discretionary docket control contributes to the expansion of a public law agenda. Many ordinary courts are required to decide nearly any case that is brought to them and, therefore, their agendas consist mostly of private economic disputes. The U.S. Supreme Court, by contrast, gained nearly complete discretionary control over its agenda in 1925 as part of a reform aimed at clearing a range of routine private disputes from the Court's agenda. As a consequence, the Court's agenda has changed profoundly, from a focus on ordinary economic disputes (contracts, torts, and the like) to a focus on public law. The correlation between a discretionary docket and a public law agenda has proven so common in the United States that we are likely to find it as well in Canada.

Study Design and Data

Canada presents a nearly ideal test of these hypotheses. The Canadian Supreme Court is an active participant in "the global expansion of judicial power," and there is little doubt that the Court's agenda has been transformed toward a focus on individual rights. Most previous research, however, has not explicitly tested alternative explanations for that transformation but has assumed that it resulted primarily from adoption of the *Charter* in 1982. This study makes use of fortunate characteristics of Canada's recent history to conduct such a test. Canada's support structure for legal mobilization began to grow in the late 1960s and continued to strengthen through the 1980s; in 1975, the Supreme Court gained nearly complete discretionary control over its agenda; in 1982, the country adopted a bill of rights, the *Charter of Rights and Freedoms*; and, in the mid-1980s, judicial liberals gained a majority on the Supreme Court. The staggered timing of these developments makes possible an assessment of the alternative hypotheses.

The Charter of Rights and Freedoms

Canada adopted a constitutional bill of rights, the *Charter of Rights and Freedoms*, in 1982, and Canadians commonly attribute enormous symbolic and practical importance to the document. For one thing, its passage culminated a long and arduous battle by some Canadian politicians and activists to establish a working bill of rights in the Canadian system. Pierre Trudeau, Justice Minister and then Prime Minister in the late 1960s and 1970s, proposed a constitutional bill of rights as part of a larger response to the growing threat of Quebec separatism. Trudeau apparently hoped that a new bill of rights could accomplish several purposes, among them protecting English speakers from French-only laws in Quebec, assuaging the fears of French-speakers in other provinces, and encouraging the development of rights-based cleavages that would unite some Canadians across provincial boundaries.

Both critics and supporters of the *Charter* claim that it has produced a number of important changes in Canadian politics and society. The *Charter* is widely thought to have transformed, in particular, the Supreme Court's agenda, decisions, and workload. Most importantly, scholars argue that the *Charter* has increased the Court's level of attention to rights claims, its support for rights claims, its reliance on constitutional reasoning, and its exercise of judicial review. Additionally, several scholars have argued that the *Charter* encouraged interest groups to proliferate and to take their demands increasingly to the Supreme Court.

From these observations, I have derived several indicators of the Supreme Court's agenda that may be expected to reveal the *Charter*'s influence especially clearly. They are 1) the proportion of the issue agenda devoted to civil rights and civil liberties; 2) the frequency of exercise of judicial review; 3) the level of support for civil rights and liberties; 4) the extent of reliance on constitutional foundations for decisions (which I expand to include all "higher law" foundations, namely the common law standard of natural justice, the 1960 statutory *Bill of Rights*, constitutional law other than the *Charter*, and the *Charter*); 5) the extent of participation in cases by interest groups and other third parties; and 6) the size of the docket.

Although Canadian observers nearly universally attribute profound effects to the *Charter*, Morton and Knopff recently have argued that the effects often attributed to the *Charter* alone are, instead, the result of active political pressure by the "Court Party," an informal coalition of rights-advocacy groups, lawyers, and judges. As Morton states, "the *Charter* itself is not so much the cause of the revolution as the means through which it is carried out." That analysis is consistent with the support structure hypothesis.

Canada's Support Structure for Legal Mobilization

Canada also affords a test of the support structure hypothesis because the Canadian support structure for legal mobilization grew dramatically between 1965 and 1990, with much of the growth preceding adoption of the *Charter*. I briefly survey developments in the three components of Canada's support structure.

Rights Advocacy Organizations. The development of private rights-advocacy organizations in Canada occurred in a relatively short space of time, roughly between the late 1960s and the early 1980s. Prior to 1970, business and agricultural groups dominated the Canadian interest group system, but after that year the number of non-producer advocacy organizations virtually exploded. Interest groups focusing on civil liberties and civil rights, in particular, did not exist before the mid-1960s, and their prominence in Canadian politics grew substantially by the early 1980s. The two principal civil liberties organizations, the British Columbia Civil Liberties Association and the Canadian Civil Liberties Association, were founded in 1962 and 1964, respectively, but only became relatively active after about 1970.

Advocacy organizations supporting civil rights also began to form in the years following the mid-1960s. In the area of women's rights, the National Action Committee on the Status of Women was formed in 1971; the Canadian Advisory Council on the Status of Women, a quasi-state organization, in 1973; the National Association of Women and the Law, in 1977; and the Women's Legal Education and Action Fund, in 1985. The major aboriginal rights organizations also formed in the late 1960s and early 1970s. Of 239 major aboriginal political organizations existing in 1993, 43 formed in the 1960s, 92 in the 1970s, and 28 in the 1980s. The Advocacy Resource Centre for the Handicapped, a leading organization advocating expanded rights for the handicapped, was formed in 1980.

After the mid-1960s, the national and provincial governments created government agencies that have acted as advocates of the new civil rights and liberties. Beginning in the mid-1960s, the Canadian provinces and the national government began adopting comprehensive human rights codes prohibiting private discrimination on a broad range of grounds; along with these codes, they created human rights commissions having jurisdiction as quasi-judicial administrative agencies to hear discrimination claims, from which there are appeals to the regular courts. Additionally, in the late 1960s, several provinces and the federal government created law reform commissions that provide continuing advice to legislatures on legal reform. Both the human rights commissions and the law reform commissions became institutional sites for liberal rights advocacy, and there has been a fluid interchange of talent and legal resources between these governmental agencies, the law schools, and private rights advocacy organizations.

Canadian rights advocacy organizations are primarily liberal or left-liberal in orientation. To a significant extent, this reflects deliberate policies by the national government to cultivate liberal advocacy organizations. The Canadian Department of the Secretary of State, under the direction of Trudeau's Liberal Government in the late 1960s, developed an aggressive program to finance citizens' advocacy organizations focusing on such issues as women's rights, language rights, and multiculturalism. Nonetheless, several conservative organizations support litigation, among them the National Citizens' Coalition and REAL Women, but they have enjoyed much less success than liberal groups because, as Morton and Knopff observe, "they are decidedly swimming against the ideological tide."

Government Sources of Financing. The national and provincial governments have developed a variety of programs that finance rights litigation and advocacy. In the decade after 1965, in a major policy revolution, the Canadian provinces created legal aid programs that finance both civil and criminal cases. Spending on court cases by the new legal aid organizations increased dramatically in the 1970s.

The Court Challenges Program, a set of funds created specifically for financing test cases on language rights and equality rights, is another government-sponsored legal program that began prior to passage of the *Charter*.

The Program was established in 1978 to finance court cases on language rights protected under the *Constitution Act, 1867*; since then, it has "supported almost every major language law case at the [Supreme] Court." The government added an equality rights component to the Program in 1985 to finance cases under the equality provisions in the *Charter of Rights*. Between 1985 and 1992, the equality component of the Program provided financing for 178 court cases at all levels of the system, including 24 cases in the Supreme Court.

The national government's Department of Indian Affairs and Northern Development (DIAND) also began sponsoring test case litigation prior to adoption of the *Charter*. DIAND began funding court cases in 1965, but the agency significantly increased its funding for litigation in the late 1970s, financing about 25 test cases before 1982. DIAND has provided financial support for most of the aboriginal rights cases that have reached the Canadian Supreme Court.

The Legal Profession. Several highly significant changes in the legal profession have occurred since 1945, with the most important developments occurring between the mid-1960s and the early 1980s. First, Canada's system of legal education changed dramatically as the importance and autonomy of law schools increased. In Canada, as in the U.S., training for the practice of law has shifted from apprenticeship, a system in which legal education is dominated by the relatively conservative interests of the practising bar, to law schools. Ten of Canada's 20 law schools were created after World War II, and the number of full-time law professors increased dramatically, almost doubling between 1971 and 1982 alone. As the importance and autonomy of the law schools increased, legal training increasingly emphasized theoretical and constitutional issues. By 1982, the year of the *Charter*'s adoption, Canadian law professors were remarkably young (the median age was 38) and generally supportive of a growing policy-making role for the judiciary on civil liberties and civil rights.

The growth of law schools also provided an institutional base for critical scholarship and advocacy on constitutional issues. Bora Laskin, chief justice of the Supreme Court from 1973 to 1984, led the push in the 1950s and 1960s for scholarly critique and advocacy. In 1951, he attributed the Supreme Court's conservatism to "the conservative tradition of the Canadian legal profession... [and] the late development of university law schools." By the 1980s, by contrast, many in the growing cohort of law school professors actively pursued advocacy scholarship favoring liberal judicial interpretation of civil rights and liberties.

Additionally, in the decade after 1970, Canada's lawyer population grew dramatically and began to diversify, and lawyers increasingly engaged in advocacy activities. The most significant growth of the Canadian lawyer population occurred between 1971 and 1981, when the number more than doubled. The lawyer population grew at a faster pace prior to 1981 than after that year; thus the *Charter* induced no unprecedented growth in the number of lawyers.

The Canadian legal profession also began to diversify by ethnic origin and sex in the decade following 1970. In 1961, 79.6% of all Canadian lawyers were from either British or French backgrounds; by 1971, that proportion had declined to 74%; and by 1981, it dropped to 68.1%. The proportion of lawyers from British ethnic origins, in particular, declined from 56.3% in 1961 to 44.5% in 1981. Ethnic minorities constituted only about a fifth of the total number of lawyers in 1961, but they constituted almost a third of the total by 1981. The rate of growth in the representation of women in the legal profession is even more dramatic than the growing proportion of ethnic minorities. In 1961, women were only 3% of all lawyers; their number grew to 5% in 1971, 15% in 1981, and 22% in 1986.

The structure of legal practice also began to change in the 1970s as the number and size of large law firms began to grow. Both the number of large firms and the number of lawyers working in large firms have grown at a significantly faster pace than the number of lawyers in general.

Taken together, these changes in Canada's interest group system, governmental financing of litigation, and the legal profession fundamentally transformed the Canadian support structure for legal mobilization *prior to adoption of the Charter in 1982.*

The Canadian Supreme Court's Attitudinal Composition

Due to patterns in the Supreme Court's attitudinal composition over the 1960–1990 period, the Canadian case also makes possible a test of the judicial attitude hypothesis. Recent research has confirmed that judges in Canada, like their counterparts in the U.S., differ significantly in their voting on rights cases. Nonetheless, what is striking about the Court's attitudinal composition is the unambiguous dominance by judicial conservatives over the entire period prior to the mid-1980s. Judicial liberals gained a majority on the Court only after 1985.

The Extent of Docket Control by the Canadian Supreme Court

Canada also presents an ideal test of the docket-control hypothesis. The Supreme Court's workload began growing in the early 1970s, prompting Parliament to grant the Court in 1975 nearly complete discretion over which cases to decide. There remain appeals as of right principally in some criminal cases, but the vast majority of cases coming to the Court are now on the discretionary docket. Thus 1975 marked a significant turning point in the Canadian Supreme Court's institutional history.

Patterns in the Canadian Supreme Court's Agenda

In light of these various changes in Canada's constitution, its support structure for legal mobilization, the Supreme Court's attitudinal composition, and the Court's docket control, what changes have occurred in the Court's agenda and when did they begin? I pursue here a data triangulation strategy, using a variety of alternative measures of the Canadian Supreme Court's agenda and workload from 1960 through 1990. The data generally tell much the same story: significant changes in the Canadian Supreme Court's agenda, on a number of dimensions, began in the early 1970s and continued at rates that remained largely unchanged by adoption of the *Charter* in 1982. There are some exceptions to that general pattern. Most importantly, both the Court's level of support for rights claims and the number of requests for the exercise of judicial review apparently rose in response to passage of the *Charter*. But, on most dimensions, the agenda transformation began at least ten years prior to passage of the *Charter*. In this section, I survey these developments, leaving a discussion of their significance to the following section.

The issue agenda. First, the Supreme Court's issue-agenda changed dramatically between 1960 and 1990 (see Figure 1). The proportion of the agenda devoted to civil liberties and civil rights grew dramatically, and the proportion devoted to tax cases and ordinary economic disputes declined dramatically. Both developments began prior to adoption of the *Charter* in 1982. Civil rights and civil liberties cases constituted 13% or less of the Court's agenda prior to 1975, and by 1990 they claimed about 60% – but the growth rate between 1980 and 1985, 86%, was only marginally faster than the 78% growth rate between 1975 and 1980. Similarly, the proportion of the Court's agenda devoted to tax and ordinary economic issues abruptly began to decline after 1975 but prior to adoption of the *Charter* in 1982.

Figure 1. Issue Agenda of the Supreme Court.

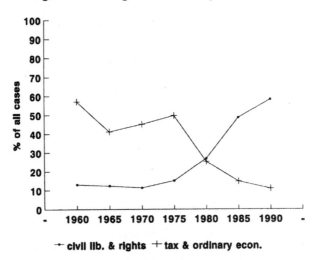

Source: Author's coding of Supreme Court decisions.
N = 1960, 77; 1965, 73; 1970, 80; 1975, 119; 1980, 119; 1985, 68; 1990, 110.

Judicial Review. The Canadian Supreme Court's exercise of judicial review increased between 1960 and 1990 too, but again, the growth appears to have been unaffected by passage of the *Charter*. Figure 2 presents two summary measures, the number of cases in which the Court has considered whether to overturn a law, and the number of cases in which it did overturn a law. The Court's use of judicial review increased moderately between 1960 and 1990, but the largest increase occurred between 1975, when the Court struck down a law in only one case, and 1980, when it struck down laws in five cases. After 1980, although the number of laws struck down increased, the rate of growth appears to have declined. The number of cases in which litigants asked the Court to exercise judicial review, on the other hand, significantly grew after passage of the *Charter*. Although the growth apparently originated in the late 1960s or early 1970s, between 1985 and 1990, the number of requests for judicial review increased dramatically. In 1985, the Court decided eight cases centering on a request for the exercise of judicial review; in 1990, it decided almost thirty such cases.

Figure 2. Judicial Review by the Supreme Court.

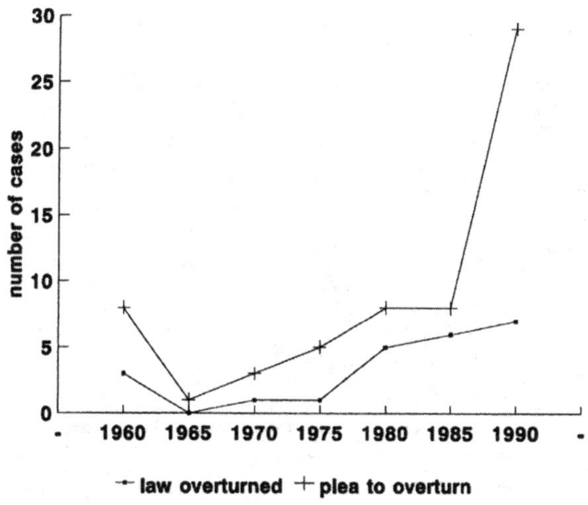

Source: Author's coding of Supreme Court decisions.

Support for rights claims. Adoption of the *Charter* may have affected the Court's level of support for rights claims but, if so, the effect was neither clear nor dramatic (see Figure 3). In the early period of the study, changes in the level of support are an artifact of the small number of rights cases, and so most of our attention should focus on the years after 1970. At the aggregate level, the Court's level of support for rights claims grew significantly between 1980 and 1985, but dropped again by 1990. Contrary to expectations, the *Charter* had no sustained effect on the Court's level of support for the rights claims on its agenda. These aggregate-level results, however, do not control for changes over time in the nature of the rights-claims being decided. Additionally, the aggregate-level results do not reveal a growing dispute on the Court in the late 1980s over which rights-claims should be supported: in broad terms, some justices favored criminal due process and negative liberties, while others favored egalitarian claims. Nonetheless, the results in Figure 3 suggest that the *Charter's* effects have been more subtle than is generally believed.

Figure 3. Support for Rights Claims by Supreme Court.

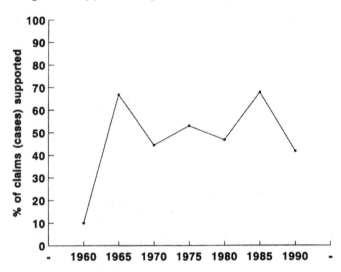

Source: Author's coding of Supreme Court decisions.
N = 1960, 10; 1965, 9; 1970, 9; 1975, 17; 1980, 30; 1985, 31; 1990, 60.

Basis for decisions. Trends in several indicators of the basis for Supreme Court decisions reveal another dimension of the Court's agenda. First, even after passage of the *Charter*, the proportion of cases involving rights claims *not* founded on that document continued to expand (see Figure 4). There was a substantial increase in non-*Charter* rights cases in 1985 over 1980; in fact, a surprisingly small proportion of the cases in 1985 were decided on *Charter* grounds, probably in part because of the time lag in bringing *Charter* cases through several levels of the judicial system. The drop in the number of non-*Charter* cases in 1990 resulted either from *Charter* cases squeezing non-*Charter* cases off the agenda or from a translation of what previously would have been non-*Charter* cases into *Charter* language. These data cannot answer that question. But it is clear that *Charter* cases themselves were only a small proportion of rights claims in 1985 and that, for much of the period prior to the late 1980s, rights claims developed in formal independence of the *Charter*.

Second, trends in the Court's use of all higher law foundations – including non-*Charter* constitutional law (primarily federalism), the 1960 *Bill of Rights*,

Figure 4. Non-Charter Rights Cases in Supreme Court.

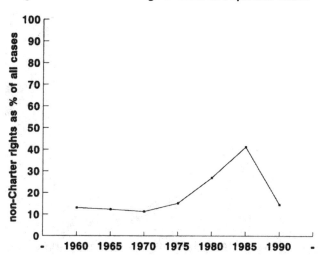

Source: Author's coding of Supreme Court decisions.
N = 1960, 77; 1965, 73; 1970, 80; 1975, 119; 1980, 119; 1985, 68; 1990, 110.

the common law standard of natural justice, and after 1982, of course, the *Charter of Rights* – are presented in Figure 5. The proportion of cases decided on all higher law grounds began to increase prior to 1982. Part of that growth reflects an increase in the number of federalism cases decided by the Supreme Court. After 1982, the proportion of cases in each of the non-*Charter* categories declined as the proportion of cases involving the *Charter* increased. By 1990, *Charter* cases began to replace non-*Charter* cases on the agenda, although even in 1990 a significant portion of higher-law cases were not based on the *Charter*. Because the use of higher law foundations for decisions began increasing as early as 1975 and, because the most important changes after 1982 consisted not of an acceleration in the rate of growth for *all* higher law cases but a shift toward *Charter* foundations from other higher law foundations, it is possible that passage of the *Charter* simply changed the foundation on which claimants based their challenges.

Types of litigants. The nature of the parties appearing in Supreme Court cases also changed between 1960 and 1990. A useful indicator of that change consists of trends in the types of private litigants that oppose government actors. I focus here in particular on individuals, who often must rely on external sources of support to reach the Supreme Court, and businesses. Over the period of the study, the presence of individuals has increased and the presence of businesses has decreased (see Figure 6). Significantly, the growing presence of individual litigants began prior to passage of the *Charter* in 1982 and the rate of growth did not increase after passage of the *Charter*.

Figure 5. Higher Law Foundations for Decisions in the Supreme Court.

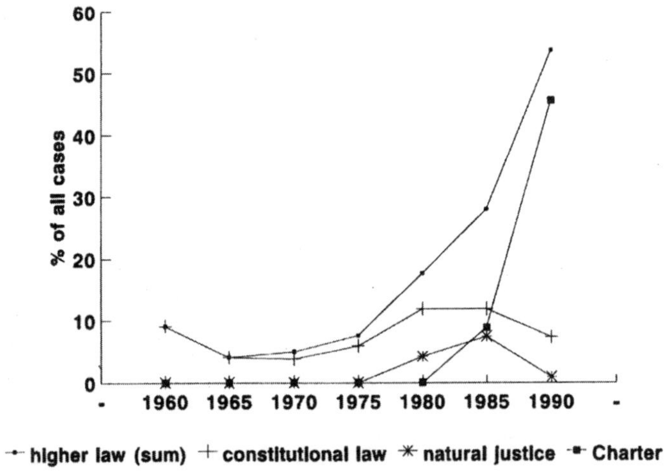

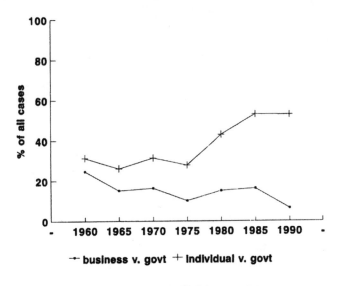

Source: Author's coding of Supreme Court decisions.
N = 1960, 77; 1965, 73; 1970, 80; 1975, 119; 1980, 119; 1985, 68; 1990, 110.

Figure 6. Individuals and Businesses v. Governmental Parties in the Supreme Court.

Source: Author's coding of Supreme Court decisions.
N = 1960, 77; 1965, 73; 1970, 80; 1975, 119; 1980, 119; 1985, 68; 1990, 110.

The extent of intervention in Supreme Court cases by third parties also has grown since 1960 (see Figure 7). Third party intervention in the Canadian judiciary is analogous to *amicus curiae* participation in the U.S. courts, and its extent is often taken as an indicator of the degree to which the Supreme Court has become politicized. Brodie found that third-party intervention began to increase prior to passage of the *Charter*. My data, too, clearly indicate that trends in intervention by third parties began prior to passage of the *Charter*. Some growth is apparent as early as 1975, and substantial changes are undeniable by 1980. As Brodie points out, however, third-party intervention by non-governmental organizations began to increase only after 1980.

Figure 7. Third-Party Interveners in the Supreme Court.

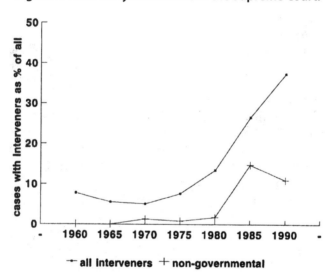

Source: Author's coding of Supreme Court decisions.
N = 1960, 77; 1965, 73; 1970, 80; 1975, 119; 1980, 119; 1985, 68; 1990, 110.

Caseload. The number of cases brought to the Court also grew dramatically over the period of this study, but almost all of the growth occurred before 1982 (see Figure 8). The Court's docket is composed of two broad categories, leave to appeal applications (over which the justices have complete discretion) and appeals by right (which the Court theoretically must hear). As noted earlier, a statutory change in the Supreme Court's jurisdiction in 1975 shifted much of the Court's docket to the discretionary leave category, thus giving the Court greater discretion over which cases to decide. As a result, the number of leave applications filed per year began to grow around 1975, accompanied by a corresponding drop in the number of appeals. The drop in appeals, however, did not entirely compensate for increases in the number of leave applications, and so the total number of cases coming to

Figure 8. Caseload of the Supreme Court.

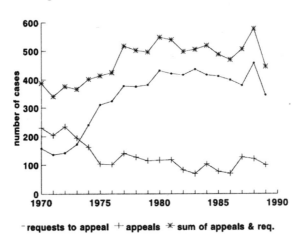

Source: Calculated from *Bushnell* (1982; 1986) and *Bulletin of the Supreme Court of Canada*.

the Court rose substantially between the mid-1970s and early 1980s. The period of significant growth ended in the early 1980s, prior to passage of the *Charter*. In short, litigants began turning to the Supreme Court in increasing numbers long before passage of the *Charter*, and that event produced no new spurt in the number of cases brought to the Court.

Discussion

The Canadian Supreme Court's agenda indeed has been transformed in the last several decades. The Court is now a major constitutional policymaker, focuses much of its attention on civil rights and liberties, increasingly decides cases brought by individuals who are supported by interest groups and government financing, increasingly faces complex disputes involving large numbers of parties, increasingly relies on higher-law foundations for its decisions, increasingly entertains requests to strike down laws, and increasingly does strike down laws.

Most observers have attributed this broadly based transformation to Canada's recent adoption of the *Charter of Rights and Freedoms* or, secondarily, to the efforts of left-liberal justices on the Supreme Court. The evidence presented here, however, suggests that the *Charter*'s influence is overrated and that judical liberals gained control of the Court too late to have done more than encourage already-existing developments. Instead, changes in the Court's agenda appear to have resulted from the combined influence of two developments: the shift to a discretionary docket in 1975 and the development of a support structure for legal mobilization.

The shift to a largely discretionary docket in 1975 significantly contributed to the agenda transformation. When the Court gained discretion over its docket, it abruptly began moving private disputes from its agenda, making way for a growth in the agenda on public law in general and civil liberties and rights in particular. This shift occurred even though judicial liberals were in the minority on the Court at the time and remained so until after the mid-1980s. The experience of the Canadian Supreme Court in this respect closely parallels that of other courts, in particular the U.S. Supreme Court, that have gained discretionary control over their agendas. Given a choice, judges apparently prefer to decide rights cases rather than private economic disputes. Perhaps this is because rights cases are more interesting and expand judges' influence more than do ordinary private disputes, and perhaps because rights cases are difficult for judges to avoid.

The growth of the support structure for legal mobilization also contributed to the agenda transformation. The various components of the support structure began growing and diversifying just prior to the start of the Court's agenda transformation, and the support structure continued growing as that transformation unfolded. Temporal priority and correlation alone cannot prove causation but the weakness of the primary alternative explanations, those focusing on judicial attitudes and adoption of the *Charter*, lends credibility to the support structure hypothesis.

Moreover, there is direct evidence of causal links between the support structure and the Supreme Court's agenda. Government financial aid has supported a range of important rights cases that have reached the Supreme Court. Legal aid, for instance, directly contributed to the growth of the Court's agenda on criminal procedure. In interviews conducted for this study, lawyers who were active in criminal defense and human rights work in the 1970s identified the growth of legal aid as the principal source of financing for criminal cases in the Supreme Court. Governmental sources of case financing also supported other types of rights cases. The government's Court Challenges Program financed virtually all of the language rights cases to reach the Supreme Court and many of the equality cases. Financing provided by the Department of Indian Affairs and Northern Development has supported nearly all of the aboriginal rights cases to reach the Supreme Court.

Additionally, both the diversification of the Canadian legal profession and the growth of large law firms influenced the Supreme Court's agenda. In the 1980s, large Toronto firms allowed a number of their women lawyers to divert time and resources to the development of a legal strategy and funding for women's rights litigation. Those lawyers created the Women's Legal Education and Action Fund (LEAF) in 1985, which has financed virtually all of the women's rights cases since 1985 in the Supreme Court.

Even the *Charter* itself may be understood as a product of the changes in the Canadian support structure that transformed the Supreme Court's agenda. A number of rights advocacy organizations directly influenced the language of the *Charter* in highly significant ways by participating in the drafting process or by putting pressure on the national government's negotiators in that process. For instance, the Canadian Civil Liberties Association, along with several other groups, successfully lobbied for significant changes in the *Charter*'s procedural rights provisions.

Although both the *Charter* and the Supreme Court's agenda transformation reflect changes in the support structure for legal mobilization, the *Charter* nonetheless has exerted an independent influence on some aspects of the Supreme Court's decision-making. In particular, the Court's level of support for liberal rights claims grew, albeit temporarily, after passage of the *Charter*. Furthermore, this growing support apparently encouraged litigants to bring more such cases, as evidenced by the dramatic growth between 1985 and 1990 in the number of requests for judicial review. As Manfredi has argued, the Supreme Court's willingness to interpret the *Charter*'s provisions broadly and creatively, and the willingness of interest groups to constitutionalize their claims through litigation, interact to heighten the policy-making role of the judiciary.

Finally, although the majority of Supreme Court justices did not actively encourage the agenda transformation documented here, some justices, particularly those identified as liberals ... certainly did. Additionally, majorities of the court made several decisions that significantly opened access to the Court's agenda. In several decisions in the late 1970s, the Court relaxed its rules on standing, allowing individuals and groups to pursue public interest lawsuits, and in the mid-1980s the Court opened its doors to third-party intervention by interest groups. These decisions surely contributed to the agenda transformation.

Conclusion

In recent decades, constitutional engineers have relied heavily on bills of rights as a means for protecting rights. However, bills of rights are not self-activating. Interpreting and developing the often ambiguous provisions of a bill of rights depends on mobilization of the law by individuals, but individuals by themselves typically lack the capacity to take cases to a country's highest court. The effects of a bill of rights, therefore, depend on the extent of organized support for mobilization of the law. Admittedly, a bill of rights may affect judges' willingness to strike down legislation or to check official action but, in the absence of adequate resources for legal mobilization, few non-economic cases are likely to reach the judicial agenda, and judges will have few occasions to use their constitutional authority. Thus constitutional reform alone, in the absence of resources in civil society for legal mobilization, is likely to produce only empty promises. None of this indicates that bills of rights are irrelevant to politics. Bills of rights matter, but only if civil societies have the capacity to support and develop them.

11.8

Interest Group Litigation and Canadian Democracy
Gregory Hein

This article is reprinted as Reading 7.5.

11.9

Key Terms

Concepts

parliamentary supremacy
constitutional supremacy
constitutional convention
constitutionally entrenched
canon of statutory interpretation
"interpretive avoidance"
"power allocation"
"power denial"
"implied bill of rights"
"equality in the application and administration of the laws"
"equal laws"
Section 33 notwithstanding (legislative override) clause
juridicalization of politics
liberal versus post-liberal constitutionalism
under-inclusive
support structure for legal mobilization (SSLM)
rights advocacy organizations
systematic litigation strategy
the Court Party
"judicial democrats"
interpretivism vs. non-interpretivism

Institutions, Events, and Documents

Alberta Press Case (1938)
Boucher v. *The King* (1951)
Roncarelli v. *Duplessis* (1959)
1960 Bill of Rights
Drybones v. *the Queen* (1969)
A.-G. Canada v. *Lavell and Bedard* (1974)
Charter of Rights and Freedoms (1982)
R. v. *Oakes* (1987)
Eldridge v. *British Columbia* (1997)
Vriend v. *Alberta* (1998)

Judicial Decision-Making 12

The subject of this chapter is the decision-making processes of appeal courts, and specifically the Supreme Court of Canada. The practising bar and the general public are interested only in the practical "product" of courts – the final judgment and opinion. However, the character and even the quality of the final "product" are influenced by the internal procedures and jurisdiction of a court – how a court goes about its business. To better understand the judicial process, we must go behind the institutional facade of courts and examine how appeal court judges actually decide cases and write opinions.[1]

Courts, like other institutions, have a particular institutional logic formed by and around their purpose. The traditional adjudicatory function of courts has moulded the internal decision-making procedures of courts in all common law countries. The original notion that the judicial function is "to find the law" led to the practice of *seriatim* opinion-writing, in which each judge gives his or her own "findings" or reasons for judgment. *Seriatim* opinions reflected and reinforced the tradition of judicial independence, which includes the independence of the judges from each other as well as from outside influences.

Whatever the merits of *seriatim* opinions in the traditional realm of private law, the practice is open to criticism in the realm of constitutional law, where judicial decisions tend to have a greater impact on public policy. The principal criticism of *seriatim* opinions is that they are often confusing. This can be appreciated by any student who has had to wade through the multiple opinions in such Supreme Court decisions as *Saumur* or *Johannesson*, both from the 1950s. McCormick has described this problem as the "anarchic independence of *seriatim* opinion writing." In constitutional law cases, public and private policy "actors" look to the Supreme Court's decisions for guidance as to what is or is not permissible government policy, and what can reasonably be expected in the future. Each opinion is in effect a new "rule" of

---

1 For a more in-depth discussion of these issues, see Ian Greene, Carl Baar, Peter McCormick, George Szablowski, and Martin Thomas, *Final Appeal: Decision-Making in Canadian Courts of Appeal* (Toronto: Lorimer, 1998).

constitutional law. Accordingly, a decision that gives five different "rules" for the majority decision is not as helpful as a single "opinion of the court."

As second criticism of *seriatim* opinions is that the multiplicity of opinions saps the authority of the court. If a final appellate court hands down a single unanimous opinion in a potentially controversial case, it sends a subtle but important message to the losing side that continued litigation or resistance to the decision would be futile.[2] Multiple reasons for the same result send a very different message.

Predictably, it was the American Supreme Court that first abandoned the practice of *seriatim* opinion writing. John Marshall (1800–34), considered the greatest and most influential of all American chief justices, persuaded his colleagues that a single "opinion of the court" expressing the majority view would enhance the authority and prestige of the then fledgling court. Marshall initiated the practice of formal conferences as a means for the judges to share their opinions, to discover common ground as well as differences, and so to facilitate the production of a single "opinion of the court." Until the New Deal court crisis, over eighty per cent of the American Court's decisions were unanimous. Since the "constitutional revolution" of 1937, concurring and dissenting opinions have steadily multiplied to the point where unanimous decisions account for only twenty-five per cent of its decisions.

Notwithstanding post-1937 developments, American Supreme Court opinions still tended to be more coherent than the Canadian Supreme Court's continuing practice of *seriatim* opinions, if simply because they were less diverse. This began to change in the 1970s under the leadership of the late Chief Justice Bora Laskin. Laskin initiated a number of procedural reforms designed to increase the collegiality of the court and to reduce the number of separate opinions. Laskin formalized a practice begun by his predecessor, Chief Justice Cartwright: holding a judges' conference after oral argument.

Conferencing was calculated to enhance the efficiency and coherence of the Supreme Court's opinion-writing. Judges can discover whom they agree with and whom they disagree with, and responsibility to draft a single opinion (and a dissent, if necessary) can be assigned. Conferencing also facilitates strategic coordination among judges and innovation in the law. If judges are writing their reasons independently in isolation, there are incentives for each judge to try to "follow precedent" as faithfully as possible. Caution is the best policy. By contrast, when judges conference before any opinion writing begins, new directions can be identified, discussed and even adopted. McCormick has observed that, "The conferencing court is better suited for coherent, systematic leadership and particularly for innova-

---

2 The textbook example of this was the U.S. Supreme Court's decision in the 1954 School Desegregation Case. The Chief Justice Earl Warren spent several years "negotiating" with reluctant members of the Court in order to produce a unanimous opinion for a decision that he knew would incite controversy and opposition in the American South.

tion," and that the jurisprudential innovations of the Laskin Court had its foundations in these procedural reforms.[3]

The most immediate effect of this reform was a reduction in the number of opinions being written. During the 1950s, following abolition of appeals to the JCPC, each of the nine judges wrote an opinion in about half of the cases he heard. For the Lamer Court (1990–99), the average was down to one in four.[4] Justice Wilson's account of the contemporary Supreme Court (Reading 12.1) confirms the attempt to build consensus and the tendency of judges to concur – often after some bargaining – with the written opinion of another judge.

Conferencing also seems to have facilitated another trend: a small but growing number of decisions delivered simply as unsigned opinions of "The Court." Prior to the Laskin Court, there had only been one such case, the 1969 *Offshore Minerals Reference*. These decisions are unanimous, and there is no indication of who wrote the opinion. Most of these cases have dealt with politically volatile issues – minority language rights in Quebec[5] and Manitoba,[6] Quebec's claim to a unilateral veto over constitutional amendments,[7] the federal government's claim to unilateral authority to reform the Senate,[8] and Newfoundland's jurisdictional claim to the offshore Hibernia oil fields.[9] The Supreme Court, aware of the political sensitivity of the issues raised in these cases, seems to have adopted a "united front" strategy. There have also been several instances of "group authorship" of single majority and dissenting opinions.[10]

Another important Laskin initiative was changing the rules governing access to the Court for civil cases. As a consequence of the Chief Justice's initiative, Parliament amended the *Supreme Court Act* in 1975 to abolish appeals as of right in civil cases with a value over $10,000. This reform permitted the Supreme Court to control its own docket, to pick and choose which cases raise sufficiently important questions of law or policy to merit the Supreme Court's time and energy (Reading 12.2).

During the 1990s, the Court received between 550 and 650 leave applications a year. It accepted an average of one out of every five (20%) applications. To consider these applications, the Court sits in three panels of three judges, appointed by the Chief Justice and changed every year. Oral argument was eliminated in the 1980s as a time-saving device. Until recently, applications

---

3 Peter McCormick, *Supreme at Last: The Evolution of the Supreme Court of Canada* (James Lorimer, 2000), p. 64.

4 McCormick, *Supreme at Last*, pp. 20, 133.

5 *A.-G. Quebec v. Blaikie*, [1979] 2 S.C.R. 1016.

6 *A.-G. Manitoba v. Forest*, [1979] 2 S.C.R. 1032.

7 [1982] 2 S.C.R. 792.

8 [1980] 1 S.C.R. 54.

9 Released March 8, 1984, unreported.

10 See *Re Exported Natural Gas Tax*, [1982] 1 S.C.R. 1006.

were screened by the clerks and their recommendation accepted or rejected by majority vote of the three judges. In the late 1990s, the task of summarizing leave applications was transferred to staff lawyers. (Staff lawyers have increased from two in 1987 to thirteen in 1998.) If a judge is unhappy with a panel decision, he can request that the Court reconsider it the next time they conference as a full court of nine judges. Occasionally, the full Court will reverse the panel's decision.[11]

The impact of this change has been dramatic. Between 1970 and 1975, seventy-two per cent of the Supreme Court's docket came from appeals as of right, and only twenty-three per cent by its own decision to grant leave to appeal. This situation was reversed after 1975. Between 1976 and 1980, seventy-five per cent of its cases were chosen by granting leave to appeal, while only twenty per cent were heard as a matter of right.[12] During the 1990s, the number of appeals heard as a matter of right edged upward to about thirty per cent. These are mostly serious criminal cases with a dissent in the lower appeal court or an appeal court reversal of a trial court acquittal. All six justices interviewed by Greene et al. indicated that they would prefer that these remaining appeals as of right be reduced or abolished altogether.[13] The contrast between the old and new Supreme Court was captured by Ian Bushnell's observation that prior to the 1975 reform, "it [was] the litigant who [was] afforded access and he [brought] the legal issue with him," while now "it is the legal problem that determines access, and the litigant is brought along with it."[14]

It is the judges who determine which legal issues are sufficiently important to merit their attention, and it would be naïve to assume that only legal considerations come into play in such important decisions. In the U.S. Supreme Court, it is well documented that non-legal factors also influence justices' decisions on which appeals to hear. In Reading 12.2, Professor Roy Flemming applies this U.S. research to the Supreme Court of Canada in a modified form.

Flemming identifies three principal hypotheses that explain how justices decide which cases to hear: jurisprudential choice, litigant resources, and strategic choice. These explanations are not mutually exclusive. Two or three can operate simultaneously. The first takes the Court's announced legal criterion of "public importance" at face value and tests for empirical characteristics associated with "public importance." These include conflicting judgments on the same point of law and impact on federal or provincial public policies. These types of characteristics are readily observable in the

---

11 For details, see Greene et al., *Final Appeal*, pp. 107–09.

12 S. I. Bushnell, "Leave to Appeal Applications to the Supreme Court of Canada: A Matter of Public Importance," *Supreme Court Law Review* 3 (1982), p. 479.

13 Greene et al., *Final Appeal*, p. 100.

14 Bushnell, "Leave to Appeal Applications," p. 488.

Canadian context, and Flemming was able to apply the hypothesis directly. (See Table 1, p. 552, for complete list.)

The litigant resources hypothesis assumes that higher status litigants are more likely to have their appeals accepted than lower status parties. For example, this hypothesis assumes that governments are more likely to gain access to the Court than non-governments, organized interests more than individuals, "repeat-players" more than "one-shotters," parties represented by experienced lawyers more than parties with inexperienced lawyers, and so forth.

Institutional differences prevent this hypothesis from being fully applied to the Canadian Court. In the U.S. Supreme Court, organized interests participate as *amicus curiae* (intervenors) in the leave process in the same manner as they do in the subsequent hearing of the appeal on the merits. They submit factums urging the Court to accept or reject the leave application. This permits American political scientists to test the litigant resource hypothesis based on the record of which organized groups intervened. In Canada, there is no intervenor participation in the leave to appeal stage, so it is not possible to test for the role of organized interests. To modify the litigant resource hypothesis to account for this institutional difference, Flemming limited his test to the status of the applicant and to proxy characteristics such as the applicant's lawyer experience or status as a QC – Queen's Counsel.

The strategic choice hypothesis assumes that judges cast their votes whether to hear a case based on how they think the case would ultimately be decided. If a judge anticipates that the final outcome would be one he favours, then he votes to grant leave to appeal ("aggressive grant"). If a judge thinks the full court would decide the case in a manner she does not favour, then she votes against hearing it. For example, in a foetal rights case, if a judge favours broad judicial protection of abortion rights; and the lower court has ruled to expand the right to life of the unborn; the judge might still vote to refuse to grant leave if he thinks that the full Supreme Court would uphold the lower court decision. This type of strategic choice is known as a "defensive denial."

Unfortunately, institutional differences made it impossible for Flemming to test for this hypothesis. The U.S. Court sits as a full panel of nine judges for both leave and merits hearings. In Canada, the Court sits in panels of three to decide leave applications and then in variable panel sizes – five, seven, or nine judges – for decision on the merits. Since a judge cannot know with certainty which judges will sit on the final merits coram, he cannot reliably predict how the case might be decided.

Flemming's study found that the most important legal factors influencing the Court's selection are the novelty of the issue; conflicting lower court decisions; dissenting votes in the lower court decision; invitations to revisit an earlier decision; and a demonstrable effect on the interests of either the federal or provincial governments. Asking the Court to correct an alleged lower court mistake did not increase the probability of succeeding. For extra-legal factors, Flemming found that the Court was more likely to grant leave to appeal to cases in which applicants have greater resources (or "status") than the respondent. The status of the lawyer hired to argue a case did not affect outcomes.

A related change initiated by Laskin was his preference for the Supreme Court to sit as a full nine-judge bench rather than in panels of five. The practice of five judge panels had long been followed and was defended on the grounds of efficiency. After the Supreme Court assumed final responsibility for overseeing the legal dimensions of Canada's constitutional development in 1949, this practice began to be criticized as introducing a haphazard element into the court's decisions. A case might be decided differently depending on how the five-judge panel was selected, a matter totally at the discretion of the Chief Justice. This was considered particularly inappropriate in constitutional cases.

Before his appointment as Chief Justice, Laskin had publicly disapproved of the five-judge panels for important cases, and he quickly exercised his new administrative prerogatives to implement his preferred policy of nine-judge panels. The results were significant. In the three terms preceding his appointment, nine-judge panels heard only ten per cent of the cases argued before the Supreme Court. In the eight years following Laskin's elevation to the chief justiceship, the average increased to thirty-six per cent, and since 1976 there have been more nine-judge panels than five-judge panels.[15] This trend has continued through the 1990s. For important or controversial cases, the Chief Justice usually convenes a coram of nine judges. For low profile, appeal-as-of-right cases, the Court may still sit as five judges. The clear norm is seven.[16] The cumulative effect of this trend has been to increase the authority of the Supreme Court's pronouncements on constitutional issues and so to make it a more influential participant in the political process.

An institutional change that may curb the Court's quest for greater collegiality and consensus is the parallel development of the increasing use of "law clerks" (Reading 12.3). A law clerk is typically a recent law school graduate individually selected by a justice to work as a research assistant. Until recently, the use of law clerks was largely an American practice. The Supreme Court of Canada did not hire its first law clerk until the late 1960s. By 1978, each justice had one clerk, at which point Chief Justice Laskin hired a second. By 1984, each justice had two clerks, and Chief Justice Dickson then hired an "Administrative Director." Today, each justice has three clerks. American commentators agree the increasing reliance on clerks has tended to bureaucratize the American Court, creating "nine little law firms" inside the court and thus eroding collegiality. There is no reason not to expect a similar effect from the same trend in Canada.

Clerks also play an important role in bringing contemporary legal

15 S. I. Bushnell, "Leave to Appeal Applications to the Supreme Court of Canada: A Matter of Public Importance," *Supreme Court Law Review* 3 (1982), p. 479.

16 McCormick, *Supreme at Last*, pp. 87, 115.

scholarship before the court, the use of which is another one of the changes in recent Supreme Court opinion-writing. Often, this material includes "advocacy scholarship" intended by its authors to bolster the *Charter* claims of certain rights-advocacy groups. Lorne Sossin, a former clerk, has written that most clerks are supportive of the *Charter* as a vehicle for legal and social reform. He adds that a subset of "programmatic clerks" are consciously "result-oriented" in advocating either judicial activism or self-restraint, whichever will assist a "disadvantaged group" in a given case.

The American Supreme Court's decision-making process provides a comparative perspective and points to some interesting parallels. Both courts are constrained by the common need to find or build a consensus that can support a majority if not a unanimous judgment. This shared objective induces strategic voting and opinion-writing in both courts. The basic options are the same: join a majority opinion; concur in a majority opinion; or write a dissent. Judges on both courts negotiate with one another, bargaining votes for wording changes, what Justice Wilson describes as "judicial lobbying." Despite the American Court's early leadership in developing the practice of a single "Opinion of the Court," such unanimity is now the exception not the rule. The factors contributing to the decline of consensus on the American Court are increasingly present in the Supreme Court of Canada: control of docket, resulting in more controversial, thus more divisive, cases being decided; the triumph of the non-interpretivist approach to constitutional interpretation; and the increasing use of law clerks.

Professor Kelly's study of the Supreme Court's first 390 *Charter of Rights* decisions (see Reading 12.4) provides contradictory evidence with respect to this hypothesis. After the initial "*Charter* honeymoon" (1982–87) which saw a unanimity rate of sixty-five per cent, the Supreme Court became more divided in its *Charter* decisions with only fifty-nine per cent of its decisions being unanimous by 1992. In the period 1993–99, however, the unanimity rate climbed back to sixty-seven per cent (Table 1). This is still low, however, compared to a rate of over eighty per cent in its non-*Charter* decisions.

Nor is this disagreement random. Kelly's analysis of individual judge's voting records confirms earlier studies that shows that certain judges have been consistently activist in their *Charter* interpretations while others have repeatedly exercised judicial self-restraint. Justice Bertha Wilson, who supported the rights claimant in fifty-five per cent of the *Charter* cases she heard, claims the record as the most activist Supreme Court justice, while Justice McIntyre (22%) has been the most deferential. Among current justices, Bastarche (23%) and Gonthier (26%) appear the most self-restrained, and Major (37%) the most activist (Table 3).

These aggregate voting records, however, obscure some fundamental differences. When the *Charter* cases are divided into two categories of criminal and "Court Party" based on the issues involved, a different picture emerges (Table 8). Some justices – such as L'Heureux-Dubé – have low levels of support for rights in criminal cases (24%) but high support for court party cases (63%). A judge like Sopinka is the opposite, supporting rights claims in only thirty-four per cent of court party cases but forty-seven per cent in criminal cases. Looking just at their aggregate or "combined" data, however, L'Heureux-Dubé (31%) and Sopinka (37%) both look like middle-of-the-road *Charter* supporters.

These findings support the legal realist view that the judge is as important as the text of the law in determining the outcome of many cases. This conclusion was confirmed in a similar study of Supreme Court voting patterns and panel assignments by Professor Andrew Heard. According to Heard, "The unmistakable conclusion of this study is that the outcome of a *Charter* claim argued in the Supreme Court of Canada depends to a very large extent upon which judges sit on the panel that hears the appeal."[17] This is a reminder why many would like to see the Court hear all important *Charter* cases as a full court of nine judges.

Another important procedural difference between final appellate courts is the relative importance that they assign to oral and written argument. In Great Britain, written argument is limited to a brief one- or two-page outline of issues and precedents, while oral argument is unlimited, and typically lasts several days. This practice represents the extension of the adversary process into the appeal courts: counsel for opposing sides do battle before passive and impartial judges. At the other extreme is the American practice of strictly limited oral argument but lengthy and detailed written "briefs." In the U.S. Supreme Court oral argument is strictly limited to thirty minutes, with a system of flashing lights to warn counsel that time is almost over. Prior to oral argument, however, the American justices receive written briefs of twenty to a hundred pages, detailing not just the legal arguments and precedents, but often relevant socio-economic evidence as well. The purpose of oral argument is to allow the judges to ask questions and to clarify facts and arguments presented in the written briefs. Despite the fact that each lawyer has only thirty minutes, the justices frequently interrupt and ask questions. Unlike the appeals courts in Great Britain, it is the judges, not the counsel, who control the course of the hearing.

Until recently, Canadian practice fell somewhere between the American and British approaches. Unlike their British counterpart, the Canadian Supreme Court developed the practice of accepting substantial written argument known as "factums," prior to oral hearing. Unlike the Americans, however, the Canadian Court allowed unlimited oral argument, often running several days. In 1972, Bora Laskin wrote that the written factum was "often subservient" to oral argument. As recently as 1986, the oral argument in the appeal of the Morgentaler abortion case went on for four days.

Perhaps as a result of this experience, the following year the Court decided

---

17 Andrew Heard, "The Charter in the Supreme Court of Canada: The Importance of Which Judges Hear and Appeal," *Canadian Journal of Poitical Science* (1991), pp. 290–307, at 305.

that unlimited oral argument was a luxury that it could no longer afford. In the years following the adoption of the *Charter*, the Court fell behind badly in its caseload. The annual number of decisions handed down dropped precipitously and there were delays of twelve months and longer between oral argument and delivery of the judgment. In 1987, the Court announced that henceforth oral argument for normal appeals would be limited to two hours, one for each side.

Today, oral argument is very different from what it was twenty years ago. As recently as the early 1980s, the justices were mostly passive when listening to oral arguments presented by counsel. Today, the justices intervene frequently with pointed questions and follow-ups. An inexperienced or inept lawyer can easily find himself diverted from his main points and the allotted time suddenly over. In an interview, Justice LaForest confirmed that, having read the factums ahead of time, the justices now view oral argument as an opportunity to "test" the perceived strengths and weaknesses of the competing legal arguments and in so doing perhaps influence the votes of some of their colleagues. Greene's interviews with the justices indicate that they change their minds during oral argument in as high as twenty per cent of the cases they hear.[18]

The Court also discontinued (except for very rare instances) their traditional practice of a fifteen-minute oral hearing for parties seeking leave to appeal. Henceforth, leave to appeal would have to be submitted in writing. Some members of the Canadian Bar protested that this reform robbed them and their clients of their "day in court." It did, but the protests fell on deaf ears. The Court justified both the elimination of oral hearings for leave applications and the new time limits on oral arguments as necessary efficiency measures. It was true that these reforms would save the Court many "judge-hours" that could now be devoted to other tasks. What the Court did not explicitly state was that these other tasks were a consequence of its new and evolving "supervisory" function. The Court was no longer primarily a "court of error," serving as a backup to provincial courts of appeal. Even before the adoption of the 1982 *Charter of Rights*, the Court had begun to change from an English-style appeals court to a more political role. The reduction of time committed to oral argument was a symptom of this change.

Laskin also rearranged the Court's schedule so that, during their three annual sessions, they heard cases for only two out of every three weeks, and no cases were scheduled for Fridays. These changes were intended to facilitate conferencing and to encourage the justices to give more attention to the quality of their written opinions. Laskin's attempts to focus the justices attention on their written opinions as the most important "product" of the Court has continued down to the present. Today, the Court sits to hear cases two weeks on, then two weeks off, from October through June with breaks during the Christmas and Easter periods. During non-sitting weeks,

---

18 Greene, *Final Appeal*, p. 123.

the judges work on their written judgments, deal with leave to appeal applications, and read the factums for upcoming cases.

A final change in the way the Supreme Court decides cases is what "authorities" it cites. Appeal court judges are obliged to support their decisions with precedents. But which precedents? If, as Professor McCormick suggests, "You are what you cite," then the Supreme Court has undergone a profound change in identity. As indicated in McCormick's figures below, the Court has abandoned its early reliance on JCPC and English court precedents. Instead, it now relies primarily on its own decisions for precedents (55.8%), while U.S. precedents have increased five-fold.[19]

Table 1-1
Percentage of Citations from Selected SCC "Courts"

	JCPC	SCC	Canadian Courts	English Courts	U.S. Courts
Rinfret (1949-54)	16.1	21.7	16.7	43.7	0.8
Kerwin (1954-63)	13.2	28.7	21.4	33.7	1.5
Tashereau (1963-73)	7.6	38.8	24.3	25.2	3.1
Laskin (1973-84)	7.7	38.4	29.4	19.3	3.3
Dickson (1984-90)	2.9	38.9	35.3	13.7	7.2
Lamer (1990-99)	1.4	55.8	27.5	8	5.6

A second important trend in citation practices is the increasing reference to legal academic literature. Historically, precedents, not academic commentary, served as the primary source of authority. Four decades ago, the Supreme Court had an unwritten presumption against using contemporary academic sources. At the end of the 1960s the Supreme Court Reports contained "barely a dozen references a year to academic texts, and virtually none to legal journals."[20] In the 1990s, by contrast, the Supreme Court cites hundreds of books and articles a year, most written by living authors. Although most references are to Canadian authors, U.S. writers now account for about one half as many citations as Canadians. This new judicial reliance on contemporary legal scholarship is most prominent in three categories of cases – *Charter*, family law, and tort. This is yet another trend that Chief Justice Laskin, himself a former professor of law, is partly responsible for starting.[21]

In 1972, Bora Laskin observed that the "more fixed and formal" internal structure of the American Supreme Court reflected its greater jurisdictional responsibilities. Most of the procedural changes in the Supreme Court of Canada since then may be understood as logical responses to its own growing jurisdictional responsibilities as Canada's final court of appeal.

---

19 These figures are collected from the data presented in McCormick, *Supreme at Last*, pp. 24, 47, 71, 96, 117, 139.

20 Greene et al., *Final Appeal*, p. 150.

21 McCormick, *Supreme at Last*, pp. 95–97.

Since the abolition of appeals to the JCPC in 1949, which marked the end of what Laskin sarcastically described as a "captive court," the Supreme Court of Canada has steadily discarded the procedures designed for a middle-tier British appeals court and adapted its procedures to fit its new responsibilities.

Laskin will be remembered as the architect of this institutional retooling. In his history of the modern Court, McCormick describes Laskin as "the Revolutionary," claiming that "Laskin changed the way the Court operated (with larger panels and eventually greater unanimity) and the way it approached its business (with more willingness to tackle law reform and more concern for policy consequences)."[22] As in other government institutions, the "how" influences the "what"; procedure shapes substance.

12.1

Decision-making in the Supreme Court of Canada
Justice Bertha Wilson
"The Judge as an Individual Member of the Court v. The Court as an Institution."
University of Toronto Law Journal 36 (1986), 227–92. Reprinted with permission.

This tension [between the judge as an individual member of the Court versus the Court as an institution] is in a rather different category from the others I have mentioned. Some judges think that the best way for an appellate court to operate is for each judge to perform his or her judicial function independently – ideally with each member of the Court writing a separate judgment. Lord Reid was a great advocate of this approach. He believed that the diversity of views expressed, although admittedly making it more difficult to identify the *ratio decidendi* of the case, had the advantage of providing greater flexibility in the development of the law. Lower courts could pick and choose from among a variety of different judicial approaches the one that seemed most appropriate to changing social conditions; the others would simply wither away Indeed, the majority of the Law Lords, when interviewed by Alan Paterson for his book, *The Law Lords,* expressed the view that between the 1940s and the 1970s the Court's attitude to dissenting judgments had changed radically. The pressure to present a united front had gone, and the right and duty of individual expression had become central to Their Lordships' perception of their role. On the other hand, the Judicial Committee of the Privy Council for many years published only one opinion, apparently on the theory that dissenting views would weaken the authority of the tribunal which, notionally at least, was only advising the sovereign on the resolution of the dispute.

---

22 McCormick, *Supreme at Last,* p. 103.

Present practice in the Supreme Court of Canada lies somewhere between these two extremes. Different members of the Court hold differing views on the extent to which it is important to develop a consensus on particular legal issues. Is public confidence in the institution enhanced by unanimous judgments? Some think so. Or do strong dissents and separate concurring reasons reflect the potential for growth and change in the system? Is there any merit in "watering down" a judgment in the interests of unanimity? To what extent should judges try to persuade their colleagues to their point of view? And why do some judges find this process of judicial "lobbying" repugnant?

The answers one gives to these questions will depend, I think, on one's concept of what a collegial court is and how it should function. For some reason very little has been said or written on this very fascinating subject. Yet no consideration of the decision-making process of an appellate tribunal is complete without it. If there is, indeed, an obligation on a collegial court to strive for a consensus, or at least to submerge individuality in the interests of fewer sets of reasons, then the dynamics of the Court's process would seem to be extremely important. So let us take a brief look at what happens following the hearing of an appeal.

After argument is concluded the judges retire to a conference room to express their tentative views on the case. It is our practice for each judge to state his or her views in reverse order of seniority, beginning with the most junior judge and concluding with the most senior. The thinking behind this tradition was to avoid the more junior members of the Court simply adopting the views of their elders and betters. I may say that whatever may have been the case in the past, there is very little risk of this happening today; the members of the Court are, as the Chief Justice euphemistically puts it, "fiercely independent." It is interesting to note that the United States Supreme Court does it the other way round, proceeding on the basis of seniority, with the Chief Justice expressing his views first.

The first tentative expression of views at our conference will usually disclose whether there is any prospect of unanimity or whether there is clearly going to be more than one judgment. We decide at this conference who is going to prepare the first draft. This will be a member of the group which appears likely to form the majority. One of that group will normally volunteer or, if there is no volunteer, the Chief Justice will ask one of the group to take it on. The other judges then set aside their record in the case until a draft is circulated. Depending on the complexity of the case and the number of other judgments which a particular judge is working on, it may take several weeks or, regrettably, even months before a judgment is circulated. When this happens the judges on the panel get their papers out again, review their bench notes and any memoranda they may have dictated immediately following the hearing, study the draft, and decide whether or not they are going to be able to concur. They may at this point ask their law clerks to do some additional research.

Sometimes members of the panel will make suggestions for amendment which the author of the draft may accept or reject. Sometimes these suggested amendments are proffered in terms that that judge's concurrence is premised on their adoption. More often than not they are put forward on the basis that the judge views them as an improvement or clarification or as additional support for the result but would be willing to concur in any event. If amendments are made, the draft is recirculated and approval sought for the changes from those proposing to concur. The changes may be dropped at this point or, if not, they may spark concurring reasons.

A member of the Court may find the draft reasons totally unacceptable and will memo his or her colleagues that he or she proposes to dissent. This grinds the process of concurring to a halt since it is viewed as "bad form" to concur with the original reasons until you have seen the dissent. The same process of suggested amendment may take place with respect to the dissenting reasons. Two and maybe three sets of draft reasons are now in circulation. It is agreed at the next court conference that this is an appeal on which judgment should be released soon, on the next judgment day, if possible. The pressure is on. At this point, if not before, the individual judge's approach to decision-making becomes very important. This is particularly so in a court with a very heavy caseload. The ideal would, of course, be if all the judges could spend as much time on the cases assigned to their colleagues as they spend on the ones they are writing themselves. This is simply not possible. As the late Chief Justice Laskin put it: "If the case load is heavy, the tendency will be for judges to concentrate their limited time and their energy on opinions that have been assigned to them; and to show generous institutional faith in opinions in other cases prepared by others." Laskin concluded, therefore, that on a busy court "there is an institutional preference to support a majority result by reasons acceptable to a majority." I have no doubt that this is correct, and it should, of course, be the focal point of our concern about overworked courts. Under the pressure of a heavy caseload the delicate balance which should exist between judicial independence and collegiality may be displaced and collegiality may give way to expediency. This is an extremely serious matter for an appellate tribunal because the integrity of the process itself is threatened. The only answer is to grant fewer leaves and make sure that the balance between the Court's sitting time and its non-sitting time is appropriate and correct, one that allows adequate time for research and reflection, for conferring with one's colleagues, and for the drafting and redrafting of reasons for judgment.

First drafts have a way of developing a life of their own as they pass through a number of different hands. This is hardly surprising in view of the tensions in the decision-making process which I have been discussing. Nor is it surprising that there are multiple judgments on a court of nine people. Consciously or subconsciously, judges bring their philosophy of judging to bear on their judgments. Yet scant attention has been paid to the pre-suppositions about the role of the judge on which our different philosophies are based, and to the process by which decisions are reached. I believe this is changing. I think the advent of the *Charter* is bringing the role of the courts into sharper focus and that one of the benefits may be a more sophisticated appreciation by both lawyers and judges of what we do. Perhaps with that more sophisticated appreciation will go an enhanced sense of responsibility and dedication to our task.

12.2

Agenda Setting:
The Selection of Cases for Judicial Review in the Supreme Court of Canada

Roy B. Flemming
Department of Political Science, Texas A&M University. This is a revised and shortened version of a paper presented at the Annual Meeting of the Canadian Political Science Association, Quebec City, Quebec, Canada, July 29–August 1, 2000. The complete paper including methodology and statistical results can be accessed at <www-polisci.tamu.edu/flemming>.

Discretion and the Rule of "Public Importance" in Canada

Since 1982, when Canada entrenched the *Charter of Rights and Freedom* in its constitution, the Supreme Court of Canada has become an increasingly important policy maker. A presage of the Court's enhanced influence was the 1975 amendment to the *Supreme Court Act* that made the "leave to appeal" process the central avenue to the Court's docket. The amendment eliminated most mandatory appeals and gave the Court wide discretion over which cases to review. According to the amendment, the Supreme Court's decision to grant leave to appeal rested on the "public importance" of the issues raised by attorneys or appellants in their applications for leave.

The 1975 amendment did not define "public importance." Nor has the Supreme Court over the past 25 years been willing to develop a jurisprudence for the public and legal profession that states explicitly how the Court defines "public importance" when it reviews requests for judicial review. In 1995, then Chief Justice Antonio Lamer summed up the Court's view:

> The ability to grant or deny leave represents the sole means by which this Court is able to exert discretionary control over its docket. In order to ensure that this Court enjoys complete flexibility in allocating its scarce judicial resources towards cases of true public importance, as a sound rule of practice, we ... do not produce written reasons for grants and denials of leave.

The late Justice John Sopinka wrote a book on appellate practice in which there were hints to attorneys regarding how the Court interpreted public importance. Leave applications heeding these suggestions, he advised, stood a better chance of being granted by the Court than those that did not. An issue raises questions of public importance, they claimed, when it involves one or more of the following:

- a novel constitutional issue
- a significant federal statute of general application
- a provincial statute similar to legislation in other provinces
- conflicting decisions in the provincial courts of appeal
- the need to revisit an important question of law

Once again key words like "novel," "significant," and "important" are left as terms of art for the attorneys to decipher, and for the justices to decide whether the lawyers' intuitions and interpretations come close to the mark.

How the U.S. Supreme Court Uses its Discretion: Three Hypotheses

How can Canada's leave to appeal process be explained? There is little Canadian research aside from annual practice notes that addresses this question. In the United States, though, there is considerable research on similar processes in the U.S. Supreme Court which also has broad and vaguely defined discretion over the cases it wants to hear. Explanations of how the Court uses its discretion pivot around three broad hypotheses. The first is the *jurisprudential choice* hypothesis. According to this hypothesis, justices apply legal considerations to requests for judicial review, and legal factors weigh heavily on the justices' deliberations. The indicators of "public importance" suggested by Justice Sopinka, for example, like conflicting lower court decisions or novel constitutional issues, according to this hypothesis might help explain how Canada's Court sets its agenda. This hypothesis does mean the process is mechanical or rigidly rule-dominated, however. Instead legal factors prompt justices to give applications for leave a second look in a process that is strongly governed by the presumption that few requests for review warrant approval.

The second major hypothesis focuses on *litigant resources*. In the United States, the status of litigants, i.e., whether "upperdog" or "underdog," is related to the voting behavior of justices in the agenda setting process. Higher status litigants, the upperdogs, generally are more likely to gain access to the Supreme Court than underdogs, although this relationship depends in part on the Court's ideological preferences. Other studies show that the presence of interest groups supporting the parties is an important influence on the selection of cases for judicial review. Finally, parties represented by lawyers who are repeat players with expertise before the U.S. Supreme Court have an edge over opponents with less experienced counsel in the Court's agenda-setting decisions. Experienced lawyers may also recruit interest group support.

The third hypothesis focuses on *strategic choice*. In broad terms, this hypothesis suggests that justices anticipate what the outcomes of cases would be if they were heard on the merits and then cast their votes on whether to grant judicial review according to whether these expected outcomes are consistent with the justices' policy views. Recent elaborations of this hypothesis argue that justices pursue particular strategies, e.g. "aggressive grants" or "defensive denials." The question that immediately comes to mind, of course, is whether Canada's justices play a similar "leave to appeal game."

While individual pieces of the literature in the U.S. gravitate toward one or the other of the three hypotheses, the three hypotheses are not mutually exclusive. A comprehensive understanding of agenda setting in Canada's Supreme Court clearly requires consideration of all three hypotheses if that is possible. An important preliminary question, however, is whether institutional differences or customs affect whether these hypotheses rooted in the American experience can be exported to Canada.

Institutional Differences between the Two High Courts

It is naïve to expect the three American hypotheses can be applied directly to the Canadian case. This section identifies two major differences between the U.S and Canada and how they limit the applicability of two of the preceding hypotheses in order to set the stage for rest of this analysis. In one instance, the hypothesis must be modified; in another instance, the hypothesis cannot be tested at all.

Organized interests are important elements of the litigant resource hypothesis. Their involvement in litigation before the United States Supreme Court is well-documented. A somewhat similar development has occurred in Canada. [See Reading 11.7.] In contrast to the United States, however, Canadian organized interests focus their activities exclusively on the stage after leave applications are granted. Interest groups rarely if ever file briefs as intervenors in the leave process. The Court does not explicitly forbid or preclude this activity; it nevertheless frowns on motions to intervene in leave applications, an attitude widely honored by the legal profession. Interest groups as intervenors consequently are conspicuously absent from the Canadian agenda setting process.

Just as it is not possible to test for the role of organized interests in the leave process, the strategic choice hypothesis cannot be exported into Canada without major modifications. The agenda game in the United States grows out of the norm that all nine justices on the Supreme Court participate in both the agenda setting and judicial review stages. Because of this custom, justices develop reasonably accurate expectations about their colleagues' voting habits or preferences, which in turn allows them to act strategically. In Canada, the situation is different.

Separate panels of three justices each process the leave applications assigned to them and place their decisions to grant or deny on different dockets for review by the entire bench when the nine justices meet in conference each month. The panels usually sit for a year before the Chief Justice reshuffles them. As a result the panels may not be the same from one year to the next. In addition, the panels do not routinely meet face-to-face but communicate instead by memoranda. The decentralized, discontinuous nature of Canada's leave process may mean its justices lack a full sense of how their colleagues might react to the issues raised in leave applications. A second difference with the U.S. is that the size of the merits coram, the court that hears cases granted leave, varies in Canada. Although the three justices on the leave panel that approved an application are typically members of the coram assigned to consider the merits of the case, the entire Court of nine justices does not sit en banc. Instead a coram may be set at seven justices (and sometimes five) rather than nine. For those justices who might want to act strategically at the leave stage, this custom increases the uncertainty of expectations or unpredictability of how other justices will vote.

In sum, the absence of organized interests at the leave stage marks a major difference between the Canadian and American Courts. It is well to recall this difference reflects the contrasting norms of the two Courts regarding interest group involvement in the agenda-setting process. It does not reflect an absence of mobilized interests in Canada that see litigation before the high court as an important political weapon. [See Reading 7.5] A second major contrast is that the Canadian custom of having three-judge panels review leave applications and the varying sizes of the merits corams create interesting obstacles for strategically-oriented justices and perhaps inhibit the emergence of leave to appeal games. As result of these differences between the courts, this analysis focuses on the jurisprudential and a modified litigant resource hypotheses.

The Empirical Sources for Explaining How Canada's Court Selects Cases

The applications for leave to appeal and their accompanying "factums" or briefs filed by the attorneys for the applicants during the three-year period 1993–1995 provided the data for the statistical analysis underlying this study. This three-year period includes the first three calendar years of a "natural court" that began in November 1992 and ended in October 1997, a period when the Court's composition was stable. A total of 1266 applications were included in the statistical analyses.

To test the jurisprudential hypothesis, Perry identified several indices and signals that indicated whether cases were worthy of judicial review in the United States. Two additional indicators were coded with regard to whether an application for judicial review involved the *Charter of Rights and Freedom* and whether a judge dissented in the lower appellate court. In general, all these indicators cluster around either legal conflicts in the lower courts or some aspect of public importance.

The second major hypothesis is the litigant resource hypothesis which suggests that parties with greater resources are more successful litigants than parties with few or meager resources. Previous research ranks the parties according to presumptions about their resources or status. Parties were thus categorized in ascending order of presumed status or resources: individual, groups/associations, unions, business, crown corporations (quasi-public businesses or organizations, e.g., the Canadian Broadcasting Corporation), municipal government, provincial government, and federal government.

The next measure of litigant resources focuses on whether applicants and respondents had attorneys who were "repeat players" or "one-shotters" before the Supreme Court. Experienced lawyers are repeat players; less experienced attorneys are one-shotters. Experience was measured by how often the attorneys argued a case on its merits before the Supreme Court for several years prior to the study period. An added dimension to the qualification of lawyers in Canada is whether they are "Queen's Counsel," an honorific title bestowed on attorneys by provincial governments. Queen's Counsel presumably have stature in the legal profession and visibility in their communities that might make them more formidable opponents in the courtroom than lawyers without this credential. Six of the nine justices during the time of this study, for instance, were Queen's Counsel before they ascended to the bench.

While these three measures are consistent with the litigant resource hypothesis, the indicators more appropriately should measure the inequality between attorneys or parties. McGuire, for example, measured the disparity in Supreme Court experience between attorneys in the United States. The statistical analysis therefore used indicators that measured imbalances between the status of the parties, the experience of the attorneys, and whether the attorneys for the parties were Queen's Counsel or not. Last but not least the analysis considered the possibility that the various leave panels might grant leave to appeal more often than others and that the criteria the panels used to make their decisions might also differ.

The following table lists the variables that were used in the statistical analysis of the Supreme Court's leave to appeal decisions.

The Criteria Used by Canada's Court in the Leave to Appeal Process

As in the United States, the Supreme Court of Canada is more likely to deny leave to appeal than to grant it. In general, the Court grants leave roughly 1 out of 5 times. By comparison, the U.S. Supreme Court agrees to grant judicial review in "paid cases" (usually civil cases) about 3–4 per cent of the time and in "unpaid cases" (usually criminal cases) about one out of 500 times. Agenda-setting in both courts despite their differences nevertheless rests on a common premise that judicial review usually should be denied and access to the courts rationed.

In Canada, while not all of the factors listed earlier in this chapter were found to be statistically significant, several jurisprudential factors countered the predisposition to deny access while others reinforced it. The novelty of an issue, conflicts between courts, plus indications of the public importance of issues were significant, for example. However, arguments resting on the *Charter of Rights and Freedoms* were not; there evidently must be more to an argument for leave than simply citing the *Charter*. By itself, a reference to the *Charter* fails to overcome the Court's tendency to deny leave. As Justice Sopinka noted, "If a *Charter* challenge is involved, it is important to consider whether there exists an appropriate record to determine, for instance, a s. 1 analysis." In other words, the grounds for the challenge must be prepared in the lower court, not in the leave to appeal application.

New questions of law or novel doctrinal issues drew the attention of Canada's justices, and they were more likely to grant leave to applications that involved such questions or issues. As the American literature amply suggests, arguments for judicial review in Canada that pointed to conflicting lower court decisions also were more likely to be heeded than arguments without this trump card. Lawyers who could claim there were conflicting decisions among provincial appellate courts were more likely to have their applications approved. As the court of final appeal in a centralized national court structure, the resolution of conflicting lower court decisions is one of the Supreme Court's most important responsibilities. These claims, it should be noted, were "alleged" and not "real" conflict. That is, any claim of conflict, regardless of whether it was exaggerated or not by the attorney, was likely to improve the chances for getting on the Supreme Court's docket. Another aspect of lower court was the presence of a dissenting vote on the lower appellate court. Dissents caught the eye of the Court and improved the odds that leave would be granted.

Six of the indicators shown in Table 1 can be treated as aspects of the public importance criterion in Canada. Three of them were positively related to leave decisions, three negatively. Applications urging the Supreme Court to revisit previous decisions were positively related to leave to appeal decisions. Arguments that showed how lower court decisions affected the interests of the provincial or federal governments also improved the chances that applications will be granted leave. In contrast, lawyers who stressed the need to correct procedural or interpretative errors by the trial court without linking them to larger questions failed to convince the Court that leave was warranted. In a similar way, arguments that were "fact specific" or simply reargued the factual elements presented to the appellate court also reduced the chances of applications being granted leave. These results are consistent with Justice Sopinka's explanation of the Court's role: "We are not a court of error and the fact that a court of appeal reached the wrong result is in itself insufficient.... On the other hand, if a misinterpretation of one of our judgments becomes an epidemic below, then we may want to set the record straight" (Crane and Brown 1998, 308). Finally, applications that were

Table 1
Variables Related to Hypotheses of Leave to Appeal Process

Jurisprudential Hypothesis

Conflict-related variables:

Conflict in *lower courts?*

Conflict between *provincial and federal courts?*

Conflict with *Supreme Court decision?*

Dissent in lower court?

Public importance variables:

Are *federal interests* affected?

Are *provincial interests* affected?

Are *broad socio-economic interests* affected?

Does issue in application have only *limited generality?*

Is the case of only *parochial interest?*

Does the application raise a *novel issue?*

Is the Court being asked to *revisit* one of its rulings?

Is the primary argument that there is a *jurisdictional error* in lower court ruling?

Is attorney's argument *"fact specific"?*

Is the application asking merely to *correct a lower court error?*

Is the application *frivolous?*

Was the *Charter of Rights and Freedoms* an issue?

Litigant Resource Hypothesis

Did applicant have a status advantage over the respondent?

Did applicant's lawyer have experience advantage? ("repeat player")

Did applicant's lawyer have advantage of being Queen's Counsel?

Institutional Hypothesis

Identity of panel that granted or denied leave to appeal

simply "frivolous," lacking any concrete reason why the Supreme Court should hear the case, were denied.

The findings for the litigant resource hypothesis were somewhat mixed. If an attorney was Queen's Counsel and the opposing lawyer was not, the advantage, if there was one, was not statistically significant. This result supports those observers of the Canadian legal profession who claim that being Queen's Counsel "does not signal preeminence in advocacy (as it does in England) but merely some degree of seniority and professional or public repute – if anything." The other two variables appeared to play a more important role in the Court's deliberations when it is deciding to decide.

Applicants with higher status relative to the status of the respondents were more likely to have their cases heard by the Court. This finding is consistent with McCormick's (1993) analysis with regard to cases decided on the merits. Party status, therefore, aside from the kind of argument made in the factum, appears to exert an independent effect on the Court's leave decisions. It is well to recall though that governments are ranked higher than private parties in the construction of this variable. This finding suggests that governments, especially federal agencies, are favored parties in the leave process, an often-repeated finding in the United States.

An imbalance or disparity in experience arguing cases before the Supreme Court in favour of the applicants' attorneys was expected to improve the chances for leave to appeal. The statistical analysis found something different. The justices granted leave more often to applications brought by more experienced attorneys for the respondents than to those where the applicants' lawyers had the repeat player advantage. The reason for this unexpected and seeming anomaly may be found in the fact that Canada's Supreme Court tends to affirm appeals more often than it overturns them. From 1991–1995, the Court affirmed an average of 57 percent of the cases it heard on the merits. The leave process is triggered, of course, by parties and their lawyers who lost in the lower courts and who hope the Court will overturn the rulings against them. For a Court that affirms more often than it reverses, this wish runs against the grain.

For an affirmance-minded high court, the arguments made by respondents' attorneys may justify taking up lower court rulings and extending them throughout Canada rather than letting them stand only as provincial law. Justice Sopinka, for example, noted that although the Court normally denies leave if the court of appeal is "plainly right," the Court may nonetheless grant leave "if a decision binding on the whole country is desired." Thus, while rebutting an applicant's request for leave, the respondent's lawyer may provide the justices with good reasons to consider extending the lower court decision to the country as a whole. Being granted leave, then, is not necessarily a defeat for the respondent's attorney. Indeed, it could be just the reverse if the respondent has interests in the case that transcend provincial boundaries.

When the individual various panels that reviewed leave to applications were all included in the statistical analysis, there was no evidence of significant differences among the panels with regard to their decisions to grant or deny applications. Overall, it appears that when other factors like legal considerations and litigant resources are taken into account the leave panels per se contribute little to an understanding of how Canada's Supreme Court selects cases for judicial review. The absence of differences in leave rates across panels is consistent with how applications are assigned to the panels. Leave applications after being vetted by the staff attorneys in the Court's Legal Service division were then assigned more or less randomly to the panels by the head staff attorney. (The one exception to this rule was applications from Quebec which were sent to a panel comprised of three Quebec justices.)

Summary of Findings

The Supreme Court of Canada selects appeals for judicial review through a process shaped by institutions and norms that differ in many respects from those in the United States. Compared to the U.S. Court, the Canadian process is less politicized. From an external perspective, it is less politicized in the sense that organized interests are not involved in the process. And it is less politicized from an internal perspective in that strategic maneuvering by the justices is difficult to accomplish. For both courts, it is important to remember that their rules, procedures, and norms reflect the courts' own particular interests, preferences, and needs. The exclusion of interests groups and the use of panels in Canada were not foisted on the Supreme Court by Parliament. This means the central feature of the Canadian process, the prominence of jurisprudential considerations in the selection of cases for judicial review, either by design or default is a characteristic of the process determined by the Court itself. The status of parties and their lawyers influence the odds of leave being granted, but they take a backseat to the jurisprudential factors derived from the "pubic importance" rule the Court has imposed on the process. Placing leave decisions largely in the hands of the leave panels, however, appears to lead to different standards or criteria for leave among the panels. In sum, the particular criteria of choice guiding leave to appeal decisions in Canada reflect the way the Supreme Court has constructed the application process, a process that excludes or filters out alternative standards or criteria that are common in the United States' Supreme Court.

12.3

The Role of Clerks in the Supreme Court of Canada

Excerpt from F. L. Morton and Rainer Knopff, *The Charter Revolution and the Court Party* (Peterborough, ON: Broadview Press, 2000), 110–13, 145–47.

When we think of courts and judicial decision-making, we think mainly of judges. In fact, there is a new set of judicial decision-makers, invisible to the public but increasingly influential. These are the clerks, the scores of recent law school graduates who assist appeal court judges in researching and writing opinions. While all appeal court judges now employ clerks, here we focus on the most influential – those at the Supreme Court of Canada.

In the years following the adoption of the *Charter*, the number of clerks at the Supreme Court have increased from nine to twenty-seven, that is, from one to three per judge. The clerks play a central role in all major court functions. They recommend which appeals to accept, prepare briefing notes prior to oral argument, and draft portions of the judges' written opinions. In effect, the clerks function as a filter between what comes into the court (factums) and what goes out (written judgments). Lawyers can no longer assume that the judges have actually read their factums, as opposed to selective summaries prepared by the clerks. Lorne Sossin, a former Supreme Court clerk, describes the new clerk-ocracy as "a research and advisory pool that is analogous in some respects to the Prime Minister's Office (PMO) and the Privy Council Office (PCO)." Sossin's comparison is troubling in light of Donald Savoie's recent book, which argues that the PMO and PCO have effectively eclipsed Cabinet in terms of power. This rapid growth in the number and functions of the clerks has effected a devolution of power from the top (judges) to the middle (clerks) of the bureaucratic pyramid.

While Sossin denies that clerks directly write their judges' decisions, he admits that they have a significant impact on them. As with "any other policy-making institution," he notes, the Court must rely on aides. "Just as the prime minister may have aides to assist him in drafting legislation, clerks play an analogous role. What's more," Sossin adds, clerks "represent the outlook of a new generation." In other words, clerks, whose average age is 27, bring new legal and policy thinking to the Court. The University of Western Ontario's Robert Martin puts it more strongly. "The clerks manage to capture the judges," he argues. "They come along with the latest fancy ideas fresh out of law school. The judges then think, 'I may be old, but I'm still hip,' so they latch on to" those ideas. According to Michael Mandel of Osgoode [Hall] Law School, one can sometimes detect the influence of new clerks on a judge's opinions. Recalling when a left-leaning student clerked for former Chief Justice Dickson, Mandel discerns a "certain leftist tinge to Dickson's judgments" that year.

Although the substantive work of clerks is enveloped in the "court's shroud of secrecy," anecdotal evidence illustrates the important impact they have on Supreme Court opinions. For example, Joel Bakan, one of Chief Justice Dickson's clerks in 1985–86 is alleged to have concocted the now famous Section 1 "*Oakes* test." Dickson, it is said, was dissatisfied with the section 1 portion of a draft judgment. He gave the draft to Bakan and asked him to rework the "reasonable limitations" section. Sensing a long night, Bakan armed himself with a bottle of sherry and set about constructing the now famous three prong "balancing" test. Thus, what Chief Justice Dickson later described as "the most important section of the *Charter*," was given its practical meaning by a 23-year-old clerk.

Another story involved Bakan and Chief Justice Dickson's first Admistrative Assistant, Jim MacPherson. The Chief Justice is supposed to have asked both MacPherson and Bakan to draft opinions for the *Alberta Labour Reference*. At issue was whether the *Charter* right of "freedom of association" protected a "right to strike" for unions. If it did, then Alberta's ban on strikes by "essential service" public sector unions would be invalid. Bakan, well known for his left-leaning politics – perhaps he is the left-leaning clerk referred to by Mandel – drafted an opinion that took the side of the unions. The more centrist MacPherson wrote a draft upholding the Alberta statute. When a luncheon meeting at Dickson's home failed to resolve this conflict, Dickson pointed to his swimming pool with a smile and announced that they would have to swim a race, and to the winner would go the judgment. Bakan thought this somewhat irregular, but was not prepared to second guess the Chief. What he didn't know – but Dickson did – was that MacPherson had been a competitive university swimmer. Apparently, Dickson was having fun, and was not really leaving the outcome to chance. The race proceeded, MacPherson left Bakan in his wake, and Alberta's anti-strike legislation was upheld – the result that Dickson favoured all along.

More recently a lawyer arguing a case before the Supreme Court tried to bolster his argument by quoting from a previous Court ruling. (Judges are evidently as susceptible to this form of flattery as professors.) He began quoting from a judgment that he identified as having been written by Justice l'Heureux-Dubé. After several moments, an agitated l'Heureux-Dubé interrupted the lawyer in mid-sentence, and exclaimed that she had never written what he was reading. After the startled barrister meekly provided chapter and verse, the now embarrassed justice withdrew her disclaimer. Of course, she probably had not written it. The more likely scenario is that one of her clerks had, and she had just signed it.

These anecdotes are consistent with recent American experience. According to Edward Lazarus, a former clerk on the U.S. Supreme Court, "the broadest exercise of what has become politely known as clerk influence occurs ... in the Court's written rulings." "During October Term '88," Lazarus writes, "the vast majority of opinions the Court issued were drafted exclusively by clerks." Only two of the nine American justices allegedly wrote their own first drafts. The others "consigned themselves to a more or less demanding editor's role."

Lazarus's description of "the power of the first draft" applies with equal force to Canada. When they write the first draft, it is the clerks who make the crucial choices with respect to key words, phrases, precedents, structure, and facts. "In the endless ongoing interpretation of Supreme Court opinions," Lazarus aptly notes, "the devil is in these details." In the U.S., and increasingly in Canada, the details are controlled by the clerks.

The clerks' drafting and filtering functions are coloured by close ties to their law schools. Supreme Court clerks are selected annually from the top graduates of Canadian law schools and serve as an intellectual conveyor belt from the law schools to the inner sanctum of the Supreme Court. The clerks on the U.S. Supreme Court have been described as a "law school conduit" as they "carry the attitudes of the revisionist academic culture directly to the federal judges.... Professors are likely to have been clerks to federal judges, and they send their best students to clerkships."

This pattern has replicated itself in Canada. For example, Katherine Swinton and Kent Roach clerked for Justices Brian Dickson and Bertha Wilson, respectively, and both became professors at the University of Toronto, the law school that sends more clerks to the Supreme Court than any other. Swinton is now a judge in Ontario, while Roach became Dean of Law at the University of Saskatchewan. Professor Wayne MacKay, now at Dalhousie University, clerked for former Chief Justice Bora Laskin, as did Joseph Magnet, now a law professor at the University of Ottawa, and Allan Young, who now teaches at Osgoode Hall Law School. Joel "Oakes" Bakan clerked for Chief Justice Dickson before becoming a professor at the University of British Columbia. Jamie Cameron, another Dickson clerk, teaches at Osgoode. The "swimming clerk," Jim MacPherson, went on to become Dean of Osgoode Hall Law School. Today he is a judge on the Supreme Court of Ontario. With the most recent appointment to the Supreme Court, the circle was completed. Louise Arbour clerked for Justice Pigeon in 1971–72, worked briefly for the Law Reform Commission of Canada (and her former law school professor, Antonio Lamer), taught at Osgoode Hall for thirteen years, served as a Director for the Canadian Civil Liberties Association, and was then appointed to the Supreme Court of Canada (where she again rejoined Antonio Lamer). Like many other Canadian elites, the judicial elite is small and cozy.

While the law school connection does not necessarily mean sympathy for the Court Party, Sossin reports that, "the clerks, by and large, shared the optimism espoused by progressive voices who have advocated more innovation under the *Charter* to redress social wrongs." This orientation was especially true among what Sossin calls "programmatic clerks." More than others, programmatic clerks are result oriented, arguing for either judicial activism or judicial self-restraint, whichever is most likely to help "disadvantaged" groups. Sossin stresses that "this applies especially to *Charter* cases."

> Rather than "striving for neutrality" in their analysis of a case, these clerks are much more likely to strive for what they consider just. What programmatic clerks have in common is a belief that the *Charter* can accomplish policy ends....

Again, if American practice is any guide, the advent in Canada of programmatic clerks is not surprising. Lazarus has described the U.S. clerks' power as "very significant" and has detailed the "very conscious and abusive manner in which clerks exercise that power for partisan ends."

Sometimes the clerks' support for Court Party interests goes beyond advocacy. In December, 1988, LEAF's co-founder and leading litigator, Mary Eberts, gave a series of lectures at law schools around the country. Eberts was received as a sort of conquering hero in the heady aftermath of the feminists' triumph in the *Morgentaler* abortion case. Emboldened by the celebratory mood that surrounded her lectures, Eberts recounted how LEAF had been able to seek intelligence from contacts inside the Supreme Court when it refused to dismiss as moot the pending appeal of pro-life crusader Joe Borowski. Since private contact with a judge on such a matter would have been a gross breach of judicial independence, LEAF's insider contacts could only have been with sympathetic clerks, some of whom Eberts would have known earlier as students at the University of Toronto.

Sossin's explanation for the clerks' partisan advocacy is straightforward and plausible. Unlike the judges for whom they work, the clerks have "studied the *Charter* in high school, university, and law school." This "formative period of their legal education has been one in which the rights of women, linguistic and ethnic minorities, refugees, prisoners and other groups are perceived to have been enhanced as a direct result of Supreme Court action. With some exceptions, clerks tended to applaud these developments and sought to extend them further." In sum, the influence of clerks has been an important factor in the Court Party's success before the Supreme Court. As in all dealings with government bureaucracies, having supporters on the inside is the ultimate form of "positional support."

...

Advocacy scholarship is brought to the attention of judges through two primary sources. The first and most obvious is the factums of the interest group lawyers who appear before the courts. The ability to cite academic literature confers authority and legitimacy on an otherwise novel interpretive position. This is the central function of the influencing the influencers strategy: "The simultaneous appearance of numerous articles all supporting the same position puts judges and legal scholars on notice that there is support for the position advanced." In *Lavallée*, for example, Justice Wilson relied not only on the work of Lenore Walker, but on three other law review articles.

Julie Blackman, "Ideas Toward the Representation of Battered Women Who Kill," *Women's Rights Law Reporter* 227 (1986).

Phyllis Crocker, "The Meaning of Equality for Battered Women Who Kill Men in Self-Defense," *Harvard Women's Law Journal* 121 (1985).

M.J. Willoughby, "Rendering Each Woman Her Due: Can a Battered Woman Claim Self-Defense When She Kills Her Sleeping Batterer," *Kansas Law Review* 169 (1989).

Note not just the focus of these articles but the fact that two of the three were published in law reviews devoted exclusively to feminist issues. The *Lavallée* case is an example of the feminist legal strategy of "flooding the market with women's stories." Indeed, in this instance, the circle is closed: a feminist judge cites feminist authors published in feminist journals to acquit a woman charged with murdering her husband. *Lavallée* is symptomatic of the interaction of judicial activism and advocacy scholarship.

While factums come through the front door of the Court, advocacy scholarship also comes in the back door in the persons of the clerks. At times, the connection between clerks and the advocacy scholarship relevant to a particular case is direct and personal. As Ian Brodie notes, sometimes "the clerks have just finished taking law school classes taught by the very same activists who are intervening in the cases." Lorne Sossin, a former clerk to Chief Justice Lamer, adds that "Clerks tend to have had their legal education more influenced by law reviews. They usually rely on the reviews more heavily when forming their opinions ... than do the Justices." He believes that the ability of clerks "to bring this other body of literature before the justice may well have an impact on the decision and the way in which it is justified." He adds that "this is especially important with respect to cases involving the *Charter* because [*Charter* issues] may hinge on arguments derived from unconventional legal sources." Sossin suggests that the clerks' penchant for using law reviews as authorities explains "the frequency with which law reviews are now cited in Supreme Court judgments."

The role of clerks as conduits for law review commentary was indirectly confirmed by a 1983 comment by former Chief Justice Dickson. After observing that scholarship was an important source of interpretation, Dickson went on to complain that "one rarely finds reference to scholarly writing in the factums that counsel present to the courts." How then does it find its way into judicial decisions? The ghost-writing role of Dickson's former clerk, Joel Bakan, has already been noted. This may explain the reference to several law review articles in the Chief Justice's opinion in *Oakes*, despite the fact that none were mentioned in the factums presented to the Court. This conjecture is consistent with Greene et al.'s speculation that the much higher incidence of citations to legal scholarship in the Supreme Court decisions than in the decisions of provincial courts of appeal is due to the greater number of clerks at the Supreme Court.

12.4

Judging the Judges:

The Decline of Dissent in the
Supreme Court's *Charter* Decisions

James B. Kelly

Adapted for this book by James B. Kelly from his Ph.D. dissertation, *The Supreme Court of Canada and the Rebalancing of Liberal Constitutionalism: A Statistical Analysis of 390 Charter Decisions, 1982–1999.*

Growing dissent marked the Supreme Court of Canada's first 195 *Charter* decisions (1982–1992, henceforth referred to as "Period I"). The rate of unanimous decisions was 65 per cent for the first 100 *Charter* decision (1982-1987). This declined to 59 per cent by 1992. The most notable trend in the 195 *Charter* decisions by the Supreme Court between 1993 and 1999 (henceforth referred to as "Period II") is the return to a higher rate of unanimity. During this period the Court has been unanimous in 67 per cent (130/195) of its *Charter* cases, and this has resulted in an overall level of unanimity of 63 per cent for the first 390 *Charter* decisions.

Table 1
Unanimity in *Charter* Cases

	Charter Decisions	Number of *Charter* Decisions Unanimous	Percent Charter Decisions Unanimous
1993	43	32	74%
1994	25	15	60%
1995	26	17	65%
1996	40	29	73%
1997	23	15	65%
1998	20	11	55%
1999	18	11	61%
1982-1999	390	246	63%
1982-1992	195	116	59%
1993-1999	195	130	67%

There are a number of explanations for this turn toward greater unanimity. First, the Court's membership was relatively stable between 1993 and 1999, with Bastarache and Binnie replacing Laforest and Sopinka as the only personnel changes By contrast between 1987 and 1992 seven justices on the Court were replaced.

Secondly, the focus of the Court in Period II was largely on procedural questions concerned with the conduct of public officials. Procedural questions are less likely to divide the Court than substantive policy issues, which arise when the Court focuses on challenges to statutes and regulations. Substantive policy issues are laden with divisive questions about the legitimacy of the unelected judges challenging the decisions of legislative majorities. The Morton, Russell and Riddell study (henceforth, "the Morton et al. study") found that in *Charter* cases decided during Period I, the Court focused mostly on statutes involving substantive issues. By shifting its primary focus to *Charter* cases raising procedural issues, the Court has reduced the frequency of judicial-legislative conflict and attained a higher degree of consensus.

The increase in the rate of unanimity has seen a corresponding decrease in the number of written opinions for *Charter* decisions. The average number of written decisions for the first 195 *Charter* decisions was 2.31. This declined to 2.05 opinions per case during Period II. The number of concurring and dissenting opinions also showed a downward trend. Concurring opinions send mixed messages to lower courts and legislative actors because they dilute the clarity of judicial decisions. For Period I, when the number of single opinion decisions were factored out (87), the average number of written opinions jumped to 3.4. The analogous figure for Period II was 3.0. The growing *Charter* consensus on the Supreme Court stands in direct contrast to the experience of the American Supreme Court where the level of unanimity on *Bill of Rights* cases has remained at 25 per cent for the past four decades.

Table 2
Number of Written Opinions per *Charter* Case

	Charter Decisions	Number of Opinions	Number of Opinions per Case
1993	43	86	2.00
1994	25	58	2.32
1995	26	69	2.65
1996	40	77	1.93
1997	23	41	1.78
1998	20	36	1.80
1999	18	33	1.83
1982-1999	390	851	2.18
1982-1992	195	451	2.31
1993-1999	195	400	2.05

Different Judicial Approaches to Rights and Freedoms

Eighteen individuals sat on the Supreme Court between 1982 and 1999. Only former Chief Justice Lamer was a member of the Court this entire period. Table 3 summarizes the voting records of the justices that sat on the Supreme Court between 1982 and 1999. Wilson remains the most activist justice to preside over *Charter* cases at 55 per cent support rate for *Charter* claimants, followed by Estey (44 per cent) and Le Dain (43 per cent). Lamer was the second most activist judge during Period I at 45 per cent, but his activism reduced significantly in Period II, moving him to fifth place overall (38 per cent). At the other end of the spectrum, McIntyre remained the most self restrained member of the Court (22 per cent), followed closely by Bastarache (23 per cent) and Gonthier (26 per cent). Justice McLachlin replaced Sopinka as the most activist Mulroney appointment on the Court at 39 per cent, but both justices declined in their activism after 1992. This trend of declining support rates for *Charter* claimants is a common characteristic of the individual justices on the Court between 1993 and 1999. Justices that remain at or below the Court average of 33 per cent along with McIntyre, Bastarache and Gonthier include Stevenson (28 per cent), L'Heureux-Dubé (31 per cent) and Laforest (33 per cent).

Table 3 provides an opportunity to re-evaluate David Beatty's suggestion that the decline in activism is the result of conservative judicial appointments by Brian Mulroney. The Mulroney appointments exhibit varying levels of activism, a pattern that casts doubt on Beatty's claim that there exists two ideological voting blocs on the Supreme Court. The difference in support levels between the most activist Mulroney appointment and the least activist is 13 per cent (McLachlin to Gonthier) whereas the distance between the analogous Trudeau appointments is 33 per cent (Wilson to McIntyre). The small distance between the Mulroney appointments and their close proximity to the Court average reinforce Morton et al.'s previous conclusion that the result of moving from a Trudeau to a Mulroney court has not been the entrenchment of a "Conservative Court" but rather "a consolidation of the Court's grey middle. As noted earlier, the emergence of a centre-dominant coalition in Period II differentiates the Canadian Court from the American Court, where ideological polarization has been sharp since the Nixon administration (1968-1974).

The growing consensus on the Supreme Court has seen the number of dissents decrease from 12 per cent in Period I to 10 per cent in Period II. The three women justices on the Court continue to be the most frequent dissenters. L'Heureux-Dubé continues to have the highest rate at 21 per cent, followed by Wilson (19 per cent) and McLachlin (16 per cent). What continues to differentiate the women justices is the direction of the dissents. Wilson's 25 dissents all favoured the rights claimant, while L'Heureux-Dubé was more likely to favour state actors. However, a notable trend that emerges between the women justices presently on the Court is the relative balance in the direction of their dissents: sixty per cent of L'Heureux-Dubé's dissents supported state actors (32/53) and forty per cent (15/38) of McLachlin's dissents resulted when the majority favoured the rights claimant.

Table 3

Judges' Support for Charter Claimant by Year

	1984	1985	1986	1987	1988	1989	1990	1991	1992	1993	1994	1995	1996	1997	1998	1999	Totals
Wilson n=4	75% n=9	67% n=11	73% n=21	52% n=18	44% n=26	42% n=37	63% n=6	50%	n/a n=132	n/a	n/a	n/a	n/a	n/a	n/a	n/a	55%
Estey n=4	75% n=8	50% n=8	38% n=10	40% n=4	25%	n/a n=34	n/a	n/a	n/a	n/a	n/a	n/a	n/a	n/a	n/a	n/a	44%
Le Dain n=1	100% n=6	50% n=9	22% n=19	33% n=7	29%	n/a n=42	n/a	n/a	n/a	n/a	n/a	n/a	n/a	n/a	n/a	n/a	43%
McLachlin n=2	n/a n=27	n/a n=27	n/a n=22	n/a n=41	n/a n=25	50% n=21	40% n=33	44% n=19	27% n=20	29% n=17	41% n=254	38%	47%	37%	35%	35%	39%
Binnie	n/a	n/a n=7	n/a n=16	n/a n=23	n/a	n/a	n/a	n/a	n/a	n/a	n/a	n/a	n/a	n/a	29%	44%	39%
Lamer n=4	75% n=10	60% n=9	44% n=20	40% n=21	52% n=25	28% n=34	44% n=19	59% n=19	37% n=30	23% n=24	54% n=19	26% n=26	25% n=19	58% n=13	23% n=15	60% n=307	38%
Beetz n=4	75% n=7	71% n=9	11% n=17	24% n=19	32% n=6	67%	n/a n=62	n/a	n/a	n/a	n/a	n/a	n/a	n/a	n/a	n/a	37%
Sopinka n=14	n/a n=37	n/a n=29	n/a n=23	n/a n=41	n/a n=25	43% n=26	38% n=36	45% n=22	30% n=253	24%	48%	35%	30%	59%	n/a	n/a	37%
Cory n=10	n/a n=27	n/a n=26	n/a n=19	n/a n=38	n/a n=24	20% n=26	44% n=38	48% n=23	27% n=19	26% n=14	50% n=264	31%	28%	57%	26%	50%	37%
Major n=23	n/a n=22	n/a n=23	n/a n=37	n/a n=18	n/a n=19	n/a n=15	n/a n=157	n/a	n/a	26%	37%	30%	34%	50%	47%	27%	37%
Dickson n=4	75% n=10	60% n=10	30% n=21	33% n=21	33% n=23	30% n=34	31%	n/a n=123	n/a	n/a	n/a	n/a	n/a	n/a	n/a	n/a	35%

	1984	1985	1986	1987	1988	1989	1990	1991	1992	1993	1994	1995	1996	1997	1998	1999	Totals
Iacobucci n=15	n/a n=23	n/a n=39	n/a n=24	n/a n=24	n/a n=34	n/a n=22	n/a n=17	40% n=16	22% n=214	31%	46%	33%	29%	54%	29%	44%	35%
Laforest n=2	n/a n=6	0% n=21	33% n=20	29% n=23	20% n=36	35% n=25	47% n=23	32% n=36	35% n=24	28% n=21	29% n=31	24% n=18	21% n=286	56%	n/a	n/a	33%
L'Heureux-Dubé n=2	n/a n=11	n/a n=21	n/a n=37	0% n=26	18% n=18	19% n=37	40% n=20	27% n=22	5% n=27	27% n=19	11% n=14	36% n=18	36% n=272	42%	7%	39%	31%
Stevenson n=17	n/a n=12	n/a n=29	n/a	n/a	n/a	n/a	n/a	29%	25%	n/a	n/a	n/a	n/a	n/a	n/a	n/a	28%
Gonthier n=8	n/a n=34	n/a n=24	n/a n=23	n/a n=35	n/a n=24	13% n=25	41% n=38	38% n=20	17% n=18	20% n=17	17% n=266	20%	26%	40%	22%	29%	26%
Bastarache n=2	n/a n=14	n/a n=15	n/a n=31	n/a	n/a	n/a	n/a	n/a	n/a	n/a	n/a	n/a	n/a	0%	21%	27%	23%
McIntyre n=4	75% n=10	40% n=10	30% n=23	13% n=22	14% n=11	18%	n/a n=80	n/a	n/a	n/a	n/a	n/a	n/a	n/a	n/a	n/a	22%
The Court n=4	75% n=10	60% n=11	27% n=23	26% n=23	30% n=26	31% n=43	35% n=29	38% n=26	23% n=43	23% n=25	44% n=26	31% n=40	28% n=23	57% n=20	25% n=18	39% n=390	33%

Note: n=number of cases in which a judge participated. %= percent of n in which a justice supported the *Charter* claimant (does not count results that were counted as 'inconclusive').

Table 4
Vote Orientation: Dissents, 1982–1999

	Number of Dissents	Total Cases	Percentage Dissents	Outcome of Majority Decisions [a]	
				Individual Wins	State Wins
L'Heureux-Dubé	57	272	21%	32	21
Wilson	25	132	19%	0	25
McLachlin	41	254	16%	15	23
McIntyre	12	80	15%	11	1
Laforest	30	286	10%	15	14
Lamer	29	307	9%	7	21
Estey	3	34	9%	1	2
Gonthier	24	266	9%	18	5
Sopinka	19	253	8%	3	13
Major	13	157	8%	5	8
Cory	17	264	7%	6	10
Dickson	8	123	7%	3	5
Stevenson	2	29	7%	1	1
Beetz	3	62	5%	1	2
Iacobucci	11	214	5%	5	6
Binnie	1	23	4%	0	1
LeDain	1	42	2%	1	0
Bastarache	0	31	0%	0	0
1982–1999	296	2829	10%	124	158
1982–1992	157	1324	12%	46	99
1993–1999	139	1505	9%	78	59

(a) Majority outcomes classified as 'inconclusive' are not counted. Therefore, the addition of 'individual wins' and 'state wins' columns for individual judges may in some instances not add up to the total number of dissents.

The change in the direction of dissents illustrates the Court's growing deference to the policy choices of legislative actors and the rebalancing of liberal constitutionalism in Period II. During Period I, the justices were likely to dissent when the majority decision found no rights violation: 68 per cent of dissents in this period supported the rights claimant (99/145). By contrast, during Period II, 60 per cent of dissents (78/137) supported the state actor. This suggests that divisions on the Court are more likely to occur when the Court rules in favour of the rights claimant.

A Double Standard for Different Types of Rights Claims?

To test whether the justices on the Supreme Court approached criminal rights cases differently from non-criminal cases, Morton et al's study created two sub-indices of *Charter* decisions: a criminal rights index and a "Court Party'" index. For the first 390 *Charter* decisions, the criminal rights index totals 213 cases and the Court Party index has 88 cases. The criminal rights index consists of all Supreme Court *Charter* decisions involving legal rights (sections 7-14 of the *Charter*) and the federal *Criminal Code* or related federal criminal statutes, such as the *Narcotics Control Act*. The Court Party index is based on a concept developed by Morton and Knopff to explain the increased use of *Charter* litigation by interest groups. They argue that the judicialization of politics in Canada – what they term the "Charter Revolution" – is sustained by a coalition of interest groups – what they call "the Court Party" – that use the courts to bypass traditional democratic arenas. Court Party groups are distinct from traditional interest groups because most are organized around sections of the *Charter*. Alan Cairns labeled these same groups as "Charter Canadians" to denote their genesis in the making of the *Charter* in 1981-82.

The Court Party roughly corresponds to Cairns' *Charter* Canadians with a number of important differences. The Court Party is postmaterialist in both its membership and in its policy goals. Morton and Knopff have described the Court Party as a being "rooted in a 'new class': the so-called post-materialist or postindustrialist knowledge class," the "equality seekers" who attempt to reform society as a whole. The issues that define the Court Party include linguistic and visible minorities, gay rights, feminism, aboriginal rights, environmentalism and world peace: "in sum, the Court Party hypothesis argues that both the adoption and the 'success' of the *Charter* reflect the growing ascendancy of these postmaterialist interests in Canadian society and their preference to pursue their policy agendas through judicial politics (litigation) rather than through electoral-legislative politics." For right-wing critics, the Court Party's success illustrates the undemocratic nature of *Charter* politics. The agenda of the Court Party involves substantive policy issues that are increasingly being decided by the courts, and for critics, the courts have neither the authority nor the capacity to decide such issues

The Court Party index is an important indicator whether the Supreme Court has interpreted the *Charter* in a manner that advances policy objectives of Court Party groups. The coding of Court Party cases involves special attention because a "win" in a Court Party case might be coded as a 'loss' in the rest of the study:

> For example, Jim Keegstra's unsuccessful challenge to the anti-hate sections of the *Criminal Code* was coded as a 'win' for the Court Party, since the impugned provision was intended to protect minorities and was defended before the Supreme Court by LEAF and several other intervenors who are

members of the Court Party coalition. For the same reasons but to the opposite effect, Ernst Zundel's successful challenge to the false news provisions
of the Code was coded as a Court Party 'loss'.

Table 5 summarizes the support rates of individual justices for the criminal
rights index and the Court Party index between 1982 and 1999. Several justices demonstrate significant differences in support between the two sub-
indices. The clearest example is L'Heureux- Dubé, who has the third highest
support rate for Court Party cases (63 per cent) but the third lowest support
rate for criminal rights (24 per cent). Sopinka is another justice who demonstrated contrasting support levels between the two sub-indices, but in the
opposite direction of L'Heureux-Dubé. Sopinka had the third highest support rate for criminal rights at 47 per cent and the second lowest support
rate (34 per cent) for the Court Party. Several justices – Le Dain, Cory and
Gonthier – showed very little difference in support levels. Wilson had the
highest level of support for both criminal rights (61 per cent) and the Court
Party (81 per cent).

Table 5
Rights Claimant Support Comparison by Judge: Overall, Criminal Rights, "Court Party," 1982–1999

	Overall Support	Criminal Support	"Court Party" Support
Wilson	55% (n=132)	61% (n=67)	81% (n=32)
Estey	44% (n=34)	50% (n=18)	56% (n=9)
Le Dain	43% (n=42)	39% (n=23)	38% (n=8)
McLachlin	39% (n=254)	33% (n=135)	57% (n=56)
Binnie	39% (n=23)	25% (n=16)	67% (n=6)
Lamer	38% (n=307)	47% (n=165)	49% (n=74)
Sopinka	37% (n=253)	47% (n=120)	34% (n=57)
Beetz	37% (n=62)	33% (n=30)	53% (n=17)
Cory	37% (n=264)	36% (n=138)	45% (n=57)
Major	37% (n=157)	40% (n=93)	47% (n=38)
Iacobucci	35% (n=214)	35% (n=111)	39% (n=49)
Dickson	35% (n=123)	41% (n=63)	57% (n=30)
Laforest	33% (n=286)	40% (n=147)	34% (n=68)
L'Heureux-Dubé	31% (n=272)	24% (n=140)	63% (n=67)
Stevenson	28% (n=29)	50% (n=10)	0% (n=3)
Gonthier	26% (n=266)	29% (n=148)	36% (n=59)
Bastarache	23% (n=31)	11% (n=18)	57% (n=7)
McIntyre	22% (n=80)	19% (n=42)	50% (n=18)
1982-1999	33% (n=390)	35% (n=213)	48% (n=88)
1982-1992	33% (n=195)	40% (n=99)	53% (n=36)
1993-1999	33% (n=195)	31% (n=114)	45% (n=52)

The individual voting patterns of the justices demonstrates that the aggregate data can be misleading because it hides important differences in how the justices approach criminal cases and non-criminal cases. The overall voting patterns of Sopinka (37 per cent) and L'Heureux-Dubé (31 per cent) would suggest that these two justices are similar in their approach to the *Charter* are part of the centre-dominant part of the Court. In fact, they are practically diametrical opposites, and lie at the activist/restrained ends of the spectrum within the two sub-indices.

The most striking aspect of Table 8 is that the Court's support rate for the Court Party index (48 per cent) is well above the overall average of 33 per cent. At first glance, the higher success rate for the Court Party seems to confirm the Morton-Knopff Court Party thesis. However, the aggregate data mask important new trends in the *Charter* decisions from Period II – trends that demonstrate the emergence of a centre-dominant Court in Canada, and important changes in the Court's approach to the two sub-indices. In a departure from the trends identified by Morton et al in the Period I cases, the Court exhibits greater consistency in its approach to rights. The level of support for criminal rights (31 per cent) is now very close to the overall rate of support (33 per cent), and support for the Court Party claims has dropped significantly from 53 per cent in Period I to 45 per cent in Period II. Support for the Court Party's agenda has declined among the individual justices, as half the justices who sat on the Court in 1992 had declining support rates by 1999 (Lamer, Laforest, L'Heureux-Dubé and Gonthier).

As noted above, Sopinka and L'Heureux-Dubé continue to exhibit contrasting levels of support for the two sub-indices. L'Heureux-Dubé has the third highest support for the Court Party and the third lowest support for criminal rights. By contrast, Sopinka was one of the highest supporters for rights of the accused at 47 per cent, but one of the lowest supporters of Court Party claims at 34 per cent. Gonthier emerged as a *Charter* conservative in Period II, changing direction from his activist approach to criminal rights and the Court Party identified in Period I cases. The most recent appointments to the Supreme Court – Bastarche and Binnie – have demonstrated some of the lowest support rates for the criminal rights, but some of the highest for the Court Party index.

Despite the continued presence of justices at the edges of activism, in Period II the Court emerges as a centrist court. The close grouping of the justices around the median illustrates that the Lamer Court is more centrist than the Dickson Court. The justices provided less support to the Court Party during Period II, a trend that questions the continued accuracy of the Court Party thesis, and demonstrates the rebalancing of liberal constitutionalism that has occurred since 1992. The decline in the success rate of the Court Party is linked to other important developments in Period II, such as the Court's greater focus on the conduct of public officials and the declining success rate against statutes. As the Court Party's agenda is substantive in nature and concerned with challenges against the legislative choices of democratic actors, the rebalancing of liberal constitutionalism in Canada has seen a decline in the success rate of the Court Party.

Conclusion

The data demonstrate the growing consensus on the Supreme Court on the *Charter* and the role of the judiciary in Canada's constitutional order. The Court has broken away from the trends established in Period I and returned to a higher rate of unanimity, a decreasing rate of dissents and concurring opinions, and a convergence in the Court's support rates for criminal rights and non-criminal cases. There continue to be activist justices, but the number has declined to a distinct minority on the Court. Furthermore, such activism varies between *Charter* areas. The decline of dissent in Period II has contributed to the rebalancing of liberal constitutionalism in Canada.

12.5

Key Terms

Concepts

oral argument
factum / brief
post-hearing conference
judicial collegiality
seriatim opinion writing
"opinion of the court"
majority opinion
dissenting opinion
concurring opinion
plurality decision
five and nine judge panels
law clerks
legal citations / authorities
"agenda setting"
jurisprudential choice hypothesis
litigant resources hypothesis
strategic choice hypothesis
"repeat player"
"one-shotter"

Reconciling Judicial Review and Constitutional Democracy

13

The readings in this final chapter raise and address some of the fundamental questions about the practice of judicial review. Donald Smiley's contribution emphasizes that the real question raised by an entrenched *Charter of Rights* is not whether Canadians shall have civil liberties or not, but *who* decides what is and is not a civil liberty. The principal effect of the *Charter* is to transfer the primary, although not exclusive, responsibility for such decisions to the courts, or more specifically, to Canadian judges. He notes that typically these decisions involve balancing competing rights or competing interests, and that every decision will have "opportunity costs." Smiley expresses skepticism over the judges' ability to make these kinds of decisions better than Canadian parliamentary legislatures. Smiley points to some of Parliament's reforms in the 1960s involving capital punishment, abortion, divorce, hate literature, and official languages. Each of these legislative reforms were widely viewed as enhancing liberty, minority rights, or both. In effect, Smiley asks what special competencies do judges have that elected legislators lack (Reading 13.1)?

The late Alexander Bickel, the leading American constitutional scholar of his generation, has elaborated this question and also provided an answer. He described the requirements for a justification of judicial review on principle, rather than habit and tradition, as follows:

> The search must be for a function which might (indeed, must) involve the making of policy, yet which differs from the legislative and executive functions; which is peculiarly suited to the capabilities of the courts; which will not likely be performed elsewhere if the courts do not assume it; which can be so exercised as to be acceptable in a society that generally shares Judge Learned Hand's satisfaction in a "sense of common venture"; which will be effective when needed; and whose discharge by the courts will not lower the quality of the other departments' performance by denuding them of the dignity and burden of their own responsibility.[1]

The potentially unique contribution of judicial review, according to Bickel,

---

1 *The Least Dangerous Branch: The Supreme Court at the Bar of Politics* (Indianapolis: Bobbs Merrill, 1962), p. 24.

is the defence and articulation of a society's fundamental political and ethical principles. In the name of individual liberty, the pursuit of self-interest is given wide range in Western democracies. The executive and legislative branches are purposely made responsive to the resulting clash of interests and groups that is the stuff of democratic politics. Amidst the welter of competing self-interests, the rush and crush of practical affairs, and the ensuing short-term perspective on all matters, it is prudent to have one institution, purposely distanced from the fray, to guard the principles that preserve the justice and dignity of that society. Judicial review offers this potential.

Bickel's defence of judicial review is echoed by the Chief Justice of the Supreme Court of Canada, Beverley McLachlin (Reading 13.9). McLachlin acknowledges the problem of democratic legitimacy raised by the Court's new role under the *Charter*, but argues that it can be mitigated by judicial decisions that are "grounded in principle and an appropriate respect for the constitutional role of Parliament and the legislatures." Chief Justice McLachlin's spirited defence of the Supreme Court's *Charter* decisions reflects the new confidence in judges as the arbiters of Canada's fundamental constitutional norms. The optimistic perspective articulated by McLachlin has displaced the skeptical "Smiley perspective" that was dominant in Canadian legal and political culture prior to the 1980s. However, the debate over the legitimacy of judicial review under the *Charter* has changed not disappeared. As Professor Patrick Monahan has observed, "The debate is [no longer] over judicial review *per se*, but rather over what type of judicial review can be justified in a democratic polity." As in all practical matters, the legitimacy of the principle does not vouch for the legitimacy of its application.

This new version of the legitimacy debate can arise in the context of a specific *Charter* decision (See Justice La Forest's dissent in the *Provincial Judges' Reference*, Reading 5.6); or more generally, in competing approaches to constitutional interpretation, such as the interpretivism versus non-interpretivism debate. (See Introduction to Chapter 11.) It has also arisen in the debate over the Section 33 "notwithstanding" (or legislative override) clause of the *Charter*. John Whyte, former Dean of Law at Queen's University Law School, has forcefully argued for abolishing the legislative override power. (See Reading 13.2.) Note that Whyte's argument shares the same optimistic assessment of judges' policy capacity as found in the reading of Chief Justice McLachlin. In a similar vein, Professor Peter Russell's equally forceful defence of section 33 resonates with the same skepticism of judicial policymaking that animated Smiley's critique two decades earlier. (See Reading 13.3.) The players and the law have changed but the debate endures.

Scott Reid (Reading 13.4) has given a new dimension to the debate over section 33. Noting the Canadian public's current disillusionment with elected governments, Reid argues for subjecting any government's use of section 33 to a referendum. If the test of limitations on rights is that of "reasonableness," what better way to discern Canadians' perception of what is or is not a "reasonable limitation" than by asking them directly via a referendum? A bill incorporating Reid's idea of linking the use of section 33 to public approval was introduced by the Klein government in Alberta in 2000 but has not yet been approved.

Another response to the legitimacy issue is found in the Hogg-Thornton "dialogue" theory (Reading 13.7). Hogg argues that in *Charter* rulings the Supreme Court rarely has the last word. In his review of 66 *Charter* cases involving judicial nullification of a statute, Hogg found that there was a "legislative sequel" to the judicial ruling in two-thirds of the cases. That is, governments have responded to judicial nullifications by a variety of means – amending and re-enacting the statute, repealing the statute or by invoking section 33 and re-instating the statute. Thus, rather than "activist" courts "dictating" new policies to governments, Hogg argues that the *Charter* has created a two-way "dialogue" between courts and legislatures, in which the latter usually have the last say. Hogg's "dialogue" theory has become a popular defence against the charge of undue judicial activism but is not without its critics. Professor Manfredi has challenged Hogg's methodology as unscientific and his definition of "legislative sequel" as self-serving.[2] Morton's response (Reading 13.7) is that in most of these 66 cases, legislatures simply did what the courts told them to do – a relationship more accurately described as a "monologue."

Another response to the charge of illegitimate judicial policy-making under the *Charter* has been Gregory Hein's "judicial democrats" thesis (Reading 13.5). According to Hein's study, the *Charter*, with the help of the Court Challenges Program (see Reading 7.3), has enhanced, not harmed, Canadian democracy by creating new opportunities for previously marginalized groups to participate in the policy-making process. Prior to the *Charter*, Hein argues, the political use of the courts was primarily the preserve of corporations and governments. His study confirms that, since 1982, rights advocacy groups have become regular litigators before Canada's appellate courts, but Hein claims that this rise in advocacy group litigation – the new "judicial democrats" – merely "levels the playing field" for previously excluded and marginalized groups. The "judicial democrats" thesis has been criticized by Professor Ian Brodie (Reading 7.6) for ignoring how unaccountable courts are and how unrepresentative Canadian judges are.

Interest group use of litigation is also discussed in Professor Ian Greene's study of judicial independence (Reading 13.6). Greene's survey of Canadian appellate court judges revealed that two-thirds perceived threats to judicial independence, and that pressure from "special interest groups" was the most frequently cited source of this threat. (Students should consider this finding in light of LEAF's campaign of "influencing the influencers" [Reading 7.2].)

---

2 See Christopher P. Manfredi (with James Kelly), "Six Degrees of Dialogue: A Response to Hagg and Bushell," *Osgoode Hall Law Journal* 27 (1999); pp. 513–27; also "Dialogue, Deference and Restraint; Judicial Independence and Trial Procedures," *Saskatchewan Law Review* 64, no. 2 (2001), pp. 323–46.

Forty-five percent of the judges interviewed agreed that interest group use of litigation was "not appropriate," but 35 percent said that it was "appropriate." Other judges cited criticism of judicial decisions by the media, government ministers, and MPs as a growing threat to judicial independence. This view is echoed and elaborated in a speech that Justice l'Heureux-Dubé gave to the annual meeting of the Canadian Bar Association in 1999 (Reading 13.8). Justice l'Heureux-Dubé singled out critics of "judicial activism" as threatening judicial independence when their commentary "degenerates into personal attacks and accusations that the judges are overstepping the proper institutional boundaries of their roles." In light of these charges and countercharges, it is hardly surprising that Greene found that the judges in his survey were evenly divided – 45% versus 43% – on the question of whether the *Charter* had created a "crisis of legitimacy" for the courts.

Canadian students should not be alarmed by these recent developments. A comparative look at U.S. experience suggests that the more political influence a court wields, the more interested parties will compete to influence and shape the exercise of that court's power. While the U.S. Supreme Court has exercised judicial review over a written *Bill of Rights* for over 200 years, it has not always had the "final word" in constitutional disputes. The history of the United States is strewn with Supreme Court decisions that have been reversed or ignored. This has been accomplished by a variety of "court-curbing" techniques: constitutional amendment, withdrawal of jurisdiction from the Supreme Court to hear certain types of issues, statutory reversal (i.e., new legislation), courtpacking and even outright defiance.

In this respect, Russell is correct in placing the section 33 override as simply another intermediate step along this continuum. In the final analysis, the debate over section 33 reflects the ambiguous nature of judicial authority. That nature, and the difficult task it imposes on constitutional judges, was captured by the French philosopher Alexis de Tocqueville's analysis of American federal courts over 150 years ago:

> [The power of the courts] is immense, but it is power springing from opinion. They are all-powerful so long as the people consent to obey the law; they can do nothing when they scorn it. Now, of all powers, that of opinion is the hardest to use, for it is impossible to say exactly where its limits come. Often it is as dangerous to lag behind as it is to outstrip it.... Federal judges therefore must not only be good citizens and men of education and integrity, qualities necessary for all magistrates, but must also be statesmen; they must know how to understand the spirit of the age, to confront those obstacles that can be overcome, and to steer out of the current when the tide threatens to carry them away, and with them, the sovereignty of the Union and obedience to its laws.[3]

The written constitution, in the end, is no stronger than the unwritten constitution. The difference is the enhanced role of judges in shaping both.

---

3 Alexis de Tocqueville, *Democracy in America*, ed. J.P. Mayer (Garden City, N.Y.: Anchor, 1969), pp. 150–51.

13.1

Courts, Legislatures, and the Protection of Human Rights

Donald Smiley

Courts and Trials: A Multidisciplinary Approach. Edited by M.L. Friedland (Toronto: University of Toronto Press, 1975) 89–101. Reprinted with permission.

This paper examines in a Canadian context the appropriateness of judicial as against legislative decision in the definition and ranking of human rights. The issue is often put within the framework of proposals for the further entrenchment of human rights in the Canadian constitution.... Most provisions related to human rights ... would necessarily be expressed in general language conferring on the courts of law the responsibility of defining and ranking rights in an ongoing process of judicial review of the constitution....

... Most discussions of legislative as against judicial decision with respect to human rights proceed according to conflicting views of what I call democratic fundamentalism.

The first view asserts that in terms of democratic theory, elected officials have better claims than courts to define and rank human rights as well as to make other important decisions about public policy. Democracy in this view is government in accord with the will of the governed, and the organs of government best able and most likely to act in accord with this will are composed of people who have successfully contested popular elections – and act in anticipation of future elections. I do not find this argument completely convincing. If we look at the operative constitution of any developed political system – the constitution in action as against the constitution of the textbooks of law or civics – we find a complex allocation of discretionary powers. Powers are wielded in various kinds of matters by judges and juries, by political executives and career bureaucrats, by elected legislatures and political parties, by the electorate, by the groups who effect constitutional amendment. And we also find different kinds of procedural rules for reaching various kinds of decisions – unanimous consent in jury verdicts, certain motions in the House of Commons and the most crucial of constitutional amendments, consensual decision-making at federal-provincial conferences and, perhaps, in cabinets, pluralities, bare majorities and extraordinary majorities as so defined, different provisions for quorums, and so on. On this basis, I would see no *a priori* reason stemming from democratic theory which would prevent a democratic community from conferring decisions involving human rights on the courts or from enacting provisions respecting such rights other than those which prevail in respect to ordinary lawmaking....

... It seems to me ... that the connection between the preferred procedures for protecting human rights and natural law is historical and psychological rather than logical in the sense that if the imperatives of natural law are binding, surely they bind legislatures as much as courts. Which of the two sets of institutions will better protect such rights is thus a matter of prudential political judgment rather than political philosophy....

... Perhaps some will agree with most of this but still maintain that, on balance, courts will be wiser and more zealous than elected bodies in defining and ranking human rights. In much of the argument for entrenchment there is the underlying premise that the community needs to be saved from the inherently liberal tendencies of public opinion because these create irresistible pressures on elected legislatures. Perhaps. It is my own impression, however, that in Canada the elected political elites are considerably more liberal than are the prevailing sentiments in their respective local, provincial, and national electorates. Again, it is my impression that when we begin to inquire carefully into those institutions of Canadian society under the direct control of the bar and the bench we will find less than a total commitment to humane values. There is a strain of absolutism in recent Canadian proposals for an entrenched *Bill of Rights*. Prime Minister Trudeau said in 1969, "To enshrine a right in a constitutional charter is to make an important judgment, to give to that right of the individual a higher order of value than the right of government to infringe it." This argument proceeds on the assumption that encroachments on human rights are always unequivocal and disinterested and liberal people will always be able to agree when such encroachments are made. Again, if we take Mr. Trudeau's statement literally, there is the assumption that under all conceivable circumstances entrenched rights are to prevail over other considerations. These absolutist premises are in practice indefensible. In the sphere of human rights there is indeed an economy, and rights have what economists call "opportunity costs," in the sense that to get something of value it is necessary to give up something else of value.

As a non-lawyer, it seems clear to me that if Canadian courts are to assume a more active role in the ranking and defining of human rights there must be profound changes in the Canadian legal culture. Canadian jurists are profoundly in the positivist tradition. But the determination of human rights in particular circumstances is in Peter Russell's terms the "delicate balancing of social priorities." I confess not to know the shape of the new jurisprudence or how judges and legal scholars are going to get us to realize it while maintaining the continuity with past traditions and lines of judicial interpretation that is surely necessary in our kind of polity. I confess also that the break proposed by Atkey and Lyon is too radical for me. But perhaps there should be a warning to enthusiasts for a socially relevant jurisprudence. This approach by its nature downgrades the technical nature of the law, and when members of bar and bench set up shop to articulate the political need and political ideals of the community they enter a world in which others make the same claims. To be blunt: as piety does not make a theologian or pugnacity a military strategist, an increasing social sensitivity among lawyers and judges is no substitute for intellectual discipline in the social sciences and political philosophy.

To return to the main argument of this paper, I quote what I said on a previous occasion:

> Apart from those times where public opinion is inflamed, the democratic legislature is uniquely equipped to make sound judgments about human rights. In my view Parliament has been at or near its best in some of the debates about human rights in the past decade, debates in respect to capital punishment, divorce, abortion, hate literature, official languages. Although the determination of the scope and nature of human rights usually involves some technical considerations, the technical content of reasoned discussion and decision is characteristically not as high as in regard to, say, defence policy or environmental pollution. Thus the major considerations in respect to human rights ordinarily involve the clash of human values, the sense of the community about what is acceptable and the broadest judgments of where society is going. Further, questions involving human rights tend not to be as localized in their incidence as is true of many other public policies and the Member of Parliament may well be more free to act primarily as a member of a deliberative body rather than a voice of particularized constituency interests. Elected politicians working within an environment of public discussion and debate are well equipped to deal wisely with questions of human rights. It is yet to be demonstrated that the Canadian judiciary can do better....

13.2

On Not Standing for Notwithstanding
John D. Whyte
Alberta Law Review 28, no. 2 (1990), 348–57. Reprinted with permission.

... [W]ith respect to the debate on whether to continue the override clause, the usual starting point has been to advance arguments rooted in Canadian constitutional principle. For instance, a claim made by Professors Peter Russell and Paul Weiler in their opinion piece on the issue is that legislative override is a uniquely Canadian feature of our constitution. What must be being expressed by this observation is that there are other elements of our constitution – other constitutional arrangements that reveal fundamental commitments – that fit well with permitting legislative override of *Charter* protections. Professors Russell and Weiler, in arguing against repeal of the override power, provide a rudimentary explanation of what those commitments are:

> ... nothing in our constitution is so distinctively Canadian as this manner of reconciling the British tradition of responsible democratic government with the American tradition of judicially enforced constitutional rights.

Another version of principled justification of the override clause is to label it as the perfect device for accommodating a regime for vindicating civil rights with the constitutional principle of parliamentary supremacy. Professor Peter Hogg, for example, has explained the clause as "a concession to Canada's long tradition of parliamentary sovereignty."

In my view these attempts to locate a justification for the override procedure in Canadian constitutional theory are wrong for two reasons. First, the principles at work in the design of the Canadian state support not allowing any legislative exemptions from court-enforced rights at least as powerfully as they support including such a power in the constitution. Second, arguments rooted in constitutional principle distract us from enquiry into the actual social goods and bads that are likely to be produced by the practice of exercising the legislative power to override *Charter* rights. In short, this sort of debate keeps us from choosing a policy that is good because it reflects the actual aspirations of political community.

Looking for the Lesson from Constitutional Theory

The position that is advanced in this paper is that the debate over keeping the override power should be conducted in terms of what will produce the soundest government and fairest society and that we should approach this question by trying to anticipate how effective courts and legislatures actually will be in making various sorts of social and political accommodation. For this reason it is not essential to demonstrate that Canadian constitutional theory requires repeal of an override power for legislatures. What I do want to demonstrate is that the values inherent in our constitutional arrangements do not require (or even tend towards) including in the constitution a trumping authority for legislatures over courts in the complex business of mediating between claims of right and the general social interest.

The basic constitutional principles that I perceive to be at work in the formal structure of the Canadian state are legalism, democracy and federalism....

Legalism

Public authority in Canada derives at least a part of its legitimacy from its legal base. What a government does must accord with what, from a legal perspective, it is entitled to do. This idea that the legitimacy of state power can be measured through legal adjudication is, in our culture, well over half a millennium old. We understand authoritative social relationships to be formed and governed by enforceable promises and the keystone of the system is that enforceability is produced through legal evaluation. In order to produce a system for legal evaluation that has some degree of formality, specialized legal agencies grew up. Furthermore, we attached to those agencies political attributes that were designed to conduce to legal or formal evaluation (as opposed, say, to self-interested evaluation). These attributes were expertise and independence. Of course, we are right to be highly skeptical about the role of expertise and formality when the legal order that requires expertise and formal elaboration is as indeterminate as it is. We are also right to be skeptical about the actual degree of independence from social forces that can be achieved simply through protecting pay and tenure, the devices that are provided by the 1867 Constitution. However, it is not important to this argument that we subscribe to the purity of formalism or complete independence. All that is necessary is to see that they are long-standing constitutional values: it is through the identification of certain ideals and values that we can determine what arguments from principle can be made.

If it is accepted that these values have been recognized in Canadian constitutional ordering then other conclusions might be drawn. The chief one is that our state structure seems to be based on the idea that formal commitments represent binding promises that restrain future power. This idea is perhaps derived from the development of the law of contract. In any event, the commitment to legal enforceability of promises extends to binding governments as well as individuals. Legalism is what makes possible constitutionalism, the process by which political expressions from one age can bind future ages unless equally formal political processes are mustered to remove the constitution constraint. In short, Canadian constitutionalism is not in thrall to the idea that populations are free to determine their own best interests from moment to moment. Judicial control over governmental authority and legislative choices is no alien concept for Canada. We are a nation in which past solemn commitments are allowed to work to the disadvantage of current preferences. For instance, perfectly clear legislative preferences about the administration of laws are frequently frustrated by the prior constitutional commitment to the separation of powers. The separation of powers is seen as a relevant doctrine to the maintenance of a commitment to legalism and the implications of that commitment are tolerated by the people of this democratic state.

My claim is simply this. As a matter of principle we have adopted the notion that there are adjudicable public issues. Furthermore, we have come to terms with these issues being *ultimately* adjudicable – not subject to legislative review and revision. If Canada wants to say about human rights claims that not only are they adjudicable at the first stage of resolution, but they are adjudicable as a matter of ultimate resolution, this would be entirely consistent with our commitment to legalism in public ordering.

However, in the context of the *Canadian Charter of Rights and Freedoms*, section 33 means, first, that what were once political problems have been transformed into legal problems but, second, that when political interests are sufficiently compelling these issues can revert to being resolved through political choice. This arrangement gives rise to a further principled argument. The idea that some problems may be adjudicated – may be made subject to legal determination – requires there to be substantive constitutional value to be interpreted and applied. It is necessary to the conception of legalism that adjudication of disputes be based on previously expressed normative standards. When there is a sense that there are no constraints, or no interpretative processes (for instance, when there is no textual basis for decision-making), no genuine adjudication is possible. Canada, in enacting the *Charter of Rights*, accepted that some political problems were capable of adjudication and at the same time, created a normative order (a text, in other words) to ensure that those issues could be resolved through adjudication. The nation expressed its commitment to, first, the rightness of social resolution being produced by the interpretation of rights and, second, the capacity of the terms of the *Charter* to be interpretable – to be the subject matter of adjudication. This assessment of what was possible and appropriate for adjudication does not fit well with the idea that the ultimate method of resolution of conflicting claims is through a purely political process. In other words, once the advantages of constitutional interpretation were accepted, as a general matter, it is not easy to see why the framers of the 1982 Constitution then saw political judgment to be a preferred form of political accommodation in each and every instance in which political interests wished to suspend the operation of legalism.

Democracy

Judicial enforcement of human rights standards poses a serious challenge to majoritarianism. The advantage of pure majoritarianism is that there is no situation which cannot be responded to and no strategy of social regulation that cannot be tried once a majority of the people wish to act.

The problem with truly entrenched rights is that they undermine the majoritarian principle. Legislative calculations of social need are subject to being substituted by courts which are not representative and are not amenable to majoritarian control. The will of the electors is not sovereign. The question is whether the shift away from majoritarianism through removal of the override power reflects a conception of democracy that is as fundamental as the popular conception of democracy – that state policies ought always to reflect the preferences of a majority of electors.

Democratic theory rests not so much on the mechanisms of expressing political preferences (or who should represent the voters in making political choices) and on who should govern, as it does on deeper conditions such as political participation, equality, autonomy and personal liberty. From the now fully developed constitutional idea that people have the right to participate in public choices it is possible to tease out a series of non-derogable conditions. For example, we know that duly elected and popularly supported governments can, and do, believe that the appropriate conditions for democratic politics include such things as censored political speech, restrictions on political participation, political campaigns that are funded by government, and perhaps most currently, in at least two Canadian jurisdictions, gerrymandering. In considering this list, it is not difficult to see the connection between the use of judicially enforced fundamental rights of speech, equality and due process and the vindication of principles that are designed to protect democratic processes.

Of course it would be wrong to suggest that the whole array of interests identified in the the *Charter of Rights* are justifiable on the basis that they enhance the democratic process. Some rights (for example, an expanded notion of personal security being protected from substantive injustice under section 7 of the *Charter*) must be explained by reference to other political commitments. However, the point that needs to be made is that the democratic principle provides a powerful pedigree for judicial control over political choices that erode some fundamental human rights.

Federalism

There are two points to make about Canada's adoption of federalism in organizing state power. The first is that the chief justification for the federal arrangement (and this is particularly true in the Canadian experience) is that it provides protection to minorities from the political choices of national majorities. Federalism is a political arrangement that is designed to blunt the force of majoritarianism because groups within the nation are recognized as having special interests that deserve entrenched protection. It is true that this mode of protection does not entail courts engaging in the same kind of social accommodation as they do under the *Charter*. Nevertheless, courts do intervene to protect specific constitutionally recognized interests. Federalism is quite simply a substantial check on the exercise of national popular will. As such it is a further instance of seeing our constitutional order as consisting of commitments that have been embraced so that, as we live out our life as a community, certain ideals or images will prevail over power.

The second point is that by looking at the history of court adjudication over federalism we might get a better perspective on the significance of the debate over the override clause. Courts have been involved in disallowing back to work legislation and Sunday closing legislation, in adjudicating refugee claims and rules for qualifying as a profession, and in setting out the modes of proof in criminal liability and the allowable strategies for criminal investigations, each of which produces some disruption of public administration. These outcomes require the abandonment of administrative processes and, sometimes, governmental policies. Indeed, some of these policies have become established within the country as the standard way of accommodating social conflict. *Charter* decisions that cause an abandonment of established accommodations will produce periods of dislocation and adjustment and could effect long term changes in the distribution of social benefits. However, the capacity of governments to regulate society for the public good has not, yet, been fundamentally hampered by *Charter* decisions. The major determinants that shape well-being in society are not frequently at stake in *Charter* decision. For instance compare the significance of any of the *Charter* cases alluded to above to the significance of a court decision that prevents a province from controlling trans-boundary environmental damage produced by pollution that is licensed by an adjoining province. Compare any *Charter* decision with the significance to a province's economic development of deciding that it is unconstitutional to ration production of a resource with a view to sustaining a viable market for the resource. Or compare the impact of any *Charter* decision with the consequence for a province of limiting its capacity to control the distribution of benefits from its most valuable natural attribute. This is not a country in which governments have never been seriously frustrated in implementing policies that make a difference to the health, wealth and well-being of every person in their jurisdiction. It is not credible to argue that removal of the override clause will produce a shift in the balance of power between political decision-makers and courts that will change the nature of our society. Constitutionalism already exacts a high price on the autonomy of electoral politics. Most Canadians see this as legitimate and fair in order to maintain the integrity of our national commitment to federalism. Undoubtedly the *Charter of Rights* has produced additional restraints on democratic politics. However, it has not made irrelevant the role of politics in shaping the nature of our society. Our experience under federalism has clearly shown us that politics lives (that political initiatives are vital and that political mobilization makes an important contribution to the well-being of society) even when courts have the authority to protect constitutional values.

As I have stated, it is not my ambition to demonstrate that the override provision cannot coherently be included in our constitutional arrangements. My goal has been simply to show that it doesn't earn its place in the Constitution because of its logical fit with the general constitutional pattern. The most basic features of our constitutional arrangements do not, as it happens, create a logical or principled argument for the legislative override of the *Charter of Rights*.

Finding a Lesson in Political Practice

… The constitutional patterns that we create are, happily, hardly ever pure. There are many visions of a good society and we act wisely when we find ways not to deny the legitimacy and place of perfectly plausible visions. Hence, one of the virtues of the override power is that it has allowed Canada to create a regime for protecting human rights and it has left room for determined legislators to maintain social arrangements that they consider particularly important.

The unfortunate aspect of this benign description of the override clause as a restrained tool, instrument of thoughtful response and balance of constitutional ideologies is its use is simply not likely to be restricted to instances that match this description. The primary reason for wishing to do away with the override clause is that the anxiety that produced the political demand for entrenched rights cannot rationally be calmed in the face of the legislative power granted by section 33. That anxiety is simply this: political authority will, at some point, be exercised oppressively; that is, it will be exercised to impose very serious burdens on groups of people when there is no rational justification for doing so.

Furthermore, the more that we succeed in marginalizing section 33 by pointing to its rare use and speaking of its deployment in extraordinary circumstances only, the more that legislative override will become associated with the intense political moments that produce political oppression.

There are two types of situations in which the *Charter of Rights* seems a positive constitutional instrument. One is when legislatures neglect to calculate the extraordinary impact of legislative measures on particular individuals. Another is when they know full well the impact on certain people but do not care enough about the problem (or do not have the time or skill to cope with the problem) to tailor the measure to avoid the injury to constitutional rights. Courts applying the terms of the *Charter of Rights* can give to individuals and groups both a forum to explain the precise nature of the disadvantage, and relief from undue burdens.

The other scenario that impels the entrenchment of rights is one in which fear and distaste by the majority for certain people leads to the oppression of those people. The Canadian historical record reveals a number of instances of political passion directed against conspicuous minorities – Japanese Canadians, Hutterites, Doukhobors, aboriginal peoples, Jehovah's Witnesses, the Acadians, Métis, Roman Catholics, communists and separatists. All of these groups have, at some point, been seen as producing more social disruption and risk than society has been able to bear and all of these groups have been governmentally burdened in order to reduce the fear that has surrounded their presence. In all of these cases the governmental assessment of risk has been facile and overstated. In all of these cases the governmental response has been more than merely disadvantageous to members of these groups. It has been brutal, community crushing, and life destroying. Political passion that is generated by the fear that there are communities whose practices subvert the fabric of our society is powerful and terrifying.

In a recent article, Professor Andrew Petter quotes the famous observation of Judge Learned Hand: "Liberty lies in the hearts of men and women; when it dies there, no constitution, no law, no court can save it; no constitution, no law, no court can even do much to help it." To the extent that this is accepted the moments of political anger and passion that I fear – the moments of political reaction that we invariably come later to regret – will not be forestalled by the removal of the override powers. There are, however, two ways in which Learned Hand's assessment of the role of the courts in applying constitutionalized human rights is unduly pessimistic.

First, the terms of the *Charter of Rights* are not totally indeterminate. Judges are not free to reflect the dominant political winds in interpreting rights. The systematic destruction of a group's expression and practices cannot easily be denied as a *Charter* violation. Judges are, of course, aware of the political passion that is around them, but the values of independence and discipline that we seek to vindicate in appointments do frequently shine through both in this country and in the brave judgments of courts in nations with a longer record of repression than ours....

The second claim to make for the benefit of judicial supervision in moments of oppression is that the calling into play of *Charter* claims reminds the political community of the costs to fundamental values of political desperation. For the political process, for the people whose rights are being abridged and for the future political environment, the process of identifying carefully and calmly the precise loss of freedoms and rights is a process to be valued above all others in extreme political moments.

It is my view that the *Charter*, in its normal course, does not substantially rearrange society. In the normal course the *Charter*'s benefits are, in any event, distributed in the same manner as legal services – preponderantly to the wealthy. It seems perverse to advocate the retention of a provision which is most likely to be used to preclude judicial intervention when that process has its strongest moral claim, and when the radically dispossessed will have no route for salvation other than appealing to courts to intervene on behalf of the *Charter* values of liberty, equality and due process.

13.3

Standing Up for Nothwithstanding
Peter H. Russell
Alberta Law Review 29, no. 2 (1991), 293–309. Reprinted with permission.

[The *Alberta Law Review*'s] first annual supplement on constitutional issues included an essay by Professor John Whyte putting the case against the notwithstanding clause in the *Canadian Charter of Rights and Freedoms*. Whyte's article is the most fully reasoned attack we have had on the *Charter*'s override clause. It is an important contribution to our constitutional debate which certainly deserves a reply from one of those singled out, quite rightly, by Professor Whyte as a defender of the override.

Although I readily confess to being a supporter of the override clause, I am not at all satisfied with Professor Whyte's understanding of the rationale for such a clause. Unfortunately, instead of carefully examining the scholarly writings of those who have defended the override, he cites only a portion of one sentence from an "opinion piece" in the *Toronto Star* by Professor Paul Weiler and myself and a few words from a passage in Professor Hogg's book on *The Constitutional Law of Canada*. The words quoted and the arguments he proceeds to knock down do not come close to providing an acceptable justification of the *Charter*'s notwithstanding clause.

Bad Reasons for the Notwithstanding Clause

The passage quoted from our *Toronto Star* piece draws attention to the distinctively Canadian manner in which the notwithstanding clause balances the British tradition of responsible democratic government with the American tradition of judicially enforced constitutional rights. I would certainly agree with Professor Whyte in dismissing arguments for the override clause that depend primarily on showing that it is distinctively Canadian. I am sure there are plenty of things that are distinctively Canadian that are perfectly dreadful. The point we were making is that the override gave Canada an opportunity to get the best out of British and American constitutionalism, the two traditions which have profoundly influenced our constitutional development. Professor Whyte, unhappily, may be right, and as English Canada moves ever closer to *Charter* worship, it may no longer be distinctively Canadian to try to strike a shrewd balance between the wisdom derived from these two parts of our heritage.

It may well be true, as the quotation from Professor Hogg suggests, that political defenders of the override have most often couched their arguments in terms of the need to preserve the principle of parliamentary sovereignty. Again, I am in agreement with Professor Whyte that the case for the override cannot rest on a simple invocation of the principle of parliamentary sovereignty. Even if one were to accept, as this writer does not, a purely Burkean standard for constitutional development and insist that our constitutional future never break from inherited tradition, it simply is not true that the Canadian constitution historically has been based on the principle of parliamentary sovereignty. No Canadian legislature or parliament has ever been sovereign, and I hope none ever shall be. Legislatures in colonial Canada were subject to important imperial controls and since 1867 Canadian legislatures have been subject to judicially enforceable limitations, limitations based on more than preserving the federal division of powers.

Equally unacceptable as a defence of the override is an appeal to simple majoritarianism. The crude utilitarian standard of "the greatest happiness of the greatest number" is an unacceptable ethical foundation for a constitutional democracy. *Liberal* democracy requires much more than giving free play to the preferences of the majority. Professor Whyte delineates a number of the "deeper conditions" of democratic government: "political participation, equality, autonomy and personal liberty." Professor Ronald Dworkin in his contribution to the same issue of the review cogently argues that democratic government should not be founded on a statistical, head-counting, conception of political equality but on a communal understanding in which citizens share equally the responsibilities of determining what is right for their political community.

With all of this I whole-heartedly agree. The override should not be defended on the grounds that appointed judges must never be able to thwart the will of a body elected by the majority. Such an argument would rest on the most simplistic and illiberal conception of democracy, a conception oblivious to the need for checks and balances as a condition of liberty and oblivious to the injustices which a majority may wish to inflict on a minority. Such a simplistic and morally shallow theory of democracy is not held by this defender of the notwithstanding clause, nor, I suspect, by most others who see its merits.

Now, having cleared away the underbrush of unacceptable arguments for the override, I shall attempt to put forward what I regard as the strongest grounds for retaining this provision in the *Canadian Charter of Rights and Freedoms*. These are the arguments which Professor Whyte does not address.

The Case for the Override

The major arguments in support of a legislative override turn on considerations about the substantive outcome of decision-making and about the process of decision-making in a liberal democracy. Let me deal first with substantive considerations.

Substantive Considerations

In a nutshell, the argument about the substance of decision-making is as follows. Judges are not infallible. They may make decisions about the limits and nature of rights and freedoms which are extremely questionable. There should be some process, more reasoned than court packing and more accessible than constitutional amendment, through which the justice and wisdom of these decisions can be publicly discussed and possibly rejected. A legislative override clause provides such a process.

At the core of this argument is recognition of the kind of questions courts typically deal with in interpreting and applying a constitutional charter of rights. These are questions not about the validity of the core values enshrined in the general language of the *Charter* – freedom of speech, fundamental justice, equality – but about the proper limits of rights based on these values. It is a truism that no single right should be treated as an absolute. This truism is recognized in section 1 of the *Charter* which states that all the rights in the *Charter* are "subject to reasonable limits prescribed by law as can be demonstrably justified in a free and democratic society." It is also recognized in decisions of the Supreme Court of Canada eliminating certain kinds of claims from the definition of the entrenched right or freedom. Thus, it is quite misleading to describe what the courts are doing in deciding *Charter* cases as "guaranteeing" that citizens enjoy the rights entrenched in the *Charter*. What judicial review under the *Charter* guarantees is careful consideration by the judiciary of a citizen's claim that a *Charter* right or freedom has been unreasonably encroached upon by a law or executive act of government. In dealing with such a claim the court must decide whether it should be upheld or whether it should give way to other important rights or interests with which it conflicts.

Consider the Supreme Court of Canada's decisions on claims based on section 2(b), the freedom of expression section of the *Charter*. In these cases the Court has determined whether the following were reasonable limits on the constitutional right to freedom of expression:

- a Criminal Code provision requiring that a trial judge, on the request of a complainant in a sexual assault case, ban publication of information identifying the complainant
- an injunction issued by a judge, *ex parte*, prohibiting striking court workers from picketing court houses
- a law prohibiting commercials directed at children under 13
- an order from a labour relations board requiring an employer to write a letter of recommendation about a wrongfully dismissed employee
- a law requiring French-only commercial signs and firm names
- a law prohibiting publication of the details of evidence adduced in matrimonial proceedings.

In the first four of these cases the Supreme Court decided that the limit on free speech was justified and in the latter two that it was not. One does not find in these cases the Court defending citizens against government attacks on what is fundamental to the right of free speech in a democracy, the right to criticize the government and advocate opposition to it. Instead, in each case the Court dealt with an issue at the margin, not at the core, of free speech and whether such a marginal claim should give way to some other value. In effect, in these cases, the Court was making decisions about the policy of free speech – how far this essential democratic right should be extended and under what circumstances and for what purposes it should be subject to restrictions.

In making the case for a legislative override in the *Charter*, one need not, and indeed should not, argue that the judiciary should play no part in policy decisions such as these. I agree with Professor Whyte that "Canada in enacting the *Charter of Rights*, accepted that some political problems were capable of adjudication...." But Professor Weiler and I and other defenders of the notwithstanding clause part company with Whyte when he contends that these issues must be "ultimately adjudicable," that once the judiciary has spoken there must be closure on these issues.

Far from it being the case, as Professor Whyte claims, that we Canadians in adopting the *Charter* committed ourselves to having questions about the limits of rights and freedoms ultimately determined by the courts, our constitution-makers in 1982, through the override clause, provided for a partnership between legislatures and courts. In Professor Weiler's words:

> Under this approach judges will be on the front lines; they will possess both the responsibility and the legal clout necessary to tackle "rights" issues as they regularly arise. At the same time, however, the *Charter* reserves for the

legislature a final say to be used sparingly in the exceptional cases where
the judiciary has gone awry.

Under the *Charter* we can certainly benefit, in ways described by Professor
Whyte, by having "rights" issues systematically ventilated in the courts.
Most often we will accept the decisions of the courts on these rights issues.
But occasionally situations will arise in which the citizenry through a
responsible and accountable process conclude that a judicial resolution of
a rights issue is seriously flawed and seek to reverse it. These are the situations in which we should enjoy the benefit of the legislative override.

For anyone familiar with the history of judicial review in the United States
or in our own country, it is difficult to believe in the infallibility of judges. In
American history, the decisions of the Supreme Court in *Lochner* and other
early twentieth century decisions denying state legislatures the power to
ensure vulnerable workers decent conditions of employment are reminders
of the injustice and harm that can flow from judicial decisions interpreting
constitutional guarantees. Already under the *Charter*, several judicial decisions vetoing legislation might be questioned for the harm and injustice they
inflict on vulnerable groups in Canadian society. One example is the decision of the Ontario Court of Appeal that in certain circumstances it would be
an unreasonable limitation on an accused's *Charter* rights to give effect
to the recent amendment of the Criminal Code protecting complainants
in sexual assault cases from being forced to give evidence on their prior
sexual conduct. [*Ed. note:* In its 1991 decision in *R. v. Seaboyer and Gayme*, the
Supreme Court of Canada reached the same conclusion. In 1992, Minister of
Justice Kim Campbell announced amendments to the "rape-shield" law that
respond to the *Seaboyer and Gayme* ruling but without using the section 33
override.] Another is the decision of the British Columbia Court of Appeal
overturning provincial regulations designed to channel the influx of new
doctors to areas of the province where they are most urgently needed, a decision from which the Supreme Court of Canada has denied leave to appeal.

Countries without legislative overrides in their constitutional bills of
rights have other means of reversing judicial decisions. In no constitutional
democracy is there absolute closure on rights issues once they have been
pronounced upon by the judicial branch. The most direct method of reversal
is constitutional amendment. But in most constitutional democracies (and
most certainly in Canada), amending the constitution is an extraordinarily
difficult process which may leave decision-making power in the hands of a
small group of people who are indifferent to or beneficiaries of the injustice
resulting from a judicial decision. The more usual method of reversing constitutional decisions of the courts, at least in the United States, is to change
or threaten to change the composition of the judicial bodies most influential
in interpreting the constitution.

Absent a Canadian-style legislative override, court-packing or court-
bashing are the devices to which democratic leaders are most likely to resort

when faced with judicial interpretations of the constitution they consider to be seriously unjust and harmful. These devices may yield relatively quick results as was the case with Roosevelt's threat to pack the U.S. Supreme Court or they may work much more slowly as has been the case with the efforts of Republican Presidents to reverse certain decisions of the Warren Court. In either case court-packing or court-bashing, involving as they do the application of raw majoritarian power to the judicial branch, would seem less appropriate devices than legislative debate and discussion for challenging judicial decisions. The legislative override has the merit, when properly used, of applying reasoned discussion in a publicly accountable forum to the great issues of justice and public well-being.

Now it will be noticed that I have qualified my support of the legislative override by arguing for its superiority "when properly used." By "properly used" I mean when it is invoked only after a reasoned debate in the legislature. This is precisely the point about the override which the Supreme Court of Canada failed to grasp in *Ford* when it upheld Quebec's blanket use of the override. The Court held that in using the override legislatures are not even required to name the rights or freedoms which are to be restricted. By insisting on an entirely formal approach to the override clause, as Professor Lorraine Weinrib has put it,

> The Court thereby defers to a legislative process devoid of its legitimating qualities of reasoned and focussed debate by the people's representatives.

The Supreme Court's approach to the notwithstanding clause, unfortunately and ironically, is a departure from the purposive approach applied to other sections of the *Charter*. The primary purpose of the override is to provide an opportunity for responsible and accountable public discussion of rights issues, a purpose that may be seriously undermined in legislatures are free to use the override without discussion and deliberation.

At this point it is essential to turn to the second wing of the argument for the *Charter*, the argument that focuses on the process advantages of the override. It is only when we recognize the contribution an override can make to the quality of democratic government that the inadequacy of the Supreme Court's ruling on section 33 can be fully understood and the merits of the notwithstanding clause fully appreciated.

Process Considerations

A legislative override does not guarantee that we will arrive at the right answers to the questions of political and social justice raised by the *Charter*. What it can do is to subject these questions to a process of wide public discussion so that the politically active citizenry participate in and share responsibility for the outcome.

The advantage of retaining a role for legislatures in the determination of rights issues is not to ensure that the will of the majority prevails. Even if one accepted a simplistic majority rule conception of democracy (which this writer does not), the decisions of legislatures can rarely be realistically equated with the will of the majority. This is especially true of legislative decisions on the issues of moral conscience and justice raised by questions about the appropriate limits of rights and freedoms. The point of maintaining parliamentary bodies in a democracy is not to ensure that majority preference gets its way on all public issues. Given the wonders of modern electronics, we do not need legislative chambers to register citizens' preferences. No, the fundamental purpose of parliamentary bodies is to facilitate the democratic ideal of government by discussion. A parliament must above all be a "talking place" – that is, after all, the very root meaning of the term. Through media coverage of legislative debates, citizens are engaged in deliberating on public issues. It is through parliamentary institutions that we move closer to experiencing a form of democratic government that is not simply rule of the greater number but that, in the words of Ernest Barker,

> ... elicits and enlists – or at any rate is calculated to elicit and enlist, so far as is humanly possible – the thought, the will, and the general capacity of every member ... a government depending on mutual interchange of ideas, on mutual criticism of the ideas interchanged, and the general capacity of every member.

Much the same democratic ideal is put forward by Professor Dworkin in his recent contribution to this journal. Dworkin rejects what he calls a "statistical democracy" whose institutions are designed simply to ensure that political decisions match the will of the majority. Instead he argues for a "communal democracy" in which

> each citizen insists that his political convictions are in every important sense his business, that it is his independent responsibility to decide what is required of the nation to do well, and whether or how far it has succeeded.

We have much less chance of realizing Barker's or Dworkin's democratic ideal, if, as Professor Whyte insists, we give judges the last word, the ultimate say, on rights issues raised by the *Charter*. To exclude citizens and their elected legislators from the ultimate determination of these issues is to exclude them from resolving questions of justice which should be at the very heart of political life. As Aristotle taught so long ago,

> It is the peculiarity of man, in comparison with the rest of the animal world, that he alone possesses a perception of good and evil, of the just and the unjust, and of similar qualities: and it is association in a common perception of these things which makes a family and a polis.

Giving judges the last word, the definitive say, on issues of social and political justice is to exclude citizens from participation in the essential activity of a political community.

In making this point I do not mean to denigrate the contribution judicial decisions can make to public discussion and consideration of rights issues. Some *Charter* critics, in my view, have gone too far in denouncing judicial review under the *Charter* as excessively elitist and undemocratic. These critics tend to underestimate the extent to which legal aid and the organization of advocacy groups have made litigation much more accessible than in the past as well as the extent to which *Charter* litigation generates action on law reform issues which are neglected or ignored by legislatures. Also, I would acknowledge that both the presentation of *Charter* issues before judges and the reasoned decisions of judges on *Charter* issues can contribute significantly to public understanding of rights issues. But I am not persuaded that these benefits of applying the judicial process to these issues are so great as to justify making adjudication always the ultimate means of resolving rights issues. Court decisions on whether restricting where new doctors supported by public medicare can practice is a justifiable restriction of individual freedom, or on whether a French-only sign law is needed to preserve the predominantly French character of Quebec may well have contributed to public understanding of these issues. But in a democracy that aspires to government by discussion and full participation of its citizens in questions of social and political justice, court decisions should not close off further debate and decision-making in elected and publicly accountable legislatures

Legislatures, it is true, may act precipitously and make questionable decisions. On occasion their consideration of rights issues may, to use Professor Whyte's phrase, be unduly influenced by "the dominant political winds." But it is a dreadful distortion to suggest that such impassioned and inconsiderate behaviour is the norm in Canadian legislatures. A reading of legislative debates on justice issues such as capital punishment, criminal procedure, aboriginal rights and language rights does not find legislators simply pandering for popularity. At the same time we should recognize that while judges are free from any pressure to curry favour with the public they are not altogether free from other institutional biases. The Supreme Court's court opinion in *B.C.G.E.U.* v. *British Columbia* upholding the power of a judge to restrict the free speech rights of workers does not shine out as a carefully reasoned and balanced consideration of that rights issue. Professor Dale Gibson's article in the last issue of this journal reveals other instances of judicial bias and self-interest in adjudicating public law issues.

In designing the institutional matrix for making decisions on rights issues it is a mistake to look for an error-proof solution. Both courts and legislatures are capable of being unreasonable and, in their different ways, self-interested. By providing a legislative counter-weight to judicial power the Canadian *Charter* establishes a prudent system of checks and balance which recognizes the fallibility of both courts and legislatures and gives closure to the decisions of neither. A legislature's decision to use the override, it must be remembered, is not ultimate. It is good for only five years. After five years it can be reviewed but not without re-opening the issue for public debate and discussion.

If we do anything to section 33 of the *Charter*, we should reform it, not abolish it. There is need to overcome by constitutional amendment that part of the Supreme Court's decision in *Ford* which permits standard-form overrides without any obligation on the legislature to identify the specific legislative provision which in its judgment needs protection or the right or freedom which in its view should not be given priority. Professor Weiler and I have advocated a further amendment which would require that any use of the override be subject to two enactments, one before and one after an election. This would ensure a cooling off period and time for second thoughts. What is even more important, it would also ensure broad citizen involvement, thus contributing to the fundamental process value of the override .... [*Ed. note*: Russell discusses two test cases: one in which the override was not used but in which he argues that it should have been; the other in which it was used but many people think that it should not have been. The first was the National Citizens' Coalition successful 1984 challenge to the Elections Act, striking down its restrictions on non-party spending during federal elections. The latter was Quebec's use of the override to re-instate its "French-only" public signs law that was struck down by the Supreme Court ruling in *Ford* v. *A.-G. Quebec*.]

The Perspective of Principle

At the beginning of his article Professor Whyte argues that the future of the override cannot be settled by resort to principle. By this he means that the case for the override cannot be a logical deduction from the "basic constitutional principles" he perceives to be at work in the "formal structure of the Canadian state" – namely, "legalism, democracy and federalism." The elimination of the override, he argues, is at least as consistent with these principles as its retention. Given that the established principles of our constitution cannot settle the issue, the merits of the override should be assessed on a more prudential basis in terms of "the actual social goods and bads" it is likely to produce and "what will produce the soundest government and fairest society."

As I have earlier indicated, I have no difficulty accepting Whyte's suggestion that we not try to judge the override entirely on the basis of our constitutional antecedents. And I agree with him that the override should be judged in terms of what will produce a sound and fair polity for Canadians. But I do take issue with his treatment of what he regards as Canada's basic constitutional principles and their bearing on the override issue.

I have the least quarrel with Whyte's treatment of the federal principle. He is right in viewing federalism as a check on national majoritarianism and pointing out that judicial decisions enforcing the federal division of powers have significantly constrained Canadian legislatures in the past. But he overlooks an important difference between judicial review based on federalism and judicial review based on a bill of rights. Also, he underestimates the impact of the *Charter* on the workings of Canadian federalism and on the unity of the country.

When courts strike down legislation on federalism grounds, normally this means that one level of government but not the other is precluded from proceeding with a policy. This is a less drastic result than when legislation is struck down on *Charter* grounds for then the judicially vetoed policy, absent the override, is placed beyond both levels of government. It is in this sense that removing the override from the *Charter* would, contrary to Whyte's assertion, entail a greater shift in the balance of power between legislatures and courts than is inherent in the judicial enforcement of federal limits. Secondly, the *Charter* does have a centralizing effect on Canadian federalism. The article by Morton et al. also in the most recent issue of this journal, tracking the judicial nullification of statutes begins to take the measure of the Supreme Court's capacity under the *Charter* to impose uniform policies on the provinces. This centralization of policy-making power, from a normative perspective, may at times have clear benefits for Canadian society. At the same time it may reduce the policy pluralism and diversity that many of us value in federalism. Finally, and from the perspective of national unity most seriously,... it is most unlikely that we could retain Quebec as a member of the Canadian federation if we were now to insist on removing the override from the *Charter*. This is not because the majority of Quebeckers are opposed to rights and freedoms but because they want to keep a reasonable measure of control over their cultural security in their own hands.

But Professor Whyte's elucidation of the principle of legalism gives me much more difficulty than his discussion of federalism. For it is here that he seems to slide into the very mode of analysis he has cautioned us to eschew and to argue, in effect, that regardless of "the goods and bads that are likely to be produced" we must be bound by the implications of his principle of legalism.

Whyte's initial formulation of what he calls legalism – namely "the notion that there are adjudicable public issues" – is not problematic. But then he goes on to assert that "we have come to terms with these issues being *ultimately* adjudicable – not subject to legislative review and revision." Here he seems to be saying that having accepted through adoption of the *Charter* that a great many public issues which were heretofore dealt with by the "political branches" are now to be subject to adjudication, we are ineluctably committed to giving the judiciary *ultimate* control of these issues. But that surely isn't so. Certainly when the *Charter* was adopted with an override, we Canadians made no such commitment. The question now before us, using Whyte's own criteria, is whether making *Charter* issues "ultimately adjudicable" will lead to the soundest and fairest system of government.

For reasons already advanced in this article I believe that in terms of both the substance of rights policy and its process it would not be sound even to try to let all the public issues which may be adjudicated under the *Charter* be ultimately settled by judges. I say "try" because that is the closest we can come to realizing Whyte's ideal of forever removing issues arising under the *Charter* from what he calls "a purely political process." The experience of the United States shows what an illusion it is to think that without the possibility of a legislative override, rights issues dealt with by the judiciary are forever withdrawn from the political process. School desegregation was not withdrawn from the American political process after the Supreme Court in *Plessy* v. *Ferguson* gave its blessing to "separate but equal" any more than Roosevelt's New Deal legislation was removed from the political agenda after being vetoed by the Supreme Court.

But it is difficult to see why even trying to remove rights issues *entirely* from the political process should result in "sounder" or "fairer" laws. Professor Whyte asserts that "the capacity of governments to regulate society for the public good has not, yet, been fundamentally hampered by *Charter* decisions." Some might consider the damage done in *Wilson* to government's capacity to provide for an equitable distribution of publicly funded medical services or in *National Citizens Coalition* to government's freedom to follow an election commission's advice on how best to provide fair and effective election laws as already a refutation of Whyte's dictum. But, let us concede that these decisions have not *fundamentally* hampered government from "regulating for the public good." The question remains why is it sound and fair to accept this much judicial damage to effective, socially responsible regulation without the possibility of legislative review and, indeed, risk the possibility that judicial decisions might go further and fundamentally cripple government's effectiveness in providing for the public good? Are the judiciary and the judicial process so inherently superior to the legislature and the processes of ordinary politics that we are justified in running these risks?

Professor Whyte apparently thinks they are. The problem with legislatures, he tells us, is that sometimes they "neglect to calculate the extraordinary impact of legislative measures on particular individuals." Sometimes too, he says, they simply do not care enough about the injury to some persons' right to tailor measures which will minimize the damage. I agree with Whyte that legislatures certainly do these things and these are precisely the situations in which we may be well served by *Charter*-based judicial review. But I would submit that judicial review of legislation under the *Charter*, in turn, has its own limitations and blind spots. Judges often fail to take into account, and indeed sometimes are exposed to the scantiest of submissions on the relationship of a challenged law to its total social or policy context. In *Wilson*, for example, the British Columbia Court of Appeal in upholding the "liberty" of new doctors to practice their profession at public expense wherever they wish in the province, did not consider the possible inequity in not extending a similar liberty to other newly graduated professionals in that province or the impact of this decision on the financing of other social programs. Judges considering *Charter* challenges to legislation and government regulation may, on occasion, minimize the damage which can be inflicted by private centres of social and economic power on the freedom and equality of the most vulnerable groups in a market economy. It is to his credit that Chief Justice Dickson warned against this possibility. But we cannot always count on such enlightened judicial leadership or on its being followed.

The art of living with the *Charter* and with its override is to get the best out of both the judicial and the legislative process in making decisions on rights issues. However, according to Whyte's principle of legalism, we must now put all our eggs in the judicial basket. A legislative back-up, in his view, is too apt to plunge rights issues back into the grubby, unprincipled, partisan realm of "pure politics." It is here that we encounter what I find most unacceptable in Whyte's argument, his disdain for democratic politics.

In his discussion of the democratic principle Whyte rejects, as I would, a simplistic majoritarian conception of democracy. I agree with him that a liberal democracy requires checks and balances and that judicial review based on a constitutional bill of rights is not inherently undemocratic. Where I differ with him on the democratic principle is on how best to enhance and develop our capacity for democratic citizenship. The attempt to remove rights issues, irretrievably, from the arena of popular politics is to give up on what democratic politics at its best should be – the resolution of questions of political justice through a process of public discussion. As I have written before it, "represents a further flight from politics, a deepening disillusionment with the procedures of representative government and government by discussion as a means of resolving fundamental questions of political justice." For me, the legislative override clause is a way of countering this flight from democratic politics. It is a signal that we Canadians have not yet given up on our capacity for debating and deciding great issues of political justice in a popular political forum.

In the concluding paragraphs of his article Professor Whyte turns to what for many may be the clinching argument against the override – the need for a judicial check against "extreme political reaction." It is in moments of "serious political repression," he contends, that we are most in need of cool judicial guardians to check the passions of democracy. Now, I have no doubt that legislative bodies can act unreasonably and fall under the sway of very repressive forces. In the 1950s we witnessed just that when McCarthyism held sway in the United States. We also witnessed then how ineffective that country's judicial guardians were in checking that repression. But more fundamentally, I would argue that a democracy which puts its faith as much in its politically active citizenry as in its judges to be the guardians of liberty is stronger than one that would endeavour to vest ultimate responsibility for liberty and fundamental rights exclusively in its judiciary.

13.4

A Better Way of Saying "Notwithstanding"

Scott Reid

National Post, September 21, 1999, A18.

The Supreme Court of Canada received mostly favourable media coverage recently when it ordered the government of British Columbia to reinstate a female firefighter who had failed the province's standardized fitness test for firefighters. In reporting the warm and fuzzy human interest story, in which Tawney Meiorin was given back her job after a three-year struggle, the real issue regarding the wider implications of this ruling was lost.

Regardless of one's personal view as to the merits of Ms. Meiorin's case, one cannot help but be struck by the fact the court did not stop by simply ruling there is "no credible evidence showing that the prescribed aerobic capacity [measured by the test that Ms. Meiorin failed] was necessary for either men or women to perform the work of a forest firefighter success-fully." A reasonable argument can be made, and has been made in case law, that any test that is irrelevant to job performance, but which is harder for women to pass than for men, represents a form of discrimination.

But the court chose to continue on and to develop an elaborate three-step process that must now be applied in designing all job-related tests, and which will be retroactively applied to all existing tests. In imposing this kind of detailed process upon employers, the court is acting more as a legislature than as a judicial body.

Such de facto legislating is now a regular activity of the court. When the Supreme Court ruled last spring that conjugal homosexual relationships of reasonably long duration must be regarded as marriages under Canadian law, the justices effectively rewrote, or mandated the rewriting, of hundreds of laws, at the federal level and in every province. The redrafting generated by this decision will affect not only laws relating to marriage and divorce, but also legislation dealing with spousal rights, pension benefits, and so on.

A court decision with such sweeping implications is, for all practical purposes, an amendment to the Canadian Constitution. This is significant, because under normal circumstances amendments can take place only when a broad-based popular consensus exists. Some countries, such as Switzerland and Australia, require a "double majority" (a majority of voters nationwide, as well as local majorities in at least half of all states or cantons) approve any proposed amendment in a national referendum. Canada and the U.S. require approval by a special extra-large majority of provincial or state legislatures. By contrast, a court-based amendment needs the approval of only five Supreme Court justices, and concerns about a broad-based con-sensus, or even of bare majority support among the Canadian people, are simply not part of the equation.

To deal with the danger of excessive power accumulating in the hands of the Supreme Court, the authors of the *Charter of Rights and Freedoms* included a provision that allows for court decisions to be overridden on occasions when they might conflict with the fundamental beliefs of the populace. This provision is Section 33 of the *Charter*, known as the "notwithstanding clause." Today, the notwithstanding clause represents the only method available to Canadian legislatures of limiting the awesome power of the court.

However, polls clearly indicate most Canadian do not trust their elected officials to use the *Charter*'s override provision. Any attempt by a government to simply re-enact a law by means of the normal legislative process will run into severe opposition in which the clause itself, rather than the relevant legislation, will become the subject of debate, with the government cast as the destroyer of rights. The result is that even when unpopular court decisions are made, politicians do not dare to use the notwithstanding clause, and so, in practice, the power of the court to arbitrarily remap Canadian law remains unchecked.

Perhaps the faith of Canadians in the notwithstanding clause would be restored if it were the people themselves, rather than Parliament or the legislatures, who were to be entrusted with the power of invoking the Sec. 33 override. Ten years ago, legal scholars Peter Russell and Paul Weiler suggested the clause might have more legitimacy if it were amended so that any specific use of the override would not come into force until it had been enacted twice: once before and once after a general election. The election would therefore become a sort of referendum on the government's specific use of the notwithstanding clause.

Earlier this year, Alberta went a step further. A bill was placed before the legislature that would require a referendum prior to any use by the province of the notwithstanding clause to re-enact legislation that had been struck down by the court. This seems to be the model to follow.

It would be an easy matter for Ottawa or any provincial government to draft a law forbidding the use of the notwithstanding clause except when authorized by referendum. Or one could go further: The law could state that if any legislation of that jurisdiction were struck down by the courts as infringing on rights guaranteed under the *Charter*, the offending provisions would automatically be submitted to the electorate for their consideration at the time of the next general election. Following such a combined referendum/election, the new government would find itself under a moral obligation to use the notwithstanding clause to re-enact all laws approved by the electorate and to let stand any court decisions not marked for override by the voters.

If it were successful in returning legitimacy to the notwithstanding clause, the referendum-based override would certainly reduce the power of the courts to make arbitrary judgments as to the meaning of vaguely drafted *Charter* rights. Yet it would not place any new powers in the hands of politicians. It is the people themselves who would be empowered.

This is only one advantage of democratizing the notwithstanding clause. Section 1 of the *Charter* permits legislation to remain in effect even if it violates the letter of the *Charter*, as long as the limits such legislation places upon *Charter*-guaranteed freedoms are "reasonable" and can be "demonstrably justified in a free and democratic society." The Supreme Court has developed a cumbersome standard, known as the "*Oakes* test," for determining whether legislation that does not comply with the *Charter* should be permitted by virtue of Sec. 1 to remain in effect. To an outside observer, it is hard not to conclude that in practice this test has allowed some draconian legislation to be exempted from the *Charter* while causing other, fairly inoffensive laws to be struck down.

At present, it is not an easy task for the justices of the Supreme Court to determine whether a law is genuinely deserving of Section 1 exemption. This is particularly true when provincial laws are being challenged, since it is often the case that none of the judges come from the province in question. Judges are therefore faced with the choice of, from time to time, erring on the side of extending the definition of rights in a manner offensive to community standards, or of erring on the side of restricting rights through the too-frequent or too-extensive invocation of Section 1.

A democratic override would bring an end to this problem. Whenever a vote is held, the electorate would be, in practice, redefining Section 1. Given that the debate would be free and the vote democratic, one can scarcely imagine a more appropriate way of demonstrably justifying what constitutes a reasonable limit on rights in a free and democratic society. Just as, according to one Supreme Court justice, rights enumerated in the *Charter* gain meaning when the courts "breathe life" into them, the electorate would be able to breathe life into Section 1.

Judicial review is a necessary component of a law-based, democratic society. But the Supreme Court needs to be made aware that it is not the *only* necessary component, and that its role remains one of legislative review rather than legislative enactment. Enacting laws to create a de facto people's veto on the court's decisions might be a good place to start.

13.5

Interest Group Litigation and Canadian Democracy
Gregory Hein
Montreal: IRPP 6:2 (2000).

This article is reproduced as Reading 7.5.

13.6

Judicial Independence
The Views of Appellate Judges

Ian Greene et al.
"Judicial Independence," in *Final Appeal* (Toronto: James Lorimer, 1998), 183–91.

This article is reproduced as Reading 5.7.

13.7

Dialogue or Monologue? Hogg versus Morton
The Charter Dialogue between Courts and Legislatures

Peter W. Hogg and Allison A. Thornton
Policy Options, April 1999. Reprinted with permission.

Judicial review is the term used to describe the action of courts in striking down laws. Lawyers and political scientists, especially those employed at universities, love to debate the question of whether judicial review is legitimate. In Canada, the question arises because our *Charter of Rights* vests judges, who are neither elected to their offices nor accountable for their actions, with the power to strike down laws that have been made by the duly elected representatives of the people. Is this a legitimate function in a democratic society? Is the *Charter of Rights* itself legitimate, inasmuch as it provides the authority for a much expanded role for judicial review?

The conventional answer to these questions is that judicial review is legitimate in a democratic society because of our commitment to the rule of law. All of the institutions in our society must abide by the rule of law, and judicial review simply requires obedience by the legislative bodies to the law of the Constitution. When, for example, the Supreme Court of Canada strikes down a prohibition on the advertising of cigarettes (as it did in the *RJR-MacDonald* case, 1995), it is simply forcing the Parliament of Canada to abide by the *Charter's* guarantee of freedom of expression. Similarly, when the Court adds sexual orientation to the list of prohibited grounds of discrimination in Alberta's human rights legislation (as it did in the *Vriend* case, 1998), it is simply forcing the Legislature of Alberta to observe the *Charter's* guarantee of equality.

The difficulty with this conventional answer is that the *Charter of Rights* is for the most part couched in such broad, vague language that in practice judges have a great deal of discretion in applying its provisions to laws that come before them. The process of applying the *Charter* inevitably involves interpreting its provisions into the likeness favoured by the judges. This problem has been captured in a famous American aphorism: "We are under a Constitution, but the Constitution is what the judges say it is!"

In this article, we argue that, in considering the legitimacy of judicial review, it is helpful to think of such review as part of a "dialogue" between judges and legislatures. At first blush, this concept of dialogue may not seem particularly apt. Given that the Supreme Court of Canada's decisions must be obeyed by the legislatures, one may ask whether a dialogue between judicial and legislative institutions is really possible. Can a legislature "speak" when its laws are subject to the constitutional views of the highest Court? The answer, we suggest, is "Yes, it can," certainly in the vast majority of cases where a judicial decision is open to reversal, modification or avoidance by the competent legislative body. Thus a judgment can spark a public debate in which *Charter* values are more prominent than they would have been otherwise. The legislative body is then in a position to decide on a course of action – the re-enactment of the old law, the enactment of a different law, or the abandonment of the project – that is informed by both the judgment and the public debate that followed it.

Dialogue will not work, of course, if the effect of a judicial decision is to prevent the legislative body whose law has been struck down from pursuing its legislative objective. But this is seldom the case. The first reason why a legislative body is rarely disabled by a judicial decision is the existence in the *Charter of Rights* of the override power of s. 33, under which a legislature can simply insert a "notwithstanding" clause into a statute and thereby liberate the statute from most of the provisions of the *Charter*, including the guarantees of freedom of expression (s. 2(b)) and equality (s. 15). Section 33 was added to the *Charter of Rights* late in the drafting process at the behest of provincial premiers who feared the impact of judicial review on their legislative agendas, and it is the most powerful tool legislatures can use to overcome a *Charter* decision they do not accept.

When the Supreme Court of Canada struck down a Quebec law forbidding the use of English in commercial signs on the ground that the law violated the guarantee of freedom of expression (*Ford*, 1988), Quebec answered by enacting a law that continued to ban the use of English on all outdoor signs. The new law violated the *Charter*'s guarantee of freedom of expression as much as the previous one had, but the province protected it from challenge by inserting a s. 33 notwithstanding clause into it. The Quebec National Assembly recognized that it was restricting the freedom of expression of its anglophone citizens, but concluded that the enhancement of the French language in the province was important enough to justify overriding the *Charter* value.

More recently, when the Supreme Court of Canada held that Alberta's human rights legislation violated the guarantee of equality by not providing protection for discrimination on the ground of sexual orientation (*Vriend*, 1998), there was much debate in the province about re-enacting the law in its old form under the protection of a s. 33 notwithstanding clause. In the end, the Alberta government decided to live with the decision of the Court. But because using the notwithstanding clause to override the decision had been an option, it is clear that this outcome was not forced on the government, but rather was its own choice based on, among other things, what the Court had said about the equality guarantee in the *Charter of Rights*.

Both these cases are examples of the dialogue that s. 33 permits. Admittedly, because of the political climate of resistance to the use of the clause, "notwithstanding" is a tough word for a legislature to use. But making tough political decisions is part of a legislature's job. In the dialogue between courts and legislatures, "notwithstanding" is therefore at least a possible legislative response to most judicial decisions.

The second element of the *Charter of Rights* that facilitates dialogue is Section 1, which provides that the guaranteed rights are subject to "such reasonable limits prescribed by law as can be demonstrably justified in a free and democratic society." In other words, Parliament or a legislature is free to enact a law that infringes on one of the guaranteed rights, provided the law is a "reasonable limit" on the right.

Since 1982, the Supreme Court has established rules for determining whether a law is such a reasonable limit. The rules can be boiled down to: (1) The law must pursue an objective that is sufficiently important to justify limiting a *Charter* right, and (2) it must limit the right no more than is necessary to accomplish the objective. In practice, the Court usually holds that the first requirement is satisfied – that is, the objective of the law is sufficiently important to justify limiting a *Charter* right – and in most cases the area of controversy concerns the second requirement, whether the law limits the right by a means that is the least restrictive of the right.

When a law is struck down because it impairs a *Charter* right more than is necessary to accomplish the legislative objective, then it is obviously open to the legislature to fashion a new law that accomplishes the same objective with provisions that are more respectful of the *Charter* right. Moreover, since the reviewing court that struck down the original law will have explained why the law did not satisfy the s. 1 justification tests, the court's explanation will often suggest to the legislative body exactly how a new law can be drafted that will pursue the desired ends by *Charter*-justified means.

In the Quebec language case, for example, the Supreme Court acknowledged that protection of the French language was a legislative objective that was sufficiently important to justify limiting freedom of expression. However, the Court also held that a complete ban on the use of other languages in commercial signs was too drastic a means of accomplishing the objective, and it suggested that the province could make the use of French mandatory without banning other languages, and could even require that the French wording be predominant on the sign. Such a law, the Court implied, would be justified under s. 1.

As we have explained, the province was not initially inclined to follow this suggestion and simply reenacted the outright ban under the protection of the notwithstanding clause. However, five years later, when language passions had died down a bit, the province did enact a law of the sort the Supreme Court had suggested, requiring that French be used on commercial signs and be predominant, but permitting the use of other languages.

Many other examples could be given of laws which have been modified and re-enacted following a *Charter* decision. The point is that s. 1 allows dialogue to take place between the courts and the legislatures. Section 1 dialogue facilitates compromise between legislative goals and the courts' judgment on what the *Charter* requires.

Several of the rights guaranteed by the *Charter* are expressed in qualified terms. For example, s. 8 guarantees the right to be secure from "unreasonable" search or seizure. Section 9 guarantees the right not to be "arbitrarily" imprisoned. Section 12 guarantees against "cruel and unusual" punishment. When these rights are violated, the offending law can always be corrected by substituting a law that is not unreasonable, arbitrary, or cruel and unusual.

For example, the enforcement provisions of the *Competition Act* have been struck down on the grounds that they authorized unreasonable searches and seizures contrary to s.8 of the *Charter* (*Hunter*, 1984). So have the comparable provisions of the *Income Tax Act* (*Kruger*, 1984). But in both cases the Supreme Court also laid down guidelines as to how s. 8 could be complied with. What was required was the safeguard of a warrant issued by a judge before government officials could search for evidence. Parliament immediately followed this advice and amended both acts so that they now authorize searches and seizures only on the basis of a warrant issued by a judge. The legislative objective is still achieved, but in a way that is more respectful of the privacy of the individual.

Once again, many other examples could be given, but the essential point is that the very language of the qualified rights encourages a continuing dialogue between the courts and the legislatures.

The proof of the pudding is in the eating, and our research has indicated that most of the decisions of the Supreme Court of Canada in which laws have been struck down for breach of a *Charter* right have in fact been followed by the enactment of a new law. In a study published in 1997 in the *Osgoode Hall Law Journal*, we found that there had been 66 cases in which a law had been struck down by the Supreme Court of Canada for breach of the *Charter of Rights and Freedoms*. Only 13 of these had prompted no legislative response at all, and these 13 included both recent cases, in which there may have been little time to react, and cases in which corrective action was under discussion. In seven of the 66 cases, the legislature simply repealed the law that had been found to violate the *Charter*. In the other 46 cases, a new law was enacted to accomplish the same general objective as the law struck down.

A critique of the *Charter of Rights* based on its supposed usurpation of democratic legitimacy simply cannot be sustained. To be sure, the Supreme

Court of Canada is a non-elected, unaccountable group of middle-aged lawyers. To be sure, from time to time the Court strikes down statutes enacted by elected, accountable, representative legislative bodies. But the decisions of the Court almost always leave room for a legislative response, and they usually receive a legislative response. In the end, if the democratic will is there, a legislative way will be found to achieve the objective, albeit with some new safeguards to protect individual rights. Judicial review is not "a veto over the politics of the nation" but rather the beginning of a dialogue on how best to reconcile the individualistic values of the *Charter* with the accomplishment of social and economic policies enacted for the benefit of the community as a whole.

Dialogue or Monologue? A Reply to Hogg and Thornton

F.L. Morton
Policy Options, April 1999.

Peter Hogg argues that the alleged illegitimacy of the courts' new power under the *Charter* is much ado about nothing. According to his theory, the *Charter* encourages a "dialogue" between courts and legislatures. Courts scrutinize legislative means not ends. If courts do try to block an important legislative objective, governments have the option of the final say via the use of the section 33 override power. The result is a democratic process enriched by a new rights dialogue between independent judges and accountable legislators. I will briefly address three of the principal problems that I see in Hogg's "dialogue" defence of the Supreme Court's activist exercise of *Charter* review.

1. Dialogue is a two-way street

Hogg uses a self-serving definition of "dialogue." Obeying orders is not exactly what most of us consider a dialogue. If I go to a restaurant, order a sandwich, and the waiter brings me the sandwich I ordered, I would not count this as a "dialogue." Yet this is how the concept is used in Hogg-Bushell 1987 study. Hogg counts as dialogue any legislative response to the judicial nullification of a statute. If a government repeals the offending legislation or amends it according to specifications laid out by the Court, this is counts as "dialogue." No wonder Professor Hogg found a two-thirds incidence of dialogue!

This lax operationalization of the concept of dialogue also obscures important differences between types of legislative response. When Parliament added a new search warrant requirement to the *Anti-Combines Act* after *Hunter* v. *Southam*, it simply did what the Court told it to do. After *Daviault*, by contrast, Parliament created a new offence that explicitly rejected the Court's ruling that self-induced intoxication can be used as a *mens rea defence* against assault charges. Similarly, Quebec's 1988 use of section 33 to avoid compliance with the Court's ruling in the "French-only" public signs case is clearly not on par with the same government's decision in 1993 to comply with the Court's ruling. Yet in the Hogg-Bushell study, these very different responses are all counted equally as "dialogue."

Hogg anticipated this response and declared that even if one excludes cases in which governments simply followed judicial directions,"there would still be a significant majority of cases in which the competent legislative body has responded to a *Charter* decision by changing the outcome in a substantive way." It would have been reassuring to have an actual number to attach to "significant majority." It is also hard to reconcile this assertion with Hogg's earlier claim that, "In most cases, relatively minor amendments were all that was required in order to respect the *Charter*." Were most of the 46 legislative responses "minor" or "substantive"? Were governments delivering the sandwich the judges had ordered or were they changing the menu?

2. The means/ends distinction does not bear scrutiny

Another essential element of the dialogue theory is the means/ends distinction. By this account, *Charter* review only impinges on the "how" not the "what" of government policy. Under the "reasonable limitations" provisions of section 1 of the *Charter*, as operationalized by the now famous *Oakes* test, judges review government policy to ensure that legislators have chosen the "least restrictive means" of achieving their policy objectives. When judges believe a policy fails the "least restrictive means" test, it remains open to the responsible government to redraft the legislation to achieve its original goal with more carefully tailored means.

As Rainer Knopff and I have argued elsewhere, the means/ends distinction sounds fine in theory but breaks down in practice. First, politics is as much about means as ends. Everyone wants equal employment opportunities for women and racial minorities, but not everyone favours preferential treatment or quotas as the way to achieve this goal. No respectable person is willing to defend child pornography, but many will argue that restrictions on it must be balanced with our respect for freedom of expression and privacy.

Second, apparent disagreement about means sometimes turns out to be disagreement about ends. Everything depends on the purpose(s) a judge attributes to the statute. The broader the purpose(s), the easier it is to find that the legislation passes the "least restrictive means" test. In fact, any half-clever judge can use procedural objections as a pretense to strike down legislation that he opposes for more substantive reasons. As examples, I would point to the very cases used by Hogg: those involving voluntary religious instruction in Ontario schools and the federal prisoner-voting cases. In both instances, courts initially struck down policies for failing the "least restrictive means" test. In both instances, the responsible governments redrafted the legislation to restrict its impact on religious freedom and voting rights, respectively. And in both instances, the courts again ruled that the new legislation was still "too restrictive" of the rights at stake. In cases such as these, the means/ends distinction becomes a charade for substantive disagreement about public policy.

Perhaps the best example of this instrumental use of procedural objections comes from the Chief Justice of Canada. In the 1988 Morgentaler case, Justice Lamer joined Justice Dickson in an opinion striking down the abortion provisions of the Criminal Code because the procedures required to attain a legal abortion were too restrictive and ambiguous. However, speaking on the tenth anniversary of the Morgentaler decision, Lamer told law students at the University of Toronto in 1998 that he voted to strike down the abortion law for a very different reason: because a majority of Canadians were against making it a criminal offence. Does this mean that his 1988 procedural objections were simply after-the-fact rationalizations to justify striking down a law that he opposed for other reasons?

3. The staying power of the policy status quo

Hogg assumes that if a government is unhappy with a judicial nullification of one of its policies, then it has the means to reverse it – either by enacting revised legislation or, more emphatically, by re-instating the old law through the use of the section 33 notwithstanding clause. "If the democratic will is there, there will be a legislative way," he declares (p. 4). If a government fails to use the tools at its disposal, that's the government's fault, not the court's.

This account fails to recognize the staying power of a new, judicially created policy status quo (PSQ), especially when the issue cuts across the normal lines of partisan cleavage and divides a government caucus. I develop this argument by adapting Thomas Flanagan's recent analysis of the Mulroney government's response to the Court's 1988 Morgentaler ruling.

Contrary to Chief Justice Lamer's beliefs, in 1988 the majority of Canadians were not opposed to the abortion policy that he voted to strike down. Under that policy, abortion was deemed wrong in theory but available in practice. (Dr. Morgentaler and his lawyers could not produce a single witness who had actually been prevented from getting an abortion.) This compromise accurately reflected Canadians' conflicting opinions on the abortion issue. In 1988, 24 percent said that abortion should be legal under any circumstances; 14 percent illegal under any circumstances; and 60 percent legal under certain circumstances.

A recently published study of abortion politics in Canada and the U.S. found that from the late Sixties through the early 1990s "the contours of public opinion towards abortion have been generally unchanged. What exists is a situation where two intense minorities have polarized views of abortion policy that do not represent the feelings of a majority of Americans or Canadians. In both countries, the majority stands to the right of the strongest pro-choice position but left of the absolutist pro-life position."

This pattern of support was replicated in House of Commons voting on the Mulroney government's efforts to enact a new abortion policy after the 1988 *Morgentaler* ruling. The new policy was designed to meet the procedural problems identified in the written judgment of Justices Dickson and Lamer. (The government mistakenly believed that these were the "real" reasons for Justice Lamer's vote.) It left abortion in the Criminal Code, but would have significantly widened access. In its final form, Bill C-43 would have abolished the requirement of committee approval; broadened the definition of health to include "mental and psychological" health; and lifted the "hospitals only" restriction.

The government's "compromise" approach was opposed by both pro-choice and pro-life factions within Parliament, albeit for opposite reasons. Two pro-choice amendment – which basically affirmed the new judicially created policy status quo of "no abortion law" – were easily defeated in the House by votes of 191–29 and 198–20. A strong pro-life amendment, which would have created a more restrictive policy than the one struck down by the Court, received much more support but was narrowly defeated by a vote of 118–105. A paradoxical coalition of pro-choice and pro-life MPs then combined to defeat the government's own compromise proposal by a vote of 147–76.

The following session, the government re-introduced a new compromise abortion policy – Bill C-43. To avoid a repeat of the earlier disaster, Mulroney invoked party discipline for his forty cabinet ministers and warned pro-life MPs that this would be his last attempt. The House then approved the bill by a vote of 140–131. However, it was subsequently defeated by a tie vote (43–43) in the Senate. As in the House of Commons the year before, the pro-choice and pro-life minorities combined to vote against the policy compromise, but in the Senate there were no Cabinet ministers to save it. The new judicially created PSQ of "no law" thus continued by default, not because it commanded majority support in either Parliament or the public.

The defeat of Bill C-43 illustrates a common dynamic between public opinion and Supreme Court decisions on contemporary rights issues. Contrary to the rhetoric of majority rule and minority rights, on most contemporary rights issues there is an unstable and unorganized majority or plurality opinion, bracketed by two opposing activist minorities. In terms of political process, the effect of a Supreme Court *Charter* ruling declaring a policy unconstitutional is to transfer the considerable advantages of the PSQ from one group of minority activists to the other. The ruling shifts the burden of mobilizing a new majority coalition (within voters, within a government caucus and within a legislature) from the winning minority to the losing minority.

This transfer is a significant new advantage for the winning minority. Just as it was impossible for pro-choice activists to persuade either the Trudeau or Mulroney governments to amend Parliament's compromise abortion law of 1969 prior to the Court's *Morgentaler* decision; so after the ruling, it has been equally impossible for pro-life activists to interest the Chrétien government in amending the new judicially created PSQ of no abortion law. The reasons are the same: the issue is not a priority for the government, the opposition parties or the public.

Indeed, the priority for most governments on such "moral issues" is to avoid them as much as possible. Such issues cross-cut normal partisan cleavages and thus fracture party solidarity, from the cabinet to the caucus to the rank and file membership. Nor do they win any new supporters among the (disinterested) majority. To act risks losing support from the activist policy minority you abandon, without securing the support of the activists you help. (After all, you only did what was "just.") On such issues, political self-interest favours government inaction over action.

A similar pattern occurred in Alberta after the Supreme Court's *Vriend* ruling in April, 1998. The Klein Government – and the Conservative Party of Alberta – were deeply divided on whether to add sexual orientation to the *Alberta Human Rights Act*. Two previous task forces had recommended against it, but with minority reports. Gay rights groups had lobbied aggressively for the reform. Social conservatives – a force to be reckoned with in Alberta politics – were just as strongly opposed. For the majority of Albertans, it was an issue of secondary importance.

When the Supreme Court "read in" sexual orientation to the *Alberta Human Rights Act*, there was a strong public outcry – especially among the rural wing of the Alberta Tories – to invoke section 33. After a week of public debate, the Cabinet was as divided as before. In the end, Premier Klein declared that his personal preference was not to invoke section 33 and a majority of the caucus fell into line.

Describing the Alberta government's decision to "live with" the *Vriend* ruling, Hogg writes: "But because 'notwithstanding' was an option, it is clear that this outcome was not forced on the Government, but was the Government's own choice." Hogg is only half right in this assertion. He ignores that the Court's decision decisively changed the government's options. The government's preferred choice was not to act at all – to simply leave the old PSQ in place. The Court destroyed this and – with the clever use of the "reading in" technique – created a new PSQ.

Prior to the ruling, the government could safely ignore the issue – upsetting only a small coalition of activists, few of whom were Tory supporters in any case. After the ruling, the government had to choose between accepting the judicially created PSQ or invoking the notwithstanding clause – a decision that it knew would be strongly criticized in the national media and that risked creating a backlash among otherwise passive government supporters. The judicial ruling significantly raised the political costs of saying "no" to the winning minority. For the same reason that the Klein government had refused to alter the old PSQ, it now accepted the new judicially created PSQ. In both instances, the safest thing to do was to do nothing.

Hogg writes that judicial nullification of a statute "rarely raises an absolute barrier to the wishes of democratic institutions." (81) He is right in his observation, but wrong in his conclusion. It does not have to be an absolute barrier. Depending on the circumstances, a small barrier may suffice to permanently alter public policy.

To conclude, Hogg's theory must be qualified to account for different circumstances. A government's ability to respond to judicial nullification of a policy depends on a variety of factors. When the policy is central to the government's program, the government should have little difficulty mustering the political will to respond effectively. Examples of this pattern of dialogue would include the Quebec government's use of notwithstanding in response to Ford and the Devine government's overruling of the Saskatchewan Court of Appeal's rejection of its back-to-work legislation.

By contrast, when the issue cuts across partisan allegiances and divides the government caucus; when public opinion is fragmented between a relatively indifferent middle bracketed by two opposing groups of policy activists – the judicial creation of a new PSQ may suffice to tip the balance in favour of one minority interest over that of their adversaries. Both *Morgentaler* and *Vriend* illustrate this pattern of response. Some of course will applaud these practical results. Others, such as my colleague Rainer Knopff, would see them as further examples of how courts are "more apt to intensify than moderate the tendency to Tupperism in political life."

To conclude, what Professor Hogg describes as a dialogue is usually a monologue, with judges doing most of the talking and legislatures most of the listening. Hogg suggests that the failure of a government to respond effectively to judicial activism is a matter of personal courage, or the lack thereof, on the part of government leaders. The fault, if there is any, rests with individuals.

By contrast, I am suggesting that legislative paralysis is institutional in character: that legislative non-response in the face of judicial activism is the "normal" response in certain circumstances. When the issue in play is cross-cutting and divides a government caucus, the political incentive structure invites government leaders to abdicate responsibility to the courts – perhaps even more so in a parliamentary as opposed to a presidential system. If I am correct, the Canadian tradition of "responsible government" is in for a rough ride in our brave new world of *Charter* democracy.

13.8

Judicial Independence and Judicial Activism
Justice Claire L'Heureux-Dubé
Notes for an address to the Canadian Bar Association Council Awards Luncheon,
August 21, 1999. Reprinted with permission.

*"Upon the Integrity, Wisdom, and Independence of the Judiciary, Depend the
Sacred Rights of Free Men and Women"*

These inspiring words are inscribed in marble in the courtroom of the Court
of Appeals of Georgia, which I recently had the opportunity to visit. I find
them particularly meaningful for several reasons. First, they remind me of
the critical task which has been conferred upon members of the judiciary.
Our duty of rendering justice has significant consequences for the lives of
those in Canada, and for the future of our society. Second, those words set
out the importance of preserving the *institution* of an independent judiciary
and the rule of law as factors necessary to maintaining a free and democratic
society. Finally, and perhaps most importantly, they link the importance of
an independent judiciary with the protection of the rights of all people.
Indeed, it is because of my passionate belief in the importance of human
rights, equality, and justice for all that I am an equally passionate believer
in the importance of an independent judiciary. Judges stand as a bulwark to
ensure that justice is done, and as those empowered with the special mandate to protect those who are disadvantaged or marginalized, the independent exercise of their responsibilities is essential to ensuring that all people's
rights and obligations are respected.

Earlier this month, the President of the ABA said that he couldn't "think
of any time in the history of the country that the independence of the legal
profession has been as threatened as it is now." In my remarks today, I will
emphasize why I believe that the independence of the judiciary is an issue
that is significant for jurists in Canada today. Attentiveness to the principles
of judicial independence is important for those who wish to stand in solidarity with jurists and citizens in countries where these basic principles stand
unrespected. In addition, within Canada, I believe that it is critical that judicial independence continue to be an issue which is an important focus for
jurists and for members of the public. Even in a healthy democracy like ours,
the need to be vigilant to ensure that we continue to have a strong, independent, and effective system of justice cannot be underestimated.

What exactly is meant by the concept of judicial independence? The
United Nations *Basic Principles on the Independence of the Judiciary*, which
have been endorsed by the U.N. General Assembly state, in Article 2, that:

> The judiciary shall decide matters before it impartially, on the basis of facts and in accordance with the law, without any restrictions, improper influences, inducements, pressures, threats or interferences, direct or indirect, from any quarter or for any reason.

This is, rightly, a broad definition, reflecting an important international consensus about the importance of a free and independent judiciary. It emphasizes that a judge must be independent of all restrictions and improper influences, free to make decisions on the basis of the law and of the case before her. Judicial independence includes freedom from *all* interference with decision-making, from government or from *any* other source. As emphasized by Chief Justice Dickson in *The Queen* v. *Beauregard*:

> Historically, the generally accepted core of the principle of judicial independence has been the complete liberty of individual judges to hear and decide the cases that come before them: no outsider – be it government, pressure group, individual or even another judge – should interfere in fact, or attempt to interfere, with the way in which a judge conducts his or her case and makes his or her decision.

Judicial independence distinguishes the process of judicial dispute resolution from political decision-making, and ensures that legal judgments are made on the basis of the application of principles of law, considering the equal rights of all those who come before the court. Decisions must be supported by reference to the values and principles of the legal system, rather than on the basis of what is popular, attractive, or expected by those who appointed the judges. Judicial independence must therefore be consistently enforced through clear principles and constant respect for them. Judges have no police forces, armies, or budgets to spend as they please to enforce their place in the constitutional order. The maintenance of judges' role as guardians of our constitution and values and as independent arbiters of disputes depends entirely on voluntary respect for their place in the constitutional and societal order. The neutrality and independence of judges is what makes our justice system strong, and leads to public acceptance of the results of decisions.

   The importance of being vigilant to ensure the independence of the judiciary is no more clearly demonstrated than by noting how, in so many places around the world, lawyers and judges are under attack. As stated in the introduction to the 1997-99 report, *Attacks on Justice*, carried out by the Centre for the Independence of Judges and Lawyers in Geneva,

> [Between March 1997 and February 1999], the CIJL found that at least 876 judges and lawyers were harassed or prosecuted for carrying out their professional functions. These attacks are perpetrated by government forces, opposition groups, or even sometimes by the business community or land

owners. Of the 876 documented cases, 53 jurists were killed, 3 disappeared, 272 were prosecuted, arrested, detained or even tortured, 83 physically attacked, 111 verbally threatened and 354 professionally obstructed and/or sanctioned. The CIJL also received reports of an additional 508 jurists who suffered reprisals in 1997 and 1998 but was unable to conclusively confirm those reports.

… this disturbing account of the fate of judges and lawyers, who are often perceived as privileged members of society, highlights the inadequacy of human rights protection in the countries we covered.

When these acts occur, the ability of judicial systems to render justice and ensure respect for human rights or for the principles of our constitution is diminished or eliminated.

Fortunately, throughout Canadian history we have been free of the most blatant attacks on judicial independence such as those the International Commission of Jurists and its affiliates have documented elsewhere. Systemic corruption, "telephone justice" as it is often referred to where governments dictate decisions to judges, and interference with the institutional and administrative functions of the judiciary have never been great concerns for Canadians. Neither have personal attacks or violence against judges been part of our traditions.

Indeed, Canada's Constitution, as interpreted by our Court, guarantees judicial independence in several different ways. It is protected through the guarantee in s. 11(*d*) of the *Charter* of a trial by an independent and impartial tribunal, the judicature principles contained in ss. 96, 99 and 100 of the *Constitution Act, 1867*, and, in a more general sense, by the reference in the preamble to the Constitution that it is similar in principle to that of the United Kingdom. Our Court has emphasized that judicial independence from government includes three guarantees: the financial security of judges, the security of tenure of judges, and the administrative independence of the judiciary.

Given the history of respect for this principle in Canada, it might be surprising that I want to raise the question of whether current discussions about the role of judges and the debate over "judicial activism" might be having an effect on the independence of the judiciary in our country. In the media, and even by some politicians, it is increasingly being suggested that judges make decisions solely on the basis of their personal preferences, without proper respect for their role in our political order. Judges are criticized personally for the outcomes of their judgments. What effect does this have on the ability of judges to make decisions independent of all influence, on the basis of principles of law and the values of our society? At what point does vehement personal criticism of judges and their decisions run the risk of interfering with the independence of the judiciary? It is these questions, and the interaction between the charge of judicial activism and the principle of judicial independence, that I will address in the remainder of my comments.

Much has changed in the last 20 years in terms of public discussion and perception of the role of judges. While previously, judicial decisions were often ignored or given little attention, this has changed dramatically. Decisions of the Supreme Court, in particular, are extensively reported and commented upon, subjected to intense public and media scrutiny, and, in some cases, comment and criticism by politicians.

The discussion, however, is not only about the merits of the decisions. The commentary on the recent decision in *M. v. H.,* to give just one example, included assertions that the Court "is in fact being guided by its own high opinion of itself" rather than the law, that "the Supreme Court is increasingly an embarrassment", that its decision "is yet another in a long and tiresome line of arrogant judicial violations of society's democratic principles". Though, of course, much of the commentary recognizes the role played by our judicial system within the Canadian political structure and not all discussion is along these lines, attacks on judicial institutions and upon individual judges are becoming more and more frequent and the vocabulary bears less and less the signs of civility. A good example is seen in the recent attacks on Justice Shaw in British Columbia where even threats to his life have been reported by the media.Unfortunately, we are not alone. As Robert O'Neill has written in *Trial* magazine, "the intense judicial criticism of the late 1990s is not simply business as usual. In several ways, the current attacks on the bench seem more troubling than those in the past.... Bench-bashing seems to have moved from the fringe ... to the mainstream ... Attacking judges ... has become an eminently reputable activity for the political and the legal establishment."

I must emphasize strongly that I am not suggesting that judges are, or should be, immune from criticism. On the contrary, discussion about the consequences of court decisions, and criticism of the reasoning process and interpretation of the law contained in them is an essential part of our judicial system. Comments on judgments by journalists, academics, law students, members of the bar, and members of the public are not only acceptable, but important in ensuring that there is reflection and comment on the work that we do. Though judges may not always agree with the content of such criticism, it is a necessary part of dialogue in a democratic society. Speaking for myself, I take commentary on different approaches to law and legal issues very seriously, particularly if it approaches the issues from an understanding of the nature of judges' roles and the legal process.

However, I am concerned that public debate is demonstrating an increasing tendency to focus on the "messenger" rather than the "message". Rather than discussing the ideas or values underlying judicial decisions or the legal methodology or reasoning used in reaching them, the debate places the attention on judges themselves and sometimes degenerates into personal attacks and accusations that judges are overstepping the proper institutional boundaries of their role. The prime example of this criticism of the messenger rather than the message is the accusation that judges have somehow taken it upon themselves to overturn legislation passed by Parliament or to make other changes in the law without respecting the appropriate separation of powers – the accusation of "activism".

What is meant when a judge is charged with "activism"? It should be noted that, for one thing, judicial activism cannot be associated with either so-called "liberal" or "conservative" perspectives. In the United States, for example, the activist charge has been pronounced both concerning the jurisprudence of the *Lochner* era, a jurisprudence concerned with the protection of the right of property to the detriment of social legislation, as well as a criticism of the egalitarian position later taken by the Warren Court. Similarly, the criticism of the Supreme Court of Canada's broad interpretation of equality rights in *Vriend* and *M* v. *H.* contrasts that which followed earlier jurisprudence in which equality rights were said to have received an unduly narrow interpretation. It cannot be limited to the defence of a particular conception of the good.

The activist judge is also often portrayed as one with an inclination towards judicial intervention and, in particular, with a willingness to change the law. Yet most people would agree that it is appropriate for judges to make changes in the common law and the interpretation of legislation or the constitution when necessary, particularly to adapt it to contemporary values. It is also often suggested that activist judges place their personal preferences above the requirements of the law. Yet such criticism ignores the process of legal reasoning and justification that forms part of every legal decision. Legal interpretation requires a judge to use arguments and sources that are acceptable within the legal community, and justify that decision with regard to those values. This accusation also fails to recognize that cases that make their way to appeal courts generally reach that stage precisely because there are no clear or already determined legal principles to decide the questions at issue. Legal texts, constitutional principles, or common law rules have no clear, unambiguous meanings that can be mechanically applied to every new situation. Appeal cases give rise to controversial and challenging issues, which are contentious precisely because already established legal principles do not give rise to a clear answer. Rather than representing pure "personal preference," differing views often reflect different interpretations of how existing principles lead to a result in a new case. The need to make arguments and justify a result in accordance with the principles of legal reasoning prevents the mere imposition of the judge's preferences.

In Canada, the advent of the *Canadian Charter of Rights and Freedoms* in 1982 and the jurisprudence that has flowed from *Charter* litigation is largely responsible for the public debate about the proper role of the courts. This should hardly come as a surprise to anyone. That the charge of activism is most often related to decisions in the area of human rights is simply due to the fact that human rights bring directly into light disputes over conceptions of justice, equality and the self. But it must also be remembered that if judges were to fail to overturn legislation that violated the constitution, and to decline to make these kinds of difficult decisions, it would be to ignore the law and commit the ultimate in judicial activism. Refusing to evaluate the constitutionality of legislation would be to ignore the principle in s. 52 that the Constitution of Canada "is the supreme law of Canada" and that any law inconsistent with it is of no force or effect. Questions of the legitimacy of judges overturning legislation ignore the more fundamental issue of when laws should be struck down. As Justice Rosalie Silberman Abella has eloquently noted:

> By focusing ... on whether judges should interpret the constitution, a conversation rendered irrelevant by this country's decision to have one in 1867 and rendered irrefutably irrelevant when we decided to patriate and expand it in 1981, we are allowing cranky attacks on our credibility to distract us from our ongoing duty to ensure the public that their right to accessible justice is being credibly met.

Canadians, through the democratic process, have decided that we will have a *Charter of Rights and Freedoms* to protect fundamental human rights, and that it will be the duty of judges to ensure compliance with those rights. Discussion of judicial decisions should recognize that fact. As Justice Stephen Breyer has written recently in the *Oxford Journal of Legal Studies*, "why then, why, one might ask ... have democratic societies increasingly tried to create independent judiciaries with final, or near final, authority to interpret basic documents that guarantee basic rights?" The obvious answer to Justice Breyer's question is that these new democracies have measured the criticism against what they see as a need for the protection of democratically structured government and of basic liberties that an independent judiciary guarantees.

The charge of judicial activism more frequently masks disagreement with the substantive merits of a case and the values underlying judges' decisions, rather than truly representing a dispute over the legitimacy of the judicial role. A good example of this is the contrast between the laudatory discussions in the media of the Supreme Court's decision to strike down the government's seventy-two hour ban on the publication of poll results in *Thomson Newspapers* and the accusations of judicial activism when the Court has made decisions on social issues such as Aboriginal or equality rights in cases such as *Gladue, Delgamuukw, Vriend,* or *M. v. H.* This difference in the reaction to these issues shows that the debate is not really about *whether* courts should strike down Parliament's decisions, but *when.* As noted by Rosalie Abella:

> So what are we really talking about when we discuss judicial activism versus restraint, the politicization or "Americanization" of the judiciary, or related concerns? We are really talking about whether we agree with a court's result and what to do about it if we do not. If we favour the court's result, we tend to applaud the approach, whether it be called restrictive or expansive. If our

> notion of justice is offended by the result, we chastise what we consider to
> be an abdication of the judicial role or an invasion of the legislative one.

It is cause for concern when discussion and debate fail to respect judicial institutions or recognize the decisions that Canadians have made, collectively, about the manner in which we will resolve disputes. It is also misleading when it is suggested that judges are now developing the law in a manner that they have not done in the past, or that there is a "clear" answer to the dispute which is being ignored by the judges.

In my opinion, criticism and reports which fail to understand the type of decisions which judges must make and commentary which gives rise to personal attacks and criticism raise concerns about the independence of the judiciary. A recent report even suggested that cabinet ministers should telephone Supreme Court judges to explain that a certain result was expected by the government in an upcoming case. How can we not be concerned about the effect of such statements on judicial independence?

Given these issues, it is essential that judges and lawyers be attentive to the importance of maintaining judicial impartiality and independence, and recognize the need for a judiciary that makes decisions not out of fear of criticism or concern for popularity, but on the basis of the interpretation of the rules of law that are at issue before the Courts. Faced with the barrage of attacks, courage becomes a more and more important prerequisite for the work done by lawyers and judges: the type of courage that Justice Kennedy of the U.S. Supreme Court described recently as "the courage required at some times and in some places to provide the proper answer to a clear violation." That is, the courage to stand up for causes that may be unpopular and the courage to make decisions that we realize may attract criticism. Judge Hiller Zobel of the notorious Boston nanny case said, "Judge must follow their oaths and do their duty, heedless of editorials, letters, telegrams, picketers, threats, petitions, panelists, and talk shows. ... we do not administer justice by plebiscite."

The importance of public understanding of the nature of our legal system and of the work done by judges also means that members of the Bench and the Bar have an important role to play in helping ensure that the correct information does make its way into the public domain, and that the public and the media understand the institutional context within which Court decisions are made and the principles upon which they are based. It is helpful when members of the profession or of the academic community intervene in public debate to remind the public of the importance of avoiding personal attacks on judges and of preserving judicial independence. When reports are inaccurate or misleading, are critical of the messenger rather than the message, or do not recognize the nature of Canadian institutions, it is necessary for jurists to intervene more frequently, in order to remind the public of the importance of judicial institutions and explain the real reasons behind the decisions. As Justice Michael Kirby of the Australian High Court has noted:

It therefore rests increasingly on the organized legal professional to defend the judiciary, to correct blatant misinformation and to remind politicians, the media and others of the precious heritage of judicial neutrality and independence which we have enjoyed until now.

And as former Chief Judge of the D.C. Circuit and former Congressman Abner Mikva stated:

Only the lawyers know enough and have enough self-interest to defend the judges in their unpopular decisions. Lawyers not only have to restrain their own judge-bashing, which they are wont to do: they have to be the voices of the judges. If we don't, who will defend the notion of an independent judiciary?

The independence of the judiciary is promoted when lawyers speak out since judges know that there are those who will step in to help explain or defend our decisions, and correct misapprehensions about the principles upon which they are based.

Judges and jurists should not be immune from criticism, nor is it expected that judicial decisions should be popular or uncontroversial. However, I hope that members of the Bar and Bench can increasingly work together to ensure that in public debate and discourse, the role of the judge and the important place of the judiciary in our constitutional order remain respected. I can do no better than to cite the inspiring words of Justice Michael Kirby:

Let it be a goal of the coming millennium that we re-teach the lessons of our constitutions and engender an informed appreciation of the judges and of their vital importance for the peaceful government of us all. Not blind or uncritical faith. Nor confidence extracted by the ever present threat of legal enforcement. Not appreciation won by clever public relations and media hype. But a deserved evaluation of faithful and honest service in a difficult profession, the alternative to which is anarchy and the power of guns.

In closing, I would like to say a few brief words about the International Commission of Jurists, since I speak today as President of this organization which has as one of its top priorities the protection of judicial independence. The ICJ is a human rights non-governmental organization, founded in 1952 by De Bevoise, and is devoted to the independence of Bench and Bar and to respect for the rule of law throughout the world. The ICJ is today one of the world's oldest and most respected international human rights NGOs. What distinguishes it from other human rights NGOs is its specifically legal approach to human rights. It is composed of and staffed by jurists. The ICJ is headed by a Commission of up to 45 members from as many different countries who are outstanding jurists and human rights defenders (they include judges, lawyers and law academics). Its 82 national sections represent all the legal systems and traditions of the world. The ICJ has consultative status with many international organizations, and has won several human rights prizes. It was at the forefront of the Montreal Declaration on the Independence of the Judiciary now adopted by the U.N. In addition, the ICJ has made a number of interventions at the UN Commission on Human Rights, and it supported the establishment of a permanent International Criminal Court (ICC) as well as the drafting and adoption of numerous international human rights instruments. The ICJ has also been very active throughout the world in promoting programs on the domestic implementation of international human rights. The Canadian section is headed by Judge Michèle Rivet, Chair of the Quebec Human Rights Tribunal. It has around 500 members, among them most distinguished jurists. I invite you to join this organization, by becoming a member of the Canadian Section of the ICJ. In joining, you will not only contribute to this important mission, but stand in solidarity with our fellow jurists throughout the world, in insuring justice for all through an independent judiciary.

13.9

Courts, Legislatures, and Executives
in the Post-*Charter* Era
Chief Justice Beverley McLachlin
Policy Options, June 1999, 42–47. Reprinted with permission.

In 1982, on a cold, windy day on Parliament Hill, the Queen signed the *Canadian Charter of Rights and Freedoms* into law. It marked a momentous step in Canadian constitutional history. Some, including many in England, viewed the step with grave apprehension. Today, it seems much less singular. Now the British have passed their own written Bill of Rights. In Africa, in Asia, in Europe – everywhere – people seem to have or to be getting constitutional bills of rights. New Zealand has a charter. Australia does not, but its High Court is nevertheless prepared to strike down laws on the basis of unwritten constitutional conventions. People vehemently defend their own particular charter versions. The British, for example, make much of the fact that their Bill of Rights does not automatically invalidate offending legislation, instead giving Parliament one year to amend the law. But whatever the mechanism for ensuring compliance of the law with the basic charter principles, in the end it is a safe guess that substantial compliance there will be.

All over the world, people are subjecting their parliaments to a higher constraint, that of the written constitution. This may be the short answer to the debate that fills so many Canadian newspaper columns about whether we should or should not have a charter. It is increasingly difficult to imagine any modern democracy without a charter that sets out agreed-upon principles governing the conduct of parliament. Constitutional, rights-based democracy is swiftly becoming the international norm, if it has not already so become. It seems fair to suppose that sooner or later Canada, whose Parliament and legislatures were from their inception subject to the constraints of the *British North America Act*, would have entrenched in a constitutional form the fundamental principles upon which our democracy and legal order are based, just as so many other countries have done or are poised to do.

This is the background against which we must set the Canadian *Charter* – a world that increasingly accepts that legislatures may properly be limited by the need to conform to certain basic norms – norms of democracy, norms of individual liberties like free expression and association, norms governing the legal process by which the state can deprive people of their liberty and security, and norms of equal treatment. No longer is democracy synonymous with naked populism. The world increasingly accepts that while the will of the people as expressed through their elected representatives must be paramount, that will should always respect the fundamental norms upon which the very notion of democracy and a civil society repose, and upon which the legitimacy of the legislative assemblies themselves is founded.

In one sense, the reordering of democracy necessitated by the entrenchment of constitutional rights norms is merely an evolutionary adjustment of the Canadian democratic landscape. Anyone who supposes that prior to the *Charter* Parliament and the legislatures were not constrained by basic constitutional principles, including fundamental democratic rights, has not studied our history closely enough. And anyone who supposes that the courts pre-*Charter* did not hear and decide on challenges to legislative powers is equally mistaken. From the beginning of Canadian democracy, courts have had the task of deciding whether laws challenged as going beyond the powers of the legislature that enacted them were valid or not. Moreover, even without a written bill of rights, courts required legislatures to conform to the basic principles of democratic government and equality. They did this through interpretation and in some cases – and this surprises some people – through striking laws down. Let me cite an example of each.

The first example is interpretative. It shows how, 50 years ago, the courts used the process of interpretation to recognize equality rights in Canada. Canada, of course, was founded amid the patriarchal notions prevalent in the mid-nineteenth century. Professions, governance – indeed, everything outside domestic work and a little teaching and nursing – was strictly reserved for men. When Emily Murphy was sworn in as a police magistrate in 1916 in Alberta, she was met on her second case with a challenge to her jurisdiction. The challenge went this way: Only "persons" are entitled to sit as judges. "Persons" means men. You are not a man. Therefore you cannot sit as a judge. Or to put it in the quaint but precise terms of Edwardian legalese: "Women are persons for pains and punishments, but not for privileges. Sitting as a judge is a privilege. Therefore, you, a woman, cannot sit as a judge."

To us this argument sounds ridiculous. But in the early 1900s it was not. Courts in England and in various parts of Canada had repeatedly ruled that laws enabling persons to do certain things – be they to practice law or medicine or sit as judges – applied only to men. Outside the criminal law, which applied regardless of sex, the word "persons," interpreted legally, meant "men." So the lawyer who challenged Emily Murphy's jurisdiction to sit as a police magistrate was on sound legal ground. But Emily Murphy refused to accept the legal status quo. She believed the law to be fundamentally unjust and decided to seek its change. She brought a case before the Supreme Court of Alberta and obtained a ruling, revolutionary at the time, that "persons" in the *Judges' Act* included women.

But that was not the end of the story. The federal government did not accept the view of the Supreme Court of Alberta that "persons" included women. It continued to deny women the right to sit in the Senate of Canada on the ground that women were not "persons" within the meaning of those provisions of the *British North America Act* dealing with the constitution of the Senate. Emily Murphy and four cohorts in Alberta sued again, this time for an order that "persons" included women. The government fought them all the way. They pursued their claim to the Supreme Court of Canada, which ruled against them. So they raised more money and took their case all the way to the Judicial Committee of the Privy Council in London, which was then Canada's court of last resort. There, finally, in a decision that has come to be known as the "Persons Case," they prevailed.

The Privy Council, in a landmark ruling that affected the law not only in Canada but in Britain and throughout the Commonwealth, held that contrary to previous law, "persons" should be read to include women. Viscount Sankey proclaimed that the Constitution of Canada was "a living tree, capable of growth and expansion within its natural limits. The object of the *Act* was to grant a *Constitution* to Canada.... Their Lordships do not conceive it to be the duty of this Board – it is certainly not their desire – to cut down the provisions of the *Act* by a narrow and technical construction, but rather to give it a large and liberal interpretation...."

In the course of interpreting the Constitution this way, two important things occurred: The law was altered, indeed fundamentally reversed; and women were accorded vast new rights they had not enjoyed before. Many people didn't like the ruling, and many people, we can safely speculate, muttered darkly about judicial activism. Sound like the *Charter*? Indeed, yes. Of course, at the time, it would have been open to Parliament to pass a new law saying expressly that women could not sit as senators. But reading the history books, one gets the sense that parliamentarians were not keen to remove from women what the Privy Council had found to be a fundamental right: the right to participate in the governance of the nation.

The second example illustrates how pre-*Charter* courts could and did require legislatures to conform to the fundamental principles of justice by striking down offending legislation. I refer to the 1938 *Alberta Reference.*

The times were hard, people were desperate, and extreme ideas held great appeal. One of the strongest majoritarian governments Canada had ever known, the Aberhart government in Alberta, determined that for the good of the people, it must restrict the press' criticism of the government's economic policies. So it passed an act, modestly entitled *"An Act to Ensure the Publication of Accurate News and Information,"* requiring critical comment to be submitted to the government for advance inspection.

Canada then possessed no bill of rights or *Charter*. It had only the *British North America Act*, setting forth the division of powers between the federal and provincial governments. Nowhere did that *Act* mention free speech. Yet the Supreme Court of Canada struck the bill down. Although the result was ultimately based on the fact that the entire scheme was beyond the legislative competence of the provinces, the Court commented on the impact of this particular *Act*. It held that there was an implied guarantee in the Canadian Constitution that protected free expression about the conduct of government. Free speech was one of the pillars upon which the very notion of democracy itself existed. Free speech, said Chief Justice Duff, was "the breath of life for parliamentary institutions." As such, the legislature of Alberta was bound by it, even though it did not formally appear in the *British North America Act*. These are but two examples. There are many others. In the area of criminal law and evidence, for example, pre-*Charter* courts modified and adapted the common law and interpreted legislation in a way that ensured that the fundamental liberties of the individual were maintained. Thus, *Charter* rights did not spring, full-grown from the head of Zeus. Canadians had rights long before the *Charter* and the courts served as the guardians of those rights. The *Charter* accepted this tradition and entrenched the role of judges as interpreters and guardians of the rights it guaranteed. Once we came to realize as a community that some rights were fundamental, there was really no alternative. As former Supreme Court Justice Bertha Wilson wrote in the April issue of *Policy Options*, "You cannot entrench rights in the Constitution without some agency to monitor compliance. The judiciary was the obvious choice."

So in one sense, the *Charter* is old news. Yet in another, it has changed things, indeed, changed them profoundly. On a micro level, it has forced us to update our laws of criminal evidence and procedure. It has given impetus to the move to require governments to treat their citizens equally, without discrimination, regardless of factors like race, religion, sex or age. It has forced examination of electoral practices, like manipulative riding boundaries and bans on polling. And it has required us to consider again precisely where we should draw the line between the individual's right of free expression and the need to protect the community from harmful expression.

On the macro level, change has been equally important. I accept the frequently-made charge that the *Charter* has changed the way Canadians think and act about their rights. The *Charter* has made Canadians realize on a profoundly personal level what perhaps they had formally recognized only in a detached, intellectual sense: that their rights belong to them, that these rights are a precious part of their personal inheritance, and that they must exercise them and vigilantly protect them if they are to keep them healthy and strong.

If this is a culture of rights, then I welcome it. The debate we see every day on the editorial pages of our newspapers about the ambit of our rights and where lines should be drawn between conflicting rights and between the rights of the individual and the interest of the community, can only strengthen our society and our sense of being partners in this Canadian venture. It is the mark of a civil society, of a healthy mature democracy, that such things are debated in the newspapers and on the talk shows of our country, and not swept under the rug or, worse yet, fought out in back alleys and trenches.

The second general way the *Charter* has changed Canadian society is that it has increased the profile of the judicial branch of government. Before we had a *Charter*, judges were marking boundaries between rights, changing the law to reflect settled and emergent conceptions of rights, and occasionally even striking down laws that violated fundamental rights. However, the *Charter*, by putting the people's rights up front and centre, has accelerated the process. It is easier to challenge a law on the ground that it violates a fundamental right when you have in your hand a document that specifically proclaims your entitlement to that right. Compared to the task faced by Emily Murphy and her cohorts, for example, it is easier to change a legal interpretation that produces inequality, like the traditional interpretations of the word "persons," when you possess a document that commits the government to equal treatment. Moreover, people's new awareness of their rights has led individuals and interest groups – and they are to be found on both sides of virtually every issue – to come together and mobilize to protect their conception of a particular right. So the *Charter* has increased the challenges to laws on the basis of rights and thus incidentally increased the profile of courts called upon to resolve these issues.

This brings us to the current debate over whether the formal realignment in powers that the *Charter* has brought about has left too much power in the hands of judges. Depending on how the commentator views the issue, it is put in different terms. Some common variants include:

- "Judges have used the *Charter* to effect a giant power-grab."
- "Unelected judges are running the country."

And simply,

- "Judges are too activist."

The idea of an overt power grab is easily dismissed. There is no evidence that judges, individually or collectively, particularly wanted the *Charter* or that, once it arrived, they decided to use it to entrench their power at the expense of Parliament and the elected legislatures. Equally easily dismissed is the idea that unelected judges are running the country. True, judges are unelected, and I believe should remain unelected, having considered the conflicts of interest and related problems an elected judge system presents. But that does not mean they cannot properly act as referees between conflicting rights and interests and as interpreters of the Constitution and the law. Nor does it mean that they are running the country.

Anyone seriously putting forth such a charge must confront the existence of Section 1 of the *Charter*, which permits the legislatures to trench on guaranteed rights to the extent that such a course can be shown to be justified in a free and democratic society. Should s. 1 fail to confirm a law, Section 33 is also available to permit the elected representatives of the community to override the courts' assessment of what the rights of the individual require.

At this point the proponents of the theory that the judges are running the country shift to pragmatic arguments. It's too hard to justify infringements under s. 1 or to use s. 33 to override judicial decisions, they argue. There is something in this. It is true that, as a practical matter, it is not easy for legislatures to say to the people, or even a small unpopular subgroup of the people, "Notwithstanding your rights, we are going to violate them." But that, I believe, is as it should be. Individual rights have substance and they should not lightly be cast aside. But the fact remains that, in some circumstances, Parliament and the legislatures can override judicial decisions on the *Charter* if the considered sentiments of the community make it politically feasible to do so. We must therefore reject the arguments that the judges of Canada have used the *Charter* to effect a power grab and are running the country.

This leaves the charge of judicial activism. Judges, it is said, are too eager to overturn laws, too ready to strike statutes down, too apt to "rewrite" laws enacted by Parliament and the legislatures. I note at the outset that there is not much hard evidence that judges are inappropriately activist, whatever that may mean. A recent study by Professor Patrick Monahan of Osgoode Hall Law School concludes on the basis of considerable statistical analysis that the Supreme Court of Canada, far from being activist, as many have charged, is rather inclined to be judicially conservative and deferential to the elected arms of government. The same study suggests that it is very hard to find instances of the Court "rewriting" laws. Given the absence of any contrary studies of similar depth, this should at least give the critics pause.

Beyond this, it seems to me that if we are to talk sensibly about judicial activism, we must define our terms. Judicial activism means almost as many things to its critics as did the parts of the elephant to the blind men in the old parable.

Some people equate judicial activism with any judicial decision that changes the law. The theory here is that it is the job of judges to apply the law as it is found to exist, never to change or update it. This theory betrays a misapprehension of what judges have always done under both the common law and the civil law of this country. The venerable tradition of developing the law through an accumulation of precedent lies at the heart of our legal system, and is the lifeblood of a socially responsive body of law. New circumstances are brought before the courts. In applying the law, be it a previous case or a provision of the *Charter*, judges examine the law and the circumstances to see whether the old law should apply or whether it now seems unjust to do so. If a careful analysis reveals that the old law no longer reflects what is considered to be fair and appropriate, it is modified. This involves changing the law. But if changing the law is judicial activism, then judicial activism is neither new nor undesirable.

Ah, the critic says, but judicial activism is not merely changing the law, but changing the law too much. There is some truth in this. Radical changes of the law can be considered "activist" by definition. However, this does not get us any closer to answering the question of whether the *Charter* has made judges activist. We are left with many difficulties. The first problem is whether the fact that a change is radical necessarily means it is bad. Was it necessarily bad that the Privy Council in 1929 ruled that the word "persons" included women, thereby opening public life and the professions to women? The change was radical, but most would argue, desirable and long overdue.

The second difficulty lies in defining "radical." One person's "sensible incremental development" is another's "radical alteration of the law." Judicial activism in this sense thus often reduces itself to a debate about whether one likes or does not like a particular judicial decision. This does not bring us much closer to answering the question of whether the *Charter* has made judges inappropriately activist.

This concept of judicial activism is closely related to what I call the "political mirror" model of judicial activism. On this view, a decision is "activist" if it does not accord with one's political or legal viewpoint. This has led to the situation where both conservatives and liberals accuse the courts under the *Charter* of being too activist. Conservatives assail liberal, rights-affirming decisions as "activist." Liberals, on the other hand, assail as "activist" those decisions in which, rather than setting aside the law, the courts ignore or read down *Charter* provisions. Thus, as Professor Lorraine Eisenstat Weinrib wrote in the April issue of *Policy Options*, "It is the deferential, conservative justices who have been impermissibly activist. They have consistently ignored the values of the *Charter* text, its political history and its stated institutional roles." With the fire coming from both quarters, what, one might be forgiven for asking, is a judge to do?

Another version of judicial activism equates it with result-oriented, agenda-driven judging. I am the first to say that if it could be shown that Canadian judges were engaging in this kind of judging it would be bad. Judges must be impartial. They must not be biased. Their job is to study the law and the facts, listen to all the arguments pro and con, and after due deliberation, rule as their intellect, informed conscience, and training dictate. The spectre of agenda-driven judging is, to the best of my knowledge, just that – a spectre. If established, it would be a terrible thing and could not be tolerated. But it is not established.

It seems to me that people too often confuse agenda-driven judging, which would be bad, with judicial consistency, which is good. In the course of their work, judges may have developed fairly firm views about what a particular *Charter* provision means or where lines should be drawn between conflicting rights and interests. It is the task of the judge, at the beginning of each new case, to suspend those views and reconsider them in light of the submissions of the parties in that particular case. Yet if the judge, after considering all the submissions, arrives at a conclusion similar to that which he or she arrived at before, that is no cause for alarm. Indeed, it suggests a rational, carefully considered approach to the task of judging.

I am left with the feeling that the vague term "judicial activism," to the extent that it is used as more than merely a proxy for decisions the critic does not like, has to do with the fear that judges will depart from the settled law – that they will take advantage of the fact that no one, except for Parliament or the legislatures under s. 33, can override them, to foist unwarranted and unjustified laws on the people. The fear is well-known to jurists and not confined to rights litigation. Long before charters of rights were dreamed of, the English spoke ominously of "palm tree" justice, evoking the image of a colonial magistrate, seated under his judicial palm tree, meting out whatever decisions happened to seem right to him in the particular cases at hand.

The opposite of palm tree justice, or what we may call judicial activism in the *Charter* era, is justice rooted in legal principle and appropriate respect for the constitutional role of Parliament and the legislatures. The law has developed rules and ways of proceeding to assist judges in avoiding the evils of unprincipled, inappropriately interventionist judging. The first rule is that judges must ensure that their decisions are grounded in a thorough understanding of the *Charter* provisions at issue and the jurisprudence interpreting it. Where previous authority exists, changes should follow incrementally – absent the rare case of where manifest error is demonstrated, such as, for example, in the *Persons Case*. While the language of the *Charter* is open-textured and leaves room for judicial discretion in certain areas, it provides more guidance to those who study its language and values than is often realized. To quote Professor Weinrib again: "The *Charter* itself provides significant guidance for judicial interpretation."

It is still very early days for the Canadian *Charter*. But already we have a significant body of jurisprudence fleshing out its guarantees. Future decisions will build on this. The first time a *Charter* pronouncement is made that seems to change the law, it may strike many as "activist." But as a body of principle develops, the foundation of court decisions on the words of the *Charter* and the stable nature of the jurisprudence will become more apparent.

The second rule judges should follow is that they should be appropriately respectful of the role of Parliament and the legislatures and the difficulty of their task. While always important, this rule assumes particular significance in cases where the *Charter* or law at issue permits two or more interpretations or authorizes the judge to exercise discretion. "Appropriate respect" presupposes an understanding of the role of the legislative branch of government as the elected representative of the people to enact laws that reflect the will and interests of all the people.

To state this role is to acknowledge the difficulty of its execution. In a society as diverse and complex as ours, enacting laws is rarely a simple process of codifying the will of the people. It is rather a delicate task of accommodating conflicting interests and rights. Compromise is the watchword of modern governance. Judicial decision-making, on the other hand, is necessarily a blunt instrument, incapable of achieving the balances necessary for a workable law acceptable to society as a whole (on this point see Professor Rainer Knopff's paper in the April issue of *Policy Options*.)

This is not to say that, where an individual's constitutional rights are at stake, the courts must always accept the compromises the legislators work out. Where laws unjustifiably violate constitutional rights, it is the clear duty of the courts to so declare, with the result that the offending law is to that extent null and void under Section 52 of the *Charter*. Slavish deference would reduce *Charter* rights to meaningless words on a scrap of paper. It is to say, however, that judging should be grounded in principle and an appropriate respect for the different roles of the elected representatives of the people and the courts.

Thus far in our *Charter's* short history, the courts have repeatedly countenanced respect for the choices of Parliament and the legislatures. They have repeatedly affirmed that it is not the court's role to strike the policy compromises that are essential to effective modern legislation. The role of the courts is the much more modest but nevertheless vital task of hearing constitutional claims brought by individuals, identifying unconstitutional legislative acts where such can be demonstrated, and applying the *Charter* we have all agreed upon.

13.10

Key Terms

Concepts

judicial activism
democratic legitimacy
Section 33 notwithstanding power
Section 52 supremacy clause
court-curbing (U.S.)
judicial independence
Charter dialogue theory
legislative sequel
"judicial democrats"
human rights
populism
republicanism
separation of powers
checks and balances

Appendix

Constitution Act, 1867, ss. 91-95, 133.

VI. – Distribution of Legislative Powers.

91. It shall be lawful for the Queen, by and with the Advice and Consent of the Senate and House of Commons, to make laws for the Peace, Order, and good Government of Canada, in relation to all Matters not coming within the Classes of Subjects by this Act assigned exclusively to the Legislatures of the Provinces; and for greater Certainty, but not so as to restrict the Generality of the foregoing Terms of this Section, it is hereby declared that (notwithstanding anything in this Act) the exclusive Legislative Authority of the Parliament of Canada extends to all Matters coming within the Classes of Subjects next hereinafter enumerated; that is to say, –

   1. Repealed.
 1A. The Public Debt and Property.
   2. The Regulation of Trade and Commerce.
 2A. Unemployment insurance.
   3. The raising of Money by any Mode or System of Taxation.
   4. The borrowing of Money on the Public Credit.
   5. Postal Service.
   6. The Census and Statistics.
   7. Militia, Military and Naval Service, and Defence.
   8. The fixing of and providing for the Salaries and Allowances of Civil and other Officers of the Government of Canada.
   9. Beacons, Buoys, Lighthouses, and Sable Island.
 10. Navigation and Shipping.
 11. Quarantine and the Establishment and Maintenance of Marine Hospitals.
 12. Sea Coast and Inland Fisheries.
 13. Ferries between a Province and any British or Foreign Country or between Two Provinces.

14. Currency and Coinage.
15. Banking, Incorporation of Banks, and the Issue of Paper Money.
16. Savings Banks.
17. Weights and Measures.
18. Bills of Exchange and Promissory Notes.
19. Interest.
20. Legal Tender.
21. Bankruptcy and Insolvency.
22. Patents of Invention and Discovery.
23. Copyrights.
24. Indians, and Lands reserved for the Indians.
25. Naturalization and Aliens.
26. Marriage and Divorce.
27. The Criminal Law, except the Constitution of Courts of Criminal Jurisdiction, but including the Procedure in Criminal Matters.
28. The Establishment, Maintenance, and Management of Penitentiaries.
29. Such Classes of Subjects as are expressly excepted in the Enumeration of the Classes of Subjects by this Act assigned exclusively to the Legislatures of the Provinces.

And any Matter coming within any of the Classes of Subjects enumerated in this section shall not be deemed to come within the Class of Matters of a local or private Nature comprised in the Enumeration of the Classes of Subjects by this Act assigned exclusively to the Legislatures of the Provinces.

Exclusive Powers of Provincial Legislatures.

92. In each Province the Legislature may exclusively make Laws in relation to Matters coming within the Classes of Subject next hereinafter enumerated; that is to say, –

1. Repealed.
2. Direct Taxation within the Province in order to the raising of a Revenue for Provincial Purposes.
3. The borrowing of Money on the sole Credit of the Province.
4. The Establishment and Tenure of Provincial Offices and the Appointment and Payment of Provincial Officers.
5. The Management and Sale of the Public Lands belonging to the Province and of the Timber and Wood thereon.
6. The Establishment, Maintenance, and Management of Public and Reformatory Prisons in and for the Province.
7. The Establishment, Maintenance, and Management of Hospitals, Asylums, Charities, and Eleemosynary Institutions in and for the Province, other than Marine Hospitals.

8. Municipal Institutions in the Province.
9. Shop, Saloon, Tavern, Auctioneer, and other Licences in order to the raising of a Revenue for Provincial, Local, or Municipal Purposes.
10. Local Works and Undertakings other than such as are of the following Classes: –
    (*a*) Lines of Steam or other Ships, Railways, Canals, and other Works and Undertakings connecting the Province with any other or others of the Provinces, or extending beyond the Limits of the Province;
    (*b*) Lines of Steam Ships between the Province and any British or Foreign Country;
    (*c*) Such Works as, although wholly situate within the Province, are before or after the Execution declared by the Parliament of Canada to be for the general Advantage of Canada or for the Advantage of Two or more of the Provinces.
11. The Incorporation of Companies with Provincial Objects.
12. The Solemnization of Marriage in the Province.
13. Property and Civil Rights in the Province.
14. The Administration of Justice in the Province, including the Constitution, Maintenance, and Organization of Provincial Courts, both of Civil and of Criminal Jurisdiction, and including Procedure in Civil Matters in those Courts.
15. The Imposition of Punishment by Fine, Penalty, or Imprisonment for enforcing any Law of the Province made in relation to any Matter coming within any of the Classes of Subjects enumerated in this Section.
16. Generally all Matters of a merely local or private Nature in the Province.

Non-Renewable Natural Resources, Forestry Resources and Electrical Energy.

92A. (1) In each province, the legislature may exclusively make laws in relation to
    (*a*) exploration for non-renewable natural resources in the province;
    (*b*) development, conservation and management of non-renewable resources natural resources and forestry resources in the province, including laws in relation to the rate of primary production therefrom; and
    (*c*) development, conservation and management of sites and facilities in the province for the generation and production of electrical energy.
    (2) In each province, the legislature may make laws in relation

to the export from the province to another part of Canada of the primary production from non-renewable natural resources and forestry resources in the province and the production from facilities in the province for the generation of electrical energy, but such laws may not authorize or provide for discrimination in prices or in supplies exported to another part of Canada.

(3) Nothing in subsection (2) derogates from the authority of Parliament to enact laws in relation to the matters referred to in that subsection and, where such a law of Parliament and a law of a province conflict, the law of Parliament prevails to the extent of the conflict.

(4) In each province, the legislature may make laws in relation to the raising of money by any mode or system of taxation in respect of

 (a) non-renewable natural resources and forestry resources in the province and the primary production therefrom, and

 (b) sites and facilities in the province for the generation of electrical energy and the production therefrom, whether or not such production is exported in whole or in part from the province, but such laws may not authorize or provide for taxation that differentiates between production exported to another part of Canada and production not exported from the province.

(5) The expression "primary production" has the meaning assigned by the Sixth Schedule.

(6) Nothing in subsections (1) to (5) derogates from any power or rights that a legislature or government of a province had immediately before the coming into force of this section.

Education.

93. In and for each Province the Legislature may exclusively make Laws in relation to Education, subject and according to the following Provisions: –

(1) Nothing in any such Law shall prejudicially affect any Right or Privilege with respect to Denominational Schools which any Class of Persons have by Law in the Province at the Union:

(2) All the Powers, Privileges and Duties at the Union by Law conferred and imposed in Upper Canada on the Separate Schools and School Trustees of the Queen's Roman Catholic Subjects shall be and the same are hereby extended to the Dissentient Schools of the Queen's Protestant and Roman Catholic Subjects in Quebec:

(3) Where in any Province a System of Separate or Dissentient Schools exists by Law at the Union or is thereafter established by the Legislature of the Province, an Appeal shall lie to the Governor General in Council from any Act or Decision of any Provincial Authority affecting any Right or Privilege of the Protestant or Roman Catholic Minority of the Queen's Subjects in relation to Education:

(4) In case any such Provincial Law as from Time to Time seems to the Governor General in Council requisite for the Execution of the Provisions of this Section is not made, or in case any Decision of the Governor General in Council on any Appeal under this Section is not duly executed by the proper Provincial Authority in that Behalf, then and in every such Case, and as far as the Circumstances of each Case require, the Parliament of Canada may make remedial Laws for the due Execution of the Provisions of this Section and of any Decision of the Governor General in Council under this Section.

Uniformity of Laws in Ontario, Nova Scotia and New Brunswick.

94. Notwithstanding anything in this Act, the Parliament of Canada may make Provision for the Uniformity of all or any of the Laws relative to Property and Civil Rights in Ontario, Nova Scotia, and New Brunswick, and of the Procedure of all or any of the Courts in Those Three Provinces, and from and after the passing of any Act in that Behalf the Power of the Parliament of Canada to make Laws in relation to any Matter comprised in any such Act shall, notwithstanding anything in this Act, be unrestricted; but any Act of the Parliament of Canada making Provision for such Uniformity shall not have effect in any Province unless and until it is adopted and enacted as Law by the Legislature thereof.

Old Age Pensions.

94A. The Parliament of Canada may make laws in relation to old age pensions and supplementary benefits, including survivors, and disability benefits irrespective of age, but no such law shall affect the operation of any law present or future of a provincial legislature in relation to any such matters.

Agriculture and Immigration.

95. In each Province the Legislature may make Laws in relation to Agriculture in the Province, and to Immigration into the Province;

and it is hereby declared that the Parliament of Canada may from Time to Time Make Laws in relation to Agriculture in all or any of the Provinces, and to Immigration into all or any of the Provinces; and any Law of the Legislature of a Province relative to Agriculture or to Immigration shall have effect in and for the Province as long and as far as it is not repugnant to any Act of the Parliament of Canada.

IX. – Miscellaneaous Provisions.

General.

133.   Either the English or the French Language may be used by any Person in the Debates of the Houses of the Parliament of Canada and of the Houses of the Legislature of Quebec; and both those Languages shall be used in the respective Records and Journals of those Houses; and either of those Languages may be used by any Person or in any Pleading or Process in or issuing from any Court of Canada established under this Act, and in or from all or any of the Courts of Quebec.

The Acts of the Parliament of Canada and of the Legislature of Quebec shall be printed and published in both those Languages.(66)

Appendix

Canadian Bill of Rights, 1960

Preamble

The Parliament of Canada, affirming that the Canadian Nation is founded upon principles that acknowledge the supremacy of God, the dignity and worth of the human person and the position of the family in a society of free men and free institutions;

Affirming also that men and institutions remain free only when freedom is founded upon respect for moral and spiritual values and the rule of law;

And being desirous of enshrining these principles and the human rights and fundamental freedoms derived from them, in a Bill of Rights which shall reflect the respect of Parliament for its constitutional authority and which shall ensure the protection of these rights and freedoms in Canada:

Therefore, Her Majesty, by and with the advice and consent of the Senate and House of Commons of Canada, enacts as follows:

Part I

Bill of Rights

1. It is hereby recognized and declared that in Canada there have existed and shall continue to exist without discrimination by reason of race, national origin, colour, religion or sex, the following human rights and fundamental freedoms, namely,
    (a) the right of the individual to life, liberty, security of the person and enjoyment of property and the right not to be deprived thereof except by due process of law;
    (b) the right of the individual to equality before the law and the protection of the law;

      (c) freedom of religion;

      (d) freedom of speech;

      (e) freedom of assembly and of association; and

      (f) freedom of the press.

2. Every law of Canada shall, unless it is expressly declared by an Act of Parliament of Canada that it shall operate notwithstanding the *Canadian Bill of Rights*, be so construed and applied as not to abrogate, abridge or infringe or to authorize the abrogation, abridgment or infringement of any of the rights or freedoms herein recognized and declared, and in particular, no law of Canada shall be construed or applied so as to

    (a) authorize or effect the arbitrary detention, imprisonment or exile of a person;

    (b) impose or authorize the imposition of cruel and unusual treatment or punishment;

    (c) deprive a person who has been arrested or detained

        (i) of the right to be informed promptly of the reason for his arrest or detention,

        (ii) of the right to retain and instruct counsel without delay, or

        (iii) of the remedy by way of *habeas corpus* for the determination of the validity of his detention and for his release if the detention is not lawful;

    (d) authorize a court, tribunal, commission, board or other authority to compel a person to give evidence if he is denied counsel, protection against self-crimination or other constitutional safeguards;

    (e) deprive a person of the right to a fair hearing in accordance to the principles of fundamental justice for the determination of his rights and obligations;

    (f) deprive a person charged with a criminal offence of the right to be presumed innocent until proved guilty according to the law in a fair and public hearing by an independent and impartial tribunal, or of the right to reasonable bail without just cause; and

    (g) deprive a person of the right to the assistance to an interpreter in any proceedings in which he is involved or in which he is a party or a witness, before a court, commission, board or other tribunal, if he does not understand or speak the language in which such proceedings are conducted.

3. **(1)** Subject to subsection (2), the Minister of Justice shall, in accordance with such regulations as may be prescribed by the Governor General in Council, examine every regulation transmitted to the Clerk of the Privy Council for registration pursuant to the *Statutory Instruments Act* and every Bill introduced in or presented to the House of Commons by a Minister of the Crown in order to ascertain whether any of the provisions thereof are inconsistent with the purposes and provisions of this Part and he shall report any such inconsistency to the House of Commons at the first convenient opportunity.

(2) A regulation need not be examined in accordance with subsection (1) if prior to being made it was examined as a proposed regulation in accordance with section 3 of the *Statutory Instruments Act* to ensure that it was not inconsistent with the purposes and provisions of this Part.

4. The provisions of this Part shall be known as the *Canadian Bill of Rights*.

Part II

5. (1) Nothing in Part I shall be construed as to abrogate or abridge any human right or fundamental freedom not enumerated therein that may have exist in Canada at the commencement of this Act.

(2) The expression "law of Canada" in Part I means an Act of the Parliament of Canada enacted before or after the coming into force of this Act, any order, rule or regulation thereunder, and any law in force in Canada or in any part of Canada at the commencement of this Act that that is subject to be repealed, abolished or altered by the Parliament of Canada.

(3) The provisions of Part I shall be construed as extending only to matters coming within the legislative authority of the Parliament of Canada.

C

Appendix

Constitution Act, 1982, ss. 1–35, 38–49, 52.

Part I

Canadian Charter of Rights and Freedoms

Whereas Canada is founded upon the principles that recognize the supremacy of God and the rule of law:

Guarantee of Rights and Freedoms

1. The Canadian Charter of Rights and Freedoms guarantees the rights and freedoms set out in it subject only to such reasonable limits prescribed by law as can be demonstrably justified in a free and democratic society.

Fundamental Freedoms

2. Everyone has the following fundamental freedoms:
   - (*a*) freedom of conscience and religion
   - (*b*) freedom of thought, belief, opinion and expression, including freedom of the press and other means of communication.
   - (*c*) freedom of peaceful assembly; and
   - (*d*) freedom of association.

Democratic Rights

3. Every citizen of Canada has the right to vote in an election of members of the House of Commons or of a legislative assembly and to be qualified for membership therein.
4. (1) No House of Commons and no legislative assembly shall continue for longer than five years from the date fixed for the return of the writs at a general election of its members.

(2) In time of real or apprehended war, invasion or insurrection, a House of Commons may be continued by Parliament and a legislative assembly may be continued by the legislature beyond five years if such continuation is not opposed by the votes of more than one-third of the members of the House of Commons or the legislative assembly, as the case may be.

5. There shall be a sitting of Parliament and of each legislature at least once every twelve months.

Mobility Rights

6. (1) Every citizen of Canada has the right to enter, remain in, and leave Canada.

   (2) Every citizen of Canada and every person who has the status of a permanent resident of Canada has the right

   (a) to move to and take up residence in any province; and

   (b) to pursue the gaining of livelihood in any province.

   (3) The rights specified in subsection (2) are subject to

   (a) any laws or practices of general application in force in a province other than those that discriminate among persons primarily on the basis of present or previous residence; and

   (b) any laws providing for reasonable residency requirements as a qualification for the receipt of publicly provided social services.

   (4) Subsections (2) and (3) do not preclude any law, program or activity that has as its object the amelioration in a province of conditions of individuals in that province who are socially or economically disadvantaged if the rate of employment in that province is below the rate of employment in Canada.

Legal Rights

7. Everyone has the right to life, liberty and security of the person and the right not to be deprived thereof except in accordance with the principles of fundamental justice.

8. Everyone has the right to be secure against unreasonable search or seizure.

9. Everyone has the right not to be arbitrarily detained or imprisoned.

10. Everyone has the right on arrest or detention

    (a) to be infomed promptly of the reason therefor;

    (b) to retain and instruct counsel without delay and to be infomed of that right; and

    (c) to have the validity of the detention determined by way of habeas corpus and to be released if the detention is not lawful.

11. Any person charged with an offence has the right
    (*a*) to be infomed without unreasonable delay of the specific offence;
    (*b*) to be tried within a reasonable time;
    (*c*) not to be compelled to be a witness in a proceedings against that person in respect of the offence;
    (*d*) to be presumed innocent until proven guilty according to law in a fair and public hearing by an independent and impartial tribunal;
    (*e*) not to be denied reasonable bail without cause;
    (*f*) except in the case of an offence under military law tried before a military tribunal, to the benefit of trial by jury where the maximum punishment for the offence is imprisonment for five years or a more severe punishment;
    (*g*) not to be found guilty on account of any act or omission unless, at the time of the act or omission, it constituted an offence under Canadian or International law or was criminal according to the general principles of law recognized by the community of nations;
    (*h*) if finally acquitted of the offence, not to be tried for it again and, if finally found guilty and punished for the offence, not to be tried or punished for it again; and
    (*i*) if found guilty of the offence and if punishment for the offence has been varied between the time of commission and the time of sentencing, to the benefit of the lesser punishment.
12. Everyone has the right not to be subjected to any cruel or unusual treatment or punishment.
13. A witness who testifies in any proceedings has the right not to have any incriminating evidence so given used to incriminate that witness in any other proceedings, except in a prosecution for perjury or for the giving of contradictory evidence.
14. A party or witness in any proceedings who does not understand or speak the language in which the proceedings are conducted or who is deaf has the right to the assistance of an interpreter.

Equality Rights

15. (1) Every individual is equal before the and under the law and has the right to the equal protection and equal benefit of the law without discrimination and, in particular, without discrimination based on race, national or ethnic origin, colour, religion, sex, age, or mental or physical disability.
    (2) Subsection (1) does not preclude any law, program or activity that has as its object the amelioration of conditions of disadvantaged individuals or groups including those that are disadvantaged because of race, national or ethnic origin, colour, religion, sex, age, or mental or physical disability.

Official Languages of Canada

16. (1) English and French are the official languages of Canada and have equal rights and privileges as to their use in all institutions of the Parliament and government of Canada.

    (2) English and French are the official languages of New Brunswick and have equality of status and equal rights and privileges as to the use in all institutions of the legislature and government of New Brunswick.

    (3) Nothing in this Charter limits the authority of Parliament or a legislature to advance the equality of status or use of English and French.

16.1 (1) The English linguistic community and the French linguistic community in New Brunswick have equality of status and equal rights and privileges, including the right to distinct educational institutions and such distinct cultural institutions as are necessary for the preservation and promotion of those communities.

    (2) The role of the legislature and the government of New Brunswick to preserve and promote the status, rights and privileges referred to in subsection (1) is affirmed.

17. (1) Everyone has the right to use English or French in any debates or other proceedings of Parliament.

    (2) Everyone has the right to use English or French in any debate and other proceeding of the legislature of New Brunswick.

18. (1) The Statutes, records and journals of Parliament shall be printed and published in English and French and both language versions are equally authoritative.

    (2) The Statutes, records and journals of New Brunswick shall be printed and published in English and French and both language versions are equally authoritative.

19. (1) Either English or French may be used by any person in, or in any pleading in or process issuing from any court established by Parliament.

    (2) Either English or French may be used by any person in, or in any pleading in or process issuing from any court of New Brunswick.

20. (1) Any member of the public of Canada has the right to communicate with, and to receive available services from, any head or central office of an institution of the Parliament or government of Canada in English or French, and has the same right with respect to any other office of any such institution where

    (a) there is significant demand for communications with and services from that office in such language; or (*b*)   due to the nature of the office, it is reasonable that communications with and services from that office be available in both English and French.

  (2) Any member of the public in New Brunswick has the right to communicate with, and to receive available services from, any office of an institution of the legislature or government of New Brunswick in English or French.

21. Nothing in sections 16 to 20 abrogates or derogates from any right, privilege or obligation with respect to the English and French languages, or either of them, that exists or is continued by virtue of any other provision of the Constitution of Canada.

22. Nothing in sections 16 to 20 abrogates or derogates from any legal or customary right or privilege acquired or enjoyed either before or after the coming into force of this Charter with respect to any language that is not English or French.

Minority Language Educational Rights

23. (1) Citizens of Canada

      (*a*)   whose first language learned and still understood is that of the English or French linguistic minority population of the province in which they reside, or

      (*b*)   who have received their primary school instruction in Canada in English or French and reside in a province where the language in which they received that instruction is the language of the English or French linguistic minority population of the province,
      have the right to have their children receive primary and secondary school instruction in that language in that province.

  (2) Citizens of Canada of whom any child has received or is receiving primary or secondary school instruction in English or French in Canada, have the right to have all their children receive primary and secondary school instruction in the same language.

  (3) The right of citizens of Canada under subsections (1) and (2) to have their children receive primary and secondary school instruction in the language of the English or French linguistic minority population of a province

      (*a*)   applies wherever in the province the number of children of citizens who have such a right is sufficient to warrant the provision to them out of public funds of minority language instruction; and

      (*b*)   includes, where the number of children so warrants, the right to have them receive that instruction in minority language educational facilities provided out of public funds.

Enforcement

24. (1) Anyone whose rights or freedoms, as guaranteed by this Charter, have been infringed or denied may apply to a court of competent jurisdiction to obtain such remedy as the court considers appropriate and just in the circumstances.

    (2) Where, in proceedings under subsection (1), a court concludes that evidence was obtained in a manner that infringed or denied any rights or freedoms guaranteed by this Charter, the evidence shall be excluded if it is established that, having regard to all the circumstances, the admission of it in the proceedings would bring the administration of justice into disrepute.

General

25. The guarantee in this Charter of certain rights and freedoms shall not be construed so as to abrogate or derogate from any aboriginal, treaty or other rights or freedoms that pertain to the aboriginal peoples of Canada including

    (a) any rights or freedoms that have been recognized by the Royal Proclamation of October 7, 1763; and

    (b) any rights or freedoms that may be acquired by the aboriginal peoples of Canada by way of land claims settlement.

26. The guarantee in this Charter of certain rights and freedoms shall not be construed as denying the existence of any other rights and freedoms that exist in Canada.

27. This Charter shall be interpreted in a manner consistent with the preservation and enhancement of the multicultural heritage of Canadians.

28. Notwithstanding anything in this Charter, the rights and freedoms referred to in it are guaranteed equally to male and female persons.

29. Nothing in this Charter abrogates or derogates from any rights or privileges guaranteed by or under the Constitution of Canada in respect of denominational, separate or dissentient schools.

30. A reference in this Charter to a province or to the legislative assembly or legislature of a province shall be deemed to include a reference to the Yukon Territory and the Northwest Territories, or to the appropriate legislative authority thereof, as the case may be.

31. Nothing in this Charter extends the legislative powers of any body or authority.

Application of Charter

32. (1) This Charter applies
    (a) to the Parliament and government of Canada in respect of all matters within the authority of Parliament including all matters relating to the Yukon Territory and Northwest Territories; and
    (b) to the legislatures and governments of each province in respect of all matters within the authority of the legislature of each province.
    (2) Notwithstanding subsection (1), section 15 shall not have effect until three years after this section comes into force.
33. (1) Parliament or the legislature of a province may expressly declare in an Act of Parliament or of the legislature, as the case may be, that the Act or a provision thereof shall operate notwithstanding a provision included in section 2 or section 7 to 15 of this Charter.
    (2) An Act or a provision of an Act in respect of which a declaration made under this section is in effect shall have such operation as it would have but for the provision of this Charter referred to in the declaration.
    (3) A declaration made under subsection (1) shall cease to have effect five years after it comes into force or on such earlier date as may be specified in the declaration.
    (4) Parliament or the legislature of a province may re-enact a declaration made under subsection (1).
    (5) Subsection (3) applies in respect of re-enactment made under subsection (4).

Citation

34. This Part may be cited as the Canadian Charter of Rights and Freedoms.

Part II

Rights of the Aboriginal Peoples of Canada

35. (1) The existing aboriginal and treaty rights of the aboriginal peoples of Canada are hereby recognized and affirmed.
    (2) In this Act, "aboriginal peoples of Canada" includes the Indian, Inuit, and Metis peoples of Canada.
    (3) For greater certainty, in subsection (1) "treaty rights" includes rights that now exist by way of land claims agreements or may be so acquired.

(4) Notwithstanding any other provision of this Act, the aboriginal and treaty rights referred to in subsection (1) are guaranteed equally to male and female persons.

35.1 The government of Canada and the provincial governments are committed to the principal that, before any amendment is made to Class 24 of section 91 of the "Constitution Act, 1867", to section 25 of this Act or to this Part,

(*a*) a constitutional conference that includes in its agenda an item relating to the proposed amendment, composed of the Prime Minister of Canada and the first ministers of the provinces, will be convened by the Prime Minister of Canada; and

(*b*) the Prime Minister of Canada will invite representatives of the aboriginal peoples of Canada to participate in the discussions on that item.

Part V

Procedure for Amending the Constitution of Canada

38. (1) An amendment to the Constitution of Canada may be made by proclamation issued by the Governor General under the Great Seal of Canada where so authorized by

(*a*) resolutions of the Senate and the House of Commons; and

(*b*) resolutions of the legislative assemblies of at least two-thirds of the provinces that have, in the aggregate, according to the then latest general census, at least fifty per cent of the population of the provinces.

(2) An amendment made under subsection (1) that derogates from the legislative powers, the proprietary rights or any other rights or privileges of the legislature or government of a province shall require a resolution supported by a majority of the members of each of the Senate, the House of Commons and the legislative assemblies required under subsection (1).

(3) An amendment referred to in subsection (2) shall not have effect in a province the legislative assembly of which has expressed its dissent thereto by resolution supported by a majority of its members prior to the issue of the proclamation to which the amendment relates unless that legislative assembly, subsequently, by resolution supported by a majority of its members, revokes its dissent and authorizes the amendment.

(4) A resolution of dissent made for the purposes of subsection (3) may be revoked at any time before or after the issue of the proclamation to which it relates.

39. (1) A proclamation shall not be issued under subsection 38(1) before the expiration of one year from the adoption of the resolution initiating the amendment procedure, unless the legislative assembly of each province has previously adopted a resolution of assent or dissent.

(2) A proclamation shall not be issued under subsection 38(1) after the expiration of three years from the adoption of the resolution initiating the amendment procedure thereunder.

40. Where an amendment is made under subsection 38(1) that transfers provincial legislative powers relating to education or other cultural matters from provincial legislatures to Parliament, Canada shall provide reasonable compensation to any province to which the amendment does not apply.

41. An amendment to the Constitution of Canada in relation to the following matters may be made by proclamation issued by the Governor General under the Great Seal of Canada only where authorized by resolutions of the Senate and House of Commons and of the legislative assemblies of each province:

(*a*) the office of the Queen, the Governor General and the Lieutenant Governor of a province;

(*b*) the right of a province to a number of members in the House of Commons not less than the number of Senators by which the province is entitled to be represented at the time this Part comes into force;

(*c*) subject to section 43, the use of the English or the French language;

(*d*) the composition of the Supreme Court of Canada; and

(*e*) an amendment to this Part.

42. 1) An amendment to the Constitution of Canada in relation to the following matters may be made only in accordance with subsection 38(1):

(*a*) the principle of proportionate representation of the provinces in the House of Commons prescribed by the Constitution of Canada;

(*b*) the powers of the Senate and the method of selecting Senators;

(*c*) the number of members by which a province is entitled to be represented in the Senate and the residence qualifications of Senators;

(*d*) subject to paragraph 41(d), the Supreme Court of Canada;

(*e*) the extension of existing provinces into the territories; and

(*f*) notwithstanding any other law or practice, the establishment of new provinces;

(2) Subsections 38(2) to 38(4) do not apply in respect of amendments in relation to matters referred to in subsection (1).

43. An amendment to the Constitution of Canada in relation to any provision that applies to one or more, but not all provinces, including

  (*a*) any alteration to boundaries between provinces, and

  (*b*) any amendment to any provisions that relate to the use of the English or the French language within a province may be made by proclamation issued by the Governor General under the Great Seal of Canada only where so authorized by resolutions of the Senate and House of Commons and of the legislative assembly of each province to which the amendment applies.

44. Subject to sections 41 and 42, Parliament may exclusively make laws amending the Constitution of Canada in relation to executive government of Canada or the Senate and House of Commons.

45. Subject to section 41, the legislature of each province may exclusively make laws amending the constitution of the province.

46. (1) The procedures for amendment under sections 38, 41, 42, and 43 may be initiated either by the Senate or the House of Commons or by the legislative assembly of province.

  (2) A resolution of assent for the purposes of this Part may be revoked at any time before the issue of a proclamation authorized by it.

47. (1) An amendment to the Constitution of Canada made by proclamation under section 38, 41, 42, or 43 may be made without a resolution of the Senate authorizing the issue of the proclamation if, within one hundred and eighty days after the adoption by the House of Commons of a resolution authorizing its issue, the Senate has not adopted such a resolution and if, at any time after the expiration of that period, the House of Commons again adopts the resolution.

  (2) Any period when Parliament is prorogued or dissolved shall not be counted in computing the one hundred and eighty day period referred to in subsection (1).

48. The Queen's Privy Council for Canada shall advise the Governor General to issue a proclamation under this Part forthwith on the adoption of the resolution required for an amendment made by proclamation under this part.

49. A constitutional conference of the Prime Minister of Canada and the first ministers shall be convened by the Prime Minister of Canada within fifteen years after this Part comes into force to review the provisions of this Part.

Part VII

General (Supremacy Clause)

52. (1) The Constitution of Canada is the supreme law of Canada, and any law that is inconsistent with the provisions of the Constitution is, to the extent of the inconsistency, of no force or effect.
    (2) The Constitution of Canada includes
        (*a*)   the Canada Act, 1982, including this Act;
        (*b*)   the Acts and orders referred to in the Schedule; and
        (*c*)   any amendment to any Act or order referred to in paragraph (*a*) or (*b*).
    (3) Amendments to the Constitution of Canada shall be made only in accordance with the authority contained in the Constitution of Canada.

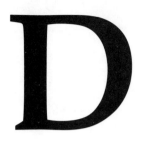

Appendix

Chief Justices of the Supreme Court of Canada

	Name of Chief Justice	Term on court as Chief Justice	Province from	Appointed by
1)	Hon. Sir William Buell Richards	September 30, 1875 – January 10, 1879	Ontario	Alexander Mackenzie (Liberal)
2)	Hon. Sir William Johnston Ritchie	January 11, 1879 – September 25, 1892	New Brunswick	Sir John A. Macdonald (Conservative)
3)	Rt. Hon. Sir Samuel Henry Strong	December 13, 1892 – November 18, 1902	Ontario	Sir John Thompson (Conservative)
4)	Rt. Hon. Sir Henri-Elzéar Taschereau	November 21, 1902 – May 2, 1906	Quebec	Sir Wilfrid Laurier (Liberal)
5)	Rt. Hon. Sir Charles Fitzpatrick	June 4, 1906 – October 21, 1918	Quebec	Sir Wilfrid Laurier (Liberal)
6)	Rt. Hon. Sir Louis Henry Davies	October 23, 1918 – May 1, 1924	Prince Edward Island	Sir Robert Borden (Conservative/Unionist)
7)	Rt. Hon. Francis Alexander Anglin	September 16, 1924 – February 28, 1933	Ontario	Mackenzie King (Liberal)
8)	Rt. Hon. Sir Lyman Poore Duff	March 17, 1933 – January 7, 1944	British Columbia	Richard B. Bennett (Conservative)
9)	Rt. Hon. Thibaudeau Rinfret	January 8, 1944 – June 22, 1954	Quebec	Mackenzie King (Liberal)
10)	Hon. Patrick Kerwin	July 1, 1954 – Feb. 2, 1963	Ontario	Louis St. Laurent (Liberal)
11)	Rt. Hon. Robert Taschereau	April 22, 1963 – Sept. 1, 1967	Quebec	Lester Pearson (Liberal)
12)	Rt. Hon. John Robert Cartwright	September 1, 1967– March 23, 1970	Ontario	Lester Pearson (Liberal)
13)	Rt. Hon. Joseph Honoré Gérald Fauteux	March 23, 1970 – December 23, 1973	Quebec	Pierre Trudeau (Liberal)
14)	Rt. Hon. Bora Laskin	December 27, 1973 – March 26, 1984	Ontario	Pierre Trudeau (Liberal)
15)	Rt. Hon. Robert George Brian Dickson	April 18, 1984 – June 30, 1990	Manitoba	Pierre Trudeau (Liberal)
16)	Rt. Hon. Antonio Lamer	July 1, 1990 – January 6, 2000	Quebec	Brian Mulroney (Progressive Conservative)
17)	Rt. Hon. Beverley McLachlin	January 7, 2000 –	British Columbia	Jean Chrétien (Liberal)

Appendix **E**

Puisne Judges of the Supreme Court of Canada

Name of Supreme Court Justice	Term served on the court	Province from	Appointed by
1) Hon. William Johnstone Ritchie*	September 30, 1875 – January 11, 1879*	New Brunswick	Alexander Mackenzie (Liberal)
2) Hon. Samuel Henry Strong*	September 30, 1875 – December 13, 1892*	Ontario	Alexander Mackenzie (Liberal)
3) Hon. Jean-Thomas Taschereau	September 30, 1875 – October 6, 1878	Quebec	Alexander Mackenzie (Liberal)
4) Hon. Télesphore Fournier	September 30, 1875 – September 12, 1895	Quebec	Alexander Mackenzie (Liberal)
5) Hon. William Alexander Henry	September 30, 1875 – May 3, 1888	Nova Scotia	Alexander Mackenzie (Liberal)
6) Hon. Sir Henri-Elzéar Taschereau*	October 7, 1879 – November 21, 1902*	Quebec	Alexander Mackenzie (Liberal)
7) Hon. John Wellington Gwynne	January 14, 1879 – January 7, 1902	Ontario	Sir John A. Macdonald (Conservative)
8) Hon. Christopher Salmon Patterson	October 27, 1888 – July 24, 1893	Ontario	Sir John A. Macdonald (Conservative)
9) Hon. Robert Sedgewick	February 18, 1893 – August 4, 1906	Nova Scotia	Sir John Thompson (Conservative)
10) Hon. George Edwin King	September 21, 1893 – May 8, 1901	New Brunswick	Sir John Thompson (Conservative)
11) Hon. Désiré Girouard	September 28, 1895 – March 22, 1911	Quebec	Sir Mackenzie Bowell (Conservative)
12) Hon. Sir Louis Henry Davies*	September 25, 1901 – October 23, 1918*	Prince Edward Island	Sir Wilfrid Laurier (Liberal)
13) Hon. David Mills	February 8, 1902 – May 8, 1903	Ontario	Sir Wilfrid Laurier (Liberal)
14) Hon. John Douglas Armour	November 21, 1902 – July 11, 1903	Ontario	Sir Wilfrid Laurier (Liberal)
15) Hon. Wallace Nesbitt	May 16, 1903 – October 4, 1905	Ontario	Sir Wilfrid Laurier (Liberal)
16) Hon. Albert Clements Killam	August 8, 1903 – February 6, 1905	Manitoba	Sir Wilfrid Laurier (Liberal)
17) Hon. John Idington	February 10, 1905 – March 31, 1927	Ontario	Sir Wilfrid Laurier (Liberal)
18) Hon. James Maclennan	October 5, 1905 – February 13, 1909	Ontario	Sir Wilfrid Laurier (Liberal)
19) Hon. Lyman Poore Duff*	September 27, 1906 – March 17, 1933*	British Columbia	Sir Wilfrid Laurier (Liberal)
20) Hon. Francis Alexander Anglin*	February 23, 1909 – September 16, 1924*	Ontario	Sir Wilfrid Laurier (Liberal)
21) Hon. Louis-Philippe Brodeur	August 11, 1911 – October 10, 1923	Quebec	Sir Wilfrid Laurier (Liberal)
22) Hon. Pierre-Basile Mignault	October 25, 1918 – September 30, 1929	Quebec	Sir Robert Borden (Conservative/Unionist)
23) Hon. Arthur Cyrille Albert Malouin	January 30, 1924 – October 1, 1924	Quebec	Mackenzie King (Liberal)
24) Hon. Edmund Leslie Newcombe	September 16, 1924 – December 9, 1931	Nova Scotia	Mackenzie King (Liberal)
25) Hon. Thibaudeau Rinfret*	October 1, 1924 – January 8, 1944*	Quebec	Mackenzie King (Liberal)
26) Hon. John Henderson Lamont	April 2, 1927 – March 10, 1936	Saskatchewan	Mackenzie King (Liberal)
27) Hon. Robert Smith	May 18, 1927 – December 7, 1933	Ontario	Mackenzie King (Liberal)
28) Hon. Lawrence Arthur Dumoulin Cannon	January 14, 1930 – December 25, 1939	Quebec	Mackenzie King (Liberal)
29) Hon. Oswald Smith Crocket	September 21, 1932 – April 13, 1943	New Brunswick	Richard B. Bennett (Conservative)
30) Hon. Frank Joseph Hughes	March 17, 1933 – February 13, 1935	Ontario	Richard B. Bennett (Conservative)
31) Hon. Henry Hague Davis	January 31, 1935 – June 30, 1944	Ontario	Richard B. Bennett (Conservative)
32) Hon. Patrick Kerwin*	July 20, 1935 – July 1, 1954*	Ontario	Richard B. Bennett (Conservative)
33) Hon. Albert Blelloch Hudson	March 24, 1936 – January 6, 1947	Manitoba	Mackenzie King (Liberal)
34) Hon. Robert Taschereau*	February 9, 1940 – April 22, 1963*	Quebec	Mackenzie King (Liberal)
35) Hon. Ivan Cleveland Rand	April 22, 1943 – April 27, 1959	New Brunswick	Mackenzie King (Liberal)
36) Hon. Roy Lindsay Kellock	October 3, 1944 – January 15, 1958	Ontario	Mackenzie King (Liberal)

*Asterisk denotes date of appointment as Chief Justice; Term as Chief Justice in Appendix D.

Name of Supreme Court Justice	Term served on the court	Province from	Appointed by
37) Hon. James Wilfred Estey	October 6, 1944 – January 22, 1956	Saskatchewan	Mackenzie King (Liberal)
38) Hon. Charles Holland Locke	June 3, 1947 – September 16, 1962	British Columbia	Mackenzie King (Liberal)
39) Hon. John Robert Cartwright*	December 22, 1949 – September 1, 1967*	Ontario	Louis St. Laurent (Liberal)
40) Hon. Joseph Honoré Gérald Fauteux*	December 22, 1949 – March 23, 1970*	Quebec	Louis St. Laurent (Liberal)
41) Hon. Douglas Charles Abbott	July 1, 1954 – December 23, 1973	Quebec	Louis St. Laurent (Liberal)
42) Hon. Henry Gratton Nolan	March 1, 1956 – July 8, 1957	Alberta	Louis St. Laurent (Liberal)
43) Hon. Ronald Martland	January 15, 1958 – February 10, 1982	Alberta	John Diefenbaker (Progressive Conservative)
44) Hon. Wilfred Judson	February 5, 1958 – July 20, 1977	Ontario	John Diefenbaker (Progressive Conservative)
45) Hon. Roland Almon Ritchie	May 5, 1959 – October 31, 1984	Nova Scotia	John Diefenbaker (Progressive Conservative)
46) Hon. Emmett Matthew Hall	November 23, 1962 – March 1, 1973	Saskatchewan	John Diefenbaker (Progressive Conservative)
47) Hon. Wishart Flett Spence	May 30, 1963 – December 29, 1978	Ontario	Lester Pearson (Liberal)
48) Hon. Louis-Philippe Pigeon	September 21, 1967 – February 8, 1980	Quebec	Lester Pearson (Liberal)
49) Hon. Bora Laskin*	March 19, 1970 – December 27, 1973*	Ontario	Pierre Trudeau (Liberal)
50) Hon. Robert George Brian Dickson*	March 26, 1973 – April 18, 1984*	Manitoba	Pierre Trudeau (Liberal)
51) Hon. Jean Beetz	January 1, 1974 – November 10, 1988	Quebec	Pierre Trudeau (Liberal)
52) Hon. Louis-Philippe de Grandpré	January 1, 1974 – October 1, 1977	Quebec	Pierre Trudeau (Liberal)
53) Hon. Willard Zebedee Estey	September 29, 1977 – April 22, 1988	Ontario	Pierre Trudeau (Liberal)
54) Hon. Yves Pratte	October 1, 1977 – June 30, 1979	Quebec	Pierre Trudeau (Liberal)
55) Hon. William Rogers McIntyre	January 1, 1979 – February 15, 1989	British Columbia	Pierre Trudeau (Liberal)
56) Hon. Julien Chouinard	September 24, 1979 – February 6, 1987	Quebec	Joe Clark (Progressive Conservative)
57) Hon. Antonio Lamer*	March 28, 1980 – July 1, 1990*	Quebec	Pierre Trudeau (Liberal)
58) Hon. Bertha Wilson	March 4, 1982 – January 4, 1991	Ontario	Pierre Trudeau (Liberal)
59) Hon. Gérard Eric Le Dain	May 29, 1984 – November 30, 1988	Ontario	Pierre Trudeau (Liberal)
60) Hon. Gérard V. La Forest	January 16, 1985 – September 30, 1997	New Brunswick	Brian Mulroney (Progressive Conservative)
61) Hon. Claire L'Heureux-Dubé	April 15, 1987 – June, 2002	Quebec	Brian Mulroney (Progressive Conservative)
62) Hon. John Sopinka	May 24, 1988 – November 24, 1997	Ontario	Brian Mulroney (Progressive Conservative)
63) Hon. Charles Doherty Gonthier	February 1, 1989 –	Quebec	Brian Mulroney (Progressive Conservative)
64) Hon. Peter deCarteret Cory	February 1, 1989 – June 1, 1999	Ontario	Brian Mulroney (Progressive Conservative)
65) Hon. Beverley McLachlin*	March 30, 1989 – January 7, 2000*	British Columbia	Brian Mulroney (Progressive Conservative)
66) Hon. William Stevenson	September 17, 1990 – June 5, 1992	Alberta	Brian Mulroney (Progressive Conservative)
67) Hon. Frank Iacobucci	January 7, 1991 –	Ontario	Brian Mulroney (Progressive Conservative)
68) Hon. John C. Major	November 13, 1992 –	Alberta	Brian Mulroney (Progressive Conservative)
69) Hon. Michel Bastarache	September 30, 1997 –	New Brunswick	Jean Chrétien (Liberal)
70) Hon. William Ian Corneil Binnie	January 8, 1998 –	Ontario	Jean Chrétien (Liberal)
71) Hon. Louise Arbour	September 15, 1999 –	Ontario	Jean Chrétien (Liberal)
72) Hon. Louis LeBel	January 7, 2000 –	Quebec	Jean Chrétien (Liberal)

*Asterisk denotes date of appointment as Chief Justice; Term as Chief Justice in Appendix D.

Appendix

Useful Websites

Supreme Court of Canada	www.scc-csc.gc.ca
Supreme Court of Canada Decisions	www.lexum.umontreal.ca/csc-scc/en/index.html
Canadian Judicial Council	www.cjc-ccm.gc.ca/english/index.htm
Office of the Commissioner For Federal Judicial Affairs	www.fja.gc.ca
Current legal news	http://jurist.law.utoronto.ca/
Canadian Politics On the Web [see Constitution, Legal System, Civil Rights]	www.nelson.com/nelson/polisci/canpol.html
Access to Justice Network	www.acjnet.org
Policy Options (April 1999)	www.irpp.org/po/index.htm
University of Calgary Law Library Home Page	www.ucalgary.ca/library/law

Rights Advocacy Organizations

LEAF	www.leaf.ca
CCLA	www.ccla.org/oth
NCC	www.citizenscoalition.org
EGALE	www.egale.ca/
CFAC	www.familyaction.org
ACLA	http://calcna.ab.ca/acl/aclr.html
ACSA	www.pagusmundi.com/acsa/

Index